Under the Rose

The Cross-Cultural Memoir Series introduces original, significant memoirs from women whose compelling histories map the sources of our differences: generations, national boundaries, race, ethnicity, class, and sexual orientation. The series features stories of contemporary women's lives, providing a record of social transformation, growth in consciousness, and the passionate commitment of individuals who make far-reaching change possible.

THE CROSS-CULTURAL MEMOIR SERIES

Under the Rose

A Confession

Flavia Alaya

THE FEMINIST PRESS
AT THE CITY UNIVERSITY OF NEW YORK

Published by The Feminist Press at The City University of New York
365 Fifth Avenue, New York, NY 10016
www.feministpress.org

First edition, 1999

Library of Congress Cataloging-in-Publication Data

Alaya, Flavia
        Under the rose: a confession / Flavia Alaya — 1st ed.
        p. cm. — (The cross-cultural memoir series)
        ISBN 1-55861-221-1
        1. Alaya, Flavia. 2. English teachers — United States — Biography. 3. Housing policy — New York (State) — New York — Citizen participation. 4. Catholic Church — United States — Clergy Biography. 5. Women scholars — United States — Biography. 6. Italian American women Biography. 7. Browne, Henry J. I. Title. II. Series.
        PE64.A48 A3 1999
        282'.092 — dc21
        [B]
                                                                                          99-35835
                                                                                          CIP

This publication is made possible, in part, by a grant from the Ford Foundation. The Feminist Press would also like to thank Joanne Markell and Genevieve Vaughan for their generosity in supporting this book.

Text design and typesetting by Dayna Navaro
Rose photographs © by Ann Alaia Woods
Printed on acid-free paper by R.R. Donnelley & Sons
Manufactured in the United States of America

05 04 03 02 01 00 99   5 4 3 2 1

For Esta
For Robert
For both my fathers—
may they forgive me

sub ro·sa (sub rō′zə). In secret; privately; confidentially [Latin, "under the rose," from the practice of hanging a rose over a meeting as a symbol of secrecy, from the legend that Cupid once gave Harpocrates, the god of silence, a rose to make him keep the secrets of Venus.]

—*American Heritage Dictionary*

Contents

Photographs appear on pages 215–218 and 393–396

See! Sweet and sound she sleeps in granny's bed,
between the paws of the tender wolf.

—Angela Carter, "The Company of Wolves"

Prologue

This book has had a long and layered history. My best enemies tried to discourage me from writing it. My best friends begged me to make it a novel. And in some sense I have, not just to please them, but because I could see no way to tell the story without all the color it came to me in as I wrote it. I did not understand why, unless we mistrust the very gorgeousness of truth, a true story need be any more dull or evasive or lame than a fictional one.

This was a problem for readers who thought, and may still think, that the stylistic boundary between true and fictional narrative should be wide and well-policed. Maybe a distaste for my style went with a disdain for my morals, with the result that when a late-draft manuscript was circulated some time ago a certain distinguished editor remarked, in the same breath, that she liked neither style nor person, the one being "too ornate" and the other "not nice people."

I believe—or, more to the point, I believed—she was not alone in thinking so. I had already been working on the book for too many years, too many years pocked with too much anguish, to make her judgment bearable. I made a halfhearted effort at getting it published after that, followed for a time by no effort at all.

Because I eventually saw a beautiful symmetry (simultaneously beautiful *and* true) between trying to make a life and trying to make the book about making it, I tell some of this tale of lost heart at the end of the book. I recall it here only to spotlight a certain sea change in the publishing universe as the book finally enters print. Not because the editor's judgment I describe will never be passed again—no doubt it will. But because I think there is a greater friendliness now toward my style and my story, a greater willingness generally to accommodate the voices of women and of Italian Americans—attitudes toward both of whom, I believe, were unconsciously coded into that denigrating put-down.

For me these voices happen to share a common chord, a common vocal idiom, which the opera titles of my parts are meant to both signal and amplify. But I have been a long time giving myself permission to be "ornate," which means to me also to be operatic, in some real sense *excessive,* to be romantic (and *italic*) in both language and emotion. I have needed a lot of help from other women, and from other Italian American writers. Why should I be surprised it is a permission even slower in coming from the mainstream world of publishing, or that small presses should have to push the envelope?

I am no less grateful for it. Publisher Florence Howe of The Feminist Press has done tremendous service to publishing in many ways, but perhaps none more so than in candidly admitting how late the Press came to printing and reprinting Italian American women, or how long she herself took to hear the resonance of voices like those of Helen Barolini and Dorothy Bryant and Tina De Rosa. Whether or not the world thanks her for publishing *me,* she has published *them.*

But romance, even Italianate romance, may be one thing and scandalmongering another. Even you may think my story about "not nice people." Or because it is true, too too true, about someone who has rendered herself "not nice" by the very act of telling it. Bad enough to commit the sins I committed. Worse the effrontery of making them public. It seems always to come back to this: *If only it were fiction!* Then I could write it and you could read it and we could all go see it, or its equivalent, at the movies (or the Met) and still be "nice people." Quite nice, in fact.

But I could no more make it fiction than I could live another life. Much has been said about "transgression" and its role in the discourse of feminism, but even feminists are conflicted on the point. Some will need to cast me as a kind of victim, a whistleblower on the hypocrisy of "concubinage" and the myth of Catholic celibacy, insisting the book ask how the Church could possibly promote a higher standard of moral, indeed of sexual responsibility, and continue to allow such wrong to be done to women. Or to men. And they are right. It's what the book is meant to ask. Or I should say, *was* meant to, before telling my life had performed the strange alchemy of transforming it, and I was more deeply self-identified as a Catholic than I frankly am now, and cared more that such hypocrisy was itself scandal to the Church.

Which is not to say that I care less now about women (and other men) who live in long-term relationships with Catholic priests. I care, and care deeply. I care about those who love priests and are forced to feel ashamed, to experience their love as "sin." And I care about the priests, not those who prolong such relationships out of a certain relish for the exploitative power that is inevitably part of them, but those who simply cannot bring themselves to leave their vocations, even for love. I care, and I believe the Catholic Church, which has to answer for all these ethically compromised relationships, should care, because everyone should.

But I have to confess a more unregenerate transgression. I have to confess that I am still grateful for the passion—and the freedom—that the Church's hypocrite secrecy made possible for me. "*We cannot all be white bread,*" said the Wyf of Bath —as true a woman as ever man made—when she told us about seducing and eventually marrying a cleric, and so spoiling a priest. In my case I don't take all the credit for the seduction (and even with the Wyf of Bath it worked both ways), but I know I can't somehow turn brown bread into white by some abracadabra of moral transubstantiation afterward, and I don't want to try.

I have said freedom as well as passion, and I mean to underscore it. Freedom: personal and political. And freedom for Harry Browne as well as for me. I can't tell you Harry Browne would have approved my pronouncing this insight on his behalf, especially in print, but I can tell you what I most deeply believe: that it was and is as true an insight for him as it was and is for me. It is one of the things this book is about. It is one of the most vexing and irreducible things it is about.

Others, even other feminists, perhaps completely understanding that as a writer I could not choose but write this (and having written it, want it to be read), may still think it hollow of me to protest my doing and writing it all in the name of freedom, if, in the end, it is a freedom still defined by love. Love for a man, a man who in this case also dominates my narrative. *Two* men, in fact, the two "fathers" of whom

I beg forgiveness in my dedicatory words. I have no excuses for this. Our lives are what they are. Mine was defined by love, and still is. Almost unbearably so. It has been, in one form or another, from my infancy.

Perhaps I am too hopelessly, too operatically, too radically Italian in this. I will never forget the time my sister-in-law the Italian feminist came back from a meeting of Italian feminists recounting an impassioned discussion on just such a theme: "*Ma, perche li amiamo? Perche continuiamo ad amarli?*"—"Why do we love them? Why do we go on loving them?" I have never heard the question put quite this way among American feminists, who I think might be vaguely embarrassed to expose, not their libidos, but their *hearts* in this way. Let me dare to think that perhaps my book, since it is about love as well as sex, is the more Italian (and Italian American) for this. Perhaps also because it is so centrally about the Church, the patriarchal yet motherly Church, the Church of love bodily and spiritual sitting in the center of that culture, geographically and in every way. Also because it is about how an Italian American woman navigates such conflicted territory here, here in one of the hearts of the diaspora, where Catholic spirituality is no better represented than among *Irish* Catholics. Like Harry Browne.

And finally because, like so much Italian opera, it is about love and politics—the politics of personal love and the politics of collective freedom. It will become obvious to any reader that I believe we live our lives in an ecology of relationships, including historical ones: that this is a definition of politics. That (borrowing from philosopher Emmanuel Levinas) the politics of freedom begins with accepting even the *self* as impossible without responsibility toward what we perceive as irreducibly different. But that we must feel this at the level of emotion as well as of mind.

And so let me also dare invoke the spirits of two women, Olive Schreiner and Simone de Beauvoir—deeply political women *and* writers *and* lovers, neither of them Italian yet both of them my patron saints—as I say this to my readers: I have written my book. I let it go, with all its flaws, into your hands, into your minds and hearts. I have been able to invent no better way to tell my story of spiritual and political freedom, of being a woman between many genders, of being an Italian between many cultures, than to be true to the experience of my own life.

Acknowledgments

A single life is inevitably a compendium of other people's lives, and the history of this book about me is also a history of other people.

Not long after Harry Browne died in 1980, I was approached by a television producer who said I had a good story. Her version was not quite the story I wanted to tell, and so I was determined to tell it myself, but it was then an episode rather than a life—the "Harry book"—and for many years that's what it remained. Thanks to Patrick O'Connor and Charlotte Sheedy, a few sample chapters got me a Macmillan contract. Soon the publishing dragons came and swallowed up whole houses, spewing out better books than mine. Cynthia Merman, then at Atheneum, stood by me, even as they roared and spewed. Joan Brookbank, my new agent, rafted me to safety on the mighty flood that followed. In those tough middle years, the late, magnificent Ellen Moers, pioneering feminist critic and midwife of difficult literary births, inspired me to go on writing, almost literally handing me when she died to her brilliant friend, writer Esther (E. M.) Broner. I bless all these wonderful people for treating me not like a writer-in-the-making, but like a writer.

As the manuscript circulated, and word got out about the story, I don't like to think what went on behind the cupped hands of people who thought it too naughty for their imprint. Rumors abounded of characters like Harry Browne being written into soap operas. I have had an absolutely unbased paranoid fantasy that the New York Archdiocese had a role in thwarting the book's publication at some point. But when a spate of new books appeared in the early 1990s about priests and women, when Annie Murphy became a celebrity, calling a scoundrel a scoundrel and proud of it, it seemed to a lot of people that "it" had been done, whatever "it" was. My contract had already died, a blessed death, as I see it now. For just as the TV producer's story was not my story so neither was Annie Murphy's or any of the other variant voices of women with priests that enjoyed their brief *succès de scandale* at the time.

Had it not been for Julia Cameron's *The Artist's Way* (because it is clearly the artist's way to have a certain necessary chutzpah) I would not have approached The Feminist Press. Had it not been for Florence Howe and The Feminist Press's Cross-Cultural Memoir Series, the story might never have been expanded into the fuller "life" it is now. If not for my editor, Jean Casella, it would never have become a "life" that I feel even tremulously proud to have written. I have told her that no one reading me has ever been so intuitive about what I intended to say and do, that when she could not see through my verbal impasses she always, *always,* inspired me to write my way out of them. Now I get to tell her in print. And to apologize for the weaknesses in me that in the end set the limit to how much better a book she could make it. As for the other Press staff, I thank them for all the care, the meticulousness and beauty, of their work, and for being part of a mission to *understand* women's writing, as well as to keep it alive and in print.

Ramapo College, its administrators and sabbatical and research committees, were an inevitable part of the process, giving me small amounts of released time—never enough of course! But they meant well and I am grateful. And I don't know who I would be if it weren't for the intellectual freedom to be who I am and have been there, or the wonderful colleagues I have lived with and loved in the School of Social Science over the years, especially Patricia Hunt-Perry, friend and soulmate across a single office divider wall. It was she who put my story up with much better peoples' in a lecture series called "My Life is My Message" in 1996, and created a turning point in my sense of claim to a life worth having lived, let alone having written. This was clinched by a grant that same year from the Geraldine R. Dodge Foundation to spend a month of blissful Vermont time writing, and being well-fed and lionized, at the Vermont Studio Center. They have a lot to answer for.

I want to thank the many people who, having loved Harry Browne and vividly remembered the West Side scene in the sixties when I interviewed them in the eighties, launched heartily into stories that have enriched the book, especially Dr. Marvin Belsky, Mike Coffey, Monsignor Jack Egan, Father Tom Farrelly, Fred Johnson, Father Phil Murnion, and the delicious and incomparable Esta Kransdorf (Armstrong). Esta died suddenly in 1995, a shock that darkened a host of lives, and lost me my wisest and most discerning reader.

Then there are my three children, Harry, Chris, and Nina, who jestingly refer to themselves as "spawn of Satan"—or the funniest and witchiest of them does, and cracks up the other two. Also their wonderful partners, Imelda, Rebecca, and Carl, who have stood by them as they stood by me. I still don't get how they did it, all of them. How they not only let me go on writing like this, for what seems decades, but rooted for me, boasted about me, casting the movie at least three different times. Thanks to the rest of my family, especially my darling sister Ann (whose poignant roses illuminate these pages), for bearing all this self-indulgent revelation—so far as they have borne it. I think they know the worst is yet to come. My husband Sandy does too, and it seems almost presumptuous of me to say thanks for a love that has already survived tests of trust and courage that would wither lesser men, and will have to survive more.

Finally, unutterable gratitude to all the people who have ever loved me in my life, my parents, my relatives, here, and there, my wonderful, devoted students, my friends, those I still have and those I have lost. And to all the artists and writers who have ever made it possible for me to think of myself as an artist and a writer.

Part One

TOSCA

1

The room I slept in as a girl stood high above the down-sloping green of what then seemed a great stretch of lawn at the arrowhead intersection of Sickles Avenue and Sickles Place. The room frames itself in my memory as a kind of Bluebeard's tower, which I happened also to share, like the troubled heroine of that tale, with my younger sister Ann. Its two small casement windows faced north-northeast, and beneath the more easterly window, as winter dawn faintly grayed the sky, I can remember two shivering girls hugging the steel fins of the radiator for a warmth that existed only in memory or desire, praying desperately that it might heat up faster, wishing the furnace had not been so completely shut down, as it was every winter night no matter how bitter, by some iron economic hand.

It was through the thinnish walls of this room that I first heard the mingled groans of my parents' lovemaking. I think I did not yet know what the sound meant, for I remember praying when my mother cried out that she was not being hurt, and striving to suppress the surge of fear and anger that welled up against my father. And yet it was here, not so many dark nights later, that I was to discover the secret pleasures of my own body, as my exploring hand rode its smooth, new swales and warm grooves to a bliss I could not believe I owned—until a car headlight might blaze a sudden dazzling track of light across the black ceiling, and my sister, alarmed by my shallow breathing, might whisper, "Are you sick?" across the ten feet between our beds, and I whisper back that no, I was fine, and drop off to sleep like a stone.

It was here, too, on a deep winter's night, amid whoops and squeals that rang like a carillon of bells off the icy street below my window, that an episode of my lonely teenage melodrama played itself out by streetlight as Knowledge dropped straight from the Tree: Janet, who lived two houses away and had been my dearest friend of summer, companion of every Glen Island beach day, whispering secret sharer of the strange, disquieting girl-mystery of the soul kiss, had given the New Year's Eve party she had promised after all, and had not invited me.

Janet's abandonment somehow awoke me to a peculiar aloneness that inspired one of my earliest stories, even to its closure with the shattering sound of the window blinds as they fell on the street scene of my wounded gaze. And I can remember thinking even then, at the raw age of fifteen, that, for better or worse, bitter or sweeter, the art of storytelling for me was going to be the art of telling the truth—meaning not, in the Aristotelian way, what *might* have happened, but what did. I could not tell tales, as others told, no matter how much I might envy the gift. Life as it came, as it unspooled itself in the newsreel of my mind, was like a script already written, already relentlessly *storied*, needing almost no touch of art except to find its intrinsic, if hidden, shape. This was a handicap at first, when "creativity" seemed by textbook definition to demand fantasy and invention, and I had convinced myself that to be a *true* artist I had to resist what came too easy and too unearned. Soon, by varying degrees of willing suspension, of wise passiveness, of acceptance of whatever gift was mine, learned or unlearned, earned or unearned, I let go of true art and allowed the storied universe to seem, to be, ever more compellingly, wonderfully, mystically what it was, what it had always been, to me.

I had not always lived in a tower. Rather, in the manner of some of those fantastic invented tales, I had been somewhat thrown out into the world—a world whose ever-widening rings started from the little earthly paradise of New Rochelle, third stop on the commuter rail lines through the Westchester suburbs of New York City. Third child, first girl, born not in hospital but in an apartment above my father's North Avenue meat market, I had been given to the light (as Italians say), all eight pounds of dark flesh and thick, curling black hair, on a burning day in mid-May 1935 that my mother always remembered as first sign of an insufferably hot summer.

My father, his *macho* secured by the prior birth of two *figli maschi*, made me his darling. They tell me that the love I returned nearly cost me my life. One day, thinking I heard the sputtering sound of his truck in the driveway and passionately eager to see him, I leaned out the window against an unhitched screen and fell two stories to the graveled pavement. My parents guessed that my fall had been broken by a cable about twelve feet from the ground, otherwise there was no imagining how I had survived it. Like Ancient Mariners they told and retold this story, astonished that the gods had not punished their neglect, astonished at my remembering nothing of it, and even more by what followed—that while the doctor, who had taken them aside, was hushedly informing them that I might never walk again, I clambered down off the examining table and limped into view. The story was meant to illustrate the arrogant simplicity of medical men in the clear presence of miracles, but telling it again and again also had a way of confirming for them that I was still alive, with every promise of leading a charmed life.

I was then two and a half years old. Six months later my sister was born, and the family set was complete. For several years we had been moving in that clambering way of immigrant strivers from apartment to bigger apartment to rented house, until we settled at last into mortgaged possession of a semidetached stucco on that oddly pointed corner, which seemed to nose its way gingerly out of New Rochelle's sprawling Little Italy, hurry past a rather interesting black neighborhood of setback houses with great Victorian porches, and tend vaguely in the direction of Scarsdale, which our Italian neighbors described very simply as "where the rich people live."

My two older brothers, Louis (whom my parents called Luigi or Luigino and we kids called simply Lou) and Carlo, had been born in Italian East Harlem, my newlywed parents having rented their first apartment from Grandpa Spagnola, my mother's father, who owned flanking buildings at 228 and 230 114th Street, just east of the Third Avenue El. My mother, Maria, born on Cherry Street on the Lower East Side, was already a veteran of several successive Little Italys before she met my father, Mario —she leaning out of the parental window one fine Mother's Day Sunday, he passing below, one single smoldering glance firing a romance that lasted nearly seventy years.

Like me, she had also been a third child, but third of ten, eight of them girls, the second daughter, but first to marry—so deep a violation of Sicilian protocol that it required the formal dispensation of her beloved father, who could refuse her nothing. But what a catch Mario must have seemed: flagrantly, darkly handsome, *very* Valentino, a decorated former officer in the Italian army, veteran of the Alto Adige campaign in the First World War, who had fought among Gabriele D'Annunzio's handpicked company of *arditi*— "the ardent ones." She, for her part, was an Arabian princess. He had been caught unwillingly in the dark thickets of her hair; her steady unwavering black eyes had bewitched his soul. But, truly, her love for Mario was master, and it was she who had been bewitched, she who was opening the long saga of Spagnola women and their fatal need for beautiful men.

And yet neither the mastery of that love, nor, when they finally left Harlem, the distance up the Boston Post Road to Westchester, could keep her from her father, and from the familiar Sicilian noise and grand passions of her home place and its glorious community of women, still everything to the girl in her. And so her world opened to me on Sundays, as we made our way back to East Harlem to visit, filling the afternoons with street music and Italian ices and stoop game pleasures overseen by a bevy of protective young aunts, until we turned sleepily homeward, blanket-wrapped, at night. Other Sundays belonged to the satellite of my father's family, who came together in the tiny rented flat of his adoring younger sister, Carmelina, on East 78th Street, above their own market. Somehow, even as children, we knew the difference between the two families with a deep tribal knowledge—that they were *Napolidaan*, not *Zeechilyaan* like my mother, and that darkly hinted hostilities lay between them, so unfathomable, so natural and perfect, so ancient, as to preclude any search, then, into their origin.

Aunt Carmelina—Zi' Carme'—was married to Uncle Sam, a sour, reclusive hulk of a man. There was this paradox about him: that though he spoke little English, there seemed to be no Italian version of his name, only that ironic appropriation of this essence of his adopted America. A boyhood hunting accident in Italy had left him with a disfiguring puncture scar in his throat, just below his jaw, and seemed to have taken a piece of his soul. He drank silently, heavily, broodingly. Yet he had an uncanny gentleness with children, like some cowardly Italian lion, and we forgave him his wound and his brutish misery. My aunt was his first cousin, a fact as normal to our kinship consciousness as the mountains of cutlets and plump, homemade ravioli on the dinner table. Their two daughters, Gloria and Gioia (whose names I think Sam had had no part in choosing), were close in age to my sister and me, and our ritual visits in good weather usually began with Carmelina lining the big iron grid of the fire escape like a birdcage with stretches of wrapping paper from the store and setting the four of us good little girls amid the basil pots, twelve feet up from the boys' noisy ball games in the street, to dress and undress our dolls.

To us it was in its way a wild zone—an outside place perilously free—and at the same time a private box on a secret family opera playing inside. Against the big window frame hung a real birdcage, my aunt's bright yellow canary catching and trilling the breeze. In the near distance, her bedroom was paved almost to the walls with a single and enormous *letto matrimoniale* whose intricately knotted white chenille bedspread we were warned never to mark with our shoes. And beyond the bed, from out of the dim interior light of the parlor, drummed the deep voices of the men hunched over the dining table, two wine carafes set in the midst of its embroidered linen expanse, the table so leafed-out to capacity that there was barely space to pass through the room. The women exploded at intervals from the crowded galley kitchen like tambourines, and then the murmuring drums would start again, *adagio*, and then the deep clunking sound of large pots, and then another high-pitched explosion, *molto allegro*, bringing up a grand finale of laughter and ringing glass. Out of this rolling musical noise would now and then come a warning burst in the direction of the window—"*State attente!*"—sign that we were, after all, being watched. And always, out of the heart of that little inner room, out of the very heat of their bodies, they seemed to pump an exquisitely killing perfume of wine and food, the scent pouring out to us on the interchange of air and driving us mad with hunger.

These few rather surreal flashbacks of early childhood memory divide themselves irrevocably from almost everything else I remember about the house in New Rochelle—the sequestered girlhood, the room like Bluebeard's tower—all of which comes from a later time. For abruptly, when I was not quite six, in the most extraordinary, sequence-rupturing episode of my mobile young life, we moved for three years to Tucson, Arizona, forsaking all grandfathers and uncles and sisters and cousins and aunts—with one, single delicious exception, which I shall save for its place.

I call attention to this zigzag of my narrative not just because disruption—displacement—became part of the essence of its meaning, but because out of these jagged and episodic fractures of my childhood there arose mysteries of self-making only to be recaptured by piecing them more curiously together. For this first rupturing move west was followed, about three years later, by another rupturing move east again, creating in its turn another two-year interim when we actually lived in East Harlem, before we reclaimed our New Rochelle house.

Or five of us did, which made it perhaps not just an interim but an interregnum. My father had been taken seriously and rather mysteriously ill out west, had been carried east by train only to be shifted from hospital to hospital and nursing home to nursing home in what seemed to my child mind an endless, baffling captivity. These were hard times, and family on both sides sustained us. For work my mother relied on my father's father, who owned a pork store just below the 116th Street station of the Third Avenue El. For a place to live she relied on her Sicilian family, moving into a fifth floor railroad flat in the old 114th Street tenement on whose stoop I had first learned to climb stairs, in the giggling aura of my young aunts.

By now these same fecund Spagnola girls had burst like novas into galaxies of family, filling the building, rattling it with the noise of children clattering and howling, of all eight of the sisters baying to one another up and down a stairwell that echoed like a silo—*Terrreeee-saaa! Carrrmeeee-laaa!*—tearing it apart with screaming family fights and sulking, neurasthenic silences and seaming it together again with the paradisal smells of eggplant and fennel sausage and red bell peppers darkly roasted over a gas flame.

It was a strange two-year matriarchate. I remember it as a wonderfully liberated time—though freedom for a prepubescent Italian girl-child, even *senza padre,* is a very relative thing, and we lived after all on the topmost floor, up (or down) four steep and daunting flights, past the doorways of all my aunts. And yet at ten years old I traveled the New York subways unchaperoned, attending theory classes at the Manhattan School of Music (because my mother, bless her, thought I was a piano prodigy), going to libraries (because she said I could read anything in print), visiting art museums (because I was already so amazingly clever with pencil and brush, clearly an artist, like my father), all of it on my own; and finally, just before we moved back to Westchester, beginning seventh grade at a rather toney junior high school to which (she would announce proudly to her customers) I had been selectively admitted by a *very* competitive entry exam, all of it her doing: she had taken me by the hand and trotted me down there, to the tests.

Even amid this curious freedom I sometimes think I took a kind of room with me, a room of my own, wherever I went—a safe, dark, inner space from which I peered unseen. Then, however, this inner room seemed much less tower than sanctuary, rather like the tiny room my sister and I shared in that top-floor apartment, one of five strung out, front to back, just like the railway cars such flats were named for—or better, as we thought, like beads on a rosary. It, too, had its little inner shrine to Motherhood, mirroring our matriarchal real-life, an *imago* that stood watch on the horizon of my daring but did not stand in its way. Their common symbol was a framed holy picture that hung on our bedroom wall, not a traditional Mother Mary with her boy-baby Jesus, but an icon of Mary's own mother, St. Ann, patron saint of childbirth (for whom my sister had been named), with a young Mary, still a girl-child and still the apple of her own mother's eye.

It was not a lovely work of art. I am amazed, as I recall it again, not to have been alarmed by the cadaverous pallor of St. Ann's face or felt my nascent artistic conscience disturbed by the acid green of her gown. But I was not alarmed or disturbed by these any more than by the drooping eyelids and elevated fingertips of her too-teacherly style of mothering. Maybe I saw myself as the absorbed and enchanted Mary, her child face and eyes turned softly upward, grateful to be chided by such a mother. And yet who knows what secret ambition might have tied me to the mother and her power to chide?

Why do I love to remember this time, this symbolic little room, this cell, so spartan and small, and, because it was next down from the front bedroom where my mother slept, so utterly lacking in privacy? Not only did it place us under her eye as we slept, but she could, and did, pass through it at will, at any hour. It had steel-frame bunk beds, a single chest of drawers my sister and I shared, and a small vanity table and mirror. Before this mirror we plaited our thick Italian hair, when she, She-Who-Must-Be-Obeyed, too overstretched at last, admitted that taming its copious, insurrectionary masses was something we must do for ourselves. Hair, after all, had to be disciplined, at least as much as our budding girlhoods did, perhaps (if measured against unchaperoned subway miles) more. And so Ann and I learned upon each other the fine art of weaving braids: the two small braids along the side, first, out and away from the temples, and then, swiftly, lest these shoot recalcitrantly back into stray hair, the small braids folded into two long, large braids at the back. Gleams of gold and russet threaded our dark brown girlhood hair in those days, both of us having had three years' bleaching in the desert sun. But mine was always coarser and darker than Ann's, and as we grew older, darker still. We can still tell the difference between the braids we cut off when we were finally bobbed, which both of us have preserved like surrogate virginities ever since.

They say our mothers, no matter how loving, elude us. They say it is the reason there is desire. I know there were times I reached for mine and caught air. She had once, of course, defined what someone has called the semiotic fluid of pre-Oedipal childhood, the very force field of life—life without definition or boundary, open, exposed, a meadow, a street, a door, a window into the sky—when experience still had no other place than *She*, no sacred space shielded from her passion or hurt or kisses or rages, which were all the daily bread and trespasses we understood; when *Mother* was no separate *She* but the *Mamma* who trembled between life and death if you had a fever and swooned if you fell and cracked a millimeter of skin; when *She* was in fact not even she alone but the collective *Mater Dolorosa* of motherly aunts and cousins, shrieking and weeping and biting into the fat of their thumbs when you were bad, as if they could punish your infant crimes on their own flesh, out of their own salt.

I speak now of the after-Mother, the woman herself, the woman I knew and did not know and would never know, who seemed always in flight—working, making, finishing the forever-unfinished—always doing some relentless god's or sorcerer's bidding, darting and flashing like an Ariel or a hummingbird. One memory print of her survives where she is still—fixed—and my own eye is the camera: Arizona, our first brief foray, and she is merely paralyzed with lonely grief to be there without my father.

Otherwise there remains nothing but photographs to read her fugitive meaning by. Cleaning house once, probably in the years when we were both in college, my sister and I discovered a cache of them, buried for so long and in such seeming secrecy we had to read them like archeologists. We guessed that my father had taken them soon after Ann was born, my mother's most difficult birth. It had been part of the family lore my brothers knew (and with arrogant, cruel intention would frequently repeat to my sister) that our mother had bled for weeks, that she had nearly died. Thus the pleaded intercession of St. Ann and the elevation to household saint, the rosaries, the novenas, the reverence of naming.

And now, oddly, out of the memory of these pictures, like the sudden opening of a shutter, vivid and black, springs a glimpse out of my earliest and most elusive childhood memory: a big, cold house where my brothers and I are briefly in institutional care—a misery of children, a distant pond, a few pale and unfriendly ducklings, a gigantic, white-tiled washroom in which I am somehow unaccountably alone, a sense of something overwhelming in the hugeness and strangeness of its seeming abandonment.

Surely these pictures had been taken then, when she was too ill to care for us herself. Perhaps the doctors had told my father she was dying. It seems very Italian— almost a cliché of Italianness—to think of the camera as a kind of window standing in death's way. I see a lifetime of family funerals, a gallery of memorial card photo images, each with its gauzy airbrushed halo, and it defines a sense scored so deep that even now a part of me knows mortality to be the true, secret meaning of pictures.

But these were not clichés, and I think now that in this way, as in many others, Italy had marked Mario differently. For he once told us that he had been trained to use his first camera as a soldier in the field, imaging the carnage of war, and now, perhaps, in the face of *this* possible death—this mortal life bleeding itself away—he was utterly beyond any cliché of mortality as defined by the burial crypt. Here the lens that sees also holds, refuses to let go. It is become his own prosthetic will, obsessive, prurient, probing a deeper mystery than fear, even than death, taking my mother's body at curious, artful, languorous angles, revealing her, carnal and silken and voluptuous even in the surrender of her suffering. These are pictures of *Maria*, shameless declarations of renewed passion, and the very violence of their intimacy transcends death, as does their willful insistence that the camera transmute her pain into beauty. Against the pallor of her cheeks he has chosen to see her ever-sad soft dark eyes as smudges of wet charcoal, her hair like Salome's, streaming black blood upon the pillow.

Accidental voyeurs, we could not refuse the messages of secret sin and penance that had been coded into these images. Nor could we unravel them. Why our mother would have wanted to die we didn't know, but there was something—a dumb withdrawal, a recoil even in her acquiescence—that said to us she did. And yet what might these same images we were looking upon now have said to her when she first saw them? What life-affirming passionate obsession did she read into the urgency with which Mario took them in such relentless and unaccountable numbers? Did they make her want to live, the warrant of something still lovely she thought she had lost?

Reading these signs years after, Maria's daughters, too, still young and unwise, wanted to live for Love. We imagined Maria our sister somehow, rising from that sickbed with her faith renewed in the image of a Love as imperious as Tosca's, a Love Dante had made so commanding that the beloved could never withhold her own in return.

And so we imagined Maria wrapping her shapely figure in thick woolens again, sacrificing day after day again, on her feet in the chill-cold North Avenue market, in that market filled with the fragrant stinks of cheeses and salt meats and damp saw-dust, with its dark pinecones still clutching their nuts like fists, with its intoxicat-ing scents of oranges in winter and of Christmas anise. She helped lift the huge, steaming sides of beef onto storage hooks in the icebox. She candled eggs in the back room till her eyes seemed to melt into her head. At the front counter she forced her-self to smile the shopkeeper's winning smile. And, oh, it was a sweet smile, they said, none sweeter, so winsome and large it transformed her melancholy face.

But still there were ominous forecasts about her breaking health. In the morn-ings she wept, we could hear her weeping, her arthritic joints ached so, and the lim-ited safety of the child who knows fear seemed to have been made more fearful.

Surely from the baseline of my infancy there had been some intuition of the mys-teriously twining roots of love and pain, even love and death. Hadn't I been marked for both when I'd been named for my mother's mother, who had died the year before I was born? In a family that deeply respected the age-old privilege of the father to name the first girl-child after *his* mother (in this case, Immacolata, the grandmother living in Italy), such encoding of the memory of my dead Sicilian grandmother into my life bore almost unintelligible significance. It also happens to have spared me a lifetime symbolically blazoned with the inviolate sex of the Madonna—a name which, in any case, was decorously tacked on at my christen-ing. Of course even "Flavia" was a cross for an American child to bear, and after about eleven years of it I cried bitter tears, begging my mother to let me give myself anoth-er name. My father had changed his—he had told us so—when as a young officer his true first name of Salvatore had made him a hayseed to the more genteel of his comrades. But my mother had told me then about her mother, how good she had been, if stern, and wise and clever besides, and said, "You will come to love your name." And I did, if not entirely for her sake.

But I had also been only five when my grandfather, my mother's father, died of a stroke, a bitter wound to the heart of child love. He was Calogero, a name even more comical to the ear of Italian fashion than my father's Salvatore, and as distinctly Sicilian as the sweet wine he made every fall and drank through a winter of Sundays with his card-playing cronies, keeping an ever tighter grip on the bottle and the deck. He had made much of us, his first grandchildren, and we had adored his dry and wist-ful humor, doled out with mysterious pennies in a cunning sleight-of-hand and accom-panied by tickles of his peppery handlebar mustache, which he wore wickedly curled and waxed to a fine arabesque.

His death had been sudden, and catastrophic. Their Mamma gone, he had become everything to his girls. They held his wake at home, as families did then, on the par-lor floor of the very tenement that stood as the congealed sweat of his stonema-son's brow. He had been foreman, my mother loved to remind us, on the construction crew of the Saw Mill River Parkway—one of the country's first grand, tree-lined parkways, which ran through the Bronx and Westchester. He had stood up to the mafiosi in the protection racket when he ran a grocery store on East 106th Street, and she, his Mary, who had thrown herself in the way when they shot him, the bullet just whizzing past her shoulder—who in that moment had become his most precious treasure—had never wanted him out of her sight.

What useless flotsam we four children had suddenly become on the flood of his daughters' primitive, tidal grief. Years later, as often as I read of the women of Troy mourning Priam in the fiery collapse of the ancient city, I would see a darkened front room eerily lit with flaming candles and enwrapped in a velvety embrasure of white flowers, a father's poor work-worn body lying still and straight amid the waving silhouettes of his daughters, their shrieking voices strung into one great piercing wail of anguish. I can still hear them, still see myself sobbing, in empathy and terror, in the room where the dark winter coats are mounded, until some pitying aunt takes me in her arms. To this day the scent of gardenias makes me want to faint.

Her father's death seemed to have become a turning point for Maria, who, sick in heart and body, had for a moment felt the meaning of her family gone. This was true for Mario as well. The terrible war had just begun, abruptly cutting off everyone here who still felt rooted in Italy from everyone still left behind. No one could go there, no one could leave there. One day, they said, Immacolata had delayed getting away. One little day!—someone was sick, she could not go so quickly—and the gate had shut like iron. Husband and wife, mother and children, were condemned to live out the war apart.

It was a moment of cruel poise between past and future. Or so it seemed, for how else could we explain the mystery of this sudden wrenching change, this cruel tearing apart of everything to go thousands of miles across the continent? If, as time went on, we began to understand it differently—to see something perhaps more ominous than beautiful at the passionate heart of those old photographs, something less unasked for than death in the urge to fly, less liberating than the will to take courage and move on—it was not because what we believed then and still in part believe was less believable: that the east seemed cold and insidiously full of hurt, that the west seemed bright and beckoning, that each of my parents, out of tender deference to the other, longed to seek the cure of the sun like amputees cauterizing each other's wounds.

But whatever it was to them, this is what it was to me: the journey that altered, ever after, the way I read the universe.

2

Mario stayed behind to sell the fixtures in the North Avenue market; Maria packed us four for the scouting trip westward, and we headed to Tucson by train to search out a place to live. I remember my sister and me hugging the window seats, watching the states unroll beside us like a vast cloth on which the feast of America was spread, cupping our hands at night against the glass until our eyes ached, sleeping curled together in our plush seats (which felt like little rooms and smelled close and spongy) as the hum and click of the track set the rhythm of our heartbeats. I remember stepping off the train four days and nights later into the freshness of early morning Tucson amid a sweeping surround of sun and cactus. I felt as if I had been suddenly given the sky.

But Maria did not see sky. Faced with the four of us amid the stark green walls of a room in a motor court, she had discovered the limits of her bravado. Stopped in full flight, she lay plunk as a sopped towel in an armchair, the tears bleeding silently down her face, while we stood with our stupefied big-baby eyes frozen beside her.

Within days we were rattling again across the prairies, switching in Chicago to the Rock Island Rocket, blazing like a railroad movie into Grand Central Station, where Maria and Mario, in whose orbit of passion we lived and moved, turned the roar on the platform into a *crescendo appassionato,* and fell into each other's arms.

But for Mario there could be no stopping now, no changing, no turning back, whatever Maria's misgivings. He had never turned back, not since he'd left Sperone, not since the day in 1921 when, in a driving rain, he had stepped onto the ship in Santa Lucia, his beloved Naples behind him, drenched in the national grief of Enrico Caruso's funeral. Within weeks, we were packed and ready, on the road like Okies, all the stuff we could fit piled into an old Dodge and a pickup. And still my mother amazed us, driving a truck. We had never seen a woman drive a truck.

Spelling them both at the wheel was a friend who had joined them for the journey, Joe Detta, a tailor from New York, *paesano,* exhilarated like Mario by the romance of moving on. Joe was about my father's age, smart, lean, hardhanded. He was a kind of immigrant Tom Joad, no wife, no kids, just a caring anarchist heart and a pure, clean passion for the road. I know he struck out for parts even farther west soon after we arrived in Tucson. Throughout our marvelous journey, even if we called him Uncle Joe for respect, we privately invoked him as "JoeDetta," in one single, magical word. He stars in some of my vividest recollections of our first days in the Arizona desert, pointing the way like a shaman to the secrets of our astonishing new moonscape.

Above all else, that journey taught us the authority of the continent. We might pretend that we had conquered every mile as we went, but the truth was that we had also humbly yielded it up again behind us. It took our little caravan about two weeks to cross the country, counted out in Route 66 telegraph poles and Burma Shave signs with messages we kids memorized frame by frame and sang out in competitive ecstasy from the back of the car before we even got close enough to read them. Every night we seemed to drop into the very same E-Z Rest Motor Court with the railroad tracks alongside, the same fifty-five-car freight train passing at four every morning. There was the occasional wayside farmhouse that obligingly took guests, where breakfast was a full-course meal around an immense table, already surrounded by men in dungarees with the size and appetites of giants, who would gently help us load our plates from enormous bowls of potatoes and grits and chuckle about how four little kids could really eat.

Food was in every sense enormous that trip—a pure revelation of strangeness from day to day, like space itself, which seemed to have taken on a fourth dimension. I couldn't have known the metaphysics I was in the presence of; I knew only that there was something about earth and sky both perpetual and friendless. I can remember waking up in the truck after nightfall, on a black stretch of barren Texas prairie somewhere east of El Paso, to see Dad and JoeDetta wrestling some huge thing in a ditch alongside the road, my brothers standing by, their faces lit with wonder in the circle of pink and orange light thrown by a crude fire, and my mother, behind them, lit with a fainter glow, watching with shaded eyes, unmoving. Ann still slept beside me.

The boys toiled up the embankment to tell me with a hush of excitement that it was a steer the men had just pulled, torn and bleeding, off the roadside barbed wire, a fence that had for hundreds of miles marked the impassable boundary between ranch and road. A butcher's child, I could not yet hate this work by which my father lived, but I was at once captivated and bewildered by the almost wordless rhythm of the hard teamwork of butchering, which I had never yet been permitted to see. Survival seemed suddenly to be more amazing, extreme, and violent than I had ever imagined. For a few days after, we bypassed the Bar-B-Q stands and ate our well-carved sirloins over open campfires like the privileged children we were, digesting the ambiguities of meat and meaning together.

JoeDetta had a way of making freedom and love seem like nothing more than your plain two hands. He waited to move on until we'd found a little rented bungalow off the main road south of Tucson, hanging on maybe a month or so until we were settled, repairing the truck's broken axle and hunting wild quail and bringing a brace back for supper, all with that innocent, unthankable air of doing what needed doing. He taught us about the stars, when the sky that had hung so bright and hot and close all day seemed to curve indifferently away from us at night like a great black dome pricked with light holes.

The older three of us had started school (albeit reluctantly, sorry to leave the day school of JoeDetta) at a little two-room schoolhouse out beyond the desert flats, and were coming back from our first day when he met us at the porch, little wide-eyed Ann beside him. I was full of my first-day story. I had just set my dusty foot on the porch step, ready to announce that the teacher had said I counted so well I could move one row over to the second grade, when Joe said he'd killed a rattlesnake, and did we want to see it?

We'd been warned about rattlers; it was their desert, really. But none of us had actually seen or heard one, and we followed him eagerly, fearlessly, as we always did, and the instant he said, "There," we froze. Out of the brush came the chattering sound we'd been told of, and my first thought was that the creature Joe had killed had miraculously come back—the desert, to me, already full of miracles enough for such a thing—but no, there lay the dead snake, flat in the footpath. What we'd heard was another, a second one, and then we saw it, magnificently coiled and arched and hissing noisily two or three yards away, poised to strike if anyone dared to touch the poor dead thing lying stiff and papery in the dust. "She's his mate," Joe whispered simply, laying a firm hand on my arm, and we backed away, leaving the dead snake untouched.

I did not ask how he knew, or how he knew she was a she. JoeDetta knew such things, and the tone of sorrow and tenderness in his voice became a key, unlocking the snakey universe and all its tragedies forever.

Tucson, in those days, still at least a decade away from the Sun Belt, was nothing more than a cow town with a college. It had had its moment of Depression-era fame, when the Feds had caught Dillinger there in a famous bank-robbing shootout. That was before he'd become Public Enemy Number One, while he still had a grip on the popular mind as an outlaw hero. For us—as for him, I suppose—it was still the romantic Wild West, its few dusty intersections lying open to the unguarded chances of fate and adventure. But the romance had its menace. Around us stretched a bleak sand sea, harsh and hostile, the tall saguaro cactus marching away in files like an occupying army to a vanishing point in the flanks of the Catalina Mountains. And everything—and everyone—on this earth, under this new and inexorable sun, seemed blond or blonding: the houses built of adobe sand cakes, the tin-roofed cement squats hunkered down beside the runoff ditches along the roads, the roads themselves, the tanned hills holding up the sky like mounds of cornflakes, even the crouching little cacti looking bleached and crisp, disguising their pulpy innards. Only we were not blond, and the Chicanos, and the Indians who sought shaded street corners from which to sell their wares, the bracelets I loved that tumbled in rippling rivers of blue and silver across their blankets.

Was I feeling what my father felt? Ten years before this westward trek, the already reinvented Mario Salvatore had invented himself again as an American. Proud, even smug in the faintly accented but flawless grammar of his American English, he had become a citizen with the zeal of a newly baptized convert entering the Church. Everything—his studied knowledge of American politics, his dedication to Republican self-reliance, even his devotion to baseball—had seemed preparation for a future symbolized by the Golden West, had made the troubles of the Old World seem ancient and inconsequential.

And then Mussolini dragged Italy into the war on the Axis side and Mario felt the shame he couldn't escape. Even his shoulder hurt again, where the shrapnel still lodged from the Alto Adige campaign. Digging in, he declared himself an American, and went to a nearby defense plant looking for work. And now, after fifteen years proving he wasn't *gangster, anarchist, mafioso, wop*, he was suddenly *belligerent, enemy alien*—new names to cut him with like a steer in the barbed wire. So much for the America of the beckoning future. He took up his pen. In righteous anger, in his fine hand and perfect grammar, he wrote his complaint to President Roosevelt. Then he went on, uncertainly tossing about for work. Maria seemed to feel even more displaced. Her naturally shadowed eyes had become deep pools of longing from which he knew tears fell at night in the dark. Should he go back? What was there for him now if he did? In his life-odyssey, you always went forward. Back meant failure. It was closed for him, closed as water.

The two of them schemed about another business they might begin independently, what they had perhaps hoped to do from the start. For a time he found work in town with a prosperous grocer who seemed to understand his plight. Afternoons, my mother would sometimes pile us into the truck and take us to visit him. We would prowl the store while she shopped, slipping comic books stealthily from the racks and sneaking off to read them because it was something he hated to see us do.

The day waned, the palm trees cast long shadows across the tiled front plaza. I waited eagerly for his workday to be done, sitting on a low little wall and watching him, the prince of my Oedipal romance, pushing the day's dust across the pink herringbone bricks with a long-handled broom.

I think it must have been then, more than ever, that he began to dream of Italy again—of mother, motherland, mother tongue—dreams that both salved and corroded his heart. We must learn to speak Italian, he told us. He schooled us with proper little black-and-white-bound composition books for vocabulary and verbs, and burst into rages when we came to our drills reluctant or unprepared. My mother would gladly have done this, and spared him by teaching us herself—she loved to teach—but no, her Italian was a despised Sicilian dialect bastardized by a generation in New York. She sewed instead, cocking an ear to our stormy lessons and attacking her machine more zealously than ever. A superb dressmaker, she had once vaulted to principal draper for Bergdorf Goodman in the palmy career days before her marriage. Now she had begun quietly to sell her sophisticated skills altering fine clothes for the wives of the rancher gentry.

And it was then that my father's Italy became a place imprinted on the platen of my soul. Forever after this, to go there meant a return somehow to a place already known and loved, a place we might have danced to on the airs of his cherished operas. His lessons were not always harsh. Sometimes he would forget to drill us and fill an hour instead with tales of home. He was a storyteller born. In a single sensual gesture of language or a hand lightly playing on the air, he could catch just that icy freshness of spring water in the heat of summer, the cool of overhanging chestnut trees, the burst of a succulent fig on the tongue, the scorch-scent of pinecones tossed on the fire to release their pearly nuts, the majesty of a long, snaking procession-al to the shrine at Montevergine as the village begged the Blessed Mother to inter-cede in illness or war. He could remember climbing the well-ribbed flank of Vesuvius to peer into her churning mouth, and he laid his boyish fear and courage on our hearts.

He would tell us about how it had been to be the first of fourteen children, run out of fingers counting them. Fourteen! I could not imagine being one of fourteen, when to be one of four already seemed so many. And he had not even been the first. Two infants had died before him. The wise women of his village had told his moth-er, the beautiful grandmother we had never known, that she'd lost them because she was too tender and hovering, too protective. *"Lascialo andá!"*—"Let him go!" they'd admonished her whenever he pressed his rubbery baby legs into her lap, eager to fly. And so, he said, she had finally "tossed him into the road" as soon as he could crawl, and he laughed, as if to say, "And so you see, now!" And so we saw.

And how proud he was of me, his smartest girl, when I said my Italian vowels roundly, and rolled my *r*s (and yet it came so easily to me!). How enchanting he was when he wasn't angry or dull or withdrawn into his grief, or boiling with some scheme that would pave his way—and ours—with gold. So I could not separate him from Italy or from love, the unresisting love of a girl-child for her father's sorrowing eyes.

But fuse that love with fear, even fear of love—a fusion like those wax images sealed between two disks of glass one sometimes sees in collections of Roman antiquities, the mysterious art that once welded them together now completely lost.

I am eight, and in love. It is dinnertime; the family is gathered around the table. Outside our house, in the yard, I know there is a desert wind rustling the cot-tonwood trees, but I can barely hear it because my brothers are taunting me, demanding that I tell the name of the boy I love. They do not mean this to torment me only. My father is already scowling. We cannot tell which of us is wounding his dark olive eyes.

The boy I love is not dark. He is as white and gold as moonlight on sand. Even his name is white: *Charlie White*. I tell it over to myself secretly, like a spell.

My father calls me to him after supper. "Who is this boy you love at school?" he asks, with just that crucifying touch of scorn on the word *love*. But the name fights back. It is as though there is a danger in my mouth, and only the whitest white silence can protect it.

"Tell me his name," he says. All gentleness has been emptied from his voice, and he says, "If you won't tell, you must never speak to me again." I know this is a game. I look at him, astonished, trying to find the playful message in his face, in a twitch of mouth or eyebrow. But I am thinking, I cannot tell, and you cannot mean to shut me away with your silence—not for such a little thing! His indifference is enthralling. Near him in the dark, I read every curve of his body hungrily for a sign. I wish I had his pen now; I could so easily draw the face outlined by lamplight, the sinuous line easily embracing the fine, sad profile, the black hair silvering above the shapely ears.

A half hour goes by. It is made of thirty separate and unbearable minutes, I have counted them, and they are forever enough. I go to him, not daring to touch even his sleeve. When he lifts his head and turns it toward me his faraway glance is tender, and a delirious sense of salvation catches at my throat.

I ask him what he is writing. He shows me a letter in Italian, to his sister Irena in Striano, a village near Sperone. I think of Italy, the village, the aunt, his sister, I have never seen, her children, my cousins. But he has not forgotten his warning. "Now you have spoken," he says, with dark and terrible finality. My brain is blinded with disbelief. More than ever now I will not tell him. I am stunned by this new power my father's love has over me, dazed by the superb and violent cunning of his jealousy.

"Write it," he says calmly.

I take the pen from his hand, meaning to resist, but the tip presses itself to the white sheet. I tell myself it is a name, a silly name, *Charlie White*, but in the wind I can hear it fall and see it break into dust and scatter and lose itself among the trees.

Perhaps less guiltily than I later thought he should have, my father began to leave a book about the house, face down to mark his place, a book with a green baize library binding plainly imprinted in white and a straightforward title like *Managing the Squab Farm*, full of line drawings of various pigeon breeds and poor-quality photos exhibiting the layouts of sheds.

All this seemed to go from print to reality like the swift turning of a movie page. We moved from our little bungalow into a bigger one on a rather bald and dusty road, oddly named Fair Oaks Drive. The house itself seemed clattery and somewhat the worse for wear, but it had a pebbled horseshoe driveway in the front, bordered with great, green, shaggy rhododendrons and oleanders that lent it a sheltered look, and in the back, shading the barn and two long rows of tin-roofed pigeon sheds, a majestic phalanx of cottonwood and eucalyptus trees.

Soon enough we children learned of the miracle of bird and egg and how they did increase and multiply, and how suddenly and ruthlessly they died, got plucked, and on the third day were sent off to be eaten. And then it wasn't long before the pigeons were joined by ducks and chickens and turkeys, making an only slightly profitable enterprise slightly more profitable. And since, unlike the pigeons, these forlorn creatures wandered about the yard pecking at the gravel and playfully attacking us, and were as often accused of misdemeanors as we were, we inevitably endeared them with names and made them our friends.

But it was not a playful business. Squab farming was hard and dirty and demanding, and Lou and Carlo were soon recruited into the feeding and cleanup when they were not at school. Eventually the slaughter, too. At first they may have thought it a perverse adventure. But it was brutal work to break the necks of baby birds, and it didn't take long for the ugliness to spread itself, dreary and awful, on their souls. I am amazed to remember how the fall of a single infant sparrow from its nest in the porch roof was a catastrophe the four of us rushed to like a battlefield medical-surgical unit, how we would take turns wrapping it in warmed towels and nursing it with an eyedropper, and when it died, which it always did, bury it in the garden with a little Popsicle-stick cross, every one of us weeping, my brothers no less than my sister and me. But this childish reparation could not lift the stone of guilt from off their daily little murders. Denial soon passed into sullen resistance, and when this roused my father's anger to sterner discipline, the two boys began to scheme how they might run away.

I would not have known this except that I had taken refuge one afternoon in a favorite spot of mine for reading, a comfortable crotch in a branch of a great cottonwood tree at the back of the yard. Like some Nancy Drew storybook heroine, I simply overheard them, hunkered down together behind one of the pigeon sheds, conspiring. Their plans seemed already far advanced. They'd built small wagons out of old wooden crates and discarded baby-carriage wheels, crammed them with cereals and tins of soup and beans, and hidden them behind the barn. They even had rifles and gunpowder-makings (my genius brother Lou having researched the formula), and a supply of .22-caliber bullets, though they swore later they would not have killed a rabbit unless they were starving. Lou had talked a friend into joining them, Billy, a neighborhood kid who shared his dogeared Zane Grey novels and seemed to have a natural hormonal reservoir of thirteen-year-old discontent. The three of them were wild when they realized I knew what they were up to. I cried desperately, not out of fear, but at the thought of their going forever. I swore I would never give them away, not even under torture, and I meant it.

But my honor was never put to the test, my father never dreaming I could be part of such a heinous plot. I lay in my bed on the screened porch, listening to the caravan creakily depart in the dark before dawn with my heart pounding so loud in my chest I thought it could wake the house. But the boys were miles away before my father missed them, and they were miles farther on before he understood what it meant. My mother begged him to be calm, but she was no match for his bellowing rage. She herself was caught between fear of his wrath and the plain, crushing truth that her sons had also left *her*. Billy's father was drawn into the search. They headed the old pickup into the Catalinas along the route he and the boys had taken the previous Christmas, when they'd braved snow to cut trees to sell on city street corners, guessing now that this was the familiar road the boys would trust. And sure enough, by nightfall they found them, huddling around their campfire high in the mountains, some twenty miles away.

Lou was thirteen, his voice just beginning to break, Carlo only ten, shy, undergrown, with a sickliness that left him still a kind of baby. I could hear the small, uneven duet of their strangled sobs even as the truck crunched into the drive in the deep of the night, and my father pushed them out into the yard and into the barn. Then their howls of pain, punctuated by his choking staccato monotone of rage. He whipped Carlo first and sent him into the house, then tied Lou to a post and flogged him again and again, until the sun rose and lay full and plain over the desert and all one heard at last was the silence, even of the birds.

I had lain through the night in a stupor of disbelief, struggling to understand. How could he inflict a pain of which he seemed never to get enough? How could he bear it? How could my mother, who would flinch at the sight of a splinter in the palms of our hands? She must have drugged herself, stoned herself to death with prayer, devised some lie of the mind, some mercifully self-annihilating belief that this was happening to *her*, that she was merely surrendering blindly to her own punishment. How did *I* bear it? You could not drive the sobbing sound out of your head, no matter how much noise you made crying into the pillow, no matter how you stopped your ears with the sheets. It was as if I were there with them in that dim-lit barn, had seen it happening. It wasn't possible, he would never have let me, and yet I think I still see them there where we were not allowed to go, not even to bring them water. I see her, whispering into her rosary, her throat tight and dry with exhausted grief, the crystal beads wedged between her thumbs, and her heart a lump of volcanic ash still too hot for the tears she wept to be wet.

When you are a child, when you are told to step over and around the corpse on the carpet, you do it. The corpse in this case was not just my father's cruelty but his misery, the livid bestial frustration and selfish panic at who knows what world lost, darkened still more by my mother's complex of self-sacrifice and guilt at somehow having dealt him this fate. The moral bearings of all these things escaped me. I needed to love my parents. I needed to forgive them. I began faintly to grasp at a solacing if still bewildering truth that there was a link between our family's lives, which had in earlier days seemed for all their tumult so much our own, and that mysterious, dim other universe of wars and national hatreds. This world, which came at us in wonderful alliterative warnings like "loose lips sink ships" and bloodthirsty jingles about Hitler and Mussolini and Tojo blithely sung in the school playground, in hearty exhortations to do your part for the war effort—which we kids translated into fishing through dirt heaps for scrap metal and turning in our brown copper pennies for white ones—had just that airy false optimism and dark undertow I still connect with the comic radio of Jack Benny and Fibber McGee. We didn't know enough to call it history, but whatever its name was, we knew we lived in it. It did not forgive. It did not explain. But it said, You don't understand, my dear little girl, because there is so much, so much, to understand.

And it seemed to speak sometimes in the nasally voice of President Franklin Delano Roosevelt, for even if he had not replied to my father's letter in his own person, there appeared the sudden fact that something in the war had changed, Italy had joined the Allies, and that the same Italians who'd been scorned on Wednesday were back on Thursday in the good graces of the American government. If with equal suddenness a place for Mario's fine Italian hand was found on the defense equipment finishing line in a plant just outside of Tucson, it did not seem so entirely amazing or far-fetched to think the president had personally interceded. Mario, vindicated, took his place painting insignias on warplanes, spending much of his day on his back or squirming around on elbows and hips, like Michelangelo under the Sistine ceiling.

Beware the wish granted, by gods or presidents. Unlike Michelangelo, Mario was steeped in a dense bath of chemical solvents and paint fumes. Within six months he was deathly ill.

He wandered about the house at first, perplexed at the willful refusal of his own body. He worked intermittently, when his strength came. He sought out healers who were baffled by his illness, and got slowly thinner and weaker.

The chores of the pigeon farm had to go on without him. My brothers told me secretly that Lou had devised a way to anesthetize the birds before killing them, with a thin needle inserted behind the skull. It was no more than a kind of delusionary triage. Even if he could get to the infant birds in time, the hapless chickens and ducks couldn't be spared, and at holiday market time dozens of them still squawked, in brutal scenes of madcap slaughter, headless and bleeding about the yard.

The most terrible death was that of a spangled Japanese Bantam rooster, whose dawn crowing had become as familiar a part of our lives as the cooing of the pigeons at twilight. We called him "Nip-on-knees" because if you got too close to his hens he would sneak-attack you with his beak at what it was funny to think of as the Pearl Harbor level of your anatomy. When his time came to die for somebody's fricassee, my sister and I suffered so vocally that my mother declared all Bantam-slaying over. She could make such ultimatums now, though she'd never have admitted—in deference to my father, would never have dared think—she ruled the roost. But he had taken to his bed, and though he still gave orders from his closed and unapproachable room, we could tell he was growing less and less able to police how well they might be filled.

Probably in response to a gloomy epistle of my mother's complaining that everything that could go wrong had, my Aunt Mildred, Spagnola sister number four, wrote us that winter. "I'm coming," she declared, and she did, arriving from the East one day like a sunrise. Maybe she was having her own life crisis, or had reached an impassable plateau in her career. Or maybe she had simply, selfishly, imagined that any visit out here, to the land of eternal sunshine, had to be a vacation. But that was Aunt Mildred; you could never tell, as she unpacked her seventy-seven halter tops, what she did to please you from what she did to please herself.

Like all her sisters, Mildred was in the fashion trades. Or like and unlike them. They say the eldest, May (really Gandolfa, the same who had never quite forgiven Maria the injury of catching a husband before her), had already destroyed her eyes beading by the time she married Dante, that improbably named pretty-boy of hers—a man I remember from my later years in East Harlem as always mysteriously pale and well-shaven, and never to be seen on the tenement stairs before noon on weekdays in his trademark soft fedora and silk tie. Next came my mother, Maria—called Mary at home—with her promising berth at Bergdorf before Mario carried her away. And then Teresa, who had followed Mary into a similarly promising career before she'd met and married her fine, patrician-looking cousin, Louis.

But Mildred, who had slapped a kind of movie star moniker over her own original Carmela and effectively passed, had outshone them all, going into fashion design and making it at the Seventh Avenue cutting edge. Not black-haired and Arab-African–looking like all the others, but sandy red–haired like Papa Calogero and hazel-eyed like nobody (in that anciently mixed-up, who-knows-what-you-will-get way of the children of Sicily, an island trod by every race since time began), she even had the high cheekbones and air of cool command that could put you in mind of Dietrich in the right light. She knew what to wear, and how and when to wear it. On her own sewing machine, fitted on her own dressmaker's dummy, she made things rich women died for. And she was still single and flaunted it.

The relatively recent buzzword for this particular form of cool was *glamour*, which had begun to denote something, some irresistibly feminine, Coco Chanel sort of something that even women who were powerful and career-oriented could have— or maybe that *only* women who were powerful and career-oriented could have. I knew she had it, whatever it was, the moment she stepped down off that transcontinental express in Tucson and set her open-toed sandals on the station platform. And I wanted it, too.

She also had a certain starry look in her eyes. My first thought was that the glamour and the starry look went together, not understanding that they were actually antithetical, as things often are that follow one another as cause and effect and so for a single confounding moment show up in the same place. We kissed and hugged and cried for joy, and Mildred said how amazed she was to see what a pack of four little Indians her sister was raising, and so on. But it wasn't long before she let out that she had met her dream man on that train, someone by the totally southern American name of Ferril Dillard, a tall, blond, beautiful Alabama soldier-boy coming west with his platoon to be trained for combat in the Japanese theater of war.

If there was one being in those mid-war days who was even more glamorous than a Seventh Avenue fashion plate, it was a man in uniform. And this Ferril Dillard turned out on sight to be really delectable, a kind of blond Elvis before there was an Elvis, with baby blues and a crooning sort of drawl and a funny joyous fatalism that was such a contrast with the rather dark kind we'd grown up with that I fell half in love with him myself. He came to visit on weekends before going overseas, and brought us things, and courted and cuddled up more and more to Aunt Mildred, and she, who was so tough and smart and self-possessed when he wasn't around, turned into a kind of backlit American Beauty rose at a garden show, and just smiled and smiled.

My father, I'm sure, had his dark doubts about what was afoot, or what might actually come of this whirlwind courtship. But he was already too sick and bed-bound to raise a fuss over somebody who had actually shown up to give Maria a hand. And if he didn't like to encourage marriage to this totally un-Italian Alabaman, even less did he like the idea of Mildred's having a fling without it. So he played resident patriarch as best he could, and Aunt Mildred, not especially chafed by his watchdogging, settled into Tucson "for the duration," as they said, or as much of it as it took.

There were moments of total misty absence of eye contact when you could tell she was thinking about *him*. But she not only loved us kids, but truly adored my mother, and most of the time Mildred was with us she was actually with us, a kind of celebrity big sister, dolled up and ready for her public, prancing around in shorts, showing off the trademark family good legs in bobby sox and platform heels. It was she who taught me about making a statement with lipstick, of which she had at least nine equally brilliant shades in expensive cases. And when she wasn't lending a hand with the shopping or the wash or the cooking, or conspiring with my mother over some fine seam on the sewing machine, she would slather herself all over in cocoa butter (the smell of it can still pull the memory of her, like a genie, out of a jar) and throw herself down in the sun in her glamorous red bare-midriff swimsuit for a good hour's tan.

And whenever Ferril had a short furlough, she dazzled him, and he dazzled her, and before you know it she was pinning together a cream-colored satin dress on the mannequin, and they were married in a quick and simple ceremony that was part of what came in those days with men going off to war. And then he went off to war, and they had a baby on the way.

Mildred never had another child. Thinking back, I can understand why. I was much too protected to be let in on the medical aspect of her condition when I was a girl, but I know she went a terribly long time giving birth. And I remember my sister and I being steered away from her until well after it was over.

She'd gone into labor the night before the night before Christmas. When we were finally allowed to see her, her face looking drained—and astonishingly lipstickless—there was all the same such a lustrous glory in her eyes that I thought her delight in her child must at least be proportional to her difficulty in getting it out of her body. It was a girl, a very tiny girl, born deep in the night of Christmas Eve, sleeping in a bassinet off to the side of her bed when we came enchanted and whispering into the room.

My mother and she had spent months playing with names, but Mildred threw it all over and completely surprised her. "Starr," she announced, when asked. Maria kissed her cheek and smiled her most winsome smile. We all smiled. The whole issue of naming, now that we had left the Old World with its heavy burden of the deaths of ancestors, seemed to be thrown wide open. And Starr, in this context, could arguably be said to have had a basis in scripture. But for Mildred as for her tribe, only the road of excess could lead to the palace of wisdom, and a single allusion to the triumph of giving birth on O Holy Night would never be enough. "Starr Carol," she corrected herself archly, looking a little, I thought, like a cat who has stuck her paw in the cream, again.

Maria expressed content by finding her least ironical smile and smiling it, and was just blowing her nose into a hankie when Mildred added, "Noel," and forced her black eyebrows to shoot up again. Ann and I laughed and then clapped our hands over our mouths. Our mother shot a glance our way and then turned back to Mildred. Jokingly, she asked, "Any *more* names?"

"Of course," said Mildred, wincing slightly as she shifted her weight in the bed. "Starr Carol Noel *Dillard.*" She pronounced it as if she had just locked in her baby's claim to a platoon of harmonizing angels, and in that full, long, magical string you could hear the self-satisfaction of the Spagnola woman who has already got pretty much everything she ever wanted out of her man, and then some.

With a few exceptions, my sister Ann figures so little in the experiences I most remember about early Tucson that I have wondered if she was still too young to be part of them, apron-tied at home while every day my brothers and I adventurously (I thought) crossed a stretch of desert to our schoolhouse, a mile away. I am sure I strove to distance myself from her babyhood—even her girlness—in my longing to be taken seriously by my brothers, whose boy-freedom I envied and whose boy-daring I wanted to emulate.

But it was a continuous struggle: the more I sought them, the more they avoided me. As we followed the footpath home from school they would dart ahead or straggle behind, roaring for joy whenever an unpredictable finger of some evolutionary anomaly called "jumping cactus" flung itself at my head and grabbed one of my thick black braids, or stuck me full on the backside through my shorts, driving me to tearful despair, as if the whole Arizona universe were conspiring to punish me for being a girl.

The family called me "Fluffy," to make matters worse. It was meant endearingly, a baby name that had hung on as such names do, and my mother used it with an especially tender affection that my little sister echoed. But still, it was a silly, lapdog sort of a name. And especially since my own body made itself laughable and awkward, it could be used against me. I could not seem to shed my baby fat no matter how tomboyishly I ran and played dodgeball and climbed trees. People might patronize me as "pleasingly plump," but I was never fooled. I had to face it. The plain fact was I loved to eat. Not all of it went to fat, of course. By the time I was eight or nine I was also bigger and stronger than Lou, who was actually rather scrawny and bookish, and I was a giant compared with Carlo, whose misery nickname was the Runt. But to my brothers, I was forever Fat Fluffky. And they knew that the moment they skewered me with that name, I would disappear, hurt and humiliated.

Only the movies brought us together. My father, who ranked Saturday matinees lower than comic books as moral minefields for the impressionable young, must have made an exception for Walt Disney's *Dumbo,* or else a restless, pregnant Aunt Mildred had prevailed over his house rule. He was right. Once we had seen that absurdly sweet and doleful, wing-eared circus elephant, we couldn't get him out of our minds or our bodies. All Lou had to do, when the four of us were cleaning up after supper, was give the signal, and we would jump together and stack ourselves acrobatically on the kitchen floor, me at the bottom holding up the other three.

My brothers made no secret of how impressed they were with this performance of supergirl strength. For a few heavenly weeks I was their buddy. Now and then they would cut me in on a devilish plot, just so I could display my quisling subjection.

Like the day we decided to poison my sister. It was really the silliest ploy in the book. Ann was six, nearly seven, and even if she was tiny and naïve, she was nobody's fool. The new bars of bluing my mother had begun to use for soaking the bed sheets out in the wringer-tub in the yard were stamped into break-off squares like a Hershey bar, but they were actually blue. When I told her this was a new kind of chocolate she was really going to like, she wasn't tricked in the least, and said firmly, "It is *not*."

Somebody, maybe my mother herself, had said that whatever those bluing cubes were made of could poison you, or at least make you blind, but I still urged Ann to try one. "Try it yourself," she said, pushing me away, sure that if it was candy and as tasty as all that, I wouldn't be in such a hurry to share it. But I held her and tried to force it to her lips, just as my mother abruptly came in from the yard and my brothers crawled sniggering from behind the couch and scurried out the door. Ann grabbed her around the knees. "They were trying to poison me!"

My mother glared at me hard, snatching the package out of my hand and reassuring Ann in a voice tight with banked anger. I had watched the boys disappear, and stood there, paralyzed, yet weirdly awake. Ann protested that I had really tried. She was right. I had, to buy an instant of my brothers' admiration. "They wouldn't have let you, darling," my mother had said. But I knew what I knew, and it was like sudden carnal knowledge.

She lay now in the safe circle of my mother's arms, her hair stroked and kissed, as I slipped guiltily out and across the yard and scrambled into the familiar splayed branch of the cottonwood tree, my own gut tumbling and aching as if I had poisoned myself. Time passed. The screen door swung gently open from the enclosed back porch where Ann and I usually slept together. I could see her tiny shape, in her little blue and white pinafore, emerge tentatively into the yard. Her feet were bare. A mass of hair had escaped from her braids and sprung into irregular loose brown curls around her dusky face. Her face was all wide-open eyes, searching the fading light.

I knew she was looking for me. It was as if I were seeing her for the first time.

I am glad not to have been a mother then. It was struggle enough to learn to be a motherly child. Nothing declared the impotency of parenting more than an apocalyptic Arizona rainstorm, when, after days—weeks—eternities of blanching and relentless blue skies and flaming sunsets, of long, blue-velvet nights flagrant with moonlight, a switch would be thrown on the universe, and rain and wind would flash across the desert, shutting down the world in a solid wall of water and erasing connection to anyone out of the reach of your arms.

My mother, who had a houndlike vigilance about danger (a sixth sense in her, literally, almost as overdeveloped as her sense of smell, which was legendary), would gladly have raised cowards, I think, just to be sure we'd hide safely under our beds like puppies when the power-rains came down. But her sons had just that bit of the blind, gambler's daring of their father that seemed to have got us to Arizona in the first place, and even something of his queer taste for rousing and then flouting her womanish terrors. When the rain exploded out of the skies that famous year of Aunt Mildred, as suddenly as the lightning plunged into that live radiant soup of September heat, the boys rallied against all cries and dove into the flashing water like crocodiles, disappearing from sight before they had left the horseshoe drive, even before the smashing rain had carromed their reckless whoops and yelps out of the air.

We women and girls stood by, arms helplessly outstretched. But not all of us wanted to stop them. I wanted to be with them, to leap barefoot and bare-chested into that air ocean and let my eyesight be shattered by the sheer force of water and the rain pelt my back like bullets, as I had seen it pelt theirs, and dart and dance into the running river of the road. Here in the house the rain hammered on the metal roof, the wind drove sudden gushes of water at the windows. We could imagine the birds in their screened refuges soaked right through their oily feathers, hunkered down into soft balls, huddling together for comfort as the rushing rain drove deep new freshets into the dirt floor of the sheds. But they were safe, and would not fly, like boys, into the wall of water.

Had she known Carlo was in danger of drowning in a gully before she knew he'd been rescued, my mother might have died, just from the sheer fact of being helpless to save him. Something just that quixotic lay between the two of them, a deep tenderness she felt for his vulnerable smallness, he with that seemingly inarticulate yearning to be her boy, her only boy—to be, in fact, her *man*. With so much of her family's strange witchcraft coded into acts of naming and renaming, perhaps there had been the magic of the patronymic he was blessed with as second son, singularly entitled to carry the name of her beloved Papa—or the elegant variation of it acceptable to my father. For Carlo, too, she would have stopped a bullet, a hundred times.

I think he knew he had this hold on her, that he lived and moved within the safety of its possession. Sickly and small, he had first survived pneumonia as an infant (one of our oft-repeated family miracles), then, with Lou, a scarlet fever that had left them both afflicted with the same fever-weakened eyesight. But Lou's owlish glasses made him look the genuine budding genius, while Carlo's lay as heavy and huge in his tiny face as the optics of a bottle fly. He clowned, he tricked, he teased, he ruthlessly taunted my sister and me, he did whatever he was told not to. He became ever more the mischievous little scapegrace as he grew. My father, his heart increasingly darkened and sore, felt baited, and even from his sickbed gave him the full brunt of a military, withering scorn. And the more he gave, the more Carlo seemed to want, to taunt him to give, as if it were a drug for which he had developed a habit, or as if it had become the dark side of my mother's unconditional and enabling love, which could deny him nothing, forgive him everything.

But that day, when they brought him home half-dead, the shriek she shrieked could have stopped your heart. The sun had already burst through the clouds again and was beating the soaked earth into smoke when the whole posse of them abruptly appeared at the bottom of the drive, Lou and the neighborhood boys lead-ing the way. Behind them walked the gas station man from down the road, Carlo lying across his arms as limp as a bolt of wet muslin. We knew he was alive. As they drew closer, we could hear him grotesquely weeping against his chattering teeth in a parody of his own impish laughter, see him wanly waving his brown little legs as if he wanted to run, as if he'd been caught and not rescued.

But he was safe, safe, *safe,* everyone reassured her! Yet she could not stop wail-ing in terror-exaggerated pain. And yet I knew she indulged her passion, her fury, and did not drop down dead at the sight of him, because by Jesus, Mary, and Joseph, and all the holy saints, even if he was half-dead, he was still alive.

The boys grabbed excitedly at their breath as they told us that the rain had already stopped pounding, and was just beginning to sift down straight through the sun-light, when Carlo had taken it into his head to breast the wild water flooding the drain ditches in streams as wide and boiling as rivers. He'd been caught, swept into a culvert pipe under the crossroad by the gas station. Lou had lunged forward and grabbed and held him by the wrists, screaming for help as he threw himself across the embankment, but without the strength to wrench him out against the force of the current. There was nothing to do but resist it, the two of them one body, arms tearing at shoulders, until the other boys came and made a chain and held them both back from the flood rushing into the great pipe. And then the garage man with his strong back and forearms had come and just reached down and yanked Carlo out.

For a few moments my mother simply took him in her arms, and, weeping, laid him across a blanket in her lap, took his head between her hands and kissed the streaky wet hair. His chest bled where it had been thrashed against the arch of the culvert, the fine brown-gold skin stripped away from throat to navel. He howled with pain coughing the foul, coffee-colored water out of his choking lungs, and she wept, we all wept, in pity for him. But he was *alive.* The saints had kept him alive.

Still, it was a deathblow, the last shimmering spike in my mother's feeling for this beautiful and cursed place—a feeling that from the beginning had never been love. Ever on the watch for signs, she lost no time in reading this one, as she had my father's slow decline, only without doubt or equivocation. Even as we moved through our own slow gulfs of childhood time, increasingly haunted by the thinning form we caught only in occasional scaring glimpses when the bedroom door was left ajar, we knew conferences were held, plans made; we felt a nameless danger, sensed a new horizon of hope.

Aunt Mildred, restless for independence, perhaps superstitious enough to be repelled by the morbid sadness of our house, had moved out and nested into spe-cial single blessedness at the back of her own shop in town until the Christmas baby arrived, and then into a special kind of madonna-with-child blessedness afterwards. She turned a small income from cutting and draping and stitching her artful fashions, drawing on Ferril's army pay and what was left of her savings, finding her niche, content to wait out her soldier in the Arizona sunshine.

She was still a mesmerizing sight for two little girls whenever she visited the squab farm. From the somewhat sprung-out armchair in the family room, our eaves-dropping perch on the kitchen, we could see, as she moved the baby from shoulder to shoulder, that she was cultivating a slightly blowsy Rita Hayworth look now, self-consciously tossing her mass of brassy gold hair out of the way, and dodging carefully as my mother careered about the room. Both of them seemed caught in an instinctive dance of frenetic Spagnola energy, rapt in jolted, telegraphic conversation filled with hushed allusions to doctors in the East.

It snowed the following winter in Tucson, for the first time in fifty years. The snowflakes floated out of a lowering gray sky like fine volcanic ash and sublimed back into the air almost before they had dusted the earth. In my anguished and mis-remembering mind's eye it is all one image—the vanishing snow, my father taken from the house on a stretcher that then lifts so lightly into the train it seems to be empty, the sighing train heaving itself away as if it could feel pain.

The farm vanishes, the birds, the splayed cottonwood tree. For a very little time we seem to be with my aunt and the Christmas baby with the lovely Disney name, my little sister and I, together, climbing up and down the dust pile in her parking lot, collecting bits of scrap metal for the war effort.

And then the lights behind the big blue sky go quietly dark.

3

My father's illness, the key that unlocks the mystery of this childhood experience of the West, is itself a palimpsest erased and told again so many times that it is no longer possible to say of it, "This is the truth."

I remember with an embarrassing rush of nostalgic joy how as a girl, even as a young woman, I imagined that I knew the truth and would always know it, that truth itself was drawn to me—loved me, discovered me the way the wind itself did, roughly caressing my face—that somehow great mysteries locked to others would open obligingly to my unconquerable mind. I dreamed dreams of flying, too, so real and convincing that I would swear I could step off the sill of my bedroom window in broad daylight and float at will, twenty or thirty feet above the lawn.

I cannot fly, nor do I know what the truth is. I cannot tell my story as linear history, as if it were a chain of cause and effect defying ambiguity, or play it like a musical score. Even to tell the truth as it was for me then—tell it and leave it alone—seems a luxury. How much truth is possible—not just within the range of my own capabilities, but within the conventions of this confessional mode? Am I allowed, slowly or suddenly, to peel away the layers of discovery in strategically timed revelations as they did in fact come to me in real time?

This is not a novel, though I might sometimes wish it were. And because it is called "true," who knows whether such mysteries and gaps are licensed by the contract between the one who writes and the one who reads what is written? I strive to recover what I felt as a child, but my story does not therefore become the diary of a child's life. It remains the self-reflective account of a woman for whom childhood is half a century old, a woman who has, for years in fact, been pondering the archeological and meta-archeological dynamics of memory and truth. And so I know, as surely you know too, that as I write I bring with me not just "the truth as it was for me then," but knowledge laid over it time and time again, each layer not merely structuring fresh feelings about the facts I already knew, forging new tools of memory with which to recover new "facts," but reconfiguring the very way all subsequent events, thought to be already explained and understood, are presented to the mind to be explained and understood again. And so it is memory's curious trick to have knowledge be not singular—one knowledge, one truth, standing straight and upright in place of memories proven false or imprecise—but many knowledges, able like ghosts to somehow disregard the law of the conservation of matter and occupy the same place at the same time.

These memory-ghosts most haunt me here, where my story veers back upon itself. The ghosts stand, immovable, not-quite-cast-out old versions, not-quite-vanished plausibilities in some curiously reflexive relation to one another. It is as if my life is an archive from which nothing can be taken or destroyed, whose mission it is to preserve all the beautiful dreams of the way things were. Or a synoptic gospel, each version equally true, or equally credible, and each somehow, in spite of conflict, still reverently acceptable as an alternative interpretation of the same life.

Plain truthseekers, take comfort. If what I have told is not everything I came to know, it is still as real, as inexorable, as history. The Arizona ur-narrative, with its infrastructure of poetic irony (my mother's illness the decisive factor in the going, my father's warplant sickening the pivot of the return), remains still both objectively true and also how it was for us then. Pitying our mother's pain, we understood our father's pity for it. Pitying our father's pain, we understood our mother's pity for it. Through it all, to our eyes as children (and it is fair to say that the four of us, collectively, lived within these meanings, and were in fact the theater in which they were played), whatever else we saw or felt, to see the seductive sheer romance of this crisis in their young marriage and in our young and innocent lives was a real and powerful way of seeing.

Even in the East Harlem years that followed, and the life resumed in New Rochelle two or so years beyond that, we could, without laying a scratch on the impenetrable veneer of this family romance, reimagine these same facts within a plausible complexity of motives. Since we had known even as small children that our father had sold his business to go west, we could now add what he could not possibly have shared with us then: the immense significance of this to him within the framework of his values. Its meaning, that is, to a man willing to admit, as time went on, how deeply ambitious he had been for wealth, for *success* as defined by the materialist American dream.

And so in time I understood that it had not been the prejudice of wartime, or even the poisonous defense plant, that had sickened my father's life, but a deep sense of failure, an underlying humiliation that could never be fully forgiven, not of my mother, not of God himself. It was difficult for us—but perhaps I should speak only for myself here, once our childhood theater of meaning had fragmented—difficult for *me* to grasp this view, for what could it mean to a young imagination already so powerfully fired with the symmetry of love? How could I understand the hard economic realities of wartime markets, let alone how he had experienced them—that when rationing came in, the meat futures he had sold in early 1942, just after Pearl Harbor, had skyrocketed in black market value and made other men rich? It added a jagged edge to a sad tale. It did not fundamentally alter its romantic outline, which memory had already enshrined beyond the reach of fact.

More knowledge would eventually come to write itself like the primal scene upon the innocence of Eden. And with it a clearing of vision, like a new planet swimming into view. At last we could see the madness of it, the madness of a man so deeply centered in his own life-drama that, like some vernacular Oedipus, he could inflict this near-suicidal wound upon himself, give up a burgeoning business in the East, the consolations of an extended family, renounce every former life-chance, inspire his wife to tear herself from her home, her loving sisters, from the city at the very heart of who she was, whose absence from her life could drain the splendor of Arizona of all its own magnificence and beauty. And this madness not just the frenzy of the gambler, sighting a new vein of life-chances, not just the madness of love (though the madness of love had been real, real and undying, still there between them to the last moments of their lives together), but an imbecilic rage at having given up what he really wanted, both ways, at having made a fatal mistake, at having somehow struck the wrong deal with life.

Rage. I know it now. I can hear its unmistakable roar. It is a sound like that of something happening in the street, something that comes slowly to your awakening senses with the choking smell of smoke, until you realize that it is the whole neighborhood clamoring to your benighted ears that your house is on fire.

I wondered how I had not seen it sooner, how it had happened that in all the over-determined, multilayered authorized versions of the family story it had only been allowed a surrogate place. And yet it was there again and again, scored on each body as illness: that same self-postponement, the same surrender that leaves the deeper desire ungratified, the true invisible worm, eating her body as well as his.

Yet remember, as you read this, how it was for me then. For all these baffling signs of his rage, I too adored him, as she did. He was a force field, a powerful black hole into which one's love might be endlessly poured. He seemed to create and consume it like God.

I adored him. He had disappeared into a train compartment, and I thought I had lost him. And for two more years, although he was there, a shadow on the well-carved Victorian porch of the Woodlawn Nursing Home, my father remained as elusive to me as an imploded star.

It was then that my mother's family took her back into the tenement in East Harlem, she and her four sunburnt, fatherless Amerindian savages, to become Mary again, as she had always been to her sisters. And as if to do some further perverse penance, she returned to work not in dressmaking, but toiling long hours at the butcher block in Grandpa Luigi's store, just as my father would have done.

Our squadron of aunts, wild with children and drudgery of their own, struggled to confine our afterschool mayhem to the limits of our fifth-floor walkup. It couldn't have been easy, and they were not always pleased with an arrangement that meant they would sometimes have the lot of us on their hands when my mother was kept late at the store, but God knows they understood it. It was opera—*La Bohème, Tosca;* it was soap opera, all the soap operas they knew, *Helen Trent, The Guiding Light, Grand Central Station.* Mario, doomed to a lingering illness, swept away as by some act of God into the healing hands of the physicians at Mount Sinai, swept into the countryside of the Bronx to be cured, beautiful, dark-eyed Mario, stand-in for all the adored and evanescent men in their eternally love-besotted lives.

I ought to make an exception for my Aunt Teresa and Uncle Louie, her husband, whom she did of course adore, with an unswerving passion. But Louie, though gentle and gently spoken, was anything but an evanescent father to my four cousins, one of them so curiously a Flavia like me. His was an affection so physical you could see it turn on like a refrigerator lightbulb when he came home at night, the instant Teresa opened the flat door. And he came home, like clockwork, though sometimes he might have to pick his way through the eight of us, bivouacked on Teresa's well-scrubbed linoleum. Still, Louie belonged to *his* family, not to us. He gave us the sight of what real fathering looked like—no small thing—but we remained spectators to this daily shower of affection. Teresa herself overflowed with the kind of endless, easy, big-breasted *abbondanza* that could not exhaust itself on eight children at a time. She tried to fill the gap, to be mother-surrogate for the sister she loved and pitied, but she could not be father too.

Our own apartment was, as I have said, at the top of the house, right under the roof, convenient to laundry-hanging and tar-beach summer afternoons. To compensate for the climb, my mother would congratulate us regularly for having "nobody walking on our heads." Once we were allowed to be on our own after school for a few hours at a time, we got to know the unmistakable sound of her swift, eager steps up that last flight. It was a wonderful, terrible sound: wonderful, because she was the lodestar of our lives; terrible, because her expectations of us were high, and her accountings stern.

It was as though as the second daughter she had received at least the second most sizable dollop of whatever made Sicilian women *serious* women—*donne serie.* May had the most, then Mary, Teresa next, Mildred after Teresa, and so on, as if the serious juice had run lower and lower as each girl had come up the line.

As the war came to a close and the post-war began and the younger sisters were marrying themselves off, this gradation grew more and more obvious, and the family house at 230 came to seem more and more a kind of allegory, with the stories set out floor by floor like something out of Spenser's *Faerie Queene.* Just below us on the fourth floor, side by side with Teresa, were Aunt May and her Dante—she the eldest daughter, he the well-combed, finely hatted shadow on the stairs. I have said that no one seemed to know how he made his living, or if he made a living and wasn't simply sponging off May's crucifying beadwork. But May was dour, silent, and uncomplaining. They had two little girls named Libby and Adele, prim and pale, who never seemed to play with other children, let alone with us, and whose trademark sound was the tap-tap of their patent leather shoes as they came and went from their apartment hand in hand with May, or with both May and Dante on Sundays.

Now and then we might hear May's ringing voice through the floor, like a muffled bell, raised to someone in rebuke. Was it *him?* Otherwise, a reclusive and hostile family silence, appropriate to a *very* serious woman, and the vision of her, perhaps once a week from June through September, leaning out over the fire escape off the apartment kitchen just beneath ours, silently drying her long, full, silvering hair in the slant rays of the afternoon sun.

But two more stories down, a single flight up from the street, lived Aunt Bea and her dandified husband Sonny with a big, white-toothed smile and the sweetest sweet-talk in New York. Bea was daughter number five. She had been baptized Rosina, and, following the lead of her older sister Mildred, had had the name surgically removed, like a mole. But just as a name, "Bea"—or as they sometimes called her, "Bee-bee"—

fit her, like a new nylon stocking with a plumbline seam. She was a honeymaker with a sting, or an existential declaration of presentness. She could have been a piece of steel shot. She had those perky, supergroomed looks that were the epitome of prettiness in wartime women. "Which of us is the prettiest?" she asked dumb little me one night, after I'd followed her and her three younger sisters, Anna, Joan, and Elena, into the galley kitchen and sat gazing in stupefied enchantment as they schmoozed and smoked over coffee after work. She knew I'd say she was, and then she'd smirk and toss her head as I blushed at being euchred into her little scheme.

But I loved to hear her boast. *"Daawrhling,"* she'd say, addressing all her sisters in the singular (and in a drawl that was classic highfalutin NooYawk), "my Sonny was *baawrhn* to dance." This would be followed by a comparison of herself to Ginger Rogers on the dance floor, while Elena, the youngest, laughed her big ringing, cynical, make-me-believe-it laugh, and Joan, eyes faintly sidelong and voice tinged with annoyance, would comment that (with her round face and bottle-exaggerated blondness) it was she people said looked like Ginger Rogers, and Bea would have no trouble granting her that. "But I've got my Fred Astaaayah," she'd remind her, meaning Sonny, her dancing fool of a husband. And then she would raise those perfectly plucked black eyebrows above those perfectly curled black eyelashes, fire up a Chesterfield, toss the match deftly into the sink, adjust her snooded aureole of black hair with her free hand, blow two plumes of smoke through her nostrils, and turn her smile beatifically on me.

But that was until Sonny gambled or otherwise squandered away every hard-earned dollar she made on Seventh Avenue faster than she could have had it printed, plus who knows what else he'd done that she wouldn't talk about. So she simply upped one fine Sunday morning (as we children, drawn by the garbled sound of quarreling, watched awestruck from the top of the stairwell), emerging from her apartment in a dramatically floating, beige satin peignoir, and cried out in that wonderful Spagnola contralto made more lush by good cognac and cigarettes that he was a *sonuvabitch bastard!* Nobody could shout the word bastard like my Aunt Bee-bee—*BA-A-STA-A-RRD*—as well-ventilated as Gramercy Park. Then she threw him out and all his bow ties down the stairs after him.

Aunt Anna, next down from Bea and also next to get married, lived with Joan and Elena (what a ménage, when you think about it) across the hall from Bea and Sonny, sharing the second-floor apartment where I had seen and will never forget seeing my grandfather dead. The parlor he'd been waked in had been closed off for more than three years now, until they decided to brave superstition and open it up for the wedding, redoing it with fancy draperies as a honeymoon suite.

But the honeymoon ended rapidly, as perhaps under those auspices was only likely. Richard, her husband, was a ruddily pink and attractive Irishman. Otherwise he was unremarkable and ambition-free, as well as who knows how spooked by the strange mores of these Spagnola women. In the end, he seemed to prefer spending his nights out on Third Avenue to coming home to his neurotic little wife and (eventually) their amazingly pale and poorly baby boy, also named Richard, who was always caterwauling with earache. Or he came home only by the time poor sad little Anna, glum and long-suffering, had long been in bed, eating her heart out. Anna, more passive-aggressive than Bea, finally obliged herself one day by having a nervous breakdown. By the time she was back from the hospital, under heavy sedation, Richard was gone.

Uncle Joey may have had something to do with this.

Seriousness was perhaps not the same kind of issue with the two Spagnola men as with the women, though it was not much of a sampling to go by. Joey was the younger of the two Spagnola brothers, the only one to come to live at 230 after he married, taking an apartment on the third floor, the one under May and over Bea. That was after V-J Day in August of 1945 and all the homecoming fuss that followed the end of the war, when he got back from the Navy. What a block party! What nights and nights of block parties! You could hear the music all over the city, way into the night. The one on our street made us kids mad with envy as we watched from our fifth-floor perch, wishing we could have been just a few years more grown up.

The stories about Joey, from wildest motorcycle days to audacious exploits in the Navy, would curl porcupine quills. He was renowned for having crashed into an El pillar on East 116th Street when he was eighteen and lived to tell about it. Just the sort of story, when the family was gathered around the table and the wine was low, to make someone sigh, "Aaaah, I could write a book," at which everybody else would nod as if autobiography were the family business. But Joey had finally settled down with his beloved Concetta to wife, found a union construction job in the Brooklyn Navy Yard, then got his own plumbing license and worked independently on the side. Hardcore down-and-dirty, he could fix anything—exactly the kind of "real man" Spagnola women seemed destined never to get in a husband.

Concetta, who called herself Mary in still another case of Italian-girl cosmetic name-surgery, was a very pretty woman—Uncle Joe would have tolerated nothing less—with the deepest, most soulful, big Kewpie-doll brown eyes I ever saw. Not even my mother's were set in such lush penumbras of soft purple. So intensely mortal were they, even tragic, they seemed to draw all attention from the small, perfect nose and little Cupid-bow mouth. And yet all these features were bound together with a flint will and uncompromising intelligence. Joey, you could tell, had been tried and toughened in the crucible of eight sisters, at least six of them smart.

Once settled into married life, Joey began little by little to define for himself a semiserious role as paterfamilias to this vertical community of women. Even had he still harbored old Sicilian standards of female virtue, which is doubtful, he knew there was no saving the sum of it his sisters had already thrown away marrying jerks. But he could protect the few still-remaining rags of family honor by making sure Joan and Elena were properly bought and paid for by decent, respectable guys before anybody took them to bed. And he could try, as best he could, to settle disputes across the halls and up and down the stairs.

I used to think it strange that Uncle Tony, who should have worn this mantle, didn't. Besides being number one of the ten, you'd have thought he had just the peaceable temperament for it, more so than Joey, who had always been the one with the short fuse. And yet here was Joey—the maverick, the trickster, the risk-taker, the guy who broke the rules and pushed the boundaries and fell on his face and picked himself up with a raunchy joke—taking charge. Joey, with the vaguely unsavory reputation as a hustler, a fixer, somebody who could always get it for you wholesale. You'd think he lacked the moral authority to boss all those bossy women.

And yet maybe that was why he could. The odd thing is that his big-talking, self-inventing sisters could never have admitted to themselves that for all the piety about their darling Papa and the lip service they paid to Duty as defined by the patriarchal culture they'd been steeped in, they had actually been liberated by their father's death and by their coming-of-age into a wartime, Eleanor Roosevelt culture, where women were being chancily slipped a license for independence. And because he somehow understood this and they weren't ready to, he still got that begrudgery of respect when he pulled rank. They would have made mincemeat of a big innocent, fair-eyed lummox of a guy like Uncle Tony. Maybe they already had, before I was there to see it.

Uncle Tony reminded me of an unfunny Popeye, tough and gentle. Family folklore had it that he'd been a forceps delivery, which accounted for his being a bit slow and a bit deaf, and maybe for a comedically challenged sort of crusty solemnity somebody I knew later used to refer to as a damaged laughing-string. You could not have dealt with Bea and Anna and Joan and Elena without an intact, catgut, cable-strength laughing-string.

But Tony was not stupid, and maybe actually had the whole thing figured out, having married a comfortable widow somewhat older than himself, an Irishwoman named Helen with two grown children, who was perfectly happy to stop right there. They had taken her apartment several blocks away, and once Joey moved in at 230, they divvied up the work. Tony took the job of keeping the old family building under repair and collecting the rents. He tried to make his job look hard, and muttered about it a lot, buffed the brass on the front-door hardware till you could see yourself in it, and kept the stoop and areaway so swept no bum scrounging around in it could have turned up a single used cigarette butt. An ice cream kid-finger-smudge never lasted on the big glass doors for more than half an hour. But nobody would ever doubt who got the better deal.

Through all the three years we were there and beyond, 230 remained the spiffiest and most beautiful building on the block. Uncle Tony saw that the stairwells were washed and the cornices painted, and the boiler always in tiptop repair, so that even the nonfamily tenants on the top floor wouldn't have to bang the pipes for heat. He made sure all the bolts on the window grilles were secure so nobody could blame him if their dumb kid fell out and got spiked on the areaway railing, sixty feet down. The tradeoff was beyond the workday: no kids under foot, no catfights, no getting caught in the middle.

But, as for me, I think Tony lost out, missing *pastacicede* in the kitchen with the girls, or sitting out in the parlor around the radio, glued to the Hit Parade and singing *"Mairzy Doats"* at the tops of our voices.

And because they weren't his windows, he never got to lean out of them, as we did, grilles or no, to get all the news of the war—or the peace, when the peace finally came—all the news you'd ever want to hear, straight up from the street. Never got to watch as the tall sculpted image of Our Lady of Mount Carmel floated drunkenly below on a sea of worshippers every sixteenth of July, her cone-shaped body covered with fluttering gray-green dollar bills, like a woman-tree made out of pure money.

4

The death of FDR had been announced in ten-foot-high letters on the street pavement beneath our tenement windows, letters meticulously painted by neighborhood boys, in a deep, reverential silence. The shock itself was stunning, and the convergence of the sudden passing of this larger-than-life being (and the only president I had ever known) with the end of the European war barely weeks later, as if he had died for it, burnished his image into temporary sainthood. Yet all of it, all of the imagery of the fatherly leader with the deeply ringed eyes, all the relentless movie iconography of patriotic sacrifice and the endless trumpeting of war bonds and victory gardens and the soothing caramel harmonies of the Andrews Sisters at the USO—all the bittersweet stuff our lives till then had been drenched in—was utterly burnt off by what we came to see within the span of that same year, as spring became summer, as summer fall, in *Life* and *Look* and Associated Press newsphotos and Pathé newsreels, that the war had ended twice in unspeakable carnage, once of the tortured and murdered Jews and again of the scorched, annihilated victims of Hiroshima and Nagasaki.

Even children saw this, saw it in the plainest and most brutal clarity, saw humanity exposed in so extreme, so unimaginable an uncomprehending innocence of suffering that we could never wake up from the sight of it again.

So in a true sense I was a different child on either side of my tenth birthday, a week after V-E Day. Till then, and perhaps for the briefest time after, I might still gather the world's moment to me as if it were my own, still rejoice in what seemed to me a bright entry into personhood, melding the end of the terrible war with my own little coming-of-age.

My mother gave me the rapturous gift of permission to see Victor Mature in *One Million B.C.* at the Cosmo on the other side of Third Avenue. I doubt she was ever sold on my father's stern principles in this matter of the movies, and with him away there seems never to have been a question of us going, beyond worrying about the cost of it. Ann would come, and my brothers, of course—they *had* to—and as for me, always the willing pachyderm at the bottom of the pile, sharing it was the best part of the gift. *She* couldn't go, sadly, not with just a single afternoon off to clean house and make pineapple-upside-down cake, but I knew when we got back she'd make sure a bit of the pleasure of it rubbed off.

The primary meaning of the movies, ever since our *Dumbo* days, had been bonding. There'd been that curious, wonderful night back in Tucson when my father had actually taken us to see *Mr. Skeffington*—a night I remember both because it *was* a night and because it was such an unexampled fatherly indulgence. Of course, it had to be a dour morality play—a Bette Davis classic about a vain and selfish wife who contracts diphtheria and loses all her beautiful hair, which I understood even then to be her punishment. But I will never forget the anguish of watching that single false curl drop silently to the carpet, my mother quietly snuffling into her handkerchief beside me as I sobbed my pitying tears into the soft, red-fox collar of her best winter coat.

My birthday movie was another story, *One Million B.C.* being perhaps the nearest thing Hollywood had come to a skin-flick since the Code. Even the Cosmo theater thought no one under sixteen should see so much flesh draped in such scanty primordial outerwear without an accompanying adult. Somehow we hadn't known this—certainly my mother hadn't—and we got as far as the queue before we panicked at the thought of being turned away at the window.

Lou is not quite fifteen and small for his age. Behind us stands a gray-haired woman in a navy-blue jacket and hat. "Would you say we're with you, lady?" he asks. Widening her dull-blue eyes, "All *four* o' yez?" she mouths back, and bounces her head four times, down the string of us. But she smiles, she twinkles, she actually seems pleased to have acquired a family. And she points out that she will have to get ahead of us in line.

Her lie relieved me to the soul. And it occurs to me now that whatever subliminal weakening of our moral fiber took place that afternoon must have taken place at that moment. Otherwise it would have to have been produced by the absolutely bewitching sight of flowing lava over a beautiful, desolate landscape that put me in mind of the Southwest, and probably was. Which is all I can bring back, except for Victor Mature himself, and the distinct, if fleeting thought that he was a much less handsome version of my absent father.

Lou was going to be headed off to Cardinal Hayes High School on scholarship that fall, and as Catholic went I wouldn't have been surprised if he told me that they'd debated the ethics of our movie matinee in his moral theology class—who, precisely, had committed the sin, what sin it was, if it was mortal or venial, and whether the little blue lady would go to hell if she were Catholic and didn't confess it, or go to hell because she *wasn't* Catholic no matter whether she confessed it or not.

Sometimes I could just not figure out the things priests and nuns typically got worked up over, like how much skin you exposed in your confirmation dress, or whether you wore a proper scarf to church instead of the make-do little handkerchief with a bobbypin, or brought in your little donation envelope for the basket on Sundays or went to the 9 A.M. mass to get properly sermonized by the pastor. I wish I'd known that scriptural saying about the gnats and elephants, since with all that was going on in the world I thought they seemed to be digesting a belly-ful of elephant as if it were cherry Jell-O.

All I knew was that before I started the fifth grade at Our Lady Queen of Angels on East 113th Street, I'd had four years of school, two public sandwiched between two parochial, and public was way out front in the standings. On my first day at St. Gabriel's when I was five, the nun-principal had struck such terror into my little body that I'd peed, hot and wet, right into the cane chair in her office, and it was as if I'd spent the whole year after that expecting the imminent loss of bladder control. Where-as I had *loved* my little two-room public schoolhouse teachers in the desert, especially the one—hardy and plain, tanned as leather—who taught third grade in the adobe school we were yellow-bused to at the edge of the Hopi reservation. She had never been bound to rules for their own sake. She had even worn jeans to school sometimes. And we'd worked *hard*—hard work being far from just a Catholic school discipline, though you'd have thought it was from the way people carried on about the difference. I loved to work—what else did you do, after all, if you were the fat, smart, artsy girl who was always in love with somebody, but nobody was ever in love with? The teacher was always asking me to draw something on the construction-paper covers of her string-tied little manuals. When she saw I could also read and count beyond my age and class, she'd put me to tutoring other kids, a bonus for me, who could see from age eight that teaching was also a better way of learning.

Then there was a month or two of fourth grade with Sister Agnes at Saints Peter and Paul in Tucson, that brief spell just before we came back east. Sensitive as I was to names, I didn't think hers beautiful enough for her. Her beauty astonished me, the young face smooth and smiling between the tight, snow-white bands, great, carved brown eyes dancing as she proudly watched me produce a perfect cylinder of Palmer *O*s, in one big looping curl like a Slinky, out of a single dip of a fine-nibbed pen in the inkwell.

Our Lady Queen of Angels, enclave of Franciscan friars in brown cloaks and rope belts and of a teaching order of the Sisters of Mercy, was sheer Lowood by comparison. In fact, reading *Jane Eyre* as a teenager, I had the advantage of a perfect reference point for the misery both of Jane and of Helen Burns, because, while I suffered myself, it was much less than my poor sister Ann, who had always needed gentleness more than I did and took any rebuke as a hurt to heart and soul. And ironically it was also her misery that in the end released *me*. Plagued with colds and earaches and terrible bouts of tonsillitis almost from the moment we were back in New York, she'd been laid up at home again and again all winter, and I had become her runner, fetching assignments home from school and carrying her finished homework back to Sister Agrippina.

Agrippina! If only I'd known the atrocity embedded in the history of that name, it might at least have given me a perspective on her sadism—for what else could have possessed her to invoke the mother of Caligula as she took the veil? One afternoon as I stood in front of her second-grade class with the news that my sister was sick again, she reached into Ann's desk for all her notebooks and threw them across the room, spilling their pages onto the floor at my feet. Then she made me get down and collect them again. I wept, humiliated, furious, both in front of the snickering children and all the way home, remembering her big voice roaring, "Sick! Sick! *Your* sister is out sick every time the wind blows!"

It didn't occur to me then how much Ann's illness might actually have been a counteroffensive in a kind of war, her only weapon against Sister Agrippina's relentless mental and even physical bullying. I knew only that Sister Agrippina was a tyrant, that my little sister was sick, and that it was mean and unjust for her to be accused of malingering.

My mother, whose outrage could be as swift, clean, and incisive as the blow of a cleaver on the neck of a frying chicken, could hardly wait for dawn to march over to the school and deliver what was known in the stairwell at 230 as "a piece of her mind." Sister Agrippina, believe me, was never going to be caught harming a single brown curl of little Ann's head or speaking to her in a voice above a murmur. But in an exquisitely twisted gesture of retribution, *I* was the one my mother pulled out. I can just hear her saying it—"*Smartest girl in the fifth grade, maybe in the whole school, you don't even know what you've got*"—as she sent me vindictively over to those godless public-school Protestants at PS 102. Let those *Calabresi,* those *capotosti* hard-boiled-egg-headed bully Franciscans eat *that* one!

Someday, oh, someday, Mother Church was going to get her sweet revenge in the shape of my own mind-numbing seizures of a religious passion, but I would never again set foot as a student inside a parochial school. Had I been able to foresee the finality of the break at the time, it would have been fine with me. I regretted only that Ann, whom I wanted so desperately to protect from all harm, had to stay behind me at the Angels, and that, now, not only was I scarily alone, but so was she.

From my mother's point of view, I suppose, Ann was still her baby, too small to make the trip she could let me take, overriding her other fears, to this farther-away school across Second Avenue and down three blocks to 111th Street. Or maybe it was some superstitious dread, some deference to the power of the Franciscans and what they might do if they got really mad enough at you. Or even a simple compromise, arrived at with my father on a Sunday visit to Woodlawn. She took such problems to him, I know, and pondered his advice, if he gave advice, or followed his orders, if he gave orders.

But personally she held no special quarter for Catholic schools, unable to stomach the child-bullying and all the endless, drumming, hectoring indoctrination. Most of all she hated the whining pleas for money. *"Non finiscono mai,"* she'd grumble. "They never stop. It's a racket, like everything else." And yet she was a devout Catholic, in her way, prayerful to the bone, and a good Catholic mother who wanted us—especially us girls—to have our white-dress first communions and confirmations and look for all the world like good little Catholic girls.

She herself had been educated to the sixth grade in public schools. She had thought school wonderful, and had longed to stay and go on for her diploma. It was the dream she would confess to us those nights when she was not too tired to talk, sitting at the side of our beds in that little train compartment of a room with the eerie green picture of St. Ann and the Virgin on the wall.

Smoothing her work-roughened hands with lotion as she spoke, working the cream into her fingertips, she would take our soft, small hands between hers one at a time and pretend to polish them, telling us about her life, about her dream of someday becoming a teacher. Then she would unroll her thick dark hair, beginning now to have the odd streak of gray in it, from the stiff net cylinder that held it in a smooth corona at the back of her head, and let it fall wavily down, and brush it and then braid it slowly and deftly for bed.

But Grandma Flavia, she said, had told her it was just too bad, there was a family to feed, and sixth grade was as long as she could wait to send her daughters to work. So Mary had had to go to work, and then to turn over her paycheck every week, untouched, and make a good case for getting any of it back over carfare. You could tell she was never going to let any such holding back happen to us. And every last bit we could get out of school, from the book report on the presidents to the topographical maps of Brazil with the little cotton balls on them, was to be got for her as well as for ourselves.

She was such a strange medley, fear and softness in her dark eyes, daring in her hands! We'd beg her to repeat the little story about the job she'd got when she was twenty, after the interviewer had said she'd write and she had snapped back that "she was looking for a job, not a correspondence." How we loved the boldness of it! And yet now she seemed to have been born to worry, as if her secret sense of the world's danger had been touched too many times since her father's near brush with the bullet. As if the blow of my father's illness, the intuition that it was meant as a reproach for some wrong she had done, had permanently darkened a part of her heart, overlaid some wellspring of natural joy in her with a stern, legislated anxiety. When she took off her glasses and rubbed her tired eyes and then looked up again, you could just catch that look, that tremulous look, flickering between courage and fear.

She worried about us, about Carlo especially, and the spite that lay like a thin glass wall of faked bravado on his childish heart. How would he survive? How would all her overachieving little brood make it through this flinty world, which seemed to grow more unbearably flinty and cruel every day? She had created a shrine of her own on the highboy in her room. She would light candles and get down on her knees before the blessed blue Virgin, or with eyes squeezed passionately shut murmur earnest prayers to Saint Anthony, he of the bare-chested and be-aureoled baby Jesus on one arm and pure shaft of lily on the other, the only true male mother of the canon. As soon as devotion to the Infant Jesus of Prague spread after the war, she purchased her own little statuette and gave away several to her sisters, lighting candles to him, too, buying all the protection she could get. Our innocent prayers were credit in the bank. On Sunday nights we were brought to our own knees to murmur the rosary together. I was hypnotized by the humming sound, the sensation of the smooth pearly beads slipping between my fingers, the sense that we were braiding our prayers as surely as if they had been the warm strands of my sister's recalcitrant brown hair.

We prayed for my father, but for ourselves as well, body and soul, since for her there was no telling them apart. I think she may have prayed for me in a special way, seeing me headstrong ("like your father") and out in the world on such a long lead. She sewed garlic cloves into my underwear. She placed a scapular around my neck and under my sweater before she sent me off to school in the morning, crossing herself at the window as I took the turn into Second Avenue and disappeared around the corner.

·

My father, she would say (she seemed never to tire of saying, with a sigh, like a hope continuously deferred, even though it might be true), was getting well. Every time she visited him without us she would bring our latest prizes with her, our gold-starred reports on the heavenly constellations, our little drawings and poems, and come back and tell us how proud he was, and how much stronger he looked. When we saw him ourselves, those spring Sundays among the apple blossoms and tulip trees up at Woodlawn, alongside the cemetery stones, he still looked limp and thin and alien, not quite ready to face us, let alone the world, but his face was growing fuller, his eyes brighter and steadier, and the tide of color seemed to be rising. Surely he felt the daunting strangeness of our having done so much growing up without him.

He had begun to write. It was something he did well and gracefully, like drawing, and had always done, but dismissively—as if it were a road not taken once and now revisited with pain. We saw none of it, except for a quip that appeared in the nursing-home newsletter. I wonder he even told us of it, it was so slight and silly: *"Mario to Vinnie: 'I lost a fortune overnight.' Vinnie: 'How'd you do that?' Mario: 'I went to bed feeling like a million dollars and woke up feeling like two cents.'"* I was a child. It made me laugh. Now I think it may have been for him something like that little sliver of an olive branch in the beak of Noah's trial bird after the flood. The Old Nick, the devil of the Neapolitan in him, was still there, that dry, faintly bitter and cynical humor that had once made him feel alive.

And it had a subtext, after all, didn't it. For the loss of a million dollars overnight might be sharper than a serpent's tooth. But there was such a thing, perhaps, as taking the venom in jesting, homeopathic doses.

It must have been that same spring of 1946 that I cracked my lip in Van Cortlandt Park, on a rare Sunday outing, a splendid day suddenly turned catastrophic. My own stupid fault. My mother couldn't stop me. "Headstrong—just like your father," she wept, exasperated. In this case the word *headstrong* applied literally, my head having led my body where my body had thought better of following. I had not lost my mimetic impulse for doing just what my brothers did, and after lunch they'd decided to take a walk along the top of a wood rail fence. But with their lean and boyishly arranged bodies they could almost float, like acrobats on a wire, balancing with a wave of their arms. I was rounder, full of wobbles, no plumper than I had ever been, but the weight was beginning to move downward onto my hips. As I felt myself fall I must have drawn my mouth in over my teeth. My chin struck the fence post just as my feet landed, driving my upper incisor straight through the soft, yielding mass of my upper lip.

"You're lucky you got no worse," said the doctor at the first aid station as he put in the stitches. My chin was sore, but amazingly the tooth had not broken. My mother held me by the arms, her eyes damp, her wet, blood-slimed handkerchief still wadded in her hand. My brothers and little sister stood by feeling sorry for me, Ann's big and anxious eyes only a little less tearful than my own.

"Will she be . . . disfigured, doctor?" my mother asked, probably wondering even as she said it if I knew what "disfigured" meant. I knew. It marked a leap in my consciousness to think what it might mean to me now. He said, "Not if she can keep these stitches in long enough to close the wound." But the lip is a tender place. He couldn't make the stitches very close or very tight. And how, I thought, as the days went by, if you have to eat and drink and smile and brush your teeth, can you possibly keep stitches in your upper lip from coming loose? I worried about this. A babysitter, once, had told me my mouth was already too big.

But the little threads tickled my tongue and slowly unraveled on their own. I didn't even have to go back to have them removed. Little by little, the tender puffiness of my lip receded into a slightly off-center little pad of fullness. Looking in the mirror, more and more as girls did, I could never bring myself to love it, though in time I found it might be lovely in a certain light, and especially tender to a kiss.

I cannot remember my father's coming home. Strange, when everything about his *being* home again is so vivid. He seemed to slip imperceptibly back into our lives as if the space he'd left had never been allowed to close. I don't remember even being glad, although I must have been. There was something secret and yet convulsive about the change he wrought in our lives—about the change he wrought in me. I felt him as a newfound love, of whom I thought present or absent, toward whom I was abject in my tenderness. But I also felt him as a new and phallic presence, a vigilant gaze, which seemed to be trained on me to a degree both lovely and unbearable. I can remember his holding up my chin to examine my still-puffy mouth wound, looking at it sad-eyed, and making that familiar old, heart-sinking *tsk-tsk* sound of his between his tongue and his teeth. I had almost forgotten that sound and the ache it gave my heart.

I can remember awakening rather abruptly to a sense that even in your own familiar house there could be a new and unprecedented division of space, here, in your own doorless railroad flat where everything lay open to the world and where, apart from the bathroom, privacy was mythical. And yet on a hot day that summer, as I scurried from bathroom to bedroom in my underwear, I felt his eyes on me, and that dark, desiring, yet hurtful look of his, that *tsk-tsk* of disapproval, followed by that even more stinging shame of a reproach directed not at me but at my mother, as if I were no longer his child, as if I were a stranger. And perhaps I was—perhaps we were both strangers to each other.

Mario resumed his place working at the side of his father, Luigi, in the pork store on Third Avenue.

How little I have said of Grandpa Luigi, for all that he was our benefactor through those troubled East Harlem years. And yet he was the only grandparent I knew past my earliest childhood memories of my mother's father. Of course, the time we spent with him outside the store was small, our four steep flights too much to ask of his poor old legs. And as for Sundays, what would they have been like for my mother without Mario, surrounded by all the Neapolitan in-laws who only pretended to love her?

I can imagine her *ansia* about this, nevertheless. And I know while she worked with Grandpa she often invited him home, and that we loved his visits—the good, genial, round, unassuming old man whose wheezing chest we could hear long before his beamish face appeared above the last flight of stairs. Chubby and chap-fallen, he seemed a wonder of the world to me. His teeth were gone and he had refused to replace them with dentures. He chewed his food with his hardened gums and laughed bigly out of that amazingly toothless mouth. I marveled at his life, which seemed to me simple as a monk's, and at his depths of salty good humor for dealing with the malign fate of war that had kept him stranded in the United States until it was over, unable to get back. For his children had made family lives here. He was alone.

He knew no English, or little. Relying on my mother at the shop had not improved it. But he had memorized a rollicking dictionary of affectionate Italian body language for kids, and could sit my sister and me on on his knees and sing us Neapolitan rhymes, and let out that big, heaving laugh that shook his empty chaps, and leave us squealing and giggling with a stinging rub of his day's growth of grizzled beard on our tender cheeks.

He could not have been more different from my father, whose *superbia* came straight from Nonna Immacolata—or so I imagined from the unsmiling pictures I had seen of her—she who had declared back in 1929 that *she* would not celebrate her son's wedding to a lowly, swart-skinned *Zeechilyaahn,* and vigorously denounced any member of the family who did. I'm not sure how I came to know this of her. Perhaps it had been one of my mother's lonely confidences, those nights when she had turned over the darkest earth in her heart's garden. I can imagine her being sorry she had told us, as if it had been a betrayal of *him,* one of those memories to lay away in the mortuary of denial, perhaps to be opened when we were grown, perhaps never ever to be opened at all. But, once told, how could it be untold? And now it strikes such a solemn chord in me that it is difficult to recover even what I must have felt in pity for my father and grandfather when those soft, black-bordered letters arrived from Sperone saying that Nonna Immacolata had died.

It had been almost ten years since Luigi had seen her. I am tempted to wonder just how deeply he felt the loss—surely less than my father, whose grief I expected to be what it was, horribly dark and solemn. And yet having only such a standard, or the remembered melodrama of my Spagnola aunts to measure my grandfather's sorrow by, how could I tell? He sorrowed. Perhaps he was mortified that he had missed her passing. He seemed to long for home more than ever. He seemed to be thinking more than ever of his own mortality. Satisfied, now, that he had seen my father through his transition, he signed over the lease to the store, and we took him to the steamship pier and waved him off.

And now from across the sea poured more letters than ever, a whole new transatlantic revival of *famiglia,* soft, sepia photographs wrapped in their fine, almost diaphanous airmail paper—who had died, who'd been born, who'd survived, who'd grown up, who'd suffered, married, miscarried. Brothers, sisters, cousins, second cousins, second cousins twice removed, with names that reclaimed all the territory of naming abandoned by my American aunts—Rosina, Raffaelo, Michelina, Irena, Rosetta, Clementina, Filiberto, Alfonso, Cenzina. New letters came from Grandpa Luigi, fired up to merchant again, eager to get into the booming postwar export trade. The iron is hot, Mario is well, no? Now *he* should come home. *Home,* they said. And he had been in America since 1921!

He promises my mother a brief visit only, a month or two, till Thanksgiving, Christmas at the latest. But it doesn't seem possible to me. My father has just come back into my life, how can he be leaving? Until it is real I refuse to accept it, until we go to that same pier again on that gray September morning and I actually see him, slumped among the massed bodies along the deck rail, searching for us in the roaring, weeping crowd on the pier, tipping his dark fedora as the S.S. *Vulcania* disappears into the mist. I could have drowned in the aching sound the ship bellowed as it pulled away. They found me hunched in a corner of the girls' bathroom at school later that day, sobbing inconsolably.

What I haven't said is that he had taken my brother Carlo with him. Because I couldn't bear it. Carlo, still undersized and baby-faced at fourteen, with a devilish shock of brown hair that got into his eyes, eyes that otherwise crackled with mischief. He had not wanted to go. Why should he? *I* loved Italy. It should have been *me.*

Yet it wasn't, and I knew why. Not just because it would have been awkward, difficult, absurd, but because in the twisted moral vocabulary of the Italian family, this was not a gift, not a reward, but a punishment. Not that they would have admitted it. No, no, no. It was protection. It was to take him out of danger, remove him from the war zone of our East Harlem neighborhood. And they were right. It was no longer just another ghetto of tough-guy Italians but the epicenter of radical ethnic change. Always a feisty neighborhood, contested turf for southern *paesani* of every dialect, for years the working-class politics of a brilliant labor congressman named Vito Marcantonio had mellowed the strife and even forged a peace between Italians and the blacks in Harlem proper, along the great Park Avenue divide. But great new migrations of southern blacks and Puerto Ricans had been thrown into the mix by the end of the war. Violent playground riots made my brothers' Benjamin Franklin School infamous. There were ugly turf-war clashes on the side streets, terrifying sidewalk confrontations. A boy could turn a street corner and find himself face-to-face with a switchblade. This had actually happened to Carlo. My parents truly feared for his life. He was tinder to a match, let alone a blowtorch.

And yet he had seemed to become so much more tractable while my father was gone, only to flare up and be restive and difficult again as soon as he was home. I am sure my mother saw this and felt helpless, just as my father saw it and felt affronted, defied. But where could they go for help? Not to professionals—this would be *vergogna,* disgrace—yet my father refused to be helpless. He was resolved. It didn't matter if Carlo were set back a term at school, or how a boy so high-spirited might feel, trapped in a strange culture under his father's constant surveillance, or he overruled such thoughts as womanish. He knew what was right for his son. And he meant well—he did—he meant to take an absentee father's full if belated responsibility. And he would teach him, finally—teach him as only he could—the lessons that must come from the great book of travel and of life.

I wrote to my brother almost the moment he left. Of course I could not see him there; I could see only myself in his place. "It must make you giddy," I said, thinking how excited I would be. And he shot back, as soon as he could put pencil to paper: "I am *not* 'giddy,' you dumbbell. Don't tell *me* how I'm supposed to feel."

The months passed swiftly after all, and the two of them came back not much later than promised, soon after the New Year. My father looked as if he had been home. He had finally stopped smoking and put on more weight. My brother looked worse, more scowling, more passive and victimized.

Grateful as I was to see my father again, I still wanted *my* Italy out of this, and hungered selfishly for its secret. I scanned everything they brought back with them, stood expectantly at the lip of each trunk, leaden with the weight of deeply embroidered linens and great lengths of Italian silk, watched the raising of every treasure as if it had come up out of the sunken *Titanic* and had some great revelation trapped in its folds. And they *were* treasures, gorgeous to the eye, silken to the hand. Yet even in my hunger I could sense something vaguely repellent beneath the aura of magic in those beautiful objects, as if I knew too well from the world of my mother and my aunts—most of them half-blind from close sewing and beading—what it meant to do elaborate, fine *ricamo* on a tablecloth twelve feet long. And so, instead of Italian hillsides abloom with oranges and light, I found myself perversely imagining aunts and cousins, girls like me, straining their eyes against the fading winter daylight to finish these *lenzuoli* and *serviette* in time, so that Mario could take them back with him and make everyone rich.

My father had bought a camera just before he'd left for Italy, this time for making eight-millimeter movies. That old itch, the photographic passion that is as much a part of him as his eyes—and it must always be the best, the latest, the technological cutting edge, like the magical timer he used to set at our picnics at Indian Lake and Sabino Canyon, so that he himself could be in the snapshots with us. He had dredged up all his old and beautiful still equipment before the trip and spread it restlessly on the table, hungering for something new. And now, one day, soon after he is back, he picks me up after school and takes me with him to the offices of Bell & Howell to buy his first projector. He converses with men who wear ties, yet roll up their shirtsleeves to their elbows like butchers; he laughs and talks shop with them as if they are his comrades. At home again, he takes out the reels he has filmed abroad and sets them up and we turn down the lights and run the silent flickering images late into the night.

He calls these places by familiar names—*Sperone, Striano, Napoli*—but they are like no Italy I have ever imagined. And they are all alike, all alike mean, war-devastated places the winter rains have left sodden and muddy. My impatient cousins pass in obligatory procession before the camera's patronizing stare, their mouths moving in soundless messages. The camera starts into a rough courtyard where the same cousins are chasing a huge, thrashing sow maddened with fear in a seasonal ritual of slaughter. They seize her and bring her screaming to the knife. She is screaming but you cannot hear her. And then the film stops and starts again, and she is hanging from a post, her blood is dripping into a pail, and we cry out.

My sister and I cry out. Carlo is silent, and I look for his eyes, near me in the darkened, flickering room, but he seems unmoved. How is this possible? What enemy of all the beauty I remembered had he met and conquered there, to be so still, so complacent? Where had it gone? What had he seen that I couldn't see, what meaning of this hideous mystery of war and after-war that I couldn't understand? He suddenly seems smaller, smaller even than he had seemed dancing there in the courtyard and flicking his handsome, wicked little face across the screen, here, now, gripping the armrests of his chair, staring arrogantly away.

Movies, suddenly, became threaded with our lives now as if they had never been forbidden. My father, the same father who had barely let them across the threshold once, threw open the door and invited them straight into the house. The metaphor is exact. First he turned the movie camera on us and made it the passion still photography had been a decade before. It seems almost too disparaging to call this premeditated orchestration of images "home movies." They were veritable cinema verité, his way of putting "home" at an aesthetic and emotional distance and re-creating it as art.

My mother humored him in this steel whim, satisfied merely that he was alive and well and back in her bed at night. She humored him even when he determined one day that he would sink even deeper into the belly of the beast, that he would beat the Hollywood film racket he had despised by joining it. He had by this time established a rather fawning friendship with the pastor of Our Lady of Mount Carmel on East 116th Street—perhaps pressed on by my mother, whose sense of the debt she owed the Madonna del Carmine for the response to her novenas could be a force. This friendship flowered, eventually, into a scheme to get parishioners to church and to the movies at the same time, movies vetted by the pastor as well as approved by the Code.

It became an East Harlem *Cinema Paradiso*, my father in the equivalent of the choir-loft projection room. Movies could be rented at a special sixteen-millimeter rate, and the church, to help recoup the expenses, would apply a small admission charge for stepping down to the basement entrance of a Sunday evening. Perhaps my father received a fee, perhaps not, but since the projector was his own, he simply took the movies back home with him, and there in our own living room we could see them for ourselves, as often as we wanted, before those round silver drums the size of pizzas had to be returned to the devil's devil they came from.

We saw movies. We saw every Bud Abbott and Lou Costello ever made, every *Road to* with Bob Hope and Bing Crosby and Dorothy Lamour swishing around in her discreet sarong, everything ever made with the Andrews Sisters in it. No

Wizard of Oz, or, God forbid, *Gone With the Wind,* which couldn't be got for love or money. Even Bogart was dicey, and the pastor was picky about anything with Rita Hayworth, let alone Garbo. But he let by the Bela Lugosi *Frankenstein*—plus Astaire and Rogers, Lana Turner, Claudette Colbert (nothing too smoldering of course), Orson Welles and Joan Fontaine in *Jane Eyre.* We had Spencer Tracy, Ingrid Bergman's Joan of Arc, eventually Saint Bernadette. We laughed, we cried. Postwar war movies like *The Five Sullivans* were killers. The living room ran with tears for days.

I fell in love with the women Paulette Goddard and Katharine Hepburn played. Someday I wanted to have all their tomboy bravado and still look as steamy as Linda Darnell. There was only one male star I loved who did not look like my father, an Irishman named Brian Aherne. The square jaw, the open, smiling face, the soft Irish eyes and burled hair seemed to possess some archetypal otherness I craved. Seemed to promise a safety and joy I had forgotten.

But I kept this love darkly to myself, my secret this time.

5

I think I must have known, at least from the time we lived in East Harlem, that my parents still owned the house in New Rochelle and had merely rented it when we left for Arizona. It had not felt that way. The break seemed to have been made with such finality. And yet here was another sign of some original *pentimento* beneath the fresh skin of paint. Perhaps it had been expedient not to rush to sell during the radically changing housing market of the early war. But in what curious haste to leave was so much left behind (as we later discovered)—old store and family stuff, photos, memorabilia, my father's sketches and drawings—the archeology of an entire epoch, stashed in cartons and chests and an old steamer trunk in the basement?

They reclaimed the house over the winter of 1947, and we moved back into it a bit at a time, slowly fitting and furnishing the stone cold rooms, with their tangy smells of freshly stripped wood and wallpaper paste topped up at each visit with the heady perfume of coffee, freshly, quickly brewed to drive out the chill the moment my father unlocked the door. That winter was indeed so frozen, so bitter and severe, that it is still used as a weather-almanac baseline. The snow relentlessly fell and fell, and then clung on, deep and hardened, through and beyond the weeks of our protracted moving. Up Third Avenue and through the Bronx my father would take us after he had shut down the store, often with the wipers on our new Plymouth churning against a light new fall of snow, past brightly lit shops pleading with January shoppers to brave the icy sidewalks and the sky-high snowpiles at the intersections. The drive grew darker and less intense along Bruckner Boulevard, and for the half hour up the Hutchinson River Parkway Ann and I usually fell asleep, curled together for warmth in the back. When we finally entered Sickles Place, layered with so much frozen snow that it crunched out loud beneath the tire chains, we would come suddenly, dreamily awake.

The rooms had shrunken, of course, as rooms one returns to after earliest childhood do. Yet it may be to this brief time, before the space of memory was refilled with rugs and lamps and chairs and all the necessary bric-a-brac of Italian American household life, that I owe my queer passion for the aesthetic of the empty house, when I felt and reclaimed its bare, precious instant of vacancy, and it was to my wondering eyes as if a cavern from a forgotten romance had been restored to me out of a frozen dream.

We were barely settled when my brothers took charge of the snowbound frontyard slope and constructed a daredevil sled jump. Lou, born leader, construction genius, ordered everyone to work who intended to use it, first bringing snow to pack, then water to pour over each carefully mounded snow layer, until it was compacted as solid as granite. Since the volunteers included not just Carlo but every neighborhood kid with half a grain of testosterone, the result was an instant circle of new friends and a jump that rose off a downhill sled run to about thirty inches high. They'd have gone higher except the slam landing after that exuberant takeoff might have shattered even the sturdiest Flexible Flyer, and eventually did a few of the less sturdy.

I helped build the jump too. So did Ann. In the end she had the good sense not to risk it. I loved the rapture of speed and the breathtaking flight into the icy air. But I quit after a try or two, before the jump had reached its full height, when the shudder that shook me as I hit the downslope racked my body with primal memories of my infant fall from that second-story window. And so the two of us, from the safe, warm, Tudor-framed tower of our bedroom above, looked down on every boy in the neighborhood—tall, short, fat, thin, black, white—risking life and limb in the service of a mad, blind, hilarious daring, not sure whether to envy or despise them.

At least *I* wasn't sure. But at going-on-thirteen a girl knows there are other risks at hand, other mysteries to attend to. That spring, beneath the same high window, where the northeast side of the house shaped itself to the steep contour of the Sickles Avenue hill, there blossomed over that once icy slope the white cascading glory of a huge and insanely fragrant juniper orange bush—a little draggled at the bottom skirt where the boys had nicked it taking the curve of the sled run, but my mother said it had become all the more bountiful for the depth of the snow that had buried it that winter. It took over the air. You could not be near it without a deep, almost delirious drinking of your breath.

It was my mother's favorite. She always called it *jasmine,* and the freight of all that is lovely and exotic and fragile was in the word. Ten years later, a friend and colleague in Greensboro, where I spent my first year of teaching, told me its proper name, and since then, juniper orange is what other such opulently endowed bushes are called. The one below my girlhood window—gorgeously fragrant, at once delicate and wildly louche in its June-day glory, with its soft aureole of bees and its fatal snow of petals in a matter of weeks—will always be jasmine. It loved to come into full bloom on my mother's wedding anniversary, in mid-June. I have seen in her bridal pictures a reminiscent spray lying across her lap.

I can still smell it. I can still feel the enchantment it evokes of something like a love of my own, of the many loves that had begun to stir me more and more in books, I can almost hear the scent rushing like noise each spring through the green fuse of my adolescent heart. To think of that jasmine now is for it to be then again. I am lying abed in the full moonlight of a June night, alive, alive, in a state of soft, obedient, liquid surrender, the window ajar, and the incense of that drunken perfume rising up to me like a lover.

Vissi d'art, vissi d'amore. I lived by art, by dreams of love. What else was there to live by, except, for a while, those old movies, and the recorded operas that made music like gods out of a machine? My father, true to form, when television sets first began to be marketed in 1947, broke the bank to get one, a big-screen Dumont framed in a walnut console the size of a coffin, creating a whole new geography of desire. From the moment it was set in its place against the living-room wall it absolutely defined the space, commensurable with nothing. Its primitive children's programming—the playschool of a new idiom for the children of the new age—fleetingly absorbed us. But it belonged to a foreign country compared with opera. Opera, ringing in ecstatic exile through the house, or pouring its fantastic heart out over the Saturday radio, signified some lost paradise regained. *Bohème* and *Tosca* for my father—and by a powerful circuitry my mother too, who swooned over Mario Cavaradossi out of an essential fidelity to her own Mario—were the very breath of cultural memory, center of a veneration more sublime and compelling than religion. I loved them, with a baffled and conflicted energy. I did not understand the words, only the sound of them somehow, and the stories were complex and inscrutable. I loved them, I think, *because* I did not fully understand them and yet their foreignness was my own and seemed to belong to me as a birthright. They *entered* me, less as sound than as imagery, darklit landscapes of incomprehensible passion, swelling the house of my mind with an idea of devotion tragic and terrible.

By now I had been enrolled in seven different schools in seven years of schooling, and in spite of being thought of by all my teachers as bright and gifted, in spite of having been trusted, while we lived in the city, to roam all over the East Side with my ready subway nickel to music lessons and art classes as well as to school, I had become rather a oddly skewed and introverted child, self-absorbed, peopling my school notebooks with faces and dancing bodies and disembodied eyes, suffering what I can describe only as a near-pathological indifference to my own visibility, as if the plumpish flesh of the body I inhabited were a kind of capsule in which I could float through the world seeing but unseen.

I had been in the first of two years at Hunter College Junior High when we moved back to New Rochelle. As schools went, it was a good place for me, a glimpse into what it meant to be a creative child while still somehow anchoring me in the real world. Hunter College was still a teacher's college for women then. It had designed this prestigious little two-year junior academy for girls as a prep school for the even more prestigious Hunter College High. Like a handful of other special public high schools in New York, it had a selective citywide admission policy, each applicant having to pass through an intense battery of IQ and aptitude tests, personally administered over the better part of a day.

I had gone there from Mrs. Streicher's sixth grade at PS 102. It was less a sign of her preference, perhaps, than of my own wavering sense of the reality of school that she had passed me over for the entrance exam and recommended instead my classmate Connie Colandro—bright, sweet, compliant Connie. But my mother was indignant. In one of those seizures of righteous fury for which she was famous, she marched me straight down to East 69th Street on her own, and when the results were posted I was in and Connie wasn't. Pity Mrs. Streicher, who also happened to be a customer in Alaya's Market. The next time she stopped at the store, crow was the special of the day, and my mother dressed it with somewhat more zest than was called for, especially since I was standing right there. But, oh, the irrepressible flutter of exultant pride, and what it taught me that day about the sweet shame of petty triumph!

Anyone but my mother might have been wary of placing me in a competitive place like Hunter, where the threat loomed of heaping even greater strain on an already oversensitized and alienated psyche like mine. The effect, as it turned out, was just the opposite. To be suddenly thrown into the midst of twenty-five girls as smart or smarter than I was, and even more talented, infused me with an ecstatic new sense of my own ordinariness. Girls like Mary Beck, who at thirteen could play "Claire de Lune" and the "Moonlight Sonata" till tears welled in our eyes, girls whose braininess and genius made me glow with the relief of a burden shared, a burden lifted. I can never remember envying their gifts. I can remember feeling only as though at last *I* had become the little sister in the protection of bigger ones, of girls who, even at my age or a little older, were awesomely worldly wise.

So I let down my guard and I took a friend almost as one might take a lover, with my whole heart, a girl who, for once, did not either fear or patronize me. She was Carole, a big, rather full-bodied redhead with kindly freckles and inappropriately stern, wire-rimmed spectacles, and a sweet maternal way that reminded me of Meg in *Little Women*. Carole seemed at least three years beyond anyone in the class in terms of physical development and already had impressive breasts in the seventh grade. She was like a mother hen, nestling me under her wing. We wrote each other long, candid, gushing letters over the two following summers, she from Queens where she lived, and I, now, from Westchester.

It was Carole, when we finally entered the eighth grade, who told me the facts of life. She could have told me in the seventh, she said, but had postponed it to spare me some of the shock she knew was inevitable. I think I strangled a cry in the lunchroom. I wasn't sure but that I might have preferred being pushed down onto the subway tracks. I did not feel spared. I think that even had I not been mute with outrage, as I was for days, I was incapable of phrasing the central question for me, which was how so savage, so animal an act could have anything to do with the transcendent emotions I had already experienced in my fantasies of love.

Had I asked, she might have actually tried to tell me. She might actually have succeeded. Perhaps my retrospect enlarges her, but I thought her very wise. As my fury abated, I sensed the greatness of her pity for me, the greatness of her sense of the pity of it all, both of us having come face to face with a knowledge she knew I did not want to know, because she had not wanted to know it either, once. But she did know, and it was as if she had made it to still another horizon, a place where you can finally take in the stunning wisdom for a girl that love can be an emotion of the body as well as of the soul. I did not yet want to know it for myself, let alone to think it was related to something my parents felt for one another. I did not yet connect it with the moans I sometimes heard in the night, now that the thin bedroom wall was all that divided my room from theirs.

Someday I would go there, where Carole had gone, if not now. And yet how merciful for so friendship-stunted a child as I was that I would be led to that crossing by a friend as motherly as Carole and as profoundly, purely, shameless. My own mother, for all her sweet moan, could never, in the shame of her body, have told me. At least not then, and then was when I needed to know.

And the more merciful, perhaps, because it had been so chancy. I should not even have continued into the eighth grade with Carole. Schools like Hunter were meant to be among the treasured rewards of city life, off-limits to children of the suburbs like me, now officially resident in New Rochelle. A hard rule, but enshrined in law. And yet there had never seemed to be any question about my staying. I had never been asked by my parents if I preferred *not* to lie about where I lived, *not* to rise in the dark and travel two hours to get to school, *not* to spend my afternoons in the dingy room at the back of the store trying to do my homework until my father was ready to close up and take me home. Whether I might simply prefer to attend St. Gabriel's in New Rochelle, as my sister did. A touch of ink on the office file and I had simply moved downtown to 326 East 78th Street, where my Aunt Carmelina's family of Alayas legitimately showed up in the phone book.

Thus Hunter had me straight through the eighth grade, in spite of the law, in spite of the lie. When it came time to think about high school, I followed, still blind and unresisting, my mother's relentless script for my future brilliant career. I lied my way through another competitive exam and began my ninth grade in the fall of 1948 as an art student under the illustrious aegis of the High School of Music & Art.

Had I actually been asked what I wanted, I'm not sure what I would have said. It was a choice like Bartleby's, and I would have preferred not to make it. I think I knew that there was no bearing to lose these fugitive life-chances, even if—especially if—we could not afford to keep them honestly. And yet I could never accept the simple expediency of this fiction. I suffered it new and stinging every fearful, sneaking day. It is a hard thing for a child to lie. It was a hard thing for *me* to lie and still believe that in every other use of my mind I loved the truth—that the truth loved me, as I thought more passionately each day. And yet I was a good child, a dutiful child. We never discussed it. I learned to nurture this strange, regrettable gift my parents had made me of a certain stupid courage and an even more certain cunning. And some little window of clarity about hard choices, which in time might have opened on a daybreak of readiness for life, instead slapped quickly shut on a dutiful daughter's abject little soul.

Carole's small window on friendship—that too seemed closed now. Friends were a danger, every one a potential informer. There were strict protocols of secure intelligence: Never to bring friends home, never to speak to them of your house or your street or, God forbid, your garden—city apartments did not have gardens. Never to visit them, lest they want to visit you in return and wonder why they couldn't, when you lived so smack in the middle of the East Side—well, *didn't* you? What would you tell them? What would you stammer? Oh, God, to be fourteen, fifteen, sixteen, and never to go to parties in the city—because anywhere you went after commuter hours was a thousand miles from home, because if you stayed too late you might miss the last train. And what would you say to friends' parents if they offered to drive you home?

No pajama parties. No sleeping over. Never, ever.

Actually, that was the only codicil of the Rule not strictly driven by the logic of the lie. Quite the opposite, since sleeping at a friend's after the theater or a party was the single most transparent, rational solution to nearly all the other problems—except the returned invitation, which theoretically could be fudged.

And yet I lived more rigidly by this law than by any other part of the Rule, just because it was not meant to be rational, and certainly not transparent, but on the face of it plain, draconian, and opaque. Opaque to me. Generations have trod and trod, understanding what it meant, knowing it was about sex. But girls were not to understand, for breaking the chivalric code to tell them would tarnish the very innocence that made them worth protecting.

Still, by some miracle of intense mutual need there were girls who did become my friends, more memorable and perhaps more loyal because they had to be so few, and because out my dark secret (somehow more ominously illegal than some of the secrets other girls kept) would inevitably pop. And then the very frisson of it would become our bond. There was Letizia, for one. I befriended her in our first year at Music & Art because she was a brilliant painter and I had to tell her so. I could not say why she loved me, since I did not feel very lovable. Perhaps, I thought, she loved to be loved. She returned the compliment with such a funny, winsome, benevolent air that it felt lavish—theatrical—like the affection of a movie star.

She loved my name, of course. Any *Letizia,* captive in this New World of names, would. And she was captive, an Italian, a Pitigliani, from Rome—"Italian Italian," as Italian Americans say. Italianness connected us, but to me it was a different kind of Italianness, a clue perhaps to the mystery I had not yet decoded, and she herself unlike any Italian girl I had ever known, a kind of Funny Girl, loping and tall, all shoulders and elbows and knees, moving her thin body both as spaciously and as awkwardly as a failed ballerina.

My father endorsed our friendship as flattering and safe, perhaps someday even useful. Neither she nor her family seemed to care a split about my sleazy little secret. *"Pouf!"* Letizia blew her breath with a laugh when I confessed. "So what?" The significance of this did not come home to me till years later. I knew the Pitiglianis were Jewish, but I did not understand that they had also been refugees from Mussolini's persecutions. They seemed so happy, even frivolous, when I met them, perhaps because they were—happy to be alive, to be together, to be going home at last as soon as Letizia's first year of high school was finished.

It seemed too hard that I should lose her as soon as I had found her. But what a sparkling good-bye-New-York-in-June it was! I made several visits to her apartment, where everything was in breezy disarray as the family packed—and shed—their American lives. Her parents, astonishingly open and kind, spoke a crisp, perfect English that struck me as both sculpted and witty, and treated me as if I were more adult than child, or just as much or as little as they were themselves. As for Letizia, I was her final, adoring American audience as well as her friend. I didn't mind. Her performance was anodyne to the pain of detaching. She had a splendid way of acting her own emotions, of outlining them, like Matisse or Modigliani, just as her own paintings did their vivid masses of color, and I was spectator to the manifest, dancing art of her spirit, trying out her gorgeous enthusiasms—I who lived in such an ambiguous world of mixed and treacherous meanings, uncertain what it was safe to love or hate.

Brian Aherne was OK, she granted, but I *must* fall in love with Clark Gable. So she thought, and so did her doting parents, utterly bemused by their wild child's cartoon of Love. They gave me an innocent permission my father—so solemn, so fearful of the seductiveness of dreaming—would never have given me. She took me with her to see *Mutiny on the Bounty.* She washed me in the geyser of her adoration of this splendid incarnation of virility. She told me that if I could not go instantly to *see* the film version of *Gone With the Wind* (which I confessed I hadn't, and couldn't), I mustn't wait. I must *instantly* read the book.

And I did, but not in an instant. Never in an instant. Long after Letizia was gone, I lingered on it—over it—under and around it. I sank and plunged and wallowed in it. I palpitated and thrilled with it. I let it burn the fingertips that turned the flesh of its pages. I buried it under my pillow at night, and by flashlight read and reread it in the dark. And at last I understood what it was Carole had been trying to tell me.

The jasmine had bloomed and gone. It was draped now in big, loopy greenwear that drooped with the heat.

I was all body, that summer I turned fourteen. I needed to move—to dance. Afternoons when no one else was home, we danced, just Ann and I; we attached every scarf we could find in the house to our underwear and played *La Gioconda* over and over again on the phonograph, until the record began to scratch and bounce alarmingly. We could not resist "The Dance of the Hours"—mistakingly calling it "The Dance of the Seven Veils" for the vision of it—with its vertiginous brilliance and sudden inexhaustible shifts of speed. I knew it was a trope for my paradoxical soul; I knew it—my body knew it—to be about the inner unconquerable stillness that somehow held back the chaotic swift flight of time and yet also about the secret ecstatic rush within the same stillness. And we were like *bacchantes,* the two of us, scarves flying, flinging ourselves wildly across the long living room, crisscrossing back and forth until we were both sweating and breathless, until the soles of our bare feet were scorched and we finally slumped exhausted to the rug.

I learned how to swim in July. My mother seemed especially vigilant these days, as she accompanied Ann and me to the beach on the Sound, one dry blue-sky day after another, and sat with her tatting on a bench above the retaining wall, straining her eyes to find us now and then in the crowd. I borrowed a book from the library and studied strokes. In my zeal for the perfect crawl, sidestroke, backstroke, I forgot time, forgot to wave to Mamma, forgot to eat. Ann stayed close, struggling with the green water, and sometimes I would grab her, and hugging and splashing and laughing, we would bound out farther to a little deeper water, and I would throw her back, again and again, until once we bounded out too deep. But I was holding her in my arms, she still unable to swim. Yet I couldn't find the bottom, and then neither of us could, flailing and thrashing the dark-green, salt-burning water; we could not get them to see us, just see us, and we were drowning, we were both of us gasping there, the black fear darkening my brain and drawing blackness down over an unending skyless minute.

Until I found it again, the muddy soft bottom, and pushed it away from my weight and threw her forward, my sister, safe. And then I remembered to lift my body and kick my found legs and move my arms, to ply them again in their smooth sockets to the shallow sandy water, to slush through the thin creamy water till I could look down and see my shining legs.

Together we found a place on the crowded arc of wet sand and sat, coughing, holding each other, trying not to cry, sputtering both of us with anger that not one of all those bathers out there—and the water had been crowded with them, hairy, big men, some of them so near—and not one, not one, had reached out an arm, a hand, to save us, they would have let us drown, right there in the midst of them, and the sun glaring down like God.

Soon after, in that same summer, I learned how to not to die of a fever that crushed me with delirium for nearly two weeks in August. And then, as soon as I was well enough to walk again, I learned how to bleed. My mother gently, blushingly, showed me what to do when it happened again.

I was thinner, I was taller. I felt strange to myself. I weighed in on the drugstore scale with a new penny and stared in joyous disbelief at the number that came printed on the little card. How had this happened? Like everything else, it had happened.

The boys in the neighborhood had picked up my brothers' name for me. "Hey, Fat Fluffky," they shouted from the street when they saw me back, bouncing the Spaldeen off the garage door.

"Not fat any more," I turned and said.

Did she say that? ". . . Normal and average. . . ."

Miss Ridgeway (who had enjoined us *never* to call her *Mrs.*), the brilliantly focused little woman who taught us watercolor in our sophomore year, was accompanying a strange man one day through the classroom studio—perhaps an artist colleague or former student. Up and down the aisles they strolled, glancing to both sides, pausing when a student creation momentarily anchored their gaze. They had meant not to disturb us. All their comments had been murmured in the same passing undertone. And just so they had approached and gone by my tablemate, Judy, and me.

But we had heard it, distinctly, both of us. We had just laid down our washes, our big Faber & Faber genuine sable brushes poised to the tips of their exquisite points, waiting out that perfect degree of dryness to apply the first keystroke of wet color that would tell everything about the perfection of our technique. "These two?" she had said, softly, but in a kind of airy, dismissive way, waving the wand of her hand over us like some inverse godmother, *"Just normal and average,"* and then she and the strange man had moved complacently on.

The look of anguish Judy and I shot each other in that moment bonded us for life. Pegasus shot down in midflight, Icarus in meltdown, could not have suffered a more mortal hurt or fallen as far or as hard. It had been one thing to be ordinary, to be "normal and average" at thirteen, taking necessary small comfort from sharing freak-space on the circus midway. Now, taking our crafts from the hands of the masters, we had—we had been taught to have—infinitely more lofty expectations of the dynamics of being, had become initiates into the sacred mysteries of matter, of chaotic worldstuff yielding to the resistless grasp of human hand and eye. Our dreams of creation were passionate and holy, even if what we aspired to touch was the least hem of Cezanne's garment, or John Marin's, or Brancusi's.

Oh, no, no. Normal and average would not do—not anymore. We had met too often in full assembly and intoned the noble poetry of our school song to the soaring music of Brahms's First Symphony.

> Now upward in wonder
> Our distant glance is turning
> Where brightly through ages
> The immortal lamp is burning—
> Our task unending,
> Defending,
> That realm above,
> Till dull and lifeless things have caught
> A beauty
> That daring dreams
> Have wrought—

They had told us a former student had composed the song, which only made it the more secretly endearing. Quaint, laughable in its way, no one would have denied how it stirred us to our depths just the same, how it challenged voice students all over the auditorium to more spectacular, bravura harmonies every time, making a thundering chorale out of our single, inconsequential little voices. I think we had come to believe we *were* defending that realm above, whatever it was.

Judy did not process the pain of this mortal wound the same way I did. Almost nothing had affirmed my existence so consistently from infancy as my little talent, that once astonishingly precocious coordination of eye and hand that had got me to Music & Art. My inner child was an artist, and I felt as my own mother might have about her, righteously outraged, burning with a flame that was not in the least hard and gemlike but bituminous, red-hot, and smoking, wishing for the power of witchcraft, for command of the evilest evil-eye, to prove to Miss Ridgeway unequivocally and forever how wrong she was.

Judy's inner artist-child simply giggled.

"How *can* you?" I implored.

"Wicked Witch of the East," she muttered roguishly, giggling again.

Judy, like Letizia, had a celluloid idol, but hers was Judy Garland. She had seen *Wizard* eight times before I met her, in the days before VCRs when seeing a feature film again and again meant catching every rerelease in every third-run little movie house all over town. She lived her life as if it shifted periodically into the screenplay, an intricate, whimsical weave of real and unreal and surreal, maddening and enchanting, hugging her Toto and trying to decide whether it was ever going to be Kansas anymore.

This was whenever she wasn't wandering in the country of Pooh-sticks and Piglet. She was big, way taller than I. Unlike Winnie-the-Pooh, whom she adored, she fought her weight with the strenuous practice of yoga and dance. But Judy could never be fully strenuous. She combined her amazonic proportions with the tenderness of a Cereal Goddess, protector of small stray creatures, preferably warm and furry ones, which she might take into her den and feed with an eyedropper until they opened their eyes and began to locate the cream on their own.

Maybe I was one. We had met in bio, where in our first weeks dishy Mr. Rappaport, in what I suspect was a ploy to deflect the crushes of his more nubile girl-students in the upper rows (every one of whom would have walked barefoot to China for a touch of his nether lip), had pretended to have a crush on *me*. It had become a running class joke that both mortified and uplifted me. For even if he didn't *really* love me—and I never allowed myself the wonder of dreaming *that* dream—his fictional fondness was kind, unmocking, a way of *seeing* me at a time when to be seen was a little like a life raft in the ocean of my bewildered and lonely selfhood. His gestures seemed so tender and genuine that they actually baffled and confused my classmates. And so they were forced to see me too, as something more than a nervous little ferret too good at math for an artist, who had maybe had one helluva good summer at fat camp.

But over that winter, in something like a female conspiracy of my mother and a pride of Spagnola aunts, there came a singular ritual of initiation into womanhood for me, and my long hair—still woven into the coarse brown braids I'd been known for—was finally cut off at the classy Richard Hudnut salon on Central Park South. For them it must have meant a great deal that I've forgotten. I remember only that it seemed to transfigure me for *him*. He must have seen, suddenly, a soulful little woman sitting there where I used to sit, a Latin lovely-to-be with an oversized mouth and dark-shaded bedroom eyes, and that new mass of soft dusky curls around her face. Looking down at me from way up on his lab-table perch, he uttered, "Oh, *Flavia*," in so melting a way that it must have checked my breathing for a full, red, blinding minute and made the big girls in the back swoon with envy.

Judy was not among them. She had befriended me months ago, after all, when I was still one of those small stray creatures needing an eyedropper. She didn't particularly care for me to bloom, or rather didn't care if I bloomed or didn't, locked in as a sort of Piglet to her Pooh. I forgave her. I didn't have to forgive her. I understood.

It was a kind of motherliness she had nurtured in the misery of a lonely boarding-school childhood before her own mother had finally, irrevocably, divorced her father and reclaimed her, brought her back home to the two-bedroom apartment they had to share with her old and dying grandparents, who were stolid, unregenerate Christian Scientists of upright British stock.

Judy wanted to dance with me now through worlds she had never been allowed to enjoy as a child, worlds whose blisses needed sharing. I didn't mind. There had been plenty of childhoods missing from my life too. I think she soon came to see—and to like—that there was some peculiar something in me independent of her waifish projections, perhaps some courage to stay afloat on my own disorienting little ocean. I took from her a certain recipe for play, for skewering reality. In exchange, she found in me some key to accepting it, some seriousness and ambition she was willing to consider respecting.

Judy lived with her mother on East 81st Street, just off Lexington, a sunny fifth-floor apartment mere blocks from where I was supposed to be living. At first she was a study of puzzlement and curiosity that I made such a mystery about where home actually was. She was thrilled with the intrigue of the awful truth. Much less so her mother, Muriel, part Cereal Goddess's Great Mother and part Mature Parent. Muriel in fact *was* the Mature Parent. In a tiny storage room off the parlor in which you could barely have fit a bathtub, Muriel sequestered herself to write a Hearst-syndicated column that offered advice on the sensible raising of children to every storm-tossed parent in the country three times a week, every week of the year. She encouraged her daughter to take this reputation seriously, probably because she was having a little trouble taking it quite seriously herself.

Yet Muriel lamented my predicament with a certain jaded total innocence of judgment. She herself was always short of money and knew what it meant to struggle on, to keep up an East Side appearance in her case while living from hand to mouth, nursing her Aged Ps through their long, slow dying. She measured my situation, and of course my parents', as a sad fact of life. Maybe she thought a striver like me would have a ballasting influence on Judy, who might otherwise fly off to the tops of honey-trees.

She wished we could spend more time together. "You are always running off to some *train* or other," she would say in her plummy near-British way. Her annoyance was only half self-mocking as she leapt up from her armchair and fluttered off to the kitchen. I loved how she looked when she strode away, always dressed in a pale-colored jersey gown of some flowing variety, as if she were just stepping off a temple pediment.

Judy chided her. It was no use. She was never ever even to *suggest* I sleep over, no matter how convenient. And Muriel would chortle in that chesty way that came from smoking too many Pall Malls when she wrote her columns.

"You know he is afraid," she'd say, speaking as blandly of my father as if she were reading a fortune cookie, "that you will bring him an illegitimate child."

So much for the opacity of the Rule.

6

In most cultures, just to be an adolescent girl is to be confused about the safety of knowledge. In me, a girl at the American midcentury, with part of my personal consciousness already under a gag rule, the confusion may have bordered on hysteria.

Self-knowledge, elusive at best, was for me over the rainbow. I knew desire, boon friend, boon enemy. I knew it as ravaging sometimes as the fever that had gripped me in the summer of my menarche. It clung like a second skin to everything I wanted to know, to do, as if knowing could not stop before the locked door of the body, as if all knowledge were carnal. Everything except the crystal theorems of geometry or the majestic and imperturbable balance of chemical equations—even book-stuff as well-upholstered as *Vanity Fair*—seemed to demand a working pretense of innocence. Innocence: the last effrontery of the newly gendering girl-mind—not merely denying to others that one knows what one knows, but denying it to oneself.

Sometimes I actually believed in my own innocence. Why not? Like some picture of Dorian Gray, I found in the mirror a more and more radiantly blank girl-hood face, a face that did not give me away, though behind it might twist the woman taken in sin, tensing for the blow of the first stone.

If I exaggerate these intersections of feeling, it is not perhaps beyond their significance to my story. I am convinced that sexual curiosity is a metaphor for all curiosity. And I believe in what has been called *epistemophilia*, which is not the love of knowledge but the love of knowing itself. This, then, may be the story of a certain defiant receptiveness to wayward knowledge, a story about my epistemophiliac way of loving to know, my slow and thwarted and even pitifully innocent way of resisting a forced *un*knowing. Mine but also maybe a bit of everywoman's.

For now that I (secretly) wanted to know everything, the capsule I had once used to wrap safely about me as I moved through the world seeing and unseen seemed to have become an imposed and suffocating bell-jar. Train trips to New York and back were carefully circumscribed, every movement had to be accounted for, every deviation from routine approved. Until I was graduated from high school and considered old enough to take a job, July and August at home were sheltered stretches of time—if "shelter" is the word for such a witches' brew of repression and conflict among Carlo and Ann and me. Friends could not visit while my parents and Lou were out working, which was always the better part of the day and evening. Not even Janet, who lived two doors away in the same semidetached row on Sickles Avenue.

Still, the summer after my junior year in high school, Janet filled a brief need for escape. On good beach weekdays I was allowed to go with her to Glen Island, a short local bus trip away. We could walk downtown to shop. I could visit her at her house if her mother was at home. Nevertheless, being her friend was like an initiation into a strange religious rite. She was All-American Girl personified. She could have modeled for the first Barbie, except that she wore her satiny brown hair in a short pageboy which she frequently smoothed with the palm of her hand, and had a cheekbone spitcurl. Janet wore her day-of-the-week panties on the right days of the week, making sure they fit discreetly under the neatly cuffed boy-shorts that showed off her long, tan, shining, smooth-shaven legs in bobby sox and penny moccasins. This was a uniform, I realized, and got my own. And when we went to Glen Island, I studied how to be coy and make myself nonchalantly invisible behind my shades, and swoon on cue at every evenly toasted lifeguard with the obligatory patch of white ointment on the bridge of his nose.

Janet, I came to see, was everything I wasn't. She was the only child at home, her parents having legally separated. She attended a Catholic girls' high school. She went routinely to confession and to Sunday mass, hated to read, ate something made of hamburger every day, never did dishes, and repainted her fingernails at least three times a week. Our conversations were like her swimming—strong to start, but a few minutes out of her depth and she made for shore. Yet behind that wide-eyed Stepford face with the pouty rosebud mouth, that babydoll way of licking her painted fingertips and touching them to her bangs, lurked a knowing woman—more knowing than anyone among my M&A circle of New York City school chums—a woman with serious boyfriends and drive-in movie dates and an authority about soul-kissing that, had my mother known about it, would have thoroughly justified her putting her house to the torch. And yet it was my mother herself who might have said of Janet that butter wouldn't melt in her mouth.

We had chores, at my house, and Janet was never an excuse for not doing them. Cooking was one, and specifically mine, but I considered it salvific. I was already learning to do a few things well, as people will who love to eat, and I not only still loved to eat but was newly enraptured by the miraculous chemistries of breads and soups. We often saved other chores for the absolute end of the day, just before our parents came home—"we" meaning my brothers as well as my sister and me, until Lou was recruited into store duty—to be done in what we termed with desperate hilarity "record time," as we raced furiously about the house with vacuum and dustcloths and sponges in the last minutes before the car lights flashed in the driveway.

The rules guarding what we did in their absence were strict. We mostly obeyed them. There were some pardonable minor violations they couldn't see to rebuke. Once Lou was gone, there were some unpardonable major ones we didn't tell.

Carlo's temperament had not softened as he grew. Certainly not toward Ann and me, whom he seemed to despise with a dull and motiveless malignancy. Being a boy he had a certain license to be less often at home. Ann and I, alone together, might quarrel and make our peace. But he would burst in on us suddenly or after a petulant lull like a stalking, and fly into a bullying, hectoring rage. He seemed to drive at us, to hate us in some essential way, to target our fresh shame about ourselves, our uneasy new womanhoods, and attack us *there*, where the mind and flesh were tenderest, first with filthy words and then physically, brutally, with his hands, hunting Ann down with some special demon anger when she fled him, pummeling me when

I stood in his way, taunting us, crowing when we wept, laughing when we screamed. And then he would dare us to phone and tell, fearless, having nothing to lose, as if he knew the only thing we could betray was our own shame. We would huddle together in our room, even there not feeling completely safe. I would try to console her outrage and pain. Sometimes I couldn't. Sometimes I could not console myself.

I read. I read to escape, but also to know. Perhaps, obscurely, to know where such demon hatred could come from that seemed to come from so much more than my brother's private little soul.

This was a universe where Janet feared to tread, and I did not try to recruit her. I took most of my lonely reading ration from my father's library, many of its volumes bound in factory-tooled leather just as they had come, one by one, from subscription book clubs. The double-column, small-print Shakespeare I had already devoured, cover to cover, taking lessons in old bawdy from its treacherous pages, discovering the powerful, the talky, the free, the cross-dressing women Janet would never have understood. When we weren't dancing, Ann and I took turns standing on the round-backed Chippendale chair pretending it was the Globe balcony and trying out our favorite parts.

I moved more surreptitiously now to Boccaccio, to Zola, both of them powder kegs from which I might have blown up my captivity from the inside. Had my father actually read them? My mother discovered a copy of Zola's *Nana* under my pillow, a weary, blue, illustrated clothbound edition from the twenties that I had turned up in a casual dig through the abandoned reliquary of the basement. She had flipped its pages, seen the sensuous line drawings, the large buttocks, the bare breasts and upturned nipples.

She looked terrified. Betrayed. "Where did you get this?"

But she knew I was no longer afraid of her anger. She was almost more astonished, I think, that such a book could be found in her house than that I should be reading it. Darkly, she said that my father would have to be consulted. But nothing happened, and I found it again weeks later, untouched, layered with a thin new bloom of dust, as I was polishing the highboy on her side of the bed.

How had I not internalized this censoring father she invoked, of whom I *was* actually afraid, whose sleeping violence kept even my mother's soul in check, who seemed transparently to stand for God? Except in my beloved Boccaccio, who opened another continent of Italianness to me, every female sexual transgression I had read of, including Nana's—especially Nana's—had been punished either by a tragic or a miserable, lingering death. Why didn't I think this would happen to me?

I plowed on like a termite, consuming virtually everything that lay behind the glass doors of the oak curio cabinet and the secretary desk, including Pearl Buck's *Good Earth,* with its scene of solitary childbirth somewhere in the hills of China, until I turned up an oversized leather-bound volume with the title *Animal Magnetism,* pontificating some strange metaphysics of the body and containing a chapter, oblique but unmistakable, on masturbation. What was this cruel disorder, it protested, but a clear sign of mental and moral derangement, especially in girls and women, root cause of other more dire and unnamable disorders?

I may have questioned the authority of my father, but I had not yet learned to question the authority of print. Perhaps I needed another tyranny, a white light overthrowing my confused conscience with its bold, dogmatic simplicity. I believed it instantly, fearing it more than mother and father together. Thrown into a panic of remorse, I hated my hands. I hated the way they had shaped angel-lovers out of the achingly warm clay of my own pleasure. I thought, *this,* then, is the real meaning of sin, that so ready, so lovely a release from my bewildering anxiety is the bomb that will actually destroy me, and not just hereafter, which I had consoled myself could somehow, someday, be rearranged, but here. Now.

It sounded almost too much like the magical, punishing Sicilian moral universe of my mother, and yet perhaps overcorrecting for this small inward bite of disbelief made me even more fierce. Faith was what I wanted, not skepticism, pure cleansing faith, mind and body, every shred of disbelief burned away, my soul fired in the kiln of purity to the most perfect ceramic.

To my mother's wary but happy surprise, I began to accompany her to evening novenas. Janet joined me in a religious retreat for young women at St. Gabriel's, where an itinerant monk lashed the certain impurity of our girlish hearts, flash-scorched them, crisped and pulverized them as if they had been nothing but used palm fronds burnt for Ash Wednesday's ashes, warning us that Christ's exquisite suffering was incalculably multiplied by each failure of ours to preserve a body undefiled.

I have no idea what Janet felt. I suspect she went home and soul-kissed her way to delirium the following week at the movies. I remained mortified. And yet I still did not know how to confess my own sin, this sin unnamed among the Ten Commandments. So I went to confession in a sweating agony one sultry Saturday afternoon in August, and told the priest behind the grille that I had committed adultery.

When I returned to school in the fall, Judy wondered about my odd solemnity, but there were subjects on which even we two were not yet ready to speak. I cosseted my new chastity. I prayed the rosary to myself on the train and stopped at St. Gabriel's to light candles on the way home from the railway station. I kept Christmas with an intensity bordering on lunacy, and my sister (who had clung intransigently to Santa Claus, well past the age of reason) delighted to follow me. Throughout the next Lent my devotions to the Stations of the Cross were unremittingly hot-hearted—I dreamed of turning to devotional art and sculpting a series of them myself. On Good Friday, I attended a three-hour devotion to the Passion and choked back scalding tears as the priest spoke Jesus's poignant *"Why hast thou forsaken me?"* from the cross.

And yet while fear drove me, fear and some diverted channel for the ecstasy of loving, I think I knew somehow that the fear was not so much fear of God as of my own defiant inner refusal.

•

Christians were the oddity at Music & Art, teachers and students. On Jewish holidays, about four of us out of thirty would show up in a homeroom staffed by a substitute. It did not seem especially outlaw to leave school quietly, once we had officially clocked in in the morning, make a dash from 135th to the subway at 125th Street, head down to West 42nd Street on our school passes, and spend the livelong day at a favorite, cheap, all-day moviehouse watching a triple bill of quirky cult things like *The Maltese Falcon* and *King Kong* and maybe a Magnani or an early Bergman, movies that took me way beyond the Cinema Paradiso of Our Lady of Mount Carmel's basement, and would never have made it to New Rochelle. No sex films, heaven forbid—the Times Square porn-flick industry was still a sinister gleam in somebody's eye—though I didn't bring conversation about them home. And we could still clock back in on Convent Avenue for the last roll call of the day.

Yet I made no long-lasting friendships with other Christians on these runs. They usually included Judy. They were fun. That was all. The rest of the year I seemed to need to cultivate attachments with my politically conscious and activist Jewish classmates. I can remember feeling oddly thrilled when a parent on the Upper West Side speculated about the Hebrew origin of my surname. Maybe it had something to do with being at an ethnic crossroads together. But I had no clue at the time to the social dynamics of "othering," and in any case, though I didn't discuss it, I was still caught up in my Catholic passion. I hadn't yet begun to imagine a theory I came to develop later on, and to find quite credible: that my father's roots, which some relative had historically traced to Spain four centuries ago, had originally been Jewish, and that his family had migrated to the Kingdom of the Two Sicilies during the excesses of the Inquisition. This notion, whatever its modicum of truth, would at some time come to seem very important to me. It is now. I still let myself be teased by the mystery of how Sant'Elia—the prophet Elias of the Old Testament—had ever come to be patron saint of the Alaya village of Sperone.

These high school get-togethers on the Upper West Side (which I am sure I explained oddly to my father, so as to be able to attend them) were, as I say, often political, or had a political hidden agenda. We would discuss enlisting in demos at the UN, or circulating petitions against HUAC witch-hunts. Or we would strategize our opposition to the loyalty oaths then being foisted on our teachers. It seemed as if the pulse of the world were in our caring hands. Coming of age in extraordinary times, jolted out of all naïvete about a warless future or the benignity of the bomb by the sudden outbreak of the war in Korea, we were the generation fated to be present at the birthing of both the peace movement and the movement for civil rights. Perhaps it was not precisely bliss to be alive or to be young, but for me it was another near-religious universe, one that seemed to recruit pure energy, indifferent to sex, consciously striking out across the color line, embracing difference, including my own.

What we didn't know we felt, and guessed, and feared. Yet I don't remember feeling fear for my private political soul, nor even precisely for my private survival. Ever since our old days in Arizona in wartime I had nursed an intuition that there was nothing that could happen *out there*, no social circumstance in the big world that wasn't capable of rupturing our so-called personal lives. In this sense, my father had transmitted a vivid political consciousness to me. But I could see, now, here, that we could struggle to rearrange the equation, not to be passive, merely, and let it happen.

My father had written to Roosevelt once, complaining of how the government had treated him. But that had been a personal act, to protest a wrong done to himself. Since then he had grown hostile to movements, movements that in any case he had always been too proud to join. Resettled now among New Rochelle's post-tenement Italian Americans, his politics had morphed into a rather supercilious, Republican worldview—a hatred of taxation, a fierce pride about self-help, unease about the business impact of the coddling ministrations of the New Deal, and a fear of what would happen to our Way of Life with the sudden in-migration of impoverished Puerto Ricans, who by now had transformed our old Italian East Harlem into El Barrio. It was as if all social help had turned sour now that he himself didn't need it anymore.

Maybe it was mere peer pressure on my side, but I like to think that I had been in some sense inoculated against my father's politics, that straight from the East Harlem tenements as I had come, my lungs still exhaled a bit of the radical live air of Vito Marcantonio, that a few brain cells still stored memory-prints of sainted anarchists. I like to think there was a certain intercultural, working-class camaraderie packed into the marrow of my bones at those tap-dance classes at Hull House on East 116th Street, where all the varicolored pigtails bounced together to the same thumping beat.

I became connected, at any rate—it was too soon, too hard to say I became "identified," "committed." My red diaper classmates were sunk into politics by the taproot, with an educated passionate intensity. Their interest in the trial of Ethel and Julius Rosenberg was not just spectatorial, like mine. The sadism of blacklisting must have come literally home.

And yet even for them it was—it needed to be—a performance of belief. In this seedtime of Beat and the sixties they wore their politics on their bodies. The girls defined the look in peasant blouses and skirts, laced sandals, scarves, dangling earrings. Everybody played the guitar, and those who didn't sang—folk songs, of course, songs with ironclad pedigrees from Woody Guthrie to Pete Seeger direct. I sang them too. I let my hair grow out again, and wore it again in a single braid down my back. I forgot about my rosary beads when I was with them. I kept my little silver Miraculous Medal and my Sacred Heart scapular in the bottom of my saddlebag. And I fell in love with Jewish boys, though their hearts were more disciplined, and they did not fall in love with me.

And then at last April approached May, M&A was ending, and *"Weeeell?,"* spoken in that long expectant drawl, was the first, exasperating thing out of Judy's mouth whenever we met in sculpture class or life drawing or the lunchroom.

Our embarrassment was becoming replete. I should say *my* embarrassment. Judy's mother hadn't made *her* a gown for the senior prom, as my mother had for me, on the impregnable theory that wishing (or more precisely, willing, praying, pleading privately with all the saints, lighting candles) could make it so. Maybe I have suppressed my own fixation on this prom-date, but I look back in wonder: who actually wanted it more, she or I?

Perhaps it would finally prove, among other mother-flattering things, that I could be the girl my father would approve her for creating. For though he routinely missed mass himself, he loved our churchgoing, smooth Sunday-morning look in gloves and heels almost as much as he despised this cheap, "teen-age" prom culture. And yet he knew the prom to be a rite of female passage, and rites of female passage he understood. I can imagine a curious mixture of dread and longing in his mental anticipation of my first symbolic moment as another man's woman.

The dress my mother made me was a checked taffeta affair in navy and gray, strangely subdued elegance for a fashion climate that favored pastel chiffons. It had a long full skirt, drop sleeves over a fitted bodice, and her hallmark featherstitching around the neckline. Pretty as it was, I could not actually see myself wearing it, which, right there, as any visualization expert will tell you, was deadly. It held itself erect on a hanger over the sewing machine like a proud beauty, straight through the prom season.

In a kind of giddy desperation, I even asked several Jewish boys to take me, moving on to another and another as each said no. Judy couldn't believe me. I couldn't believe myself. I remember something wistful and long-coming in their rejections that seemed to make them painless. And yet it was if I had been inviting them as a favor to somebody else.

Judy said we should go out anyway, the two of us, though neither of our special prom budgets had included the contingency of an *un*prom, and I knew it was not a category of expense my father recognized. My mother must have persuaded him that it was the only possible balm for my grievous disappointment. Only whatever we did, she said, was going to have to get me back to the New Haven RR in time for the train.

It was a perfect prom night. Hitting the darkening street after a movie at the Carnegie, I know we both felt that same stab, like two Alices forced to keep this side of the looking-glass. There was something as ripe as strawberries in the air. Across 57th Street the Automat was still bustling—we'd been there before the show, gloriously nickel-and-diming our dinner, popping up and down from the marbleized table as each new food fancy struck us, aesthetically overdosed on bright brass and the magic of pie wedges and radiant meringues behind shimmering convex shields of glass.

"We're kinduva couple, aren't we," I observed, rather dolefully, as we made for the subway. Judy giggled agreement. We were: short and tall, wearing our rhyming blue cottons with the waistlines we pronounced *"awhmpeer,"* the simple dresses we'd cut from the same pattern and then stitched independently, mine under my mother's expert eye. We had matching shawls to keep off the night air.

We took the A train down to the Battery, stood up all the way, frantic with laughter as the updraft on the subway car ballooned our skirts. We took a ride on the Staten Island Ferry, still just a nickel each way in 1952, across the bay and back.

We let the wind on the deck fling our hair into tangled streamers and whip our dangling copper earrings till we almost lost them. Judy took hers off and I screwed mine in tighter, as tight as I could bear. We still had the deck to ourselves—no other prom-nighters yet, making their own romance of the cheap sea ride. The salt spray the flywheel kicked up flicked into our eyes and mouths. We faced the wind gasping, hugging our flapping shawls tight about us. We laughed about how much better this was than going to the prom. We have never changed our minds.

Judy's grandfather was already gone. Her grandmother died that summer. This was sad, but an enormous relief too, and Judy and Muriel slowly unraveled themselves from their Christian Science cocoons and shook their damp bright wings in the sunshine like a pair of butterflies. After so intense a confrontation with her parents' too implacable faith, the Mature Parent was now exploring other religions. Once, she asked me to unravel the long tale of my multiple namings, how I had been christened Flavia Maria Immacolata and then added two more names, Anna and Rosa, at my confirmation, and what this all meant. Poor simply Judith Ann Lawrence felt severely disadvantaged. In retaliation, she dubbed me "Fluffy Mary the Immaculate." I winced.

"Your Catholicism," Muriel would say. "It's about the bleeding Jesus Christ, if I may say so, isn't it. Death, death, death." I had rather thought it was about the Virgin Mary, St. Ann, etc., etc., but she had a point. There was that crucifix too, and all those bloody Stations of the Cross.

I had been about to leave for the railway station and she held me, growing thoughtful again. It was as if I were a wise child who could deal with profound questions—nothing in her of that secret intent to outwit me I sensed in so many well-intentioned adults. She seemed to enjoy what I was, where I was, without the need to impose higher standards, greater expectations. Enough of these in our lives—in hers no less than mine, maybe more. She smiled. She said, as if to assure me I was not entirely responsible for the murky history of Catholicism, "Much to be said for confession."

I kissed her good-bye, thankful for the gracious exit line. Judy had me by the hook. "Oh, Fluffy Mary," she pronounced, "*do* be careful going home."

That fall, Judy decided to continue studying art, part-time, in New York. I actually envied her, though I was the one entering Barnard on scholarship. There had been remarkably little fuss about what I would actually do with my life, when it finally came down to it, because I didn't make the fuss I might have over where I would go to college to learn how to do it.

For, all credit to the power of my mother's immovable certainty that gifts like mine and my sister's shouldn't be wasted, it had been understood that I would go to college, always, and when I graduated M&A with honors, it had been understood that I would attend a very good school. My own researches into what this meant for me (Syracuse, Bard, other colleges with strong arts programs) became ultimately irrelevant. I could see this the moment my brother Lou, new Columbia College graduate, dispatched the wisdom that Barnard College, across the street from Columbia, would be quite acceptable. This reassured my uneasy father, who could feel me slipping away, and who could easily paint the dangers to my bewildered, conflicted mother of any school I could not commute to from home exactly as I had to high school—same train to the 125th Street station on the New Haven line, same bus to the West Side, different transfer, to the Broadway bus going downtown instead of up.

My mother hated to see me disappointed at not continuing my art, but there seemed to be no right answer to the question, "What will you *do?*" For I saw myself with long hair, alone, in a loft some day, painting, sculpting, writing poetry. Unfortunately, so did they. So did *he*. It was decidedly not a pretty picture.

My mother felt she had lost her fight if she hadn't made us both happy. "Wouldn't you rather be a teacher?" It was her idea of bliss.

My poor father had his hands full, between the two of us. I said, OK, OK. I will become a chemical engineer. I meant it. And yet he might have known he was in danger. Who but a perverse and wayward daughter, out to break your heart, would go straight from a high school sculpture award to a college degree in chemical engineering?

Ah, but at least there would be no more lies! Other Barnard women got on the train in Larchmont, in Pelham and Mount Vernon. They looked so beautiful to me. So fine. How could Columbia boys write "Cattle Crossing" on West 119th Street, where Milbank Hall looked out over the tennis courts?

I almost instantly lost my faith. No, that's wrong. I almost instantly let myself see it, that last sweet shred of it, in another, more ironic perspective. When I wrote my first essay for Miss Tilton's freshman English class, it had been supposed to be a paragraph, two at most: "Describe something. Anything," she had said. "Let it be carefully observed." I had described a rosary.

When we met in our first conference, she seemed very guarded, impossibly shy. Her bony hand twitched nervously before her thin, schoolmarm lips. But behind that well-fringed fluttery lid in a deep eyesocket there was a fine, gray-eyed gaze.

She placed my paper before me, quizzically. I stared at it. It was typed, as she had asked, double-spaced, as she had required, folded neatly, obligingly, lengthwise down the middle. There was nothing else on it, no marks, no comments. Nothing. I looked up in despair.

"Hmm," she said, apologetically.

Reflective, pregnant pause.

"I think you can write," she said. "But try this assignment again."

At first I was stung, insulted. It had been the rosary, obviously. Italian Catholic girl, not fitting Barnard stereotype, being hammered, if ever so nicely, Massachusetts-ly, into the intellectual mold. But it was too late to resist. I already loved her, and seemed to know what she was, who she would be for me, from her brilliant questions in class, from the way she had of silently, patiently stroking meaning out of a text, out of us. And from her streaky wood-grained hair and skin-and-bones body in dry, dark blue spinsterwear.

She was right: the thing had been carefully observed, but I had not observed the mind observing it. I knew this, suddenly. I loved knowing it.

7

Lou had graduated from Columbia College with honors, ambitious to be a doctor. But it was one thing for an Italian American kid who'd worked summers, nights, and weekends trimming cutlets and sirloins, scraping blocks and sweeping up sawdust in his father's butcher shop, to apply to medical schools, another thing to get into one. Try telling a medical school admissions committee in 1952 that nothing could be better training for hip surgery than dismembering a side of beef.

After sweating out rejection after rejection, he was finally admitted to Long Island University Medical School. This was exceptional, a coup. Most of the aspiring doctors among his Italian American classmates, including his best friend, Mario, would have to go to Italy to train. Mario used to drop over with Lou's other buddies on holidays and flirt with me, in a careless, God's-gift sort of way. God gave me fair warning, I think, the day Lou and his friends came in and found me on my knees scrubbing the kitchen floor, and Mario said in what sounded like all seriousness that "it was just the way he liked to see a woman."

Lou himself would never have said such a thing. At least I thought not, and I loved him the more for it, the more because I already felt for him something approaching awe. Coming out of his teens he had grown into his own kind of good looks— never tall, but square-jawed and handsome in a tough, Georgie Raft sort of way, athletic, physically powerful, a strong swimmer. A lifeguard for a time, he had made varsity track. Judy was mad for him. If he'd had the time and money to date that other boys had, I thought you'd have to peel the girls off him.

But there was another side to Lou, a kind of sleeping beast, given to lightning surges of feckless anger. He would abruptly pull away, come back as suddenly as sunlight after a storm, tenderhearted and all duty and discipline again, every inch the first son. The truth was, for all his determined push toward medicine, he'd actually wanted to be a geologist. But *they* wanted a doctor. He'd resisted at first, cried when Mom pleaded, and in the end obeyed, as I had.

As for Carlo, duty had never been his strong suit. He'd finished New Rochelle High School academically just getting by, doing some things well in typical fits and starts, periodically showing up in the principal's office. He was a jokester, good for a laugh, good for a good time. He could crack you up if he didn't go all sarcastic and mean. But his soul seemed too blocked with anger to care what anybody thought. He finally earned enough money doing summer jobs to buy himself a motorcycle. My parents gave him a struggle, but he won.

He loved to cut a swagger on his bike, like Uncle Joey before him. "He even *looks* like Uncle Joey," my mother would say. She tried to accept, to vocalize acceptance and make peace, to make herself believe that now that the discussion was done it was done. But I know she died every time he vroomed off and careered around the curve of Sickles Place toward Lockwood Avenue. I know she had a vision of him dead, smashed and bloody under the El like Joey, but not coming back.

Carlo and Lou both built their bodies with weights. It might be either of them I could hear heaving and grunting in their bedroom across the hall, the leaden rings clanking as they pressed, followed by the sudden thud as they brought them to the floor. Carlo used to stretch himself on a horizontal bar, longing to be an inch or two taller. He'd dreamed of becoming a pilot but the dream had died when he'd found himself blocked by his bad eyesight, and it only made him more bitter. Why, besides being short, did he also have to be blind? Lou's bad eyes had hurt his vanity but Carlo's hurt his soul. Whenever he put his motorcycle goggles on over his glasses, and then the black leather fitted helmet and tight black leather gloves, he put a meanness on him you could've walked into, if you'd been reckless enough.

So you could sense it was coming even before he got in with a bad bunch and slammed into trouble with the law. It was kept very hush-hush, even at home, but there was a court appearance. The judge went easy—seeing he came from a good family, as my parents said—and made a point of repeating. But the experience shook him, turned his ambition around. He began to work hard, suddenly yearning to know what it was he was good at, finding, amazingly, that it was math, calculus, geometry, trig. He was beginning to see himself, who he was. He must already have been preparing to take his community college degree back to Tucson and try for an engineering B.S. at the University of Arizona, by the time I entered Barnard. He amazed us. He amazed himself.

Ann would have been entering her second year at New Rochelle High School by then. She was smart, diffident, artistic, scared of her own talent, lagging behind it. She'd begun in her soft, shy way to be just as beautiful as her sweet baby looks had promised—my mother, without really meaning to be hurtful, had come to describe her to people as "the pretty one" of the two of us. She was right. Ann seemed never to have had to pass through my awkward ages, to suffer being all doughballs, as I had before I'd finally shed my fat, or looking into the mirror and seeing nothing but mouth, teeth, eyes, nose, all too big for my face. Her hair, cut short a year or two after me, had kept all of its fine curl and softness of color and hand, while mine had lost its chestnut lights and gone almost blue-black. A little vain of her tender, brown-blossom eyes, she would refuse to wear her glasses and squint toward you on the street until you got close enough to be seen, and then her gaze would take on that strangely liquid, vulnerable look of someone straining through tears. I loved the long brown lashes that needed no help to curl like a doll's, the mouth that had never been swollen with scar tissue like mine and that bowed perfectly when she smiled, dipping up into her dimpled cheeks.

I was a rough Maggie Tulliver to her sweet Lucy Deane, I suppose. Or so, when I read *The Mill on the Floss,* I liked to think. And yet I doubt Maggie ever wanted to hug Lucy as I did Ann. If conscious envy ever tainted my envious-seeming comparisons, I don't remember feeling it. Except once, when we were drying off after a swim and Ann, who was possessed by an exquisite parochial school shyness even with me, let down her towel for a moment, and out flashed a killing glimpse of two perfect breasts, pearly and round as the Venus's at the Met. Till then I had grudgingly accepted my own cone-shaped pair, their areolas as big and brown as those of a fertility fetish, now I despised them.

But Ann could never appreciate her own beauty. She'd have been appalled to know how I felt about her desirable, innocent, wary sexiness, which she only feared. She had developed no miraculous moral muscle out of the banal cruelties of our childhoods. She'd been told too often that she was the cause of all our mother's pain to make it to the first grade of self-love. The summer reign of terror with Carlo that had left me sore had left her scarred.

By now she and I had necessarily grown somewhat apart, even in our shared tower, our twin beds placed long ago on opposite sides of the room. Even had she known how much I'd suffered the lie I'd lived all through high school—and how could she? I had hardly let myself know it—she had every right to envy me. Of the two of us, I was the one whose achievements drew praise (the choice my father had made between his boys, repeated), the one whose talents had to be nurtured, for whom sacrifices had to be made to educate, whose life-center was the great Emerald City of New York. I'm sure she saw how wearing it was, the toll it took in sleep, how it explained my neglect of her and excused my distant crossness. I'm sure she imagined I had something unattainable for her. I'm sure she did not for that reason want it any the less.

She had become increasingly attached to my mother, in some sense my mother's refuge. How we hated to see the store consume them, mother and father both, day and night, consume *him*, especially, who had made us conscious of so many better talents. My mother hated it too. It exhausted her. Things had not always gone as they had wanted, as *she* had wanted. Dad's heart was not in his work, she knew that. It might be brutal, degrading work, but no, he had never allowed it to degrade him. It was only the hand that fate had somehow perversely dealt him. Her heart swelled as he spread out paints and fine sable brushes on the dining-room table to letter signs for the store windows like an artist, so they could see out there the artist he really was—so his own children could see it.

But how hard it was to stay above the blood and stink of slaughter, above the wheedling and whining and carping of customers and the arrogance and greed of vendors whose every chicken-scratched bill for eggs had to be vetted. Always to be playing the master butcher, keeping up the façade, acting as if *he* had been the misplaced surgeon. It left little energy to spare to love her. And she hungered for love, savored Ann's willingness to stay close, to be the good girl, to scale back ambition.

Me she had fought for, not always against my father's wishes, but against his fears, and had paid the price on both sides. I had fewer rules to obey, yet chafed continually at the ones I had, wanting fewer. I was the Fisherman's Wife in the fairytale, never satisfied, she the fisherman pleading with the Big Fish to be generous, to be kind. *He* didn't see all my sulks and storms. Didn't I understand how she'd fought not to have me trapped as she had been as a girl, as she was now, as Ann was becoming? Nurturing my gifts had seemed so simple, once. But now my future mystified rather than emboldened her. She stood at the last frontier of her expectations. She thought then that she could not follow me into the dark wood.

But who can completely understand these things? And she had fled from understanding. There was no understanding, when the banked fire of his inner rage once again sublimated into illness, and he sulked down, crippled with sciatica, curled into inanition on the bed, on the couch. He would sit alone, watching the Army-McCarthy hearings on television, whole days, transfixed before the flickering screen or prowling sourly about the house, when she would have to deal with the store, when Lou would have to rush from school to help her as soon as he could get away. What could she do but pity and caress him, who seemed so beached in his anger and pain, to forgive him, even when his violence might erupt against Ann because she, poor girl, could not tolerate the unholy beast of red-baiting that somehow salved his soul? When Ann's innocent objections baited him like filthy words, and he had struck her, taken the golf stick he had been toying with on the living room carpet, taken it with all his fury to her back and legs, as if she were the one who had brought down his world?

He was a great wounded animal, sensing danger, always sensing the danger of his loss of mastery, the danger in our pushing boundaries. In my pushing them. Didn't my mother now have to make a show of servility to protect me—to protect us?

She too had told herself a treacherous lie of the mind—it had become habitual, as her perpetual look of weary grief betrayed. She believed that the old fault somehow was hers, that it was hers now to make it right.

But she still adored him. So did I, so did Ann, so did we all. There was such solicitude for our well-being even in his tyranny. The promises he made of small, material things we longed for were always fulfilled. So, in spite of the petty codes my mother enforced for his sake, we forgave him, forgave him his rages, rare as earthquakes, as sudden and unaccountable as the cyclonic rainstorms of the desert. And always, otherwise, there was that theater of undying love between them, that illusion of cloudless skies, and she so happily, so proudly, beside him, consoling, softening his pain, making beautiful things to wear for him to see her in, to approve, touching herself behind her fine, shapely ears there, and there, with his favorite perfume.

The fire that destroyed the store must have started in the back, some faulty electrical circuit overloaded as it struggled against an Indian summer heat wave to cycle the gigantic freezer. All the stuff in the back room—the stored egg cartons, the tightly wrapped and closely stacked rhomboids of brown paper bags, the great rolls of wrapping paper, as thick and round as if someone had cut the columns in front of the library into firewood, the gigantic balls of twine for tying roasts, the full coal scuttle for the stove where the sliced steaks had been seared for a quick lunch, and wolfed down with a piece of Italian bread torn from a loaf the size of an arm and a cup of boiled coffee right off the grate, where hands numbed from holding frozen flesh for hours could be warmed—all of it seemed to have been put there just to feed the smoldering flames. And then the fire had exploded, burst into the flue of a stairwell at the back, and threatened to engulf the apartments and the sleeping families upstairs. But they were able to escape before the firemen came, screaming their alarms through the night, destroying with their hoses what little the fire had spared and carrying off whatever meat had not been already roasted, and some that had.

The shock first. Then the stunning aftershock, that fire had made the decision they could never have made themselves. The insurance, not enormous, was enough. Enough to think. Enough to make decisions by. Enough, finally, to say no more to this hard business that had put us through life. There was little to salvage—nothing at all from the back room. There were a few fixtures from the front of the store, two faintly wounded oak blocks that had given most of their lives already, every face they could turn scraped raw (my brother, night after night, leaning into the steel sanding brush with his full force lest a single smear of that day's blood be carried over to the next), a pair of paper-roll dispensers with their wrought cast-iron knots of decorative flowers. One had been for waxed paper, the pristine inner wrapping for folding directly against the meat, the other the finishing wrap, a satin-white coated paper my father had used for hand-lettering his window signs. I had loved this paper. Always it had seemed an infinite blank page for drawing, for writing novel after novel for a lifetime. These became our salvaged treasures, along with the majestically carved, bell-ringing cash register, a delicate spool of red-and-white twine that had stood on the long marble counter behind the glass display cases, their images repeated in the silver mirrors that ran the full length of the wall. The mirrors had been smashed. A fragment of marble remained. A scale. These few things came through, and took on a museum kind of afterlife in the basement of the house on Sickles Avenue.

I had begun to write again. I had used to tell fanciful stories as a child, and illustrate them myself. At twelve I had started a Brontë-ish Yorkshire moors romance, which my indulgent teachers at Hunter had thought promising. But until my teens I had not written my life—and *this* life—our lives, never. I couldn't dare. It would have been the last audacity to tell such stories, to retail all this tangled family misery and inwardness, all this conflagration of the soul. And I couldn't also because it was too inwardly ravening and full of gross undigested cubes of pain, like raw meat at the grinder.

My commitment to engineering had lasted about a month into college chemistry. I had of course floundered on, postponing organic, continuing math. Midway through a course in the theory of equations in my sophomore year, I had simply stalled. There had been no question of my somehow going back to making art, slipping such classes past my parents. Apart from the additional cost, studio art was not on Barnard's educational agenda, considered too "servile" a subject by the John Henry Newman standard of a classical liberal education. The registrar would not even give graduation credit for courses taken in Columbia's East Hall. One of the professors there saw a bit of my work and invited me to take his sculpture course, free, but I started and dropped it, unable to commute and write papers and study till my eyes stung, and sculpt too. Just the same, I used to go around to East Hall sometimes, at the corner of 116th Street and Amsterdam, to visit Judy, still studying there.

She was happily painting away. She'd say, "Funny how you're so good at art and me at writing, and we're both doing the opposite." It was true. Her mother was a writer. Her father had been. It ran in her blood.

"We never do what's easy," I said. But I looked at her happiness and thought afterwards that I spoke only for myself.

One difference with writing was that Barnard cared about it. Miss Tilton, commenting on something I'd written once, said she thought artists made the best writers. I presumed she meant fallen-away artists. "Something about composition," she guessed. "Seeing it whole." I didn't know. I knew things—experiences—had a shape.

The first story I wrote for John Kouwenhoven's creative writing seminar was not about my family, or was only obliquely. It was about me. Or it was about a young college girl named Gabriella, with a summer job as an artist in a small costume jewelry factory near home. I had had such a job.

After years as an ugly duckling, Gabriella has metamorphosed into a surprising beauty. She is not used to this, and acknowledges it only because the other women in the factory, already distanced by the advantage of her education, communicate it in cold, envious compliments that make her feel self-conscious and strange. She tries being friendly but they hold back, suspicious, and she grows increasingly isolated and lonely. Every day, her boss, divorced, in his fifties, comes by the little studio she works in alone to cheer her up. He takes her out to lunch. Then to dinner. In the dark, afterward, in the front seat of his parked car, he romances her. They never really make love, and he never presses her for surrender.

The romance lingers. Fall comes and she returns to college. Saturdays, he takes her on long drives into the country to see the changing leaves. He sends her flowers. He tells her he loves her. She loves him, too, a little. She feels safe in his kind of loving, but also vaguely beached in it, as if she is asleep, as if it is an endless summer from which nothing has stirred her. Her mother, who has watched her come and go in his big silver Cadillac, wonders what is going on between them. What *is* going on? Gabriella realizes that she doesn't know and must at last confront him. He confesses he is impotent. He begs her not to leave him, but she does, renouncing his summer love, his passionless world of summer without end.

I called it "The Door Out of Innocence." I suppose Mr. Kouwenhoven could see how, even for a girl's story, it might fit into the master narrative of American coming-of-age fiction. Being discreet, he didn't ask whether it had actually happened. I imagine there were a few laughs in the faculty lunchroom about the door not being opened quite wide enough. He gave it a B+.

I was encouraged. I dared to reach back now to the passionate depths of my childhood in Arizona, searching out the hidden roots of the life we were living at home, a life so hauntingly anguished and violent at times and yet so utterly frozen that none of us could look it in the face. I wrote about the squab farm. I told about my brothers' beating. I wept. I seemed to write it, word by word, on my own body. But Mr. Kouwenhoven didn't get it, just didn't get it, he said. He pick-picked at little details. He gave a B- to an undigested bit of my soul.

Both stories—the second with more strategic and secret care—had to remain hidden from my parents, who would first have killed me and then killed each other if they'd known what I was doing. The whole idea of my writing, which to them meant prima facie the likelihood of revealing family secrets, threw them into a steely panic. Not just my father, an educated reader who theoretically knew that this was what writers did, but my mother too, who held with an even fiercer passion to the principle of *omertà*—the guarded and sacred silence of southern Italians surrounding all things within the walls of *la famiglia*.

And yet they did not ask to read what I wrote. Perhaps they were too self-absorbed, my father in bed more and more now, still structuring tragedy out of the mysterious catastrophes of his life-drama, my mother working hard toward her equivalency diploma, because something needed to be done—how else keep all this together— keep us in school? And there had always been a certain sacrosanctness in what took place between me and my teachers, which perhaps they preferred to guess than to know. But though it might be a long way off, what might someday land between covers was another matter, and I can remember the bizarre clash I had with my mother the day she found Ogden Nash's *Bad Parents' Garden of Verse* atop a pile of books about to go back to the library, and flew into a rage simply over the title.

So they helped me preserve my innocence for them. But I was not innocent, not in any of the ways they would have wanted me to be, and maybe not in any way. I hadn't yet slept with anyone, of course, but I had wanted to, longed to, dreamed of doing it, many times. The confessional would have burned with my adulteries.

But my father had been right about keeping me at home: commuting to school and passing every night under his roof did hobble one's love life. It hobbled one's social life. I could see it quite easily from the college man's point of view. Without a car, what was he supposed to do with a girl who lived in New Rochelle, New York, which was barely still in the state, for Chrissake? How was he supposed to get home once he got me there? He wouldn't get me there. If I was lucky, he would drop me off at the 125th Street station about eleven and wait for the train, then see me onto it with a peck on the cheek, careful not to rouse himself before the lonely trip to upper Broadway. And he would not do this often.

But, oh, how they would murmur as I passed them on the mid-Broadway island, firing them a glance like Giovanni Verga's hungry *Lupa*. Tom Galvin, a young college poet who made the Catholic students' club one of his haunts, featured my flashing ankles in one of his poems, with a suggestion, perhaps, that I was a moving target, but I was impressed. He was a wonderful poet. He wrote incessantly, a model of dedication to the craft. Uncertainly half-Catholic, he was also a bit too professionally James Joyce with his wire-rimmed spectacles over his shortsighted eyes, having come to about chapter 4 in Stephen Dedalus's struggle with writing and faith and sex. He actually invited me out one night, then took me to the railroad station in a taxi. On the way he placed his hand gently on my thigh. When I quivered, and asked him not to, part of me meant it. It was the part he heard.

"*The elephant is slow to mate,*" he muttered, in a considered, lapidary way, like a life sentence, staring at me as he withdrew his hand. I stared back into his glasses, a deer in headlights, a hurt, stung panic at my heart. "T. S. Eliot," he said.

Well why didn't I at least kiss him? I don't know. I was scared, conflicted, a pagan little virgin. *Vorrei e non vorrei.* That terrible beautiful line in that cruel and beautiful opera, it had been written for me. I didn't love Tom Galvin, and he hadn't yet awakened any other recognizable passion. I could do nothing in cold blood, not even in cool blood, least of all chance my body to a stranger, a real person and not some phantasm I had cranked out of my own mental dreamstuff, someone who was not impotent, not impotent at all, but who knew just how and when to be kind.

My mother would have understood this keeping back, this fierce maiden integrity, from inside her own chaste-hearted shame. She might also have understood it from inside of *my* shame, knowing it to be different from hers, that it had always been different. But she had refused, and it had opened a new gulf between us. She had taken me to a doctor to treat an unaccountable pain at the tailbone end of my spine—a cyst, but he had not accurately diagnosed it, and had had me come back, night after night. His nurses applied compresses to it and warm, buzzing electrical devices, but the pain went obstinately on and got worse. One evening after an appointment, when I was waiting for my mother to fetch me home, he surprised me, sternly announcing, "No more of this, young lady, let's see what's really wrong with you." The nurses had gone and we were alone. He had me partly undress. He roughly bullied me into the examining stirrups and explored me savagely with his hand.

I didn't know it was criminal to do such a thing, alone like that in his office, I knew only, as soon as outrage had cleared my mind of the sheer blackness of terror, that it was *wrong.* I had stupidly complied. But then he was a doctor—what was I to do? How could he have done this? And when my mother had finally come and seen me white and terrified, *she* was furious. But furious was not enough. Why hadn't she killed him when I told her? Why instead had she fled with me in baffled anger as if she flinched from it—she, who had always been so righteous and bold? Why hadn't she *killed* him? I myself wanted to kill him. Why hadn't she protected me?

Yet as if my mother's ethic of self-blame had passed into me, I drowned and denied what had happened, telling no one. Not Ann, not Judy, not even my two best college friends, Anita and Joanne.

They were Italian girls, like me—full-blooded Sicilians, actually—and like me they commuted to school, though by subway from Queens. Intimate as we had become,

I felt daunted, subdued, by their superb sense of maiden intactness. Such magnificent creatures!—always perfectly groomed, perfectly turned out, an inspiration to be beautiful whether or not I was any match for their glory. Wherever they went—wherever *we* went, for we would often meet at lunchtime and spend the better part of the day together—heads would "swivel," as Anita jokingly, even self-mockingly described it, to take in her sumptuous Lollobrigida body and dark, close crop of thick Lollobrigida curls, and Joanne's astonishing aureole of insanely rose-colored hair. They considered me the brainy one of our peripatetic threesome, but we were still a threesome. Judy—now deep into the Greeks for her inspiration, and I think a little jealous that I had struck out for new territories of friendship on my own—called us the *Thesmophoriazusae,* for the women in Aristophanes's comedy who forgather in honor of the Great Goddess and perform secret, feminist sex-rites.

She was not far off, for it was surely their Sicilian devotion that got me to the Catholic Newman Club, to all those lunch hours and soirées where they knew they could legally flirt with Irish and Italian sons of immigrants under the chaplain's benevolent eye. What kept me going there, besides Tom Galvin and a few wary flirtations of my own, was something, some stirring thing I began to sense in Father Daly's homilies on Christ's collective body, as a politics of mutual responsibility. But being friends with Anita and Joanne was not an inspiration to intellectualize one's spirituality. It was a little, in fact, like discovering a couple of my Spagnola aunts in a time warp. That same self-drama, that hair-trigger laughter and tears and love of glamorous clothes and beautiful men and the romance of romance. That *attitude.* I loved it—I shared it—knowing we were a bit anomalous, even a bit scandalous, in the world of understated black-garbed Barnard feminism.

The in-betweenness of commuting was some excuse for this half-defiant, girlish alienation, but it was only partly to blame. It may be true that alienation, however expressed, was part of the essential gestalt of fifties Beat. Yet we understood without having to speak of it that this too, somehow, was a subculture not ours to claim, that there was something in it in fact that despised us a little, and, for us, in return, something just that too much too strenuous in trying to be what the college seemed to want to make us—oh-so-worldly-wise, and if politically conscious, conscious with a secret air of being safely monied and above all harm, above all risk.

With more personal ambition than either of my friends, less interest in hurrying to be manned and married, I acutely felt the halfheartedness of all but a few of my teachers toward my future, and returned it. Only Eleanor Tilton, under whose tutelage I had deepened and grown as a student of nineteenth-century literature, seemed to intuit that something Italian in my makeup deserved cultivating. It was she who had introduced me to the Sicilian Verga, author of *La Lupa,* had watched me flower as I had discovered D. H. Lawrence discovering and so powerfully translating him, so magically interanimating my two literary worlds of language and longing. She never told me she disapproved of my friends—she was above such sanctimony. Yet for her, perhaps, as for other would-be mentors, though it might be differently signified, there was an Italianness to approve and disapprove. There was Maristella Bové, Barnard's new director of Italian studies, for example, a recent aristocratic emigrée and paragon of cultural refinement, an Italian Ingrid Bergman compared with my flamingly full-breasted Mae West girlfriends.

But Miss Tilton was not so taken with "class"—in any sense—as to miss how easily the binaries of Italy north and south and pre- and postwar immigration might caricature such difference. She knew I was already studying Italian, learning to read it and even speak it with a quick comprehension and fluency that astonished even me. She spoke to me one day of a visiting foreign student taking a history degree on a special fellowship from the University of Rome: "I think you'll like her." She may even have said, "I think she will be good for you," though I have possibly imposed that bit of conscious didacticism. My guess is that she saw no swifter route to the completion of my education, for Margherita Repetto was an active socialist, daughter of a Socialist member of the Italian Parliament.

We arranged to meet. No one answered when I knocked on her dorm room door, but then I heard a chanted *"Allo!"* from the far end of the hallway, followed by Margherita's little body, wobbling with precarious speed and virtually invisible behind a tall stack of books—the entire holdings of Butler Library on Hart Crane, as it turned out. A midterm paper, she explained breathlessly. I was awed. A small bouquet of flowers, a handful of the first anemones of the season, was trapped in one fist, her room key in the other. She managed to negotiate the lock without my help, which she brusquely refused.

Inside, she dumped the books on her bed. Filling a glass of water from the sink, she placed the flowers in it atop her bureau, and pausing reflectively, gazed wistfully into their great black eyes, saying: "Flowers are so curious—so strange." I cannot explain what this phrase wrought in me, except that she uttered it in such deliberate, studied English, striking such a tone of old and weary grief, that I somehow saw those astonishing clusters of red and purple velvet as I had never seen them. For this I immediately loved her—for what seemed to me a tragic wisdom, that could summon such fugitive beauty out of a distantly remembered sadness and joy. I longed at once for the love and approval she would never return, the love, the approval, of the Italy of my desire.

Damian—*Damiano*—seemed to appear in my life, perhaps just before Christmas in the middle of my senior year, like a darkly radiant annunciatory angel.

It was the day I gave my first recitation of Italian poetry, and opened for myself a fleeting career acting classical literary theater at Columbia's Casa Italiana. The poem was a medieval lyric by Iacopono da Todi—a long, dire, vivid melodrama of the Crucifixion, operatic, full of multiple, anguished voices and images of dark passionate suffering. I loved it. I *sang* it. I had found Italian. And, finding it, I had somehow found my own voice.

I could see him at a small distance afterward, fixing me from head to heel with the haunting, unblinking onyx gaze of a crucified Christ. He brought me a small glass of red wine. "You were very good," he said.

He was tall, taller than any man in my life had ever been. He towered over me, olive and dark and seductive, a long Valentino metaphor for Romance languages. This was in fact his field. He was brilliant in it, as I discovered, unconscionably, egotistically so, very near to finishing a master's degree on existentialism in three literatures. He was also *Napoletano*, born and raised in Mussolini's Italy in a village near the historic town of Caserta, scant miles from my father's Sperone. His own father was gone—I was never sure where. Venezuela, was it? Or some other country of the dead? His mother, migrating to America after the war, had raised and educated him and his younger brother on her own. He later showed me photographs of himself before he'd left Italy, wearing the dark shirt and short Italian pants of a boys' paramilitary brigade. Even at thirteen there were those same deep, pinioning eyes, staring angrily into the camera against the sun, refusing to be blinded.

Perhaps I could only adore a man as brilliant as Damian, and as cruel, as careless of his power. I didn't understand this then, I simply adored him, with a sudden, fatal, hungry, inexorable passion. When he came to see me play Nerina in Tasso's *Aminta* and told me, my face still flushed with delight and triumph, that my interpretation had been ravishing, yes, but deeply flawed, when he said I'd carried off my role as a confessing adulteress in Machiavelli's *Mandragola* like a slut to the manner born, when he told me I was stupid as a cow, when he said I was the most rational and intelligent woman he'd ever known—I loved him *because* of this, because he could be so suddenly, unbearably cruel, so unbearably kind. Because of his unspoken Italian certainty that I would suffer—that I would gladly die—for him.

And I would have, if perhaps not gladly. I imagined it. I found myself composing Romantic verse drama, captivated at the time by the lurid poetry of Shelley's *Cenci*, staging my own self-murder in the suicide of my heroine, flinging myself down a granite staircase in an ecstasy of self-heroicizing self-surrender.

His mother was as tall as he, a warrior woman. She had his eyes. She adored him, too, it was plain, plain as the incestuous terror in those eyes the moment he brought me to meet her. She thought I might actually have won him, so proud she stupidly imagined me, and yet in truth so secretly trembling in his power. Why did this twisted labyrinth of operatic Italian emotion make me feel so alive? I felt alive. I did my best work ever. Surges of genius flashed through me like galactic implosions. I felt tremendous, invincible. And yet tragic, tragic as the Lady of Shalott with the curse upon her. I wept inwardly, in a fury of baffled freedom.

Spring came. On the great bluffs overlooking the Hudson, Damian kissed me, amid the unspeakable spring beauty of the Cloisters. He told me he loved me. I so longed to believe it, so believed it, that I could not see for the cloud of unknowing that wrapped my sight, that made the beauty of the lady in the great medieval tapestries there, the chaste and beautiful lady and the whitest white unicorn in the universe, swim before my eyes amid the green, the jasmine green of the world.

And when he took me to a romantic senior dance and, afterward, pressing me down on the bed in his room and, lifting my soft yellow gown, said, *"Let us do this now, let us finally do this"*—and I had wanted to, yes, but not now, not yet, *vorrei e non vorrei*—and he had stood over me as I lay there on the edge of the bed and lifted me roughly by the thighs and pushed himself as far as his first hard thrust would go till I cried in pain—I had welcomed him in the surrendering agony of my mind.

Damian left for Paris the August after I graduated. A year passed, some of it in misery, before I followed him to Europe.

It is a long time, a year—long enough to bury your heart like a bone in the garden, long enough to imagine it bloom again.

Long enough to transform the book of loving-to-know into the book of love.

Part Two

LA GIOCONDA

1

Perugia, October 1957. I had been nearly a month in Italy, and until this singularly fateful afternoon had felt nothing like such joy—not since the S.S. *Giulio Cesare* had docked in the Bay of Naples and dropped me for the first time in the hard lap of my father's homeland. Oddly, I can remember all the prescient little details, racing to the headquarters of the University for Foreigners, darting up and down the city's toothy hills in my new Italian heels, muttering a girl-ish prayer: *Please God, don't let me be late again, not for Luigi Barzini.*

And those miraculous new shoes!—carved by some ingenious Italian sculptor out of a deliciously edible-looking buttercream-color leather, unbelievably sexy, unbe-lievably soft. Leaving aside the fact that I could have run an Olympic 100-meter dash in them, they did things for my legs, a fact duly confirmed by the owner of a white Fiat who slowed down just long enough to pronounce judgment. It didn't even occur to me at the time that I wasn't supposed to love it. No *macho* had ever filled me with such a sudden bliss of entitlement, a conviction that all this—all this *Italy*—belonged to *me.*

Damian had met me when I'd arrived in September. He had actually come to the pier like a facsimile of an eager lover. For months I had longed to see him. For more months I had dreaded it, for weeks, for days, up to the very dawn the ship pulled into the harbor and slumped shuddering into the pier. But there had been noth-ing to dread. I had instantly and unequivocally detested the sight of him.

Fever blurs the scene, mitigating my indifference. I had caught the Asian flu—the *asiatica*—on board. Tiny Santina Dimichino, my father's cousin, eyes shaded by an elegant gray Borsalino, is waving a huge white handkerchief and crying, *"Flavia! Flavia!"* my name suddenly new and beautiful in her mouth. Damian fades away, there is barely time for me to smell the salt of the Santa Lucia harborside or take in the bay awash in morning light, before Santina and I and cousins Gino and Maria, and a poor driver friend who has lent the car and is glumly crushed against the steer-ing wheel, are all of us squeezed like bread stuffing into a tiny Cinquecento for the trip to their apartment, and I understandably go blank.

By the time I come awake, the city is gone, and I am in my Zi' Irena's garden in Striano, thirty miles away. Two beautiful cousins, Alfonso and Carlo, are taking turns plucking ripe purple figs from the orchard and feeding them to me from their hands. Striano is a teeming world of cousins, many of them young, some of them the handsomest beings I have ever seen. But also the poorest. My cousin Anna, Zi' Maria's daughter, is ashamed to expose her poverty to me, thinking I will judge it. She cries, *"Ah, Flavia, come siamo combinati!*—how we live!"—blushing as she leads me up the metal stairway to a makeshift apartment where five of them struggle to live in a drying room of the family's old spaghetti factory. They are kind.

Unbearably so, my every wish their command. But I know that, with my soft American face unmarked by suffering, what they feel cannot all of it be love.

So it was that after about three weeks with my cousins I had been rather glad to come away to Perugia, where new Fulbright grantees had been invited to be prepped for what was, *sub rosa,* really a year's duty as paradiplomats for the Eisenhower State Department. And so it was that on this strangely sublime October day I had already been in the hilly Umbrian city a week—time enough to know I would always be late for afternoon lectures, time enough to have learned to sprint up those last few marble steps and, with my aerobic heart still pounding, let the blinding shade of the portico chill the sweat off me before I made my red-faced entrance through the front door of the lecture hall.

But even as the familiar cool grabbed my hair, I could hear from deep inside an echoing riff of American laughter, unmistakable as bebop. In the frame of the great door, space and time collapse. My face abruptly meets his face shining above the thick black pillar of his cassock. Somebody shouts, *"Canceled!"* and he fractures the news back at us like some bad archangel: *"Barzini has died! Barzini is risen! Barzini will come again!"* Laughing, laughing with relief—for I have not missed the lecture after all—I let the momentum pivot me into reverse again. Somebody says, "Meet Father Browne." Our eyes join in a sudden clearing of haze.

I did not know I would love him. I thought I still loved someone I had left behind me. That day meant nothing more to me then than a reclaimed afternoon, a few sunny hours to sip vermouth under a yellow umbrella, to sail like an American fleet out to the Corso and into the bay of the piazza, Father Browne and the three of us: a young California composer named Paul Glass going to Milan, Anna McGill, a weaver from Milwaukee going to Florence—and me, a master's year in English and comp lit at Columbia behind me, taking my Fulbright to Padua to read literature and politics at the university.

This Cagney Irish priest named Browne was Father Henry J., a Catholic University professor on a research grant in immigration history, just arrived from New York. Paul had staked a personal and instant claim to him. I could see why: the movie star presence, the face a miracle of cunningless animal brightness like a feral child's, the electric violence in his wonderful hair. He had a bristly military brush cut, black sketched with gray—more fur than hair, really—jump-starting from a sharp widow's peak and surging back over that splendid head, which was set as squarely on his thick shoulders as a prizefighter's. And he was funny. Before we'd even ordered our drinks he was off the runway like a Cessna in an updraft, everything Ful- or half-bright, the underbelly of every American careerist in Italy in his gunsights, soaring away as the laughter crashed. The timing infallible, one resistless jolt after another. My brain spun. I laughed as if he'd invented it, as if a depth charge were rupturing some deep archeology of Italian-woman seriousness crusted down in me like a buried sea of Sicilian salt.

He asked me if I was from New York, and still daubing my eyes with a finger-tip, I nodded yes. "Well, actually from New Rochelle," I corrected. His burst of laughter was ruthless—the stab-laugh of a comic with a ready punchline. His face came at me in a pitch of forehead that stopped at a pair of black eyebrows like skid-marks, tiny hairs at the tips seeming to sway like antennas. He croons: "Forty-five minutes from Broadway. . . . And oh what a difference it makes." I hear myself say that I still go to the dentist in East Harlem. I hear him roar again. Everybody roars. He is on to me. When he asks, *"Di dove?"* in Italian, I know he means it just as Italians would: from where have my people come, from what inhospitable bony piece of southern mother-soil did they tear their roots? Mine is a New York story and he obviously loves it. And yet he seems also to love having me feel safe in his laughter, unraveling that old familiar worm of Italian girl-child shame like a knot. I notice that his eyes under that jagged fringe of eyelash break light to pieces. I beam him a reassuring smile. *I see what a difference it makes,* it says. *I see what a difference it makes to know the difference.*

He grins back. "Great teeth," he says.

John, the love I had so ironically left behind me in New York, had so much wanted me not to leave him, had begged me not to. I had inescapably pictured his suffering a thousand times, the image of mine before he'd rescued me, hunting me down like the hound of heaven. Somewhere out on the Atlantic crossing, I thought, I must have swallowed his wounded eyes, and they were liquidating inside me now like capsules of cyanide.

He'd been a fellow student in the Columbia master's program, a Greek American writing his thesis on Forster. When I thought of him, sometimes I'd think of *A Passage to India* too, of Forster's lyrical digression on the Adriatic, the Mediterranean, on an Italy perfectly poised between East and West. It had seemed a promise of return somehow, a reference point of safety. But now I saw it had become a trick, a mental trick, an evasion, because sometimes in reality—if this were reality—I felt nauseously unbalanced, dazed, agoraphobic—missing to myself. As if I were here in Italy inside a dream somebody else had dreamed, moving against an architextile of incompatible centuries. I felt it now, even now, electroplated in the gold of this Perugian sunset, as if the four of us were huddled together at some twentieth-century mike, plugged into time like a wall socket, waiting to hear what we would say.

Father Browne said he was going to the Vatican Archives in Rome to look at U.S.-Italian immigration documents and "find out what those guys were *really* thinking about." I felt the self-satirical bite of this and laughed, but I also found myself watching him as he spoke, as he stretched back against the rear legs of the café chair with the cassock buttons on his chest straining, and from time to time pushed his square jaw up and out, and then shoved a restless forefinger behind his stiff Roman collar and gave it a little tug. He whipped somehow into a flashback of growing up Irish in Hell's Kitchen, as if a true historian had to start with Genesis, with the kid who played sandlot baseball with another kid on Tenth Avenue—a kid named

Rocky Consaniero, with an *eeeeaasy* centerfield arm, who could throw you out on a base hit every time. *Consanieeero,* he said, dragging it like a poet.

"*Baseball* got you here?" Paul couldn't believe it. He drove his hand through the tracks in his Santa Monica beach-bleached hair and went on about Vivaldi and opera. Anna followed, speaking out of her own cowl of dark hair like a sibyl, remembering the colors she used to go back to look at, again and again, among the Italian paintings in the museum. And now—"Look at *this,*" she pleaded, waving her arm as if she were lifting a curtain off the piazza's palette of sunset on old stone. A flash of longing to paint came over me. For a drowning instant I was almost dizzy with the memory of my own hands.

But Father Browne had suddenly turned the conversation to food, and was amazingly describing his first Italian family dinner—"*eucharistic,*" he called it, uttering the word with a disbelieving awe. I too am there, but the family he is describing evanesces, and instead I see my father, rising with imperious, almost fearful dignity to carve the roast, gracefully moving the knife against the whetstone of the long sharpening steel, swinging them across each other with a frightening skill, a rasping and hypnotic sound, slicing the air repeatedly in a movement swift as light. I feel the last bliss drain from my body, down my legs and through my beautiful buttery yellow heels, in a sudden insane bafflement as to what has bracketed this place to my life.

Absurdly comes that unbidden visitation of love again in a line of poetry: *Amor che a nullo amato amar perdona. . . .* I knew my Dante now. Long passages by heart. This is what his Francesca had said: the law that had commanded her to love her lover, Paolo, forever—the law of love. But I had known it, it seemed, all my life.

The priest with the golden eyes cannot read the drowning message in my mind. I see him again, envy him, connecting *this,* this dream, with everything he has left behind him. I think you could trace a perfect line, like a cord, running from this piercing quattrocento sunset beauty back to his mean Hell's Kitchen streets.

I do not know him. I do not know him at all.

Luigi Barzini did come again, days later, bringing his famous bittersweet take on Italians, the one he would eventually make a book of, imaging his countrymen with a eye to the future cultural export trade. I did not think he was speaking to me. He breezed in and out, taking his aura with him, leaving us to the mercies of a windy academic from the Education Ministry who led us down the byzantine byways of the Italian university system for more than an hour.

I was downhearted. But I was not always downhearted, and didn't always resent our forced introductions to an Italian culture I barely recognized. And I didn't always injure these magnificent October days in Umbria, stringing themselves so obligingly out on the week like glistening blue beads, with my little grief. We could still stroll along a Corso backlit in orange autumn sunsets, as the sun-warmed streets turned cooler and the lecture halls colder, as the lectures on Christian democracy got more and more drowsy. Father Browne could still make us laugh. On good days

I could even make *him* laugh, as in the class in conversational Italian where I needled him about his Church Latin accent, and he beamed as if I were finally catching on to the basic malicious subtext of human relations.

There was this funny thing about him, that he had at least ten years on most of the scholars in the Fulbright cohort, yet lacked our pseudocynical boredom, pent-up, postadolescent offspring of Beat that we were, trying to pretend to be above shame at being citizens of the country Italians called *"Usa,"* in a word that was the third-person singular of the verb *to use,* above berating our national psychoses around McCarthyism and Little Rock, our mindless devotion to psychoanalysis and Valium, as if we shouldn't have to be accountable for them. Father Browne was no chauvinist. But his peculiar fractured reverence not only closed the age gap between us, it introduced something harder to name. Was it that sense of history? That urgency, not precisely missionary, to engage the world? He seemed to have an expectancy about him, a sense of the future along with the past, that made him seem younger than we were, as if he had actually swum out ahead and was lying poised and smiling out there on some big cresting wave about to break.

He joined Paul and me at the National Gallery one day, split between flattering my best Barnard art history spiel with his attention and skewering the other Americans wandering through the galleries saying immortal things. Paul stood in front of the paintings he liked, taking deep, meditative breaths, as if Pinturicchio could be inhaled like a reefer, until he finally lagged so far behind that we lost him. When he didn't appear outside, we decided he could catch up with us at the café.

It proved a major move: the first time I had walked with Father Browne alone, woman with cassocked priest, on an Italian street. We were unavoidably self-conscious and took an outdoor table in spite of the chill in the air. "Macy's window," he said. "He can't miss us." Neither could anybody else, and that was the point.

"So tell me about John," he coaxed, when the waiter had served the Campari. My father used to say, quoting his mother, "The tongue goes where the tooth hurts." I didn't need much coaxing. I fumbled in my bag for the cablegram that had demanded I come home, wired to me aboard ship. The paper, so tightly folded for so long, had already begun to crack at the seams. He opened it as gingerly as an archivist, then passed it back. "Sounds ambivalent to me."

"You don't know John," I said. He hadn't seen the letters. Pleading, menacing. Four of them.

He drove an incredulous hand through the electric fur of his hair. "Does he have *any* idea what this means to you?"

"What does it mean to me?" I said, wearily. Too wearily for him to believe it. I said, "It keeps changing."

"Because of him?"

"Yes," but then, "because of *me* too. Because the why I wanted to be here in the first place isn't why I came—or why I want to stay."

He said he thought Barnard women were very complicated. I took a breath and looked away, and when I looked back, I said, "Let me tell you about Damian." He settled back and I told him about the disrupted romance, the fellowship to Paris, the unanswered letters. About waiting—for weeks, for months. I began to feel choked, clearly somehow not done with it.

"Would you prefer a booth with a curtain?" I had to laugh, but what flashed on my mind was the role I'd played in Machiavelli's *Mandragola,* the silly, sex-hungry confessing adulteress Damian had said I played so well.

I told him about the single letter that had finally come from Paris after nearly six months. "I guess you only need one," I said. I began to cry. I couldn't help myself, everything suddenly sluicing back at once, that heartless, despicable good-bye letter, my own demented grief, all the nights sick-hearted with doom, the letters I'd penned back like whole epistolary novels and then torn to pieces without sending. I remembered how my mother had suffered, unable to bear to see me in so much pain. She begged my father for help, and the two of them met me in the city and took me out to dinner at an Italian restaurant on Broome Street—what other kind of restaurant did Italians go to? But I was a madwoman, besotted, possessed—it was Italy scorning me along with Damian, and every word on the menu danced in my eyes like a cackling he-devil.

I finally said, "It's taken me a long time."

"Not that long."

I winced a little. "Psychic time," I protested, trying to laugh. But he was right. I felt naked.

He waited, and when I said nothing, he simply said: "Doctor John."

The ice tinkled at the bottom of my Campari. "But you know what?" I said. "Even before John, when I already knew Damian didn't matter anymore, Italy still did." I lifted my eyes to the darkening, emptying piazza. "Sure I wanted to prove something, coming here. But not *just* to prove something." I looked straight into his face and took a deep, clearing breath and spread my hand out over the piazza as if I could hold it. "I still needed *this.* I needed to *know.*"

Father Browne tilted his chair back precariously and smiled and lifted his black eyebrows. "Say no more."

But no, that wasn't it. He didn't understand. "I *owe* John," I said.

"You don't owe him *this,*" and his hand went wildly out this time as mine had. But I wanted—needed—my kind of absolution, permission not to stay but to go, and that hard square hand was tearing again through the rough brush of his hair, refusing it. He gave me a steady brown look. He said, "You'll never forgive him if you have to give this up now and go home."

I thought I could never forgive myself if I didn't.

"You're going to have a hard time understanding this," he came back, rather sternly, "but, believe me, guilt is a wasted emotion."

I thought he was taking a chance, banking like that on his authority.

John had said it was over between us if I didn't come home. He seemed to be daring me to disbelieve him. But who *was* this John? Not the gentle comforter whose sweet summer mouth, remembered, made my lips burn to be kissed. And yet I loved him. I thought Father Browne's maxim about guilt detestable, something that would have slipped like spit off Damian's tongue.

Yet America was so far back to go back to.

I scored every day on the wall as another a failure of nerve—of love, of loyalty. I hugged sleep like a thief. In my little garret room in Signora Brancusi's *pensione* at night, I would pull the sheepskin cover over my ears and swear I would pack up and go back in the morning. But morning would come, with that same daily crash of a zillion bells, a cold clean as baptism against the window, already iced with a daybreak so lemon-white you could smell it. And then the bells would diminish into echoes of echoes until the dust motes trembled, and the street, with the blacksmith's shop below, would begin to stir and clang.

Then Nannì the housemaid would tap and shyly enter the room with a swift noiseless flick of the door latch and a cup of syrupy coffee chinking in her hand.

Nannì is as dark-toned and the muscles in her arms as roped as some country cousin of mine from the hills of Vesuvius. Nothing like the fair *Perugini* I have met along these pearl gray streets. She has told me she comes from the mountains. She has let me imagine how it might be to trade the haunts of the ancient Etruscans for a wage. Her thick hair is as black and smooth as polished wood, but the fine taut skin is too papery over the cheekbones and the petals about the eyes too dark for her to be young. She is swift-moving, elusive, her thoughts seem outside of time. When she smiles, the smile sweeps her face and vanishes as if it had never been smiled. When I see her I think no creature so beautiful was ever condemned to household slavery.

And I know there is no turning back.

I liked to refer to Signora Brancusi, the mistress of my Perugia *pensione,* as the Madonna of San Bernardino, after the church whose cold bells crashed me awake at five every morning. I learned that her husband had died soon after the war, leaving her to trade gingerly on his reputation as perhaps too zealous a devotee of the regime that had got them into it—not altogether a burden, apparently, since his bequest had included this five-hundred-year-old *palazzo,* star-listed among Italy's minor historic sites.

Still, she was an anxious businesswoman. Her stinted hospitality seemed to favor a few resident boarders, mainly widower businessmen or well-connected bachelors of a certain politics. Signor Vannucci was one. His flamboyant walrus mustache glowed at the edges, as if he snorted paprika. He had a habit of stalking me in the dim hallways leaping out of the dark and whining, *"Ah–haaa, la bella signorina ameri-caaaana!"* And then he would sweep open the door with a wave of his arm and that superannuated bachelor smirk of his that made no secret of what he would like more than anything in the world.

In this respect, I was the perfect addition to the Madonna's ménage: educated American girl, likely to bring male boarders to dinner on time and respectably dressed, a paying customer, of course, yet too new at this to make a fuss except perhaps about the cold. Under her watchful eye I was careful to slip my linen dinner napkin into its tortoiseshell ring for every meal. I loved and feared those meals, long and byzantinely ceremonious, held at an enormous banquet table with huge wine carafes at either end which seemed mainly for show, and unfolding like melodramas under the high, vaulted ceiling of the gloomy dining room. The room was banded on all four sides with a mural, painted in tones of deep blood-red and black, of leaping, pawing, prancing horses, great muscular male figures bursting their blazoned armor astride them, their helmets adorned with phallic plumes the size of trees.

I puzzled over this painting, clearly too lacking some essential quattrocento innocence to be contemporary with the *palazzo*. And then one midday, as we were waiting for the fruit course, I noticed the date in a corner—a little crosshatch of Roman numerals parsing out to "1936"—and my surprise was out of my mouth before I could check it. The Madonna raised two plump layers of chin away from her rising bosom: *"Ahhh, mia cara signorina! These* are the *gloooories* of the *hiiistory* of Italy"—pronouncing the Italian words *"gloooria"* and *"stoooria"* with such grandiose rhyming that all the bespectacled gentlemen leaned back, a little stiffly, stemware poised, and raised their eyes as if she herself had been soaring into the upper reaches of the room.

I thought, *Of course: Mussolini.* I did not say it, except to observe, cautiously, that the glories seemed exclusively military. Nannì, with salvific timing, entered the room with the fruit bowl cradled in her arm, and began her slow loop from chair to chair. Signor Vannucci leaned across the table and slipped a few more drops of *bianco* discreetly into my glass, at which I dropped my eyes to avert conversation, and he returned to flaying his quartered pear.

But I confess his surgical precision entranced me. I mortally envied his apparent Italian birthright of making such a clean, perfectly peeled quartering with knife and fork, never once touching the pear with his hands. He speared an exquisitely carved morsel, and just as he slipped it under his mustache and swallowed, he leapt on my attention: *What did I think of Perugia these days?*

Innocent enough question, I thought, to have been nursing so long, and I began in my increasingly nuanced conversational Italian to shape a textbook reply: *I had lately been quite enjoying the enchanting views from the walls—*

"Ah-haa! So, signorina, that *was* you I saw!"

My pear oozed messily into my plate. He seemed to relish my look of alarm, poising a small, wet triangle delicately on his fork before lipping it in. "Yes, *you*," he said, "strolling along the *belvedere* yesterday evening with that *birbaccione* of a little priest!"

When I recounted the story to Father Browne the following evening, he said, "What's he mean, *little?*" Then we ran through at least seven synonyms for *lowlife*, Irish as well as English, trying to translate *birbaccione.*

We were too heart-pure to think of ending our evening walks merely because people had begun to notice them. We paused on an overlook of a northwestern hillside and watched the magical dusk sift down from a deep indigo sky.

"*Bir-bach-y-ooo-neh,*" he repeated, obviously relishing the sound—and the significance. "I bet they save it for priests."

We resumed our walk along the wall. I was reminded of something I'd already told him about my Neapolitan father, the sheepish gratitude toward the priests at Mount Carmel after he'd come through his illness, yet always that prowling, gingerly, animal, anticlerical nose for danger. Now he told me laughingly about the typical gesture of Italian men on the streets, cupping their hands over their privates when a priest went by. I had never seen it—the intelligence was somewhat unsettling—and he shifted artfully from anticlerics to clerics, fascinated with my experience as a Catholic at a major secular university like Columbia: "You know, Jack Daly and I go back to the seminary at Dunwoodie together."

We'd spoken about Father Daly, the Columbia Newman Club chaplain, how he'd been as close as I'd ever come to friendship with a priest. "My father away from father," I mused. "Irish father great improvement over Italian." That was going too far, but he let it by. When he asked me what Daly thought of Damian, I said, "He never got to tell me. Damian and Newman Club didn't mix."

"See what you get?"

I laughed, not ready to concede that failure of religious discipline was what I'd been punished for in that instance. But he was already onto another theme. "Daly's not much of a heavyweight," he said. "I don't suppose he stirred up much intellectual debate—"

"Does that include sword vs. epee? Until Newman Club I hadn't known fencing was such a Catholic sport."

"Not Catholic," he corrected. "Monarchist."

I remembered that somebody from Newman Club had once told me to read Chesterton and Belloc, converts, very High Church.

"Did you?"

"No. Does James Joyce count?"

"Not if you're clearing for orthodoxy."

"Maybe that's something only Irish and English Catholics worry about."

He winced. "What do Italian Catholics worry about?"

"Love," I laughed. "What else?"

We both laughed, but it struck me rather absurdly that for me love would never be a joke. I told him then that I'd finally written to John, and he gave me a quick, artless hug as if he'd coached me through a major field event. It wasn't possible to look into that beaming face and cry.

"One thing popular prejudice fails to appreciate about confession," he said. "It's faster than psychotherapy, and a helluva lot cheaper."

At the entrance to the *pensione* he turned suddenly stage Italian and tipped my gloved hand with a kiss. "Watch out for the old fart at the dinner table."

I shushed him, mortified. "Jesus, we'll shock the bourgeoisie to death."

"Mercy killing," whispered the *birbaccione.*

•

Suddenly departures were everywhere, that simultaneous sense of ending and beginning. Sam Kaner, a hairy recluse printmaker from San Francisco who had set the session record for most orientation lectures slept through, had already left for Venice without saying good-bye. Olivia and Betty, two fresh-faced sopranos hard not to think of as a duet, lingered outside the university portico to tell us they had an apartment waiting in Trastevere. "Please come see us in Rome," Betty begged me. "We'll even invite *him*," she teased, nodding toward Father Browne. "We don't mind sharing."

The edge of innuendo was innocent. They were two child-women, feckless targets soon enough for a posse of Roman adventurers. They regarded Father Browne as something of a personal bodyguard, though standing there between the two of them—Olivia tallish and blond, Betty petite and dark—he looked more like a muscular Puck on a casting call for *Midsummer Night's Dream*.

Our last full day, when I showed up at the Duomo for a final group outing to Arezzo, Browne was alone, leaning on a borrowed Fiat in the middle of the piazza, cassock gone, a red-checked flannel shirt tucked into black clerical trousers, black beret tilted jauntily over his brush cut. Paul and Anna, supposed to join us, had been delayed. We were to go on ahead and meet them there. Gallantly swinging open the door of the car, he said, "Four's too many for this phone booth anyway."

The day danced. The landscape slid backward, a scroll of Tuscan artwork, fruit and olive orchards and stripped grapevines that sketched spidery pen-strokes on wine-colored washes of field. The rough wind whipped the leaves of the olive trees gray side out until they became great manes of silver hair. I remarked that it was just like the paintings, the scenery I'd seen in back of all those saints—every rock, even the uncanny earth purples. "I thought they made it all up when they made up the madonnas," I said, and he said, "Maybe they didn't make up the madonnas."

In those days before the *autostrada*, Perugia to Arezzo was a long, punishing ride. "Let's sing river songs," he suggests, and we sing our way through his amazing repertoire of songs for jollying away the driving time, the Missouri, the Mississippi, the Wabash. We swing into mountain songs, sunshine songs, city songs. We seem both to know "Chicago" and "Noo Yawk, Noo Yawk" all the way through, both of us stall on exactly the same line of "A Foggy Day," right after the British Museum, and both brazen it out, making it up. After a time, he says, "It must be Hartke's fault that I've got such a headful of show tunes."

He has that way of cutting straight to a name. But I have already learned the first and most draconian Browne's Law: Do not ask *Who?* Conversation will be derailed. Have faith and in a moment's miracle it will be revealed to you that this Hartke guy who loves musicals is the director of the theater program at Catholic U. and that his star recent graduates, Phil Bosco and Frannie Sternhagen, names also recently dropped, are students of Browne's who had threatened to boycott American history forever if he didn't come to their shows. "Green room parties always used to end with rain songs," he says. "Wanna sing—?"

"Pleeease," I beg, sung out. "No rain songs."

A pause filled with the hoarse noise of the engine, which could be in our laps. "Jeannie Davis did great rain songs," he says.

The car is rolling into Arezzo by now, like a toy riding smoothly on a narrow, glazed-leather ribbon of road. "I wonder if she'll get to Naples for Filomena."

Before I can check my flummox I blurt, "Who?"

He parrots me: "*Who?* Filomena? *Saint* Filomena?"

I am sure he knows precisely how maddening he is. "The woman who's going to Naples."

"Oh, Jeannie. Jeannie Davis. She's the student who got the Maria Goretti award." He cuts into a side street just short of the Piazza di San Francesco and pulls to a stop, yanking the hand brake hard. "But they made her give it back."

I am not sure why I am still giggling when he asks me if the sign that says *Vietato di Sosta Assoluta* means No Absolute Parking, which he explains should be no problem if we're only planning to stay a couple of hours.

But the glorious Piero Queen of Sheba, plumb as a blue obelisk, is sadly enmeshed in scaffolding. We catch a poor tantalizing glimpse of her and slip out of the Church of Saint Francis into the bedazzling piazza again, where Paul and Anna are suddenly coming toward us, taking the great stones in long, loping American strides. They walk right past us. "Catch you up later," Paul says, mysteriously. Anna is in blue sunglasses, grinning.

Maybe they think it's a joke that we look like an ordinary tourist couple. Father Browne seems unruffled. He calls peremptorily for the little red guidebook and flips it open with a priestly gesture of the red marking ribbon, his beret rabbinically fixed at the back of his head. According to the prophet Nagel, he announces, the town can be visited in half a day. "Excellent," he adds, beaming. "Plenty of time for lunch."

In the little side street *Buca di San Francesco*, we order chicken with garlic and rosemary. I finally beg him to finish the story he has left dangling and tell me the secret of Jeannie Davis and the Maria Goretti award. Not the Maria Goretti part, I reassure him. She, every Catholic girl in the fifties knew, had gone to her death resisting a rapist, forgiving him with her last breath. The obligatory—and swiftly certifed—three miracles had just made her a saint, instant role model for restless fifties teenagers, "fraught with significance," as the Mature Parent used to say.

Paul and Anna have chosen this moment to go by. We signal them through the window; they wave airily back and move on. "What are they up to?" I am trying not to feel annoyed.

Father Browne is forgiving. "I think Glass is still casting me as Spencer Tracy in some Catholic movie."

"*The Bells of St. Mary's?*"

"That's Bing Crosby."

"Just testing. You looking for a nun?"

"Sure," he says. "Bergman's been nixed since *Stromboli*."

"I've got the eyebrows."

"Zoom to eyebrows." His eyes are finding mine now, heading straight into the danger. But he has made me laugh safely and veered away again. He pours the last bit of *bianco* out of the wine carafe evenly between us. Irresistibly, I am touching his hand. He turns his palm upward and we clasp. Something just then crosses his smiling eyes and passes. "Now, about the Maria Goretti award," he begins.

I pretend not to have seen it.

2

Perhaps in the stern economy of love, no one who has ever loved is free. Love lost is still love. Yet in that single fugitive Italian moment I think I came as close as I would ever come to freedom. Traveling northward alone, heart-whole and refreshed with America and my American love behind me, I opened to Italy like a child loosed in a meadow of strawberry desire. The train ride that carried me through the landscape of the mountainous northern countryside might have been set to the music of *La Gioconda*. Veils flying, I seemed to dance my way into a railway-carriage romance—some perfect story from the world of the Orient Express.

I am seated in a second-class compartment, alone. The train is thundering through the beauty of ravines, blanking into tunnels, bursting into sun-soaked valleys, sweeping along resistless hillsides adrift with scattered sheep like pills of wool. I am suddenly, chancely beset by a student from Udine, returning home.

For a moment he hesitates in the doorway—tall, pale, poetic, food for my demon hunger. He finds my eyes, folds himself gracefully onto the seat beside me and turns his Botticelli face to mine. I know I have dreamed his sapphire eyes. *Pian piano*, we speak. *Pian piano*, his lips, sublimely perfect of outline as those of a cinquecento portrait, are brushing my cheek. We rush through long, gasping Apennine tunnels of protestation and surrender. At the end of my journey, as the train pulls from the station platform of Padova carrying him onward to Friuli, our eyestrings quiver a last good-bye.

I know exactly what this is. It is Love. Love so free and pure and objectless as always to discover its fragrant occasion. The ancients called it "the lust of the eye," well understanding that vaguely erotic heat, continually fed and watered by the ebb and flow of sensation. That disorder centuries of travelers have caught simply moving through the live broth of Italian air. My sweet *Friuliano*, plucked from the flux and returned to it, we shall never meet again. My sorrow is as self-indulgent as my desire. My desire closes over it like water.

I had been assigned a room in Padua at the university dormitory for women in Via Eufemia, called La Casa della Studentessa. The *direttrice* was a forceful woman perhaps in her late thirties—it was hard to tell—a nunnish air of unflappable piety seemed to have cryogenically trapped her in a permanent middle age. To my dismay, her first pronouncement when we met, in a very authoritative contralto, was a declaration of war on freedom. My being older by four or five years than most of the other women in the house made absolutely no difference. There were to be no exceptions to the convent-style rules, which permitted us to leave no earlier than seven in the morning and come back no later at night than ten.

Steward of sixty virginities, I supposed, she was going to be able to account for every one of them on the Day of Judgment. My first week, when I wanted to go everywhere, do everything, seemed a hell of house arrest. And yet it was not so much what I couldn't do as how I was watched lest I do it. This wraith, this smoothly pale, hollow-eyed *belle dame sans merci* seemed to be everywhere I turned. I began to imagine a hair shirt under her sexless dark woolen garments. She made me want to say dirty words at the dinner table.

But the filthy air of the pitiless Po Valley in winter soon leached the fight out of me. The fever and chills of the *asiatica* returned, and there would be no night-prowling without the will to prowl. Still she watched me like an attack dog. A few moments' breach of the curfew would be passed to her by the obsequious *portiere,* and her chill by the next mealtime would have dropped several degrees centigrade.

I was determined to tough it out. The rooms, which looked out over a garden, were lovely. Designed with that amazing Italian genius for integrating simple, modernist spaces into intricate old ones, they occupied a new section of the Casa created as an annex to an astonishingly beautiful sixteenth-century *palazzo.*

My suitemate, Silene, a pre-med student with a sanitary sensibility, was alarmed by my predilection for showers even on the days the hot water was turned off, but she came to rather like my American pluck, perhaps because we were both a little older than the others, and feeling captive to this dragon's keep. Silene had suffered a crippling bout with polio as a child, and limped through her life now in a perpetual shell of pain and humiliation. She needed a pet creature. Tenderly, she made one of me, who had wandered in from the wild and would gladly take food from her hand.

And yet for me Silene was the magical one, haloed with a strange beauty. She hobbled across the room on a clumsy prosthetic shoe, eyes down lest she catch you staring. If you were any self-respecting Italian, of course you *were* staring, and of course she *would* catch you, and wither you suddenly with one terrible hot glance from her pain-stricken eyes. The other women in the house feared and reverenced her—as (I considered) men with cupped genitals did priests. They assumed her stricken life gave her gypsy powers, and she treated the imputation with suitable cool. Evenings after dinner they would come to her table trembling and giggling, and plead with her to read their palms. One night she confronted me as I looked on and demanded to see my hand. She traced the lifeline cautiously. Something terrible, she said, awaited me in my middle age.

Loredanna, a staggering beauty, was watching. "*Caspita,* Silene! *Middle age!* Give us the love lines!"

Silene raised a witchy eyebrow over an even witchier wall-eye that sent Loredanna curling back into her chair. But she instructed me to fold my fingers into an easy fist so she could count the number of creases on the fleshy outer edge of my palm.

"*Quante cotte!*" she shrieked.

Cotte? Cotte? I looked up at a circle of scandalized faces, all of whom knew, as I didn't, that it meant "love affairs"—literally, "cookings." Loredanna roared with joy. Silene sank back, her face blotched with embarrassment, not having intended to make such a public announcement of my scarlet career.

•

But my freedom, such as it was, was poor and sick as well as lonely, and no promise of future "cookings" could redeem it. The Italian government had not sent me the stipend supposed to supplement my travel grant, and the Fulbright Commission in Rome claimed to be diplomatically paralyzed. My ear ached, my old flu dug down into a hard cough. Vittore Branca, the professor designated my mentor at the university, had no time for me. I cooled my heels in his front office, watched by a depressingly pasty, bespectacled *assistente* with tufts of wiry hair in his ears, feeling intellectually abandoned.

I took long walks through the town on weekends, along old streets slimy with industrial acid rain, beneath hunching, spongy stone porticoes that seemed to have sucked up ten centuries of damp. Even on rainless days the sky hung down like a soaked sheet. Silene, for all her tenderness, seemed not to think of me when she left for home on Fridays, and I knew better than to expect invitations into the *sanctum sanctorum* of these bourgeois families, protecting the saleable virginity of daughters with a fierce, patriarchal zeal for privacy.

Weekdays I worked in desultory fashion, taking notes on texts in the university library, passing afternoons in bookstores collecting books on the Risorgimento and buying cheap paper editions of Mazzini and De Sanctis and Croce and Momigliano, the critics whose nationalism I had come to study. I would take my silkily wrapped purchases into Pedrocchi's, Padova's landmark café, and unwrap them slowly and lovingly over a single espresso *lunghissimo,* reading a little, watching the people, and letting the text and the town run together.

One more gray day in November, tired of waiting for that perfect combination of weather and boon companion, I junketed alone to Venice on the morning train and boarded the first vaporetto zigzagging up the Grand Canal. My eyes danced as if they had been created for this sight, as if the beloved Ruskin I had homed to in graduate school had made every Gothic stone a friend. Even in flood, laid with pedestrian planks, San Marco was a glorious event, and I went out to the dark street at the back and came in again, just so I could see it with that famous epiphany of astonishment he had written into *The Stones of Venice.* But I soon left it behind me just to stalk the dim alleys and hang over the palings of bridges, marveling how even the sunless light between the *palazzi* could strobe the surface ripples into such brilliant, varicolored glass, how, in the dark, echoing *campi,* the shushery tongue of the *Veneti* could trap the very rustle of water in their speech.

High on the bliss of civilization, longing to share it, I made the wild decision to look up Sam Kaner, the crazy Fulbright printmaker with an address on Giudecca. I had been about to give up on the third ring when he suddenly threw open his flat door. I had roused him from sleep. He seemed hairier than ever, and stood there stark naked except for a paint-stained sweater tied around his waist, the sleeves dangling over his privates. By the time he recognized me and invited me in, I was already halfway down the stairs, like some hapless Doris Day, promising to come back at a better time.

I returned to the Casa that night exhausted, full of a new universe of wonder.

In my mail slot at the desk I found a long letter from John, already two weeks old from the date, by now for me an ancient historical treatise on the many ways to say good-bye. It had hound-dogged me across the Italian spine until it found me, standing dumb and cold in my coat and gloves, just back from Venice, in the center of that splendid marble rotunda of that beautiful house, around and above me on every wall swirling infinitely untraceable arabesques of sixteenth-century vine leaves. I read the letter through once without stopping, then page by page crumpled it as I counted out the twelve marble steps to my room.

The gypsy-eyed Silene was waiting for me, alchemizing a tiny pot of espresso over an illicit blue alcohol flame. She offered me some of her brew. I tried to explain my complex melancholy in the tongue that seemed to have created it.

Lending me the scrutiny of her inner eye, she took an oracular, cross-legged pose on the bed. Padua, she said with suitable satire, was known as the city of three "withouts." She even enumerated them: the saint without a name, the meadow without grass, the café without doors. "And you, my dear," she added, beaming me a sudden bewitchingly silver smile, "must be the fourth."

Father Browne read between the lines of feigned cheerfulness in my first letter, his return note a masterpiece of crabbed block-printing so maddeningly telegraphic only an archivist could decode it. I made out that he was being ginger about John, offering the sort of other-fish-in-the-sea kind of consolation that Silene would have clucked over. This was followed by a suitably cautionary tale about dinner with Olivia and Betty "plus pasta carbonara & reports of groping bouts with oversexed music masters." Ever the careful moralist, he admitted his evidence was limited to Rome. He could understand why I might feel hobbled by the house rules, but as for himself he liked the convent safe-house on the unimpeachable general principle that you should never give a sucker an even break.

He was living, he said, in what he called his "digs" in Montemario, a priests' residence rank with the privileges of the visiting clerisy. His latest dilemma was whether to indulge in the luxury of a car. He had an offer of a rather conspiciously large used Fiat 1100. Of course, parking would be no problem at the Villa, and if I did come down to Rome for the holidays, "we could make a quick run to the Castelli to see *Ichs-più-due,*" which translated "X-plus-two," disparaging Communist code for the incumbent Pope.

The post office made two deliveries a day, six days a week, virtual e-mail. When I asked him what he thought of my looking for a job to close the money gap, he snapped quickly back: "Too bad you're only half-bright and can't leap snakepit of guinea bureaucracy. Commission here ladles gravy tills cups runneth over. Go ahead. I promise the head office won't hear it from me."

I angled for a job teaching English at a student-run cooperative called CRUE, which offered university students cheap evening instruction in foreign languages. Sergio, my interviewer, was a big tousled chain-smoker, prematurely old. He said my accent was too American. Dino, sitting beside him, disagreed. "They'll *love* it," he said. He beamed me a fine set of teeth, tar-stained from consumption of ruthless Italian cigarettes.

Dino Portalone proved a strange and wonderful migratory bird, a refugee Sicilian who had lost his mother to the war and been sent north to be raised by foster parents. He had adored Americans with a mindless passion since the Allied invasion of Sicily. "They have *balls*," he'd say with an apologetic little shrug for the rudeness. "Even you." He had made a certain local fame for himself running a truck into Hungary during the 1956 uprising and smuggling people out through Austria—three days of hard driving without a break, wired on coffee and adrenaline. I said I thought *that* was balls.

In CRUE, my circle of friends suddenly widened. It seemed to happen in a single blinding burst, like coming up out of water. In a snapshot taken that December at the university parade for the *Festa della Matricola* where I am jammed together with fifteen other foreign and Italian students on a flatbed truck, racketing down the Corso, I look as if I have the bends. Someone has stuck a medieval shovel hat on my head. For some reason my hair is in braids, and I am staring away, over a sea of other shovel hats, as if I had received a concussion. The wine was relentless. I can remember barely making the ten o'clock curfew at the Casa that night, carried in on two pairs of international arms.

Also in Padua that year were two other American Fulbrights, who had not made the Perugia orientation: another priest, Father McManus, a Jesuit physicist from Iowa with vacant, glassine eyes and bad breath, who twanged on incessantly when we met about the provincial little clerics at San Antonio where he was quartered; and a dry Italian American from Cleveland—also, oddly, named Dino—a man of few words, and those few funny and endearing.

This American Dino was as skinny and tall and hawk-nosed and homely as his Italian counterpart was short and robust and handsome. Behind his Midwestern affability he wore a steel plate of sexual defenses John Deere couldn't have got through. My selfish passing thought was that he was exactly the protective big brother I needed. We plotted a day-trip to Mantua together to see the Mantegna frescoes. The tour bus, which left at 6 A.M. and returned at 11 P.M., put us one bad hour either side of the Casa curfew. I explained it to the Dragon Lady. Highly irregular, she observed. Very radical. Really, *signorina,* quite the last audacity.

American Dino's idea was that I should take a short-term lease at one of the big apartment blocks out the Via Venezia, where all the American medical students lived, but once out there I found a fleet of concrete pylons where everything screamed transience and flight. The medical student who showed me his apartment sat side by side with his nervous wife on the edge of a brown couch that coffee could safely be spilled on, passing a nervous baby back and forth between them. She thought the natives insolent and boring. He was clearly sore at having had to come *here* for his medical degree. I thought as I left of those signs suburban developers had begun to post on highways back in the States: "If you lived here you'd be home now."

"They're like American displaced persons," I tell Dino over espresso in his own wonderful flat, high above the Piazza Garibaldi in a new ten-story building at the center of town. This building is known locally as the Tower, part of a renewal program for this otherwise derelict section of the inner city. The developer has clearly got the land rights in exchange for preserving a scrap of ancient Roman wall surviving on the site, and working it imaginatively into his modernist façade. A row of brothels maintains a low profile on the opposite side of the road, still doing a brisk trade with mostly American GIs from the NATO base in Vicenza. Between them and the Tower, a canal-fill project is messily underway. Giotto's famous Arena Chapel frescoes are a few hundred yards across the street.

Dino has already told me that as far as he knows there are no vacancies. I allow him to stand in his stockinged feet, his arms crossed, looking as stolid as Ohio. He is gazing out his enormous picture window, eight stories up, his hawk profile sketched hugely against the glass, watching the workmen below shovel clay into the canal.

"Housing is tight," he says.

He paces the window, puts his hands in his pockets. Crosses his arms again.

"I'll talk to the super," he says. I feel a rush of admiration for his command of Italian politics.

Father Browne's first question is whether a special Royal Mountie Division all named Dino has just made a landing on the Adriatic. Then a dry reference to my tales of riding around the *Circonvallazione* on Dino's ear-splitting Vespa.

When I tell him I will be seeing my Naples relatives for the holidays, via Rome, where, besides meeting friends, I must find and strangle the bureaucrat who has frozen my living stipend, he offers me some cost-cutting travel in his new Fiat. Mapwise, he suggests meeting halfway, in Ancona, and in the end I am a pushover for his telegraphic-style promise of "*spaghetti alle vongole* at seaside, and ride over hills & through woods to Grand-mater's house all roads lead to & Barnard vs. Ministero Estero title match."

My heart misgives me as the train rides the coastline against an aluminum-gray sky, rushing past the Adriatic, repeating that little mechanical fear in the hammering rails. But before I can grasp my own *timor*, there comes the flashing steel station awnings, the screaming hydraulic jolt, the body that didn't want to stop not wanting to start again. But it does, and he is there, advancing across the sand-colored waiting-room floor like a black bird on an alien beach. It has been long enough for his crooked grin to have gone strange, but his hair still shakes out light, and he comes radiant through the resistless air, bringing the incomparable gift of his pure and seamless joy to my muddied fear and daring.

So would it ever be.

That night, after settling ourselves in different hotels (he having set my bag down in the lobby of mine with a Duck-Soup leer and tip of the ash off Groucho's imaginary cigar), we met for a trencherman's duel at a lovely white grotto of a place on the embankment, where the air was saturated with wind and sea, and the fine shimmering wine so astringent that tears smoked on our ice-cold cheeks. He mimicked me as I deftly spooled my spaghetti strands on the bobbin of my fork. "How do you *do* that?" he demanded, and tried again, but each meticulously spun forkful slithered back into a long unmanageable ribbon as soon as he trained it toward his mouth.

He leaned back in defeat. "You eat something beautiful." And he was right, because I think if God could eat pasta He would have eaten it as I did that night. I had suddenly never felt more conscious of my happiness or more content to beam like a star in the light of his gorgeous approval. I suddenly embraced my old romance with food as if I had been meant to take the world in through my mouth. Our electric knees accidentally touched. Clearly we were met here to begin again from the beginning, before the Fall.

The weather had changed by the time we stepped outside. The chill wind had calmed and the streetlamps now traced a silvery path along the wet pavements toward the boulevard. We could hear the shushing return of our own voices against the silence. We wandered through Ancona to a place were the street suddenly opened into the meadow of a soccer field, half-rounded with a terrace of whitewashed concrete benches. Suddenly he broke away, flinging out his arms and flying across the silver pavement, shouting, *"It's the Greeeat Whiiite Waaaay,"* stretching each word the full length of his black-legged strides, leaping easily onto the low white wall and beginning to dance the lightest light-footed soft-shoe I have ever seen in my life.

Old years of solemn and serious childhood drop from me like shreds of weary cocoon. I forget the operatic dark underside of dancing, the heartbreakingly secret veils. I strut, I laugh, I sing "Singin' in the Rain" at the top of my voice, and we navigate the rainpools and pitfalls together, doing our Gene and Cyd, our Fred and Ginger, all the tap-dancing fantasies ever trapped inside our legs, leap the banks of white seats, break the peace, defy the law, dare the *carabinieri,* say no to the dark beyond here and all the terrors of this night and all the other nights to kingdom come.

And then we pause in the piazza halfway between our two hotels and kiss like two scared and exhilarated children tossed up out of a rabbit hole.

"Goodnight, Mrs. Calabash," he says wistfully.

He is still standing there when I turn back.

"I finally got you to do a rain song," he says.

The next day, hurrying through the long way across the spiny and devious Apennines, we stopped in Foligno for lunch. In the dry bright daylight I saw there was something peculiarly sober in his brown eyes. He leaned awkwardly into the table and began to speak, in that same always headlong and heedless way, but now from somewhere speech had never come before.

He was running, too, he confessed. Like me. Running away. In his case it was from the New York cardinal who had last year recalled him from his professorship at Catholic University in Washington. It was clear that the recall had been meant as punishment. It had also been meant to be both authoritarian and unexplained, what cardinals could do, what cardinals did. I wondered if he had been blacklisted for his politics, but already he seemed weary of confessing, of struggling again to explain it. He simply took my fingertips lightly across the table and held them, and we lingered there, watching the moving sunlight paint slant shadows across the green courtyard beyond our window.

I knew I already loved him. But I had lost my little daring. We both had, and couldn't speak.

We moved on at last toward Rome. Passing Spoleto, we lost the sun. By Terni, you could no longer measure distances, and we stopped quickly to see the falls in a dusk that seemed to gather inside the water like soft violet rain. Pushing faster, we fled along the Via Salaria, white-banded pines flying past us into the liquid dusk. The dark rose and rose and finally closed. At intervals there came the approaching headlights turning the fast-flickering trees into a thready pulse.

Did I go on unremarkably breathing when he confessed his love in the dark, so timidly I thought he was weeping? The dark leapt up and met the stars, the stars had spears, and yet Rome still hurtled toward us on the wide curve of Earth.

I know I closed my eyes and leaned toward him over what seemed a vast basin of space, leaned my face across the universe. I let my cheek touch his sleeve softly, touch only the black stuff of his sleeve.

3

I seemed to be drowned in bewitchment and yet burning, ardent, awake; at once furiously, joyously bewildered and calmly sure that this was good, that even my impotence was a sign of its goodness. But why—how—had I let this happen to me? Hadn't I had cherished my brief heart-whole freedom from love? The storms of the past two years, even for someone destined for huge and unforgiving emotions, had been crippling—bursts of intense creativity that then dropped me into victim-like lethargies and left almost no room in my wearied affections for serene work or friendship.

It was no use asking what I wanted. I seemed to have been drawn to this danger like a gambler, as if I had been destined for it. In any case, I was not in the habit of consulting my wants, not for my life. I had never made anything but minor course corrections in paths already mapped for me by the wants of others. What had my infantilized selfhood ever been taught but how to achieve—a year of school, an exam, a degree, an award? Love, however inconvenient, had at least offered a horizon, a relief from the suffocating near distance and the banality of thwarted self-invention.

Even in Italy, for all the glory of its staging, I had somehow felt my personal reach contracted, and my farthest horizon getting through a day—a week—a month. Love had now changed everything. Love charged with fear as well as joy, and the familiar and empowering dynamics of secrecy, a combination as inexorable for me as it was barely conscious—inexorable *because* it was barely conscious. What should have been sobering instead became the trigger of my daring.

But then there was the question of what had happened to *him*. Who was *he* now, to himself, let alone to me, now that he was not a laughing god, father-surrogate to my wise child, serene guru of the spiritual praxis of comic detachment? Now that the same cheerful visibility of priest and woman that had once made a statement of innocence told a lie—here in Rome, the worst of lies?

He seemed to settle the question the moment he met Margherita.

My foreign student friend from Barnard had recently returned to Rome and invited me to spend Christmas week with her family. Marghe had always had a way of making me feel frivolous and self-indulgent, of fixing me with that sidelong socialist look whenever she thought me hopelessly benighted and bourgeois. She did it now, her eyebrow significantly arched, the moment I suggested she meet "my friend, Father Browne." She agreed to dinner, nevertheless. We traveled by streetcar along wet, glistening streets, busy with Christmas, to an *osteria* in Trastevere. It had been two days since I had seen him by this time. The instant I laid eyes on him I was in love again, entranced by his undimmed brilliance and beauty.

Over *carciofi alla giudea*—those artichokes crustily toasted in the Roman Jewish way—the two of them sparred on the subject of Christian Democracy, Red Margherita complaining that the government since the war had not rebuilt enough damaged churches, Father Browne suggesting how much more aggressively the present government should have been conducting its so-called opening to the Left, both clearly bent on proving themselves historians to the bone by their complete inability to be surprised by anything, least of all each other's opinions. I could see them getting closer by inches, too fundamentally seditious not to end the evening comrades.

She is enchanted, obviously. She is laughing—that unwilling, melancholy laugh of hers, as if laughter were a sacrament, too holy to waste. He is the reason there is laughter, and utterly irresistible. And though I have told her nothing—nothing more than that we have traveled down to Rome together from Ancona—she has known me long enough to know that I am on the edge of doom. "From Ancona?" she repeats, caustic ash-blond eyebrow raised over fine ash-blond eye. It is a long way to have traveled together—alone. She does not want to be too judgmental—too Italian—but—

She alludes awkwardly to *rispetto umano*—human respect—as if it is something we have already violated. And then he and I laugh, American-wise, separately resisting her meaning, together letting our pretense of innocence fly in its face.

It was Margherita who also finally put the Pitiglianis into context, for I was to see them as well, to see Letizia again for the first time in seven years. "*Perbacco,*" she says, "you don't *know* who are the *Pitiglianis*?" They were among the proudest, oldest, most politically impeccable dynasties of Roman Jews. I could not explain to her that this was the self-same Letizia who had once proselytized me into the religion of Clark Gable's transcendent mustache, with whom I had sustained a seven-year correspondence effusively illustrated with silly cartoons on both sides.

I was alarmed. I was not sure I could utter the word "priest" in the presence of such a family without a train of unmanageable consequences. Not that I expected them to be ruffled by the innuendo of such a friendship. But I was unnerved now by Margherita's *rispetto umano,* and it was the innuendo itself I dreaded. So I did not even consider bringing them together. Still, our time in Rome was growing short. I accepted their invitation to dinner, and he and I arranged to meet afterward, at ten o'clock precisely, in the nearby Piazza delle Belle Arti. "I'll be waiting in the Fiat," he promised as we spoke in hushed tones by telephone. From there to the Repettos' apartment, we would have perhaps fifteen minutes alone.

The cartoonists' reunion was joyous, the dinner festive. Letizia had grown taller than ever, and big-bosomed. ("It's the grapes," she said, "it must be the grapes.") All the Pitiglianis, including father, mother, and sister Anna, were as easy and welcoming as I had remembered. But I could not get that absurd rendezvous out of my mind for more than a few minutes at a time, and then it would tear suddenly out of the dark like a poltergeist and take me violently by the hair. Centuries of civilization had not been wasted on Letizia's father, who I am certain sensed my agony, and in an ironic, avuncular way that at the time reminded me of no one so much as Sigmund Freud, tried drawing me out on the interesting theme of surviving the gauntlet of the Roman street. Letizia, inspired, launched instantly into a hilarious account of how Roman men had a phrase for every kind of female beauty, including "*Sempre bella!*"—"Still beautiful!"—for her middle-aged mother.

Our howls of laughter had barely died when I glanced again at my watch. I still smart at how I betrayed my eagerness to go. At ten on the mark I kissed and hugged the four of them good-bye, and without even waiting for the elevator raced down the marble steps and out the street to the piazza. I found it almost by its sound, its hushing sound, which came from its greenery heart, still thick-leaved and rustling in this mild midwinter. As I approached, the trees looked massy and dark, and drank up street light the way the jungle might drink moon.

I circled the park, once, twice, scrutinizing windshields recklessly, trying to silence the notorious tap-tap of my heels. I prayed. I circled again and again. On the final turn I took a swift wide swing past the piazza *pissoir* through the cloud of bad air, and nearly collided with a strange man just doing up his buttons. "*Bella,*" he whispered.

But he had been there; he swore it.

"But where *were* you?"

"Right there, sitting in the car, waiting till nearly midnight. Where were *you*?"

Around it went, in that furtive phone call from the Repettos' the next day. It was absurd, incomprehensible, that we should have missed each other.

I began to harbor a superstitious dread of the power of Rome. My scheduled visit to the ministry reinforced it. I can still see those endless cold marble corridors and great fortress doors, the huge rooms occupied by solitary, small, inconsequential, and helpless functionaries, who sat at long tables and knew nothing.

I fled to Naples right after Christmas, to my cousins, who had begged to see me again. It seemed suddenly unremarkable that *he* should be going there too. That beyond the unrelenting surveillance of the Eternal City we could meet—that we *would* meet. That we could finally talk.

If the city of Naples were actually an amphitheater, with the docks of Santa Lucia as its proscenium stage, my cousins' apartment would have sat somewhere in the Family Circle, high on the hill brow where the meandering length of the Corso is traced by stone terraces. But of course I had been out of my senses with fever that first visit in September, dropped like a sack from the ship into their waiting arms, and I could not tell the cabdriver how to get there.

"Sal-i-ta Tar-si-a," he repeated doubtfully at the station, pulling at his cap and fingering a street guide. But off he took, and several circuitous turns later abandoned me at the wrong end of the Salita, which is exactly what it says it is, a climb—a hundred stone steps straight up—before it actually becomes a street with houses. The evening was unpleasantly warm, the last rays of the sun beating on my back, my bags heavy. But I dared not pause even to wriggle my feet in my heels. I climbed.

At the top, I found myself in a narrow and fetid little alley that continued to slope upward, cramped with small houses on both sides, doors and shutters open darkly

to the street. Naked children flew off like sparrows, thwarting the evil eye by staring me down from a distance. Squatting beggars were as bewildered as they had every
right to be: what was a perspiring and overdressed young woman doing on *this* street,
murmuring apologetic *buona seras* to their silent wretchedness?

The Salita had by now become a strange allegory, unfolding a past and passing
era of class ascendancy. The street grew gradually wider, and the still-shabby
buildings more imposing, until they transmogrified imperceptibly into crumbling
palazzi with tightly secured carriageway doors and blind windows or walls at the
level of the street.

When I arrived at their great door, my cousins rushed down to slip me in, and
nearly abducted me upstairs to their flat. Santina, the tiny one, taking my wet hot
cheeks between her cool hands to kiss them, cried, "Are you sick?" And when I felt
obliged to explain how I had gotten there, all three of them groaned in mortified
disbelief. "You came *that* way?" Gino asks in pained bewilderment. Maria murmurs
a prayerful "Santo Dio," and glides softly away to fetch the *caffetiere* and the ceremonial cuplets.

Santina and Maria are both handsome maiden ladies, much too self-
consciously past their prime. They are complementary: tiny Santina, well-muscled,
her face all eyes and mouth, is restive, on the *qui vive;* Maria, taller by inches, is
round with a silken, elegant roundness, clucking and giggling and cultivating a
general princess serenity and slow mildness in the face of her sister's indefatig-
able energy. Gino is their middle-aged baby brother—which in this culture does
not deprive him of his entitlement to rule. He too has never married, with obvious good reason, for he has got the better bargain of two women who cosset him
as if he is their mutual husband. He is still brooding now like a sad old child over
my unseemly approach to their house. *"Brutta figura!"* he moans into the aromat-
ic steam of his coffee, as if he is reproaching himself. His melancholy gray eyes glis-
ten. His sisters, on either side of him, pat his knees reassuringly.

Part of me dreads two weeks of their well-meaning subterfuges, in which the three
of them, I know, will dissemble their own poverty in continuous bounties. Maria
has already refused to let me sleep anywhere but in her own voluptuous bed,
made up in her mother's crisp, parchment linens, among the few precious family
things the war has spared them. The meals are scant, and exquisite.

In the morning I wake in the soft cocoon of Maria's eiderdown to the unimaginable noise of the Neapolitan street. Maria is bustling in to tell me it is glorious
weather, excellent for airing, and she flings open the casements to drape the
bedsheets proudly on the windowsill, in the public eye. Santina whisks in behind
her, calling it "Christmas summer." She beams it to me on her huge black eyes like
a previously arranged gift. The sky is a glaze of the most unutterable blue for days.

When *he* finally phones from his hotel, it is the morning of New Year's Eve. Gino,
out late the night before, is still in bed. Maria, answering, has heard the male voice
and is all a-flutter—"These girls, since the war!" She drops her eyes in what seems
a coded signal to Santina, just stepping in from the veranda with her watering can.

This spying father-tongue. There is no way to hide the gender of *amico* as I explain to them that I have arranged to meet a friend at Santa Lucia at midday. Their approval consists of vaguely chilly smiles and flickering eyes. I cannot tell if they betray censure or envy, but as I leave, I feel some mystery of arrested girlhood pleading in both their faces, and who knows what mystery pleading in my own.

But the noonday sun on the sea is without mystery, a bullet-hail of photons that shatters the avemaria blue surface of the bay into a glittering tray of spilled turquoise chips. On the street the open-air cafés make a ballet of dazzling, orchestrated musical color. *Please God, let us not miss each other again.*

He is there, the high noon tinseling his hair. Bodies fly around him, flashing like dancers, splitting him to bits. He is squinting into the sunshine. Panic stabs through me—will he see me here on the other side of the street before he dives under another canopy and I lose him?

"*Harry!*"

I have said his name. My God, I have actually *shouted* it. How easily, I think, it might become, by itself, a cry of joy or alarm.

Maybe it was the sunlight on his crisp, animal hair, or the muscular bravado of his motorcycle-dodging sprint across the street to me, or the light, conspiratorial way he smiled that made it all too much like somebody else's story—me too much Brett to his Jake at Pamplona—making daring seem so easy, so inconsequential, as if it were happening in art rather than in life.

When he went ahead of me, disappearing into the hotel doorway with that brisk, resolute stride, I thought, How did we come to this? And yet I followed him, more out of fear than desire—an illogical infant panic at his vanishing. And then it struck me, as the elevator rose, how coolly one can negotiate the lobby of a hotel for the first time. Perhaps only for the first time.

Behind that door the room was dark as water. There was no more art for this. I let him draw me to him into the powerful circle of his arms, my mind stopped as if with water, and in this ecstatic flood my hands moved, my lips were wet and spoke and stopped speaking, my hair floated. I thought I was reaching for an island beyond and beyond me, a destination yet an element, a circumambient space, but my own inwardness drew back at the edge of it, the hurt childhood will resisting. He said, "Don't be afraid," but I was afraid, and his will met mine level and relented.

And it must have been then that I was lost, when he took nothing, when I thought I was still my own, because nothing I had not given had been taken, but I was lost.

We sat together on the edge of the bed. I held his head between my hands; I pushed my hands through his hair. I did it more gently than I had seen him do it himself, but again and again until I knew when I left him the smell of his hair would still be in my palms and in the creases between my fingers. I kissed his mouth and his wet eyes. He kissed mine. He held me. He gave me his naked, helpless delight, his headlong, careless delight in that small gift. He gave me the grace of his delight, made me the naked gift of it, without power or shame, without the need for conquest.

•

That night, back at the Salita, my maiden cousins draped their large bosoms in silk and lace, and plunged tortoiseshell combs deep into their satiny hair. "Dress!" they urged. "Now you must come with *us*."

A party among friends—a signora and her nephews—it was Capodanno, after all, the vigil of the new year. Gino, emerging after two full hours of toilette, made a splendid escort, authority in the very scent of his cologne. "*Festeggiamo*," he said— "Let us celebrate." Said it plain as print, as unremarkably as if he planned to enjoy himself on sufferance. As we stepped into the street, he paused and looked at me squarely. "*Sei bella*," he pronounced. His sisters' eyes met for an instant, lips twitching—it was going to be a wonderful evening!

And so it was—a time warp, a ceremony of innocence for this late bourgeois world, imaginary balm for my lost soul. The night was clear and mild, and the spacious balcony of the signora's apartment gave a full view of the city high above the Corso and down to the darkling bay. We took our coffee in delicately enameled cups and dotted our pastry crumbs from exquisitely embroidered napkins. We sipped liqueurs from the tiniest of little rose crystal glasses, and the night wore on, Maria tinkling light operatic airs on the piano. I began to think it might be a night without Neapolitan irony, until the signora's nephew began slyly to notice the accent I had acquired in the north. I had no wit, or time, to respond. A report like a gunshot came from the street. I asked if there would be fireworks. "You will see," he said.

Gino strolled out onto the balcony to survey the starlit twinkling city, puffing his chest like a reviewing general when I joined him, orienting me with a directional arm to the lights of Santa Lucia. I felt suddenly disoriented and faint as I thought of myself there with Harry, saw us together there as though I were not here, looking out. Gino called me back: "Can you see?" And I tore my eyes from Santa Lucia. I could see, there in the haze, the faint double outline of Vesuvius and Monte Somma.

Here and there a burst of lightning brightened the face of a single *palazzo* and died, leaving a slender, rising thread of smoke to leach its way into the whitening sky. The hour approached and the explosions came more and more impatiently. We heard a crackling from below us like machine-gun fire, and then on the mark of midnight a sudden thousand explosions booming and flashing together. The city roared. The sky broke, the air broke, a hundred steeple bells clamored and crashed. The women leaned briefly out to see and their shrieks seemed scrawled on the wall of noise like graffiti. Streets came into sight for a moment and were gone. Multicolored lightning blazed up, died away, the smoke plumed up and spread and thickened until it had erased Vesuvius and canceled out the bay. "*Vieni!*" I knew Gino was crying, trying to draw me inside, but I could only see his lips move, and I gripped the railing.

In a moment the Salita would disappear, and the Corso, and the nearest church tower, and even the street below us. Everything, drowned in a single, blanched pall of smoke that stung the eyes and left a blind blankness that still brightened in single booms, an instant at a time. It was as if I had made this happen. Each burst tore through me and thundered in my chest. I could feel myself shout his name into the sonic booms, noiseless against the dense sound-shattering air. When I swallowed I could taste the gunpowder in my mouth.

I expected a rain of Neapolitan sarcasm when I reentered the expectant room. I was not disappointed. The gray-eyed signora said, "How does the signorina like our celebration?" and handed me a napkin to daub my stinging eyes.

"You think *this* is something," said Santina. "You should've seen Naples *before* the war. Then we were still throwing last year's china out the window." Gino smirked. Maybe they could go in the kitchen and get me an old set of plates?

I smiled as best I could, dipping my napkin into a glass of water and touching it to my eyes. Actually, the thought of their skin-deep patina of respectability was comical, and in its own way endearing. In their hearts they were all, even my gentle maiden aunts, cocking an obscene Neapolitan elbow at everything that had ever humiliated them—the stinging memory of the war, the volcano that could spew them out like melon pits in the morning. "*Me ne frego,*" is what the ersatz thunder said—"I jerk myself off at you."

Santina passed me a welcome glass of spumante for the toast and patted my arm with a wicked, conspiratorial chuckle. A tingling swallow and I was laughing too—laughing, and lovesick.

Sinking back into a velvet armchair, I felt suddenly very battered and lonely. Maria, though still lovely in her twilight-colored dress, was beginning, I could tell from the darkening petals of her eyelids, to feel the strain of smiling. Santina, vivid as ever in her red-plum crêpe de Chine, her eyes glossy and wide, was still engaged in intense conversation with the gray-eyed signora, her white, animated hands flitting like moths between the chain on her breast and the flute of sparkling wine on the table beside her.

Tales of a thousand aunts and a thousand operas had already taught me there was no Italian woman without her melodrama of passion. What had theirs been? I longed to ask, but felt a shame deeper and more outlaw than any that might have robbed them, once, of their genteel girlhoods.

How could I have known that war, poverty, all the sheer commonness of suffering had made respectability not a conspicuous luxury, not a pretense, but a need, a veil for hideous memories? That sanctimony would have been the luxury? I might have told them and been forgiven. I might have told them and been saved. I know this now. It has not made me wish I had known it then.

The treasure of our separate onenesses still safe, the two of us, Harry and I, were in some ways as firmly bent on keeping our selves intact as on exchanging them for some new thing. During all of the rest of our stay in Naples, we met twice more in the public space of Santa Lucia at sundown, walking about until the dark settled down. We sat in his car, facing the bay, almost silent with fear, with joy, facing the concave blackness over the sea before us with its occasional thread of moving light.

It is as though we were plotting, and perhaps we were, though there were moments when it was as if we had remade the world, invented a whole new relation—beyond guilt or power, ours or others, beyond seduction or surrender—and had already discovered between us some single transcendental persona that would transfigure some eventual carnal act with innocent selflessness.

In this curious world, with its ambivalent taste for desire gratified, maybe all secret lovers feel a similar complicity, as if they alone could plot the perfect, unpunishable crime. With us there was this difference only: that our desire, by more canonical standards than even the ordinary world's, *was* a crime, and we felt this—felt it as a kind of violence, both within and against us; felt it with the compelled cunning of outlaws. We would do this thing, but we would not do it carelessly. And to do it carefully, beautifully, perfectly would become a project with all the disciplined lunacy of beauty itself. We would turn our extremity on our selves, the selves that acted in the loveless world, shattering our old egos the way a precise blow to the face of a diamond will shatter the diamond, along its fault, into a dozen perfect faces.

In some curious way, our desire itself was complete. From the moment of our inward surrenders we seemed to have invented patience, too, as poised and complete as utopia. It was a visionary desire that made the universe pound in the senses, but that did not fret or itch or sweat or grip the belly at midnight, that wanted yet contained, that needed, yet overflowed. It was a longing with all the fullness of a gestation. It had weight, ponderous weight, inside its almost palpable lightness.

There would be time.

For now, we simply schemed our exits from Naples to coincide exactly, so that we might be together for the several-hours-long drive north to Rome again. Our one last piece of theater under the gaze of Naples was to visit the cave of the Cumaen Sibyl, priestess of Apollo, oracle of the gods who spoke before God spoke.

There was something of the pagan pilgrimage about it. We were both conscious of marking the opening of the new year with the solemnity of an epoch. But if it was *anno Domini*—year of our Lord—it was also pagan time, year unreckonable, and so not time at all. Crouched in those chambers of holy, incinerated lava dust was something more primal even than the old Church, than Vergil or Aeneas or the golden bough. Something we brought that was already there, in that womb of mind before words.

To remember it now is more like dreaming than remembering. A cave chamber, the earthen ceiling punctured with holes that drop decisive little columns of daylight into the sacred dust. We choose a single pool of light and stand in it together, faintly touching, shuddering with love, breeding erotic energy the way it is possible to imagine rocks breed radiation. When we move apart and enter separate columns of light, we can still feel ourselves encircled within a larger field. The guide, watching us, has wisdom in his sexless, senescent gaze, and seems to be tracing the very line of our perfect fault.

This memory has a mind to dislocate itself, to go as it should out of the line of ordinary time. No sooner do I recall it than I seem to lose it again. Did it really happen then—there—where I have just sequenced it? Or was that another time, under another spell? A slithering and wayward memory that will not be civilized, that resists the line, not to be led to, nor from.

But it remains. I am the virgin sibyl, the She-unto-herself, fiercely fixed and integral. Harry too is Himself, an unrelenting identity. But singleness is passing away. We are Harry and me, there, innocently decoding the inscription on the Avernian rock, reading without irony of the descent into the underworld.

He is hunkering down, absorbed, taut black wool hugging the tense muscular line of his buttocks and thighs. I lean toward him, a curve of compliance and attention, lifting my loose hair away from my enchanted eyes and ears.

4

F*estina lente,* prayeth the Saint. *Hurry slowly.*
The return journey to Padua was long and absurdly lonely. Part of me still hovered in a sentient, bridelike expectancy, my own flesh incandescing in my imagination as though I had fallen in love not just with his body but with my own.

Yet I found I still lived—as one is said to live at a particular address. I functioned as if the universe had not upheaved. I prepared for a new term of writing, reading, independence. I finally broke with the Casa and took my own apartment at the Tower.

When Sergio the *portiere* handed me my key and I let myself into that tenth-story L-shaped room, I felt as if I had walked into the sky. In its Italian way it was as lovely and cream and mauve and dove-colored as my soul's secret state of romantic enchantment. I had worried about furnishing it, but every furniture need was met with built-in amenities: a tiny fully equipped kitchen, a four-seater dining banquette, bookshelves on every wall, a draped bed alcove with a bracketed shelf and pad for sleeping that could be lifted up and out of the way in the daytime. And lest this simplicity seem too ascetic, the bathroom offered a hedonist sanctuary, paved like a Venetian chapel in a total, sleek, continuous skin of tiny purple mosaic tiles that captured every shade of twilight in the *Valpadana.*

I felt bewitched, transported to a land where it was always afternoon. In another dimension of time I could account for a thousand years of history from my spacious balcony, including all three of Silene's "withouts," San Antonio's nine cupolas on the horizon, the wide-open Prato in the middle distance, and Pedrocchi's, the café without doors, directly below me. No ordinary student, radical or otherwise, could any longer afford to buy coffee there in 1958, but the magic of the place could still burn its electric radiance into the cold of a January midnight. The little Arena Chapel, where Giotto, for a price, had painted the usurious Scrovegnis out of Dante's hellfire, was just out of sight to the east—to see it I had to climb two flights to the roof. But I didn't have to move an inch of langorous anatomy from my snap-down cot in order to frame a vast unearned piece of the southwestern sky, with its everyday pastel mornings and passionate sunsets, in my own window.

Silene was awestruck. She did not complain that I had come by this lovely place via the same unholy route as all my other American privileges, but I would not have argued with her if she had, being too awestruck myself to feel deserving. Still, she did not kill my joy. She made me a housewarming gift of a little silver *caffetiere* like her own. She limped gleefully from balcony to bathroom to playhouse kitchen, where she paused just long enough to monitor the hissing pot. Then she limped back to the balcony, stepping out the glass door in spite of the cold to savor the glorious view. At last she fluttered down beside me at the table. She was nobody's fool and could tell I was in love. "Now, you are *without* nothing," she said absurdly—jealously—generously, as if she herself had granted my wish. We drank our licit coffee with the same pleasure we had once bestowed on her dormitory pot, troubled only by the bewildering choice of points of view from which to sip it, and watch the clouds, the purpling sky, and a rising evening star.

I described these things in all their gorgeousness to Harry, as the mail rushed back and forth between Rome's Montemario and Padua's preservationist Tower with a frequency that might have alarmed even a jaded postal bureaucrat. It eased my guilty happiness to share it with him. But in the end, to be young is to take the good of life pretty much as it comes. If I imagined myself meeting the challenges of living abroad with heroic resourcefulness, if I worried about money and sold English lessons and performed miracles of budgeting to cover expenses, and reluctantly but gratefully accepted the small money gifts my parents made me from time to time, none of this unsettled my delight in my stunning privileges—indeed, it was what made delight possible.

After all, quite apart from my studied, somewhat leftist politics, I had probably owed my training in small self-denying economies in equal proportions to my mother's phobic terror of penury and my father's struggle to be rich, which went together hand and glove. One of the strangest books in my father's strange library when I was a girl had been an unforgettable little hand-illustrated Depression-era volume called *How to Live on a Dollar a Day*. It had also been one of the most captivating, making desperate, heroic economies like that seem not only ordinary but desirable, as if the *best* world were also the meanest, in which you had to struggle to survive. I was quite prepared to believe it, then, that to be capable of the arrogance of following your bliss required the even greater arrogance of thinking you had any bliss coming.

Yet I think there was already something in my conscience kin to those Italian women workers of Lowell, Massachusetts, who'd wanted "bread, but roses, too." If I was getting more than my share of roses at the moment, I had an early inkling that I wouldn't always, and I am glad to have obscurely felt that one's social conscience should always leave some grace beyond the reach of Marx.

From the time of my Arizona childhood, when the gift of a little silver bracelet with a turquoise stone in it had seemed to me the pinnacle of treasure, I had thought things of this particular blend of sky and sea possessed a special grace—an air of pure excess. I am not sure how I had come to own an angora beret of this translucently lovely color while I was in Italy—I can imagine it a gift from one of my canny Spagnola aunts at our parting—but now I told him to look for it when he looked for me in the women's second-class waiting room at the Pisa railway station. I said it would be the first thing he'd see.

And so it was.

But the first thing I saw was how crystal, how fragile he looked, as I suddenly happened to glance up, straight into his shining eyes, into the reflected image of my blue-green behatted and besotted self, and a seizure of pure joy blinded my body.

•

We separated decently on the fourth floor of our Pisan hotel, at a certain curious intersection of carpet, trying to keep our balance and speak necessary words in spite of the dizzying voltage arcing between us. We met in the lobby and went to dinner. We ate and drank. I cannot remember what, for once. At the door of my room, both of us trembling, he left me, promising to return in an hour. I followed his lead, and for all the thickness of my heartbeat smiled inwardly to think of us perhaps obeying rituals outlined in Catholic marriage manuals.

But no foresight could have prepared either of us for the wonder of each other—for me to see at last his lovely, sinewy body faintly gilded by the yellow light slip between the creamy, sweet-smelling sheets and fold them apart again for me—for him to watch, as my satin slip fell, how I snatched it suddenly to my breasts again, amazed by my own nakedness. I remember, then, having time to think a Shakespearean Cleopatra thought: *Ah, this is how it feels to carry a man's weight.* And after, more than anything else, the exquisite simplicity of it astonished me, the resistance that had melted away, that had so miraculously liquefied.

I was sure he would want to return to his room for the night and was preparing myself to let him go, but he said, "I just *got* here," as if the very suggestion were absurd, and I felt such a confused sudden rushing together of passion and gratitude that it burst out in a swoop of self-mocking laughter. After all, he added, it wasn't like communion and then *ita missa est.* And recovering rather hereticly, I said that it had seemed like a sacrament to me.

And so we simply fell asleep in each other's arms, and slept together what lovers call sleep, waking at intervals in a breathless, vacant haze, awed by the sheer naked heat of each other's bodies and in a state of transcendent astonishment at our perfect fit.

We climbed the famous tower. We had to stop often, laughing at our poor love-winded lungs and the cramp of unaccustomed thigh muscles. We leaned often against the handrail to watch our breaths steam in the cold, laughing breathless at the thought that this poor tower seemed to have been precisely engineered to eroticize the Pisan landscape. We faced each other from opposite walls of the well-rubbed stairtower poised in an unblinking lovesickly gaze. We stood framed in the upper arches, drinking in the still-brilliant green of the Campo Santo stretched below us, the deep upon deep of absolute blue above us, the rose and gold of the city between. All of it as plain, plain and unwonderful as the face of heaven.

Four days we wandered, through the bell towers of San Gimignano, through Viareggio, all gray winter beach under a pale sky. People told us the pine trees were dying. On to Rome again along the coast. We no longer dared to be seen together in our old haunts. We parted so rank with love, so weighted, so bloated like corpses with the thought of parting that we simply floated up, numbly, stupidly, back into the world.

Italy bloomed now like an enlarged landscape of myself, and I walked through it omnipotent, feeling empowered to bring everything dead to life. I began to write again, stories, poetry. I began to want to sink my hands in sculpture and went to the Accademia in Venice to enroll myself in a studio course. There was no urgency in this. The river that seemed to flow fast through me was yet a river of heavy water, and Harry's face hung like a reasonable moon above the horizon of my mind. Until our next meeting, time would be no more than a single sheetlike transparency.

But when we did meet, in Siena, my brain was like glass and could take no imprint. I remember little more of it than a few sunlit façades and the unearthly green face of the cathedral at night. We found when our bodies touched again that our hunger had become a living, ravaging thing. When the morning finally came to part again, he lay on the bed as if he were bleeding slowly to death, and I lay on his breast feeling his deep, strangling sobs pass through me. Did I really expect nothing from him, not now, nothing more than this? And when I said I did, when I swore it, nothing more, he wanted me to want more, wanted me to demand it for myself, and the guilt that so looped itself was pitiless. That morning our pain together became the blankness of the railway station where he left me.

But not now, not yet.

There were still lies to write home, craven bits of mendacity to my sister, who had once been confidante of all my childhood lives. Until she had left Barnard to begin training as a nurse the year before, restive with both a sense of calling and a need to get away from home, what minutest emotion hadn't we shared? I thought she was doing well. I thought she had already done well. But now came something different, difficult, evasive in her letters, a hint of some kind of a crisis. A mention of illness . . .

What could I possibly tell her now? I begged her to confide in *me*. I wrote long, compulsive, desperate letters that abjectly dodged everything truthful I might have told her yet pleaded in their way to be read as confessions. Terror of the new dark in my own life would sometimes sink me like a felon, wake me sweating in the night. But I couldn't tell the truth, not even to her, now least of all to her, and if not to her then to no one. I faked lightheartedness when I wrote to her. Her letters confided her sexual fears to me. I tried to console them. I said I thought making love was not some sacred ritual but "a pleasure, like laughing." I couldn't tell my thoughts from Harry's anymore. The multitudes I contained were his. Some of them. The weariest smug wisdom about accepting the joy of love and the pain of parting was my own. I said, "If you really love you will never feel alone again." What a lie of the mind, if I believed it, when the truth was that I had never felt more alone than now.

In some ways my letters didn't lie. I wrote often and passionately, and at least in this way told her the truth about loving *her*. But loving Harry was a contract of silence I would have died sooner than betray, even to her, and yet she was the only human being I knew who would have understood it completely.

Then for weeks in February came a dire, long gap in her letters. My mother finally wrote. Ann was sick—depressed—had lost a great deal of weight. They had found no medical reason, they said. She was in hospital, and from my mother's self-crucifying tone it was clear they thought she was somehow starving herself to death. How baldly her illness screams itself now as the guilty and unconscious outrage of self-postponement scripting itself on her body. And yet *anorexia nervosa* was not only not a term widely used, the disorder itself seemed to be inarticulate to the pundits of medicine. Like my parents I was baffled. I couldn't believe in the possibility of her dying, but still a sort of terror of my own disbelief seized me, as if somehow she might die while I was here and I be unable to save her because, following my own happiness or wallowing in my own tragedy, I could not bear to go now and heroically face down the haunting demon in her life.

Under this new terror my letters became even more frequent and passionate—and less truthful. They pleaded with her to get well, only get well. Seeing them now as I write this they nevertheless remind me how lies can sometimes speak the truth. They were coded like dreams, begging for pity, saying as transparently as they could without saying it, *I am in love . . . I am making love . . . My love and I are forced to part. . . .*

But what was the truth? What truth was there to tell? By now Harry and I were both of us stuttering refugees, helpless to tell our meaning even to ourselves—unable to be together, unable to part, displaced persons, banished from home and emotional safety without the language to speak our frightened courage in. At times it seemed to me that we would be like the people the war had uprooted who had never again found home, but who had found the daily grit to be lost forever. The world seemed big and wanderable. Even before we met, hadn't it been a place for us of floating boundaries? What nation did either of us belong to now? What race, what blood? History, I began to think, had created whole new worlds of transformation where a certain nomad readiness was all.

Perhaps Harry, older and by training more prudent, could see the folly of this better than I. But I knew that this emotion had taken him too unguarded for even him to see it clearly. He lived in a secure structure of belief. He believed, with a conviction that made *me* want to believe, not just with my body, with my unconscious pagan gift for wonderment, but with my whole mind. He belonged—or thought he did—and feared the power he believed in and belonged to. But I sometimes wonder, if I still had our letters—the letters he later had us both so prudently murder, by the book, by the candle—might they have foretold his slowly growing less and less fearful? Of his gradually learning the self-reliance that is corollary to the insufficency of prayer?

I would watch him sometimes sitting in his shirtsleeves in a hotel chair or pacing the balcony in his shawl, breviary in hand, performing his matins and vespers as if we had come together for some spiritual retreat. Apparently God followed him right into the bedchambers of our most abandoned intimacies. I thought clearly this was no implacable God if still He stayed His lightning.

But this sanctum of his inner life I never touched, no speaking of it, no daring to speak. When I first saw him pray, I felt a brooding, inarticulate sense of my own otherness, a loathing of whatever cause there was in me for his desire that could justify the incantations he might be pronouncing against it. In time, this was superseded by a simple sense of paradox: I imagined a stark conflict in his loyalties that he was praying for some metaphysical intercession to resolve. At length I came to understand how little I had to fear from his prayers. And looking back I knew that whatever this demon love had originally sprung from, it had quickly awakened his essential inner anarchist, the steely, defiant little Harry-devil that only the hardest of hard lifetime disciplines could possibly have trained to petition authority before questioning it, let alone to question before defying it outright.

Had he been willing to stoop to the level of his potential earthly confessors, those worldly lawyers of canonical chop-logic, he might have found a ready answer: to them, it was all very simply, reductively "glandular." This is lust, my friend. And lust, well, lust is what we might call the "purest" sin. Hadn't Dante said so? Quite forgivable, to a point. Everything forgivable to a point.

Even love? Ah, but love was an infinitely more complex question. After all, what *was* love? And where on the subject had the Everlasting ever unequivocally spoken? Was it in the charge to those in the religious life not to succumb to the lure of "particular friendships"? And yet wasn't it true that such friendships were problematic less because they were inconsistent with celibacy than because they were incompatible with an entireness of love for God and all of God's creatures?

Did Harry in love feel less love for God and God's creatures? Was I not God's creature?

This much I knew: If Harry had ever been satisfied with the thorny and ambiguous pronouncements he'd been taught, he wasn't now. If he prayed for anything, I believe it was not for a way out of this but a way to make it holy. How could he have known it might come by its opposite?

In March, I met him again for a trip together through the south of Italy, both of us seeking distance and anonymity, leaving behind even the land of my father's fathers, where men who might have been cousins, small and lean and dark and inward, a sinister effrontery in their glances, sprang out of dark corridors of streets as if from a private sowing of dragon's teeth.

But there could be no Italian anonymity. Everywhere we stopped we had to resign our separate passports overnight to the *Questura*. We took two rooms, always, indulging in absurd and transparent pruderies so that we might still find our way to one another at night, and smother shame in the pleasure of each other's bodies, sleeping uneasily wherever the sound of lapping water and the scent of orange groves drifted toward us under the great moon.

The roads became more lonely as we left the coast and headed inland toward Eboli. The great writer Carlo Levi had said Christ himself had chosen not to venture beyond this place, but we did, making our way through winding and precipitous mountain roads to villages the map had made seem near but that for us stretched farther and farther away as we approached them. Along the roads peasant women leaned toward us squinting into the slanting afternoon sun, their heads wrapped in tight black bandannas, their backs bent under great nests of firewood wrapped in long linen rags. Trailing behind them were barefoot girls with hair wrought into thick, smooth naked braids, their faces all eyes, swaddled babies cradled in their arms. A universe of women until we found the men, all of them, it seemed, in the dreary piazza at Potenza, standing idly, sinking their small bodies under black greatcoats and capes and shading their eyes with the wide brims of their hats. And though it felt as if we had already come a thousand miles, in every direction the mountains still stretched, brown on brown, and sketched on them ahead of us were still the faint lines of roads we had not yet taken.

Nothing seemed welcoming, everything sad and reproachful. We pushed on in the dark, filling our driving hours with unconvincing bursts of song. We shared cigarettes to stay awake, their red tips glowing as we passed them hand to hand. Exhausted and unnerved, we slept at last in Cosenza. The next morning in the parking lot we saw a small, dwarflike man in a blue attendant's uniform and cap bobbing from car to car. He beamed us a gap-toothed smile in a day's growth of beard, and Harry dismissed him with a toss of small change. It is hard to remember whether with my mother's pagan fear I sensed some sign, some premonition of danger.

> *March 4. Dearest Ann, Life is not the cruel set of choices you seem to think. There are many chances to retrace your steps and change your mind. I think I once thought very much as you do, that life was a moral rack— that so many people stood to suffer, that you yourself would be ruined, despicable and remorse-stricken for the rest of your life, all because of a single choice, a choice whose complexity seemed to be beyond understanding. But I think now that you must have an honest faith in your power to take what is to come. Dearest Ann, if you were always to imagine the worst you would always stand still. Don't be too presumptuous, leave some of the consequences to God. . . .*

The roads, gray and pocky, seemed raw nerves never meant to be exposed. Children stood in listless clusters along them, begging with their eyes. For a time we saw almost no one, only silent empty villages where no birds sang, and Mussolini's old slogans still flaked from granary walls. We stopped at last in a little whitewashed hotel in Taranto, on the coastal underside of the Italian boot, and in the morning walked the bay, letting the guilty stench of poverty burn itself off in the sunshine. The town was a bit of bright hard gold caught between the blues of sky and bay. Standing at the edge of the docks where the water lapped the fishing boats, looking down into shelf after shelf of white rock bathed in the most crystal aquamarine of the sea, you could not have believed in original sin.

Then Harry walked ahead of me to the hotel and left me briefly behind with the car. When he reappeared, I was in tears.

I could barely explain what had happened. If Harry himself had not caught sight of him leaving, he might have thought I had hallucinated him: that little man again, so much like the other one, I thought he *was*. I tried to explain how he had confronted me, dancing over to me in his blue-black trenchcoat, staring into my face with his crackling eyes, "asking if you were a priest," and I was not prepared to lie, I had said *yes*—

Harry's sick pallor so flooded my soul with remorse that I couldn't tell him the little man had also said, as he danced off, *"And you?"*

A cynical heartsickness overtook us. When we finally entered Bari it was as though we had silently agreed to numb ourselves with pleasure. We took an opulent suite at the Grand Hotel of the Nations, its bath fitted with what must have been the biggest, most sybaritic bathtub in the *Mezzogiorno,* bath towels the size of bedspreads. Everything in the room was dazzling white and on the same godlike scale, the bed itself a vast bridal playing field, a room that instructed you what to do as music instructs you how to dance. We bathed long and voluptuously and made frenzied ritual love into the dusk, then slept paralyzed. We awoke at twilight, raging with hunger, and went out prowling the waterfront for food. Everywhere behind the smug bourgeois façades of this once wealthy Adriatic city the night seemed to lie hidden, smelling of monarchy and old lust and *lire* worth a dollar apiece on the foreign exchange.

Keenly awake now, following nothing but the seamless, starry course of chance, we found a small restaurant on the boulevard and an exquisite supper of *merluzzo,* fresh from the sea. Afterward, at a strange little theater wicket in a side street, we purchased the last two seats for an after-hours musical farce that starred the brilliant Roman clown Toto and a troupe of the American June Taylor dancers featuring a redheaded Amazon beauty named Candy, the very swish of whose muscle-swollen dancer's thighs made the mostly male crowd moan. The Baresi had sold their souls to have this revue for a single night, to see Toto bolt about the stage like a loose id and finally drop himself into a giant wooden chest he called "La Cassa del Mezzogiorno" after the government's subsidy program for the impoverished south, explaining in the flawless logic of southern Italian politics that "everything that went into it was guaranteed to get back to Rome."

The next day we found the morning side of Bari, as paradoxically, startlingly candid and innocent as if it had been whitewashed by the austere Norman patron saint San Nicolò himself. His cathedral, stark enough to pass for Protestant, was an absolute admonition to all lust, and in the streets of the old city everything was as clean and proper in its place as a dolls' village, shops full of puppet makers who looked like Geppetto, whitewashed walls strung with the endless jointed wooden bodies of a thousand Pinocchios.

That much more strange, as we were leaving, to see the little dwarflike man again, the one in the blue coat, glancing at us as he dodged the cars in the piazza.

Dearest sister, My coming home plans are uncertain. Summer ship departures are already completely filled. Don't worry about my turning up too

*soon and spoiling your plan to have me find you fat again. Father Browne
has told me that his friend Father Wilde has visited you in the hospital. He
said it was hard to get you to laugh. . . .*

North out of Bari the roads suddenly whitened treacherously with snow, and sleet sputtered and froze on the windshield. Harry hated driving in snow—the very thought of it unmanned him. As the road forced us inland from the coast, we edged forward barely fifty miles in a raging blizzard, stopping at nightfall in the village of Serracapriola, where we took what was offered, in this case a pair of cold chamber-potted rooms over the kitchen and the bar, respectively, of an old family-run inn that looked as if it had not enjoyed a good day since the eighteenth century. We ate a starveling, ill-cooked supper at a bus stop across the road, had a quick drink at the bar, and parted uneasily for our rooms.

Mine was over the bar. It had a bed that looked like a slung hammock filled with four greasy comforters and a pair of tough gray sheets the damp clung to like a thin film of skin. In the queasy pendulum shadow of a naked fifteen-watt light bulb you could still smell stale bodies. Such a nauseating sense of the squalor of common suffering came over me that even in the semidark I fled to Harry's room, which was easily as frigid as mine, the cold an absolute affront. I found him looking sheepishly out from under his own greasy comforters. He still had on his beret. Though he had removed his overcoat he said that this had shown an alarming lack of foresight. He launched into a lengthy repertoire of cold jokes until he had me laughing through my chattering teeth.

We couldn't have bedded together that night if we'd tried. I touched my lips lightly to his eyes and borrowed a pair of his heaviest socks for bed. He told me to make sure he didn't sleep through the alarm.

The cold grew even deeper during the night, stinging my back right through the thin mattress. The blankets were useless. At dawn, headachy and unslept, I slid my feet from underneath the whole glacial pile of covers, trapping Harry's socks. I didn't even feel them go. We were twenty minutes farther on before I missed them. "Wanna go back?" he asked drily.

And then it was suddenly spring again, a pure blue radiant sky. We might have dreamt that squalid, sleety dream, I thought, as I looked east and saw again the silver Adriatic across fallow brown fields. Sitting beside him in silence, I searched the guidebook to see how far we were now from Ancona.

We bent inland once more, leaving the shore for the road to Rome. One last night in Aquila, no more desperate laughter, only the incubus dwarf-man sitting on Harry's chest in the dark, his eyes like burning headlights.

Guilt, that wasted emotion, has mass. It obeys physical laws of motion and gravity. It watches you like a spy from inside your own soul.

Harry returned to Montemario. I took a hotel room alone for the single night I had to be in Rome waiting out my train, making contact with no one. In the mercifully mild weather, though in a kind of lonely dread and hunger, I walked the Via Veneto and stopped at an outdoor café. A blond American beauty sauntered by, her buttocks floating in her turquoise blue dress like a pair of helium balloons. Men literally leapt from their chairs to follow her. I felt something as close to envy as I had ever come for her sexy, indifferent power.

In the only afternoon of that obscure Roman estrangement, he and I met once more, at the morosely named St. Paul Outside the Walls. He drove up with an unfamiliar deliberateness, and I got in, and there we sat, side by side in the parking lot in that searing spring daylight. And there he told me what I am certain every priest-lover has eventually told the woman he loves, that he could not belong to me and Mother Church.

It didn't feel like the first time he'd said it, and if it sounds almost funny now it was because it sounded almost funny then. My weary grieflessness seemed to disappoint him. I must have said, yes, I understood. Mother Church. Somewhere where he couldn't see me I was refusing to understand, but I had lost the place. It wasn't in my heart, I knew that, because I could feel my heart quite well. It must have been some place deep in my body, down where the pain made a great hole that the dark caved through like water.

No falling out here. No falling off steep-down gulfs of liquid fire. When the roar spoke, it said, *Forgive me.* I heard it faintly. Oh God, how my heart hurt, hurt with shame, hurt with pity because he seemed to have rehearsed it through. I am not sure if I was lying when I said, "I forgive you." I am not sure now.

Ita missa est. The mass is ended, go.

He dropped me at the Tiburtina station. The walls of the underpass had a ghastly wet sheen as if they had seen grisly ceremonies. Other travelers moved beside me or across me or against me from another part of geological time.

From Padua, I wrote to my sister of what I had now new-learned of love. Peace to Dante forever. I said in my fresh wisdom that love was a power that should never become a constraint to another to love you. Somehow, somehow, I could still marry this wisdom to our family opera, meld its hard, existentialist courage to be alone with a singular woman-courage to sustain "a union which is forever." My God, how deeply I was still in love, still speaking "of a man who does love you, and yet cannot find it in himself to give you that forever," coming this close to my secret. "Do not try him," I said. "Accept."

I told her to never to doubt that real love can exist, "though it is often thwarted."

I told her the man who eluded language would be her true lover.

There will not come many into your life, I said, and, remember, you cannot always embrace them, because they are going somewhere else, and have only a moment to give to you, only a moment.

The pages are not tear-stained. I do not remember if I wept.

W hen I could feel, I felt motherless.
I mean this to be literally true, but true also in the sense he had given it, as if he had declared the Church mother—lover—only to him. Then what was it to me? I wanted, still—wanted and did not want—to be included in that collective "body of Christ" he in his politics seemed to image so brilliantly. I still believed in a good and infinite God, a God of answered prayer. My consciousness still asleep, the question I asked about my exclusion was not yet a source of insight into Catholic sexism, just a source of pain.

In every other respect it was a choice I understood, accepted, respected, squaring with some deeply rooted ideal of priesthood—of male selfhood, in fact—that had needed no Church to conceive as too lofty to be swayed by the temptations of mere mortal female flesh. It was a thousand Damians and Johns, a hundred renunciations, operatic and existential together—by very definition "the mistake that had to be made." It was literature. It was Henry James. It possessed all the distinctive lineaments of the grand moral impasse, of the choice once allegorized so magnificently by the Renaissance between sacred and profane love. It was almost too easy for me to isolate certain such choices from their context in doubt and backsliding and contradiction and laughableness and plain carnal messiness and give them the status of tragedy.

Perhaps I am too satirical. My loss wasn't laughable then. My mother might have taken me for the image of my father when I was confident and proud, but in love I had always been her child, and never more so than now. Harry could do absolutely nothing I couldn't ultimately forgive. I quite literally adored him. Even his least nail parings had become as clean and incorrupt to me as if he had been sainted. This *peccadillo* of his, this—this merest failure of nerve, this bit of arrogant certainty about what he really wanted, which was in the end painful to no one but me—*me*—a she-person of small significance, how could this change what I felt or spoil my love? It was *his* suffering I felt the meaning of, his torment, the terribleness, the awfulness, the implacability of *his* choice. Mine the fault for having loved him, mine the fault for having presented the lure that had made this choice necessary—faults I could forgive myself only because he had been so lovable. Otherwise I was ruthlessly unforgiving. I took his guilt the way a bodyguard would take a bullet, the way my mother had when she threw her own body between her father and the Mafia.

And there was so much I didn't yet know—the distance he had come to have come at all to this penitential avowal of fidelity to Mother Church. Italians called him *sbotonato*—unbuttoned—yet his openness was in its curious way a façade, and behind it a deep reticence, a corpsman's loyal silence. He had not yet revealed to me—at least not in words—the depth of his humiliation at the cardinal's hands, still less the complicity of others he had trusted. How could I have known, who knew so little? In those infant days of my own ego, what did it mean to me to have a public persona at all, let alone a public persona publicly rebuked? And if I didn't know, how could I understand that original swerving in a perverse revenge and then the guilty swerving back again? I knew only how to know how to forgive.

Harry had once confessed his surprise at how young I was—he had thought me more than twenty-two. I had never asked him why. Was it the dark-encircled eyes? the luxuriant voice? the loosened sexual hunger? Or was it a trick to mantle his own shame—that if he had only known he wouldn't have—?

But, then, what *did* he know of me? What could he know of how this love for him had changed me and made me old, old as whoring? What did he know what stations of fear and wounding I had had to cross, like minefields, before I could surrender myself to any man, let alone to a priest. A priest! Before him, priests had seemed unhuman, not precisely repulsive, but of a flesh without salt or scent. I remembered now—it seemed to me that I had had at first to overcome just this repelled indifference, this subliminal loathing, before I could even touch him. Surely it was *this*—not desire but desire's opposite—that had made my tongue dry and my heart leap when he approached me. But soon—I had forgotten whether suddenly or by imperceptible degrees—I had even forgiven him this, the first forgiving that had led to all the others, and soon he had crossed over—or I had—and we were loving what had been strange in a land of fragrant, familiar, savory flesh.

Now I knew his body as tenderly as my own but with a higher, more numinous knowledge, knew it golden-white with its filigree tracery of fine, dark hair on the wide, deeply scored chest, knew the roughly muscled thighs, the calves like turned marble, the ankles, slender, bluish at the bone, the unmanly small, well-shaped feet and fine even toes, more beautiful than my own. I knew the silk and velvet genitals, the hard magenta satin of his erection, the single plane of belly and breast that lay so squarely and hotly on me, the crook of the knees where my own legs fit exactly, the strangled sob of climax, the master-craftsmanship of shoulder and arm that took so perfectly the weight of my head and the deep, orchid-colored bruise it forced through the paper skin—the only mark I ever dared leave on his body.

All this came back to me in a radiant desire no more alien to me now than the smell of my own body or the taste of my salt. My old fear reproached my new lust. I tried to encourage it to cure me.

American Dino asked no questions, but he knew something was wrong the moment he saw me. He suggested we go sightseeing to Venice together. The canals were swollen, San Marco terrifically flooded again. I was in no mood for new catastrophes, I told him, so we settled on old ones—the local Mantegnas, just restored since the wartime bombing of the Church of the Sepolcri. Even their ravaged beauty filled me with pain. Neither of us could in fact bear to stay long, and we fled for relief back to the temple of the blue Giottos, made more astonishing now by the thought of what they'd been spared. Still, nothing showed up very well, to tell the truth. My eyes were bad from the inside.

As fate would have it, we met the whining Father McManus as we left the chapel, the Jesuit Fulbright physicist who had missed Perugia. We couldn't shake him. He was starved for American conversation and we felt obliged to invite him up to the Tower for coffee. To the look I shot Dino, *Your place or mine?* he signaled mine, understandably, knowing it would be the only way eventually to get him to leave. We politely waited out the sunset from my balcony, but even when he and Dino were finally gone, the hum of that twangy nasal drone still hung in the air like whining smoke.

It was time for me to sit down and write a letter home, and I opened it with a casual allusion to McManus: *If my voice seems to have a certain Midwestern twang,* I wrote, *it's because of this priest. . . .*

I was about to learn something about the illusion of geographical distance as well as the speed of international mail. It wasn't a week before I had a return letter from my father, four solid pages thick, back and front, in his smallest, firmest, finest Italian hand. In religious jargon it was a screed—A Father's Diatribe Against Priests—a thundering, blistering, vituperative blast in the voice of the wrathful God, which just happened also to be his. I couldn't read the first page through before I was trembling so violently I felt faint. I carried it into the purple bathroom and tore it into confetti and flushed it down the toilet, which had an explosive power-flush that burst like a depth charge. I had to hit it again and again and again, as tiny, ink-smeared fragments kept frothing and cackling back on the surface of the water.

Then it was my father's voice that wouldn't leave. For days, for nights, I screamed back at him from inside my mind. *What do you know? What do you know about priests, or women? What do you know about me? What have you ever done but sabotage my joy, hurl your old hatreds into my young life, as if fatherhood gave you the right to destroy my little sunrise because you couldn't see it?*

But his curse had already done its malignant work. It was as if I had eaten the most delicate sweet, only to be told it was made of oil of rat and saliva of snake. No use retching up the contents of your belly now that the tainted stuff has already passed into your bloodstream and through the pulsing ventricles of your heart.

But there was this, too: that even if my soul dry-heaved at my father's connecting this nauseating Jesuit with me, it had also held up a mirror, a grotesque snapshot of the truth, of the tainted, spoiled sweetness of my Harry-love. It was the cold and twisted image of the voyeur, but a voyeur who has done routine professional detection and knows the shape things have a way of taking.

In this darkness of my soul I felt a new and colder bond with Harry. But a bond with my father, too, tinctured with hatred—the bond of like to like in our common lust of the eye. Images fired him, and the fetish of virgin flesh. My bank of child memory still remembered his romance with the camera. And now out of the depths of repressed knowledge came to me in nauseous sharpness a day in Tucson when he had turned the camera on my brothers and caressed their young bodies with the coiled finger of its mechanical retina. I had been shushed and sent away when I tried to see, but I had seen enough—two boys, naked, humiliated, whimpering, instructed not to cover themselves with their arms; naked, beautiful, bars of pale flesh striping their taut, well-tanned bodies, hard, polished buttocks shining in the afternoon light.

Spring seemed only to exaggerate Padua's moldering grayness of damp and stone. It was a sapless life, but it was my life for now, and I turned my face to it. I started sculpture classes at the Accademia in Venice with a wan enthusiasm, then gave them up again, renounced them, as if they had been Harry, too, in a pain that was like giving up my hands. I returned to the literary university, where my elusive Professor Branca, l'Illustrissimo, had resumed his renowned course of lectures on Boccaccio's *Decameron*. It was like watching a man play chess with an absent opponent. For weeks he sat, an hour or more at a time, several times a week, publicly ruminating on the book's plaguey introduction, taking tantalizing, fugitive dips into the stories, tickling the intellectual appetite for those comedies of clerical lust and female desire.

On such themes, I was not what one might have called disinterested. I could feel—oh, I could feel—but I couldn't think, and the play of memory and desire over the passionate score of Boccaccio's text only invited acute, disorienting seizures of my own sense of lost love and pleasure. At that particular moment I didn't think beauty either sweet or civilizing, and lust seemed a very unfunny thing. Sudden tears would pierce through my chest. The odor of Italian sweat, which by now I thought I had grown used to, distracted me like a faint premise of death.

When I glanced up from my notetaking, it was absurd to find myself—or the face and body my sorrow mortally inhabited, which happened to be sitting here on this day in this room in this century—fixed perhaps in some cool, lascivious gaze of blue, northern Italian eyes. I imagine that the look I returned at such moments was sad and inward rather than vexed, perhaps in the voluptuous spring air illogically inviting. But I could no more imagine myself desiring another man, let alone making love to one, than I could imagine suicide—which to tell the truth I couldn't imagine at all. A nunnish reserve, a punitive schedule of work, but the earth still seemed too full of strange promises. My *no* was to sex, not to life, and in my heroic state of celibate resolve I was sure life was possible without it.

There were moments—incredible moments—when my grief at losing Harry was burned off in a cool flame of moral exhilaration that I had actually renounced him—declared him free of me! Nothing seemed to break through that conscious wall of monumental selflessness to tell me: true. And you, fool, are free of *him,* too.

I took up a few loosened threads of my social life again, and went to a CRUE-sponsored international spring dance at the local community hall. You could easily pick me out of the smoky crowd: the dancing nun, wearing the high-heeled strip sandals and the black Marilyn Monroe dress with the tight-fitting waist and low, square-cut décolletage. I danced all night—all the night you could dance in. Unlike the other women students, especially the Turks from Istanbul whose brothers and cousins policed them ferociously, I had no curfew now, and was still lindying in my stocking feet long after they'd gone to bed.

The lights went out on Italian Dino and me doing the last dance, but we were both so endorphined by then that neither of us could bear to call it a night. And when we finally stepped outside, what a night it was!—moist as a sponge and full of polka-dot stars and the big promise of spring. He wrapped me in his Jimmy Dean leather jacket and we sped out of town on his air-grinding Vespa, me hugging him with one arm and with the other hugging a half-full bottle of Fundador tight in the fold of his jacket. We traced the network of roads along the Brenta, stopping in a shadowy piazza in Abano Terme. And there, to the music of a plinking fountain, we sipped Spanish brandy and talked abstractly of loyalty and love, and I took off my stockings as well as my shoes and spread my bare toes lusciously on the cold, damp stones.

He had his ties, I knew it. Neither of us named any names. We connected somewhere between islands of wayward desire. I was half in love with the way the lamplight fell on his crinkled Sicilian hair and shaded the brave thrust of his jaw. I never said the word *priest,* never spoke of Harry. And if at sunrise the kiss we kissed good-bye at my Tower door was not precisely chaste, it was also not meant on either side to be alluring.

If April can breed lilacs out of London, how much more easily out of the warm decay of Italy?

When Harry phoned, when he said, simply, "I'm on my way to Padua, don't go away," what could I do but laugh—with astonishment—confusion—joy?

"I'm starting early," he said. "I'm going to drive without stopping. Except to pee. Unless there's a freak snowstorm in the mountains, I should be there tomorrow afternoon."

So much for my steel morale, my tinsel renunciation. All I could feel was desire, coursing through me with the insane blinding high of a drug. And then the peace of a childlike gratitude fell on me, the peace of all the forces of destiny.

I left a message for American Dino with Sergio the doorman that I would be away for a few days, completely forgetting that Dino had the key to my apartment and permission to come in when I was gone. There was no time to think. Harry arrived even sooner than I had optimistically calculated—or else I had lingered in the purple shower too long, rediscovering the pleasure of my skin. When the apartment door buzzer sounded I was still drying and powdering, and had to wrap myself quickly in a towel and stand behind the open door to let him into the foyer.

In rushed the cold of this last spurt of winter with him, trapped in the folds of his coat. The balcony window dropped a beam of lemony afternoon sunlight on us like a spotlight. The door rushed shut, the towel fell, and we fell together, crazed by the sense of distances crossed and iron resolves exploded and differences obliterated—cold/warm, dry/wet, clothed/naked—his strange passionate mouth on mine, until as we drew apart we saw that from shoulder to knees my bare body had left a powder white imprint on his clerical trench coat, like the Shroud of Turin.

The pleasure of our coming together again was shattering. When I could speak, I told him, "This is what you are priest of." I, too, felt like its priest. I was filled full with the power of my own imagined beauty, my sex seemed in the dark to have sight and thought, the landscape of our bodies to open like some visionary shore. Sleep was only the intervals of delirium during a fever, desire overpowered us like victims. Night came, light came, night came again. We ate uncaring of taste or appetite, slept again in an animal sweaty clasp, blacked out and dreamless, and woke into startled passion again. On the third day we realized that our tangle of arms and legs in the narrow bed had begun to kill sensation, and spread a pair of blankets on the floor. And I was teasing him there when the door buzzer crashed through me like a gunshot.

What happened in seconds replays itself now like a slow-motion nightmare, and yet my blood beat so wildly then I thought it would burst in my paralyzed brain. Behind the crimson divider curtain, hanging between us and the door, I heard Dino turn the key in the lock and the door slide heavily on its hinges. I watched the horrible suck and flutter of the curtain inward from the draft. A single warm wand of afternoon sunlight stretched like a giant index finger over the floor and under the curtain and onto the tips of Dino's huge, thick-soled American shoes. The shoes stood very still, as if they had ears and could hear breathing, if we breathed. And then it came to me that the shadow of the two of us, locked together, lay outstretched on the floor of the foyer beneath the curtain, caught in that same finger of sunlight at Dino's feet.

The whole scene might have been caught in an f-stop. Before Dino could move I had leapt to my own feet and clapped a blanket around me. Harry dropped swiftly into the butterfly chair and pulled something over his lap.

"*Flavia?*"

Dino called my name, timidly, just as I reached the drape and slipped past it into the foyer. He had, if anything, the meanest flash of Harry's legs. I made some poor, barefaced excuse for being home. Dino backed away with that endearing doggie look of his, as if he wished he could be a dwarf but was condemned to be a whole continent of mortification. Then he disappeared for a week with an absoluteness that could only have been deliberate.

But the shock had a tonic effect. We decided to seek the sexless safety of public visibility again, to get out of Padua altogether and head for Venice, where the only person who knew both of us was Sam Kaner, and he was just a recluse printer living on the Giudecca.

It was a bright, cold, fine gift of a day on the Grand Canal. It was as though I were seeing Venice new again, the newness of Harry seeing it for the first time. But the city already had a history for me, as we stopped at the Accademia so I could show him where my sculpture classes had met, and from there wandered my favorite sinuous little alleys with all their repetitive displays of glass figurines.

We lunched late on seafood and crisp Veneto white. By sunset we hit the open piazzetta beneath the Rialto with dancing feet. Fired now with the romance of Venetian water, the daring of the city open to our unguarded secret, we hired a gondola to take us forward into the mouth of the Grand Canal. The late afternoon sun painted the waves with a buttery gold as we passed halfway between San Marco and Santa Maria della Salute, where the city of Venice marries the sea. Barely twenty feet away another boat came toward us, heading for San Marco, a kind of gypsy gondola with no cabin, only a standing oarsman who loudly greeted our mustachioed gondolier. The boat glided by almost before we saw it coming, cutting the silk lagoon, weaving our wake into a crosshatch of wavelets. And in it, unmistakable in deerstalker cap, earflaps loose over a nest of wild hair, was Sam Kaner, recluse printmaker. As the gap between us closed, we could both see the awakening flicker of recognition in his eyes.

"Father Browne!" he shouted with plain, unabashed delight.

Everyone was always glad to see Father Browne.

6

Harry never tried to explain how he had come to renounce his renunciation. I didn't ask, perhaps believing that for him as for me, under the Italian heaven, a certain fatalism was not extravagant. If there is a providence in the fall of a sparrow, why not a destiny in a desperate drive across the Apennines, against all odds and canonical injunctions and in the face of a demon need, stopping only to pee?

But this destiny gave no promise of absolution. On the downside of joy, in our itchy midnights, our separate failures haunted us intensely. We had crossed a gulf between innocence and experience, not just through sex, though that had transformed us too, but because we saw ourselves in the grip of forces not ourselves, and dubiously God by any standards either of us knew, something beyond our capacities to reconcile with any order or future we had ever imagined.

But there were vexing differences between us. I had always been swept by emotional forces I didn't understand, or understood too late. Not Harry, who couldn't be said to have just now discovered himself as a sexual, susceptible being—who had often laughingly told me he'd known what he was in for after his first foxtrot at a Hudson Guild dance when he was fifteen. Apparently to be such a being and a priest had never seemed impossible, only interesting, and nothing in the bromidic wisdom of the Grand Masters of the major seminary had ever discouraged this rather hubristic idea of self-mastery.

My God, how veteran, how weary the Church was about sex and "love"! It had all happened before, every bit of it, no new sins under the moon or the sun. All the roads others had traveled before you had been mapped and codified, even down to the exquisitely timed tricks of contraceptive *interruptus*. What if you needed a few more than the standard issue of cold showers until your glands slowed down? Penance, after all, covered a multitude of sins. It would take more than a few grains of testosterone to define an "impediment" to Holy Orders.

I imagined Harry at Catholic U.—women everywhere, loving women, admiring women, adoring women. Had they been merely a severer test of the theory of the cold shower? How often down in D.C. had he kicked the traces between friendship and flirtation doing a rain song? Yet these dangers had never really daunted him, it seemed—not until he met real temptation during a postgraduate summer doing routine parish duty in the Bronx. Her name was Gloria, convent-educated daughter of a fruit peddler on Arthur Avenue. She had materialized like a long-repressed fantasy, archetype of the dark, forbidden Italian girls who had first stirred his blood on the streets of Hell's Kitchen. Once he had spoken of her to me, there was no hiding that she'd represented an awakening for him. But the firewall had held, and he had passed the supreme test of priestly fatherhood and married her to another man.

Now he didn't like to speak of such things, not anymore, of desires either of us had had before our desire for each other—not mine, not his, not Damian, not John, not Gloria, not anyone. I had once quoted him John Donne—"Twice or thrice had I loved thee/ Before I knew thy face or name . . ."—and he would spoon the words back to me in homeopathic doses whenever the still hungry little epistemophiliac would long to know more and more. I think he was a bit afraid to see the past by the light of the present, afraid he might find himself looking too squarely into the face of his own denied and inchoate emotions.

I was afraid too, with the difference that I couldn't help but think a little jealously of the beautiful Gloria and the chanciness of time that had advantaged me over her, ripened me here in Italy and given me the idiom of my own beauty the same way it had given me the idiom of my tongue, guaranteed he would have the incarnation of all his weaknesses—the time, the place, and the woman, all together.

And yet it was the sublime accident of all those weaknesses I also loved, which in surges of tenderness I felt also to be his strengths, even the hint of Catholic bigotry in his New York–Irish faith, with its taproot sunk in his mother's pietistic devotions to the purity of the Virgin and all the sexlessness and dailiness of candles and early morning masses. I thought of my mother, whose rosaries were a kind of contract with her own private protection racket, whose novenas, like payments made on time, were like promissory notes to be exchanged for favors on demand. Was she really so different from his mother—also named Mary—who had bought a different kind of protection, with no guarantees for the here and now, but with the certainty of a glorious hereafter, son for Son?

I loved him for the dangers he had passed. For having come from and outreached this kind of tribal faith, for the web of company-man loyalties he yet wore so lightly, for the iron brotherbond of the chivalry of God he rattled with his historian's Olympian laughter, for the love he would not let go of for his true father, Father John "Doc" Monaghan, who as his first true teacher had mixed social justice with catechism and English, lifted that pious Irish dailiness off its knees, and sent him out to the Catholic Worker and ministering into the world. I did not love him for loving me. I forgave him for that. I can never remember a moment, despite my early ignorant and primitive Italian notions of what it meant to be a priest, ever wishing that he had been anything else.

Gradually I tried to piece together the story he had begun to unfold so cryptically in December, though it never came to me in the good sequential order of the historian (it wasn't "history" for him, and it never would be), and intuiting all of it would have been a little like putting together a thousand-piece puzzle without the picture. But this much I got: that in 1956 Francis Cardinal Spellman (who would always be "Spelly" to his diocesan recruits, men like Harry who were officially ordained into his service) had recalled him from his professorship at Catholic University. Suddenly. Summarily. Without anything a noncleric would think of as explanatory due process. Simply pulled him up and set him down, indefinitely, to teach social studies at the New York preparatory seminary known as Cathedral College. It was high school duty, plain and simple, and Harry never, ever said the phrase "first-year civics," but the outrage was like a knife blade just drawn out and still smoking with blood.

Easy to say in his pious universe, perhaps, that as a good priest he should count his blessings, that he'd already had plenty of bonuses others hadn't: applause, prizes, academic lionizing. To say that humiliations like this came, after all, with the bargain he'd originally struck when he'd offered his obedience to the cardinal in exchange for the security of a lifetime appointment in the ecclesiastical civil service. Not easy for him. I suspect obedience had actually become an issue when, with time, he'd discovered himself to be utterly without ambition for a place in the hierarchy, when he'd found that for him rising through the meritocratic academic ranks at Catholic University was ambition enough, when he'd become something of a career maverick and a star in his own right, outside the world of purely ecclesiastical approval or disapproval.

But that seeming independence must have been precisely the problem, for Harry had intellectual ambition. He'd apprenticed not just to the priesthood but to the priesthood of radical knowledge, a role I gathered had been handed down to him, father to son, as it were, as part of John Monaghan's legacy. What had fired Harry's imagination had been *history*—history that rewarded all the midnight oil, the cold showers, boy and man, the sacrifice of every male energy still left past the adolescent thrill of *Argosy Magazine* adventures and the Boy Scout macho of the Boys' Brigade. And I could see how his mission as a historian of the Church itself might well have come to be in some sense to define—if necessary, redefine—how a priest ordained might make obedience to the Faith compatible with obedience to the Truth, a challenge that might sometimes require admitting just how big Faith (or slavish institutional loyalty) stood in Truth's way.

It was not a mission unique to him, least of all in the transcendently cynical Catholic Church, with a name and a bureaucratic niche for every possible ambition including the *advocatus diaboli,* or "Devil's Advocate," whom in another breath it called "Promoter of the Faith." As an official recorder not just of past ecclesiastical greatness but of past ecclesiastical foibles and mistakes, in some sense that's just what he was, or what he thought himself to be, the DA whose function it was to call out even faithful fakes and phonies whenever they were discovered to be parading around in the buff.

You could forgive him, then, for deluding himself into thinking he had carte blanche to poke around in the messier truths about the redoubtable John Hughes, first New York archbishop, whose official biography he was writing—his ill-disguised drinking problem, his better-hid "special friendships." Or permission to raise Cain organizing the faculty at C.U. Or maybe even sing a song or two too many in the Green Room, who knows? I believe he never fully knew what he'd been punished for—perhaps all of the above. The canonical cops, somewhere, had booked him on presumption—presumption of something they were under no obligation to explain. It had hit him in the softest underbelly of his ego. It had only served to prove he had one.

People who loved him saw him suffering. One of them told him, "Harry, get yourself a Fulbright. Go to Italy." How could the cardinal mind having him over there in Rome, right under the eye of the Cardinal of Cardinals? Better to travel than to burn.

And so, as I now saw it, he had come away wounded and still burning, away from the romance of history to the romance of Italy, away from "Spelly," away from New York, away from the United States and its works and pomps—for now—into his Roman digs at Montemario where he would do his research and take his American priesthood *stilo italiano,* have his car, his hours, his freedom of sorts, lick his sore ego without too gross a test of his loyalty—in fact, for all intents and purposes, affirming it.

I don't think he actually saw me, or saw me consciously, as some ultimate test of that loyalty. Not until, after falling in love, he had kept falling, not until in the wretched south, where Christ had stopped, some demon Christ had bolted and reminded him how big Obedience still stood in the way.

And I could imagine that for a time renouncing our love, our passion, had felt good—hadn't it after all, in its way, felt good for me? That it had made him feel clean and innocent again, clean as the sacrificial lamb, the sacrificial child, the child he'd been back at St. Michael's, more saint now because he'd been the sinner, more welcome as the prodigal son returned. For that little time he'd had it back—had been again the boy he'd been when he'd been Monaghan's boy, when the chastest of man-boy love had been his greased lightning, when he'd turned out twenty-five articles in five years and been the campus darling at C.U. and the Labor Day firebrand besides—had all this back and that pure clean state of remission of sin, that deep-down freshness only the Catholic knows walking out of the confessional dipped in crystal absolution and baptized again in the eternal milk of sacred love.

He'd had it all back. And it had not been enough.

Would this be enough? The unspoken question added a certain poignancy to our mutual tenderness, even by mail, as if we were looking back now from a future when our love, our little love, our Great Love, would have shaped itself into an episode, a memorable *liaison dangereuse.* And in Padua, as the sun of May cooked the vegetable damp of the Po Valley into *minestra,* the present seemed a very uncertain mix of something about to be over and something about to begin.

Harry in Rome had a sharper sense of turning point. May was crisply hot and clean there, he reported, the beaches welcoming, the smell of tourist money already on the morning. Friends from Washington, who had all booked ahead swearing to celebrate a Roman holiday with him after term time, were on their way. Father Robert, the fellow historian and old seminary chum who'd been recruited on my behalf to visit Ann in the hospital at home, was expected any minute. Harry wrote to me to say it was time to destroy our letters.

I ached. I couldn't. Even granting him that unbearable retrospect, when our somehow orphaned love letters might lie under the damning scrutiny of some future

Church historian's gaze, I couldn't. He showed me how. He described how he had bundled mine, every one, into his briefcase, alongside his notes from the Vatican Archives on the American hierarchy's so-called Italian problem, and headed out to Anzio with the briefcase beside him in the Fiat.

It was a brilliant beach day, but it was early, and he found himself driving alone along the shimmering dunes. The beach looked smooth and wide and empty, the Mediterranean for miles a spread palette of blues. He stopped at a stretch that reasonably offered to remain secluded for a while, took off his shoes and trudged barefoot, briefcase in hand, through the just-warming sand, till he was within about a body's length of the sea's trembling edge. There, as the sun rose higher and the water slowly breathed nearer, he reread the letters one by one, every word. Then, as he finished, he tore each one to bits and cast it on the green and purple swells and watched the bits float asunder like a tiny expeditionary fleet.

I had the Lido, but resisted. I put it off. When I understood that if I were going to do it at all, I could no longer put it off, I took the letters by the bunch and, choking back tears, ripped them to pieces and sent them the way of my father's diatribe, down the mauve commode.

I had no more excuses for thinking myself a victim, not innocence, not the passion of the moment, not ignorance. He had swerved from me once. It had had finality, and I had survived. Life had proved possible without him. In the eyes of Holy Mother Church I was now his authentic concubine, complicit in his sin.

Now a new era had begun in the power rotations of love—for what is love but an indefinite contract to suspend calling power by its true name? I had granted him the option to equivocate, which meant the option to walk away again if he chose.

I did not expect him to choose to walk away. I did not expect him to choose. Had he proposed we marry I think I would almost certainly have declined. I cannot tell if this was out of some grand philosophical attraction to my freedom— or his. I know there was that still-lovely false radiance of self-abnegation. Long before Harry ever quoted me those famous lines about sacrifice that he had pat from the Catholic marriage ceremony—that "only love can make it easy, and perfect love can make it a joy"—I knew plenty about love and sacrifice, knew it, as one might say, from my mother wit. This perfect love of ours had now made it possible for me to prove it. This perfect love, for which all other loves had been mere rehearsals, would demand by its very nature the greatest sacrifice. By just this sign would I know it.

American Dino was on his way to his kinfolk in Terni, and gone before May was out. As for me, my summer plans were still unclear, and I hung on. Ann seemed much better, better enough that I did not have to cut short my stay, and I was otherwise not eager to be home, or even to rush off to a final visit with my Neapolitan cousins. However much I might want to see Harry, there was a question whether

I should be in Rome at all and too obviously in his way now that Robert Wilde was there. Meanwhile, my obligations to CRUE English classes and to the two or three people I privately tutored in Padua made an easy excuse not to part from my little Tower studio until I had at least wrung the last day from the month.

Silene, casting ahead to how she would feel when I was gone and deciding she would miss me, broke the family rule and invited me to spend a weekend in Schio with her parents. They were kind, but, as I expected, very possessive of Silene, their only child, and a little wary of her friends. Schio itself was a Swiss-like little village high in the Alpine foothills, still in the last tenacious grip of winter. A drive into even higher foothills took us through crisp white mountain fastnesses, where we caught the first yellow and white wildflowers forcing themselves bravely through the snow, and I picked and pressed one into my Orlandi dictionary.

I came back to the spring soup of Padua, and lingered about a week into June. Italian Dino, trying to cover his boundless Sicilian parting emotion with a transparent glaze of Veneto irony, handed me my last CRUE paycheck and invited me for a Campari-soda. Two of my favorite women—the gorgeous husky-voiced Loredanna, and Silvia, a wisecracking blond with a cheeky, sidelong grin—took me for our last supper to a *pizzeria napoletana* hidden in the arcades opposite the Palace of Reason. Dino showed up again as we were finishing. He joined us for a good-bye spell of sentimental midnight meandering through a chain of echoing piazzas, the four of us arm in arm singing *"Quei mazzolin di fioriiii . . ."* at the tops of our voices. Until the women dropped away, one by one, kissing me and me, *modo italiano,* on both tear-streaked cheeks for the last time. Dino walked me back to the Tower, dark, late, sorrowful. There being something in the way for me put something in the way for him, which was, after all, just as well.

But what seemed hours later we were still in each other's arms, weeping. I couldn't bear for him to leave me, and we lay still clothed and clasped tightly together in the black alcove where Harry and I had spent such inexpressible days and nights. Through my compliant need Dino could still feel my resistance. With that steel self-discipline I had sometimes arrogantly felt was too much—too much—but was glad of now, he said, "Tell me what you want," and pulled back, quenched himself, when after a heart-stopping silence, my brain swimming with this alien desire, I whispered, "No."

We still couldn't part. It was my fault. He had become for me in that single white night what almost every man in my life was later to become, my refused rescuer, my renounced salvation. I clung desperately to him, and he clung to me because I did, and we spent hours awake and suspended. As dawn approached, my last dawn in Padua, my last sunrise over the Cappella, I begged him to come with me to see it. I drew him out of the apartment and into the stairwell, barefoot, where we started up the the hollow silent darkness toward the roof. It was only two flights of terrazzo staircase, but emotion and exhaustion had turned my legs to paper, and I stopped on the landing just short of the rooftop door, panting.

He paused too, expectant, on the landing just below me where the stairs turned, leaving us perhaps seven steps apart. Above us the half world of heaven had begun to brighten, and a slice of light between the threshold and the rooftop door glowed down on us a cold neon blue.

I don't know how long we just stood there, staring at one another, leaning against our opposite walls, listening to our answering breaths.

I left Padua the next afternoon. Dino, before going away, had promised to help me to the railway station with my bags.

I think he rather wished he hadn't. For one thing, it had become one of those insufferable June days when the heat by noon is white enough to cook flesh. But he came back anyway like a good soldier, erstwhile rescuer of fleeing Hungarian heroes. He helped me to a taxi. He swung my bags coolly aboard the train. He did not seem to sweat. I sweated. I stuck to the platform like a slug, feeling puffy and white from lost sleep and heat and grief, and grief, and grief. And the panic of going, which seemed to attach in train stations to some primal dread. When we kissed good-bye I could feel my face varnished in a lacquery ooze. It was a public kiss, as though we had already parted.

"In America next time," he promised staunchly, and I smiled somewhat bravely, climbed aboard, and leaned out the compartment window. I saw him squarely planted there as the train pulled away, eyes locked on mine, until he was a tiny, distant, swimming blur.

7

I have never liked thinking of myself as an artful photographer—that old war between truth and poetry, I suppose, perhaps that old inner war between my father and me. I hate the artificing distance of picture-taking when I am in the moment, though of course I regret, later, what I lose.

But sometime during my first Italian weeks in Naples, well before I understood the meaning of *trenta mila lire,* I remember at my father's urging going with my cousin Gino to the waterfront and being yanked with him into a greasy little alley to buy a camera on the black market. It was my first serious camera, a Zeiss Icon, and the only one I have ever loved. I can almost mark the day I took my first pictures with it—mark, not remember, for it is one of my grievances with cameras that they remember what I then let myself forget. The first frame was not my own, but a picture taken of me by one of my handsome country cousins, Zia Irena's sons—perhaps Carlo, who from the start had lavished me with punishing attentions, or was it Alfonso, with the girlish mouth and liquid gaze? I was still recovering from my staggering flu, but it was a bright, mild day with a warm scent of leftover summer still in it, and my aunt, mindful of her accountability to my father, had said I might just climb out the big bedroom window onto the faintly tar-smelling roof for a bit of sun.

I took the camera with me, and stretching myself comfortably amid the yellowing tangle of vines, I framed the fig trees and grape arbors and furzy hills with my hands imagining the pictures I might take, when Carlo (or was it Alfonso?) joined me, saying I was looking so well again, really, I ought to have a picture of myself, just as I was, stretched out there on the roof.

And there the saga begins of pictures various through trips various, whenever I remembered to bring the camera with me, whenever I remembered—or overcame my resistance enough—to use it, or someone persuaded me to pose for posterity. Very often Harry was that persuasive someone. He snapped me in piazzas, at fountains, on pedestals and benches, leaning on tombstones in the Appian Way, running along the Calabrian beach with the wind in my hair. They were for him. It was as if locking these moments in the camera's eye were a kind of homage to them. He couldn't be in the pictures—Lord knows the last thing he wanted for posterity were exhibits of his days alone with me. But he could be their invisible creator.

Well, not so invisible, really. Absolutely no judge of a vertical vs. a horizontal subject, he seldom got the frame right and often cut off my head at the crown or my legs at the calf, or got the camera strap in the way or his thumb in the picture, or misjudged the light or the focus. He would fumble with the light gauge muttering, "Gimme a Brownie any day," and then he'd smile wickedly and say, "Say 'cheese'," knowing I hated saying "cheese" with a passion.

That summer, when I finally got to Rome, the first thing he did was sweep me up with two other nice Catholic girls to Nemi's annual strawberry festival. It was a Father Browne excursion and photo op extraordinaire. Besides me, there would be singer Olivia, looking for a day's respite from a torrid affair with her singing coach, and Alicia, a vacationing nurse from D.C., who had once tended Harry through a minor operation. It is a mild and gorgeous June Sunday, and Harry and I, having spent nearly six weeks apart, must not let our glances intersect or our bodies touch for an instant. Today we will practice the sublimation of love into strawberries— strawberries and lemon, strawberries and white wine, strawberries marsala, strawberries and *panna,* strawberries and pain. Like everyone else, we shall drift into the sunny piazza, twisting and turning on the spit of the air in the unnatural light, strangling passion under the umbrella trees amid a rush of faces that floods space like a sudden release of Technicolor balloons.

But the camera, remembering nothing of my secret anguish, remembers what that anguish might have easily erased like noise drowning music. It remembers that I took a seat in a puddle of sunlight by a wrought-iron fence, that behind me the strawberried terraces fell away to the splendid lake, that near me was a child, about two years old, bouncing a large ball again and again, and looking back gently to see if I were watching. He had a large round high forehead and a thin, soft layer of silvery hair that shone like a halo of smoke. I felt for the sweetness of his look something more insane than love, as if I had suddenly birthed him. Before me, in the public gardens, everyone with whom I sustained this cosmic moment, sons and daughters, lovers and mothers and fathers and babies, seemed to sway lightly in the dappled sun.

"Let me take the two of you," Harry offered suddenly, breaking my rapture and slipping the camera from my shoulder.

And so there we are in the album—squintily smiling because he has snapped us in the direct rays of the afternoon sun—*Madonna con bambino.* He is there too, as usual, having also unwittingly caught his own shadow throwing itself blackly across my strange baby and me.

Those few brief days in Rome had already been a circus. I had met the redoubtable Father Robert, and we three had begun to scheme a trip to Sicily with Alicia, in spite of the braising June heat. Then Jeannie Davis showed up. *The* Jeannie Davis.

You didn't have to know why she had lost the Maria Goretti award. She was a stunner—peachy-cream complexion, pouty pre-Raphaelite mouth, fringed aquamarine eyes, all set in a surround of honey hair atop her bosomy body like a flower in a china vase. I held my breath when she was asked whether she was interested in a trip to Sicily, but she said, no, she needed time to research her pamphlet on the Italian devotion to Saint Filomena.

If it was a sin to feel a sudden outpouring of affection for this Filomena, I sinned. A few more years, poor thing, and they'd drum her officially out of the Church calendar as a fiction, but she was still a card-carrier that summer. Whenever she was pictured, it was always as a mysteriously iconic type of Alexandrian Greek who looked, in fact, a little like me. Her name, which meant "the loved one," had been found scrawled on the wall of a catacomb, giving her dim, provocative ties to all the strange goings-on in the primitive Church.

Jeannie's plan was to make directly for the little village in the Campagna where the cult of Filomena had defied the centuries. She was not feeling especially brave about this, with good reason. She had never been to Italy before, with or without the Maria Goretti award, let alone to a remote mountain village known for worshipping another obscure martyred female. When Robert announced he would not be going to Sicily after all, but would be staying on in Naples to study antiquities while Harry and Alicia and I pushed on, Jeannie couldn't help expressing relief that he would be there, ready to rescue her if she needed rescuing.

"Don't worry!" Robert reassured her, Harry reassured her, Alicia and I reassured her. "We'll be back together in less than a week."

I worried. I worried about the unfamiliar stirrings of jealousy in my craven heart. I could see how meaningless they were: Jeannie was one of those utterly pious devotees of Harry's who drew the *thou shalt not* so tightly about her that I think an erotic glance from him or any other priest would have crusted her like a leper. But I was a tumult of new emotions. I felt myself inseparable body and soul from a man who now belonged to everyone, and who withdrew farther from me the closer he came. Who had to. How could I understand my own panic as I watched another woman, a splendid, desirable woman, blush and stammer in front of him as if she were in the Divine Presence, let alone understand the shame she felt at being desirable at all?

And now there was Robert, whose visits to Ann while she was sick had already made us presumptive friends: Harry's longest-going-back chum and boon companion, with him from day one at the seminary, ordained the same day in 1944. Was there ever going to be any way to disguise ourselves to him? He was, besides, such a puzzle of self-protective mischief that he might as well have been a CIA agent playing a lean and balding classicist somewhat indifferent to his appearance—he had Henry Fielding's Parson Adams right down to the Greek text in his pocket.

Robert was also balding, nearsighted, and deaf in one ear, with a tendency to correct for sound distortion by opening his mouth and tilting his head. A fine head, of course, allowing for the tightly wrapped skin, which had a tendency to go pink in the sun. He was understandably shy. He did not expect attention. But he plainly worshipped Harry, and though he clearly took something vicarious out of the adulation Harry received, especially from women, he also used to disappear and reappear on the sudden, as if he had periodically to reestablish his autonomous existence. Once at the Foro Romano he vanished, causing both Harry and me a wave of panic, until Harry rediscovered him in the public *gabinetto*. When the two of them reappeared, strolling arm in arm, Robert was beaming as if they had just played out some old scatological shtick.

Jeannie's air of naïveté, on the other hand, was the genuine article. Her first blaze of joy and nerves on arrival, when she'd seemed to rather demand an entourage, had been a case of coping with the first stages of Italian sensory assault and getting from here to there without having a nervous breakdown. By the time we all arrived in Naples she was ready for the plunge and determined to go it alone, until the two padres offered at least the ride to Filomena's village and she accepted.

Harry later described the scene where they'd left her: a piazza, a little stuccoed church on a hill, many many steps, the mountains falling away behind, a gaggle of women in black dresses and snoods ecstatic to see her, ready to close osmotically over her as soon as the two priests left. Jeannie, like some feckless Rose Red in a fairy tale, had turned a last plaintive look back. Leaning into the window of the car, she'd said, "If you get a call—even if you *don't* get a call—come *fast*."

Robert appeared quite unalarmed about our tour of Sicily, implying a previous knowledge of the safety of threesomes. Comradeship with women might not be Robert's particular cup of tea, but on principle he seemed to like the idea that Harry had topped the misogyny of the Church by reversing it. If sex, like death, destroyed a priest, you might say that the idea of sex saved him.

This was a new universe for me. Even Alicia, as skinny as a stick and as chaste and aseptic as clean-room surgery, seemed to elevate sexuality to the realm of pure forms. As a nurse, as Harry's nurse once, she had grounds for an intimacy of sorts, but Alicia was not one to take a mean advantage of intimacy. Laughing out loud at the body, as Harry did—as Harry made her do—put the whole nasty carnal human condition at a bearable distance, and could almost magically lift away the awful mortality of flesh. Of course, like Jeannie, she'd have been absolutely shattered if he'd touched her. Not to mention damned surprised, since, unlike Jeannie, she was plain and Polish and a woman who didn't expect moves.

And this last set of facts may have helped more than anything to make it a gorgeous, comradely run through Calabria and Sicily at full tourist tilt, halfway around the island, across the central highlands to Palermo, and back to Naples again via the overnight ferry, just in time for Alicia to make her flight home, Harry and I so lustful the whole way, and Alicia so blithely above it, that her afternoon naps were a dare to make quick love, peel our sticky bodies apart again, and return to innocent cigarettes, lemon ices, and map-reading on the veranda.

Still, though this punishing desire made us fitfully indifferent to her sometimes, Alicia inspired respect, even fondness, and she and I got on as women, both of us grateful to have whatever it was we had. And the three of us were splendid together, sharing all our swims and tours and prowls through village marketplaces and seaside fish stalls, and our voluptuous trattoria feasts of scampi and calamari and *cassata siciliana.*

Harry had started a beard in Naples. A grubby fuzz by Paola in Calabria, it had become fur by Siracusa and Papa Hemingway by the time we crossed the island to Palermo, the heat so intense as we drove through the highlands that even the air blowing through the car window could have incinerated an iron lung. Alicia offered to give him a professional pre-op shave as soon as it was cool enough to sit still. Lolling together at last in the cool opulence of the Villa Igea, she sat him down and softened his beard with warm, wet washcloths, took it down to an Amish fringe, then a Vandyke, then a Teddy Roosevelt with sideburns, finally a simple mustache. At each stage Harry would jump up to look at himself in the mirror and stage a routine that had Alicia and me in pain. "Remember I have a *razor*," Alicia would manage to choke, though she was the epitome of grace under pressure. Harry wore the mustache and an ascot to supper in the decadent dining room of the hotel. He shaved it off in front of the mirror the next morning, the two of us looking mournfully on, like acolytes.

On the ferry to Naples we fled to the deck from our sweltering compartments and slowly inched our way to the bowsprit. And there we stayed as night came on and the other passengers dropped below, the three of us cuddled sleepily on the cold slick bench with Harry in the middle, dozing and waking as the ship dipped and rose until it was dawn. The ship's lamps were haloed in fog as the thick spray shot up in the dark all around us, misting over the stars.

I visited my cousins in the Vesuvian hills for a day or two. When I got back to Naples I phoned Harry and Robert's hotel room repeatedly. No answer. I was diffident about leaving messages. Frustrated, I concocted a way to send Harry a wire, something vaguely needy like, "Where the hell are you?" and dodgily signed, "Filomena," the loved one.

Still no word. Finally after several more phone tries, Robert picked up. "We *just* got back," he said, breathless. "P-poor Jeannie. She was d-d-desperate."

He handed Harry the phone. "We got this frantic wire signed *Filomena*," Harry told me. "We drove straight out. Jeannie was a maniac. She nearly went into cardiac arrest when we got there. *'Miracolo, miracolo!'* It was the only Italian she'd learned all week." He laughed out loud. "You'll never believe this," he said. "Jeannie told us she never sent any wire. She couldn't even cope with the phone."

I waited to tell Harry what had really happened till Jeannie had already fled back to the United States full of her story. "Jesus, don't tell Robert," he said. "He and Jeannie are set to start a whole new Filomena sodality when they get back to C.U."

There was a lot not to tell Robert. I doubt he had much to say about my joining up with the two of them in Paris, a couple of weeks later, for a trip through southern France and Spain in a rental car, when Harry puffed me as fluent in five modern languages and I, too selfish to think beyond another chance to be with him, had us pictured as a Graham Greene version of *The Sun Also Rises*, two priests in civvies and a woman in desperate love, schlepping to Pamplona.

After sixteen hours on a train from Naples, I can remember lighting like a moth on the platform of the Gare de Lyons and spotting Harry loping toward me, leaving Robert and bounding down the platform in that to-hell-with-him way, just like a lover. Poor Robert. And yet, no matter how heroic he was about us, he also demanded a sort of heroism back, being skinny and deaf and bald and half-blind from reading incunabula. I loved him, on Harry's account and his own. In theory.

In practice, I—we—must have hurt him continually. It was hard to tell. Once he said to Harry that he had never seen him so attentive to anyone. *Attentive.* He must have made some fairly deliberate choices about what he would close his eyes to or hear with his bad ear, but that was his way. Because he said nothing, you thought he could see and hear no evil, when chances are he saw it all and stored it up, as they say, in his heart.

There was that one terrible night just outside of Perpignan when we couldn't find a hotel, and the car was too suffocating and Robert's snoring too loud to sleep in the car. Harry and I slipped out and finding a reasonably soft spot in a roadside ditch a few yards away, curled up together in our coats. We opened our eyes in the gray chill of dawn, and there was the fearful sight of Robert standing over us, aghast, looking down at what must have been the fearful sight of the two of us, clasped together in the dirt.

From then it was clear he'd become the wife, the piece of the Holy Mother Church Harry had married, and I the other woman. Even Harry's snapshots of me that trip tell the story of my dismal sort of sensual torpor. I felt hopeless about us in a way I had never felt with Harry's women, in a way I hadn't felt since St. Paul's Outside the Walls. Robert's stern, sad, pitiful hurt, that peculiar male hurt of his, only mirrored my own hurt back to me.

The morning after Perpignan was Robert's turn at the wheel, something to dread even at the best of times, and this was not one of them. He drove like a spastic, pushing and lifting the gas pedal and steering in nauseating, seasickly jerks. I could hear myself groan through a fitful doze as he passed through Nîmes and Arles without stopping, and the price of our all being wretched that morning was that we got into a stupid quarrel about missing the Maison Carrée. Harry stepped in and it was everything I'd dreaded, to hear him take my side against his friend.

It was a form of dread I would learn to live with, cope with, slowly train myself to bear, until it had come to be so familiar I think I lost my taste for life without it. But then it turned everything dark. And it was in that sense a momentous journey, a memory of Spanish mountainscapes filled with a God more menacing, more just, than ever El Greco had warned of.

On top of it all, the beastly rental car broke down repeatedly. We had already been held up with two costly repairs when the odometer suddenly stopped working in Barcelona. Robert was trying to figure out how to say "fix odometer" in Spanish when Harry said, "Are you out of your mind?" It was the one bittersweet grace of that sorry trip, that they could return that car some thousand miles short on the mileage charge.

Which they did, with relish.

And then they left together for the Holy Land.

There had long ceased to be any question of my staying in Italy for another year. Whither thou goest I will go. In any case, it was time, and I booked a flight, my first ever, for early September, announcing my homecoming exactly a year to the day since I had left.

Hostage for the remaining month to my spinster aunts in Naples, who watched every move and reported to brother Gino the according state of the family honor, I settled back in Naples to sketch everything that would stay still for at least thirty seconds. I sometimes pictured myself a remake Lady of Shalott, taking the world in my magic mirror and weaving cartoons of it. One such sketch, of a fishwife in the Salita courtyard shouting the morning catch and pulleying it up to the third floor in a rope basket, I posted to Harry in a thick, passionate letter care of the family in Perugia he'd be visiting before he went home. He never got it—a strange mischance that haunted us both for years.

We foiled the Vatican demon one last time, and met for a single whirlwind tryst in Rome. I was glad on short notice to find space in a rather proper little *pensione* near the Via Nazionale, and when Harry somehow made it past the desk surveillance and burst into my room gloriously tanned and splendid to set eyes on, he stunned me with joy. Remembering the propriety of the place we held ourselves in check. And then he calmly took a ring from his pocket and slipped it easily, perfectly, on my left-hand ring finger.

"It's an Alexandria stone," he explained. He'd got it in Cairo, cheap, maybe hot, off a guy in a turban.

"Very romantic," I laughed as soon as I could find my breath—not quite intending to be ironic. My eyes must have been very bright.

"Depends what you think is romantic," he said, smiling a little wistfully. I was holding the ring to the overhead light, a deep, many-faceted, amethyst-colored stone mounted with high drama on four thin, pink-gold tips, and he took my hand and tilted it toward the window, showing me how differently the ring shone in another light.

This was too much. I laughed again. "An allegorical ring, is it?"

"Blue outdoors, by daylight." He took my fingertips in both his hands and kissed them. Then he leaned forward and put his whimsical mouth on mine, and wordlessly, in that single, beseeching moment I forgave him everything yet to come, forever.

A sudden peremptory knock on the door—I leap to open, but the concierge has already unlocked and swung the door ajar. His eyes are spinning—he waves his fat, sweaty hands over this dubious transaction between Harry and me—"*Vergogna, signorina!* For shame! We are respectable people here!"

Which abrupt pronouncement blessed our little ceremony with just the perfect witness of respectability it called for.

He flew to Ireland with Robert at dawn. From my hotel bed I listened for the plane's roar as it passed away over Rome. I had two more weeks of Italian boy cousins obsessed in their own ways with obstacle love, vying for my attention when I visited them in the country, bringing me gifts of watermelon and figs and laying them in my lap like offerings, and then, when I returned to Naples, finding excuses to see me there.

Carlo had sultry smoking eyes and a mouth that burned my cheek when he brushed it against my face. I tried to forget that here in southern Italy first-cousin marriages were often dispensated and that he might have something more bourgeois in mind than pure incest. I made dates with him I seemed to have no energy to refuse. One afternoon he met me in the park near the university, and kneeling down before me where I sat on the grass, he presented me with a first edition copy of *Dr. Zhivago*, just smuggled out of the Soviet Union and published in Italy.

Somewhere in an alive place in my heart the thought that he would intuit the momentousness of this novel for me touched me very much. That evening we returned to the Salita and the two of us wandered about the dim, cool apartment doing small chores for my aunts. In the shadows of the rear bedroom, as we set fresh linens in the press, he tried to kiss me and I did not try to stop him.

But at that moment Zia Maria surprised us together precisely as she suspected she would. Carlo was mortified, I blushed, but was glad. We had the perfect kinship romance, Maria and I. I believe she fantasied me as her own child sometimes, her virgin birth. Naturally, in her soft, gentleladyish way she blamed Carlo for our peccadillo and packed him home.

Maria. Somehow you knew, as she continually polished her soft white alabaster hands with glycerine and rosewater, that she was preserving them as a metaphor of her ecstatic soul, that beneath her mask of exquisite respectability beat the most soaring, operatic heart, capable of glamorous, magniloquent, singable sins. Cousin Carlo would not do, we both knew it. Whatever my life still held, if for her sake it was to be an installment romance, the next episode would have to be set not here in Italy, but in America, in New York.

Good-bye, Maria. *Addio, Italia mia.*

I wonder now if in my eagerness to embrace this brave new exile I let myself know how new it would be, this New World of Harry's America, of Harry's New York.

Part Three

THE GIRL OF THE GOLDEN WEST

1

Unlike my own family, very unlike my own, the only move Harry's had ever made (before the second generation's diaspora to Washington Heights, and the third generation's to Brooklyn's Park Slope) had been from one tenement building to another within the same West 35th Street block of New York's West Side, never leaving the parish boundaries of St. Michael's.

Sinking a taproot into your parish was fairly writ into Irish canon law in the days when Harry's world was making Harry. By which I understood why, even in all his own later wanderings, he could never really leave his home place, how the home place had, in the end, left him, devastated by the draconian law of Robert Moses–style urban planning, with its land-grabbing West Side tunnel entrances and heartlessly sweeping urban removals, animated by the principle that every tenement neighborhood was ipso facto a slum. The old Irish haunts had been reduced to a single pub on the west side of Tenth Avenue. St. Michael's had been left standing, a parish church almost without a parish, amid a wilderness of wandering access roads and warehouses.

I knew that his parents, more than a bit baffled by what had happened to them in their last age, had been relocated to Ravenswood on the Long Island City side of the East River. They lived now in a public housing project built cheek by jowl with the East River generating plant of Con Edison, under the shadow of the Queensboro Bridge. It seemed to help me to know such things about Harry and his family, as a shift for actually knowing them, for who knew when I would?

To know other things, too: family stories. Like the fact that Harry and his father were both Henrys, from a long and redoubtable Irish line of them. That Mary, Harry's mother, had called her husband "Hen-ner-y," in three syllables, while Harry she had called, well, Harry—thus keeping the two of them straight and perhaps opening a certain Oedipal seam in the bargain. Henry *père*, I was to learn later, had been born and raised in the country village of Timahoe, which at the turn of the century lay in the county just south of Dublin still known by the despised British name of Queen's, a name it was only too happy to shed for the Gaelic Laois (pronounced "Leesh") under the Republic. But he had not been there for the independence celebrations, having migrated in 1905 after doing perfunctory military duty in the Royal Irish Constabulary and escaping honorable and unscathed. His adventurous turn seems to have found its limit once he stepped off the boat onto the West Side of Manhattan, for he appears to have gone no farther.

I gathered from Harry's piecemeal bits of family intelligence that across the wide dividing sea, along with his powerful, huge frame and "fresh" complexion (as the de-mob officer wrote who signed his discharge papers), Henry had carried a certain begrudging pride of descent from a memorable line of mind-speaking Brownes, who in the generation before him had tended to be scholars of sorts. In fact, both his father's father (another Henry) and great-uncle John, both of them probably too ornery and Parnellian to be priests, had been schoolmasters, well known around Timahoe for a rather bullying style of pedagogy. Henry had left two older sisters in Ireland to carry on the family tradition of public truculence, preferring for himself, apparently, the attractive black sheepishness of becoming nothing more particular than an American.

Mary was his singular achievement, his pearl of price. You could tell this even from their wedding picture, which I eventually came to see. He is seated, tiny Mary beside him, the top of her head, standing, arriving just to the top of his sitting down. She looks perfectly made and irresistible, a porcelain Gibson-girl doll with soft piled hair and leg-o'-mutton sleeves, skin so translucent you want to touch it, and light, piercing eyes that are a promise of a tongue equally piercing.

She was older than Henry, Harry told me. She must have been proud of the edge of seniority it gave her between them for she always boasted of it. But she also refused ever to be exact about her age. She had come over a little ahead of him, passing through Ellis Island arm-in-arm with her sister Maggie. Both of them had quickly "gone into service," as they say, Mary to the patrician Squibb pharmaceutical family. And it was there, among the other things she learned, that she learned the gentleman-pleasing gesture of holding her master's jacket down in the back as he slipped into his overcoat, a trick she was later to teach her son the priest by mock-reverentially holding down his.

Soft as I am for a love story, I never learned when or where the two lovers had met, except that it was somewhere in the tough Five Points. No one ever doubted it was a love match. The equally smiling eyes on both of them in that 1915 photograph tell how happy they were to be wed. But while Mary was becoming a devoted wife, her sister Maggie was continuing ever the devout spinster, a permanent clinger-on, as I gathered from her still relentless and somewhat unforgiving presence in the family circle when I met her, and I wondered whether there'd been dicey times when the couple had put to each other the question of who exactly was married to whom.

There'd been four kids, six counting the lost twins, arriving in rapid succession and clearly without any godless notions of planning. Harry in 1919 was the third surviving, John and Kay before him, the twins having died in infancy. It was a staggering thought, this tiny woman giving birth to five children in four years. My own mother, a devoted Sangerite (with a well-powdered diaphragm in her bureau drawer), had spaced all of hers at least two years apart. It is hard to imagine the state of exhaustion and bewilderment of Harry's parents even then, when he was born, and baby Billy still to come.

Billy was to be the last of that first generation of American-born Brownes. Harry confessed to having found himself wildly jealous of his baby brother, on whom his mother, he thought, too absolutely doted. And so all through their growing up, Harry would tease Billy with Mammy's long string of saccharine pet-names for him—*Darlin' Billy, Billy-boy, Billy-o-fer-the-Mammy-o*—just to put him into a froth of embarrassment.

From the first day I'd known him, and over many the long Italian car ride or midnight conversation after, I'd picked up the scraps of this family narrative as Harry in his maddening way had tossed them to me, forgiving him the ill assortment because most family histories come, even to the families themselves, in a blotchy patchwork of group memories and fantasies and willful forgettings caught between the real and the fabulous. So too had mine. I loved the epic poetry of the dead twins, a kind of mythical Castor and Pollux to the two generations of twins that were to come in Kay's and her daughters' generations. But until that awesome day when I was first presented at a family gathering as "a friend of Father Harry's" to sister Kay and Uncle Frank and their three girls, plus brother Billy and Aunt Helen, and that even more awesome day still when I at last met Mammy and Maggie themselves *in propriae personae*, they had all seemed rather mythical to me.

These first encounters were too swollen, too charged with a certain self-mortifying angst, for me to have noticed the absence of Harry's older brother John. And yet I could tell he already had a special place in the family dreamwork, just from the way he flashed across Harry's accounts as a big-brother presence named Jackie on the rowdy streets of Hell's Kitchen, back when. "Jackie" was to become for Harry a metaphor of everything it meant to grow up poor and cold and ill-fed and, eventually, sick in a big Irish family in an old-law tenement in New York. Yet Jackie's was, quite literally, another story, a story that had lost its bearings, its frame of reference in anything like the present. It was to fall to the generation of Kay's children to rediscover him, the lost uncle, still living—living a kind of life—in a Rockland County hospital some forty miles outside of New York.

The twin girls, Catherine and Frances, were already nineteen—years older than when I'd first met them—when they learned about him, and about how he'd been put away after his mental breakdown at twenty or twenty-one. Grief-stricken, appalled at the secrecy that had so long erased him from their lives, Frances went to see him in all the earnest courage of her loyalty. She came back in a dumb, blubbering rage, knowing that what was done couldn't be undone.

Harry had a special hell to pay for this, even though at the time of Jackie's bursts of wild violence he'd been younger than his nieces were when they'd gone to see him in Rockland. Priest of the family, glorified son, glorified uncle—and yet to their minds he had actively conspired not just to bury his poor, mad brother alive but to bury the fact of burying him. They didn't put it so cruelly to his face, and Kay, with her own accounting to make, was perhaps too fair-minded to have stood for them doing it to hers. But they set their mouths in anger just the same, and made no secret of their right to hold him accountable.

But this was to come. In our first years together, I was still as ignorant of this story as the twins were. He had not told me, just as he had not told anyone in his priesthood life, because there was something in it that baffled and muted him, for which he could find no words. How could he explain to his nieces that their disappointment was in direct proportion to their wrong expectations of him, when he couldn't explain or admit it to himself? When all he knew was that somewhere in the obscure violence of his own soul there was this original sin, this fratricidal murder, bound up with his identity as a priest in a nexus so deep and secret it was unspeakable? Knowing nothing, I knew nothing of how it had transformed him at that vulnerable age, the difference it must have made as he passed through the vale of priest-making. I knew nothing of the need to forgive him, nothing of his need for self-forgiveness, nothing of this complex, other Harry—unknown and *other* even to himself—who had had no obvious part in our love, except to have had every part in it, to have been the third man always beside us.

Not to speak of it, not to analyze or strain to fathom it: that was his way. And by the time I finally heard him confess his anguish and understood as much of it as I dared to understand, it had become my way not to analyze or fathom it for him. I could only experience his sorrow as if it were my own and pass on the mystery of forgiveness and take him in my arms.

These are perhaps confusing layerings to tell, or try to tell. But life comes to us this way, or comes after us this way, whether in its moments of bewildering unconcealment or in the peculiar distortions of retrospect. And the truth of how I came to piece together these conflicting fragments, the story of how I came to know them, to know *him,* this man of shreds and patches, is part of my story too, and may have to be told in some of the conflicting fragments in which it was revealed.

What I find so strange now is that the Harry I knew then, as I looped back over the Atlantic just ahead of him, or as I slowly became inserted into his old life in New York, though he is a different Harry from the Harry of the morally tried boyhood I would come to know (a Harry less complex and conflicted, even in some sense less mortal), still seems even in this curious backlight to be just as true—and certainly no more mythical. Strange, that is, how *this* Harry's story, without John's broken mind in it, retains all the resistance and credibility of a simpler, more essential truth.

And so I see him still as I saw him then, as a kind of wild duck starting up out of the rough brake of the New York Irish Catholic working-class, a brother, yes—Jackie's little one, Billy's big one—a bit of an idol to Kay, apple of his mammy's eye, a queerish miracle mystery to his da. Surely knowing the expectations of priestly vocations in such families, this life flows with equal logic into the priesthood, effortlessly, almost weightlessly. The smart and winsome child, the boy who worked hard and grew ambitious not because ambition was his nature but because he could not live without praise, because he loved to be loved.

How could you not love him? From the time he was ten he was already amazing to look at and promising to be more so, a transfigured satyr with that wild dark hair dipping forward against the ivory-white forehead like a tooth. And yet besides this his wonderful mind and flypaper memory and that uncanny gift of fluent, goodly speech the nuns virtually worshipped at St. Michael's. And what a biddable, blessed cheerful little angel Sister Dorothea thought him! Of course, Mammy knew both versions. She had him nailed for a "house devil, street angel," so that he'd grown up knowing there were at least two sides to every myth, including his own.

Nuns' darling by the time he graduates St. Michael's, *this* Harry then becomes the familiar protégé of John Monaghan (was there a fatality in the name of John?), and Monaghan, his teacher at Cathedral College, becomes the kind of father a man can be only when he is not your father.

I never met Doc Monaghan. I never met Harry's father, whose reality was no less real for having come to me—forced by the circumstances of our relationship—exclusively by picture and report. And yet even before Henry died in 1960, it was as if there'd been a kind of death in the last few years of his life. Even then, Harry used to quote mother Mary's summary take on him as though it were a eulogy: "The old man, he always came home."

Pop Hennery was no Doc Monaghan, maybe, but he taught Harry a thing or two, and not just how to carry a growler of beer and ever after be angrily wary of the drunk-making pub. He had been a roustabout longshoreman on the docks in the twenties, tall and tough and commanding, known then for taking his drink and holding most of it. When the Depression struck, he found himself a dry-dock loading job at W. & J. Sloane's on Fifth Avenue. And as the family's needs kept growing he'd moonlighted the night watch at the Sheffield milk plant, where just before dawn he could pick up a bonus pint or two and bring them home to the kids.

I imagine his life sliding into a grind, his taking harder to drink and toiling drunkenly up the tenement stairs early mornings, whining bits of ballad on the arms of a pair of buddy longshoremen. And I can see Harry turning in his sleep, hearing his father's noisy clatter and trying to think only of the sweet gold cream atop the chinking milk bottles in his father's greatcoat pockets.

The old man, he always came home. Mary could say that much for him at least, and in hard times it was much to say. They saw that his eyes had begun to water and the veins darken along his nose, but he'd kept the fine aquiline features and the titanic stature that made her seem a twinkling little dwarf beside him. The hair went dashing white. He still had his glibbish brogue and fine if well-banked wit and smooth manners just this side of truckling, and all these finally landed him a job as a doorman at the Hotel Times Square—a presence smiling or menacing at the entrances and exits of the somewhat rich and famous. Until there came the unforgettable day when, as a proud old man who'd worked every day of his life, he was dismissed with a high-handed telegram that simply instructed him one morning not to report to work.

The telegram was dated February 28, 1951. He and Mary preserved it to the end, in the same box with his honorable discharge and his birth and marriage papers. There was a perverse old-country Browne pride in this. There was also a calculated new-country Browne sense of the dubious justice of present social arrangements. It was a reminder, in case anyone in the family might ever need one, of the mortifications to which one was always subject in the service of the Great. It had been a still-green memory in 1956, when Cardinal Spellman spoke the command that brought Harry back from Washington. The command that had changed all our lives.

•

I sank tentatively back into my own world, now side by side with Harry's. Ann was a benediction, her joy in seeing me healing for both of us. We held each other, her body almost too thin to hug, swaying and weeping, resolving in tears whatever there was left of my guilt at the pitiful sight of her and the hurt she must have harbored from my selfishly long absence.

I was furious when she told me that despite the obvious benefit of other treatments, the psycho-medical men were still hammering at "sexual repression," and touting the sex cure, as if the nineteenth-century notion of hysteria had never died. I phoned and lambasted her doctor, who lambasted me back, accusing me of trying to control her. It was true, I was an insufferable little expert, but I was right. "Is it better if *you* control her?" I said. I was intuitively right, on the authority of *her* body, which in a strange irony I understood, I think, better than my own.

What misery lurked in the ruling narratives of women's lives! How long it was to take for me—for us—for all of us—to understand them, to even begin to begin to understand them, let alone to disassemble their ancient and elaborately worked Chinese puzzles.

I remember once, as I was reading William Morris's lovely fantasy, *The Wood Beyond the World,* having a sudden, acute recollection of my father's admonitions in my college years against reading my own life by the light of fiction. We'd come to a fearful deadlock. Some inner salt had seemed to muddy his olive eyes and he'd launched into a coded speech on the perils to female virtue lurking in the undertexts of novels.

I had begun to study Italian at the time and to become absorbed in the culture of Italy just before and after the First World War. I thought the idiom of his pronouncements very Italian of a certain class and era, befitting a man born in the last year of the nineteenth century—someone in fact who'd scripted his own early life by the light of a fin de siècle D'Annunzio romance and now could imagine his own daughters swooning at the feet of some ardent but unprincipled lover and destroying the family honor forever. Naturally, I dismissed both his literary criticism and his criticism of life. *Middlemarch* and *Adam Bede* (I told myself then) had no such incendiary power over the flammable passions of young women.

We were both wrong, blindsided by our differences. How could he have known—how could *we* have known—that the danger to women was "clear and present" as well as "always, already," that it came less now from the pale fire of old novels than from the blue screen of the new American sky? That it had dropped on us like invisible fallout from Nevada test sites? That it had slipped into our media milk through the flickering altar he himself had stretched across the wall of our living room, and nuked our innards and burned off our last rags of tomboy-girl self-love? That the warriors of the Cold War (with his willing complicity) had captured the Rosie-the-Riveter woman-power of my mother and my deliciously remembered Spagnola aunts and turned it into a bitch-goddess? That on the rape of her fecund body they had fathered a new homefront of perfect Stepford vestals, keepers of the flame of consumer quietism, obedient to the law of small, daily, conjugal desire, trained (and if resistant, drugged) into becoming the vaginally receptive, vulnerable candy simulacra of desire embodied, every *I want* punished as the outlaw and insufferable witchcraft of female ambition?

Without the helps, in due time, of the women who would tell us this, this and more, what lever was there for wrenching this all-about-Eve world out of orbit, and from what position of sufficient distance? And yet Ann and I were both trying to do this, somehow, to resist, to *scream* resistance, to speak out of the authority of our bodies, out of the authority of our queer, contradictory, incoherent choices.

Wasn't it logical to do it together? But we were not logical.

No, not together, better not together.

My God, what an efficient little liar my love had already made me, the kind that wastes no attention on inconsistencies. Everywhere I thought: *This,* now, surely, *this* is the moment to tell her about Harry. But the telling stuck in my throat. I didn't know—I don't know now—if it was for his sake or hers or my own.

When Harry arrived from Ireland ten days after me, he immediately phoned me at home. His words were guarded, but his voice as delicious and intoxicating with fresh brogue as a pour of Bailey's Cream.

"I'm sure you want to hear about the slaverin' deference of the Irish to their priests," he warned. It didn't matter, I told him, I could have sat at the open line in utter lunatic silence, though my heart rushed thinking of my mother on the other side of the kitchen wall listening to me laugh like a woman in love.

A dark and stormy night, he tells me, the depths of County Cork, himself and Robert on the road without their collars. It is pissin' rain. They find a lady publican glad to offer them a whiskey but caught short of beds for the overnight. She sends Robert to a cousin's house a half-mile away and puts Harry up in a cot alongside one of their regulars, snoring off the drink.

"In the morning the poor dear discovers we're the holy anointed. '*O, Faaather!*'' she wails to me, crossing herself all the while. '*Can* you *forgiiiive* me havin' you sleepin' wid *sich* a one—and *him in the better bed?*'"

I am hunched over the phone suppressing a convulsive laugh as he goes on: "I have pictures of me and Robert kissing the Blarney Stone to show you." And I ask why I need any pictures if I have a thousand words? But my chest suddenly hurts when he says, "I bet I won't know what to say when I see you."

"You have to meet Ann," I had said to him. There was no need to sell her on the idea. Ever since Robert Wilde's visits last spring, any priest-friend of mine had become a priest-friend of hers. We went together to see Harry in his residence at the Cathedral College Faculty House, Riverside Drive and West 108th Street, as elegantly sacerdotal a place as ever inscribed an invisible *Fear Women* over the door. He seemed to explode into my sight, dancing that lightfoot way of his down the curved staircase like a memory of dancing, and for a dizzying moment I could barely stammer introductions, my heart pounding just to see him. But also to see him so different, so forbidding, so forbidden again, so untouchable.

He called her "Annie." She loved him instantly. Perhaps in her special emotional acuteness and need she could feel something powerful between us and wanted to be inside of its safety. She reached him, too, only partly for my sake—softened something in him that was typically a little impatient with illness. I think her strangely disarming patch-together of fragility and grit made a claim on his spirit.

And so it happened that with a certain instinctive reluctance on his side, and a certain mutual dread of the Italian family mystique he understood only too well, Harry became Father Browne again, and Father Browne became a "friend." Bit by bit he slipped into the good family graces. At last my father allowed him to be invited home with us to dinner. And so the very serpent in the garden of his daughter's virginity supped at my father's table.

Harry was astonishingly easy and unceremonious that night, serpentine from beginning to end, never letting on that he felt the iced scrutiny behind my father's velveteen hospitality no matter how acutely he did. He ventured his bumbling Italian so that Mario might correct it and dodged reminiscences of Italy to tell amusing stories about his trip to Ireland. Then he opened the rich gold seam of New York memories, East Side and West Side, our side and his side, until my mother had tears in her eyes from laughing that big, singing, pleading laugh of hers.

"A piece of bread," she said to me softly in the kitchen as we cleared, her noblest Sicilian compliment. But my father didn't know what to do with that unerring alarm of his about priests, which already smelled something rank between Harry and me, and was refusing to surrender to this conspiracy of infatuated women. Inwardly, darkly, I could feel my will growing against his like a fist, and I took the wall.

But even I could see, when I found some mental distance, that a year had changed him. He had felt Ann's suffering like any parent, as something written remorselessly on his own body. But he had also felt it selfishly too, as a wordless reproach to his fatherhood, a theory her psychiatrists and doctors had not discouraged, no matter how it stung him. For the past few years he had watched in morose bitterness as my mother had picked up the shattered dream of her girlhood and struck out for a new life as a teacher. It was poignant how her preternatural innocence could protect her from duplicity. In the ruse of convincing him that there was nothing self-realizing in this for her, just what had to be done out of dire necessity, she had convinced herself too. Now, he had finally seen it as a good thing—good enough for him—and had decided to go back to school for *his* degree.

There was male ego in this decision, of course, a determination not to be outdone. But the unforeseen double effect was that this venerable patriarch of fifty-nine had abruptly morphed into a lowly college student, at the feet, and in some sense at the mercy, of professors who might have been his children. You could sense that hairline fracture in the old tyrannical self-certainty we used to tremble under at the dinner table.

And then, how he wanted me to love him, as warrant of his old possession, to come back heavy-laden from Italy with the gift of my grateful love. In this I softened to him a little—out of the law of love. But it wasn't enough, it could never be, never satisfy the hunger he had to be adored as we had once adored him, and now, as the day of the superior young dawned, the hunger he had for his lost significance.

Ann was already back at school, allowed to share an apartment at Columbia with several other women, as I had in my first graduate year. Now, when I said I would be moving out too, he tried to shake the old thunder. I had become his last stand. "You were perfect when you were seventeen," he claimed, absurdly—this was one day in the midst of a tiresome quarrel about my freedom. I knew precisely, with a kind of witchlike intuition, the day he was remembering: I *was* seventeen, and he had asked me to read to him from "Tintern Abbey," and something—what was it? some similar incestuous wish for innocence? some near-erotic desire for "what I was once," as if it could be perpetuated forever?—had passed briefly between us. I wondered now: Could there really have been a time when to please my father I would gladly have become "a dwelling place for all sweet sounds and harmonies"? And now, was there anything I could want to be that wouldn't hurt him?

"Look at your mother," he demanded, meaning as a model of a woman fulfilled. I didn't dare laugh, though I thought he must be desperate. "My life begins where hers leaves off," I said arrogantly, and his stung face mirrored my arrogance to me as he silently watched me climb the stairs to my room.

I learned to drive. He didn't try to stop me. I thought he didn't know how anymore, on what authority. When I finally found an apartment I could afford on the salary of my new job at Olivetti New York, he actually offered me the car to move. My last night home he even offered his help to drive me down with my few belongings. I could tell he was bracing himself to see where I'd be living, whether outer darkness could be a real place.

The apartment was on West 24th Street in Chelsea. My mother came too. We drove down and entered the building with a funeral solemnity. A nip-waisted, middle-aged woman left her ground-floor apartment with two leashed terriers just as we crossed the downstairs lobby with our shopping bags. I could sense my father's body-alert. The woman, rather voguishly dressed for her overweight, had on a felt hat with a long, rakish orange feather. Doggie paws strained and scratched and her heels clicked across the tile as she passed us without a glance, trailing a scent of patchouli, and it was as if before his eyes his wayward daughter had been transformed into a plump and superannuated whore.

He waited till we were inside the apartment, and then, in one final, desperate outburst of repressed dementia, he went wild. I thought I had seen rages. That night awoke primal memories. In savage, bellowing fury he hurled cartons of books across the floor, sent shopping bags full of kitchen things crashing against the cabinets. And then he struck me so hard across the face that I reared back into the wall. My mother shrieked, pleading for him to stop, but he didn't stop until he was done, until he was exhausted, until he was victorious, until he was defeated, until he was weeping.

•

The Greek super seemed to understand father-daughter tragedies and returned my deposit and crumpled the lease. But the taste of my own blood in my mouth had hardened my heart.

When I refused to go home, my old school chum Judy and her mother, Muriel, put me up temporarily in their rambling flat on East 81st Street. "Here comes Fluffy Mary the Immaculate again," Judy said with a sardonic humor I found surprisingly welcome. I appealed to my godmother Zi' Carmelina for further aid and comfort, going to see her on nearby East 78th Street, where I had mythically "lived" in high school. She too found something comic in all this—my father, she said, was like some buffoon old man in the *commedie*: always imagining naughty things, which was just the way to make them happen. *"Baci e pizzicchi non fanno buchí,"* she said— "kisses and pinches don't make holes." And she passed on this time-honored scrap of Neapolitan wisdom with a cackle that shook her great shelf of bosom, as if she were remembering some test case of her own girlhood.

She tried to intercede with her brother, told him frankly that he was wrong, that he should encourage my independence. He grew becalmed and penitent. I grew becalmed and more impenitent than ever.

In any case, I mused heretically that God must be on my side, since I found another place almost as soon as I reopened the *New York Times*. There were four rather steep flights up, but it had two rooms and a small kitchen, and was in the park block on West 88th Street with four huge windows facing south. Its separate bedroom even had a door, as the apartment on 24th Street hadn't. I gathered up my things, kissed Judy and Muriel good-bye, and moved in the first week of December. "You extraordinary baggage," drawled Muriel, plummily. "Keep in touch."

Harry had been living at the Faculty House since September, worrying hints in the air of a forthcoming assignment to a parish. It might be anywhere in the city. I remembered that he had told me of spending his summers before Italy at St. Elizabeth's in the Bronx. Sadly far away.

My phone was installed the week before Christmas. Harry's inaugurating first phone call opened briskly enough: *"Arise, my love!"*

It was still the darkest dawn of the longest night of the year. I lay there in bed letting the chocolate of his voice flood silken brown color behind my eyes. "You're going to have to be awake to believe this," he said.

I didn't believe it.

So he told me again. St. Gregory. Gregory the Great. West 90th Street and Amsterdam Avenue. Two and a half blocks away.

2

E ven leaving me out of it, the sheer synchronicity of dropping Harry Browne down on West 90th Street in the winter of 1958 is amazing. For you could have counted the time in weeks since the city had announced a massive new redevelopment project for the West Side, known on the books as the West Side Urban Renewal Area, or WSURA, and on the streets simply as the Plan. A vast and utopian scheme, it was inspired by two identifying features of "urban renewal" planning at the time: first, that much of the "Area" in question was a slum and, second, that there was no slum urban planning couldn't fix.

The Plan would, in the end, do what it set out to do, and change the face of a major part of New York; but it may be no exaggeration to say that the reaction to it would also transform the way cities were re-visioned in the United States for the rest of the twentieth century. And for us, Harry and me, it became the spatial equivalent of an apocalypse. Everything that happened to us afterward bore its profound and indelible mark.

Strange that even Francis Cardinal Spellman, by most accounts as canny a reader of signs of the times as ever wore beretta, had missed this one. There was no possibility of his having been guided in his choice of Harry's parish assignment by any immediate concern for the future of the neighborhood. The last thing he would have wanted was to waste his prize diocesan historical scholar on the flapdoodle of local politics. The boxy pseudo-Renaissance palace of St. Gregory the Great, with its stacked church and school and rectory and its quiet and solitary penthouse on the top floor, was clearly intended to be another Father Browne exile. Only this time, directly under the chancery's vigilant eye—just the place for a wayward genius to complete that long-awaited official biography of Archbishop John Hughes, first prelate of the first Archdiocese of New York. No excuses this time, no complaints about the long commute. Cathedral College, where Harry taught his "first-year civics," was a five-minute walk away.

I could imagine Harry's first protocol visit to the chief when he got back. The cardinal would ask him about Italy, working his way to the delicate subject of the Church's treatment of Italian immigrants. Harry would enthuse about the wonderful source material in the Vatican archives. The cardinal would say, "Nothing . . . embarrassing, I hope?" and Harry would laugh, a bit wryly, recalling what he had once dug up about Hughes. "Nothing we wouldn't be willing to admit."

There would be that benign smile, a twinkle of the small, round, gold-rimmed glasses. Spellman would certainly want Harry to know he trusted his judgment. "Time Italians got their justice, *non è vero?*" he'd say, as if, for him, history was a little like Queen for a Day. And then His Eminence would press the balls of his fingertips together into a prayerful little tent, purse his lips. "And publication, Harry? I know you academics always find the subject a bit touchy—"

"Not at all, Your Eminence. You know me. I already have at least four articles ready to go—if I don't get burned out teaching first-year—"

"And the Hughes, Harry? When will we see the Hughes?"

For a while there was a kind of chancery truce. Harry sketched out his articles, at first conscious of the Plan only as a distant rumble of thunder. Up the spiral staircase in his two-room eyrie on the roof, five stories above the street, he mounted a vast web of interlocking steel bookcases and lined the walls and the hallway with the books he hadn't unpacked since he'd left Catholic University. Then he opened his notes from the Vatican and went to work, turning out four scholarly essays in no time, without sweat, without apparent effort, without seeming to need feedback or reassurance from anyone, least of all from me. His urgency for print appeared so normal it was hardly noticed that he didn't touch the Hughes.

I looked on enviously, torn between pursuing some kind of career that would make adventurous use of my now-fluent Italian, or fulfilling my parents' dream for me and completing the master's degree that would bring me closer to college or university teaching. I discussed these choices with Ann, but she was no one to be looking to for help, seeming somehow to be waiting on *my* guidance, and, absent that, to be headed down what seemed to me the rabbit hole of classical archeology. I took a steno course in the evenings. I set aside my thesis, that heady nineteenth-century influence study of Arnold and the French philosopher-critic Ernest Renan, and dropped my already brokenly explored Risorgimento theme from Italy. My poems, my stories—all my other writing—I stuffed dolefully away in boxes, too thin-skinned to bear more than a sting or two of rejection. Harry had a theory that you never took an instant to suffer—you just checked the manuscript for dogears and put it in a clean envelope and shot it out again. Good advice to have given me then, and maybe I would have taken it, but even he was not ready to give me advice. It implied too much, something beyond what was already too much—to have been in some sense the cause of the tearing sacrifice of my family self.

I absorbed the beneficence of his nearness without any hotness for future certainties. He would come to my apartment for supper, or after, and slip into my narrow bed with me for a few comforting hours. We might sink into sleep, and then in the dead of night start awake and find ourselves both on the lip of tears, he as full of self-recrimination as I was full of fear. Again and again in my predawn nightmares my father would throw open the door and discover us in each other's arms. I never knew whether the sun might not rise on two miserable, craven souls caught *in flagrante*.

But the sun did rise, every day, on whatever it was we had, or did.

Early in the new year, armed with the secretarial skills that seemed infinitely more saleable than any academic or artistic accomplishments, I let myself be lured away from my glamourous life in the secretarial pool of Olivetti's accounting department by a young Euro-playboy named Filippo Theodoli, who supervised the Olivetti and Alitalia accounts at a fancy ad agency on Madison Avenue. Theodoli loved my Italian, my French, and my looks. He promised me the moon. He gave me a job that would touch the creative heights, I discovered, of placing four-by-four ads in *Gourmet* for the Barbizon Plaza Hotel.

Harry, meanwhile, was enjoying his own glamourous berth as assistant to St. Gregory's patrician pastor, Monsignor Joseph Flanagan. Flanagan one day proposed he interest himself in something he typically cast in question form as "this urban renewals group?" as if it were a mere nuisance, sparing himself a meeting and unwittingly inching Harry closer to the great new issue on the street.

Each private pastoral visit to me in *my* little fifth-floor eyrie at 45 West 88th posed its own burning issue: should he remove the Roman collar before I buzzed him in downstairs? on the second-floor landing? or all the way at the top as I let him into the apartment? But then, as the door closed behind him, he became Harry, guileless and winsome as an archangel, with that wind still blowing through him like an electric storm from some upper air, as if he'd just landed on the roof and actually stepped down to my door.

He'd tell me what he knew, that the powers were going to shuffle everybody around out there over an area of twenty square city blocks, from 86th to 96th and Central Park West to Amsterdam Avenue. They were going to tear a lot of stuff down, gussy up the side streets, leave nice brownstones like the one I lived in pretty much alone, and do a whole new luxury number on Columbus Avenue. And they wanted to "involve" people, he said. Very enlightened.

Pasta and Gallo red and Harry at my table, giving me lessons in first-year civics, giving me lessons in another meaning of love.

"Do you know what is a 'leading citizens' group'?" he'd ask. "It's two rabbis, two ministers, a Catholic priest, and the principal—excuse me, the *headmaster*—of the Walden School." Having tossed off this piece of flotsam cynicism, he would propose we read the signs of the times by the ever-ready light of the Catholic Worker: "What'll happen to the people who are gonna be booted?"

He told me that in some weird sense, Flanagan had been right to think of the committee he'd sent him off to as just another public relations gig. But Flanagan couldn't have cared less, and Harry cared. Cared that whatever the do-good intentions of the inviting professionals, the parish was being conned into little more than an appearance of public support so that the city could look progressive and the developers get on with the *real* agenda, which in New York was real *estate,* which was making the West Side Urban Renewal Area profitable again for themselves. And what they needed most of all was the potential market frenzy of a Plan that looked as if it were moving down the Upper West Side like a melting glacier.

Public involvement—public support—a mere codicil in the so-called democratic process. Could it ever make a wedge big enough to stop a glacier?

The single-frame flash of new names across our conversations became almost as maddening as when I'd first known him. Foley, Coffey, Ratensky, Rafferty, Mollen, Davies. I obeyed Browne's Law, did not ask "*Who?*" and waited for the footnotes to catch up with the text.

•

First came Foley. Jack Foley. The city's official WSURA organizer, an Irish Midwesterner, recycled career Navy man, hired from out of town by the Housing and Redevelopment office to organize the leading citizens. His job had been to pull together the respectable folks, the ones with established constituencies and real estate to protect, and make the process "look good and go smooth." I think he really thought he wanted to do that.

And yet you might say that Foley cut the wedge.

In fact, by the time Harry and I first talked about it, Foley had, all unbeknownst, been working on cutting it for several months. He had already come up with the idea of advising the leading citizens' group, the Park-Hudson Citizens Committee, to hire another organizer, whose charge it would be to organize a few not-so-leading "affected citizens." For purposes of procedure he proposed that these would form an advisory subcommittee. Park-Hudson, the parent, would then process their advice, take or leave it, and pass their recommendations on to Housing and Redevelopment. H and R would in turn pass theirs up to the City's reviewing council, the Board of Estimate, and democratic due process would be served.

Right?

Coffey was Mike Coffey. Michael J., the organizer Foley hired. Another Irishman, social worker, a next-generation Molly Maguire from the anthracite fields of eastern Pennsylvania, dreamer, country boy who hated suits, artist at heart, atheist, anti-clerical from his mother's milk. He'd talk to anybody in the way of work, which explains the perverse instinct that possessed him to talk to Father Flanagan in that same early winter of 1958/59.

He thought Flanagan impossible, holed up in his mazy rectory fourth floor above the church, with no feeling at all for his parish, clinging for dear life to the illusion of ecclesiastical hauteur embodied in the last pastor's fine furnishings and walls full of high art. Above the church, above the school, above it all. An obvious skinflint, too—he could see that even before Harry gave him that crack-up one-liner about Flanagan keeping the rectory heating bills down with a vigil light in front of the thermostat. The place was freezing.

He and Harry loved to talk about it afterward, about how chance the convergence of things had been. Even I got to know Mike's tough-guy, bright-eyed mug pretty well in succeeding months, and to know why he had to be forgiven for the long strategizing nights that began to be Harry's alternative to nights with me. The irony was that Mike had given up on St. Gregory's just before Harry got there, and moved on to Father Pat Rafferty, the pastor of Holy Name at West 96th and Amsterdam. Rafferty, a well-meaning sort, had offered him a few leads, but just didn't see himself as a voice of the people. It was on one of Coffey's drop-in visits, still trying to light his fire, that Rafferty mentioned the new assistant over at St. Gregory's, a guy named Browne with a reputation as a pretty good talker.

As he made his way back to St. Gregory's that night, figuratively to carve the wedge, Coffey could not really have told you who it was more needed whom.

•

But that was how St. Gregory's school auditorium became the site for the first major public hearing on the Plan. It was a big night. Sam Ratensky, then head of Housing and Redevelopment, couldn't—or didn't—make it, but Milton Mollen, his next in command (later to become central to the developing scenario), did. Jack Foley and Mike Coffey were there, and a couple of planning technicians whom they must have tagged as having a passing acquaintance with people-ese. I thought, as I edged into a folding chair, that they looked pretty confident for people who had no right to.

Of course they had the high ground, so to speak, and the proscenium between them and the bleachers. They had their easels and pretty pictures, and their brochures with color-wash drawings of well-shaded, traffic-free side streets and Columbus's new high-rise boulevard with little stick people going in and out of glistening shops.

I was naturally beginning to see things as Harry did, and beginning to be able to throw "poor-people removal" rabble-rousingly back in the faces of the predatory salesmen of "revitalization"—in my mind, at least. I now knew all about the devastation of Lincoln Center, the neighborhood just to the south of us, where tens of thousands of poor people, most of them Catholics, had been displaced, sent to the outer boroughs, as the value of the real estate they were living on shot up. By any other name, this had been the real West Side story, not the Leonard Bernstein version just readying for its famous Broadway run, a liberal heart-wringing fantasy that was to lift the original permanently out of history and market its amazing and disappeared ethnocultural stew as a timeless Romeo and Juliet romance.

Of course I was still trailing a few clouds of Westchester and mollycoddle and the Italian Fulbright thing myself, a bit too obviously educated by the Barnard crème de la crème and finished by the European Grand Tour, but I was all the same jump-restarting my Music & Art political apprenticeship and picking up my new New York political literacy from things like Stanley Aronowitz's first SANE antinuclear meetings plus a canny routine reading of the *New York Times*. In this learning emergency, I was also frequently suspending Browne's Law. But there were lots of people at that public meeting even less in the know than I was, seeing for the first time the astonishingly radical scope of the Plan and hearing the class breakdown of the overhauled neighborhood in the code language of whatever number of units at whatever amount of rent. You didn't have to be Milton Mollen to see that four hundred new low-rent apartments out of a project of nine thousand was going to mean a radical change in the character and complexion of the West Side.

And yet no one dared harbor any illusions about a popular groundswell of protest out of this new urban mix of Irish and black and Hispanic and dirt-poor, of Catholics maybe too scared or tired to fight any more and hugging their old parish a little sourly, begrudging the upstart Puerto Rican newcomers whose lot they were thrown in with. And these all indigestibly tossed together with the old Jewish garment union organizers and Holocaust survivors and children of Holocaust survivors, still jostling with the old Irish regulars in the wake of McCarthy for control of the local Democratic Club. Maybe they had clung to the familiar turf, but their kids had gone to Teaneck and Great Neck. Now which side were they on?

The excitement was breathable as people scraped to their seats at 7:30. Flanagan, in his cassock and pink cummerbund, hair freshly hennaed for the occasion, fluttered around the edges of the noisy room like an aging altar queen. Harry was unselfconsciously working the crowd, shoving the gunmetal folding chairs aside to get at people he knew. He looked cool, brilliantly in his element, yet he still had that way that tore my heart of pushing urgently on his collar now and then, and swiping his hooked index finger along the inside as if it were finally getting to him.

Once or twice he caught my eye and smiled. Mostly he steered his glance away. I tried to do the same, straining to get the knack of this public thing—whatever it was. I was learning to cultivate my own distance, so that I could bear the pain of Father Browne's indifference, and he was learning to cultivate the indifference I had to bear. In front of me, in a state of rapt admiration, sat four teaching nuns, still dressed in the thick fluttering habits the Vatican was destined within a few years to whisk away.

March 1959. By what mysterious alchemy the time was about to become something it wasn't yet, I don't pretend to know. All we knew was the thrill of a big futuristic scheme, even if it wasn't pure or courageous enough to be called visionary. All we had was a stubborn, insubordinate resistance, equally thrilling, a body language that said, "Don't tell *us* how to read a glossy urban renewal prospectus." Plus certain comfortable meeting garments that I later came to know as the dress code of the Upper Left Side.

It was a toss-up, that night, who in the end gave the city more fair warning of the trouble it was in for—the faithful remnants of the Lincoln Brigade, who acidly inquired what Foley could possibly mean by "humane relocation," or the old ramrod-straight Irish ladies in their dusty rose head scarves, who warned that the city would be "takin' their dead bodies to Brooklyn before they could get 'em alive out to Queens." After that night, to a certain dumb astonishment among the experts, the "affected citizens" shaped themselves into a somewhat loose and baggy coalition, ponderously christened the Provisional Council of Independent Organizations. Housing and Redevelopment head Sam Ratensky, the story goes, called in Foley to complain and Foley turned around and called in Coffey.

"I did what you told me," Mike explained. "Was I supposed to tell the affected citizens not to get too affected?"

In the next rushing weeks of awakening springtime, I began to take the feel of city life again for the first time since my East Harlem childhood, as I never really had while I was commuting to high school and college. I struggled to fit my own history into the history of the city I had begun to read as a *planned,* a made—even a sculpted—environment. I went to see my old dentist, still plying his trade on Third Avenue. How many times had I come and gone from there without seeing, or wanting to see?

East 114th Street had been "slum cleared" into nonexistence. I could vaguely remember the family discussions among the Spagnolas still living there when the offensive came through, about what a paltry, insulting sum the city, with its surly powers of eminent domain, was offering them to get out. Of course number 230 was gone, all of them were gone, all the serried five-story brick tenements that had been passed through three generations of Italian families. No more ornate copper cornices jutting out like dark, censorious brows over window eyes, no more beveled glass doors and brass doorknobs that Uncle Tony had used to polish as if under military orders, no more railings along the brownstone stoops molded into rigid bouquets, framing the step-down "airways" with their summertime boxes of geraniums we didn't dare to pluck.

The street itself was gone—the one that I'd used to look out over from the front window on the fifth floor, the one that the brass band played through on feast days, that rang with the sound of block parties after V-J Day—paved over and smoothed out into a windy prairie of concrete, from which the great brick flat-blocks of the new public housing projects rose like silos.

Gone Our Lady Queen of Angels, gone the Spagnolas and Rizzos and Russos, scattered like milkweed across the Bronx and Queens and Westchester and Bergen and Rockland Counties, pretending to put down new roots but sending out only seeds, the old ones coming together for weddings and funerals, *basta*. It was almost too easy to predict even then, as I passed these old haunts of my mother's Sicilian family, that I wouldn't see most of my aunts and cousins again until somebody died—my darling Aunt Mildred first, and then the beautiful Concetta renamed Mary, Uncle Joey's wife and eternal sweetheart, carried off too young, both of them—and that I wouldn't see relatives again until Joey himself died, and then almost never again after. Uncle Joey's post-relocation odyssey had taken them to Greenwood Lake, then Warwick, New York, and finally Perth Amboy, New Jersey. Once Mary was gone, home meant less and less to him—a place to strike a good real estate deal on, that was all. Uncle Joey died in the South Bronx because his own house in Perth Amboy was too far away to die in. They took his cancer-riddled body to St. Raymond's cemetery—the one family spot the city hadn't renewed—from a funeral home near his daughter's house off the new Bruckner Expressway.

So many places given, so many taken away. New Rochelle, Tucson, East Harlem, Padua—perhaps I had grown a footpad for a foot and couldn't put roots down any more. It suddenly seemed important not to lose this place before I could begin to know what it meant to be home.

I made gestures of commitment toward the space I lived in—a plant or two, a breakfront cabinet and kitchen table and chairs my mother had no trouble parting with, a few odd pieces picked up in the used furniture shops on Amsterdam. To recreate a semblance of my Padovano paradise I used the cabinet as a room divider for a little dining alcove. The kitchen was as small as the one at the Tower in Padua, but not so pretty. Sink, stove, refrigerator, and cabinets were all contained in one six-foot-long white-enameled wall unit. Overhead, up a long shaft, was a domed skylight. It made a bright well of light out of this otherwise dingy space, and you tended to forget the soot it collected until a gob dropped into the soup. But at night, even if you couldn't see the stars, there was a bit of poetry in being reminded by the glass ceiling that they were there.

The bathroom had a skylight, too, lending it an incandescent glow even by day, an effect I enhanced by painting the walls the color of soft old brick and hanging a shower curtain with a riot of bursting roses all over it, so that I could do Edith Piaf, if I felt like it, to my own pink image in the mirror in the mornings.

And many were the nights *en rose* when Harry faced that mirror, too, not waiting for the day-glow of sunup lest he be spotted. He had community visibility now, and while 88th Street off the park was pretty transient and anonymous and middle class and, yes, non-Catholic in every one of these social categories, and while people might not necessarily find it surprising to see a priest out on the street at odd hours, he chose to be careful—if you could call it careful to do the equivalent of jumping off a major bridge with water wings.

Careful or not, there were some of the loveliest Saturdays, when he'd come early and we'd push our luck and just love-nest all day. About midnight he'd slip groggily out, maybe turn east toward the park and around the block past the Walden School, swing alongside the uppity façades of Central Park West for two blocks and around again up 90th to Columbus Avenue, and then stride past the graveyard-shift stoop-sitters on the Columbus-to-Amsterdam tenement block to the church. The old elevator had a tendency to rattle alarmingly as it slid up to the rectory. But Flanagan slept heavily and didn't really ask questions—or asked so many that you couldn't tell them apart and didn't have to. And in any case, Harry, light-footed, perhaps a bit too lighthearted, would trip up the spiral staircase to the penthouse on tiptoe.

Life went on, replete with daily bread and daily wine, a triumph of dailiness over anxiety and indecision. This much I knew: the glitz of advertising was for me a life sentence to the typing pool, punctuated at the approximate rate of once a week by some sleazy ad space salesman's college try at passionless seduction. Full of good if unfocused creative energies, I picked up my master's essay again with one hand, and with the other, in the form of elaborate notes in a small black loose-leaf binder, began a novel about my mother's family in East Harlem. I opened a job file at Columbia and began to send around inquiries for a teaching appointment.

On the other side of my street lived a number of striving actors and singers and musicians—as you could easily tell the moment the warm weather came and the windows went up—some of them stripping the plaster off their brick walls and redesigning their living rooms around pole lamps. Guided by an instinctive desire for privacy, I leaned toward the unsophisticated decorating zone of drawstring drapes. The super lent me a ladder for hanging them, and Harry, shirt-sleeved and risqué in my daytime window, helped me mount the track. But gorgeous weather made dreary work of sewing twenty yards of fabric, and the ladder stood by the window for more than a week.

Then Harry's friend Father Hartke brought a touring Catholic University production of *Oedipus Rex* to town, and gave him tickets enough for Ann to go with the two of us. It was a lovely, sweet, and mild night—Ascension Thursday, I remember; such little liturgical landmarks mattered now—the kind of night when, walking along the park under the trees with people you love, you can't remember why you have not lived every moment of your life in the city. Ann, you could tell, adored Harry, too. The truth still seemed too much of a burden to ask her to share, but I know she would have forgiven us anything that night.

The first thing I noticed when I got back to my room at midnight was the strange, hard brightness of the lights, all of them on, then the ladder by the window, gone. And then I saw the alien, staring, indifferent, heart-sickening disorder.

It was easy to tell what I had lost. Italy, all of it. Every piece of jewelry except the ring I had on. A new pair of hand-cobbled red pumps I had been saving to wear to some wonderful event. My camera. My Olivetti portable, succedaneum of my inner life. Whoever had done this had simply lifted out the page I was typing and carried away the typewriter. The clock radio. A ripe avocado in my fruit basket.

I found the ladder in the bathroom. The burglar had pried off the skylight dome and dropped himself down from the roof, leaving two big dirty footprints on the terra-cotta wall. Leaving, he'd just moved the ladder under the open hole and gone up the same way he'd come down, my stuff apparently wrapped in the shower curtain. I could picture him going out over the roof, like a Santa Claus with roses.

"Drugs," said the cops. "They're all over. Good thing you weren't home."

The Wilsons, my down-home Texan neighbors across the landing, had been. Ed had told me when I moved in that with a name like mine he was sure I'd be a belly dancer. Now he seemed to enjoy repeating idiotically that he'd heard a lot of commotion, sure, but (as he explained to the detective—there were apparently some things Ed *didn't* miss), he thought Flav was just having a helluva fight with her boyfriend.

Directly below me lived an actor who went by the stage name of Brother Theodore, a Holocaust survivor who had turned the tortured agony of his real life into a bloodcurdlingly funny off-Broadway monologue. He'd seen nothing, of course, having been out doing his gig in the Village when the burglar struck. Many a dark and stormy night his garbled rehearsals had come through my floorboards. I'd thought it amazing what in New York could pass for a stand-up comic. But in spite of the wild hair and fierce, Dracula eyes, he was a gentle man, and when he invited me to dinner, and out of sheer terror I refused, he invited me to his show instead. Harry shared the barrage of paranoid and haunting dementia with me, slumped down in his seat, wearing a neck scarf disguise.

Thus was I ritually initiated into the West Side "crime mentality," a cynical source of bonding among people in all walks of life—some who you would not have thought had anything to lose, others who had lots—who offered the free exchange of cautionary fables at dinner parties. I had never before been victim of a theft. I began to see the compelling logic of the monastery and to wonder if an altogether possessionless life, if it were possible, mightn't be the more livable. Still, I was relieved that the building owner seemed concerned enough for my safety to bolt a heavy steel cage down under the dome of each of my two skylights.

The experience, in the end, seemed to put a bridge over troubled family waters. My parents came down from New Rochelle, my father scowling, my mother looking ashen-faced and terrified and staring up at the footprints under the skylight. I don't think they went away satisfied that I wasn't about to be raped or murdered in my bed, but they came back the following week and made me birthday presents of a phonograph and an Osterizer, two more wonderfully stealable things.

But now it was *my* West Side, too; I had paid my dues. And I joined in its special wakefulness. The struggle was in the air. I took out my paints and drawing crayons and went up and down the blocks, demanding that the local kids sit for me, staring every surviving gargoyle on every brownstone façade into permanency, lest it be carried forever down the flood of renewal.

My own future seemed also to be expectantly approaching. I plowed into the revisions on my thesis, conscious now that it was my only ticket out of the world Theodoli was only too happy to leave me stuck in, picking up his slack as he raced off to Monza. Working in the Butler Library stacks one night I ran into Robert Crozier, an old graduate seminar classmate, still plugging away at his monograph on Thomas Hardy.

Bob had been John's best friend in that primordial year before Italy, and now we suddenly, wordlessly realized there was no John to connect or divide us, though I couldn't say, of course, what still did. How could anyone have been more married than I was to Harry? And yet a tenderhearted man, a certain touch, and that damned alarm would go off, screaming at me to get out now before it was too late. And it was as though all Harry's magnetism abruptly polarized, and I was seized instead by a dizzying fear of him—someone to flee—and I would as abruptly respond to the urge for flight as if he were a fire, a plague, a crime.

No one could have been more tenderhearted than Bob. Only when I invited him up to see my apartment, I had forgotten about the nude drawings I'd done of Harry the Saturday before, on impulse, as we'd been lolling around naked in a blazing heat wave, and had taped along the full length of the wall behind my work table.

Bob remained characteristically cool. "Anybody you know?"

I stammered, offered the distracting glass of iced tea. The thought struck me that he might have seen Harry and me together around Columbia, visiting Ann. I was convinced there was no mistaking that prizefighter body. Bob was magnificent. "Quite well hung," he remarked on the way out.

And then something happened that offered to change everything without my having to stir an atomy of heart or will: my activated career placement file turned up a job offer from the Woman's College of Greensboro, North Carolina.

I considered turning it down. I was a creature of politics now, as well as of love. It was a dispiriting time to have to leave New York, for both reasons. On the political side, reform was in the air. The summer pulsed with it. Carmine DeSapio, titular czar of New York's powerful Democrats, had just become the bogeyman, the reason-for-being of the whole Democratic Reform movement. It mattered only at some undigested level of my nascent political consciousness that he was Italian. For now, he was a cartoon enemy, New York was really Gotham City, and a floodlight was burning on the midnight sky, crying for Batman and Robin.

On the *upper* Upper West Side, the Morningside Reform Democrats, challenging DeSapio's old New York guard, had already sent William Fitts Ryan to Congress. In our neighborhood, the one-upper West Side, the ancient separatist covenant that had kept the old Irish and old Jewish Democrats from each other's throats was slowly yielding to a contentiously hyphenated political compromise called the FDR–Woodrow Wilson Democrats, over which the Reformers were struggling to gain control.

And now they were all faced with the beast just coming to birth out of urban renewal, the hydra-headed people-monster sprung from the Provisional Council of "affected citizens" and the city's meddling with the popular will. There was at least one historian with the clairvoyance of hindsight, musing on these things from his rectory penthouse, who thought this might become the way to make history.

I knew his energy boiled. He didn't have to tell me, "This is what I was meant for." This was what he was meant for. Those who can, do.

People looked at Harry, then—Cardinal Spellman did—as a man who'd outgrown the streets, risen above them: "Dr. Browne," Ph.D. historian, Fellow of the Society of American Archivists, author of two upscale parish histories, twenty-nine scholarly articles, and the definitive study of the Catholic Church and the Knights of Labor. And he was all these things, and loyal, too—that baffling part of him, "married to Mother Church," reluctant vassal, but vassal all the same. Capable of churning out that big ecclesiastical biography as doggedly as any zealot, if his pride hadn't been stung.

But who dared to say now that the flock of a live city parish wasn't more important than the biography of a dead archbishop? The cardinal hadn't—yet—and even if the sky wasn't yet falling on Irish New York, Spellman's continuing silence suggested that he wasn't on principle against somebody's saying it was.

And anyway, it was a historian's struggle—the struggle of a true historian of the Catholics of the city of New York—ready now for that pure canonical *delectatio morosa*, that delicious revenge of frying the rapists of Hell's Kitchen on their own griddle, the planners who had disappeared his street for the Lincoln Tunnel so that ad men could speed their BMWs to Upper Montclair, and who had disappeared ten thousand more, so that they could hear the symphony at Lincoln Center. Enough was enough.

Reluctantly, I decided to take the appointment in Greensboro, for a year. Harry gave me obviously ambivalent encouragement. It was my career. Under the continuous meltdown heat of my apartment roof that summer, we spread our Saturday sheets on the floor and daubed ice cubes on our bodies, and talked of what was past and passing and to come.

My knowledge was still full of gaps and discontinuities, but it was also a kind of test screen for making course corrections and trying predictability of outcomes.

"We have to put down some roots." I knew he intended the political *we*, though the political was personal, even then, and it had a sad, ironic edge, in light of my being about to go away. "To find a way to say we shall not be moved."

I repeated, as if it were a promise, *"We shall not be moved."*

The Provisional Council had been looking for a new name, something to capture imaginations, give some identity to this shapeless, ornery Urban Renewal Area. Harry had been poring over old maps at the New-York Historical Society and discovered a Dutch farmer, Jacob Strycker, who had owned everything from the 96th Street inlet back to the park. We tried Strycker's Inlet. We threw it away. We needed something bigger. "Strycker's Bay?"

It had a resonance. Strycker's Bay. Perhaps, in the end, it gave its name less to a place than to a time. But like Kip's Bay, a newly named neighborhood on the East Side, it sounded authoritative, respectable. The Strycker's Bay Neighborhood Council.

Harry had just turned forty on July 15, 1959. He had become a forty-year-old priest in love, in love with me and in love with the city, his old life ruptured like a vital organ inside him. This is what they mean, I suppose, by climacteric.

When Milton Akers, the principal—pardon me, the *headmaster*—of the Walden School, became the chair of the Strycker's Bay Neighborhood Council, Father Browne became chair of the housing committee. Within that committee the whole future of the Plan would be hammered out, the wedge that stopped the glacier, with Father Browne's body behind it. The first thing the committee did was to double the number of planned low-income units to eight hundred and make it a demand.

Because in the summer of 1959, the sixties had already begun.

Locals knew her in their downhome way as "Mrs. Frank," by her acquired status as Frank Armitage's relic, but my doleful landlady had apparently ventured enough pluck when he died to redo the second story of their rambling black-and-white frame Victorian near the Woman's College into two furnished apartments. She rented one of them to me that fall, as I guessed she had to a new university hireling every September running.

The other, its door directly across the upstairs hall from mine, had been more steadily tenanted by a childless, middle-aged couple, he a salesman, with a great paunch and a salesman's perpetually beery look of glaciated benevolence around the mouth and eyes, and she his Jack Sprat converse, thin and timid and sad, a yet unwidowed Mrs. Armitage of sorts, with an intimidated dark-eyebrow look that laid a kind of funeral awning over the wet burial of her eyes.

Just before retreating into downstairs semiseclusion again, Mrs. Armitage handed me an old mortice-style key, saying they didn't actually set much store by locking up. Obviously more than a daunting thirteen-hour train ride separated North Carolina from New York. I locked up anyway. I put my bags on the floor and my body on the bed—Mrs. Armitage's bed in Mrs. Armitage's house—and in the sleepless dark of my first night in Greensboro heard the alien sounds and smelled the alien smells of the South, and felt with furious sorrow the mastery of my love.

It seemed to have happened so fast—Harry and I finally, soberly, convinced that this was necessary, if it wasn't necessarily good, Ann, still at Barnard, agreeing she could take over the 88th Street apartment and split expenses, a flattering first job, considering my M.A. would not be official till January. The Woman's College, a branch of the State University of North Carolina considered fairly "progressive" for the South, was respectably academic enough for local women to get a good liberal arts degree without paying a pile for it. *White* women, I should say—progress had not gone *that* far. Black women, if they could afford it, went to nearby Bennett College. Looking back, it is actually easy to see the brewing dynamics of change. As civil rights consciousness awakened, these and a number of other schools must have made Greensboro fairly yeasty for a Southern college town, though deceptively flower-garden pretty and full of evidently well-brought-up students of both colors and sexes, in the days when there were only two of each, with well-monitored proximities between them.

A few years into the sixties and the Woman's College would no longer be strictly either for women or for whites. But from the day I kicked its dust off, I have frankly never thought to ask whether such general convulsive change had any trickle-down effect on faculty working conditions. I know that in 1959 the nearest thing to doing bent-back labor in the tobacco fields had to be teaching entry-level English: five courses a term, sections so sprawled out over the week that the only morning I didn't have an eight o'clock was Sunday (the standard for newly hired women—the one man they hired that year slept late); under orders to assign a paper every week to our three comp classes and one every two weeks in our survey courses, averaging about seventy-five a week stretched over two fifteen-week semesters.

I may be exaggerating my serfdom, considering what adjuncts do now in American colleges and universities and what they do it for, but even in 1960 $4,500 a year seemed a slim, poorhouse wage, tending to imply that eating was as secondary as sleep was tertiary to the work of reading, grading, and making intelligible heuristic commentary on whatever glimmers of intellectual light we—canonical sharecroppers of the close-reading faith—could pry from the sleeping minds of Nature's own. The telephone became my lifeline—Harry or Ann, ten blessed stolen escapist minutes every few nights—just to cut the solitary drudgery into tolerable segments. It nearly consumed my little wages. Four roundtrip air tickets, Greensboro–High Point to LaGuardia and back on breaks, took the rest.

My hair visibly grayed. I could almost stand in front of the bathroom mirror and watch it turn. As the fall sank in agonizing slow motion into winter, I could foresee almost nothing to make the long time bearably sociable beyond the occasional Saturday night thirty-people drunkfest at the remote country cabin of some obligingly lonely assistant professor. It was not a dating culture: there was little to do, virtually no one to do it with, and too much gossip if you did. The two charmingly effete men in Romance Languages, who became the nearest thing to male friends I had, logically fled Greensboro every weekend. And yet for some reason, scrutable only to the swampy unconscious of a small Southern college town, I came to be known as the Scarlet Woman.

This bore absolutely no relation whatever to the fact that, in some sense, I was. Facts didn't come into it—not what Harry Browne would have called "true facts" at any rate, as I learned when I learned about it at all, which was not until Greensboro and I were well parted. The only way for anyone there to have known about Harry and me would have been through me, and I would have lied my way through a witch-burning.

It turned out, apparently, to have been a fantasy kindled in the smarmy imagination of a departmental colleague named Jimmy Painter, the kind of small man with a twitchy, lecherous nervousness I could imagine peeping under the drawn shades of first-floor bedroom windows without even having to bend. But that was in hindsight. Early on, perhaps wistfully blindsided by his curious surname, I thought him a rather harmless hypocrite, fearful of women, yes, and perhaps a tad too fond of barking me down at faculty meetings. But it was only later that I would learn of his deep-down, divine, and absolute Baptist certainty that no papist like me, fresh from the strumpet decadence of Europe besides, could be anything but a flaming daughter of the whore of Babylon.

It is probably a mercy that I didn't know this while I was still in Greensboro. All

I knew then was what Amy Charles, who taught Metaphysical Poets, had rather drily leaked: that I had in fact been hired as the English department exotic *du jour,* that they had even got a certain *frisson* out of my Columbia University connection —a politics and history–conscious degree that was, in this New Critical heyday, suspect, if not actually culpable. Yale was still and forever the mecca the Southern "Fugitive" cultural aristocracy and their disciples turned to pray. Amy may have had a tendency to paint with a broad brush, avoiding unpleasant specifics as to personalities, but still I gathered it was safer to be a witch in Salem than to be a good-looking, loud-laughing, Italian-speaking woman of twenty-four in the hinterland, with a large sensual mouth and a bodacious Levantine tendency to kiss people at the drop of a glass of bourbon.

Not that in a dry college town in a dry state you normally dropped a glass of bourbon anywhere but along the human esophagus. Alcohol was sex and sport, recreation, titillation, song and dance to university Greensboro, the single sin all adults had a total dispensation to commit. And it was Amy, whimsically lapsed Pennsylvania Quaker, whose bourbon and branchwater I came to drink more often than anyone else's, and so managed to put an occasional fine personal buzz between me and that knot of daily, almost unaccountable pain.

She was a passionate woman, of a peaceable sort of passion, slow and heavy of movement, with a large shelf of breast, and hair and eyes the color and depth of loam. She lived in a pure Boston marriage with a terse, no-nonsense musicologist named Betty Cowling in a big old house that seemed to grow the clutter of two lifetimes of antiquarian scholarship, Amy's on the saintly Elizabethan poet George Herbert and Betty's on the checkered history of the viola.

To my hungry mind and heart, they were Greensboro's blessed answer to Gertrude Stein and Alice B. Toklas, and their house the nearest thing to a salon within the cultural limits of the Carolina piedmont. As the year went on, I came to be invited regularly to their wonderful house parties. They were mostly for women, and they were filled with music, since Betty of course could be easily got to perform without any boring need to be coaxed. The two of them could conjure up a respectable feast in a trice, providing a howling acrostic definition of *trice* in the bargain. But whether I made one of a party or dropped in singly for supper, it was Amy and Betty who were home to me, offering a little respect for my accomplishments, a well-placed word of astringent wisdom when I needed it, a dusty green-tweed couch, and a small, beloved unkempt terrier to worry my feet. And Amy simply had no truck with the Jimmy Painters of the world. I think in her dry, seen-it-all way, she even came to love this wandering papist whore, and I loved her back, savoring her genius for turning paper-scrip gossip into purest gold reserve as it passed through the mint of her mind.

Yet it still vexes me how the "Scarlet Woman" thing ever got going, considering that there were very few men at the college who weren't gay or transparently terrified of women. May Dunlap eventually broke me the story about Painter, though she had no clue how to explain it. May was our resident expert in Restoration Drama, a downright Manichean combination of Columbia Ph.D. and faculty tenure, I thought—a kind of double agent, gleefully attracted to intrigue. She was also a high Anglo-Catholic, obsessed with a dreadful longing to become a Roman and near-desperate for the confidence to make her momentous decision. This inevitably became a source of bonding between us, as if I were already there, on that strange, untroubled shore. Little did she know! She would euchre me and a few others into Sunday-night suppers—lamb chop, well-peppered Carolina rice, amply flowing bourbon—followed by group sessions on the Ouija board. Maybe the power of common boredom was enough to explain how three or four pairs of unwilling hands could balance on that moving cup, and night after night raise the same restless, beleaguered spirit. The spirit actually had a name—Agnes—and nothing better to do, it seemed, than admonish poor May to give up her foot-dragging and cross over to Rome.

I thought this extrasensory propagation of the faith hilarious at the time, but it was clear May didn't. And it crossed my mind that had she known what a corrupt Roman Catholic I really was, she might've been less easy about imperiling her soul with our friendship. Yet I was desperate too. Her friendship, like Amy's, was a blessing I couldn't refuse. And what a darling, in her own terminally blond, plump, Hummel-doll way, as vivid a comedic and feminist person as the women she favored in her scholarship, like Aphra Behn and Elizabeth Inchbald and Lady Mary Wortley Montague, women who kept bawdy secrets (or didn't quite keep them) and wrote reams of snotty verse in reply to various smug and learned Augustan pomposities like Alexander Pope. When she came to New York on sabbatical the following year, I eagerly wanted to see her again. And it was then, with her unerring sense of drama, that she dropped the Scarlet Woman on me.

I think we were sitting in Columbia's Philosophy Hall lounge at the time. The memory is vaguely muddied by another story she was telling me, about a friend confessing to being a lesbian, which itself seemed suddenly reminiscent of something I had recently read in Henry James, and in that moment all of it, all the secrets of the confessional, real and fictional, ran inextricably together with the repressed image of my sinner self, like the shadow of a woman in a darkened room, and I must have just then said I was—that I had long been—hopelessly in love.

"You're very mysterious," she said. "Is he married?"

"Something like that." It was as near as she would ever come.

But she had her punitive little gambit ready. "Everyone thought there was something about you, even then . . . " And it came out.

Scarlet Woman. My God. Now I think of it as something out of Wycherley, or Sheridan. But then it must have set back my recovery from Greensboro another two years. Absurdly, I think I never forgave May, who had at least had the nerve to tell me.

I had been so lonely, and it had all been so puritan really, all my time there. Nothing but the unfairness of it could have galled me as much as it did.

I suppose you could have called my bright red dressing gown scarlet. I remember throwing it over me late one Sunday evening after a hot shower, my hair still wet, not half an hour back from the airport through a frightful, driving rain. A knock at my apartment door, my colleague Pierre (Romance Languages) suddenly there, looking slightly, crisply drunk and appealingly melancholy through his streaming face and hair. It did occur to me that if I felt sad and lonely, only a few flight-hours from New York, how must it have felt for Pierre from Strasbourg? Yet I sent him away without even asking him to take off his wet raincoat, or offering him a cup of tea. I will never know how long we both stood there, dripping, grappling with the exquisite dilemma of what to say, he not daring to speak what conceivable lonely suffering could have driven him out into the dark and rain to find me, I praying only that that damned red nylon wrapper wouldn't bare a centimeter more of me than anyone else in Greensboro might vouch for by broad daylight.

But liquor was quicker, everybody said, and it was, obviously. On this point I was schizoid, love-hating the hard stuff, but still resolutely, innocently Italian about wine. Once, making up for a missed eight o'clock in freshman comp, I held a house gathering at my place, and a student helping me serve up the cider noticed a bottle of marsala in my kitchen cabinet. Afterward an outraged colleague told me I could be fired for having offered her a taste. Jesus, that was it. *Fire me*, I thought. *Please, fire me.*

It didn't help to be reading Flannery O'Connor, starting with "A Good Man Is Hard to Find" in our first-year anthology and on from there, as far as I could. I respected the hard authentic rub and scent of Southern life, yet it seemed so brilliantly terrifying and cruel of her to exile the souls of her characters beyond society and call only that dark void by the name of God. Her religion divided us. I felt as if all the chilling authoritarian metaphysics of the South had gone into the making of a searching, intelligent, and unutterably suffocated Catholicism.

I'd also begun to read William Carlos Williams, because here in something like the heartland of American poetry, with a great, gentle, and gently satirical poet like Randall Jarrell in our own department (a lovely, sad man who brought Rilke to read when he came, as we all did, to duty at the registration table), poetry seemed so humane—vital—necessary. Jean Stafford came on a conference visit, bringing with her a sudden tidal launch of snow—two feet of it, maybe more. We had to plow paths through it to get to her readings. But it soon melted past credibility. Sitting in a library carrel on those endlessly sunny Greensboro afternoons, I would look out to the college lawns even midwinter hadn't faded, then beyond them to that place of Williams's poem called Paterson. I had never seen it, never heard the roaring Great Falls. I saw it now as a need, a city on the landscape of my mind where God might still inhabit the streets.

I loved my students—especially the fateful marsala girl, who I remember had to take time off from school to help her family harvest tobacco back on the farm. She and her best friend had been salutatorian and valedictorian respectively of their tiny rural graduating class. She'd called me weeping, late one night after they'd had a terrible row, begging me to let her change her term paper topic to "the *true* meanin' of *frayundship*."

It was not her fault I hated Greensboro—teaching had, for the first time, actually come to seem a professional skin I could live in. And yet long before I actually said I would leave when my contract expired, escape had shaped itself like a dream on my hungry soul. Only Amy's gentle, brown-eyed sorrow at the prospect of my going could have made me think even passingly of retracting. And yet it was strange how heavyhearted I felt once the decision had become irreversible. It had been lush and succulent here, an Eden to the senses, a place, I thought, understandably fixated on original sin.

Only Harry, the comfort of those few hurtling visits when even my sister, and every other thing beloved and unbeloved, were driven out of our lives for a few passionate hours, could have helped me understand this experience in a way I myself couldn't then, and maybe even to bear it with more inner patience and grace. Years in Washington had made him sensitive to the currents of Southern life. He was the kind of acute news-devouring historian who knew something crucial in the world was brewing, that Greensboro, the South, was an important place to be now—now that something interesting would be coming out of that old-time religion, something indeed already coming, already making its way toward us, with the desegregation decision and the rise of Martin Luther King. He knew I would soon regret what I'd missed, and be rolling pastry for the humble pie of my blinkered insight someday.

But I was hopeless, trapped in my own version of provincial bigotry. I saw, heard, even made part of the rumbling local racial discussion, I paid attention enough to think even of writing for publication about it, but I couldn't wait to be home, back on the West Side. I ate up Harry's news about how the Provos of the Provisional Council had given smooth way to Strycker's Bay Council as the voice of the people, about how he and Mike had stayed up all night over a quart or two of Cutty Sark drafting its constitution, until the sun came over the penthouse roof and shone plain green through the empty bottle glass.

The political is personal. Everywhere. If I had my bourbon and branch in Greensboro, Harry had his Scotch on New York's West Side. In fact, that one night of constitution writing opened up a whole new drinking era for him, who had never drunk the hard stuff before. Never. Not since his boy days when Pop's ugly touts had, he thought, turned him off it forever. He'd begun to look back now and see himself—the only guy at Catholic U. who could boast of getting and staying drunk on pure Coca-Cola—as an insufferable teetotaling prig. It had come to him in Italy that drinking could be a form of scholarship, requiring a certain residual sobriety to retain the competitive expert edge on region and vintage. Likewise now with J&B versus Dewar's: he had a lot of making up to do for the study time he'd lost.

And the personal is, of course, also political. Queer how Scotch would come to symbolize for him the good fight on the West Side, and even the new social liquefaction of the sixties. It's what made Mike and Harry both love to retell the story of that all-nighter together, I think, reliving just how their mutual creative Irish demons had been unleashed. Mike told the story shyly, Harry arrogantly, as if it proved what a commoner he really was, not the little "milord" better than his father he'd had himself pegged for in his smug adolescence. For him that long Strycker's Bay night became the hell-harrowing from which he rose to the people, to being his father's son.

His father must already have been dying then. Harry said that if they'd had the money, and Mam and Pop hadn't been dumped out there over the river, doctors might have caught the cancer and given Pop another twenty years. Housing wasn't enough.

But that was later, when he'd put his feelings into a shape he could deal with. On that morning in March when his call woke me out of a Southern spring night's deepest sleep, he said he was sorry. Then he told me his father was dead. All we could do was cry together into the phone.

A climacteric in all ways, in that same month of March three things had happened in New York politics to transform the debate about the Plan.

Two of them were public policy events: the City publishing the Panuch Report—appropriately pronounced "panic"—an independent blue-ribbon study claiming the one thing that would either make or break New York was immediate attention to good, affordable housing; and the State passing the new Mitchell-Lama law, named for its two drafters, promising fifty-one million dollars in loans for building it. The clinching third was the man to get behind the program: Robert Wagner, Jr., son of a legendary New York senator and a Regular Democrat who'd come up through the ranks into an appointment as acting mayor. With his special chromosome for political genius, he'd also managed to make himself the quasi-darling of Democratic Reform. And now he was vocally, publicly, pledging good across-the-board housing as a priority of his City administration.

It was a hat-trick windfall, "totally incredulous" to the Strycker's Bay man or woman on the street, and to our own Philosopher of the Penthouse a bloomin' miracle, a Transfiguration, with the politicians suddenly lamenting things like the plight of people in single-room occupancy that only sociologist intellectuals used to worry about before. From Greensboro the possibilities sounded breathtaking, a tornado of pronouncements from every weather-layer of government spinning into the vortex of the city: Robert Moses, King of Slum Clearance, happily swept away into the Tolkienesque planning world of the New York World's Fair, as new names like Weaver and Felt and Hortense Gabel dropped down from the TV sky, as up from the sidewalks sprang fighting clerics like Father Gusweller and Father Browne, as WPIX interviewer Gabe Pressman discovered them and a whole new world of entertainment.

Oh, those early morning telephonic bulletins! Those honey aubades of love, shading by degrees out of my southland dreams into Mission Impossible press clips, self-destructing on Ma Bell's electronic air!

Yet there had been no warning, nothing humming along the wires of the universe, the night my thin, funereal neighbor lady clamored at my door and called me quickly to her apartment across the hall. I shakily called the ambulance. She stood trembling by, hands open on her streaming cheeks, fingers half over her eyes, as if it mightn't be true if she couldn't see it. I knew her husband was gone, though it was the first time I had ever actually seen a man in the grip of death. He lay on the couch as if he'd been suddenly trapped in glass, the dilated empty eyes still staring astonished from his puffy face, the evening paper lapsed onto his great chest, the news of all the world come to this.

That same day the students from Greensboro and Bennett Colleges had begun their famous sit-in at Woolworth's lunch counter downtown. Something had died everywhere in this city. Something had been born everywhere in the world, a new generation launching the struggle. Nothing in the civil rights movement would ever be the same. It may have occurred to me fleetingly that it was not the time to leave here, that I should stay, see what would become of this place as the ladylike, lily-white traditions dividing all these colleges came to shreds, as the metaphysical dreams of Southern religion met the exploding realities. But I couldn't wait to go, *I couldn't wait.* And to my rabid urgency even the embattled racial politics of June 1960 seemed only another reason to get away.

With more to hold him in New York, more that needed him, Harry still tore himself out of the West Side when I gave the signal, and drove ten hours straight to me in the used black Ford he'd just bought from his friend Father Wilde.

He arrived in the dead—no, not the dead, the *alive,* the sweet-smelling jasmine-juniper-orange-scented holy and soft Southern live beauty of the Greensboro night—and I let him guiltily into my room in proper Mrs. Armitage's house, and hungrily into my body in proper Mrs. Armitage's bed, before he'd even had a chance to wash off the chilled sweat he was damp with. At dawn the local headlines were far too preoccupied with other news to note the Scarlet Woman's departure to the Outer Banks with an AWOL New York priest.

4

A week of the salt freshness of sun and ocean at Nag's Head, together on that crooked finger of sand poked into the stormy belly of the Atlantic, and a year's hunger filled. Hunger of every kind, it seemed, since food itself was restored as a metaphor of joy, and we gorged ourselves on crab and bluefish straight from the sea, savoring it like released prisoners, as if our ten months apart had actually been in stir.

And then, excepting that now we harbored a more empirical fear of the occasional routine penance to be done for our happiness, we passed back into our West Side life almost as if it never been interrupted. I awoke in my skyey brownstone penthouse as if I hadn't been waking for months to the scented Carolina air and birdsong. And if my heart pounded in some nameless existential panic, some dread of the beating wings of time, there—still—again—was the brilliant New York daylight and the cooing of sophisticated pigeons on the window ledge, and Harry's voice from his penthouse a few blocks away, as intoxicating as bootleg bourbon and warm as the sun on my back at the beach, soaking into my body, into my skin, evaporating dread.

And for those few hours a week when we gripped each other in the night, in the crushing intimacy of my single bed, what fear was there? What could we feel but our own transcendence and the insignificance of time? What did natural law matter any more than canon, or civil, or criminal? We defied it. We defied gravity. If parting here was the price of heaven hereafter, then to hell with heaven.

But the days were still days. Cold War days, besides, terrible *On the Beach* days, full of looming common images of well-positioned nuclear missile silos and movie fantasies of nuclear winter, when SANE searched for larger and larger West Side apartments to meet in, when the macro-panic was swelled by each micro-soul, when vague personal dread might be smothered in nights of extravagant consolation—for others as surely as it was for us. We couldn't have been the only lovers to imagine ourselves stumbling naked through the Lincoln Tunnel, never again to be divided, the city in flames behind us.

Never to be divided. It came back to that singular thing, always. And yet sometimes it did occur to me to wonder whether all this romantic transcendence was anything more than a delusion, gilded cover for a mean failure of nerve, a pretense of daring made heroic by pushing it to the edge of doom. In our dreams we could defy the nuclear holocaust. Waking, we couldn't even defy the poor mother for whom Harry's priesthood shone as the last seam of brightness on the edge of her fading life. Still, it was better—wasn't it?—to keep the lie and the love if the lie and the love went together?

Wasn't it?

Once upon a time, back in my advertising days before the Greensboro penance, I had walked into my account executive's office on a brilliant June morning to find a handsome Englishman waiting to see him, just sitting there in the sunlight. An ad-space saleman from *Travel,* well-tanned, lean, long-torsoed as a runner, weathered, as if some windy tropical beach had bleached his hair and turned his eyes that unbearable shade of gray. When he looked up at me it was as if I were bathed in a shower of gold. But what must the gift of my eyes have done to him?

He was too much, too much. *Ah, don't do this,* I thought, but I didn't say it. And he came at me that day, he came at me with such a strong, sad, passionate, convicted urgency. Mid-June, solstice, Harry briefly away. I was bad, miserable, restless, hideously sorry for myself. I wanted to end this suffering. I wanted so much to be rescued. And here was the Angel Gabriel.

I don't know what I told him—it didn't seem to matter. He told me of his English divorce, his escape to the States. We arranged to meet at his Lexington Avenue apartment. We were both of us sick, nauseated with desire—sick, I think, the way a drink will make you sick if you have been taking a drug to stop drinking.

"Four years," he said as he lay there, waiting for me on the bed, staring blankly into the ceiling. He had been watching me undress, but suddenly his eyes seemed to burn, and he shut them and turned away. "Four years," he said again. It was as if the memory of her grew inside his body like a tumor. "We made love every single night."

My hands were still fumbling with the last buttons on my dress, a ridiculously innocent chemise with a small pattern of bright yellow daisies. I could feel the stinging start in my eyes. "I know," I said stupidly.

Christ, it was as if we were a pair of collision victims, rushed to bed by ambulance in this June evening daylight. A single pull of anesthetic and that damned love would come up on us like a meal still undigested in our stomachs though we struggled to choke it down, to force it back, so as not to hear ourselves saying, *Please, God, I want something better than this, I want something else. Please, I want what I had, not you, beautiful as you are, not the sight of you across this lonely bed, in this lonely sickroom—*

His phone rang. He picked it up. And in that spot of time it flashed on me that I was still alive. Alive. Awake. I quickly redid the buttons on my daisied dress and waved a silent good-bye. He stared, bewildered, unable to speak over the live receiver. I let myself quietly out of his apartment and back into my lie, my love, while I still had it.

Say I was in love with love. Barring God, what better thing?

And not barring God?

Harry had the comfort of the Church's age-old assurance that the sacrament remains pure even when the priest who performs it is tainted. And even as a taint, almost the worst that could be said of this sin of "concubinage," as they so daintily called it, was the word itself, a wreckage of twisted metal in the mouth, a tortured thing that canceled everything human in the relation, that evoked some loathsome disease, or the poisonous curare to cure it.

Because as a sin it was tiresomely ordinary, really, wasn't it. Gossipy Church history was full of it, full of the snigger of it, a mine of cynical bromides and hackneyed jokes, like the one about the monsignor who prayed so selflessly for a Church without celibacy, "not for ourselves, dear Lord, but for our sons." Or the doughty archbishop who, when asked if he had ever fathered any children, replied, "None to speak of."

Between us it was hardly always a laughing matter. If he didn't say his matins and vespers anymore in my company, I think he still said them, and behaved generally like a man in a state of grace. Was I then the only one who had fallen? I knew he was glad I was pointed now to that scholarly career, marching inexorably to the Ph.D. Barnard College has just offered to make me a teaching assistant, a small thing, but a comfort. Something to his credit, perhaps, that at least he had not stood in my way.

Yet it was not long before I was a West Side addict activist again in what that same summer's tourist ad campaign had dubbed "Estival Festival" New York, with Columbus Avenue as noisy and sticky and smelly and puddle-wonderful as the Sesame Street they said was modeled on it, with STRYCKER'S BAY NEIGHBORHOOD COUNCIL a freshly painted storefront sign just off the northeast corner of West 86th Street.

Democrat fever stirred up by the conventions, the coming Nixon-Kennedy television debates, the elections, the clubs amok with factionalist activity, political rivalries, hot, daily urban renewal bulletins, meetings everywhere, all the time, about everything, no innocent bystanders allowed.

I was neither innocent nor bystanding, but I made no speeches, only swelled the scene, especially at council meetings where Harry was the hub, many of them held at night on the park corner of my block at the Walden School auditorium, where coming up the street I could actually smell the tobacco smoke before I could even see the glowing orange haze of it through the windows, or hear the smack of Harry's gavel.

By day, when I wasn't teaching or buried in the stacks at Butler, I had the council's storefront office to play in. It was hard discipline to say, "Don't go again—not today." But when I did go, and he was there, what a rush just to see him, his eyes star-spangled as I came through the door.

But Strycker's Bay had more than Harry now. It had Esta.

When I first saw her, with her huge smoldering eyes and thick black upswept hair, she was sitting wreathed in cigarette smoke on her new job behind the reception desk, like some smiling Siva in a cloud of sacred incense. I believe a stab of instant fear went through me—not something I felt often anymore. Between Harry and me, we thought of *him* as the jealous one. It was a terrible thing, I'd tell him, a savage throwback. And yet why was *I* so above it all? Surely not out of some serene confidence in his love. And yet possessiveness about him had seemed irrelevant, almost from the beginning.

But—but—but—here was Esta Kransdorf, and here she would always be, day in, day out, under his eyes. Always lovely, with that skin like tawny old ivory and those brilliant dark topaz eyes, the kind of beauty the more seductive because it wasn't artless yet wasn't always thinking about its art, that didn't pretend innocence, abandoned all pretense and demanded candor, that made mysterious, cruel, bittersweet promises—

Ah, I had obviously fallen in love with her myself—why shouldn't he?

I suppose she didn't know quite know what to make of *me,* with all those uppity Columbia degrees and pedigrees. A bit of a vamp, too, from the looks of me— the legs, the lipstick, all that thick, untamable hair. Madly in love with Father Browne. But who wasn't? That much we had in common.

Maybe we were both the kind of bewitching women who knew we had best be friends, toughly enough tried-in-the-crucible to know we were both hopeless lovers of love. Not quite instantly, we gave one another the OK.

But Esta didn't come easy. You had to negotiate those unspoken inner politics. What'll you do, she seemed to say, if I make it good for you coming through that door? I'll write for you, I'd say. I'll draw for you. Not for me, Esta seemed to say. Not even for Father Browne. For the people. For the cause. And in my heart, I'd say fine. For the People. For the Cause. In my heart, with my heart, for she'd have known the difference.

Well, something of my brilliant career in advertising was to prove useful. I designed Strycker's Bay's first letterhead and the masthead for the newsletter, even helped write the newsletter regularly, created the entire first "Why Strycker's Bay?" brochure. I was prouder of that than of my master's essay in two languages.

Esta thought I was great. "Grrreeaaat!" she'd say approvingly in that peat-smoked voice of hers. She meant it, or I believed she did. She made me *want* to do things. Not just for her, not just for Harry. She made me *want* to write benefit letters and design posters and charts and mimeo handouts for subway exits. When I dropped in with my Saturday sketchpad full of watercolors of neighborhood children, she made me want to make more, and give them all away.

With Esta—how can I put it?—there was *something* about *everything.* All of it, each little bit of it, seemed to come wrapped in a unique aura of meaning, to be more important than itself, not just now but in the whole sequence of time. It was as if by some fluke of DNA she had inherited history and carried it with her like a title. Just over thirty and she already had a past, less a personal past than a kind of species past, a midrash of cultural memory: parents who'd escaped the Russian and Polish pogroms to become union organizers, their desperate remnant of family left behind to be murdered in the Holocaust. She'd been Red from the diaper, of course, blossomed into a young Red mama, organizing welfare mothers out of the East Harlem projects where she'd lived after her marriage broke up. We realized in a joyously sisterly moment of poetic irony that her projects were the ones that stood now on my renewal-annihilated childhood street.

Always *engaged,* in the deepest, most political meaning of the word, a natural intellectual, Esta had moved with instinctive tact among the writers and artists on the blacklists after the McCarthy debacle. She'd gone to London to assist escapees seeking work and safety there in the mid-fifties. She'd known Doris Lessing, had shared with her the very London apartment house of *The Golden Notebook.* She'd spent a year in Paris (definitively Sartre and de Beauvoir's Paris, then) aiding the Greek resistance movement, and there had had the one great love of her life. She begged me to tell no one of it, ever. But how is it possible? How can I tell who she was to me, and not tell?

He had died in her arms. "We were together for twelve months," she said, her face suddenly, wearily soft. "One magnificent year. We made love like insane people, every night."

As tenderly as I knew how, I said, "I know."

The world turned into winter 1960/61. John Fitzgerald Kennedy, after a breathtaking election race, was headed for the White House, Nelson Rockefeller was in Albany, Robert Wagner gearing for a campaign to secure himself as mayor in the 1961 campaign, wondering if the Reform troops would support him.

Urban renewal politics, all of it, hung in these mighty balances. New housing, certainly, but for the rich or for the people? How much relocation? Would displaced renters be allowed to come back? How long would it take? And could they afford it? Who would actually build, or even own, the housing? Profitmaking developers? or nonprofit housing corporations and cooperatives?

Then there was the question of control of the process. Some pundits said it didn't matter what happened in the City, it was the State legislature that counted. Others that you couldn't do anything without the City's Board of Estimate behind it. And what about the Feds, the loan programs? If you wanted leverage, where was the best place to put the lever?

The *New York Times* cried, "On with the Plan!"—typically walking that fine *Times* line between the good liberalism of promoting housing (the only way to "stem the flight to the suburbs") and the good business of stroking the developers who'd thrive on any rentals the market would bear. The irony was lost that the developers they were stroking were the same who'd made flight to the suburbs possible ten years before by building Lefrak City and Levittown, and who in the bargain had broken up all the old politico-ethnic enclaves that had once made New York City politics the predictable animal it wasn't anymore.

But the developers were going to need more than the support of the *New York Times* to navigate the next few political whirlpools. For one thing, under the new state Mitchell-Lama law, there was now a profitability limit on new rental housing, a limit that tended to favor people at least at the upper spread of what's called middle income, some of whom not only voted but even read the *New York Times*. A few for-profit developers were going to have to pretend to like the constraints they were under, in the end, whether they liked them or not.

The other swirling whitewater was Relocation, and it was also a piranha pool. In theory, few policymakers minded if developers drove a few poor people off prime real estate for the sake of "progress," especially when they were the poorest of the poor. But that didn't mean they couldn't be *nice* about it. After all, the well-off who bought bedrooms in those new glass towers in mid-Manhattan still needed to sleep the sleep of the just. Even the world of the well-off seemed to have such needs, then.

When the City pols named as the new Director of Relocation Bronx leader Herman Badillo—a rising Hispanic who'd come up out of the postwar immigration—it was a sign, but a sign with several possible readings: yes, an emerging Puerto Rican leadership; yes, a possible new sensitivity to Puerto Rican community needs. But what if it was a way to co-opt Puerto Rican support for a "humane" relocation process that in the end would be anything but? It raised hopes. Expectations. The Puerto Rican community—bumped uptown, bumped out of town, bumped once too often—was finally claiming turf. One way or the other, Harry said, it was time Mike Coffey brought some real Hispanic leadership into Strycker's Bay.

He did. And the instant they joined, via a couple of business and church organizations, the ante in this game of housing poker went up, and the eight hundred low- to middle-income units the Strycker's Bay Council had asked for got pushed to a thousand, with revolutionary talk of demanding even more. You could tell president Milton Akers didn't court trouble. There were ethnic and class wars at those meetings, and he would pass the gavel to Father Browne, who chaired the linchpin Housing Committee, because *he* could take the flak. And give it back. "Enough with these windshield-wiper surveys," Browne would say, skewering the public officials who'd ooze up and down the sidestreets in dark gray Caddies doing tenement triage. "Damned planners can't even get out of their limos to see what shit people are living in. Time," Browne would say—always careful to mix "shit" and Latin in the same speech—"to start factoring in the *vox populi.*"

He was wonderful, another being when he was up there, no one sure just when he might forge on the smithy of his soul some slight but jolting impropriety. He was onto the newsmaking power of a phrase, beginning to see how the publicity shots were called and getting bolder about calling them. But he was no loner. Everybody, he said, had to get informed, to be a part of it. And then they had to get downtown and *make* the news, not wait till the news came up and hit them.

He was no bully in St. Gregory's pulpit either, but he had the more sophisticated parish Catholics completely dazed, the urbane style of the Church history scholar slipping his radical message past their defenses. More than ever they seemed to think Sunday-morning homilies worth getting up for. Now that I attended mass pretty regularly myself, I could spot them—the European emigrés, the artists, writers, lawyers, media people, technicians, entrepreneurs, beginning to calculate just what mass-rotational schedule Father Browne was on and coming to hear him preach. I think they wanted to believe their own ears, that somebody in *their* church, in *their* neighborhood,* in the Year of Our Lord Nineteen Hundred and Sixty, was actually talking about forging a new coalition of Catholics that would bring Irish old-age pensioners, boozy World War vets in SROs, black welfare mothers, Puerto Rican families with eight kids, and themselves, together in a single cause.

Monsignor Flanagan had let the genie out of the bottle, that was clear. But he was too nonplussed and outmaneuvered to know what to do about it. The weekly take was up. That was enough. If some folks didn't like it, they could find somewhere else to go for their preaching besides St. Gregory the Great.

Journalist Joe Lyford lived on West 92nd Street, an old brownstone side-street block, in a building he actually owned. He had already published a study of how black and Puerto Rican children got miseducated in the New York public school system, well-intentioned and, in these times, well enough received.

But now he was doing his journalist thing again, hanging around, gathering up the story of the Plan, which in his keen way he knew was going to define urban planning politics for another generation. Ultimately, he did get to tell the story, in a 1966 book called *The Airtight Cage,* still the best close to the ground account anybody has ever given of urban renewal on the West Side, maybe anywhere.

But as a property owner on a derelict street, Joe was also in the deepest sense a participant-observer—and the first to admit it. He watched his block degenerate and complained bitterly and vocally about it: buildings emptying, people losing faith, all this interminable politics of income numbers and relocatee rights adding up to nothing more than more delays. He became one of the new voices beginning to gain a hearing at Strycker's Bay meetings. Not as a knee-jerk property-owner, like some, intent only on protecting their investments. He'd been there and back already, and knew what was at political stake. But Joe also knew the City would blame every planning delay on community politics, not on its own bureaucratic sloth, and he didn't want downtown to have the right to fiddle while owners like him abandoned their buildings in despair and the West Side burned, literally burned.

Nevertheless, Joe Lyford wasn't just a journalist. He was a guy, an attractive guy, with a craggy-looking, Bill Holden face and sad sheriff-blue eyes, a recent divorce, and a perfect alibi for traipsing around with single neighborhood women like Esta and inviting himself up to their apartments for interviews. "He's pretty nice-looking," I'd say, offhand-like, to Esta. "What's he after?" And when Esta's eyebrows would shoot up as if I'd said something shocking, "I mean, politically."

She'd set her mouth on a cigarette and light up. "Basically it's the story of the people in the community against the—*goddam*—bureaucracy," that softspoken "goddam" poised between an intake and an outblow of smoke.

"People?" I'd say, implying that this was a rather vague use of the word in the present climate.

Esta would smirk, a knowing, un-huh-so-you-like-him-too kind of smirk. "He's a writer," she'd say. "Whaddyawant?"

But Joe's position was not that of the typical lonely writer. It was becoming a groundswell. Many building owners were, like him, new, buying into the community because they liked it, making an investment of their life savings on faith. Some of them cared about the social meaning of the housing calculus. But they doubted, sometimes, whether they'd get through this whole thing alive, let alone whether their buildings would still be standing if the rehab funding stalled by the numbers game didn't show up fast.

The crime rates were mounting daily. Citizens were coming forward, every one of them real, every one of them "affected," hurting even, every one of them a character out of *Guys and Dolls*. Like Alice Joannides, the brassy-haired, brassy-voiced representative of the 87th Street Block Association. At open public meetings, she'd screech out: "*Father!* Listen, Father! We can't wait no more! We got neighborhood body counts." Julia Matlaw, opposite of Alice in every way, a bespectacled Texan from West 94th Street with a smooth pageboy of streaky gray hair, would call polite attention to the recent news stories describing West 84th Street as the capital-crime capital of the West Side, a gangland free zone the police had lost control of and admitted it. "Won't be laaawng," she'd observe in her mildest drawl, "thaat's gonna be uuus."

And there was Peggy Horton, an education writer from Central Park West, who'd come to hot-weather committee meetings with her huge boobs barely contained by spaghetti straps, and plead, "*What's* holding things *up?*"

The question was transparently simple: how did you work the press—that is, take their attention off the "delay" issue and turn it on to real problems, like the plight of the homeowners and the suffering of poor families in squalid housing—and at the same time put just the right kind of pressure on State (Republican) and City (Democrat) officialdom without alienating either side, but still play them off against each other so they'd compete to take credit for getting things off the drawing boards and onto the streets, while also assuring a stable, predictable timetable for relocation, giving displaced people "priority" in returning to new housing once it was built, guaranteeing decent treatment for everybody, brownstone owners included, and ending up with a fair distribution of the final housing numbers for everybody concerned?

Needless to say, whatever the answer was, it was the Browne strategy.

Needless to say, you counted blessings whenever possible, so that the midwinter day that "priority" was officially guaranteed became a true red-letter day, time in the storefront to celebrate.

Not that activists needed a major triumph to celebrate anything at the time. Midnight after almost any big meeting or media boost, you could find just about everybody at the Tip Toe Inn in small bunches or en masse, trooping in through the nice, warm, steamy glitz of that wonderful place, Father Browne graciously, unobtrusively arranging it so that I might sit next to him, as in "Flav, sit here."

The drink would flow, the talk would roar, and in the midst of recounting some brain-splitting hilarity at the Board of Estimate, or doing some ruthless sendup of a City official, or telling us about what he'd said in the clips on the cutting-room floor of the Channel 4 evening news, Father Browne would remind me he was still Harry, touching his electric thigh to mine. His energy had always been aphrodisiac. Was his new power now? I wondered whose were the practiced eyes around that table who noticed the telltale shades of purple and pale I passed through.

The party would often end long after I'd left it, the political insomniacs finally packing it in, or Harry would simply elude them at last, and artfully dodge his mazy way through the glass-strewn side streets to my door, to my bed. Slipping in, and now, because I was newly expert, testing his old Doc Monaghan–inspired command of Victorian verse, he'd say, "Come again, sweet love," and I would very gladly oblige.

Maybe it was a narcolept gene for escaping an increasingly bewildering reality, maybe just those long, dreary, sunless days in the Butler Library stacks, but it seemed that winter as if I endlessly craved the anodyne of sleep.

So I remember with particular vividness the February night I lay awake, mad as hell at the endless grind and shriek of snowplows, after a paralyzing two-foot snow-fall hit the Northeast. Sanitation commissioner Paul Screvane, out to prove in this election year that a Wagner administration could meet any challenge, had mobilized the snow removal to end all snow removals—perhaps almost literally, since this was probably the single most egregious extravagance in a series of management extravagances that eventually broke a City budget ripe for breaking, and brought it to bankruptcy.

But elections are won by short-term, not long-term foresight. As the commissioner sent out his overtime and doubletime crews that night, building gray mountains of snow on every city street corner, no one seemed to care how much it cost, or how the side-street canyons so amplified the roar of gnashing metal and motor that you could still hear it ten blocks away. When the sun rose, the streets were clear.

Thus did Paul Screvane, aka Paolo Scrivagna, call attention to himself. Being also the politically correct Italian shade of ethnic, thus did he also secure himself a slot as deputy mayor on the ticket that fall, with Irish Bob Wagner as mayor and Jewish Abe Beame as comptroller, and close the frame on the perfect, traditional New York ticket in those days, certain to bring Regular Democrats successfully through the challenge of Reform.

And thus did he entwine our political fates, his and mine, for the very same Italian reason.

May 1961. I had all but forgotten my eardrum agony. My birthday arrives on a brilliant day in midweek, school almost out, and Father Browne has just offered to take me to lunch. The symbolic, new, renewal-announcing ginkgo trees are in full green, I notice, as we leave the Strycker's Bay streetfront and stroll toward Amsterdam Avenue on the south and sunny side of West 87th Street.

"*Faahther?*"

It is a genteel sort of shout not quite wanting to be a shout, from above and across the street. "*Flaayvia?*" It is Peter Paul Meagher, leaning out of the second-floor window of his brownstone on the north side. He gestures. He needs to talk. He is told where to join us for lunch. "My treat," he promises, drawing in his head.

Paul (which he prefers somehow to Peter, I think Irishly sensitive to peter jokes), devilish handsome, as Harry might say, with a noodly mop of toasted curls hanging over winsome and wettish Irish-retriever eyes, was a Strycker's Bay regular from Alice Joannides's block, a practitioner of various arts of the marketplace, going through a midlife crisis. He had last-ditch political ambitions via the

FDR–Woodrow Wilson Democratic Club. He was looking for his main chance.

In a few minutes he had danced into the corner diner to find us, and slipped alongside Harry into the booth, smirking under those melancholy eyes in his characteristically ambiguous way. Paul, I had long since decided, was a poet, doing penance to some particularly malign god by a stretch in real estate. He *cared* for words. He cherished them, even in his small talk. He hung on Harry's glibness like a birthright, and one-upped me whenever we met with quotes from Yeats and Joyce and Shaw and Wilde and my own new late-nineteenth-century Scottish Celt, Fiona Macleod, just to be as confoundedly whimsical as possible. He had a way with women, who found his disingenuous raptures on their loveliness appealing. He had a way with me—no less effective because it kept a chaste distance, as if he had acutely sensed something possessive in Harry's way of standing or sitting near me—something bespoken, a charm against temptation for a lapsed Catholic making a career of being at once romantic and cynical.

He had a proposition, it seemed, actually intended for me, but addressed with that infallible Irish political acuity of his to both Harry and me, in the third person. "How would Flayvia like to be in politics?" We must have looked at him as if a double comic-strip balloon with a huge question mark inside had just shot up over our heads.

He explained that in the coming mayoral campaign, bound to be a sweep for the new Reformers, the last Regular club downtown, the Chelsea-Clinton Democrats, was up for the cracking in the race for district leader. It was a great neighborhood, he said. He was right—it was the last remnant of Harry's old Hell's Kitchen plus half a mile of neighborhoods, still scattershot with good old Irish pols like Eugene McManus, the district leader Paul wanted to oust, and with first- and second-generation Italians who'd hung on and on and seemed to have no particular quarrel with having McManus hang on with them.

But as Paul pointed out, there was a special hitch in the City Charter, some weird relic of a bygone, turn-of-the-century feminism, whereby duly elected district leaders (a euphemism, really, for party power brokers at the ward or "district" level in New York) had to come in two-by-two, as to Noah's Ark. If he were to mount a district leader ticket, then, he would have to pair up, and find a suitable female candidate to run with.

"And you want to give it the ethnic double whammy?" guessed Harry.

"Thou hast said it," said Paul.

I thought they must be kidding. *Me?*

I could think of nothing but the liabilities. I wasn't exactly your typical Italian American, was I. And a helluva queer mix of poetry and politics between the two of us.

But they were still waiting, turning those two pair of brilliant, funny, smiling Irish eyes on me.

What the hell.

"You're going to have to remember to call me *Flaahvia*," I said.

5

I still can't believe we went through with it. Can New York politics really have been such a party in those days? Paul even arranged with a photographer friend for studio poster shots of us, so the whole neighborhood could see our big beaming faces from the bus.

I had to declare district residency, of course. Ann seemed glad enough to take over at 88th Street again, rent-free this time, while she worked a summer job and prepared for her last year at Barnard. The Reformers set me up, also rent-free, in a toney townhouse on West 22nd opposite the Chelsea seminary, a painless political contribution for the moneyed owners, I supposed, away in the Hamptons for the summer.

It was a lark of larks. Except for the watchful custodial couple living at the street level, I was Alice through the looking-glass, with the run of the place. And what a place! Each of the three upstairs floors was furnished in a different period, a little world of its own, and I could wander through all this decadent, careless elegance from world to world, choosing where I would "live." I settled on the middle floor, with its rain-forest green and art-nouveauish and potted-palm air of having last been decorated in the twenties—you could almost picture Zelda Fitzgerald in it, resting her dancing feet. The strict rules against visitors (enforced by the custodial couple, black, tall, and upright of aspect) I took in stride—if things got too lonely or claustrophobic, after all, I could escape uptown. But I remember one simmering early August night during the final week of canvassing when I just could not get away, and in the deepest dark I let Harry quietly in, and at earliest dawn let him quietly out again, and the next day, the custodial couple rebuked me as if they'd caught me on camera.

I'd had it coming, I suppose. But it felt rather sterner than necessary at the time, and seemed to clinch a feeling I had of not being taken quite seriously. Why I should be was another matter. I'm sure Paul's rich Chelsea backers thought him liability enough, and indulged me merely as his poster girl, certified ethnically correct and harmless. I had tried to alert them to the risks they were taking—an outsider with a weird, Hispanic-sounding last name, too young, and maybe a little too sultry-looking. Even if they believed me Italian, and that by itself was a long shot, the Italian American working-class and trades people on those hallowed Clinton side streets would check off everything on that list against me. Add my upscale education and it was a set of political liabilities nobody could overcome.

But they wouldn't listen. Paul wouldn't listen. The extent of his strategy was to put me into the hands of a veteran campaign activist who owned another townhouse in that same seminary block. She reminded me of a less kindly Greensboro Amy Charles—hospitable, big-bosomed, that same Gertrude Steinish smooth brown hair parted down the middle, the dry pretense of cynicism as she swept about her apartment in soft, drapey housedresses, making lapidary utterances.

"Don't you think, *Flaaahvia*," she'd say, in an earnest, parental tone as a few of us assembled dinner, "you'd do better *not* to wear pearl earrings *and* a pearl necklace?—I mean, at the *same time?*" Or "*Flaaahvia*, do you think when you get your *pee aitch dee* in English you could remember to say 'Paul and *me*'?"

But I was a sponge for correction. I wanted to do some good and didn't mind being used, maybe even a bit abused, to do it. I diligently canvassed Clinton's ethnic neighbor hoods, up and down dusty tenement staircases or shining elevators, amazed at how easy it was in the West 50s to go from shabby to glamorous on the same street. Every signature on every petition, I knew, was a potential snap-trap: the slightest deviation from the name or address on the registration rolls and it would self-destruct in the mean and grungy back rooms of the New York Board of Elections as if it had been written in disappearing ink.

And oh how I struggled to be Italian. Paul, accompanying me around to show the locals, once took me into the close, garlicky-smelling flat of a restaurant family on 56th Street. The men, wineglasses in hand, sat around a small dining table, waiting, while the women stared as I passed the inner sanctum of the kitchen. My God, it was a time warp—I was a little girl again, back on Zi' Carmé's fire escape. Worse. It was the old summer jewelry factory, where the workers hated me for going to college. It was my Italian cousins in Striano, with their thin-skinned pride.

"*Alaya?* What kind of name is that?" asked one of the women sitting squarely on a straight-backed kitchen chair, and turning her sphinx look on me as I stood nervously in the doorway. I leapt on it: "*Napoletano*," I said, clumsily beginning to unpack the family history of the odd, non-Italian spelling, a story we used to tell with a certain bitter laugh at home because my father, as a raw immigrant, had changed it from the Arab-looking southern Italian *Alaja* to something more "American." Lou, Carl, even Ann, had already officially switched to *Alaia*. I'd resisted.

"It *is* Italian, believe me," I said, "real *napoledaan*—" pushing my luck a little.

One of them caught the hint of familiar Neapolitan sound in the soft *t*. "*E'vui, parladah italianah?*"

"*Certo. Come no? E Lei?*"

An exchange of glances around the room. One woman says, "Beh, we don't really speak *Italian*. We speak the dialect. You learn Italian in school?"

Another: "Aren't you Jewish?"

McManus's supporters had spread the word that I was Paul's Jewish girlfriend, trying to pass. Paul actually had a Jewish girlfriend, my height, long dark hair. We could easily be mistaken from a distance. For these people, Jewish was bad enough, but *Gessù, faking* Italian . . .

We managed to get enough signatures by the August 7 deadline all the same, with some to spare—out day after day, up and down those hot July hallways. People would sign—indifferent housewives; playful, obliging out-of-work actors; eager-to-be-helpful motherly old ladies in the nursing home on 55th Street; hardnosed, scrutinizing lefties in rent-controlled apartments on way, way West 57th. It was a wonderful thing, really, as if for all kinds of ordinary people putting your signature on an election petition was the exercise of a birthright, a sacred democratic privilege.

But Dennis "Dinnie" Mahon stood sentinel over the Board of Elections like a dragon, and Dinnie was as tough a tough old-guard veteran Regular Democrat as they came. With perfect irony, he was also from the Upper West Side. He'd go to regular Sunday mass at St. Gregory's and parley with Father Browne on the sidewalk afterward. God only knows what Harry told him. Whatever it was, Dinnie spared me a scathing, while Paul he publicly dubbed a "drifter," wardheeler code for carpetbagger in East Side–West Side–Mamie O'Rourke's New York. His petition checkers knocked out every other name, till they had us just below the margin to qualify for the ballot.

So it didn't matter that the City Club guardians of good government had endorsed us, or that we'd got a halfway decent blurb in the *New York Times* election issue, or that Paul had already plastered Ninth Avenue with those five-foot posters, my face going uptown, his face down, so you could see either of us from both directions for a mile. It didn't matter that on one of those smothering street nights in August I'd conquered a sweating panic to climb Screvane's campaign soundtruck, sticking my oozing face into a microphone to speak my little Italian bit, the last word of every phrase bouncing back to me from the loudspeakers like a sonic boom—we never made it to the voting booth.

Paul's political career fizzled after that. The "drifter" label followed him for years. I think he considered himself lucky to land a subaltern position in the Department of Real Estate in a later mayoral administration. As for me, I said farewell to Zelda, picked up my few things from the elegant old townhouse, and moved back uptown to my little 88th Street tower where I belonged. I was secretly delighted. Not to retreat from politics because, public panic notwithstanding, I'd discovered (ace college minor in government that I was) that I rather liked the action on the ground. But the true source of my delight had been a serendipitous encounter, one canvassing afternoon, with our dread opponent, third-generation undertaker and Regular Democrat Ed McManus, Chelsea-Clinton District Leader (male). I had chanced on his Tenth Avenue studio that day and found him in, a nattily dressed, tall dry twig of a man with an oversized pile of red-orange hair. He had actually come out of his back office to shake my hand and wish me well and chitchat about the political weather. Behind that smooth undertaker voice of his I could almost imagine a rather sweet and practiced Irish tenor.

Not that I had any illusions that he took me—a mere political girl—any more seriously than the folks who were paying to get me elected. But from his side of the war, this was fair enough. He had no need of animus against somebody who'd given him nothing to fear. Besides, canvassing his neighborhoods had inspired a respect for him I hadn't had when I'd started. I knew he took care of people—they'd told me so. I knew he protected poor families from rent gougers, brought in public works projects from downtown, stayed on the good side of the biggies to keep them ready when needed, and generally kept up George Washington Plunkett's great Tammany wardheeling tradition on George Washington Plunkett's home turf. I could still despise the Citywide machine he worked for and hate the subservient role of women in his political culture. But I could also think of him as a good man in politics—as good as he could be in his time and place and culture. To my amazement, Esta agreed. "Damned self-righteous Reformers," she'd say, whenever she heard them go after politicians like him with their glib, knee-jerk, middle-class liberal sanctimony.

So when the news was out in November that McManus, unopposed, had officially taken the district again, the three of us, Harry included, drank him a hearty toast.

My profile as an academic had clearly not enhanced my political career. But what about vice versa? As a specialist-in-training on the intersections of politics and culture, couldn't I theoretically take my downtown experience up to Morningside Heights?

Possible in theory. In practice, a firewall divided the two worlds. I wasn't long in discovering that, at Columbia, possession of even the loftiest academic credentials (not to be aspired to by females generally, let alone by me) was in itself no license to publish political thoughts—not about real-and-now as opposed to exotic historical politics at any rate. As for Barnard, the only political discussions at Deanery lunches were over changing Barnard University relations and what they might do to Barnard's autonomy in tenuring its own faculty.

Oh, they were a sleek and insulated group of literary women I swam with that season, feeling like a misshapen guppy in a school of goldfish. There was a certain pungent irony in my being assigned to cover the weekly Barnard subsection of Professor James Clifford's graduate course in the eighteenth century, arguably the most political literary era in the history of mankind. Yet even this Barnard job had been political in a certain sense, hadn't it, an ur-form of affirmative action. In some dark cortical layer of their minds as well as my own, I suspect I was still one of the vulgar *Thesmophoriazusae* I'd traveled with in college, never to be allowed to forget how, as a student once, I'd jumped the evolutionary ladder from *Reader's Digest* to *Sewanee Review* in a single shedding of skin.

I sometimes think my political involvement was unconscious therapy for this still-sickening sense of otherness I felt among my blueblood Barnard colleagues. Stubborn at the bottom of my soul there lay a scummy, defiant little *nostalgie de la self,* something that had to do with my body, my hands, with a solid existential world, with a somatic Mediterranean sense of physical-metaphysical reality. It had made me mad as hell to see the college go all high on "ahht" the previous spring, when they'd joined a university-wide Arts Festival—galled me, when only a few years before, when I was an undergraduate who wanted nothing more than to go on sculpting and painting, they'd denied me degree credit for art courses. Now I couldn't credit this pretense of new sensibility. Even in the larger university you could still see and feel the contempt for the messiness of studio art, just the visible tip, I thought, of a general contempt for bodily messiness and the grubby disorder of the underclass. The same that made Columbia and Columbus Avenue the equivalent of alien planets. The same that would silently divide Morningside Heights from Harlem until the uproar that finally flamed the firewall itself in the Columbia riots of 1968.

I didn't understand this then. How could I? I was a mass of confused and thwarted ambitions that included wanting to be part of the upper heavens. I wrote an essay about the festival for the *Barnard Bulletin* that struck just the correct self-transcendent keynote, aptly citing Thomas Mann on art as religious vocation. I told the story of how in Venice in 1958 I had renounced sculpting—told it in the third person, as if it had happened to somebody else, so I could pay due homage to letting go of my own "dilettantism" without seeming self-serving. I never stopped to ask why writing it still made me cry.

This curiously overdetermined essay somehow got into a *Mademoiselle* campus journalism competition, and actually won in the faculty writing category. When the award got noticed in the campus press I had a flicker of local celebrity. One hot afternoon of that following Chelsea-Clinton summer, just after Paul and I had deposited our petitions at the Board of Elections, I ran into a student editor from the *Barnard Bulletin* on College Walk. "Got anything new for us?" she asked, eager to ride my little crest into the fall term.

I explained why I'd been too busy to write. In an instant of wayward inspiration I suggested that maybe my electioneering adventure might make a good interview. She gave a quizzical shrug—not even polite, I thought—and moved on.

I followed her with my eyes as she picked up her pace along the herringbone bricks, past the campus sundial, headed straight into the firewall.

We'd founded a Reform club in Clinton that summer, the JFK Mid-City Democrats. It became our little legacy, surviving and thriving well beyond our inauspicious stand for district leader. Even without candidates for the district, it could endorse the Wagner-Beame-Screvane slate in the 1961 election, and enjoy a shared flush of victory when they won. For the following national by-election year, Paul and I stayed involved, as the club upped its profile and brought in congressional hopefuls looking for its blessing.

There were two Reform contenders in that interesting primary race, Bentley Kassel and Mark Lane, both fairly new on the political scene. In-house debate at our fresh new Mid-City clubhouse on 56th Street seesawed, as Paul threw in his lot with Kassel (whom I thought a lightweight, with his typical knish-eating photo op on the Lower East Side), and I argued the case for Mark Lane, who'd begun to make his name in antinuclear evangelism. My new influence with club members astounded me. It also made Harry slightly uneasy, I could see, as if he'd spawned something wonderful and a little out of control. It made Paul furious. Publicly we debated. Privately, often with Harry and Esta, we brawled.

"Kassel is *slimy*," I'd say. "Just out for Kassel."

"You think Mark Lane *isn't?*"

"He has the courage to stand for something."

"*Courage?* Cheesuss, he's a lefty snake."

"C'mon, he's an idealist."

"He's an idealist lefty snake."

"So Kassel is a snake in the middle of the road. So what?"

"D'you wanna win? Or d'ya just wanna ring up credit in Commie heaven?"

"Red-baiting, Paul. Watch it."

Esta would roll her big eyes in semi-admiring exasperation. "Oh boy, here she comes—Joan of Arc." She'd begun to call me that whenever I went over the top, with only a hint of knowing how many polysemous levels her metaphor worked on.

Harry, meanwhile, would usually wait until things had come to an impasse between Paul and me. "Flav's gotta do what she's gotta do," he'd say with seeming impartiality. But he was still restive. He didn't torpedo my idealism like Paul, but he saw some craziness in Lane I couldn't see. It was that sixth political sense. Mark Lane came over as a kind of cuddly firebrand in those days, a Red teddy bear with glasses. All his future half-desperate careers—first as media bugbear, then chief Kennedy-assassination conspiracy theorist, then Jonestown exploiter, and finally purveyor of the tobaccoless cigarette—were still hidden in the womb of Time. I actually liked him. I liked his sensual mouth as well as what came out of it. I thought he had a political gift, that there was something of the true teacher about him, the strayed rabbi. I think he invented the opening line about the Cold War, "Suppose peace broke out in the morning?," a line he followed up at SANE activist meetings with a real political analysis, asking pioneering environmentalist questions about what we'd still have to do with all that poisonous nuclear buildup. Maybe he was crazy, but he was right.

He lost, of course. I lost. But years later, when the convulsive grief we all felt over the shattering of Camelot had begun to anneal itself and Mark Lane's persistent, passionate quest for the sinister subplot of the Kennedy and Oswald and Ruby murders had begun to feel like a public nervous breakdown, Harry would love to rag me.

"There he is," he'd say, as Lane's pug face and tousled hair, looking sadder and sadder, appeared on the TV news, with a microphone pushed crudely into that mouth. "There's your guy."

There is a bit of something erotic in political courtships, always, that may have lent my affection for Mark Lane an edge of sexual disloyalty, for Paul as well as for Harry. They had both, after all, begun to own me.

But Harry might have spared his jealousy. My longing, my desire for him, body and soul, had become a disease, so intense, so intensely *suffered,* that it seemed to empower me with strange, witchlike faculties. Sometimes I thought that if I just turned my unguarded glance quickly in his direction I could risk sending him up in a fiery blaze of clerical garments.

A meeting—sitting in the Strycker's Bay office—standing on a street corner as a meeting broke up—suddenly, without warning, I would feel something like an ecstasy of transport into the presence of an archangel, a lover as "pure, terrible, and handsome" as the dream-lover Simone de Beauvoir once fantasized in the sublime visions of her sultry adolescence. I can still see him, the radiant wild face bent in greedy conversation, the cocky, combative stance as he shifted his pocket hand from side to side, fast-talking out of the side of his mouth like some Cagney with black, burning-bush eyebrows. If he would only once glance my way—

How was it for him? Can I get inside his skin to tell you? count the risks he took to see me or measure the passion fueling his fearless scheming? Perhaps I was too conscious of my own danger, felt too extremely the pathos, the tragedy, the powerlessness trapped in the power of my own victim-passion. Yet I remember one fugitive night together, me still drugged with sleep as he left in the dark. I had to get up early for class. I begged him, as he left, to wake me in the morning. Don't worry, he promised, he'd be out and around, he would come by and buzz me.

The buzzer rang precisely on time. That was all. I got up, dressed, flew past my mailbox, catching sight of a little note stuffed inside, a piece of scrap paper folded in four, and unfolded, a scrawled line from the *Song of Songs*: "Arise, my love, my dove, my beautiful one." He seemed to be inside his love, master of it, choosing it again and again, like pure joy.

Surely sometimes I felt like that too. In the face of the Holy Ghost I could say: I want this. *This.* All of it. It is everything I want. But my courage was full of sinking, a day of confidence, a day of misgiving—or days, I should say, several out of every month, as we played our impromptu games of pregnancy roulette.

And yet, more than I wanted this secret lover, I wanted a baby.

A difficult obsession to understand. A difficult obsession to escape. More primitive than desire. A kind of haunting—shapeless, random, incoherent. Infants, swollen bellies, everywhere. Men who stalked you like live penises.

Like Sergio.

Where had he dropped from, so ferociously intent on rescuing me? Darkly Arabic, tall for a Sicilian and slender as a dancer, proud, composed, with a reserve as ancient as oracles. He had Italian Dino's thick-woven African hair, those same olive eyes with their curious inner light. I would never have thought "police" to think of him— though why not? Even in a silk suit he had the bearing of an Italian officer, reminiscent of my father as ardent, irresistible *ardito.* When he told me, with that earnest, urgent confidentiality of his, that he was tracking the mob with Interpol, I thought, *Yes, you could be the Law.* Something too pure—too puritan—in you to be doing crime rather than stalking it.

He demanded I marry him. I mean, *demanded.* We had taken two walks together along Riverside Park, perhaps gone out to dinner. I encouraged him that far, fascinated by his troubling fusion of cynicism and purity. But he did not understand the pulls of contradictory impulses, even those he was made of.

"*Now,*" he said, the hard curve of his jaw working in the scattershot shadow of the trees along the park. "You must return to Sicily with me. *Now.*" At first I laughed. But he was absolutely in earnest. "I will be good to you," he promised, with all the guilelessness of a culture beyond mendacity, as ancient as Aphrodite. "You will learn to love me."

I said, "I love someone else."

He would not rest until he had interrogated it out of me. Whom did I love? What kind of man was this who would not sacrifice everything for me? *Sposato*— Married? That was nothing—*Niente!* What obstacle would a true love not overcome to make me his—as *he,* Sergio himself, was prepared to do? He became Dante— Mario Cavaradossi—D'Annunzio—father—everything inexorable and resistless to my soul. He bled the tears of righteous self-pity out of me. But not the truth.

Yet still he would not go away. I begged him to, but he stood his ground, as if it was, literally, *his* ground, right there on my 88th Street sidewalk. "I will wait for you. *Here.*" I fled inside, upstairs. When I looked out, there he was in the twilight, leaning against a brownstone railing on the opposite side of the street in his dark glasses and exquisitely cut gray silk suit, slowly lighting a cigarette. At night under the street lamp he was still there, at dawn as I peered out from behind the shade. It was monstrous.

But in the full morning he was gone. Released from his spell, I felt suddenly needy, empty, cold. I slipped outside, venturing beyond my house arrest into the soft spring day, drawn to St. Gregory's as if it were sanctuary. I had no idea if Harry would be there—if someone comes, I thought, I will simply ask for Father Browne. As I slid onto a wooden bench in the vestibule, another priest threw open the carved-oak office door with the leaded-glass crucifix in the window—the new assistant, Father Dick Doherty, already notorious as resident madman. Leaning his face rudely into mine, "W-w-ant a *marry-ahj?*," he asked, stuttering the same Spanglish question he would have put to any dewy-eyed, marriageable young Latina on that bench. I backed out, dumbfounded, shaking my head. I fled back to 88th Street. There was Sergio, back at his post.

He looked up, startled, as if he hadn't expected to see me, and silently torched me with a long, searing stare. I let the heavy outer door of the apartment building slam behind me without looking back, but once upstairs I stole to the window again, and took in the slim, mysterious figure. He was blue-suited now, still pulling on a cigarette—through the open window I could almost taste the pungent scent of his Gitanes. He lifted off his shades and looked up. Those eyes, relentless, dark-encircled like my mother's—it was as if some awful racial memory had been stirred. I drew back praying, *Oh, God, go away.* I wept—deep, dry sobs—wishing in some punishing way that I could act on this ruthless, unaccountable pain.

In the morning he was gone forever.

Who could say where Harry was, the morning I went vaguely, desperately, in search of him? School? Office? Hearing? Meeting? Planning Commission? City Hall?

By now, the inner circle of the Strycker's Bay Housing Committee had been admitted into the offices of new coalition mayor Wagner, carrying social-problem statistics to him hot and fresh as New York bagels from the calculators of state housing lobbyists at the office of the New York Teamsters local. So Harry might have been there. Or he might actually have been in Albany, lobbying the state legislature and Governor Rockefeller direct, playing Republican against Democrat, both ends against the middle, if need be.

For the sense of urgency was building in this, the unofficial year of the rat, as the deadly scourge of the civilized centuries began its populous onslaught on the rapidly-being-abandoned tenements of the Area. Rats! They crawled over dustheaps like cats. By broadest daylight, they flashed across side streets and into sewers and alleyways. They crossed human paths with increasing impudence, refusing even to take the wall.

The cry went up against Governor Rockefeller's delays in signing emergency funding legislation for emptied or emptying buildings. One day, Father Browne uttered the immortal words, "Rocky is a ratfink," into a video news microphone, and shocked even himself at his leap in notoriety. Board members would rush back from the restrooms to hear him whenever his turn came to speak at a hearing. The whole city, from television reporters to the Board of Estimate, seemed to have discovered the Pied Piper himself in this "Gunsmoke" priest with a buzzcut.

I went to some of the hearings—when I could. But like any good mistress, I was really his escape from them, a few hours of delicious, even delirious relief. We would get sloshing drunk together sometimes and just roll around on my living-room rug like puppies. "Eight million people heard me today," he would say, chuckling over some city-shaking sound bite in what even he knew was a silly, megalomaniac haze. The eight million were on the other side of the scale, the 1960 census headcount of the population of Greater New York. On this side, apparently outweighing them all for tonight, was me.

And having, I thought, also done some weighing, I turned toward him, away from my own longing, and kissed his mouth and his heavy-lidded eyes and the length of his glorious sweet body, until he shivered. Kissed him, as if to say, *You are my love, my love, and there is no need to choose.*

6

Sol Steiner was as good a pharmacist as ever risked losing his Columbus Avenue drugstore to urban renewal. So when his wife, Lily, heard about a planned new nonprofit housing cooperative with retail store space, she volunteered her fine accounting hand, making sure that down on the street level someday, after his old building was dust, Steiner's Pharmacy would still be up and Sol would still be running it.

The housing co-op in question was Strycker's Bay's own, a pilot nonprofit, low-income community project the council had agreed to build because it meant not just trying to sell the dream of inexpensive good housing to commercial developers, but having people cut the dream to their own specifications and make it come true. Whatever ratio of potential disaster in such creative, bootstrap development, it was motive enough for anybody. It still is. But then it was new, and the idea caught fire so fast that even the kitchen-layout fantasies seemed to belong to the whole West Side.

Of course even a people's co-op still needed a board, which is where Lily Steiner came in, along with Sylvia Garth, Paul Meagher, Father Browne, and me. For Paul and Harry it was a stellar housing credential: one of the first nonprofit developments on the renewal map. For Sylvia, doyenne of the School 95 PTA and a woman with an eye for a leadership vacuum, it was a definite ratcheting-up of the public good she could do (and the credit she could get for it) at the small price of the occasional use of her apartment for meetings—and what Harry considered a mighty thin occasional trickle of scotch. On that last score, Lily, as big and brown and big-hearted as Sylvia was tiny and blond and pinched, didn't mind driving home the contrast when we met at her place and courting Harry's favor a little by treating the cold bottle of J&B in her immaculate Kelvinator as if it were his personal stash.

And why me? Well, why not? Maybe to keep them honest, and—who knows?—from the farsighted perspective of Harry Browne the historian, to someday become an Ishmael of this white-whale adventure, and tell the tale. I had my own reasons, of course: extra time with Harry, maybe a chance to vote for the irrefragable principle of the partitioned kitchen sink. I was flattered the other three agreed to have me, though I am still not sure why. Evidently they themselves couldn't remember when they voted me out, as soon as the corporation was solvent enough to pay its directors a salary. Father Browne they waited to vote out until the checks were actually being written.

At any rate, I had the pleasure of blockprinting my own name on a co-op posterboard display in the Strycker's Bay storefront. Esta tacked it up on the wall above her desk, following with a certain elevation of black eyebrow over squinted brown eye.

"Hmmm,"she explained, lighting up and deeply breathing.

Now Esta was the perfect professional. She knew that people buying into the Strycker's Bay Co-op for the cost of something like five hundred dollars down were buying insurance on the City's promise that, when all was said and done, they could actually find an apartment on the West Side they could afford to come back to. And she was doing maybe more than anybody to get the message over, as families came nervously in to ask about it, day after day, night after night. But she had some major doubts about what all the names on the oaktag were in it for.

Not me, of course. "Would you tell me what Joan of Arc would be in it for?" And of course not Father Browne. She didn't dare say she thought they were using him. "I just hope he keeps his eye on the ball."

"Which is . . . ?"

"Which is poor people's housing. What else?"

Well, they *were* using him, but so what, when there was in the end the quid pro quo of 180 units of cheap, pretty good housing for people, including some sizable enough for big families. Plus getting to argue with architects and builders—my God, even getting to choose the architects and builders to argue with—not just about kitchen sinks, but about bedroom sizes and refrigerator locations and closet space and toilet seats and whether or not to have laundry hampers built into the bathroom walls.

For me, the gratification was hardly all delayed till ribbon-cutting. Not only could Harry and I actually work together, but we could work together as equals, with similar access to the essential principles. He could actually defer to me without seeming to indulge a weakness, to my sense of design, say, or my capacity to imagine life as it might actually be lived in a certain shape of articulated space. There was pleasure in this quite apart from the undying thrill of his public company, though they went together. It was no small thing to be, like everybody else, comfortable—self-fulfilling—as well as pleasured in his public company.

They didn't think it a small thing, either. It wasn't just the rush of his approval—or even the contagion of his visionary housing fever—that glued us together, otherwise as unlikely a band of comrades as ever met in a good cause. It was his brilliant, radiant company. We all wanted it—Peter Paul and Bernie, Sylvia's husband, as much as Lily and Sylvia and I. Paul loved him. Paul, who'd spent half a lifetime training himself to be mealymouthed, would open up like a zipper the instant we converged at Lily's elevator.

"*Flahvia* [nod], *Fahther* [nod]," he would greet us in his mock-patrician manner, the play of incipient laughter about his mouth, those long Irish eyelashes like hummingbird wings, beating his impatience to laugh. "And what, pray," he'd ask (already laughing, as if Harry jokes required a running start), "are the eminent theologians up to these days?" And then the two of them, in utter disregard of my ladylike sensibilities, would rattle out as many of the latest sick and dirty jokes as they could cram in from the lobby to the sixth floor.

Upstairs, Harry would fine-tune for Lily, and request kosher scotch for two. Lily, after all, was a serious person. She'd let him go on, of course, confessing, once, that he reminded her of somebody she—well . . . So, you could tell, letting him go on was a little like letting herself be tickled. Anyway, she'd developed her own Father Browne addiction, that was clear. I'll bet that even after they fell out (because by then Father Browne had proved himself a radical and a traitor whose passion for low-income rentals had thrown everything out of balance), she cried her eyes dry before she took up with Sylvia and her vindictive battalion of stern partisans of middle-class property values. I'll bet she still spoke of him (as one speaks of the dead) as someone she'd loved and hated herself for loving, a kind of nice *goyische* rabbi who'd got himself mixed up with bad company.

But these were still the best of times. Nothing could have had the headiness of pre-austerity New York—even the Mets were a gas. As the baseball season opened in spring 1962 you could actually see the energy bubbling up around "the Wag's" new Reform administration, see it beginning to produce action in the urban renewal time zone. Wagner's housing assistant, Hortense Gabel, announced a mini-renewal of the West 84th Street block, devastated since the recent riots, that promised to be a preview of the whole West Side project. Barely two weeks later came the mayor's major reorganization of all housing-related agencies, with Milton Mollen as head of the new Rent and Rehab Board and Gabel as administrator. The Gospel according to Mollen came down (defended by him personally in the letters column of the *New York Times*): No more purely luxury apartment developments.

It was a temporary stunner. The City seemed to be doing everything short of giving the city away, except—except that it didn't quite stand up when you put the lens to it. The balm of more middle-class rentals, yes, but there was still nothing in it for the poor. And now the State, just as ambivalent as the City if not more so, was offering subsidies to developers for putting a few middles in otherwise high-rent projects, as if this gesture were enough. And yet at the same time they were offering the City the right of "receivership"—the right, that is, to take over derelict buildings and speed up new or rehab housing, possibly within real low-rent range. A sample was going up on West 103rd Street, a model of small, low-density public housing with none of the features that had given the mammoth high-rises a bad name. They planned to dedicate it in May. A similar project was on the drawing boards for West 94th Street, right within the Area itself.

So, it wasn't all good and it wasn't all bad. Hope damnably seesawed with frustration. Bureaucrats typically seemed to thwart everything promised by the agency heads. On April 15 a Community Service Society report appeared with a sorry count of the number of people who'd already been displaced, displaced completely—meaning they'd slipped through all the relocation nets and absolutely lost their "priority" rights to come back.

One way or another, there was breaking news daily. Sometimes we'd get it ahead of the press, by insider telephone. Sometimes Father Browne's gang would simply carry the word up with them from some downtown meeting. Sometimes we'd have skirmish by press release, a case of Strycker's Bay trying to doctor a piece of news fast enough to head off a coup by the administration, as when we heard a rumble that the City would take over the Area in a single sweep, but the development itself would take place in three stages, north to middle to south, beginning at 96th Street.

"Good. Three stages is good."

"Three stages, three stooges—what's good about it? It means everybody downside runs outatown, while-U-wait. It means property values in the primest real estate have time to skyrocket."

"Which means a project like the co-op, bang in the middle, hangs by the fingernails."

"But it still gives us time to push our own agenda, not just take what's plowing down Columbus like Godzilla."

"Sure, but now the Wag is talking 'constructive' citizens' participation. What the hell is that supposed to mean?"

Long pause.

"You could read it either way."

"Let's read it my way," said Father Browne.

Father Browne's way was to heat up his confrontations with Hortense Gabel on network television, Sunday morning encounters that became so regular people began to call them "The Harry and Horty Show." The relocation issue got so hot downtown, rumor had it that Badillo as director wasn't going to be enough. The City was about to form a whole new Relocation Department. But, Christ, who'd take that on? Who'd even touch it?

What dumb bravado to have scheduled my doctor's orals at a time like this. I can remember feeling a deadly autopilot combination of pure angst and pure gambler's nerve at the same time, as if both my mother and father had married their most typical worst natures in my soul. In flashes of lucidity, I told myself to keep my expectations real. I wasn't going for the pennant, I was just out to make the team.

But it meant that at the very moment urban renewal news was sending temblors through the neighborhood I had to get out and virtually move into the library. The social envelope never pressed more cruelly on what Jacques Barzun was promoting as "the life of the mind" than it did for those desperate last few weeks of April. There seemed endless reading still to do, even in my own specially defined areas. Shakespeare was one. ("Focus on two plays," they said. Oh, sure. *Focus.* There were enough variorum editions plus scholarship and criticism to fill a small library just on my two plays, *Othello* and *Henry IV, Part I.*) Renaissance was another area, comparative Italian-English. (Expect Shakespeare and Italy. Opera? Maybe, maybe not. Better know it anyway.) Also eighteenth-century English and nineteenth-century comparative, Italian-English-French.

My examination date happened to fall with curious synchronicity on the alleged 398th birthday of the alleged William Shakespeare. The night just before the exam, I dreamed a precise and prophetic dream, as if the collision of intense study with anxiety had abruptly tapped a brainstore of clairvoyance I'd seemed to have come less and less in touch with since girlhood, when I had twice uncannily foreseen the questions on high-school algebra tests. In this dream, I am sitting at the exam table in Room 606 (just as I would sit in the morning), surrounded by all those leonine, bespectacled professors (just as I would be in the morning), when below the window bursts a furious rattling noise that swallows every question. Suddenly I am a Tea-Party Alice—"Room Change!" shouts the chairing Mad Hatter, the professors toss their heads and shoot me madhouse looks and everyone stands up and moves lockstep down the corridor, pushing me like a prisoner under a bayonetting of questions.

The next morning, in the real Room 606, I was a limp rag on a chair. Professor Clifford (eighteenth century) presided. The examining professors, Johnson (Shakespeare), Valency (Renaissance), and Woodring (nineteenth century), all nodded respects and sat. I think I had just got launched on a response to Dr. Johnson's guileless little question about Verdi's *Othello,* my inward eye scoping curiously down the past as I stared absently beyond the faces and the polished seminar table to the great, breezy, sunlit rectangle of window at the end of the room, when a jackhammer suddenly split the air—cracked it like a nut—and the tranquil spring-green light and the graciously malevolent humanist waiting silence shattered into a million bits.

Of all the days in all the eons of philosophy and doctors of philosophy, the Fathers of the University had elected this one to begin construction of a massive footbridge over Amsterdam Avenue. They had already summarily demolished East Hall, my old art haven, and replaced it with the modernist new School of International Relations, tribute to the existence of a political universe. Now they were about to join it forcibly to Philosophy, where around this table of polished oak, in Room 606, we were still dreaming our Shakespearean dreams, and Dr. Johnson was about to worry poor Desdemona's handkerchief one more time.

The jackhammer stopped. It started. It stopped again. It started again, the questions continuing just the same, till Professor Clifford swung up out of his seat swearing, and slammed down the window behind him. This was no help at all, anymore than moving down the hall to another room, still under interrogation, just as my nightmare had prophesied. But even prophetic soul hadn't warned me that Professor Valency would slyly put me just the question I had asked him not to, as in, "Flavia, what question *shouldn't* I ask you at the exam?" "Oh, please, Professor Valency, when we get to Ariosto, please don't ask me to remember the names of the characters in all the subplots of *Orlando Furioso. Please.*"

Somehow I passed. Not a first, but that singular stride all the same. And now it was back to another season on the streets, where things had already happened so jackhammer fast I needed a replay. But it was more like a game of double-dutch: you just jumped in wherever they were, wherever they were pushing out the urban-renewal envelope, which happened, that season, to be to 2,500 units.

Meaning 2,500 units of low-income housing. Up from a thousand. *Way* up. The new delegation of Puerto Rican organizations had finally taken the upped-ante to the floor of the Strycker's Bay Neighborhood Council. It tore people apart.

"The City will *kill* us. Wagner will never buy it. You call this '*constructive*'?"

"Without it," Father Browne argued, "priority is bullshit. There won't *be* housing for people to come back to."

"They'll never buy it downtown."

"They'll buy it downtown if the community is behind it."

But the "community" wasn't behind it. Not the community of Strycker's Bay, anyway. Even Harry's salty moral suasion couldn't carry the craven-hearted with him, and the new West Side Tories were immune. "It's going too far. The balance will be tipped."

It began to get nasty. "What 'balance'? You got some magic margin that 'balances' the poor at one in *nine?*"

Herb Stember, Rutgers professor, Strycker's Bay's unofficial resident social psychologist and delegate from 87th Street, tried to mediate: "You can't just ignore this concept of 'tipping.' Ever hear of catastrophe theory? We have it in families," he said. "We have it in neighborhoods. It has to do with attitudes. In the end, it's a subjective thing—"

Browne, trying to stay objective, snapped back, "OK, you wanna talk sociology? Let's talk sociology. We're talking *racial* tipping, right? You tell me. We got race in here, religion in here—class—fear." I watched him agonize. How do you say it, after you've been nice all you can be nice? Do you call people phony liberals, trying to shame them? That doesn't work either. In the end, the more you agonize, the more days and nights and weeks you strategize, stroke, bargain, bash, the more the opposition simply dodges behind the clock: "It'll hold things up even more," they yell. "The City'll cancel the whole thing." And they won. Browne couldn't bring the council with him.

Alliances came unraveled in the muck. Lily and Sylvia, turning coat by Harry's book, feeling vindicated by the council vote, still took Father Browne's public position badly. For them, the housing co-op hung in the balance. Wasn't this something like sabotage? The meetings at the Steiners' and the Garths' weren't love-ins any more.

And the exponential rise in the number of meetings meant fewer nights for Harry and me to spend in each other's arms and more restless nights when we had them. We made plans to head for the Outer Banks in June. We canceled. We made them again.

And then in mid-May the Puerto Rican Citizens' Housing Committee bolted the council and published their own unequivocal demand: 2,500 low-income units in the West Side Urban Renewal Area. *Basta.* That tipped it. The net of support suddenly began to widen. Other organizations had to take a stand, come in or stay out. The NAACP wavered, waffled, backed away. The FDR–Woodrow Wilson Democratic club turned into a circus. On all sides, club members yelled, bullied, harangued. There was bedlam when Father Browne showed up to speak, the old

Catholic-Jewish divide a class divide now. It had opened like a faultline in a quake. Some of them publicly snarled at him that he was an anti-Semite.

And yet to my amazement, to all our amazements, they took the cold plunge and majority-voted to support the biggie. The Reform Democrats who'd won it for Wagner were going to cash in at least one of their chips. They joined the Committee for a Fair Urban Renewal with the breakaway Strycker's Bay rump group, Father Browne at the helm.

They targeted June 22 for a big rally. Holy Name auditorium. Forget the Outer Banks this year, Harry told me. Songs, he said. We need songs. Lyrics. We need lyrics.

Amid all of this, Ann graduated from Barnard. We tore Harry out of the Upper West Side long enough for the three of us to go to dinner at Pierre au Tunnel and celebrate. She was looking so well, so happy. She was done with Barnard, but had found her place. She was in love with the classics, she laughed, over the heady aromas of well-peppered steaks and jewel-red wine, by the light of the wavering candle on the table. She told us about wanting to do an advanced degree at Tufts, maybe get to Italy for archaeology. Wonderful! Italy!

But we two were mad—beyond mad. We switched from Italy, tried to catch her up in the song-lyrics craze. Later, after we'd said goodnight and given her as many gingerly hugs as her thin little body could absorb, we dogged our obsession, just the two of us, back at my place.

"OK. Listen, listen," I hushed him. I sang:

> East Side, West Side,
> All around the town,
> Urban Renewal's upon us,
> All the buildings are coming down,
> The new ones will be luxurious,
> To hell with Mamie O'Rourke—

"—She can be re-lo-ca-ted—to the outskirts of New York."

Fantastic line! "Great!" We kissed violently and I wrote it down. "Now let's try—what? 'Smoke Gets in Your Eyes?' Naaah. How about 'Bill Bailey'?"

So it went. Harry finally fell asleep. I filled up page after page of new words to old tunes that people at the rally, bless them, were going to sing, or Father Browne was going to make them. The words got passed on to Esta. Esta typed them onto a stencil. Nick Kisburgh of the Teamsters' office downtown ran them off, armloads.

The rally was scheduled for 7 P.M., timed to get people in and out by daylight. At four o'clock the telegram came from City Hall to the Strycker's Bay office, but I didn't know it. I was standing in the back of the auditorium handing out song sheets when Harry glided in, looking a tad too smug for a rabble-rouser. He leaned into my shoulder as he passed me by. "We got it," he whispered. For a single stupid minute, I wasn't sure what we'd got.

But of all the sweet moments Harry was ever to have on the West Side he'd come home to, the West Side he'd got back to loving with a passion—it and the eight million people it came bagged in—that moment was the sweetest. Bright-eyed, gleaming with sweat and expectancy, he climbed the steps of that dinky little proscenium stage to a thunder of applause, and holding up the mayor's telegram with its promise of the full 2,500 units of low-income housing, he got to speak that line no Upper Left Sider could ever resist the irony of: *"I have here in my hand—"*

The house rippled, rumbled, roared, and came down. The pols came up and rattled, everybody cheered and stomped. My song parodies hadn't been meant to be sung to the tune of victory, and had a somewhat different tang now, but we sang them anyway, and of all the lyrics I've written for fun and profit in my life, none has ever come back at me with the same zesty blast as the songs we shouted off our mimeo handout on that hot June night. After all the speeches and songs were over, Father Browne took the mike again and declared it "the greatest meeting the West Side ever had," sending everybody home with that acceptable hyperbole and the ring of a thousand clapping pairs of hands in their ears.

You couldn't get into the Tip Toe Inn that night. Never had the Jewish West Side been more in love with Mamie O'Rourke, or vice versa. Never would they be again.

7

Harry, listen.

Somewhere in this wilderness of paper you've left me, I know there's a copy of that song sheet. Who else but you would have kept it—less out of love than for the archival prowess of the thing? And yet my name isn't even on it. Where are the things I left a mark on?

There's the co-op, sure—all those apartments we filled family by family, each in its way a little memorial to a shared passion. But I'd been dumped long before the board's names got bronzed into the lobby wall. And that old oaktag I hand-lettered for the storefront? Gone, trashed—just like those great Ninth Avenue posters from the district leader campaign. Lord, I looked so wide-eyed, so ready for anything. And so bloody scared.

We called the co-op "Turin House"—named it after the Turin Lane we'd found on an old map, a street the first city grid must have buried—buried more than once, probably, until the co-op came along to bury it again, saving just the name—maybe home a century ago to a band of hardy Italians used to the bitter winters of the north, or so we liked to think. Remember how pleased we were that a kind of monument to our sacred, secret little memory of Italy would stand on Columbus Avenue for maybe another hundred years?

Somewhere I bet there's a file box marked "Strycker's Bay, 1960–62," in it everything you ever saved of mine—a brochure or two, a fund-raising letter, a few press releases, something for this old earth, rolling round, to remember me by—if only my name were on them! But I didn't sign things in those days, didn't even think of it—all those watercolors I painted, trudging through the neighborhood, and gave away! No, I haven't forgotten Airtight Cage, *page 125—and how Joe Lyford gave me credit for the "East Side, West Side" lyrics we sang that amazing night. How you loved to razz me for that: the very best line and the only one that ever made it to print had really been yours. And my name's not even in the index.*

So why does it matter now, if it didn't then? If it was enough for me to see you on the street, on the altar, on the dais, just out of reach, just beyond me, doing what you had to do, if it was enough then to know you were everything to me, no matter who else knew it, if I could hold you in the dark, in my arms, in my body, whispering your name?—

Two people knew who Harry was to me.

One was the Teamsters Union's legislative liaison, Nick Kisburgh, who split his work time between a shabby seventh-floor office on West 14th Street and a cubicle under the stairs in the Albany State House. I extrapolate to say he "knew." We never actually told him—at least *I* never did, and Harry was a bank vault. Nickie simply had a mind like a land-mine detector—plus a voice like stonecut gravel, which he'd drag you across just saying, "Hello, doll." A single wisecrack from him could give you a migraine.

I silently assumed he knew. The tradeoff was never having to pretend, never having to make believe I was some pol moll, or, heaven forbid, some great selfless crusader out to get burned at the stake. Nick had no holy principles to protect, either by keeping our secret or by lying to anybody else, but he knew *we* had holy principles to protect, or that Harry did. He always called him *Faather,* with a gently reverential whispery hoarseness in the long *a.* About us, he kept his opinions to himself. About us together, that is. About us separately—that was another matter.

"Honey, you're no political genius," he'd remind me. "Stick to Shakespeare." He'd pop a gem like this as I puzzled over some complex demographic statistics we were preparing for a meeting, trying to crack his code: *O.W., I.M. R.*

"Dickens," I corrected him. "George Eliot, Matthew Arnold—*that* lot."

"I thought you said Shakespeare."

"Shakespeare is a sideline. I've given my heart to the nineteenth century."

He howled like a loon. "You got a trade deficit, kid."

He didn't mean it as an insult. It was my seeming unworldliness he loved me for. He himself was a great reader, and had once even dreamed of being a writer. It kept him ahead of everybody, corkscrewing his wiry little body into a recliner under a couple of strategically placed lamps on a Friday night and reading all weekend, taking beaky little dips into his scotch supply, letting his eyes go bleary and his beard hard, hang-all the difference between night and day. When I first met him, he had a studio loft apartment in Penn Station South where I could imagine him doing just that, not a big place, but filled to the ceiling with books. They fell out of the shelves, tumbled over each other, lay on their sides in stacks. Yet he knew just where they were; they seemed to come to him when he called, like pets—or Pucks—or Ariels. He'd have made a great Oberon, or Prospero. He looked like Caliban.

"Is this 'infant mortality rate'?"

"Rrriiiight." Christ, he was patronizing.

"And O.W.?"

"Out-o'-wedlock, baby." His leathery little face would be sticking into mine—*"Outtawedlock"*—cigarette-stained teeth leering. "The little bastards."

Disconcerting, but ultimately harmless. He couldn't help himself. By a code I think he'd refined working for Mafia bosses, he was rude, not cruel, to women. And not on the make: he wouldn't have laid a finger on another man's woman except in revenge.

My hunch is he didn't want to lay a finger on any woman but his own. Her name was Anne with an *e,* a tall slender dry subtle wisp of a woman who filled the poetry gap in his life. She was an enigma—sultry and Mother Superior at the same time. I'm not sure why the monastic metaphor comes to mind, except that she loved Maine and would just disappear up there for months. You knew they loved each other in some screwy passionate way, yet it was as if they were under a rule, a discipline. Harry and I would puzzle over it. Was she pulling away? Was it some kind of separation? Why, then, did she write him those long, lyrical letters?

While we were speculating in our privacy about their sorrow, they were probably just as vicariously speculating about ours in theirs. When Anne finally came back from Maine, they moved uptown into a lovely big 95th Street apartment with pools of sunshine shimmering off its freshly lacquered parquet floors. Nickie, showing it off, showing off his Anne (though that spindrift woman, she would never really be *his*), invited us both to dinner—a ceremonial event, a celebration of two couplings, really, though not a word was said of love. We ate what seems in retrospect a liturgical meal: filet mignon, so rare it was still bleeding, wild rice. We had Bach on the stereo, plus the elusive, sublime happiness of four blamelessly star-crossed lovers.

Perhaps Anne's Maine connection inspired us to think about heading north that summer after the Holy Name rally, to make up for missing what had become our almost-ritual flight to Kitty Hawk in June. Esta was also going to the Cape, and that we should follow rather than try to dodge her tells half the story.

Because Esta was the other one who knew. Like Nickie, I suppose she knew before we told her, without really having to be told, but unlike Nickie, her knowledge and her response to it were framed not by a code of honor but by a code of protective love that said, *For God's sake, don't stand out there in the cold. Come in, the both of you.*

Whatever it was experience hadn't taught Esta about "the struggle," instinct had, including the wisdom that it was fueled by love. Not just "love thy neighbor" love, which, for most people she knew, couldn't be trusted past the garlic breath of the beloved neighbor, but the kind of love that would swoop down and block your sunlight, as sudden as the beating of dark wings. The kind of love you fled, and rushed to, that broke your heart, broke your brain, stopped your breath, that made you throw yourself into fire. The history of the struggle was full of such loves. What if they didn't always last the forever they invented for themselves? For their small forevers they made transcendence possible, and without that, what was the struggle? To love was to learn how to die. To love, to learn loving, was to learn what to die for.

Not, Heaven forbid, that Esta would ever have said such a thing—never out of her own mouth. Even out of somebody else's mouth, sentimentality embarrassed her. She needed to see herself tough as well as romantic. To see us as claimants to her instincts. She'd much prefer to say, *Come in, for Chrissake, don't just stand out there in the bloody cold like a couple of jerks.*

She did say it. And we did come in. We came in and sat down on her sofa one night and, calm and tearful, told her we were lovers. She listened, her eyes going wet and glossy as black olives, and then she kissed us both. From that moment she became the mother of our love. Still, she had one cardinal rule: *first,* the struggle. And one other cardinal rule: *last,* the struggle. Love was beautiful, oh yes. But love, the special love, was doomed. You couldn't have it both ways. In that respect she was a little like the Catholic Church.

The stopover at the Cape late that summer was more free-form than we'd expected. Esta hadn't really been able to explain about us to Hannah, her housemate at the cottage they were sharing—how could she?—and Hannah, Jewish, divorced, a jaded postgraduate in the course of true love, didn't quite know what to make of this—this—*priest*—this cocky activist priest at that, with rather an elegant bimbo in tow. Esta never ever called him anything but "Father." She had a way of almost lisping it: *Faathaa*, like a prayer. Our stopover turned out a bit like three celibate women and a Nun's Priest caught in a weekend Canterbury Tale.

Funny, but not fun. Not for any of us, I think. I felt compromised and fake, the relief of Esta's knowing warped into a triangle of fakery. I felt cold. I remember wishing at night that Harry could hold me in his arms. But he wasn't Harry. He was Father Browne, a celebrity in a loud shirt and bermudas and flip-flops like every other middle-aged day-tripper in Provincetown, with a straw hat pulled down to keep the sun off his nose—already a blotch of white zinc—a ruthless clown who could lash you with barbed wisecracks until you hurt. "Father," I said, just like everybody. *Father.* I wonder if it sounded like a prayer when I said it.

When the two of us finally headed north alone, I couldn't shake the feeling that we'd now created a permanent third out of our declaration to Esta, a spy named Father Browne, more afraid than ever to be seen with me, Harry's unsheddable public shadow grafted to our once-innocent private selves. The weather, which had been glorious on the Cape, grew cold and rainy. We thought it was against us. Then we rented a cottage in Boothbay Harbor, a cottage we'd never have found free but for the weather, and recklessly stretched three days of mingling shine and shadow into five.

It was a lovely little keep of a house, with rooms and furniture almost as tiny as if they'd been built for children, a house so small we never had to raise our voices even to call to one another from upstairs to down. With our own store-bought provisions and the cottage's built-in supply of literate novels and sophisticated jigsaw puzzles, we pottered about inside, glancing out of the windows at the soft blank eyelid of the horizon and the weathering sea lacing the rocks below. It was as if we inched ourselves open, let ourselves into each other as only lovers can do, and only in a long, slow, patient indifference to time. At night, in the dark and the howling wind, Harry would tell me about the Boys' Brigade of his teenage Hell's Kitchen summers. He'd tell me how he'd learned to build a fire, and teach me how to build one, and we'd watch my blaze catch and flare and go steady in the little stove on the hearth. And then he'd put me to sleep with old campfire stories, like the one about the chanting ghost crying out in the dark of night, *"Who's got my golden aaarrrmmm?"*

I slept like a child—we both did, lying abed late in the morning, soaking in the slowly rising enchantment of gray light inside and the pearl sky and mother-of-pearl sea beyond our window. We never spoke anything to one another but words of kindness and of love.

This was not always how it had been. Picture me on a street corner, waiting to meet him for dinner. In bed, late at night, waiting for him to call. In any of a dozen different places, waiting for Harry—Harry is coming, he is not coming, he is promising to come. Why am I waiting? What am I waiting for? Why am I doing this to him? Why is he doing this to me? Why am I standing—sitting—lying here like this when I could be reading—writing—painting? When my mother misses me—

when I could be spending time with her—or Ann, or Judy? When I could be having a baby, married to someone else?

Broadway in the upper nineties: a four-cigarette wait. I am burning, tortured in a fire so purgatorial I know there will be no need for purgatorial fire hereafter. I have already used the corner phone five times—to call the storefront, the rectory, the clubhouse, Goddard-Riverside Community Center, Esta. Esta says he had planned to meet Paul, who has a temporary office above the high-ceilinged bank building at the corner of 96th Street and Broadway. I go there. I climb the interminably long, steep staircase, pronouncing *why* at each step, sick and ashamed to be tracking down the lover I should not love.

And Harry is there. He is standing with Paul at the back of the huge empty loft, both of them caught in a single aura of pinkish light that makes violet waves of the blueprints spread on the desk before them. At the sound of my heels crossing the bare wood floor, Paul looks up, lifting his eyes and squinting into the dark, Harry looks up, knowing my step. For an instant we are enmeshed in each other's gaze. Paul sees the two of us as surely he has no wish to see us, two lovers, naked, exposed as lovers in an instant very approximate to hate.

And now here was this quiescently passionate truce, this acceptance of the sea, our tears—the ones we wept and the ones we couldn't weep—carving deep cavernous grottoes in our hearts for the wind to moan in.

Fiona Macleod—the strange double-sexed persona and lilting pseudonym of a restless Anglo-Scot named William Sharp who'd given a woman's name to his secret creative life—had leapt out at me once in one of those library-stack encounters Harry loved to call "serendipitous research," when I was looking for books about the Victorians in Italy during a Columbia graduate seminar. For it had been Italy in 1890 where Sharp discovered the creative female self he'd secretly renamed, and Sicily where he'd taken himself to live, and to die.

It seems only too pathetically obvious now why, beyond the Italian connection, Fiona Macleod should have so enchanted me. But I didn't look too deeply into it then, seeing only—and accepting—some curious embodiment of *la forza del destino*. Because from the moment I pulled down that slim little book about him, a book in Italian by a scholar named Anna Benedetti, I knew in my heart that I had found my man, my woman, and my dissertation subject all together.

At a reception for Ph.D. candidates that fall, I got about as drunk as I had ever allowed myself since Greensboro. Flushed, surrounded by male colleagues, feeling as radiantly powerful as I could feel on this nearest thing there was to my own intellectual turf, "OK," I said. "Mark my words. I'm going to be finished in two years."

Professor Carl Woodring stood watchful by, casting upon me the benevolent light of a mentor a good deal more absorbent of his scotch. *"Faaan,"* he said, wonderfully, in Texan. Everyone else laughed in disbelief, each with his own reasons to think me reckless—in some instances the mere fear that they themselves would never finish, which covered certain geniuses with four children and mild-mannered bachelors with the complacency to think it unseemly to hurry. Department star Jim Marolo, they said, still wasn't done after eight years. John Rosenberg had just finished his masterwork on Ruskin after ten—to enormous acclaim. But *ten years?*

"Fiona Macleod," I said. "Scoto-Italian. Start counting."

Babe Ruth pointing to the bleachers was less audacious. A lot less, seeing as he was both Babe Ruth and up at bat. I was neither. The job I now had at Hunter, the sort of thing one did as an all-but-dissertation, though it had its rewards, meant more non-tenure-track slave labor, five courses, piecework wages.

Now that I was working on the East Side, I found myself spending more time with Judy, my ever-loyal high-school friend, and her mother, Muriel, ever the Mature Parent. Still and ever the classic mother and daughter, classical even, tall and handsome as goddesses, they were now just as embattled, struggling over whether to continue to live together. Judy was still painting, plugging away, post–East Hall, at the Art Students League, a little smug still that she was doing her art while I was only writing about it. She'd had an affair with a brilliant painter named Charlie at Columbia, running over to his tiny apartment on West 114th Street to discover both the joy of sex and the gratification of painting heavily with a palette knife. But Charlie was over now, and she'd moved on to docile, attractive John. Muriel thought him a sloth. She was frantic, in her guarded way. "Why does she take up with these *weak* men?" she'd say to me. And then she'd flutter about in her well-draped garments and come up again, in her reflective British manner, "I suppose they're just like her faaather." When these discussions got started, Judy would usually stalk primly away. I felt curiously above it all, like some very old creature, beyond frivolity.

But one did not underestimate Muriel. One day she put a book in my hand. "Here," she said. "Read Erich Fromm." And then, "Poor, *poor* Psyche." She gave me her thumbnail take on the myth of the girl who could only have her lover by night, in the dark, until . . .

"Read it," she repeated.

No, one did not underestimate her.

That term at Hunter I met Al Goldman. Tall, dark, phallic, impeccably suited, and clearly in every way cuts above me in the peon pecking order. He sauntered Englishly into the secretarial section of the chairman's office one afternoon, chatted with me about freshman comp and the student autobiography he'd just been reading, which started out, "I was born of poor but Jewish parents—"

Maybe he liked the way I laughed. He wondered, worryingly, if I thought there was a *future* in my appointment as a lecturer. Damn him, to bring up the future like that.

He invited me up to his place, a one-bedroom conveniently near the college. I had half a feeling it was on the same toney little corner of the East sixties, over the same toney little coffee shop, as the gray-sky-eyed Englishman's of three years ago. It seemed a queer way to prove I'd been treading water all this time.

The apartment was small but fully and expensively furnished. I sank jealously—

guiltily—into his much-too-voluptuous couch and pillows. *Gemütlich,* he called them half-disparagingly, when I said I liked them. They were new. A wave of raging, unresolved pain transfigured the room when he told me the other handsome bachelor furnishings were all he'd got out of a bad marriage. Was it my pain, or his?

It was still too early to go out to dinner and we ordered up club sandwiches from the coffee shop. It seemed so Lexington Avenue. "My season in the East," I murmured, still hugging the pillow, as he made espresso.

"What season is it in the West?" he asked, an edge of contention in his voice.

"Call it the Golden West, my friend," I laughed. I tried to interest him in urban renewal, but concrete politics bored him, and the man who would later write books about Elvis and *The Story of O* did not take his boredom lightly. Beneath the patrician gloss boiled an urgency he held uneasily in check. Even talk about his recently finished dissertation on Thomas De Quincey didn't divert him, though he'd clearly found something about De Quincey the outlaw, the drug-taking "opium-eater," the plagiarizer, that vibrated with his own inner recklessness. "Stole most of his stuff," he tossed out. I thought he was trying to shock me into admiration. "Like Coleridge." But something had already shut me down to him. *Vorrei e non vorrei,* I thought, fatally attracted to his sense of his own potency. But it was a drawn blade.

His scent for the outlaw in me, however petty, attracted and vexed him. "My problem's simple," he said candidly, in an obvious gambit. "She took off with another guy. My fault, I suppose. Doesn't matter. I'm mad as hell." He waited for me, expectant, seductive.

But I felt throttled, alarmingly Catholic, at that moment. Just sitting there in his apartment drinking his coffee and holding one of his *gemütlich* couch pillows in my lap seemed like adultery. I stared off and away, feeling through my body the hum of his air conditioner, which blocked the lower half of his window and filled the room with a watery noise. Outside, the swinging traffic signal was barely visible in the frame of drowning twilight. "Sometimes I think I see dwarves on street corners," I said. The allusion to Anna Karenina wasn't lost on him. Nothing was. I shot a sad, dark, desperate look into his blazing eyes. *Rescue me,* it said. His eyes shot their refusal back; *No.* And then, *Maybe.* And then their own dark, exasperated demand: *Jesus, from what?*

Esta threw a party that November for her thirty-third birthday. "Invite your friends. Invite everybody," she told me. I invited Goldman. He showed up before Harry, and the instant he came in, picking his way toward me through the beat on Esta's new stereo and the waist-high plates of noshes and the dense cigarette smoke and the roar of West Side political gossip, I knew I'd been a fool to ask him. He was dressed in a vested English tweed, nothing lacking but the monocle to declare he was Lord Peter Wimsey arriving at the scene of the crime. But I was dressed, too, in one of the few dresses in my life I can never forget wearing, a halter-topped, wasp-waisted pale-green silk swirled lusciously with green roses, a dress they rightly called in those days a "sheath," and me the blade inside it.

Goldman went instantly on the attack. "You look a little Puerto Rican," he said, though his almost unguarded smile said "deliciously." He made himself a drink. I'd already been drinking—I felt hot with fear and need and wayward desire. From the kitchen, Esta bombarded us with looks.

Harry came through the door, sending me a glance that might have been the fireball epicenter of a nuclear blast. If I'd died at that moment they couldn't have peeled the dress from my corpse. I did die—Goldman's face, hardening into mine, held something like a mirror to my mouth. Abruptly, acutely, he said, "Why did you bring me here?" But by the time he veered around to see what had stopped my breathing, Harry had turned away.

"Good-bye," he said, putting his glass down, very simply, very smoothly, as if he said it all the time. There was a small, self-conscious delay as he searched for his hat. *Jesus,* I thought, he'd come in a hat. I followed him to the door and out into the hall in an agony I couldn't have explained even if his face hadn't been shut like a wall. "One at a time," he said, and disappeared into the elevator.

It had happened too fast for a scene. I went back and helped Esta in the kitchen, paying passing notice to my friend Judy, also invited here from my other life, and here she was, carrying that life with her like a private spaceship, batting her long-lashed baby blues at everyone, even at me, looking goddess-big as always and statuesquely gorgeous and shamelessly on the make. I paid attention to Harry in the usual and appropriately inattentive way, and he did the same. Something weird and contrary floated between us, but we hardly spoke, we could hardly speak. The party roared on, filling the apartment like high tide, flooding into corners, pushing past doors into closets, into the bathroom, into the bedroom with the coats. It must have been two in the morning when the tide ran out, and Judy and Harry were missing.

Ah, but they were not missing, only in the bedroom with the coats. Harry was on top of Judy, and Judy was arguably struggling. He denied everything later, with the blissful moral amnesia and unruffled expectation of forgiveness of the man who is no longer drunk. Judy, for her part, the moment she was released from his grip—and she insisted it had been *his* grip—got up very huffy and principled, brushed herself off, and said, "*That's* a priest?" Then she walked out, never to return to a party of which he was a part, and never forgiving me for having taken up with him.

"That is *not* a nice man," she would say. In a friend who had soberly reminded me she was another woman, it was a judgment I rather approved of.

We needed a break. Harry and Esta and I agreed we'd bolt for Florida right after Christmas, she and I first, lest we inflate Father Browne's now-legendary prowess on the West Side rumor-vine. So she conned a barricuda of an old Chevy from one of her admirers and, tail fins flying, we two headed south, stopping only for a quick visit with my brother's wife, Frances, before we met Harry at the Ft. Lauderdale airport on New Year's Eve.

Lou and Frances had got married the year I'd graduated from college, the year of my own Damian debacle, not auspicious for love. They were newly estranged. But I felt deeply for Frances, who'd done my brother no harm as far as I could tell.

I hadn't seen her in years. Their two children, Diana and Carlo, I had never seen.

They still lived in their tract house near the base in Jacksonville, where Lou had been a resident naval medic. Frances's father, deep-dyed *Napoletano* from Brooklyn, a fine upholstery craftsman in his time, had moved down to live with them. He had just had a disabling stroke and now sat brooding like a twisted household god in a corner of the living room, desperately swinging his useless arm.

It was a pure quagmire of family misery, as if a tribe of Arthur Miller Italians had been impressed into a Flannery O'Connor novel. No one needed to complain for me to hear the roar on the other side of silence, to too-palpably feel all the cruelties of time and age and good love gone bad. For Esta as for me, it was too much to think we were on our way to a romp on the beach. A surge of useless, protective love for my babylike four-year-old nephew utterly cheated me of any of the relief of pulling away.

A cooperative sky hung over us, wet and gray, as together, in long silences followed by bursts of conversations, we tried working it out of our systems, Esta and I, like a couple of family therapists in training. It was near dark before we realized just how dense the fog had become, moving imperceptibly off the ocean and onto the two-lane coastal highway, beginning to wrap our Chevy like a plastic bag. Esta, driving, suddenly couldn't see road signs.

From behind us came a pair of haloed headlights, looming suddenly up out of the darkening soup. A car bigger and more tail-finned than our own whipped past and shot ahead like a visitation from another world. Esta revved up, and for the next twenty minutes she hung on to that pair of pinpoint rear-end lights like a water-skier on a cable, taking curves she couldn't see, the two of us cheering, afraid only that the lights might somehow melt into the fog's mouth like twin red jujubes. But the other car finally did overreach us, and the white muck closed. Not even a pair of headlights coming the other way.

And then the dawn of our stupidity suddenly broke on us both. "Sure," Esta muttered. "Everybody's crazy enough to do eighty in this shit."

We crawled into the next town. We dropped gratefully into the first motel whose blurry pink neon shone faintly through the dark web of fog. Neither of us could sleep, imagining what might have happened if those red taillights had gone over a Florida highway embankment into the sea. But it made a great story to tell Harry when we picked him up the next day—so blazingly bright a Florida beach day you wouldn't have taken the existence of fog on faith. We paused in Miami, Harry at the wheel now, took one look around at the hot bourgeoisie, and kept going until we'd slipped the mainland and were onto the Keys. On Key Largo we toasted in the New Year with Key lime pie and Esta's special reserve champagne, hidden in the boot. But now that we were already out on these step-stone islands into the Caribbean, the romance of being ninety miles from Cuba was irresistible, and we didn't stop again till we got to Key West.

And there we played Papa Hemingway and gang, ate turtle steaks and hung around locals listening to the amazing Portuguese-American-Creole patois of the island.

Not much time left now to enjoy it, but the sunshine was splendid. Of course this only made Esta nervous. "We can't *all* go back to the West Side with a tan," she said. It was a reasonable piece of discretion. She and I lolled about, soaking up the rays, while Harry got himself a jaunty straw to protect his face, covered the rest of his body with a bedsheet from the motel, and sat uncomplaining by the pool, reading, where I painted him into posterity with my handy portable watercolors. "Don't worry," I reassured him. "I'll tell them it's Jackie Mason."

We heard New York was a freezer on the radio news. We dragged out our stay for as long as we could, figuring that with the three of us taking turns at the wheel going home we could do an overnight marathon. We were too happy to want to leave. For the first time in our lives together Harry and I were able to let down our guard in front of someone else, and Esta, missionary forever, seemed to enjoy it almost as much as we did. We all got a little crazy drunk our last night, less alcohol maybe than moonlight and stars and honeysuckle pouring aphrodisiac juice over garden walls and the romantic association with a celebrated man who looked a lot like the celebrated man we were with.

"We'd make a great ménage à trois," Harry suggested, as we stumbled through the streets in the silvery semidark. *"Faaathaa!"* Esta burst out, authentically shocked. For Esta, maybe it was first, the Struggle, and last, the Struggle, but in the middle, she was straight and true as an arrow. Of course, as he swung his wonderful arms around both of us so that we stumbled even more awkwardly than ever down the street, she didn't take him seriously, and neither did I.

Eighteen-month-old Sonia Rivera, West 94th Street, died of rat bite that winter. Esta insisted I come with her to the church chapel, where the child was laid out.

Afterward, she said I did not look well. I chalked it up to a terrible feeling of sorrow and helplessness. Another child we could not protect. I didn't confess the panic at my heart that maybe Harry and I had let down more than our emotional guard on the Keys.

The Strycker's Bay office had no bathroom, and time after time, when I was there, I wondered what Sol Steiner must be thinking as I ran into his pharmacy up the block every couple of hours to pee. Esta said not a word.

The doctor in the HMO on 86th Street treated me like a disinheriting uncle. First he asked me if I were married. Then, he broke me the results of the rabbit test.

"You're on your own," he said.

It wasn't till I was out on the street again, awash in New York's dazzling winter sunshine, that I understood what he meant.

Mario and Maria, my parents. Formal wedding photo, New York, June 16, 1929.

Mario behind the butcher block, about 1930.

Picnic at Indian Lake, New York, summer 1939. Family portrait by self-timer: me, Mario, Maria, Ann (in Maria's lap), Carlo, Lou, Grandpa Luigi.

Tuscon, Arizona, 1943. Me with Band-Aid—a small bike accident—playing "Hawaiian" guitar with my sister, Ann. Note the crepe paper hula skirt.

Harry Browne's confirmation, 1928.

My combined First Communion-
Confirmation, post-Tucson New York, 1945.

Father Harry and Father Robert (Wilde,
left), photographed on a vacation excursion to Luray Caverns in Virginia,
October 1947 (three years after they
were ordained together as priests in the
New York archdiocese).

The "Thesmophoriazusae": Joanne, Anita, and me,
outside Brooks Hall, Barnard College, 1954.

Rooftop, Striano, Italy, September 1957. Snapped by Carlo (or was it Alfonso?)

Posing for Harry—and posterity —on the Via Appia Antica outside of Rome, spring 1958. I sent this picture home with a note that said: "I feel deeply connected to these three dead Roman ladies, even if one of them is a man."

September 1957. Father Harry Browne giving the Centennial Sermon at St. Michael's Church on West 34th Street—about a week before I met him in Perugia.

Harry casts a shadow as he photographs me with a friendly baby, Nemi, June 1958.

Student float, "Festa della Matricola," the Italian University students' annual parade, Padua, 1957. Big American Dino, in glasses, in front of me, looking at the camera.

Poster-girl for the district leader race, New York, 1961.

Storefront, Strycker's Bay Neighborhood Council (east side of Columbus Avenue, just north of 86th Street), 1962. Those are my hand-lettered signs on the windows.

Part Four

La Traviata

1

Sunshine is almost all I can remember, every irresolution burned off in a sudden clearing of haze. I felt too heroic to be daunted by fear. I couldn't have walked in plainer white happiness if I'd been a snowmaiden in a grace of angels. This was less a moral condition than a factual one—perhaps a fact of purest biochemistry. Considering the alternatives—which I did not even think of doing—it was a bliss of ignorance.

I told no one but Harry—another symptom of my ardent resolve, since I neither wanted advice nor wanted to have to refuse it. Harry drew back in meek bewilderment from the spell of my certainty. We knew I would have to leave the West Side, but there was still time to scheme, time enough for me to invent futures like a novelist. And it was *my* scheming, not ours.

I continued that spring to teach at Hunter mornings, and afternoons to work at Strycker's Bay, where Sonia Rivera's barbaric rat-bite death haunted us like a harbinger of plague. The neighborhood was shaken with fear and torn with controversy over who should be held accountable. The tension rose. A new pastoral assistant at St. Gregory's, Father Tom Farrelly, wrote to the *Times* accusing them of ignoring the story and lambasting the public officials whose bureaucratic delays, he said, were being paid for in the lives of babies. But little Sonia Rivera herself haunted me intimately. I could not get the sight of her out of my eyes: a child poised forever between infant and child lying in baby lace and bonnet on the white satin of her bier as if it were a bassinet, tiny eyelids sculpted over sleep-seeming eyes. Deep, unmistakable magenta puncture marks in the crook of her plump, milk-white arm. Her pale young mother, lighting candles and keeping unbroken vigil beside the little body, looking straight at us as we approached through the otherwise empty, twilit church. She was unable to speak, some half-accusing hellfire cooking in the deeps of her eyes. Suddenly my mind was with child. Across it flashed the curious superstitious thought that motherhood was not safe.

My parents had plans to spend the summer in Italy—my mother's first trip, my father's first in fifteen years—a chance piece of destiny that seemed to fall in with my own. I innocently offered them house- and dog-and-cat-sitting services while they were gone. They eagerly accepted, too relieved to scrutinize my motives. Only my father, when I came home as they were still packing, detected my thickening middle with alarm. I threw him a diversionary bone about "the good life," but my heart raced. He gave me a curt comeback and a filthy look. What else could he do? Loose summer cottons made the evidence ambiguous, and my mother's attention was captive to all the last-minute madness of departure. They were already in mid-Atlantic, well beyond the reach of such anxiety, by the time my dear skylights passed to another West Side dreamer and I attached myself to the womb of my childhood house to grow two new lives.

At night, alone, the very dark I lay in seemed less dark for my inner light. I bred long future vistas, of traveling to Italy in August just before my parents returned, of going north to my friend Silene, now providentially degreed in pediatric medicine. Ann, also in Italy now, would be taking her Tufts field courses in classical archaeology in Naples, where in fact my parents were about to see her, engrossed in her demanding program. Little by little I would let her in on everything. She would be there for me, I knew it. Silene wrote: I could stay in Schio with her parents until the baby was due. Here, only Esta need know anything, and my baby would be born where it had really been created—yes, love child of love land, *patria d'amore.* Yes I said Yes I will yes—

So far it all seemed delusionally practicable. The after was still a blur, but no matter—I would come back, I would go on, *Madonna con bambino,* fearless, sanctified, complete. And if ever the question intruded itself, *"What about Harry?"* there was a simple answer ready: Harry is my love, Harry is the father of my child, Harry has absolutely nothing to do with this. Not that I meant to repudiate him—Lord, no! Only I would never again be the maiden in the tower or Mariana in the moated grange, waiting for rescue. I had other fabulous prototypes now. I had Hester Prynne and Gaskell's Ruth, I had Tess of the d'Urbervilles—all the maid-mothers and phallic women who had ever seized my imagination, who had ever closed the mysterious circle of myth and become untouchable and entire, evolving beyond the courtship dance or the reach of desire to their own new spiritual reckoning.

I wonder if other mothers remember this first stupid rapture of self-sufficiency, this relentless mute integrity of motherhood. No one else could believe it, or understand how it could have nothing to do with fathering. I plead the authority of experience. Quite apart from the intense tenderness for Harry that now commingled with my old passion, I believed I needed no other source of closure for my destiny. And I do not say this was good, or good for me, or even good for Harry, because, though I know there were many times in our five years together when he must have feared this baby like a doom, he must also have longed for it in another part of the tangled forest of his heart—longed for it like that thunderbolt message from heaven, the sign that would burn the path and part the waters and declare for him where his manful duty lay.

I stole his sign and made it mine. I let it fill me with a conviction so powerful, so daunting to both of us, that, if the obvious question, *"Didn't this change things?"* ever rose to his mind, I never heard it—because I would never have allowed it to pass his lips, or passing his lips, pass through the solid membrane of my plenitude. *His* mother could sleep secure.

At the moment there was little time and place for mother-thoughts on the West Side, except in the aggregate, except in the rhetoric of social justice. Even a Sonia Rivera must inexorably evanesce into something larger than life, larger than a single life or a single death, into something great and mysteriously changeful blowing in the political wind, as the great tidal season of civil rights witness moved on us like a hailstorm.

The great national March on Washington in August was mobilizing, calling for a gigantic rally on upper Broadway in June. There was absolutely no question, for the organizers or for him, that Father Browne would be a principal speaker. Only whether Spellman would let him—Spellman, still keeping cryptically silent about Harry's having deflected for more than three years now his ecclesiastical historian-biographer's mission in order to help man the urban-renewal barricades.

But there was no time to lose. There was, they said, no time even to ask. And remarkably, after the fact, Spellman did not say a word.

I was already too visibly pregnant now to be seen on the West Side. Harry kept me in touch by telephone, and after the June rally we stole hurriedly, riskily off for one last week together in Nag's Head, North Carolina, only pausing along the way in nearby Elizabeth City to purchase the simple gold wedding band that would make an honest woman of me.

After that trip we kept carefully apart. I settled at home into a kind of fairy-tale confinement with a chihuahua and two cats. There were no acrobatics of evasion: our New Rochelle neighbors, as always, kept to themselves. My brother Lou, now an orthopedic resident at a teaching hospital in the Bronx, appeared sometimes and stayed long enough to eat or sleep. But he was so intensely focused on his work and distracted from me by his latest girlfriend that I actually had to sit him down one day and ask him to take a good look.

He opened his eyes wide. Then he shut them again, completely, as if he wished he could sleep away what he had seen. Then he growled, "Who's the father?" with an Italian brother's primitive rage for honor. He was ferocious when I refused to tell him. I stopped his *"Why?"* with the fire in my eyes. He said the father ought to be held accountable. When I said I had no intention of holding him accountable, he told me I was a bigger fool than he thought. "And selfish. Incredibly selfish. What about Mom and Dad?"

"C'mon, Lou. Let's not talk selfish." It was hard to forget those two fatherless kids in Jacksonville, or the philandering that had murdered his marriage. This made him silent. After that, being a doctor made him tolerant and, to the limits of his attention, caring. It was a comfort just to have him in the house sometimes, even though for real prenatal care I went to Dr. Belle Jacobson, the miniaturized demigorgon of tough love who'd become our family doctor over the years. The day I walked in with my belly leading, Dr. Belle raised her tiny black eyebrows over her granny glasses, asked me if I were really ready for this, and when I said *yes,* took me in like Mama Bear. I never feared for an instant that she would betray me to anyone, least of all my parents.

What more did I need? I ate little and paid no rent, and, as the tales say, laid by for the future. I found it required no special commitment of thought or energy for a baby to grow in the warm petriculture of my belly. At nine each morning I opened the secretary desk where my father's leather-and-gilt-bound copies of Boccaccio and *Animal Magnetism* still stood fast behind glass doors, and, hour by quiet hour in this cool parlor alcove, casement windows to the left and right of me, small, dumb creatures curled in chairs beside me, I wove my dissertation like a tapestry on a loom, like a pregnant Lady of Shalott.

And Harry, my errant Lancelot, was on his travels. Having slain a preliminary civil rights dragon or two on the West Side, he'd tossed up his options. After a clerical summer junket in the Holy Land, he would either return in time for the March on Washington in late August—seeing me once, quickly, surreptitiously, before I left for Italy—or miss the march and rendezvous with me in London for two weeks before coming back to work at Cathedral College in September.

Perhaps in my detaching semi-dream state I was less aware than I should have been that Harry *had* to be in Washington, witness to a gathering that held promise even then of becoming the crucial civil rights event of the decade, and that now, as the great rally where Martin Luther King was to make his famous "I have a dream" speech, has taken on the historic stature of one of the events of the century. But if Harry agonized over his choice, I never knew it. Not then, not later. For the end of August 1963, he told me, he had chosen London, and me.

There were times when I might have imagined the postcards and airmail notes Harry sent me from Israel in July as messages shot into my tower by crossbow, but a summer in my parents' house was anything but medieval. A day's writing, an hour of sun in the afternoon garden with its fruiting plum trees, a small walkabout and a quiet supper, and I would stretch my sleekly blooming body for the evening before my father's altar-sized walnut console, relic of the religious awe surrounding television when it was new. And there one warm night in July I saw a rerun episode of "Gunsmoke" that almost smashed all my infant mother courage. It had a subplot I can only describe as the story of a woman taken in adultery—pregnant, and trapped in a remote prairie cabin alone when her time comes. Her baby is the fruit of her sin, her lonely, writhing, shrieking childbirth agony the price she must pay for it. There was no mistaking this. The camera stalked her obscenely, exposing her again and again in the humiliating bodily spectacle of her labor, cutting suddenly, manipulatively away and back again so you could never prepare or protect your eyes. I could not protect *my* eyes. I thought her sweat would wet the tips of my fingers if I reached out and touched the screen.

It didn't matter that only feet away, between the covers of Pearl Buck's *Good Earth,* was the doughty image of another woman giving birth alone, bravely cutting her infant's umbilicus herself with a shard of pottery—the first childbirth I'd ever read of as a girl, in its way perhaps the secret underpinning of my little bravado. I seemed to have forgotten it utterly. I lay in a kind of induced amnesia, a paralysis of newly suspended disbelief, until long after the television program was over and the "Gunsmoke" adulteress was dead. When I lifted myself up, finally, in a deep, sick dread of foreboding, the baby moved worryingly inside me. But I could no longer speak to it from the terrified loop of my mind, which I prowled wildly for every idea of childbirth I might have stored in years of being daughter, niece, aunt, cousin, student, reader, conscious epistemophiliac spectator on the world's forever goings-on of birth, copulation, and death.

Nothing came to me but a film they'd shown us in college once—an audience of mixed Columbia men and Barnard women, a film oh so carefully, so differently and documentarily cut, so voice-overed and antiseptic, the female genitals an eyeless face in a white snood, the birth instant nothing but a blind purple mouth spewing up a softball. Yet I remembered some of the cooler women betting how many men would faint when the head crowned. Remembered bitterly, because I could not explain how I had come so far and never fully imaged to myself the potency of the pain hidden inside my bodily joy like its very seed of meaning. I felt betrayed. I thought Harry, who knew everything, must have known—must have known, and feared, and fled, and left me to deal with this alone. I wondered about my innocent, self-induced stupidity. Maybe it was a good thing, a trust in my own mother's unfailing mother love, which had brought me into the world in the same painful way and seemed to have forgotten. I prayed. I think I prayed for that trust to come back and heal the bleeding gash across my brain.

But even in the solemnity of that mother-prayer, I lay under the bed lamp in a ferocious, ragged sweat of humiliated femaleness, in such a new sense of enmity with my own belly that I was unable to touch it. And yet the baby stirred again in a countergesture of amity with me. There would clearly be no sleeping for either of us. I twisted the snake arm of the lamp, scanning the bookshelf on the wall above me for something to read.

This was the same room where I had slept as a girl, where the lights from the cars making that hard turn into Sickles Place had swept arcs of tantalizing light across the ceiling, where the scent of my mother's jasmine had stirred my girl heart. It had been Ann's bedroom last, before she'd left for graduate school, and all the books she'd once collected as a student nurse were still there on the shelves she'd mounted for them. I think Grantly Dick Read's *Childbirth Without Fear* must have deliberately planted itself in my line of sight.

It was of course the answer to my prayer. I pulled it down. I read it all night. It saved me, in the way such evangelical tracts are meant to—if giving me back my fearless motherhood again can be said to have saved me. It saved me for Harry. It saved me for all those who might ever have worried their hearts over me out in the world alone, having my first baby. Saved me for my mother, for my sister. Saved me for that future I dreamed I could foretell and control.

The summer fled. I did what I'd come for. I wrote. I gestated. I took the dog to the vet for her shots, and ended up chasing her like a squirrel when she jumped my arm-hold, running half a mile down North Avenue all bouncing belly and breasts, laughing and crying and cursing the Mexicali God of the Chihuahua. Whatever the hypocrite it made me feel, I called Harry's Mammy, still living by herself in Ravenswood, because Harry had asked me to, and because I loved her, now more than ever. On my own mother's well-oiled Singer I fashioned myself a wardrobe of flowing maternity dresses for my travels. And I finished a complete first draft of the story of the double-speaking William Sharp, whose obsession with childbirth spoke like a woman to me.

Then I telephoned Esta and asked her, simply, if she would meet me at the airport on the evening of August 24. Nothing else.

I tried to see myself as she would see me, as I waited for her in the BOAC departure lounge, struggling to keep my maternity blouse with its bold print of black-and-white peonies from too-visibly creasing between my belly and my breasts —wondering just what tart, unsparing thing she would say as soon as those gun-barrel eyes of hers met my shining ones, as soon as she'd seen the wide-brimmed straw hat and the shameless tan and the general radiant glow of the unrepentant heretic.

"You're pregnant," she said, as if *she* were telling *me,* still in full stride across the blue carpet, even before she'd sat down beside me, nodding in pretend wonder at things taking precisely the course she'd always known they would. She smiled as she folded herself lightly down, her lips taking that familiar Buddhic curve of wisdom. She was still a little breathless. Her charitable eyes were wet—perhaps with love, perhaps with a fear I dared not read there. Years later, she would recall this moment. "My God, how brave you were," she said. "Stupid, but brave." She had not forgotten a thing.

We dropped down to the little ersatz pub the British kept hidden in the terminal in those days, complete with dartboard and dark corners, and I ordered my first glass of Guinness, which Harry'd told me the Irish always gave their pregnant women. I was in such a sentimental haze of love-longing, I hardly noticed I hated the taste. I felt his presence already, as if that litany of grade-school prepositions he loved to recite—*about, aboard, above, across, after, against, along, among, athwart, before, behind, between*—didn't need nouns and verbs to be predicated.

I told Esta how long we'd be in London together. "Then he's back in New York. All yours."

She roared at the absurdity of this. "Mark my words," she said. "He'll need shock treatments to keep from jumping off the Queensboro Bridge." She had me laughing. I wanted to tell her how exhilarated I felt, like an astronaut full of Jack Kennedy moon-launch fever, but I didn't, and she didn't tell me what a lunatic I was when I laid out my plan.

"What about your folks?"

"They're probably on their way home right now."

"And your sister?"

"She's in Italy. Esta, things have really worked out, believe me. She's on her archaeological dig in Naples—right there if I need her."

She looked at me hard. "We're talking about your sister." She took out a cigarette and lit it, very deliberately, took a deep drag and blew it away. "Well, you can always come back if it gets too tough."

But that was the hitch. "Not without spending two weeks in quarantine. Health regulations. They don't give inoculations to pregnant women."

"*Cheesus.*" She took another pull at her cigarette. "It's gonna be a long, lonely wait.

Got anything to keep you busy?" I tapped the Olivetti typewriter case at my feet. She knew about the revising dissertation. I tried to smile. "Scared?" she asked.

"Now I am." She asked about money. I thought I had enough. In an emergency, Harry said he'd wire more—it would probably have to be through her, OK?

And then she suddenly said, "What do you know about babies?"

I sighed into my sagging Guinness. "Send me Spock," I said.

We kissed. I was launched. The flight being near empty, the stewards whiled away the night-long crossing by treating me like a celebrity, bringing me food and wine and pushing my armrests alternatively up and down, plying me with blankets, correcting the shades when we hit the midnight dawn, serving me coffee when I sat up, calling me to the window to see the first British landfall. Still a little jealous of my lonely bravado, I wanted to scorn their solicitude. Then they handed me down my typewriter and vanished as if I had dreamed them. I passed through the customs barriers alone.

In this sour London dawn it suddenly seems so long since I have seen him. His face is below me, open, waiting to catch my nearsighted attention, and my eyes seem to rush to its brightness and to the red shirt he is wearing as to a whimsical brush stroke on the gray abstraction of the terminal. I take him in as fearful tongues take eucharistic wafers. I come down. We meet. We kiss lightly, decorously, once. We ride the bus silently into the city because we cannot speak.

Our bed-and-breakfast, on a crescent-shaped drive in Paddington called Sussex Gardens, is a crouching white bulldog in a row of crouching white bulldogs. The concierge, a tall Polish emigrée with deeply hennaed hair, seems not to have expected a "wife" so young, or so six months gone with child. There is a flurry of motherly concern for my comfort before she leaves and closes the door to our room.

It is not a pretty room, its carpeting and draperies threadbare and bottle-green. Harry's kiss has an alien taste. His urgency is frightening. But I know he is frightened too, his taste the taste of his own fear. We undress, shivering, peeling away strangeness. We sink together into the sagging hammock of a bed and plummet, weeping, into sleep.

When I finally came awake it was as though I had passed into another dimension, into an unbelieving joy so immense it felt like pain. The drapes were not completely drawn, and a pallid wand of light, reaching across the little length of room to where we lay, was all the visual clue I had to tell time by. There was the slosh of cab wheels on the rainy street, a smell of damp, old dust. Evening. It had been morning. It was evening now. Harry stirred. A rush of desire enfolded us like a sea wave. Gropingly in our awkward half-sleep we coupled, and, bodies burning, slept again, slept till it was morning, without hunger and almost without speech.

But when we woke, we talked. We ate. We talked. Grisly London weather! I wore my raincoat to breakfast. "Tea," Harry advised. "Pots of tea." It was tribal advice. Out of that London pot must have poured a thousand New York teatimes, as Harry, tongue loosened, recapitulated all the milky-sweet brewings he'd drunk from a glass at a cold enameled table in a 35th Street tenement kitchen. Back when Mammy was all middle-aged fat and flannel against the bitter winter mornings, firing up the stove to melt the frost off the tenement-flat windows, and brewing strong tea to warm her boyos. "Never short of Sheffield's, o' course," he remembered. That was when he told me about Pop, and the bottles that chinked like bells in his pockets.

I told him how well Mammy had sounded when I'd phoned. "But she still calls me Claudia," I said. He let out that big rupturing laugh of his, throwing his head back to give it room. Besides being Mammy's true projects friend, doing her marketing, bringing up her mail, fixing her iced tea in heat waves, Claudia was black. I knew the name substituting was a good sign, of Mammy's feeling innocently friendly toward me. Harry looked at me, a little scrutinizing. "You could almost pass right now." My backyard suntan. I laughed. "If *you* call me Claudia, I'll kill you."

He reached his hand to my rough black hair and smoothed it gently—something he never did in public. I'm sure he saw me quiver. His lower lip trembled a little, like a child's. His eyes were brimming. I knew he was thinking about what was coming at home: the civil rights witness. There was no way, then, you could *not* think of it. But his mind, like mine, was everywhere else too—on us, on his mother, on how he'd missed bringing her out to Rockaway Beach this year on her annual Assumption Day trip to "take the waters." It was the only little service she ever really asked of him the year round. Maybe he was remembering that one time two years ago when I'd gone with them and combed the beach for shells with his three nieces, like girlfriends. As we'd wandered off, I'd looked back to catch Mammy waddling barefoot to the water's edge, her big skirt swooped around her hips, wading calf-deep into the brine, then cupping her hands and dipping up some ocean and ladling it over her arms. A white towel lay across her back like a shawl. From under her hat, you could see the little knot of white braid poking. And then she'd looked up and out over the sea. "Looking toward Wexford," Harry'd said afterward. We both smiled now, as if we were there again somehow with that sea-blinded girl from the wild Irish coast, sitting under a striped umbrella on a sunny, windswept beach in Rockaway.

But we were not on a beach. Not Rockaway, nor some remote spit of the Outer Banks, nor some desolate cabin in Boothbay Harbor. And that was the wonder of it: here, days and days together, hand in hand together, in a city. A *city!* Even prudish London norms of public behavior seemed permissive to us, who had never even allowed ourselves to hold hands on the street, let alone lean in that eager, familiar spate of talk across a table in a restaurant or press our knees together in a pub booth, violating all codes.

My one piece of real work, the reason I'd proclaimed to others for coming here, was to search out the still-living daughter of the woman William Sharp was supposed to have loved sixty-five years ago. She had not been his wife. Scholarly rumor was that the daughter had actually been Sharp's love child. Old, now, old enough to have her crotchets, she had already been approached by another American scholar and refused to see me. I appealed to her through her solicitors, with whom I had had a hopeful correspondence from home. I pleaded my case again. But she was absolutely stolid. There was no getting past her refusal.

I felt the setback keenly. In all my scholarly naïveté it had been so unforeseen. Disappointment made the dull weather duller. I bemoaned it. I bemoaned everything, the unrelenting cold rain, the dresses I had so carefully readied for this little honeymoon showing nothing but their draggled rain-soaked hems below my coat. But Harry, blithe through all of it, made me blithe. Off to the British Museum we went to see the rhinoceros goddess, and celebrate my disconcerting fertility. We ogled mummies, wandered through room after room of luminous wax faces from Alexandrian tombs, one of whom looked like me. Sometimes he went proper. "No public kissing," he would remind me, when I impetuously violated the rule. I thought what years of public shyness, priest with woman, he must have overcome the day he just as impetuously reached over and laid his warm hand trembling on my belly, when through my thin dress he saw the baby move.

How much better to have quarreled, if only to make parting more bearable. We were like two adventurers, laughing at the folly of loving each other but unable to part in anything but pain. Our disciplined old passion seemed to come unleashed and tear us to pieces. At night, in my arms, he would cry, *"My wife, my wife"*—repeat it, over and over, in breath so hoarse and solemn, so intense against mine, that I had no choice but to surrender, to marry him again and again as though one marriage could never be enough.

Such night storms united us. Daylight, when all we had was reason, betrayed us again. When all we had were selves that walked together and apart. His singleness had the name of priesthood, which everyone understood. Mine had no holy name—who then could understand it?

We stopped trying to understand. We sank blindly back into Genesis, letting the womb of that groaning bed take us, consume more and more of our few remaining days as if we were breeding some great fetal destiny under its red plush cover. Awake, we would still laugh, at the clumsy bed, the eternal rain, the awkwardnesses of making love with a fishbowl between us. Harry, feeling at the wall of my stomach would find a foot. "My God, he's doubled in size!" It was definitely *he* by now, no more waffling on pronouns. Inexplicably we dubbed him Sam. Why? Something faintly funny in all languages? Something Old Testament, perhaps? Samson? Yes. Samson. "Out of strength, sweetness." I needed such courage. Such faith in both strength and sweetness now.

We had prearranged our flights so that neither of us would have long to wait alone. We struck out from the hotel to the airport still a couple, smiling for the concierge, as if to say: My *dear*, would we *now*, after such a reunion, ever *dream* of parting again? I believe we actually thought we had invented this sham for her. I have a letter that reminds me we said quite a decorous farewell at my boarding gate.

"Don't look back," Harry said.

"I won't," I say. "Don't you either."

But he did, and I was gone.

2

I had seen it coming, from the moment the plane took flight from London over a sea of dirty clouds that smothered the continent all the way to Milan. Then the train had passed through a sodden, amazingly inhospitable landscape I couldn't believe was Italy. Silene met me at the station in Rovigo, leaning unevenly on her umbrella like a cane, a wan, self-effacing emblem of pathos. We were halfway up the mountainside, to Schio almost, before she'd said a word.

The whole thing was off. *Sweet Jesus,* I thought. *What will I do now.*

Just inside the doorway of their marbled vestibule her father bowed inscrutably and vanished, her mother offered a limp hand and two dry cheeks to kiss. *"Non sto bene,"* she announced—I am not well. But she was as vigorous-looking as I remembered her, handsome in a ruddy, weatherbeaten way. Was she covering for her husband, unable to face me himself?

Silene, still struggling to be helpful, said the parish priest had suggested I stay in Recoaro, a mineral spa nearby—anonymous, full of hotels. *Fathers,* I thought. *Taking their stand against bastardy.* Her mother must have seen me flinch. She seemed to need to convey a caring she did not feel. *"Come ci pensa, tua mamma?"* she asked. What did my mother think of this? I was almost furious with the stupidity of her question, yet crushed with a sudden wild flashback of impossible tenderness, the sensation of my mother folding me in her arms.

She saw the rising tears, saw my struggle to quell them, asked with sanctimonious piety if I ever went to church. The irony was almost unbearable. I could feel the laughter creasing straight through the pain in my heart.

Recoaro was a summer resort, even now, in September, already dead. Silene had already booked me a single at the off-season rate, a room that might have been a cell. She left me there and drove away. I wandered alone along the desolate Corso that evening, where rustling leaves eddied into small heaps in the deserted gardens and belvederes, and went to bed supperless, sleeping a violently dream-filled sleep. The crash of morning church bells startled me awake, vibrating the little body curled tremulously in my womb, sharing everything.

I left that afternoon, with a note for Silene saying I was going to Vicenza to be near the lying-in hospital. I did not intend to think kind thoughts of her. But as the bus wound down the familiar mountainside I remembered how we had once picked yellow cowslips there together among the last melting patches of snow, how I had pressed some into my Orlandi, the ponderously boxy little Italian-English dictionary I always carried—even now packed somewhere in my bags—and I thought I could almost forgive her for the sake of that faintly gold-stained page.

·

The *padrone* of the Albergo Due Mori, up in Vicenza's old city, coolly offered me a small upstairs room in a separate hotel building called the Palladio, about a quarter mile away. I took it, my uncertain gratitude too laced with despair and exhaustion to refuse, though it meant that for *pensione* I would have to cross the wide marketplace piazza three times a day.

Nothing but the hotel signboard bespoke the great architect. The building's plainly un-Palladian restuccoed façade hunched down on a flinty alley whose cold chastity the sun never violated. I felt a vaguely virtuous sense of resigned acceptance as I entered its damp domain. There even seemed something fitting in the presence of a monastery next door, the *Oratorio dei Servi,* its front a patchwork of ancient, blotchy, tea-colored stucco. Out of this eyeless sentinel the sheet-metal voices of the monks flowed from dawn till dark, chanting penitence the full length of the dim street. Now and then the boyish, gaunt bodies the voices came from flew by the hotel in chains of brown cassocks and saucer hats as uniform and mechanical as toys, eyes fixed to the street, ears sealed against temptation—much too young and soft-cheeked to be so celibate and melancholy. And yet, discovering medicine everywhere, I discovered it also in their hair-shirt lessons in the puritan essence of this culture, a culture I had remembered with the stupidity of a rank tourist as a benign, motherly place, ready to embrace me in its infinite *pazienza.*

At night, in my high little room, I dreamed fearful dreams—dreams of giving birth to mutant mouse-babies, of a little girl whose long waxy blond braids, horribly mutilated in the course of my dreaming, were a sign to me of my inability to protect her. All seemed dreams of my lost faith in the power of mothering. I thought even Nature herself, mortgaging every spare millimeter of morale to the parasite in my belly, must have meant me to come crawling back in the end to the fatherly protection racket, begging the shelter of the tribe.

No, motherhood was *not* safe. How absurd I had been to have expected Silene's family to find me pitiable! I blamed myself, lacerated my baby-soul, sobbing my shame in the dark. I wept tears until there were no more tears. I sobbed dry, racking sobs until there were no more sobs. Until I struck something as hard and blind and irreducible and outlaw as ever.

Perhaps Nature had made sure of this, too, that lacking protection I would reinvent it. A husband? Of course I had a husband! *Per carità!* Would I be pregnant without a husband? Dear man, so *fortunato* to have a wife like me he could trust alone, even in this interesting condition! A fiction of respectability as pathetically tissue-thin and romantic in its own way as some *ardito* dream of valor in the field, as warming to the soul as those steely chants of the Servi, coiling around my ballooning body in the cold air. Yet I imagined I could maintain it—keeping busy, staying healthy, appearing discreetly thrifty, purposeful, serious, ever *la donna seria*—maintaining the fraud that I was here *because* I was a woman of resources, not because I lacked them. Above all, I had to invent what comes free with true "respectability": that armor of immunity to a shame I knew would torture me, here in this culture of my father's, with a torture as exquisite as burned skin.

Did I also have to pretend I had no need for mothering, no need to be *coccolla-ta,* as the women here said, when it was what I needed most? What was *need* to me, which I stoically defined by what I could get? I needed doctoring and could get it, at the Casa Eretenia lying-in hospital, where I signed up immediately for prenatal care. I convinced Dr. Soldini, the chief obstetrician, of the thickness of my skin—or perhaps he was not convinced. Dry, ironic, smilingly impassive, he called me *"la zingara americana"*—"the American gypsy"—when he met me. I laughed. He told me, warmly, almost tenderly, that I laughed with my whole face like a true Italian, and for a single unguarded instant his sudden excess of tenderness raised choking tears to my eyes.

He was kind. But I did not often laugh with him—or cry. The hotel chambermaids were kind, too—young women from the countryside, displaced persons like me who did not resist befriending, performing small mercies like spraying the room in the morning to keep off the hostile swarms of mosquitoes that otherwise plagued my sleep by night. In the spacious Bertolliana Library, about a mile's walk away beneath Vicenza's endless porticoes, I found a corner for writing next to a large many-paned window looking out over a green and airy courtyard. The attendant was kind. He volunteered to hold my papers behind his desk at night to spare me trudging them back and forth with me every day.

It was enough. It was almost enough. It gave me the fragile courage to bear the muttering stares on the street—visible pregnancy being almost as damaging to Italian testicles, apparently, as priests. I wrote to Ann, guardedly confessing. I tried to tell her laughingly of the Italian taboo against the public *donna gravida,* but my poor letter must have baffled her, its plea for help strangled with the cheer of my fake self-reliance. But I *knew* she would come. I *prayed* she would come. I prayed at night, with the sickening stench of repellent still hanging in the air and the drone of the Servi cutting through the wall like a band saw, lying on my narrow cot like a pregnant corpse, my hands clasped over a little blue *madonnina* medal Harry had given me, tears trickling slowly into my hair.

I sometimes told Harry in my letters how hard it was to write, not always able to repress the need for his pity. Yet I wrote, archly joking about the Vicenza hotels serving up piazza pigeon in lieu of the roast cat its citizens were said to be famous for, describing the threatened bus and tram strike and the posters that denounced the local ruling family, the Marzottos, for refusing to negotiate with transit workers, replaying him the American news as I got it, Italian style—the civil rights struggle in Alabama, Kennedy stealing headlines over Cuba. It relieved my heart to report small personal triumphs like my blossoming friendship with the chambermaid. Her name was Rosetta, a small, pale, undernourished war baby, who one night after supper walked inadvertently into my room and found me in tears. "She wept too," I wrote, "then went to her own room and brought me back her new little radio to borrow. And then she sent the downstairs maid to cheer me up."

I felt the healing balm of Rosetta's girlish sweetness, telling him of it, the pleasure of almost loving her—for whom had I loved but him in all these weeks?—

because behind the fragility of her shy good manners she was tough enough to let me cry. "For her, the war isn't over," I told him, meaning the NATO base here was too flagrantly another occupation, for what did it matter this time that the army was American? They did what soldiers did with girls, some of them girls of fifteen, she said. Some of them girls who might have been her friends. Her sisters. Herself.

I can still remember the night Ann came. It was Friday; all of Vicenza smelt of *baccalá*. "Look at you!" she said. *"Jesus Christ."*

"Who knows?" I laughed, almost hysterical with joy to see her. She blushed. We hugged, long, tearfully. We talked the night away in the old way of girls sharing a bedroom. I had been afraid she would ask who the father was, not knowing what I would say. But she didn't, and I repaid her immense tact a little by not telling her how terribly thin and overwrought she looked, or sounding too needy when I asked how long she could stay.

"Days, just—maybe five or six. How long will you need me?"

Oh, Ann.

And then I wept, the deep tearing sobs I hadn't let myself in weeks, and she held me and wept too. I had always played the comforting big sister to Ann's need, however badly. Now the role reversal lent a faint first bitterness to the balm of her comfort. It was an utterly involuntary reflex. When, finally exhausted, we fell asleep together in my narrow bed, she felt like part of me.

But the next morning she was wicked with nerves, and there were bitchy scenes between us, before and after breakfast. We truced just before I left for the library and she made off for the train station. She said she was going to meet "a friend." I had no right to ask, but I knew it was a man. When I returned from the library at midday, the bedroom was still strewn about with stocking rejects, and tumbled, indecisive dresses and shoes.

I already missed her. We had agreed to meet at supper—*Oedipus* was playing at the Teatro Olimpico that night, and I'd begged her to come with me. But our *pensione* suppertime at the Due Mori arrived without her, then curtain time at the theater. I was determined not to be frantic. I left her ticket with the *padrona* at the front desk and went on alone. But when the play broke for intermission, Mary finding Jesus couldn't have felt more joy than I did, seeing her standing there on the outside porch of the theater, smoking. And yet she seemed to look straight at me without a sign, jumping in alarm as I approached her. "I'm blind without my glasses," she explained nervously. I did not ask why she'd have come to the theater without her glasses. She looked rosier than she had when we'd parted in the morning, and deeply into herself.

We saw the play out in silence. As we walked back to the hotel together, mine were the first words between us, asking if she'd had supper. She'd caught the end of the sitting, she said. "The *padrona* was very nice about it. I was the only one there," she added. And after a reflective pause: "With the two of them."

My heart stopped. She knew how self-consciously I suffered the surveillance of the owner and his wife, who would typically trap me in their stern, questioning gazes at the supper table. Perhaps they'd heard about my nightly episodes of weeping; I'd been ashamed to ask the chambermaids to say nothing.

Our synchronized heels rang on the damp flagstones under the porticoes. Over my waves of nauseous panic, Ann slowly bled her confession. The *padrone* himself had asked who my husband was—meaning what he did. For a jolting instant I thought the worst. But *that* was impossible—Ann still didn't know. But what had she said?

"What *could* I say?" She turned full face to me and stopped. I saw that behind her heavily painted mascara her eyes looked bruised. Pity flooded my heart. I knew she really had to know, whatever the risks. I had to tell her the truth—we had to scheme this thing together.

"I'm using his name at the clinic," I said. And then I whispered it like a single breath of smoke into the night air. She lit up, smiling an angelic smile. She squeezed my arm tenderly. "I love you," she whispered back. And then, "I love *him*."

That night we undressed by the dim light of the bedlamp and slipped into our mutual pools of forbidden love. Hers was Alfonso, the youngest of our Neapolitan first cousins from Striano, the one with the poetic eyes and dimpled chin and the prettily curved mouth like a girl's. It had been the typical Italian brushfire romance from the instant they'd met in Naples. Now he was going to a business school in Bergamo, not far from Padua, and she confessed a little sheepishly that when she'd made plans to come north it had actually been for him as much as for me.

She felt utterly doomful about their being first cousins, terrified by all the medical lore she'd absorbed about inbreeding. There was another culturally relative side to such things, I said—Zi' Carmelina and Uncle Sam had been first cousins, after all, hadn't they? I held her thin, cool hand in mine, trying to be the reassuring big sister again. I did *not* tell her that my heart had already vaulted to what the codes of southern Italians like Alfonso would make of *me*—that among the sins they defined for women were some a lot blacker than consanguinity. That the one I'd committed had already tainted the sinner's sister.

I seemed to have eyes for seeing in the dark that night. Even the dark had eyes, looking back at me: the squinted, detective eyes of the *padrone*, Alfonso's eyes, unforgiving, full of sinister suspicion—interrogating, scrutinizing eyes as multiple and bulging and lidless as a fly's under a wall-sized microscope. Ann, meanwhile, slept deeply, almost innocently, her body still and cool in the dark beside me. I didn't dare risk waking her even by turning in the little bed. But my body burned, flayed with shame.

By morning I was resolved to leave the hotel, to remove myself forever from the humiliating gaze of the owners. I recruited Ann into my plan. On Monday morning the two of us set out to look for rented rooms in Porta Padova, the American quarter. A blond, bright-looking girlchild sitting opposite us on the bus reminded me of the little girl I'd dreamed of with the waxy, mutilated braids. I felt a sick wave of panic. Dear God, was every child my child? Or was every child *me?* Ann felt me trembling, and held my hand.

We discovered we could rent nothing, virtually, without a year's lease. We wandered disconsolately about, until a café proprietor, seeing we were Americans looking for rooms, unhesitatingly offered us some in the hotel above his café. And I thought, better this indifferent greed than the sleazy meddling of the Due Mori. I told him we'd be back tomorrow.

But the moment we announced we were leaving, the *padrona* of the Due Mori threw up her hands in a picture of penitent hospitality and pleaded with us to stay. She wept. I wept. Ann wept. For the same price as my cell-like little single at the Palladio, she offered the best double in the main hotel with balcony and private bath. There was absolutely no resisting her. It suddenly didn't seem to matter whether my humiliations had been real or paranoiac; they were merely incontrovertible—and therefore to be ignored.

Harry must have been bewildered by my letters, which had begun excoriating the signora in resolute high dudgeon and ended in equally resolute friendship. He must also have been very relieved. "I have to trust people a little," I told him, "even if I have to invent my trust now, out of the whole cloth." Between Ann and me, there was a certain mutual pride in our little triumph, but there was also relief. I knew she would go soon, that I would be hopelessly dependent again. And "however cruel in the abstract it might be to need it," I told Harry, the help I might get from judging, gossiping strangers would still be help. Once we were settled, I packed Ann off on a two-day trip to Bergamo, with an unequivocal warning to say absolutely nothing to Alfonso about Harry. Anything else she liked, but *that* was something no one sharing a drop of my father's family blood should be trusted with, man, woman, or child.

Silene made a surprise appearance, her first, while Ann was away. She looked for me at the Palladio, then, after a long trudge back across the piazza, limped up the sweeping marble staircase of the Due Mori, arriving exhausted, and brightening just a little too visibly when she saw me comfortably ensconced in the balcony suite. I meanly supposed she was thinking these were not the proper wages of sin. "Everything here in twos," she remarked, alluding to the "two moors" in the hotel name, on a street named *Due Ruote,* meaning "two wheels," and handing me two letters, which Harry had long ago mailed to the Schio address. I laid them among my cache to read later, and when she expressed genuine puzzlement at his writing so steadily, I protested that he *loved* me, my heart full, even as I saw her face go suddenly muddy and hurt. "But how can he love you and do *this* to you?"

I had to forgive her, I thought—how could she know, knowing nothing, what was keeping us apart? And yet even as all the wonder of him rose in his defense to my mind, and some of it to my lips, I found myself forced in my heart, to ask: Was he doing this to me? I found myself twisting, twisting, my lovely Alexandria stone around my finger, feeling shamed and exposed.

Silene must have intuited my hurt, for she illogically launched into a guilty apologia for her mother, who was *troppo gelosa,* she said—protective—overprotective. She could not explain at first what it was her mother was protecting her from. She stared instead in a kind of absent embarrassment at her own hands, pale and shapely smooth, and lying, at that moment, helplessly in her lap—the hands of a woman, I thought, with tapered fingertips and elegantly arched nails. And it came to me startlingly that I had never before thought of Silene as a woman.

She was halting and defensive as she spoke again, as she confessed she had been seeing a married man. "*Mia mamma*," she said, "she got—you—you and me—confused." I swear it was like seeing that kidskin mother-face and those dewy-wet eyes again. *Come ci pensa, tua mamma?* Like hearing the bells crash in Recoaro.

Silene was still staring at her hands. She whispered hoarsely, "*'N'importa*—it doesn't matter." And then she looked sorrowfully up and reached out to touch me. I felt the penitence of her touch. "*'N'importa.* You're much better off here—alone—without my parents. Life with them would have been *insupportabile.*" And then she left, my heart now full of her pain as well as my own. And yet, it mattered, I thought. It *mattered.*

My hands trembled opening Harry's letters. I read them as hungrily as always, but even the love in them seemed old.

There were three of them, after all, not two. The third was from my mother, and I read it with a confused hunger. A slight thing—my mother in every way. It said she'd been surprised, even a little alarmed, not to find me at home when they got back, but she was very glad that I was well and getting my research done. She wondered if I knew what had happened to her dentures.

The mosquitoes were rampant that night. In my punctured sleep, I cried and laughed, my bittersweet dreams a needlepoint of mothers, of dentures, of sisters, of Silene in love.

Harry and I had at first agreed that I should space my letters carefully and not have them come too often through the Strycker's Bay door slot. So I made a kind of journal of a few thin sheets, and would single-space the news in tiny elite type from edge to edge every day, sometimes twice a day, and post him a thick packet at the end of the week.

Now he complained he couldn't wait a week—the Schio fiasco had upset him, the telephone was alarmingly expensive, things seemed somehow altogether dicier than we'd anticipated, the seas between us deeper than water, and he was in just the state Esta had predicted. "*My heart is aching me to tears,*" he wrote from the back of the Strycker's Bay storefront one night after a week without news. "*Now I know what even a few days without a letter means.*" He meant for me as well.

We schemed a dozen ways to get mail to him more often and still guarantee its privacy. The neighborhood post office was out—Esta asked him how it would look for a local celebrity to be making daily trips to an anonymous P.O. box? There was the Penn Station depot downtown—but what if they couldn't give him a lock box and he had to ask for his mail in person every time? He was willing to chance it. Every day for two weeks running he swore he'd get to 34th Street and check it out.

It dashed us both that we hadn't foreseen this problem—one of the few that was actually foreseeable. We were a study in desperation. How had we so stupidly mis-gauged our nerves? Whatever had made us think the sordid business of having a baby "O.W." would somehow become less sordid in Italy? That trading my Italian family for somebody else's would somehow save our skins? Why didn't we know—why didn't we *know*—that Harry, the Harry of that "wasted emotion," would be trading those easy dreamless sleeps of his for a pair of scorching psychic pincers? That instead of beaming me his own life force, the devil in his mind would be devising insidious little flash-frames of Flavia in danger? That he would think, waking, "*It's midday there—how is she?*"—at suppertime, "*It's midnight there —how is she?*"—and all day, every day, be imagining the mediate air filled with cries that would reach him too late.

It was a crash course in our own puniness. It was also deep training in empathy for both of us, for while he was struggling to imagine himself into my life, I was imagining myself deeper and deeper into his. I would think of him hurrying out of his cluttered rectory penthouse every morning, the foldout bed left unmade, so he could be sure to pick the mail up off the Strycker's Bay floor before their devoted sweeper-upper and general caretaker, Walter Boone, got to it ahead of him. He'd told me about such mornings in one of his letters, the whole scene unfolding, as Walter came in behind him just as he was bending down to scramble up the mail.

"Wait'n' for somethin' importan', Fathah?" Walter chuckling, his eyes widening. We both wondered how often Walter had spotted those unmistakably striped pale-blue envelopes before Harry could whisk them into his jacket.

"Walter, please, willya get me a coffee? Black, no sugar?"

And then he'd hand Walter a bill and scuttle to the back of the shop, tossing the mail casually onto the desk unopened. Walter would *nudzh*, "Anythin' with it, Fathah?" So he'd ask for a cheese danish and throw him another couple of quarters, and Walter would catch them like a moving toll basket on his way out the door.

Esta had been reproaching him about his new weight, he told me. She called it sympathetic pregnancy. I could see him standing at the desk in the back, the file cabinets between him and the plate glass storefront, fumbling to tear the envelope open, feeling his knees get shaky, sitting down, thinking, *There's an anthropological term for this. . . .*

The letter might be one of those fat jobs, four days of Vicenza day-by-day with pictures, beginning, "*My sweet love . . .*" He'd hear my voice, the tiny type beginning to swim, and skip ahead to the reassuring entry marked "*Wednesday a.m: Ann left for Bergamo this morning, with plans to return tomorrow night and stay a little longer. . . .*" Then skip again to the end, impulsively kissing the corner where the X-kisses from Sam "through belly button" trailed off the page like an umbilical cord, lay the sheets together so as not to make any new creases, and push the whole thing into his inside jacket pocket just before Walter reappeared. Esta, coming in right behind Walter, might catch that last gesture and the shining look in his eyes. She'd take the luncheonette bag gently from Walter and hand him the broom, alerting him to the litter on the walk outside, then watch as Harry struggled to take the lid off the paper cup without spilling coffee on the rest of the mail. Yanking author-itatively on her jacket, sitting down, lighting up: "Everything OK?"

He thought so, Ann was there. "I didn't get to read it through."

"Go ahead. I'll cover for you."

But the sight of the fresh danish, unfolded from its waxed paper, suddenly made him feel the opposite of hungry. "Shit, Esta, I don't know if I can take a couple more months of this."

She blew out a long sigh of smoke and cut him sharply with her agate eyes. "Work," she said simply, firmly. "Bob Allen reach you?"

That was the NBC producer. He had. "I'm lined up for a 'Religion and Humor' panel."

"Religion and *humor*?" she laughed. "That's funny already."

"Maybe I'll get to tell the one about the Jew and the hunchback."

Esta, thinking they're finished if he tells nothing but Jewish jokes: "The FDR club will crucify you."

"I'll take at *least* two thieves with me."

Larry Eldridge popped through the door before he could tell her which two. "Father Browne in?" Esta, still laughing, pointed. Eldridge handed her the broom, which he had just found lying unmanned on the sidewalk outside. And then he launched straight for Harry: "That fuck Garth—"

Larry, a lawyer working for Strycker's Bay, intense, with boyish curly hair start-ing to thin and shining spectacles over shining eyes, doesn't stand on ceremony as he breaks the news about Bernie Garth, Sylvia's husband, now lawyering for the co-op board. "He's bringing suit," he says, furious. "He's bringing suit against the 94th Street low-income housing co-op. The greedy sumabitch." He paces the floor, growl-ing, outraged. He knows Harry is too. But he also knows Harry is caught between the rock of abandoning the Strycker's Bay Co-op and the hard place of sticking it out and dealing with his former friends' paranoia about him and Meagher some-how representing a Catholic underclass plot. "Let him sue. We'll show him." More pacing. "Dammit, Father, there's a *war* on."

But the infighting on the co-op board is also only a symptom of a bigger prob-lem, which is holding the City to its promises on low-income housing. Strycker's Bay *qua* Council has now got to resist buckling under pressure from the kind of middle-class property-owner mentality Garth brings to Strycker's Bay *qua* co-op lawyer. But it's not just Garth and his moneyed brownstone clients. It's downtown. It's the Housing Department. Every time a new planning memo goes out, the sacred 2,500 seems to get a little more eroded.

"Hell, a war you can fight. How ya gonna fight this? How ya gonna get people excit-ed about this little bitsy nibbling away?" Harry's been reading Saul Alinsky's *Rules for Radicals* again, he's told me, looking for a way to translate this thing into terms he can get hold of now that Mike Coffey has moved on to other organizing horizons.

Eldridge is not ready for philosophical insight. "Man," he grumbles, leaving. "It's law on law now."

"*Man*," Harry grumbles back, "you're depressing me. Come back with your show cause."

When Larry is gone, he swears to Esta that he's going to get to those planning pundits on his own. She reminds him to get a haircut first. Harry's buzzcut is going—his hair beginning to sweep his collar.

"How much should I cut off?"

"I liked it short. "

"You're outvoted by my mother," he thrusts, as he gets back to his desk.

"Oedipus, schmeedipus. Remember, it's early closing day at the barber's."

His letters were home movies. I could see him at his desk, eaten up by phone calls and half-finished resolutions on land costs to the housing committee. I could hear Garth calling him, having the nerve to call him, to crow about Paul's losing to Eugene McManus, *again*—Lily Steiner calling four times, in a swivet over relocation delays on the Strycker's Bay Co-op site.

I knew he'd only been five minutes late that day for his class at Cathedral College, where, as usual, he threw out the lesson plan and talked urban renewal and land costs and eternal vigilance and attacked the Tory bias of the *New York Times*. "All the news that fits, they print," he'd instructed his mostly baffled first-year civics students, "and don't you forget it." He'd done payback on that demotion from Catholic U. ten thousand times by now.

The Rector had hailed him as he fled through the lobby toward the exit door trying to be unobtrusive: "We need your catalogue copy for next year, Harry. The printer can't hold out forever."

"Tell him to make it up. I'll sign a waiver."

He'd got to the barber just before closing. Haircut accomplished, attacking Broadway against the light, I could see him groping for the letter in his jacket pocket, squeezing it a little.

When he'd crashed through the storefront door at a run, Esta was leaving.

"Your hair looks great."

"Oedipus, schmeedipus," dropping into her desk chair to read the phone messages.

"Save you some trouble. Milt Mollen called. Jack Foley called. Two memos on your desk to sign. Bad news: Foley just saw the submission on Social Services that went to Washington in July. Strycker's Bay isn't even mentioned."

"That means no funding, those shits."

The kindly reference was to Herman Badillo, Mayor Wagner's new Relocation czar, and Tom Wolfe, heading up the Goddard-Riverside Community Center, now working hand in glove to get the special D.C. blessing away from Strycker's Bay.

"Foley said he'd get you a copy. The good news is things are looking OK for his manpower grant." Pause to pat his hand. "Go read your letter."

We'd finally come up with a mail scheme, one that of course relied on Esta. I'd address my letters to her, marked on the back flap with a slashed circle, the international road sign for No Entry, she'd carry them to the storefront and slip them to him with a memo or in a deli bag.

Letters to me, he'd just continue to drop into mailboxes anywhere from Yonkers to City Hall. Writing them was another thing, stealing time in snatches—at midnight, say, in his room if he could stay awake, early in the morning at the back of the shop, between his new Saturday classes at the Dunwoodie seminary, short, telegraphic letters dashed off in his typical block-printed hand with a skipping blue ballpoint he pressed on so hard that he embossed the paper.

They were sea biscuit—I could live on a few lines for days, capsules of instant New York that bloomed Technicolor when you dipped them into your mind. A word of love caressed me like a brush of his knee, or his lips. A word of anguish drew blood. That afternoon he'd started a letter to me: "*Back only weeks,*" he wrote, "*and it's the race of rats like I never left.*" He told me how many times he'd had to put off reading mine—always some tenant with an eviction notice, or a desperate mother trying to get her kid into St. Gregory's, or a member of the Housing Committee, or Garth or Meagher or Lily Steiner on the phone—"*I actually haven't had an hysterical conversation with Lily since 11:30 this morning.*"

It was after ten-thirty that same night by the time he'd got back to the rectory to find Flanagan sitting in the rectory lounge by himself, half watching TV and half reading *Time*. "Har-*ray?*" he'd said, with that faint disapproving sniff, like a parent who's been waiting up, and his typical question-mark declarations. "I see you finally got yourself a haircut?"

Flanagan's own head looked as if it had just been lacquered with maple veneer. Harry, biting his tongue, had gone for the liquor cabinet, as the pastor began a rant about the racial situation in Alabama. *Those* people were pushing things just a *bit* too *far* too *fast,* if you asked *him*—ranting right through the eleven o'clock news, making it impossible either to follow the headline stories or to leave. Before long, Harry'd found himself starting to doze in his chair and shaken himself awake, apologizing with a sudden, jerking arm motion that scattered the ice in his glass and forced him to apologize again.

I could see him, the spiral staircase clanking under his steps, slowly withdrawing my letter again from his breast pocket, once upstairs stripping quickly, flopping onto the unmade bed, yanking over the accordion lamp, unfolding the letter and drinking it in slowly, his throat aching with unspent tears. Ah, yes, *couvade,* he'd remember. *That's the word for it.* And he'd fall asleep with the light on, still clutching the letter to his chest.

Harry never seemed to feel the awesome differential between how much we wrote and the significance of what we were doing. I would apologize for smothering him in trivia and he would ignore it, making me feel as if it was world-shaking just to nurture Sam, which Lord knows I might have done in a coma. He called my letters brilliant, took in every little sketch like a wire photo from the front, as if he were making up for all the honeyed words he'd once scattered on the purple

Mediterranean—now, no matter if from some perspectives it was even more dangerous to save them. He carried them with him everywhere, till they bulged his pockets and became checkerboard origami, soft and crumpled and sweat-stained.

I had time to write, compulsively. Some days I spent hours giving a minute account of what went on in the other hours, not even leaving out my dreams. His compulsion, of course, was the opposite—a busyness that hardly left him a minute. Every plea to slow down, even when he made it to himself, panicked him with the terror of slack. "I feel crowded and rush by things," he told me once, the heart cry of the activist with a soul—always that hunger, always that longing for an imaginary peaceful time that never was and never would be.

> *Sunday—Going all morning. The West Side Young Adults and Teachers chasing me & now West Side Equal Rights starting again. Want to sit with you in peace & harmony & and know we are part of each other all over again. . . . Tuesday/ Wednesday? You can see how screwed up I am timewise. . . . Tonite was out with Jack Foley—a little dinner & drinking—to celebrate what looks like $80,000 grant for manpower and vocational guidance—which I steered him into & for which final approval was being held up by establishment until a guy named Moynihan in Wash. who was renewing it turns out to be an old PAL boy from West Side of NY!! A great story of being nice to everyone since they may be useful in future. . . . I promise to be better on letters. How much you are in my heart. . . . I'll write soon—within day— again to make up. All my love—all my life—*
> *Harry*

I kissed his letters, and cried on them. They could take it. They can now. He had an archivist's instinct for what would last, so that the ink is just as blue, the paper almost as white and crisp, as when I first slipped them from their envelopes with trembling fingers and was with him in a Columbus Avenue time warp.

He'd gone out to see Mammy that particular Sunday afternoon, looking for a little respite from the noise. They'd had a bread-and-butter ceremonial Irish tea, and she'd recounted the story I'd told her from the New Rochelle summer, about me chasing the Chihuahua, enjoying it even without the bouncing belly and breasts that made it hilarious. He put his feet up and drowsily watched TV till she turned off the set and let him doze. It had been midnight by the time he'd got back and unlocked St. Gregory's street door to let himself in. A police car hummed quietly to the curb and two officers climbed out. "Evening, Father, wanna give us a hand?"

By the streetlight you could see they had Father Terence in tow, a new assistant who had far outdistanced everybody on staff as a regular drunk. They unfolded him gently from the back seat of the car and lifted him to his feet on the sidewalk. "Father's had a slight accident," they explained. Father Terence's knees gave way and Harry took his right side. "Is he hurt?" "Naah. Totaled the car, though." They slogged him through the street door to the elevator. God, Harry thought, he weighs like a corpse, and yet he's all bones. Stupid bastard.

But he felt a surge of protective love for him, too. Terence was a sweet guy, sober. But Flanagan was ready and waiting for him now. Soon as the accident report got downtown, the system would close in and cart him away. He propped him up in the elevator, let the two policemen out, rode him upstairs, and put him to bed. It took nearly half an hour, Terence resisting like a bad child. Harry was so wired afterward he couldn't sleep, and went back to the tube.

Jim Jensen was in the midst of a special report from Alabama. Rednecks had just firebombed a black church in Birmingham. The dead and injured still hadn't been counted.

Nonviolence would be finished after this.

My heart is aching me to tears.

3

I dreamed I was with Ann in an enormous church, full of rooms and mysterious corners. You were there, busy with other dignitaries up front, while Ann and I waited, wandering through great baroque rooms with enormous clocks. There were children filing in and out, blacks separated from whites. You were always one room away—I could catch glimpses of you sometimes just turning a corner, but I couldn't call out because of the distance, and being in a holy place—

"He says he can't come right away, but he will. He says he wants to see you." Ann had wakened me, coming in about midnight from Bergamo. We sat facing each other across the two little beds, in a soupy puddle of yellow light from the bed lamp.

"He took the news *really* well," she said, excitedly. She fumbled as she lit a cigarette, then kicked off her shoes and began rasping her stockinged feet together. I reached for the ashtray from the typing table. "But he was wondering . . ."

"Wondering . . . ?"

"You know. Whether Harry—well—couldn't just *leave*—or something—"

I stared straight into her face. "You mean you *told* him?"

I gave her time.

"Well, I thought . . ."

"Remember, when you left, I *said*—" But it was no use going on. I was as bewildered as I was furious.

"No—*no*—I didn't tell him . . . *that*," she stammered.

I was more bewildered than ever. "Then why, just now—"

"I thought you *wanted* me to say that."

Jesus.

I collapsed into bed, mute with frustration. We didn't talk again until morning. She cried hopelessly. When I said it might be a good idea if she *didn't* stay till Sunday, she protested how sorry she was, so I recanted, and we hugged, both of us crying. I still didn't know *what* she had actually told Alfonso, but I felt certain that whatever it was it would be down to Striano in the morning, and around the globe by nightfall. There was nothing I could do about it now. I was feverish with misery. I *wanted* to talk with her, walk with her, I wanted for us just to be sisters together. But I also wanted her to go away—to leave me calmly alone to work.

Three aching, dark, wet days we dragged on this wretched truce. The sun came out the morning she left. I felt all the emptiness I had expected to feel, none of the relief.

•

*I don't want to cry tonight. Yet it is so quiet and lonely here in my room,
with the clock ticking. There are sounds outside but they don't seem to belong
to me, only the desolation belongs that comes from inside me. . . . I dream
like a child that you will appear, and like a child I imagine that if I stay
in my dream long enough it will come true.*

Time became a machine, a linked chain of weary days, one by one by one. It was
as if I were waiting for transcendence in some banal state of banked terror. When
would the baby come? Where would we—*we*—stay, where *could* we stay? Surely not
here at the hotel. I wondered how soon the truth might reach my parents—
whether I would know it when it did. I wondered if, instead of some dreadful, upheav-
ing change, there would be after all only a day and another day and another
forever. Esta had said, "Go on working, it's the cure," and though little by little the
second draft of "Sharp William," as Harry called him, had seemed to grow, still I
felt stalled, silenced. *"The book is like a baby,"* I wrote to Harry, straining to describe
the ennui of my miserable fullness: *"Sometimes you have to lie there patiently, and wait
until it is ready to push itself out."*

Silene sent me a mysterious note about a family crisis, and kept her distance. The
weather turned ugly again, the premonitory fear I lived with seeming to take on its
own menacing reality outside of me. I tried to read. Harry had given me a novel
about the priesthood when we'd left London: Morris West's *The Shoes of the
Fisherman.* At first I had postponed reading it. Now I dragged it out, afraid to finish, eager to prolong a sense it gave me of a certain Harry-presence in the night—
or so I thought. But my resistance became clearer afterward, when I was done—
resistance to closure, in fact, for the book left a strange residue, like a haunting, a
residue of *priesthood* in all its special canonical tact and freighted history and
peculiar, calculated moral economics—something bodily real, something demanding not to be worn, like cloth, but lived in, like flesh and viscera, with eyes and
limbs—a male mother still sanctimoniously wagging a finger at my grief and lifting a chiding hand, saying, "You—*you*—are still Outside the Walls."

And then one evening at supper the waitress snapped at me and I broke down
and wept like a punished child. I sat there at the table weeping, in an agony of paralyzed disgrace, until I found the strength to bolt out of the dining room and up
the marble stairs and throw myself on the bed and let the deep, wild sobs tear at
the baby-self inside me. The *padrona* was beside me in an instant. Gently, she took
my hand—both my hands, grown absurdly soft and useless—between her big
competent, work-toughened ones, saying, *"Signora,"* very softly. *"Signora.* Stay
here until the baby is born—why not? And afterward too—you *must. Per carità!*—
a baby disturb the hotel? *Ci mancherebbe altro."*

I thought afterward, my heart blissed with relief, that it had been *she* always, already,
lurking there, the ominous looming thing I thought I had dreaded, now holding
me, holding my safety in the toughness of her hands. I thought, *The miracle of it,*

as this mother comfort overcame me with such a strange serenity of insight, without surprise. I thought, *Always, out of strength, sweetness. Always.*

But Emmi the rude waitress, privately rebuked I supposed, towered over her guilt, made artwork of her penitence, unable to endure it otherwise. She declared herself my personal slave. She knew I loved freshly squeezed orange juice for breakfast—*e come no?* Her boyfriend was a chef at Daniele's in Venice and knew everything Americans loved. *Ma Si figuri, Signora.* I will buy the oranges and squeeze them myself and bring you the juice on a tray with my own hands. She brought me a slice of wedding cake from a Saturday afternoon reception downstairs. If I missed a meal, she brought me milk. *Anything*, Signora. *Any* hour. Room 19—you see?—and she would take me out into the hallway and point out her room.

She was inexorable; I could not refuse her. She invited me to a film-festival screening knowing full well that in my last month's halfwit torpor I might sleep through it. As it happened, the child star of the film, hardly more than six, sat only a few seats away, and held me awake watching him watch himself, captive to his pretty upturned profile in the light-flecked darkness.

Rain fell nearly steadily now, in waving sheets across the piazza. One night, just before supper, it broke through the hotel roof. "*Disastro!*" cried the poor chambermaids, sloshing their mops and buckets furiously up stairs and down corridors. I had been thinking of a trip to Padua, and had to put it off again. Why did I want to go at all? Did I think Dino, Sicilian missionary of freedom, was still waiting with his Vespa at the station? But at the first sign of a break in the clouds, I hurried my routine morning specimen bottle to the clinic and caught a train that got me there before noon.

New York–style urban renewal everywhere, and the joyless beat of bourgeois prosperity. They had finished paving over my canal. A brash high-rise hotel stood where the old brothels had been, making my wondrous Tower already look diminished and old. I lunched nervously in a glitsy new stand-up fast-food trattoria. I searched out the old phone bank in the *galleria*. The *gettone* dropped, a woman answered—of course he was married now, and would come on cold and distant. But the moment he heard my voice he shouted, "*Miracolo!*," and my heart absolutely vaulted. "*Carissima!*" he said. Oh my God, how tenderly he said *carissima*.

He said they had been about to leave for Rome. "Ah, I am holding you up," I protested, suddenly alarmed again. But he repeated, "*Miracolo!*," and there was no disbelieving the joy of it, that sense of deliverance from a destiny too terrible to think of. We met in Pedrocchi's immediately. I tried to disguise my belly behind the immense black marble table, but it was impossible, and the moment they saw me they howled with delight, Dino kissing me passionately on both cheeks and virtually handing my face to Annamaria to kiss. "*Ti ricordi, Annamaria?*" Even she seemed glad, genuinely glad—*allegra ma non troppo.*

I told them what I had told the *padrona* and they pretended to believe me.

Amazingly, they said Dr. Soldini had delivered their own new baby, Gigi, at the Casa Eretenia! We toasted everything, exchanged phone numbers in a frenzy, hugged, kissed. I was swept back to the station in their car. It began to rain again as the train raced back to Vicenza in the dark, the fast drops dancing across the compartment window. Back at the hotel, I stripped off my wet things, set a hot cup of tea beside my typewriter, and punched out the news. I had my protection now.

Silene reappeared, brushing aside all curiosity about her family crisis with her familiar air of martyrdom, apparently resolved to deal with it in stoic independence of me. I wondered if she'd broken with her lover—how, if at all, I might have contributed to her decision—but I would never know. She told me to look after my health. I was looking pale, she said. She disappeared again.

It continued to rain. Ann wrote, depressed: her Tufts program was turning out a monumental disappointment. But I had little comfort for her, blocked by guilt and my own need. I found myself desperately longing for my mother. Sometimes I imagined myself back in her womb. I remembered tendernesses toward me I had long forgotten, that I had not allowed myself to remember when she had approached too near my paltry little freedom: how she had stroked my fever-burning hair, night after night, the summer I was sick—the summer I became a woman—never leaving my side, seeming to lure me with her tender honey voice back into the safety of a world I must have feared nearly enough to die for fear of it. When she wrote again, I almost swallowed her letter in hunger—one of her typical catchall New Rochelle dispatches, superficial, cheerful, innocently concerned for me, making me wish I had told her everything.

More rain, steady and dense.

Dino and Annamaria, returned, invited me to Padua for a few days. Esta, on hasty notice, left for a week in California, not a thought to the mail, and Harry's letters warning me bunched up at the hotel while I serenely went on, from Padua, stuffing Esta's mailbox with reports on northern Italian urban development. When the Vajont Dam suddenly burst in Udine and whole sleeping villages were swept to doomsday by an unstoppable blind crush of water, Italian television flashed a blanching flood of news film around the planet. Harry went insane. It was days before I could reassure him that not a hair of our heads had been touched—that the soggy train ride from Padua had left me with nothing more worrisome than a nasty cold.

Nausea? Sì.
  Diarrhea? Sì.
  Febbre? Sì.

Dr. Soldini seemed unruffled. "Something you ate, *magari*." But he muttered something about my vagrant husband and booked me into the hospital, where I remember a fluttering of nervous nuns in white-winged bonnets as I scrawled Harry a few days' worth of reassurance with an IV in my writing arm. When I got back to the hotel, still shaky and fatigued, the blanched look on Emmi's face told me how sick

I'd been. Ann arrived, thankfully on cue, knowing it was time. She was quivering with anxiety. In a tone I hadn't taken with her since we were girls, I told her she was going to have to treat me like one of those poor wrecks she used to kill herself for when she was an RN in New York. She could get even with me later.

"And if Alfonso wants to come and see me, fine. If he has any highfalutin' moral dilemmas, tell him to forget it." Sure enough, at lunchtime on Sunday, the two of them appeared, smiling, with flowers, and when Alfonso left that night, he kissed my hand with a romantic flourish. I let go of all my fear of him for Ann's sake, for the sake of that elegant dark face, so sweet—so much like my father's when he was young.

Monday was so serene that had I really been a gypsy I might have known it for a sign. By dawn on Tuesday the entire female corps of the hotel—Emmi, *padrona*, cooks, laundresses, chambermaids—were marching to the rhythm of my contractions. I was whisked back to the white-winged bonnets at the Casa and carefully maneuvered into a shuttered labor room, where I was left to work. Ann was splendid. She hovered beside me everywhere, coaching, encouraging, supervising my disciplined breathing as if to deliver this child perfectly meant as much to her as to me, steering curious nurses away, instinctively grasping my stubborn need to be alone, even closing the door gently when she thought the clamoring cries of other birthing women might disturb me. But it was not long before I entered a hyperventilated altered state in which I knew only that she was there—nothing else—when I felt her thin cool hand touch mine or press a wet cloth softly to my face. I opened my eyes, once, as she was preparing to slip out for a moment and heard a sound like a terrible rushing of wind—the sound of her arm simply brushing the lining of her coat sleeve.

Then I heard nothing, and light and time became a steady, luminous, transfixing gaze like that of the window beside me, crisscrossed with elusive faces. The only recognizably male outline was the doctor's, a shadow cut like dark paper into the gauzy screen of twilight. It was growing dark when I knew the baby was crowning, and suddenly out of some mysterious murmuring dusk, beyond the womb of space, a midwife appeared, a dark lady with stone-black eyes, sublimely hideous, with hair that clung to her head in tarry clods without beginning or end, wheeling me into delivery, stroking me like a priestess, coaxing me with the certain, delicate touch of her hands, and I gave up my secret burden to the world feeling no pain or panic, only a lightness, a tingling, a bursting through to the light, as if consciousness had gone inward once, and now I were my own newborn, coming up out of the amniotic sea. And then consciousness broke again like a second wave and spread itself on my skin like water, like heat and sunlight and freedom. "Bebbi-boy," I heard her say softly in English, and then, in Italian, "*Che bel negretto!*" No cry, only a gargling noise that seemed to come from an animal mass of purple flesh and wet fur suspended before me in the air, and then the beautiful dark bebbi-boy lay suddenly in the crook of my sweating, quivering arm and seemed to laugh, and I felt his weight, and only then did I feel my own.

There were frontiers of naming to cross. Harry, which she pronounced "Arri," then Mario, for the patriarch whose heart would break. I had to spell the surname for her.

Dr. Soldini arrived. Midwife and baby vanished. With swift and expert cruelty he removed the afterbirth and I felt real pain for the first time. I was tumbled into a fresh bed, exhausted, Ann's the last face I saw before I drowned in sleep. "*Cable him,*" I whispered, as the white air closed.

Trapped in our transatlantic time warp, Harry on that same Monday had opened my first hospital letter, a week old, with its crabbed and crooked intravenous scrawl, and nearly blacked out.

He'd been at the back of the office, he explained to me afterward—a typically mad Strycker's Bay day. Instantly, he'd torn off a sheet of yellow foolscap to write me and was down the first side of it before both phones rang. Esta punched her hold button and threw her voice back to him over the file cabinets. "Some guy with an English accent, making a TV special—something about Puerto Ricans on the West Side." Harry was already soothing the other caller, a semihysterical neighborhood storekeeper with his relocation notice, but he broke off: "Tomorrow—here— OK?" He could never turn down a camera.

Two women had just then edged quietly through the storefront door. The older one, black hair smoothed behind her ears, brass crucifix gleaming in the V of her cardigan, insisted in broken Spanish on speaking with Father Browne and lit up like a vigil light when he appeared from behind the files. He led them to the urban renewal wall map, and was pointing out the green cubes for proposed public housing sites in his standard melange of Spanish and Italian when the door crashed open: Alice Joannides, Strycker's Bay rep from West 87th, blue wedgies, blazing hennaed hair, flowered housedress wrapped in a fashionable coat. "*Somebody* got to do *something* about that boarded up brownstone, one thirty-four." Her voice broke sound barriers.

"What's up, Alice?"

"*RATS!*" throwing out both arms to the size of a Rottweiler.

Esta instantly wanted to call the Health Department. "I go away for a few days, and what happens." It was not a question. Alice turned on a blue wedgie, saying "*sheeet*" on the Health Department, checking herself: "Pardon me, Father," as she opened the door and crashed out.

Harry's watch had stopped. "What time is it, somebody?" Panicked, he turns apologetically back to the two women: "I'm late for class. Tomorrow. Please. *Domani. Mañana. Por favor.* No, Wednesday—no—*mañana.* We'll get you on British TV." And he hurtles back to his foolscap sheet for one last line to me: *Never got back— hectic as hell here—my heart is with you—my hand touches you—*

In the dead of hospital night, I woke startled, and in pain. Ann was gone. Out of the dense antiseptic smell of silence came a murmur of voices, then a single nursing sister hushing a woman as she prepped her for labor. I heard her say, "*Ahhh, Signora,* if only you could have *your* baby like *l'americana!*" before I sank back into sleep, my heart full.

When I awoke, an impossibly bright morning, the same heart was pounding with joy. Dr. Soldini was scanning me, solemnly nodding his head.

"You came through," he said.

I smiled at him with my whole face. "Sicilian gypsy," I murmured, replete. Had he thought I might not?

"You came through," he said again, with a hint of rebuke. "I'm glad, for the sake of your husband." He lifted my hand and patted it. "*A chi tocca, tocca.*" It could happen to anyone.

When Dino and Annamaria appeared, their arms full of flowers, I repeated what Dr. Soldini had said and Annamaria flashed Dino a look. "Ah, *sí*," said Dino. I pressed them, impatient. He spoke first, then Annamaria. Emilia Marzotto, of the family that owns Vicenza?—I remembered the union posters about the defiant tram strike against them. "Their only child. Dead in childbirth."

"Here, only two days ago."

"Of course no one told you."

Surely Harry knew such things happened, as priests do, perhaps as priests do better than anyone. But when Tuesday came for him, he still knew nothing. That afternoon, when he bolted into the storefront fresh from second-year history, the British TV team was in the shop unloading equipment, setting the camera up so it could sweep the sitting area by the door. The place seemed mobbed. The two women he'd invited back were sitting radiant on a pair of folding chairs. The older one, gold-toothed smile in full bloom, stood up when he came in.

"They wouldn't say a word until you got here," said Esta. They had brought a tiny girl with them, maybe two years old—Harry admitted he was new at this. She looked a little like a miniature Esta, her eyes only bigger and blacker, smoky hair pigtailed and beribboned. They had set her on Esta's desk, and two dusky round doll's legs stuck out from under her fluffy white skirt, ending in two doll button-shoes. She'd been playing intently until he came in, apparently, with a ballpoint pen topped with a plastic rose. But when she saw him, she'd lifted her child face and turned him such a bold, wondering look that it went straight through his chest like a flung spear and stopped, shuddering, at his backbone. *Every child becomes your child,* he'd thought, tearing his eyes away to shake the outstretched hands of the television crewmen. He turned back and laid a gentle hand on the tight thick hair over the warm little head, as soon as he could bear it.

"Cameras rolling yet?" Esta asked slyly.

"Don't tell me I wasted that entrance," he quipped.

She advised him to warm up fast, before the local Puerto Rican leadership got there. Ever since they'd taken a principled stand on the 2,500 units of low-income housing, Julio and Diaz, the two Strycker's Bay organizational reps, seemed to be pursuing their own agenda. Esta was feeling cynical about them—suspected they might be courting Relocation chief Herman Badillo for jobs on the City payroll. But she flicked Harry her *Don't say anything you'll be sorry for* look. Dan, the producer, cleared the edge of Esta's desk, suggesting Father Browne sit there, "—like *that*," and Esta began to lift the little girl out of the way. "Oh, no," Dan stopped her. "We're not that pure."

And so it had gone, Harry pulling a W. C. Fields about being upstaged by a kid, but wriggling closer so as to put her in full camera view, until she'd suddenly reached for the paper sticking out of the jacket pocket, part of his secret Vicenza letter cache, and he'd slid his hand in to protect it. And then Julio and Diaz arrived, and almost immediately got into an argument with him about what cameras do to social movements. Dan said they wanted to take a camera into the street before it got too dark to film, when the door boomed open: Alice Joannides again, yesterday's identical outfit except for a pair of pink satin mules with pompoms.

"I *shot* him!" she crowed.

Esta, honestly panicked: "Christ, Alice, who'd you shoot?"

"That fuckin' rat!"

"Four legs or two?" Harry asked.

"Pardon me, Father," said Alice, attending to him for the first time. Hands on hips, eyes narrowed into wicked little slits, she added, "What you think? Maybe I shoot another landlord?" Then she noticed the crew.

"Smile, Alice, you're on 'Candid Camera.'"

As the crew gathered up, Esta threw on her coat, readying for home. She leaned into Harry and whispered, "Call me, as soon as you hear *anything*."

Everybody gone, dark, the circus over, only a few minutes before the seven o'clock housing committee meeting, Harry slipped to the back, fumbled my letter open again, gave a quick glance to my last self-portrait with belly, started a new foolscap sheet: "*My love, please have all bad feelings pass and banish blues with brownes—*" Before he knew it he was running over the other side with apartment-hunting schemes in Washington Heights or Queens for when I got back. He looked up to see Pete Slevin, barkeep of Columbus Avenue's renewal-doomed McGlade's, nosing over the top of the cabinets. He brushed him off and wound up the letter: "*My darling, sweetheart, I hold you—cling to me—*"

Later, the meeting over, one of the committee people heard Harry say he'd missed supper, and called his wife to tell her to take the cold chicken out of the fridge. That was already near midnight. So it was past one in the morning by the time he got back and found the cable waiting.

ARRIVED TUESDAY FLIGHT 1650 SWELL. FLAVIA SAMO ANNIE

He simply stared at the message till he fell asleep. When he woke up he just lifted his eyelids and stared at it again. *Samo.* That meant it was a boy. He'd had a son all day and hadn't known it. *What color are his eyes? Is he strong? Will he be a great man? A happy one—a beloved one?*

He counted back against the time difference. Ten minutes to five there meant ten minutes to twelve here. He'd been in the office, before the BBC shoot, with Roger Starr, Mayor Wagner's rent and rehab man, and two West German housing experts. He'd even asked Roger Starr for the time.

He faced his Wednesday morning civics class and called Esta and asked her to cancel all his appointments. Then he went out to see his mother.

4

Esta didn't send me Spock until November, when the baby was two weeks old and I was already insane. My breasts hadn't produced. "It's the type of breast you have," Dr. Soldini had said, suddenly turned enemy. "What type is that?" I'd snapped back, and then I'd burst into inconsolable tears. It felt for me like the end of the world, so much so that I spent our entire first precious transatlantic phone call blubbering Harry my grief.

Silene tried to console me, saying she liked the control one had over feeding with a bottle. She also advised a firm feeding schedule—never give in, she said. But stern as she was about feedings, when I asked her to vaccinate the baby so we could meet American regulations and go home, she grew absolutely wild. How could I even *think* about putting virulent germ plasm into an infant so—so—newborn? So vulnerable? And she wouldn't stop there: "You! Remember how you cried about your breasts? Did you think how your own shots now would have contaminated your milk?" I was confused, for what was I sparing him if *he* had to get vaccinated now instead of piggybacking on my immunity? But I decided against quarreling. "*Ebbene*," she went on. "You see everything happens for the best."

The *best!* With sterile bottle feedings to organize, and formula to warm in hotel room in the middle of the night! How could she say that? It was already Chinese laundry: radiators, tables, chairs, draped, day after day, with diapers and crib sheets. And how did you keep a week-old infant from waking hotel guests at two in the morning? I found a little bottle warmer for the night feedings, but there were times he would cry through every Spock test (hungry? wet? cold? hot? a sticking pin?), and Silene be damned, Soldini be damned, I would take his blanket-wrapped, springy little body up and snuggle him into bed in my arms, feeling the lovely sweet warmth of him, the fragility of him, I would loosen the top of my gown and put his tiny red mouth to my breast, still so swollen and streaked with blue, and hold him close, and feel the yielding release of his anguish, and of mine, together.

Ann and Alfonso had both stood up as godparents when he was baptised in the Casa chapel, then he'd gone back to Bergamo and she to Naples again—to what was, by now, my unspeakable relief. To *her* relief, too, I am sure, our wild swerve of emotion having exhausted us both. But true relief was impossible for me. New motherhood under the best of circumstances must be a form of semitotalitarian torture. Here, alone, with no one I could absolutely trust, I was in dread of ever having my child out of my sight. Emmi, sweet Emmi, stood guard sometimes while I slipped guiltily out of my room to wolf a meal or shop frantically for a tin of formula. One afternoon I violated the ritual *quarantesima*—the forty days I was supposed to go without the touch of water—to have my hair washed, only to be scolded by the *parrucchiere*, and then marched back through the streets with my mess of hair in curlers when Emmi popped in to announce a desperation feeding.

It was all so manically unreal, a sleep-deprived sentence to terror. My once carefully crafted letters to Harry became mere scraps—bulletins—cablegrams—as hysterically unreadable as if I were still hooked up to the IV. And the worst of this lunacy was that it seemed to be not just personal but national, an absolutely collective obsessive sacrifice of adult sanity to the well-being of the *neonato*. On top of this, to be the mother of a newborn child wishing to go home to America was prima facie to have become an absolute menace to Italian public health. Even taking full account of my own skewed worldview, I will always contend that this was pure, objective, verifiable fact. First, Silene, who had had me about to commit bebbicide by breastfeeding smallpox. Now I must prowl about everywhere, looking for vaccination. An ungodly howl issues from the Committee of Public Safety: "*Ma il bambino, il bellissimo bimbo, il bamboluccio!*" and the entire medical expertise of the peninsula assembled stands firm for the guillotine.

"Dr. Soldini has refused outright," I told Harry. "Passed the buck back to the clinic pediatrician. Annamaria says she'll ask hers, but she doesn't feel good about it." Silene was, of course, immovable; I knew she would be. If it had to be done, she said, somebody else would have to do it, somebody willing to make the merest pretense of a scratch and then note that it didn't take. If I tried to suggest that American immigration officialdom might insist the take be positive, "*Ma, Ges-su,*" she would say, syllabifying: "*Se-i paz-za. Si-e-te paz-zi tut-ti.*" You are *all* mad, the lot of you, you and the rest of the North American continent. She may have been right. Yet here was this unyielding fact, that it stood between me and going, and it would never have occurred to her to lie, however little the danger in it. I didn't dare ask her to. I'd asked her to give official witness to Harry's sworn paternity before a municipal official the week before, and even that had put her in a dead faint for days.

Furtively, I telephoned the American base. The American military MD was quite cool about it. No problem, they vaccinated newborns there all the time. But he also coolly refused to do it for me. "Civilian personnel are treated in emergencies only. Regulations."

On the other side of the immigration wall, Harry waited. He rushed through Sunday masses out to his mother's the day the "Religion and Humor" panel aired, just to see for himself, he said, how his way of throwing his best wisecracks over his shoulder, past the range of the chest microphone, had cost him his TV career. There were only two things in televisionland, he told me, that could pull him out of a soporific couch slump: one was a shaking half hour on the Vietnam War, and the other a five-day-old baby in an insurance commercial.

For the first time in his life he saved the real estate section from the *New York Times*. He couldn't believe the rents. He wondered he'd never thought of looking at it before this, just to see what apartment hunters were up against. Esta forced him to rethink making a commitment to a lease without me. He admitted to having maybe six hundred dollars in hand by the end of November.

"Tight, but it should hold you. Try a hotel efficiency, maybe East Side, downtown, near the Village—nobody'll recognize you there. You might still find something before the Christmas rush."

Then it was back to work: an application for grant funding to the Lannenburg Foundation, the Strycker's Bay annual report. "Today's Election Day—you voted yet? And call Kisburgh. He sounded depressed."

Nickie was kvetching about minority quotas on the Downstate construction site when Harry's friend Kevin Kelly of the Catholic Interracial Council called on the other line, so he dropped Nickie to get filled in on the upcoming conference in Washington, D.C., Kelly begging him to co-chair a panel on race and urban renewal. He'd already made crazier commitments, like agreeing to host a citywide urban renewal forum for the first week in December, just when—just after—

At least that is what we were both hoping now, if I could get the vaccination. He looked at his desk calendar and saw a Strycker's Bay benefit that same week, a Police Athletic League benefit a week later. *Christ.* Plus he'd just given his midterm exams at Cathedral, five long essay questions instead of the eighty objective short answers they were used to, easier to make up but way harder to grade. Now there were four whopping bundles of papers ahead of him—another one of those famous all-nighters just before he had to leave for Washington.

The following Sunday morning he added another batch of papers from the seminary to those still untouched from the college, dumped them all out of his briefcase onto his penthouse bed, already paved with old copies of the *Times,* and left them there. Then he divvied up Sunday masses with Tom Farrelly, ran out for a luncheon talk with a group of folks Congressman Hugh Carey had got together, to talk about federal aid. After that, given the hard choice between seeing Mammy or a benefit matinee for a dear friend's new nursery school, he opted for the matinee, and by the time he got back it was too late to start grading. So, half-asleep, he scribbled off the letter to me that told me about all of this.

When he was finished, too bushed even to clear off his own bed, he went to the guest bedroom next door and fell on top of the bed in there, dusty and grim, maybe, but at least there were no *Times*es—a blessed prairie compared to his slum. The dampish spread reminded him of the big cold bed we'd once shared in a roadside cabin in Vermont. And then he told me he'd awoken fuddled and panicked, thinking he'd probably missed a phone call from Vicenza.

Finally there came that single white sleepless night between Monday and Tuesday for finishing all eighty-five of his exams at once. Farrelly, under instructions to stop all calls, stopped all but one: a triumphant announcement from Esta that the City had just declared nonprofit housing sponsors would get cleared land. *Cleared land!* That was like winning the lottery for any developer, let alone a nonprofit, able to save people at least $2.50 a room a month. She berated him: "Finish your damn papers so we can celebrate."

He sank back to his stone pile. But it was OK, maybe it was all OK, maybe it had been, all that time on the beat, all that time with Bob Wagner down at City

Hall, begging, cajoling, whipping together the good numbers, while the mayor schlepped around his office in his bedroom slippers. Maybe even worth the humiliation of going from graduate seminars at C.U. to first-year high-school civics, so he could teach 'em what he'd learned, that the mayor of New York really does rule like a Byzantine emperor. Oh, yes, they'd have those 2,500 units yet.

Farrelly let Esta through one more time to tell him that Goddard-Riverside Community Center, their rival nonprofit, doing their own housing—and doing well by doing good, as the cynics used to say—had just printed up their tenant list, with not a single relocated family on it. "We'll have some fun with that when the news hits the streets," he promised, and his adrenaline put him through the night. He rushed past the scowling Rector in the morning, turning his grades in almost on time.

That Wednesday evening, after Esta left for home, he locked up and slipped to the back desk at the storefront, hoping to get a good news letter out to Italy before he made off for the Catholic conference in D.C. A slight drumming on the window glass jerked him alert. He stood up to see somebody cupping his hands to peer inside, somebody who saw him and waved. It was Father Farrelly. Harry buried his foolscap in an expert little maneuver and let him in.

Farrelly followed him to the back. "Time to do that playground letter?" He was their "Spanish" priest, though he was as Irish as the day is long, a tall, gliding, egg-shaped man with a baby face. From the start he'd brought an illusion of order into Flanagan's regime by sorting out his responsibilities and Harry's as something like inside and outside sales. But ever since the Sonia Rivera rat-bite case he'd caught the fighting–City Hall fever and become the sorcerer's apprentice.

It seems that two old-law tenements were scheduled for demolition next to the church, and the fate of the site was still undecided. St. Gregory's was clear: they wanted to make it a playground for the schoolkids. How did they argue this?

OK. No shareable playground nearby.

Right. Kids can't even stretch their legs at recess.

And you can't make a play street out of West 90th—not with the horse manure half a foot deep most of the time.

Right. And there's no plan to do away with the 89th Street stable—

Cheesus, no, not if Jackie Kennedy needs someplace to ride when she's in the city—

And the horses gotta follow the same one-way traffic pattern as the cars, around the block and into the park—

Riiiight.

"It's great what you can do with horseshit," Tom quipped, snapping their modest proposal with satisfaction. "I'll have somebody at the rectory type it up and get Flannelhead out of the countinghouse to sign it." Harry watched him leave, amazed at how smoothly, how gracefully, Tom closed the door and glided out, glancing up and down the street before stepping out into sidewalk traffic.

Harry slid back to his foolscap. Through the thin wall, he could hear the Chinese laundryman next door loudly quarreling with his wife, but couldn't understand a word. *If he clobbers her with a flatiron I'll never be able to testify to anything.*

He wrote to me on International Inn stationery from Washington on November 15 to say how surprisingly poorly attended this important interracial conference was, in spite of the keynote speaker from the Southern Christian Leadership Conference. He'd been hard at work on some race and urban renewal statements. "Just drew up about 8 resolutions after 4-hr session," he wrote, "& am tired." He was hoping they'd do some good, although "I was expert only because of surrounding ignorance." The opulence of the setting galled him. "In this joint with a pool under a glass bubble in front of it they are on the theme of 'Poverty, Religion & Race,'" he said. "Don't know how much it's all worth. What a prophet Nickie was about how they'd turn the poor into another industry."

To his amazement they adopted every one of his resolutions. It struck him as pretty ironic. As far as the scholarly world knew, he hadn't published a word in over a year, and yet these few words might make more of a difference than any he'd ever committed to paper in his life. But success only seemed to make him more pugnacious. After a few drinks at the banquet he got into something of a brawl with Bill McFadden, who was down from the City Relocation Office. McFadden accused him of carrying this poor people thing too far. "Yours is just the kind of candyass bleeding-heart bullshit that's going to drive developers away from the West Side."

"Gimme Jimmy the Greek odds."

"You know it as well as I do. There won't be a single private developer looking at those public housing figures is gonna risk his beanbag on luxury rentals on Columbus Avenue."

"Mac, you don't know *shit* from Columbus Avenue. And you don't know *more* shit from developers—"

"You listen to me—"

"And you don't know *most* shit from urban renewal, if you think a few measly units of poor people's housing is going to lower the value of prime land to some greedy New York realestatenik."

"Ya know, Browne. You're the enemy."

"That depends which side you're on, Mac, doesn't it."

He left Washington feeling terrible, in spite of his triumphs. They were putting Band-Aids on this race thing. He tried to stay focused on housing. On Sunday he took a ride out to Evergreen Gardens, a Mitchell-Lama–financed success in the Bronx. He'd been asked to pay a kind of pastoral sick call on the Ruizes, a Cuban family relocated out of the parish. He was lousy at missions of mercy, but Mr. Ruiz thought he might have cancer and was afraid to go for tests, and Mrs. Ruiz had especially asked for him, not Father Tom. He couldn't help feeling distracted, suffocated, by the little apartment once he got there, with its brassy clutter and heavy ruffled curtains and Technicolor holy pictures above vigil candles.

He wondered if this—this bureaucratically calculated, constipated little space for cramming all of a family's living and dying into—if this, after all, was the measure of everything he was fighting for.

Silene came down with the mumps. She wouldn't even risk talking with me on the telephone. She sent her colleague Dr. Toniolo for the little Arri's weekly checkup, right to the hotel, a big Abe Lincoln of an Italian, forced to crouch his great height over the beaming babe as he lay on the bed grabbing at air. "*Che bel bimbo. Che splendido, che magnifico bambino.*" He scooped him up in both huge, articulate hands and held him to the light the way a collector might hold a cinquecento Baby Jesus. I felt as exultant as a madonna.

But there was no time to waste. "*Dottore,*" I pleaded. "Could you—*per caso . . . ?*" *Ma. Per carità, Signora. Im-pos-sibile.* He pulled himself up to his full towering height above me, his Mount Rushmore profile pinked with horror at the thought of insinuating disease toxins into angel flesh.

My last resort was the town Ufficio Sanitario, where they gave smallpox injections routinely. "*Dio ci benedica,*" muttered the poor staff doctor, recoiling at the dangled baby as if I had requested infanticide and cursing this American fetish for vaccine. But I was desperate now. I pressed him, even at the risk of being officially branded an unnatural mother. To my astonishment, he gave way. "*Molto leggermente,*" he said, doing a nimble little finger ballet in the air and lowering his voice. "Very lightly. So we may—simply—be able—to say—it was—done—"

Ah, just the subversive attitude I had been questing for! Not immediately, no, we had to give little Arri every advantage. But taking all factors into account, including the lag for checking the take, it looked like Friday the twenty-second was the latest possible date for the shot. My departure was already set for Sunday, the first of December. So I cannot forget where I was on Friday the twenty-second of November, the day my *magnifico bambino* was vaccinated.

I had been holding him for hours. He'd been cranky and restless almost from the moment the doctor had touched the needle to his arm, and I was sitting on the edge of the bed, holding his tender, fretful little body and rocking him gently in the pool of lemon-colored light from the bed lamp. Emmi surprised me, slipping so shyly into the room like that, without knocking. Her face was white.

Jack Kennedy is dead, she said. Jack of the smiling eyes is dead. Shot dead in Dallas. And she burst into tears.

When he heard the news, Harry wrote, he just got in the car and drove straight out to Long Island with the radio on, crying like a kid. His mother, a pile of frozen grief, was sunk into the brown couch in front of the TV. He dropleafed himself beside her and took her plump, cold hand in his and held it, something he never did. They sat motionless like that for hours, like everybody else in America. The screen seemed to suck confusion out of thin air and churn it up and spit it out in granite images.

He hadn't worshipped Kennedy, but he'd loved him. Irish Catholic, same age, bridger of class, cracker of jokes. And he'd once had an older brother. . . .

It didn't feel like a single death, not even a symbolically American death. It felt like a kind of genocide, as if an entire generation, Irish, Catholic, and American, had been murdered. Maybe it even felt like *his* death. Strange how scale had lost all meaning. "Now we must think of our country's future," he wrote to me, a strange new trembling in his tone, "which in such a funny way is little Harry's future—"

Words themselves seemed to buckle against him.

But it was his last letter to Vicenza.

It was the last letter he would ever have to write to me for the rest of our lives.

Part Five

UN BALLO IN MASCHERA

1

I do not remember how I confronted my parents with the reality of my father-less child. I do not remember telling them. I cannot remember any of the imme-diate emotional consequences of this confession, then or over the next few months, except that I was allowed to visit them, with the baby, virtually every Sunday. The blank astonishes and vexes me. How can mere "repression" describe such a calcu-lable erasure of ring upon ring of emotion? It is like leaving a black hole in the place where my childhood ended.

Perhaps one of my brothers cleared my path to them—maybe Lou, having in the summertime we were together constructed a grudging respect for my courage. Or Carlo, now an accomplished electrical engineer traveling all over the world. He had taken a job in Frankfurt, Germany, while I was in Italy, troubleshooting NATO defense installations there. He'd been friendlier, more approachable, since he'd begun to find himself in his profession. And now there was this anguish of the assassi-nation we'd experienced—shared—from our common European distance.

I determined to write to him as I left Vicenza, telling him as much as I dared about the baby. Without hesitation he asked me to make Frankfurt a stopover on the last leg of my return journey. I was amazed to have got this openhearted and unexpected invitation from one of my father's sons. I felt it in my need as an unimag-inably generous kindness. His care while we were with him there still fills my heart, and then the unbearable gentleness with which he lifted me and my little blue baby carrier aboard the Lufthansa flight home.

Did he beg my father to be charitable?

My father. I try to grasp what my little crime meant to him, and to my mother. Was it something like a death in the family? A small catastrophe, perhaps, compared with the nightmare's edge of national doom. The King, after all, was Dead—blasted away by broad daylight—and then the assassin, and the assassin's assassin. What obscen-ity wasn't as public as television any more? And what was I but a bit of the Apocalypse on the doorstep, a jostling, a crowding into the sanctuary of the bad-ness that had darkened the world?

Christmas, 1963. I am reminded of the "*In Memoriam*" Christmas that so "bleak-ly fell" for Tennyson once, after his dearest friend died. Maybe it fell less bleakly for us—after all, the nearer "death" in this case was also a nativity. Possibly my parents let themselves feel this, allowed the new year to come flowing on in hope, not hope-lessness. But in the blank pages of my mind are months—months—of that new year utterly past recollection of what they felt, or what I felt for them. We lived. We went on living. And if I cannot remember that first visit home, I can remember the last—or I have the color snapshot of us that remembers it for me: the wide-eyed child sitting on the carpet of my father's house—the same I danced on as a girl—myself kneeling behind him, his baby feet turned out like a doll's, the pure white of his love-ly, embroidered Italian baby smock brilliant against the sky blue of my dress.

Perhaps it is Easter Sunday, for he is surely five months old or more. *Bel Bimbo* we called him then, touching neither of the live explosives of his Christian names, "Beautiful Babe," a nickname that though it was eventually minimalized into "*Bim*," had come down in a straight descent from the Abe Lincoln doctor who'd held him high in the palms of his two hands that day in Vicenza and delivered his canticle of Italian praise. And he was *bello, bellissimo,* his tiny arms confidently out-spread, fingertips gripping mine, his face a Buddha of brightness, bald and gild-ed and as insouciantly beautiful as a Botticelli. Flashbulb overkill has haloed us with darkness and slicked our foreheads with shine. But what joy we exude! It would be false to call it false.

This single image: dropped into snapshot burial after our weekend visits abruptly ended, and forgotten in the sweet mercy of forgetting. Mercy for me, mercy for my mother, who must stop filching her guilty little grandmotherly pleasures from disgrace. *She* had embraced us: surely I cannot have twisted this by wishing it. But visit by visit she withdrew, perhaps, taking her speaking part from the pen of my father's courage. For my father had a puffed up Cavaradossi courage—the courage to walk away when I came into the room with my baby in my arms. And when the letter arrived from the family in Striano, that inevitable disdainful let-ter cutting him like a whip, he had the courage to break his own heart and say I should never come home again.

There is, then, that single Sunday image to stand for all those Sundays, and I took it away with me from my father's house, leaving no trace.

When I slept, I dreamed my mother's anxieties and felt somehow inside her skin, twisting in pity, in remorse. Waking, I didn't think of her. I thought instead of Harry's mother, whose Sundays with her own dear *boyo* would go little by little, now that he was spending more of them with us, whom I could even pity in a kind of future-past for never ever seeing or dreaming to see the beautiful grandson already ban-ished from her sight. It surely was no coincidence that we had settled for a place at the Astoria edge of Queens. Just over the Queensboro and Triboro Bridges from the city, yes, but also so near the Ravenswood projects that sometimes, when he came to see us, Harry could actually stop for a cup of tea with Mam.

Yet for all its proximity to Manhattan the apartment we took might have been in Nebraska. Part of a sprawling complex called Astoria Gardens in the neighborhood of Long Island City's 20th Avenue, it was set on a piece of the island the Triboro seemed to have sliced away and cast adrift in the East River. Immediately to the north was a strip at least a half-mile long, edging the sound and cutting off all north-ern access to the waterfront, and within the immense, fenced acres of this strip, an unscalable fortress of Consolidated Edison generating and storage facilities, including a chain of towering blue-green gas tanks the size of pantheons.

It was like taking a backward leap in housing time, when the GI Bill and the booming housing market just after the war made no prissy concessions to the environment in any sense. And yet this still modestly priced, plain brick, low-rise apartment enclave managed to stretch back-to-back-to-back the full length of several blocks without overwhelming the small one- and two-family townhouses on the neighboring side streets. Maybe the "gardens" were once verdant, though I doubt it. They consisted now of a few leggy shrubs and spidery, starveling trees around small patches of gray-green grass. The grass had been trampled rather than trained into submission. Kids' feet had worn arcs of bare dirt that corresponded precisely to the lines of sight from the apartment windows.

The ad we'd seen in the *Times* ran every week, week in, week out: in a complex of that size *something* would always be open to rent. The morning I went to see it, I stood in a queue at the office between what seemed to be two identical mothers with several rubbery children in varying stages of tumble, one with cash to pay the rent and the other pleading for more time to pay it, plus three elderly women ahead of us, all from different parts of the complex, and all with the approximate same complaint about the noisy neighbors next door. When I got back after checking out the vacancies, the tenants ahead of me now were making exterminator appointments or asking to have somebody let the telephone man in. And there I gladly signed a lease on a one-bedroom third-floor flat at 20-21 24th Street.

I was under the roof again—"no one walking on my head." From my living-room window the view to the river was crosshatched with clotheslines and spoked with chimneys and intricate webs of antennas. But one flight took me to the flat, tarred roof where I hung my baby diapers to dry in the windy sunshine, and from there the flat blocks descended row on row to the river in a single dramatic sweep, like orchestra seats for whatever astonishing sunset might be caught in the great black wings of the Hell's Gate Bridge.

As for those awesome Con Ed monuments to the power of power, breathtaking in the sheer grandeur of their ugliness—people cope with proximate manmade dooms, I suppose, much as they do with natural ones, like live volcanoes and earthquake faults. Here they simply turned away from the 20th Avenue frontier and lived their lives to the south, east, and west. On fine-weather Sundays they would wend happily down to the sprawling, green embankment by the Hell's Gate and play and picnic in the giant shadow of its half-moon girders, and sometimes, lying with their kids on a blanket there, or walking their dogs, gaze out past the Triboro, and down along the curve of the East River, to the sprouted Manhattan skyline, beyond the beyond.

Which left 20th Avenue a kind of urban desert, a wild zone, where tall weeds and sumac saplings grew in jungle profusion between the fence piles, and the pavement lay as broad and desolate and sun-blinded as a Southern California boulevard at high noon. Other mothers with strollers strolled more populous routes. Grass grew blithely between the cracks in the sidewalks. Traffic avoided it—the cars one saw there were probably lost. But my little Bim and I, who were altogether rather pleased with each other's solitary company, seemed to find something happy in its desert blankness. And there as the seasons wore on we took to wandering in this archetype urban wilderness, dwarfed by monster pipes and coils and cables that looked like magnified sets from *The Bride of Frankenstein.* And there, one fine day in his second April, my amazing *bel bimbo* looked squarely through the cyclone fence and squarely back at me, and said, simply, "dynamo," the premier polysyllable of his speaking life.

Of all the times I can remember as "times," as episodes, this may very well be the happiest. We had few money needs, then, or so it seemed. We cobbled together the rent and the telephone between what Harry and I made teaching. Hunter College had fit me in again, part-time, for the spring term of 1964, and the English chairman at Pace hired me on the spot for a couple of evening sections of comp. Until I could afford a regular sitter, my Zi' Carmelina rescued me, watching the baby for the few hours I was teaching. In open defiance of my father, I should add. She had refused to turn me away.

Zi' Carmé and I were deeply *simpatiche* by nature, just how deeply I had not known till now. My mother had only recently told me—maybe because talking about Bim's birth had somehow called up memories of my own—that when I was just newborn, Carmé had come all the way to New Rochelle to see me. She had made the long train ride from New York and then the long walk from the railway station in the grilling sun of that May heatwave, only to turn heel the instant she learned that they had named me *Flavia* for my mother's dead mother instead of *Immacolata,* for my father's and hers. And yet she'd utterly relented when my parents asked her be my *madrina.* She had stood up beside the baptismal font with complete self-forgetfulness and love, swearing to care for me if ever came the need, and meaning to keep her word.

And she had. Past the memorable fire-escape Sundays of my earliest childhood, the bond between us had deepened in innocent increments nurtured by seventh-grade schoolday afternoons in the dimming little second-story apartment on East 78th Street, doing homework with my cousins till my father came to fetch me home. Then those first years of teaching at Hunter before the baby, when I had taken to dropping in just to see her. We would always converse in Italian—I longed to keep mine alive, and her English had never been good. But her *Napoletano* was enchanting; folktales and proverbs and scraps of arcane poetry had a lilting grace in her mouth beyond my father's. Often I would find her alone—Gloria long married, Joyce at work, Sam in the store. She would chortle with joy to see me, peering through the peephole in a door thick with years of encrusted paint, and then clatteringly unlock it to let me in.

Oh, she was ever a girl, some freshly self-concocted face cream an inch deep on her flawless skin, still tight as polished ivory over her cheekbones, lovely in spite of the thickening, tightly corseted body, the shelflike bosom you could almost have rested a plate on. Perhaps she had stepped fresh and scented from the bath when I arrived, and now stood in the tiny galley kitchen over the *caffettiere,* brewing espresso for the two of us, her whitening hair new-washed and coiled, the towel still draped fetchingly around her shoulders. We would snatch a few moments together while the baby still slept perhaps, and she would regale me with tales, sometimes lyrically, sometimes boastfully, sometimes lifting a hesitant, secretive veil in maddening bits on what seemed a powder keg of family secrets: her peccadilloes, yes, and, yes, my father's too, oh yes, if the truth were told. There were things—done—so that—to do this to me now—

I did not press her for details. My aunt and I had grown so close that I seemed to take in her daring, even her wise sibyl-like dream-reading witchcraft, by intuition. I knew that this magical woman was affirming my life. This was truth enough for now. Sometimes I would even edge away from her fearful stories thinking it was for my mother's sake, conscious, too conscious at times of leaning into the volcanic mouth of some unbearable truth. Was it for my mother's sake?

Enough. What she had said was already enough—too much. She had silenced Uncle Sam's feeble admonitions. She had stood up to the brother she adored. She had welcomed my outlaw baby and me as if she had had training in the Italian Resistance.

When I could finally afford one, my index-card plea for a "mature" baby-sitter in the Gardens office was answered by a tiny, sad, sweet woman named Tess, who padded her husband's small disability income a little by working for $1.50 an hour. Tess seemed to have developed a stoop from the habit of humility. Even I, not especially tall, could see the top of her head, where her crisp gray hair grew out from the crown flat as a pie plate. In a curious way she reminded me of some of my mother's sisters, particularly my elusive Aunt May, and shy, withdrawing Anna. It almost made me cry to have her look up at me through glasses so thick it was as if the eyeballs were painted on them, thinking of their eyes, too, ruined by years of piece needlework.

But blind as she was, Tess had a kind of sonar for babies. And the tact of a duchess. She never pried, she never patronized, she never held my ways as a mother up to her standard and found them wanting. She was there when I needed her, precisely when I needed her, took perfect care of my adorable child, and assured me that minding him was so easy she was almost ashamed to get paid for it.

Tess's Eddie had emphysema, the legacy of his wartime factory job. I never met him, though we spoke of it sometimes. In all her comings and goings from my place I'm not sure she ever met my Harry more than once. That was the way it was. I was married, as far as they knew, and as far as I knew, like her, every one of the women of the Gardens had a proper husband, every child a proper father, every family was respectable and hard-working-class. Maybe they weren't. But gossip wasn't Tess's thing, and it certainly wasn't mine.

And it wasn't Terry's either, when Bim graduated to the big, blowsy brunette who said, sure, she could fit him in among her semi-legal day-care babies. Terry never said a word about the private lives of any of her mothers, and yet she never let me leave her apartment without a cup of coffee and some staggering intimacy about her own. She taught me not only that you could trust some people with your life as well as with your child; she taught me that you could work as hard as hell at looking sexy—makeup, eyelashes, cleavage, the lot—and still be as frigid in bed as an Aleutian island. Or so she told me, maybe thinking I was educated enough to advise her. She was on her second husband, she said, still trying desperately to make love like a woman.

What a stubbornly durable lot they were in those Gardens, women who for all I knew might have produced their children by parthenogenesis and mostly seemed to take the real existence of their respective men on the purest faith. A world of struggling mothers and invisible husbands and general respect for other people's private hardships. Nobody shocked at my leaving an infant several hours by day or night to go to work, because if they didn't do the same thing themselves they knew others who did. No rigid textbook standards of maternal perfection because they had learned mothering from their mothers, and it had always been hard. Some of them seemed sad, lonely sometimes, hungry for something—maybe I seemed the same to them—but never bitter, never envious, open to a good idea, a good laugh. Women like Tess and Terry found my tolerance for hours of reading a little alien, yet they respected my education without letting it intimidate them. We bonded by what *did* bond us: toilet training and baby fevers, recipes, supermarket prices, bad movies. Silence was given where silence was taken. Beautiful women, laughing, crying, smart and wise and funny. They didn't know they were helping me forget.

Or perhaps they did.

Not even Nebraska. Try another planet orbiting another sun, try Harry as Captain Kirk beaming himself to us, slipping out of the city under cover of darkness, usually, stuffing his notched black bib with its white celluloid collar into the glove compartment as he crossed the Triboro Bridge. A caution bred of sheer habit. Even on his rare daylight visits nobody in the Gardens noticed him. This was not a *Times*-reading planet. Nobody expected to meet the priest they had just seen flash by them on the TV news advancing, without his collar, up the tenement stairs. And no problem if Father Browne got longer TV exposure on Sunday mornings. Those multiple-pundit panel shows were meant for Westchester bankers. In Astoria Gardens, people went to church.

It was a world. It was a world in part created by sewing machine, in this case my mother's portable, which she had not asked me to give her back. My favorite creation was a tablecloth of flaming red cabbage roses, which I spread seductively over our little dropleaf table for Saturday night suppers, as if it were our own little garden. Until we could afford to buy a crib, Bim slept in his doll-sized carrying case from Italy. Until we could afford to buy a bed, we slept in greedy closeness on the old foam-rubber couch, one of the few things besides books that had actually survived the long Italian detour from West 88th Street. Later, we bought a Castro convertible that thumped when we opened it and thudded when we closed it in the morning. The floors were thinner than the walls. We finally bought a rug to drop it on, but the old couple downstairs still banged the ceiling with the broom every night, just as the TV news came on in both our apartments.

Back to the teaching grind, of course, at least five courses a term at low pay, without possibility of tenure and without a dream of asking for it. I managed: the household, the baby, the bills, the laundry, the marketing. I built the kitchen shelves and endtables myself—there seemed time to do everything then. I took my watercolors with me on walks to the park. I continued to revise my dissertation. My father's grudging grace extended to the use of the old family Plymouth for a time, the same as my mother's had the sewing machine. I would drive into Manhattan on workdays, deposit Bim atop Carmelina's gigantic *letto matrimoniale*—the one I'd been warned off as a child—and leave him happily thrashing his tiny fists and studying the antiquated ceiling fixture with his hungry eyes. Later, when Tess sat for me at home, I would catch the Astoria-line train at Ditmars Boulevard and ride to work on cars clean and bright enough to seem the last civilized branch of the New York subway. Life seemed so absurdly, fearlessly livable. I walked carelessly home alone in the dark. I left the car, when I had it, unwarily parked, even unlocked, on the street outside the door.

How effortlessly we slid into parenting, working, do-gooding, into taking our daily bread from this ersatz family life the satellite world of Astoria Gardens made so easy, so sufficient. Confronted with the givens, we had found the only livable life. We didn't think of ourselves as victims, or even as victors—we didn't have to. We didn't have to think of ourselves at all. The tolerable alternative, if there was a tolerable alternative, had simply not yet been revealed. It became, in fact, more elusive every day, just as the other givens became every day more certain: love a "fact" as relentless as sunrise, priesthood not something to be shed like a suit or a collar, but bone of bone, flesh of flesh. Because the canon law said, "Choose!" so did the rest of the world, so astonishingly ready to accommodate the canon law—but who chooses between eating and breathing?

Harry chose Fatherhood, compleat. Call it middle-aged *timor mortis,* but he took such a piercing joy in the miracle of having a son, at having reclaimed a piece of his humanity from the junkpile of renunciation, that he seemed to come to parenting with a wilder urgency and acuter concentration than was common— maybe by some standards than was even decent—in a father. He seemed to have invented a new icon called Harry with Child. His happiness had all the heightened reality of art, a shamelessness, a pure disregarding shamelessness, that he rushed to, blind as a magnet, as if Bim's birth had activated some deprived infancy in himself, some sublimely uncensored id. That very first Christmas he'd gone to F.A.O. Schwartz on a wild buying spree, realizing all the fantasies that he could afford. None of his gifts was meant for a baby, really, unless it were a baby going through all the stages of childhood at once. Or he'd put him through strange rites of passage, like slipping him into a brown paper grocery sack, feet first, to watch him kick it off with his booties, just so he could crow that, now, *nobody* could ever say "the Browne kid couldn't punch his way out of a paper bag." And then he'd lift him over his head like a trophy, while I stood by laughing so hard it hurt.

One day in February he arrived at my door with a complete layette. A sensible thing, a layette, more sensible than a life-size Pooh bear or a brown paper bag. But this layette had come from Mary O'Neill, children's author, an old friend of Harry's from his Washington days. She lived on the West Side now, and hearing he was at St. Gregory's, she'd shown up at the rectory. "*For some needy parish mother,*"she'd said, handing him the package. "*You decide.*"

It had happened a while ago. Harry had mentioned it to me, offhand, in one of his letters to Vicenza. "Should be you," he'd said then. And I'd said, "No, that wouldn't be right." And that was where we'd left it—until the afternoon he'd come in and dropped the package, literally at my feet.

I was mortified. "I can't take this."

"Why not?"

"Because it was meant for some poor mother on the West Side."

"Slight change of venue. Poor mother *from* the West Side."

"Harry. Please. Take it back."

"Believe me, Mary O'Neill would be tickled pink."

"This is taking the lilies of the field too far."

"You can't take the lilies of the field too far."

For days, I left it just where he had put it down. Every time he came and went I begged him to take it away, but he refused. I thought I knew why I resisted: some unspoken criminal sanction violated, concubine that I was. But he was absolutely immovable. Exasperated, I finally lifted the package from the floor to a shelf in the linen closet. Desperate one day, I tore open the wrapper and borrowed an extra diaper and baby shirt. Slowly, I progressed to lemon- and lime-colored snap-ups with booties, then to crib sheets when we got a crib. Strange how it felt as if my moral fiber had not weakened.

We never spoke of it again. Bim wore and outgrew everything in the package. I laundered it carefully, folded it perfectly, and passed it on to Terry, for another needy mother like me.

2

Summer of 1964. One of the hottest in human memory. Housekeeping overkill alternates symbiotically with dissertation frenzy. Bim learns to sleep to the ceaseless tak-tak of the typewriter. On the issue of hot showers vs. cold, Tess is uncertain: "Eddie says cold is better, but hot feels so good when you get out." I swear only an air conditioner can keep my brain from boiling under that tar roof, and calculating the cost at pennies more per pound than brisket of beef, I plunge. Two sizable men bring my new Fedders upstairs, risking life and future fatherhood just taking it across my slickly polished living-room floor.

Beyond the beyond, the world is reeling from "Negro" to Black Power. Three young students, Michael Schwerner, James Cheney, and Andrew Goodman, ominously disappear while canvassing voters on a major registration drive in Jackson, Mississippi.

Harry would forever remember it as "CoFo Summer," when the Medical Commission for Human Rights, drawing on volunteers from all over the country, teamed him up in July with Marvin Belsky, West Side M.D., on a counseling and support mission to Jackson. For people who knew Marvin as the soft-spoken Army doctor who'd once stood up to redbaiting before the Army-McCarthy hearings, he was nothing less than a Jewish Superman, complete with Clark Kent sandy hair and glasses; they wouldn't be surprised to catch him stripping down in a Broadway phone booth. I thought the two made a well-matched odd couple, Marvin with his wistful seriousness and carnal knowledge of life's hurtfulness, Harry with his noisy, instant, illogical, bittersweet sense of metaphysical absurdity. But frankly I worried as they set out by train and joined up with a black woman, a nurse from D.C., just as the search for the three missing student-organizers was about to climax. Before they even got to Jackson, it was a sure conclusion that the black nurse was safer going it alone. It was another question whether *they* were. When their hosts in Jackson discovered they'd been sent a lefty Jewish doctor and blackleg Catholic priest, they couldn't believe it.

They gave them assignments right there in town, keeping a watchful eye, until Harry and Marvin pleaded to join voter-canvassing rounds. They needed to be out past dark just once, driving back with a pair of glowering pickup headlights glued to their tail, to begin to learn what scared meant. Another time, out with two black students, Harry driving, a state trooper pulled the car over in broad daylight on an empty country road. The four of them sat frozen as he approached the car. Outside, in the woods, a terrifying silence. The trees dropped heat. The trooper, his face like a backhoe, laid his sweat-greased hand on the door, holster creaking, and peered inside the car. "*What yaw business heeah?*"

Nobody answered at first. Even Harry checked himself, in disbelief how unprepared he was for this. They'd had public confrontations, but on town sidewalks before plenty of witnesses. Sitting ahead of them in the police car was another large man, not in uniform, thick sweaty arms folded and stacked like firewood, unblinking eyes staring them down. Marvin piped up to say they were on a medical counseling mission, his voice so high-pitched Harry pictured him trying to explain later—if there *was* a later—the precise physiology of the tight scrotum.

The trooper demanded IDs. "Wheah y'all takin them two niggahs?" Harry muttered something about getting back to Jackson, but he was thinking, *Am I really giving this bastard an answer when what I wanna do is put his teeth down his throat?* But he was also thinking that with the official search for the three missing students exploding, there *had* to be some heat on guys like these. He was thinking about what the two kids in the back were thinking.

Time was the buzz of racing pulses inside the car. The trooper shifted the contents of their wallets from hand to hand like playing cards, putting things back in order slowly. He slapped the door again with his massive, juicy hand. "Y'all bettah find yoselves some trouble up North t'fix." He saved Harry's wallet for last. "We don't need no doctahs and no *preestes* 'round heah," he said. "No more'n we already got."

That was it. They pulled away. They drove on in a single envelope of silence, letting the hot breeze blow the smell of fear out to the molten sheets of open field on both sides of the road.

Finally, "This is the kind of day you get a real burn," Harry said.

They headed back toward Jackson singing rain songs on the sweet-scented roads. That night Marvin and Harry slept in the house of movement leader Aaron Henry, under an armed guard. There was only one bed for the two of them. "Don't be surprised if I hug you," Marvin said as they turned in. "Don't be surprised," Harry said, "if I hug you back."

Harry didn't talk about it much when he got back, not till later. Of the three students whose bodies turned up in that culvert outside Jackson on August 5, two had been from our own West Side neighborhood, and the ruthless heat pelting Broadway that month had an awful bite of anger and grief in it. As time went on, he might do his little ritual *shtik* with Marvin and friends, describing himself as "the guy Marvin slept with in the summer of '64," and Marvin would hunch his head down and protest that "it was all off when he found out I snored." But otherwise it was too much a memory of fear for either of them to play for laughs.

For Harry, in fact, it was too much a memory of courage not his own, the single image incarnating the whole thing not the blundering trooper, but the silent black man who'd sat outside Aaron Henry's bedroom door that night, calm and steady, with a shotgun across his lap.

Esta came over for her first Astoria Gardens visit at the end of August to watch the Democratic Convention in Atlantic City on Harry's old black-and-white TV, recently relocated from the rectory penthouse and positioned on my just-made, free-form coffee table.

Esta was glowing, Harry intense. Bim was squirming from my lap to his. West

Side Congressman Bill Ryan finds his way to the microphone, and in a thundering, magnificent moment, moves that the convention unseat the all-white Mississippi delegation and replace it with the delegation of the Freedom Democratic Party, led by Aaron Henry.

And all our meandering trails had come to this one, sharp, significant point.

It was as if there could never be another time than *now*—the time we were living. We thought we'd forced destiny itself, too rich with joy and pain to be teased by expectation.

In some sense we were prisoners of history: the very revelation was at hand. We had only to await it. Yet perhaps "awaiting" is not the word for a set of destinies so alive, so actively pursued. We were *having,* not waiting to have. If in some sense we were prisoners, we were prisoners not of our choices but of our unwillingness to make them.

Not that we were blind to our "problem" in the conventional sense. And in the conventional sense our problem grew only more complex, more concrete, as the public persona of Father Browne grew larger and more visible. If ever priest was inseparable from ministry, it was now. If ever in danger of scandal, now. Yet to avoid the scandal meant abandoning the work. And the work couldn't be abandoned.

I had so much less to lose than he, less to risk, insofar as such things are calculable. Or so I thought. "Career prospects"? Perhaps. Teachers who might have been glad to see me successfully launched. Yet it didn't seem important to be "launched" in any sense that had to do with personal ambition. Perhaps my work suffered— who can tell? Perhaps something in my creative life was quelled, aborted in the spirit. I suffered, being unable to share with others the life my work came out of. I preferred not to lie, though practice had made me almost good at it. I preferred not to be mysterious. Not to be thought of as some kind of intellectual nun who'd renounced love and family, when the truth, the truly awful, wonderful truth, was that I had renounced nothing except the freedom to say "*I have renounced nothing.*" It *seemed* I had renounced nothing. Perhaps the secret cells of my body knew I ached to fly, to dance, to go where friendship takes you, to give myself whole to life, not divided discretely into parts.

And then I hated being the dark family secret, not just someone who'd lost, who'd abandoned the tribe, but who'd betrayed it. I thought of my father sulking in his tent, weighted by moralities he knew were false, false to his own act, as I now obscurely knew, his conscience buried under the stone of his own selfishly grieving heart. I thought of my mother sharing his life sentence with him, of my mother's child and her child's child, both set beyond her reach by a wall of stolid, stupid respectability. Predictably the wall had not even protected them. The news of my shame had spread from Alfonso like a virus, to every sister and cousin and aunt in the Italian diaspora. At my Uncle Sam's funeral (where, in spite of my love for my Aunt Carmelina, I dared not be seen), my recently immigrated cousin Anna— the same who had once begged me to pity their postwar degradation in Striano—

approached my stricken parents and, in the very faces of the assembled family, smilingly mock-congratulated them on the birth of my son.

Still, even their cruelty didn't make me feel clean to be quit of them. I couldn't be. By the very nature of the family in all its Italian complicity, I spread contamination. Ann tried to spare me when her engagement broke off. Perhaps the seed was already planted in her soul that she had escaped something rather than lost it. But I could hardly face her when she came home, carrying her shattered happiness in her eyes.

It was like getting used to an amputation. The wound hardens but it always hurts. Even after my father's prohibition was laid down, I continued to drive every few weeks to New Rochelle, loyal as ever to Dr. Belle, and then to the baby doctor she passed me on to. I girded myself. I sped up the new highway that now plowed straight through the city's heart, and took the off-ramp at Main Street, prepared to count the landmarks of my childhood: St. Gabriel's belltower, the old railway station, Bloomingdale's, the RKO marquee, the brick-and-cream Federal-style library with its single forbidden copy of *Ulysses* in a locked case.

Sometimes, with my baby asleep in the seat behind me, letting myself be lured by a wayward impulse, a piety of the kind that brings people with flowers to graves, I would take all the small, familiar turns to my father's house and make an inventory as I drove by: the Tudor-style façade poised against the hillside, deceptively towering and tall, the plum tree peering over the well-trimmed privet hedges at the back, the pebbled driveway, two round sandstone markers at the curb, nippled like brown breasts. The sprawling jasmine bushes below my window, the spidery syringa making its way up along the lawnside hill to the romantically arched front door. The roses my father had planted to bury his illness and grief.

And then I sped back to the city.

Or rather, back to my little satellite, which took its flashes of Harry's vivid, glamorous light like a moon. Our lives too had their studied and deliberate apartheid. His world, once ours, became more and more his, my entries into it more and more oblique and ritual, the strict public decorum stricter than ever.

A rally, a meeting, a benefit dinner. We looked, but we did not touch. *I* looked. I listened. I heard Father Browne on radio talk shows with Barry Gray, caught him on WPIX-TV news clips with Gabe Pressman, basked in half-hour news documentaries with Joe Michaels or Harry Reasoner, the monitor of his self-creation into that bright-eyed, glib, tough, brilliant political cartoonist ("Harry Reasoner, meet Harry *Un*Reasoner"), shooting that mouth off over the magical white notch in the collar. Making it happen. Mine and not mine—everybody's. Enough. Wasn't it enough?

I had Bim in my world, didn't I? My little *"bel negretto,"* his hair turned to purest spun gold now, his face so bright and enchanting that strangers stopped on sidewalks just to look at him. The fatuous reverie of motherhood stops me in my own tracks, just to remember.

"*Look! Look!*"

Surprised by joy, I can see Tess crouching beside him, whispering, "Go to Mommy—go!" It is his first birthday. I have just come through the door from teaching, and Tess is lightly propping up his arms at the far end of the room. He is all scintillating eyes and laughter, finally lunging away as she says, "*Go! Go!*" My God, the liturgical little bastard is *walking,* on his first birthday to the day—actually taking his first lone steps on his rubbery fat legs, his hands stretched out toward me—staggering—swaggering—sauntering across the room and into my arms.

Wasn't that enough?

Enough, and more than enough. Mine was a satellite world—a little world, secondary but entire. It rolled around the real world, a relay station for playing back the real world, like movies.

There was the welfare mother movie: Melinda Rodriguez. Oh, I identified with this one—a pastiche of Harry's and Esta's retellings. And Johnny. Everybody had Melinda and Johnny stories.

Johnny was in fact her third, dusky, runny-nosed. He'd followed Esta into her building when he was three. After she'd gone out again, he'd propped the door ajar, then lugged a wooden crate from the grocery store to boost himself up to the elevator buttons, and ridden up and down all day. Then he took to following her down to the Strycker's Bay storefront, just moved to the northwest corner of Columbus and 89th, holding Esta's hand so he could tell Melinda he hadn't crossed the streets by himself.

Years passed. He was five in 1964 and he still hung around. Esta said, "Look. If you're gonna hang around, you gotta work." So she handed him a broom on the first day he was big enough not to be toppled over by it.

Nineteen sixty-four was the year of the first "welfare cheating" headlines. These made Melinda furious. She began to look on Strycker's Bay as training camp, with Johnny as her recruit. She did not usually make war, but she was warrior material, a tall, shapely Rican beauty with a mass of redwood hair and bright hazel eyes, and fine, even teeth that shone in a range of electrifying smiles. It might take some doing to stand up to those sweet-talkers she fell for, but damned now if there were gonna be any more babies. And even more damned if the ones she had weren't gonna get fed.

And not just the ones *she* had. Melinda could see the big picture: she was not alone. Welfare mothers needed to speak up. Welfare mothers needed organizing. She consulted and strategized, not just with Esta and Father Browne but with Fred Johnson, the social worker the manpower project had hired to work with the families of street kids. She spent whole afternoons at the Strycker's Bay storefront, pacing the floor like Cleopatra scheming an offensive on Rome, Johnny bopping around her like a one-child minefield. "*Man,*" she would say, striding across the worn linoleum in her short skirt and impossibly high platform heels, legs shimmering, eyes flashing, warming to her favorite theme of the male parasite. "*Man,* ain't NO guy gonna get into MY life no more unless he can FILL my refrigerator."

And then Harry's voice from over the back files, unable to resist: "Hey, Melinda, how big is your refrigerator?"

As the weather got colder some of the other organizing mothers would come into the Strycker's Bay office sometimes just to keep warm. One of them was Georgia Jefferson, who'd already organized a group of tenants on 93rd Street. Sometimes she and Melinda would meet with Esta and Lainey Bertram, a volunteer from Richard Cloward's social work program at Columbia. Not quite ready to leave when business was done, they'd hang around for a half hour and think about going home, leaning on their elbows, staring out the plateglass window.

Like the day they saved the baby. Esta was waiting for Harry to make his way back from class, remembering he had an appointment with the principal at St. Gregory's and hoping she wouldn't be getting home too long after her two little girls. Out the window she could see a woman standing on the corner, standing very still, next to the wire trash basket and the lamppost papered with Johnson-Humphrey posters.

It was that drag end of the day, the steam had begun to clank faintly in the radiators, nobody had yet turned on the overhead fluorescent. The three women sat on a trio of folding chairs, Esta behind her desk. Her line of sight was clear. A small, dark child seemed attached to the woman's leg. For an instant Esta let her glance slip to Melinda's Johnny as he slid down the fender of a parked car. When she looked back, the woman and child stood frozen in exactly the same spatial relationship to the wire trash basket and the stickered lamppost. *WALK!* the traffic-control light commanded, but they didn't. Esta had a very simple code for reading the street: lampposts stood still, people moved.

"Hot dawgs again tonight," Georgia murmured absently.

"Lainey," Esta said softly. "Look at that woman. Out there on the corner. What's she holding? Looks like a bunch of curtains."

Lainey, curious, got up, went out. Melinda, staring now, slowly uncrossed her long legs and stood up. Georgia leaned forward and strained into the murky street. The streetlights suddenly went on.

When they let Lainey back in, her face had gone white as paper. "It's curtains, all right," she said. "Those scratchy ninon kind? There's a baby wrapped up inside." Melinda was out the door like an antelope. "The baby is blue, honest to God," Lainey choked. "I couldn't tell if it was still breathing." She turned to watch Melinda, the cold pumping in through the open door. "I couldn't get her to talk. I don't think she speaks English."

Melinda had coaxed the little group inside. The thinly clad little girl was still clinging for dear life to her mother's leg and Georgia leaned over and pried her gently away, setting her trembling on her lap, hugging her little body warm. Melinda helped fold back the curtains on the infant in her mother's arms. It couldn't have been more than a few days old. It looked puckered and ghastly, barely breathing.

"Food," Esta said hoarsely. She turned to Lainey, digging into her handbag for money. "Run over to the luncheonette. Get food. Tell Jimmy whatever you have to."

"This baby is *reeeal* sick," whispered Melinda.

Georgia got up, shifting the pale child easily. "I'll call Roosevelt."

Esta punched into the other line and dialed St. Gregory's. Father Browne had just come in. Esta cut him off in mid-apology. "Never mind, come fast. Bring your car. No. Trust me. Your car."

The woman clutched her infant with a cold ferocity. The dialect was unfamiliar. Melinda seemed to be putting her whole body into the effort to communicate. "You won't believe this," she said, when she finally turned to Esta. "She's come all the way from Brooklyn. Had the baby in a hospital there. They sent her home. But the landlord put a lock on the door."

"Christ," Esta said. "What hospital, Melinda? Find out what hospital. Has she told you her name?" The woman looked up, terrified.

"Illegal," Melinda said. She laid a comforting hand on the woman's arm, coaxing loose the frozen protective grip. "It's OK." When the woman spoke there was barely a voice behind the moving lips.

"How in God's name did she get here?"

"She just got on a bus."

"A *bus?*"

"Don't tell me they're routin' buses straight to Strycker's Bay from *Brooklyn* these days," Georgia said. She let out a slow, satisfied chuckle.

Lainey burst in with her arms full of paper luncheonette bags and her face full of victorious joy. "Jimmy sent over *everything*," she crowed. Mission accomplished, she lifted "everything" out onto the desk piece by piece: five tuna fish sandwiches, two hot teas, two hot coffees, containers of whole milk, a can of evaporated milk, its lid already punctured and covered in foil, slices of buttered bread, whole apples, cups, napkins, and straws. Enough for a mass meeting. Lainey handed around the food while Esta got on the phone to Brooklyn. Georgia gently unwrapped a sandwich for the girl, by now rolled up in a kittenish ball in her lap. The black eyes came up soft as cookies as she began to eat in little testing bites. Esta, on hold between hospital extensions, watched Melinda down on her haunches, urging the woman to eat. "Is she nursing?"

She wasn't sure. "But the baby's had diarrhea pretty steady. . . . " She gestured toward the fabric bundle and Esta took hold of a loose end and felt it rasp between her fingers. They exchanged a hopeless flicker of eyes.

"Lainey, boil some water," Esta demanded, absurdly. "Do *something*," she begged. "Fucking hospital bureaucracy!" As she heard herself use the F word, she thought she was going to *become* Browne if he didn't get here fast. She slammed down the phone. She felt ferocious. "Where is that *fucking* ambulance?" She yanked down her sweater, scanning the darkening street.

Lainey leaned out the door in search of ambulance lights just as Harry's car skimmed front end first into the curb. He and Buddy Murphy, one of Fred Johnson's street-gang protégés, flew out on both sides like Batman and Robin. Melinda drew them inside. "*Es Padre Browne, de San Gregorio, aquí*," she explained to the woman, whose face lit up faintly for an instant. Harry touched the curtains nervously and Esta recognized that peculiar something in his eyes having to do with babies, laced with panic.

Lainey broke in, shaking her head. No ambulance yet. But behind her, outside, a small crowd had gathered, Georgie Thompson, the local street philosopher, up front. Behind him was the girl who worked the pharmacy counter, and behind her a circle of ordinary folks huddling together and staring through the plateglass window into the storefront where the light was on now. Somebody pushed forward, a neatly wrapped package in both hands, somebody else took it from him and passed it, and on it went hand over hand till it got to Lainey, who gave it to Melinda. Melinda looked at the package. It was a cotton bedsheet, still in its cellophane sleeve, from the drygoods store up the street. She shook it open and refolded it to about the proper size of a baby blanket, and the woman loosened her iron grip just enough to curl it smoothly around the nylon swaddling.

In the simplest Spanish, Melinda explained what was happening, that Father Browne was taking her and the baby to Roosevelt Hospital. The baby was very sick. The woman nodded. There was no time to lose. The woman nodded again, shuddered.

"OK, Murphy," Father Browne said. "Let's go."

"*La niña,*" said the woman, yearning toward Georgia, who was still sitting like a black madonna with the sad little girl in her lap sucking a milk straw. Georgia came alert and in one single dextrous motion that scattered wrappers and cartons like autumn leaves, she picked up her handbag and lifted the child onto her arm and herself to her feet.

Esta gave Harry an earnest look. "Melinda and I will wait. Call from the hospital." Melinda lifted the quivering mother to her feet. A dozen pairs of hands reached out as she made her way out to the car, wanting to help. "Outtadaway!" Murphy shouted.

Melinda: "What about somebody to handle the Spanish?"

Murphy: "I can handle it," and he dove away, flashing his black leather elbows through the little crowd on the sidewalk.

Esta shook her head. She had to laugh. "Irish J.D. turned Hispanic M.S.W.," she said.

Georgia, still hugging "la niña," was the last to settle into the back seat of the car—the springs heaved as if they were onloading a couch. Three kids, one of them little Johnny, authoritatively slammed the door after her. Up against the car window, the black-wafer little-girl eyes stared out. The motor gunned, the car aimed into traffic. A small battalion of street kids had already pushed out onto Columbus Avenue and were waving oncoming cars to clear passage, shouting, "*Fadderbrowen! Fadderbrowen!*"

The silver Ford crossed the intersection just ahead of the changing traffic light. It sped like a bullet down the avenue and disappeared, as cars and buses and trucks and vans closed swiftly and indifferently behind it.

3

There was a classic War on Poverty joke—about the bum who walked into the Office of Economic Opportunity in Washington one day and gave himself up—that seemed to compress a lot of the hidden contradictions in the program, including the hidden cynicism in its "target population."

Who, after all, was the enemy in this war? You could draw some embarrassing parallels between what they were calling "Vietnamization"—the increasing use of local ground troops in the accelerating conflict in Vietnam—and what the OEO referred to in the inner cities as the "maximum feasible participation of the poor." It seemed well-meaning in both instances, with the implication that authorities wanted to make it a people's war, as if any true solution had to be the people's solution. But in the end what it implied was that it was their *problem,* too. And that it might just stay that way.

I knew that for Harry, the OEO joke wasn't any funnier in a gallows sort of way than the truth, that a tidal wave of poverty money was about to pour in and create a whole new species of pernicious, sniveling parasite called the "poverty pimp." It was a personal issue, too. No matter how much he loved the limelight, he dreaded seeing Father Browne become just one more Great White Hope of whatever color for the poor. Somehow you had to make real space in the program for organizing *people,* for making the poverty money work *for* organizing, not against it. The thing urban renewal pundits called "citizens' participation" had to be kept from ending up a phony institutional grab-bag, with do-gooder social agency spokespeople—the reverend oldies no less than the ones that mushroomed up overnight—carrying off public money for just patronizing the poor.

This made for more movies.

"We have to have a people's lobby," he would whisper into our living-room ceiling at night, the unsleeping city to the west, beyond the window, lighting the midnight overcast with a faintly hellish red glow.

I would agree.

And the only way to have one, he would say, is to organize it, back at the curbstone, and then have *them* carry the message to the Congress and the OEO.

Yes, I would think, seeing the word in my mind's eye as "kerbstone," as he would, because he loved to use Ye Olde New York spelling when he wrote it just so people would sit up and notice. "How do you talk about pretty little 'grassroots,'" he'd say, "where the only place people ever see grass is on a traffic island?"

Congressman Bill Ryan, at least, was sympathetic. Harry might joke about his being an Irish Protestant trying to pass for Catholic, but ever since the Freedom Democrats, I knew he really thought Ryan was a saint. Ryan would visit Harry at the storefront when he was in town. Harry would appeal to his sense for what would fly in the halls of Congress. "How do you explain that it doesn't have to be middle class to be a community?" Ryan thought you had to just keep on saying it. "Keep coming down," he'd say, meaning to Washington.

"But they oughta be coming up here," Harry said. "Who ever sees anybody on the streets except you? The Feds avoid this scene like the pox. It took us three years to find out where the federal housing office was, right here in Manhattan—the one the City planning honchos were always blaming for holding things up."

"And I hear you've been raining on 'em ever since."

"Yeah, *'After me, the deluge.'* And now everybody's sitting there, drowning, at their little desks, saying, 'Don't make a wave!'"

But if federal bureaucrats dodged the West Side, nobody else did. The "target area" swarmed with white academics looking for "relevance," especially VISTA and Peace Corps volunteers, some, like Lainey Bertram, who were also on Columbia's social work internships. They hung around Strycker's Bay mixing it up with the "feasible participants," waiting for Father Browne to show up like Third World guerrilla paparazzi watching for a sighting of Che.

Harry was Strycker's Bay president now, out to keep the pressure on the City in this mayoral year to deliver on their promise of 2,500 new units of low-income housing. The latest artful dodge seemed to be the "skewed" rental—a few subsidized cheaper apartments in higher-priced or moderate-income buildings. Holding audience in the back of the shop one day, he explained how he'd just been denouncing the scheme as official three-card monte in a speech before the Board of Estimate. "We will not be *skewed* again," he'd warned as he left the public mike. But big Georgia Jefferson comes along right behind him and quotes him in those well-rounded flutey tones: "*And as Father Browne says, We shall not be screwed again!*" and brings down the house.

Everybody howled except Georgie Thompson, who was rocking softly on a folding chair up front. George was another feasible participant: black, Korean War vet, raised in the South—no one ever really knew his full history. The government sent him a monthly disability check care of the Columbus Avenue pharmacy three doors down from Strycker's Bay.

"Hey, you jokers," Esta said. "George wants to know who can define the War on Poverty?" There was a nervous scraping of chairs. Knowing George, you knew it was a metaphysical question.

One of the VISTA kids tried: "It's like spreading things out a little." He moved his arms in the air, signing largesse. "Empowerment," a young woman chimed in. She was twenty-two maybe, long flat brown hair, short denim skirt, and she stood up solemnly and looked straight at George from across the store: "Participating in your own destiny."

Esta, a little embarrassed: "It's like saying, you can't dump on us anymore, you gotta give us back our dignity. It's like saying poor people have dignity too," she tried again. "Right, Father?"

But Harry wouldn't touch it. "Whaddyasay, George?"

The rough brown jaw worked, the eyes flicked doubtfully over the array of white faces. He blinked and turned his gaze out the plateglass window again. *"Dignity,"* he echoed. You couldn't have said for sure if it took a question mark.

The phone rang. Everybody went back to position as George, looking like a collapsed carpenter's rule, unfolded himself, stood up, and let himself out the door. Esta flashed him a quick salute from her hunch on the telephone shoulder-rest and watched as the sloping Army jacket and the grizzled head of nappy hair moved slowly past the window and out of sight.

George. He'd been around for years. Even I'd got to know him, back when. He was the definition of *lumpenprole*—wherever he went the Lower Depths went with him, doorway to doorway in good weather, hallway to hallway when it got cold, smoking whatever butts he could scrounge from the street, his fingertips stained black from pinching them to the bitter end. He smoked so much that every time there was another fire in an SRO, somebody claimed George had slept under the stairs that night. Esta swore he trailed an aroma of burned-out building behind him like a slipstream.

But there was a deeply educated kind of wisdom in him. He would borrow a pen and a sheet of foolscap sometimes from Esta and sit there, writing poetry. Harry thought he should at least have been paid as a poverty consultant. But George said he preferred to keep his independence. And when he sat in the storefront like that staring at you from behind those opaque red eyes of his, you'd swear he could call the next shot in the war, whatever it was.

Some deep uncertainty about the universe had finally got to him. That night he came back, the light on in the back of the shop telling him that Father Browne was working late. Harry responded to his tap and let him in.

"I need your help, Father," he said.

The two of them sat down behind the file cabinets. Harry waited.

"Dignity," said George again, with finality. Harry tugged on his collar. "I've seen a lot of poor people in my time," George went on. "I've seen 'em fat from eating beans and skinny from eating dope." He paused. "I seen women hustling. Seen kids hustling. They looked tough. Scared. Sometimes they even looked bloody. I ain't never seen 'em look *dignified.*"

"We wanna change that," Harry said.

But all this talk about change had got George thinking about his life, he said. Even his death. Or maybe— well, suppose things changed so much around here that he'd need an ID to pick up his check?

"You mean you've got no ID, George?"

George shook his head loosely. "They have robbed me of everything, Father."

"You should apply for a new Social Security card."

"OK." He paused thoughtfully. "But what about now?"

"What about now?"

"Well, folks would believe *you* if you said I was who I was . . . who I *am.*"

Harry yanked open a desk drawer and pulled out a piece of stationery and slid it instantly into the typewriter. "Say no more." And he rapped out a letter on Strycker's Bay stationery vouching that its bearer was, by his, Father Henry J. Browne's, say-so, George (*Middle name, George?*)—George Thompson, Army veteran (*Honorably discharged, George?*)—Army veteran honorably discharged, citizen of the U.S. of A., entitled to all the rights and privileges appertaining thereunto. He signed the crisp white sheet with his Parker, folded it, tucked it into a Strycker's Bay envelope, and handed it to George.

"Right on," said George, and he shook his hand as if he'd just got his Ph.D.

I thought about George and his existential Ph.D. I thought about him being a spoiled poet, about how he'd got educated, probably in some two-room country schoolhouse in North Carolina, under the stern eye of a black schoolmarm who in a juster world would have been pushed on to *her* Ph. D.

Romantic maybe. But if the fairness of it all in those days wasn't on the mind of somebody teaching freshman comp at Hunter (while being pushed on to *my* Ph.D.), it wasn't ever going to be. They were reinventing the teaching of writing to beginning college students then, seeing it as the only way to stop the revolving door of open admissions if you didn't want it to go on revolving—that is, flunking the same students out next year you welcomed in this year—and some people didn't. The Hunter program was actually one of the best, overseen by a passionate scholar named Marlies Danziger, who vetted her staff like a combination major league coach and officer of the British Raj. It almost repaid all the countless desperate hours I put into grading when she told me that the advice I'd written on a student paper was worth its weight in gold. And it certainly helped override Harry's reproaches when he'd come in at 2 A.M. and find the desk lamp still burning and me still reading papers—or asleep in the chair over them, my neck corkscrewed and my mouth open and the air rank with dead cigarettes. He thought I was compulsive.

"What's compulsive?" I'd say, threatening an attack gambit out of sheer exhaustion. But he was right. I *was* compulsive. Most of the time I felt anger at myself for not having the skills, or frustration and disappointment because my students, so wonderful otherwise, were too slow in bridging the gap to standard English. "It's a dead language," I'd mutter only half to myself. He'd heard me.

"Give them short shrift," he'd say. "Get on with your articles."

I did that, too, adapting two pieces on Arnold out of my master's essay. I also handed in my finished dissertation in the spring of 1965, only a year behind my bold-faced cocktail-party promise, ahead of all the men and half the women who'd started when I had. Pretty good for a new mother, which I had never expected to be when I'd pointed to the bleachers.

Actually, I'd been driven, haunted, by the scholar at Duke who'd got there ahead of me, the one whose tracks I'd crossed in London in 1963 looking for Edith Rinder's daughter. Clearly I *was* ambitious, if competition, or just the threat of it, could drive me like that. And yet the odd thing was that I had no interest in scooping anything merely factual about this strange bird known both as William Sharp and Fiona Macleod. What had captivated me had captivated *me*: that curious duplicity, the man secretly taking the literary identity of a woman—becoming a kind of priestess of art, or meta-art—simply to become his own *other*.

Then there was that fascination with Italy, and that obsessive sense of *place* altogether, the chameleon capacity to register everything, to *become* what surrounded him. He was a *shaman*, of precisely the sort he loved to write, with a certain kind of boundary-less self and polymorphous shaman sexuality I found strangely beautiful, and in no way baffling. Was it because of Harry? The secrecy, the magic, the flamboyance and audacity, even the elusive *persona*—all of it seemed profoundly to do with *his* life. And with mine. Dare I say it had been a little like writing a memoir? I understood the concept of scholarly distance, but in the end it wasn't distance that gave life back to the dead, was it?

Harry, driven by his own compulsions, had also been writing, three articles for the *Catholic Home Encyclopedia* that year, on Archbishop Hughes, Terence Powderly, and the Knights of Labor, pumping each small stipend into the household kitty as it arrived. Yet amid all the public dust he kicked up, people hardly noticed he was a history scholar. *I* hardly noticed, everything about him seemed so palpably and visibly *right now*, so out there on the street, with no equivalent for that academic non-event known as "slipping silently into print." Late nights of strategizing brought results by daylight. Cause almost instantly met effect, input output. In time and motion terms what he did was probably no more efficient than what I did, maybe less, but you didn't see the waste. The challenges he was meeting—feeding the hungry, clothing the naked, sheltering the homeless—*counted* so much more, that the scholarship he thought should be my highest priority seemed self-indulgent by comparison.

So I followed him whenever and wherever I could, to Reform Democrat meetings during the Lindsay mayoral campaign, to peace rallies and Strycker's Bay movie benefits, like a Father Browne groupie, I suppose, but not just to be where he was (though there was that), but to be where it was happening. I myself learned to evangelize the gospel of "people doing for themselves," got to be what he called "a somewhat expert" on skewed rentals and 221(d)(3) mortgage insurance and vest-pocket public housing. I got to think of it as *my* life, *my* mission too, till there were moments when William Wordsworth or Tennysonian prosody or "The City of Dreadful Night" seemed no more than intimations of immortality from recollections of another existence.

I suspect even Harry's closest colleagues thought Harry had sacked scholarship for the streets, and he didn't want me to—to think it, or to do it. Not that he discouraged my interest in what he did, but I think just counting my footnotes made him horny. He couldn't wait for me to turn out those long, meaty typescripts, loved to feel the heft of them in his hands. He died to see me published, even in those esoteric little academic journals that had fewer people reading them in a year than attended a Strycker's Bay meeting in a single night. I seemed to be working some utopian Ministry of Truth for both of us, keeping a freehold in some receding intellectual continent, maybe even preserving some potentially endangered family chromosomes.

There was a line of Tennyson's "Ulysses" I used to quote to myself: "*He works his work, I mine.*" The satisfying ring of partnership in it, tonic for heartache. And yet— it was not so much like that as if . . . as if I worked *his* work and he mine, so intensely, so vicariously, did either of us value the other, like some *yang* wanting to be *yin*, and some *yin* forever longing to be *yang*.

Talk about followers, though. Now John Peter Grady was a follower, world class, and a virtual leprechaun, who ran a preschool for disadvantaged kids in Harlem, and did missionary work for nonprofit housing in uptown parishes like Tremont and Washington Heights. Harry'd love to describe how he'd popped his fur knob of a head into Strycker's Bay one day in winter 1964/65 looking for *Faaather* Browne, drawn his wiry little body in behind it, and before Browne knew what hit him, made the offensive team, and was headed with him down to D.C. on Washington's Birthday 1965, along with Esta, Fred Johnson, and Tom Purcell, a law student from St. Gregory's.

It was a big day, a critical day, organized to lobby strategic House Democrats and officials at OEO for a community action pilot grant to support people's organizing on the West Side. Only if you were flowing with history, it wasn't the day you wanted to be out of New York. They left the city in the predawn, just before the news broke that Malcolm X had been shot to death in the Audubon ballroom.

But the best-laid plans had planned the big day: Browne scheduled to speak at a National Urban Action Forum at nine, back-to-back with famous organizer guru Saul Alinsky—Harry's first time sharing a podium with his favorite radical-rouser. Then, with the help of Congressman Ryan, they were all going to spread out, stroking the pols.

Grady, a hard-drinking Irishman, had planned to ease a dull early-morning ride down the New Jersey Turnpike with a six-pack of beer and two airplane bottles of scotch in his coat pocket. It was no use Esta warning them that Harry was going to blow it up there with Alinsky, or Harry invoking his own iron rule never to start drinking before five. Grady looked at his watch and pointed out that it was past five already, and long before the Delaware Memorial Bridge, the two in back were mixing boilermakers while the three in front winced every time the car swerved a little and the empty bottles clinked under the seat. Fred, resolutely sober, still risked slipping a disc to catch a string of jokes coming out of the back seat that all ended with what the bishop said to the actress. Grady would let out a glass-shattering whoop at the punchlines and slap his thighs and stomp his feet right into the rattling cache of beer bottles on the floor.

Esta passed around what was left of her Thermos of coffee when they finally got to Washington, and Browne made such a smooth transition to the morning conference session you wouldn't have believed what he was transitioning *from*. The first letdown came when the speaking schedule got rearranged. Alinsky, who had another appointment, took the mike, and Browne, who had planned on opening for him, had to follow. He quipped his way to the dais, straining too hard, got a benevolent smile, and was just beginning to recover (topping Saul's tales of Mayor Daley's Chicago with stories of faceoffs with the new New York housing chief known as General "When-do-we-move-in-the-troops?" Lazarus), when Alinsky's wristwatch alarm went off, and he stole back the show just making his exit.

Then the news began to spread about the assassination. A terrible gloom came down, made worse by bewilderingly unclear news reports. The five of them fanned out through the Capitol Office Building on schedule, but with a hangdog sense of having an agenda completely crushed by the monumental weight of national and even global *angst*—not just Malcolm, bad enough by itself, but everything: the movement, the war, even the latest conscientious-objector witnessing by Cassius Clay, just beginning to make people uncomfortable with his Muslim identity as Muhammad Ali. A few policy aides-de-camp, hungry for "the word," wondered how widespread Browne thought the Catholic left antiwar movement would become. He quieted them, all right, by asking them to look at the pretty pitiful Catholic record on civil rights, maybe hoping he'd be wrong.

Things seemed to have gone so sour that it was stunning to learn a few weeks later that they had actually enchanted key Congressman John Fogarty, and that the stories about the West Side "Back-of-the-Stable" movement were still making the rounds of the executive washrooms at OEO. By May, Strycker's Bay was getting invited to appear before the House housing subcommittee. Five months later not only had they got a quarter-million-dollar development grant, but, coup of political coups, the money was going to bypass the normal route through the City bureaucracy and speed to them straight from Washington.

Browne and Grady considered *that* worth a boilermaker, now. Even Esta did.

Think of this all of this as the backdrop to my defense in May, which had also fatefully coincided with my thirtieth birthday, beyond which the counterculture had recently declared every living person done for. Three years before, my nearly aborted doctor's orals had been held in the same room on the sixth floor of Philosophy Hall. Three years later, almost to the day, it would be Columbia in student riot, 1968, and for a while, above those now complacently well-sunned herringbone bricks, there would be no doctor's orals.

But Time, as opaque as ever, gave us nothing more than a beautiful day that day, a sunny campus on a hushed, breezy mid-May afternoon. I had had no prophetic dreams, and no inner alarm had warned me about the neurasthenic Professor Chilton Williamson, the Barnard historian, bursting my complacent bubble of doctoral omniscience.

Professor Woodring chaired, affably moving the questions clockwise around the six professors at the table. Williamson came last, when all the nice things had already been said. In his polished captain's chair directly to my right he seemed to have suffered through every word, twisting like an eel in agony.

"So what about this woman—this *Italian* woman?"

I gulped a little high academic air. "You mean the one who inspired Fiona Macleod? She *wasn't* Italian," I said. I took great care to get my correcting voice right. "She was also a Scot, or rather Anglo-Scot. Wife of a Scottish friend. They *met* in Italy."

He seemed to thrill like a hummingbird, his head cocked. "Yes, *that* woman."

I didn't know how *not* to take his question seriously, however rude his drift. It was one of the million times I've wished for a millidrop of Harry's mother wit to say something disarming and funny. If only I'd known then what I know now: that around the halls of Philosophy, in anticipation of my study, Fiona Macleod had already become a circulating professorial dirty joke. Instead, I said, simply, seriously: "I—we—don't know . . . much."

"There *was* a child, wasn't there?" My rival's theory about the Rinder daughter being Sharp's was clearly making headway. I had never learned the grounds of it and was determined to stress the guesswork. "Elizabeth and William had no children. She—Edith Rinder—had one child, yes, the one I mentioned before—" I made a gesture in the air toward something, *supra,* and felt foolish.

"The one you tried to locate?"

"The one I *did* locate," I corrected. And I launched into the story of my quest for the living relic, the wise child who had kept "the truth" locked in her heart all those years. I told them about how I'd been balked by the literary detective who'd found her first, and for whose sake she'd put a pair of stony solicitors between us. It made really quite another book, and I found myself describing the thing as if I were writing it on the afternoon breeze.

"And you *stopped* there?" he interrupted. "You never saw or spoke with her?"

I shook my head. I never saw or spoke with her, never got the ocular proof. "Should I have gone over the garden wall?"

In that single audacious moment my life passed before me, pausing vindictively at August 1963, me in London, big with illegitimate child, scheming in vain to confront that obstinate suspected offspring of William Sharp's suspected adulterous affair. How I had despised her then, a crumpled old lady flattered by some male scholar's sedulous attentions, hugging whatever dirty little secret still lent her some power to start quarrels with. I despised her more now.

Williamson hung on. "You shouldn't have stopped there."

"But, don't you see," I said, "that it didn't really matter? That all this secrecy—this evasion I was up against—"

He interrupted me again, emphasis added: "*You shouldn't have stopped there.*"

Professor Woodring walked me out to the hard waiting bench in the hallway with a gallantly ambiguous smile, and left me to brood about facts vs. mysteries, about Edith Rinder's once baby girl—whose? Who knew? Did *she?* And by what trail of evidence now grown cold? *Cold, cold as thy chastity, my girl.* Left me to brood on my own mystery: a baby boy, born in Vicenza, 1963, duly recorded by an American consular "Report on the Birth of an American Citizen Abroad." I remembered how the officials had actually demanded his father's address, and there'd been all that panic about exposure, an exchange of desperate letters between Harry and me. In the end he'd told me to give them his 90th Street address as 142 instead of 144—"142 will be torn down in a year." Ever the historian's historian, imagining some pimply future Church history scholar grubbing after *his* dirty little secret someday, that glimpse of the primal scene for his sublimated itch, and coming up with a parochial school playground.

Facts and mysteries. Facts and reasons. I leaned back on the bench and breathed in the cool hallway smell of negative capability. They were taking a long time.

Professor Woodring finally emerged out of the hallway darkness, greeting me with that sad, ambiguous smile. "Congratulations, Doctor." He didn't tell me Williamson had denied me a first, not then. When he told me later, he blamed himself for having called attention to the rule that the committee had to be unanimous, almost inviting Williamson to voice his opposition, and no hectoring could change that fix on certifiable knowledge. But my disappointment was an afterthought by then. Harry was already calling me "*Dottoressa,*" in his wonderful, half-mocking way, and making me feel as if my brilliance transcended any Ph.D. In a few days we were lying on the beach at the Outer Banks, our first time since 1962.

Our *very* first time with the baby. Harry was a riot of prudence, wearing dark sunglasses the whole time. Plus a particularly inconspicuous checkered sports jacket to Sunday mass at Our Lady of the Sea. He refused to remove the glasses when I took his picture with the baby just outside the church. We got a baby-sitter one night and went dancing, and Harry did his famous jitterbug, clowning all over the dance floor until the place nearly came apart, and never once took off his shades.

I dropped in to see Professor Woodring when I got back, fit and tan and happy. He looked so sad when he told me the awful truth about my orals that I was almost ashamed of still feeling so good, as if I must have lacked the requisite ambition if I couldn't have it properly dashed. I was raptured when he invited me for drinks at the Faculty Club. His tall, cool Texan wife, San, was there, pretending to be happy to share him with a girl graduate, though behind her glasses I know she trained me with a killer eye.

San Woodring has a special place in my canon of Columbia saints and saintlings, a woman on whom nothing was lost. Nothing. She knew a woman with a secret. It was a triumph of Southern grace over curiosity that she never asked me point blank about mine. But what if she had? By now, I was also a doctor of how to divert curiosity without satisfying it. There was not a chance of my revealing anything—not, at any rate, anything you could have called a *fact*.

Call it a survival skill. Fiona Macleod had taught me a thing or two after all.

4

Harry had had every reason to be nervous at the Outer Banks in June. Besides that spate of appearances in Washington, he'd made more than the usual number of spots on New York television, and on May 28, barely a week before our trip, the *New York Times* had made him "Man in the News," and included his photo—Roman collar, no sunglasses—looking tough and troubled under his bristling hair.

The *Times* piece was a long essay on New York's "housing priest," sparked by the opening of the first vest-pocket public housing in urban renewal history, on West 94th Street. The story behind the story was the end of the quest for the Grail: as a final imperial gesture of his administration, Robert Wagner had declared once and for all that those 2,500 apartments out of the urban renewal 9,000 would be reserved for the poor.

But the story behind the story behind the story seemed to be the *Times*'s long war with the Chancery. For Harry was painted, with broad brush, as an institutional maverick, a priest whose gritty irreverence bordered on the outlaw, who set the hierarchy's teeth on edge and showed up—perhaps intentionally showed up—the pockmarks in the cosmetic façade of the New York Catholic Church. It singled out Harry's jab at Catholic Charities' "vested interest in poverty" as though it were the only attack he'd made on the social service industry he typically loved to describe as "doing well by doing good." It picked up a remark before a Strycker's Bay audience about the Church seeing him as a "heretic" without a hint that quips about his professional risk taking were part of a performative style, a way of reassuring the council's mixed constituency that he didn't take orders from anybody.

In short, not only did it underestimate Father Browne, it underestimated the Chancery. Cardinal Spellman had actually ceased to bother him by now. I smile to think what Harry might have told a reporter who didn't have his head in that *Times* warp, for apparently there were some things that made the New York Church look even better than a Hughes biography.

Of course, the real irony lay in what the *Times* didn't know about the razor edge Harry was walking. And yet even now, now that everybody knows, even the *Times*, there is still that bit that nobody knows. Not even I. And that is, what he might have said if the Chancery had actually confronted him, rebuked him for pushing the boundaries? Would he have said that he'd been waiting, waiting for just such a sign—waiting, maybe even hoping, for Spellman to shake his fist and give him the pretext he needed to declare his freedom? Wouldn't it have been all he needed, in fact, to rise, pure and defiant, above the Church's anger, a martyr in the people's cause? Mightn't he have had it all, then—the notoriety, the charisma, the eight million people—me—and a baby named Harry, too?

Joe Lyford, whose West Side Story book featuring Father Browne, *The Airtight*

Cage, was about to appear in print, would have known how to pitch the real story about Harry and the Church, the story about the subtler manipulations of power and image. He would have sat Harry down and started with a quote from his book, with somebody saying, as somebody there actually does say, "*If Father Browne did-n't have his collar, the City wouldn't give him the time of day.*" And he'd have said: "So, whaddaya think, . . . Harry?"—though he'd probably still having trouble calling him Harry—"True?"

"Absolutely. It's my power base."

"You mean the power of the Chancery—the institutional power of the Church?"

"Sure, there's that. There's that whether the *Times* likes it or not—whether *I* like it or not. But there's more than that. There's the power base of the parish, down at the 'kerbstone' with the people. You don't really do anything *for* people without being *with* people, in touch with them right where they are. And this means that sometimes the people have to be against the Church—the institutional Church—because sometimes even the Church is against the people. And *this* is the struggle you have to stay with," he'd say. "The struggle that makes sure the Church stays with them, that it remains what it should be: the Church of the people. Always that, always, when it's being truest to itself."

Joe Lyford might say the Church doesn't look like this to everybody—that it did-n't look like that to him. He might toss out its long record of greed and hypocrisy, of treachery and ambition and power. And Harry would laugh at being set up for a disquisition on Church history: "Watch out, I'll launch into one of my guaran-teed sleep-inducing seminary lectures."

And he'd launch anyway, but not into *that* lecture. He'd talk about how institutions die without people, how the Church lives on the knees of the old lady with the rosary, or the sweaty longshoreman crossing himself on the dock, or the bent-back farm-worker fingering the cross on a chain around his neck, or the exhausted mother with seven kids wondering in confession ("in confession to *me*, mind you") how she's going to keep from having her eighth. He'd say, "Sure, bishops forget this, and popes. Power corrupts. And, like they say, *corruptio optimi pessima.* Which means, roughly trans-lated: the bigger—and better—they are, the harder they smell. But even parish priests can smell." And he'd call Flanagan to mind, with his thermostat vigil light, grum-bling about the take every Sunday.

"But every renewal of the Church in history," he'd say, "has come from the peo-ple, from listening to the people. Like John XXIII—" That was the Pope whose Ecumenical Council, called Vatican II, had thrown open the windows to the "fresh air" of reform in 1960, had changed the way the whole Church saw itself in the twen-tieth century. "And a good cleric, bishop or pope or parish priest, knows his histo-ry. He knows there's always going to be institutions. Kill this one, it'll be replaced with another one, maybe worse. Keep this one clean, keep its priorities straight, kick it in the ass once in a while, and you've got a good, time-tested machine for taking care of people's needs—all their needs—mind and body and heart and, yeah, soul if you want soul."

I can imagine some people reading an interview like this and saying it didn't sound very revolutionary, or not revolutionary enough. And yet I think of that wonderful blessing before meals Harry'd picked up somewhere: "We have meat and some have none. God bless the rev-o-lu-ti-on." When he first heard it, he said, "I wish I'd said that," and he did. All the time. He believed God did "bless the rev-o-lu-ti-on." His kind of revolution, anyway, which was to subvert and survive.

That was a soundbite Lyford would have jumped on: " *'Subvert and survive.'* Is that a principle?"

Harry hated being pinned down on abstracts. "There are very few principles."

"Do you think Cardinal Spellman would agree with that?"

"Spelly? Sure, Spelly more than most. And I should know—" And now that he was on his turf again, he'd launch into *why* he should know—because Spelly, in his case, had a lot to answer for. "And there's still plenty he could do to me if he wanted to." But he'd say that people who didn't understand how the hierarchy worked would never understand that Spellman *didn't* want to.

And then he might tell the story he'd once told me, or told in my hearing, about Spellman, about when he was first writing the Hughes biography. "Spelly cared a lot about that. People have some cockamamy idea he quashed that biography, but that's bullshit. I was conferring with him on a visit up here—sometime in the early fifties. *'Your Eminence,'* I said. *'There's evidence that the archbishop was a drunk.'* *'What evidence?'* says he. *'Well, so-and-so says so, and such-and-such.'* And then Spelly purses his lips and tents his fingertips, just like this, and looks at me like the Infant Jesus of Prague, and says, *'I wonder what they're saying about me?'* Now there's a sense of history. I'm not ashamed to be loyal to a guy like that."

And Lyford might say: "So maybe he'll boot you upstairs. Promote you. Make you loyal. Get you out of his hair that way." And Harry would laugh and say there wasn't much chance of that. But, if you wanted to talk in the abstract, now, yes, *that* would be the real temptation, the Get-thee-behind-me-Satan-and-push kind—at least for somebody else in his position.

"Not for you?"

"No. Never. And you know why? Because I want to have *real* power, not just the appearance of it. And for the kind of thing we're doing here on the West Side of New York—the kind of thing that demands that a Catholic priest be one among equals—you know, *that* would be the kiss of death. I could say good-bye to whatever power or influence I have. Just the same as if I walked out of here and left the parish, left the Church. It sounds ironic but it's true. Everything I do here depends on people believing there's nothing in it for me. On there *being* nothing in it for me. The collar does that for me—just the collar. Whatever power I have, it's in the collar, this little piece of celluloid that gives me a pimple on the back of my neck. No red sash, no red beanie, nothing. They may not like it, but they trust it. They meaning people, plain folks, not just Catholics but Catholics included, believe it or not—let alone the City, the State, the Feds. Sound familiar? *If I didn't have my collar they wouldn't give me the time of day."*

•

And then, when he came home to me, lying there in the dark, the red light pulsing in the distance atop the Hell's Gate, his sweet voice surrounding me, not with
poetry, or not *pure* poetry but the impurest, sweet nevertheless, I might have
whispered—

*And then, Harry? What about me? What about us? Does it help much to say there are
very few principles?*

Chastity isn't one of them.

God knows. Unfortunately, the Church doesn't.

The Church didn't exact a vow of chastity from me, remember? I'm not a monk.

You're nitpicking. You know what I mean.

Celibacy? It's just an expression—like the blow in blow-job. The Church has no
illusions about it.

The Church is a bloody hypocrite.

You're right. It's a glitch in the canon law. "Priesthood is an impediment to marriage."

*I know: the Seventh Sacrament—the one that keeps you from having all seven.
Keeps any man, that is. Women don't get to choose—they get only six in any case. Queer
isn't it. Holy bloody matrimony: the only sacrament that's also a sin.*

Well, no. If you put it like that, priesthood—Holy Orders—is the other.

Right. Jesus, why? Does it really make sense to you?

It wasn't always that way. Some time in the twelfth century—

Oh, please, not that lecture again.

Don't knock it. It's not everything, but if you don't know it, you're lost.
Somewhere along the way somebody said you couldn't mix a concern for souls in
general with a concern for particular souls—and particular bodies.

You don't believe that, do you?

I don't believe it *now*. I *used* to believe it, or I accepted it—same difference.

Not the same. Not the same at all.

The same for seminarians. Same for a lot of people. It's convincing. Now I know
they've got it ass backwards. The *only* way to have a concern for souls in general,
a *real* concern, is to have a concern for souls in particular. Doesn't have to be a wife.
Doesn't have to be your own child. But it better be somebody.

How'd the Church go so goddamn wrong?

Not the Church. It's not an article of faith—*yet*. The goddamn canon lawyers.

*Nitpicking again. You know, sometimes you're just like a Jesuit. Or a canon lawyer.
How'd the goddamn canon lawyers go so wrong? Women, probably. Fear of women.*

Probably.

Women. The second oldest profession, the first oldest second-class condition.

Well, if you're back to the garden, there's snakes.

What?

You forgot snakes. They get a pretty bad rap, right up front.

Snakes don't have to get "purified" after they have babies.

Just kidding. Don't get mad.
I'm not getting mad.
Maybe you're getting even.
I wish I could. I can't. Marriage isn't how. Marriage stinks. I think I've always thought so. I think so now, more and more. Do you know what a feminist I'm becoming?
I know. Teach me.
Hell, I'm learning from you: "Subvert and survive."
You got it. Anyway, believe me, someday the Pope will catch up.
Like you always say, "Not for ourselves, but for our sons."
If only John XXIII had lived a little longer. *Juan Two Three. My maaan.*
What do we do now?
Pazienza.
You'll stay a priest.
Once a priest, always—
—Yeah, sure: "—Said the bishop to the actress." And once a feminist—

Grady set up a series of neighborhood meetings in the Bronx—on housing, social renewal, general civic consciousness-raising—and took Harry around to them. Audaciously Harry sent me on ahead to meet with Bishop Pernicone, at Our Lady of Mount Carmel in the Belmont section, and pave the way in my best ceremonial Italian. The bishop was polite and *simpatico,* though he may well have wondered just where I fit into the picture. I went to one of the meetings, where Harry pitched them the Social Gospel, *"doing where you're at,"* urging them to take advantage of the present favorable climate and help meet the need for low-to-middle-income housing by forming nonprofit housing sponsorships like Strycker's Bay. "That's the *true* Gospel in the U.S. of A., Year of Our Lord one thousand nine hundred and sixty-five. *That's* where the holy word is at in the American urban jungle in the middle of the twentieth century."

Strange how they seemed to hear him and not hear him—to *feel* him as a symbol of something, a charismatic priest vaguely luring them toward the promised land of peace and justice. Afterward, unwilling to let him go, a few parishioners plus some of Grady's friends from Tremont took us to an old wood-paneled pizza parlor off Fordham Road. Above us, all around us, were the glass-shaded Tiffany lamps everybody was beginning to be hot for, but that this old pub had never replaced. There was scorching pepperoni pizza in our mouths, cold beer mugs to touch our lips to, a cold night with the promise of winter in it, six or seven of us, mostly Irish Americans, crowding warmly into the big brown booth. There was lots of talk of Vietnam and the nuclear threat, of draft-dodging, of folks they knew who'd done it or were thinking about it, of Northern Ireland, liberation theology, some Jesuit named Daniel Berrigan who was beginning to make a serious name for himself in the antiwar movement.

I got amorously drunk—the only way I ever got drunk, really. I got sad. Harry, one public Harry among so many—so many—sitting opposite me, untouchable.

I tried to touch him with my eyes. I got to thinking of baby Bim and the baby-sitter back in Astoria, as midnight came and went, thoughts of the sort Freud would have called retarding to civilization. We finally left Grady and his friends still sipping beers, and Harry took me—took *us*—home. Even in the car dark, the shyness, the untouchableness, lingered. I felt only that familiar rush of love and terror crossing the Triboro Bridge, as he slid his collar and bib off his chest and let me help him slip it into the glove compartment.

That night, Time hung and swooped like a bridge. I think the thoughts Harry thought, the thoughts I thought, were here and now, not straining to see any farther just yet, not ready yet to track the path of the Social Gospel as it had its impact on our own lives.

Marriage: everybody was doing it. Best friend Judy had married and unmarried and married again, this time a rather celebrated writer of science fiction. My brother Lou took the plunge for a second time, and instantly relocated to California and the Sun Belt water-ski frontier. Ann, done with brooding over Alfonso, diffidently announced her engagement to a graduate student she'd met while she was working at Columbia Law School. He would have to do a year's service in Vietnam first. They'd be married when—they resolutely said "*when*"—he got back.

We celebrated, she and I. I visited her in her rambling shared apartment on West 111th Street. She was as thin as ever, still with that bittersweet aura around her life. I could tell she was letting go of more than Alfonso. She was letting go of me, and a life too sweated with superwomanish emotional stamina, which vicariously terrified her.

"I *love* Harry," she said. "Don't get me wrong. But you *are* a wife, whether you call yourself that or not. You've *got* a marriage. You're absolutely faithful and devoted. You just can't talk about it. I'm different. I want to talk about it. To be *proud* of it."

I didn't quite trust her analysis of me. But I hadn't read enough Simone de Beauvoir yet to get my head around my own practice. I worked on it. I began to picture them, the famous de Beauvoir and Sartre, living their fiercely independent integrities in their separate apartments, in their separate spheres, and gradually made it an iconic image of a *true* marriage of minds. I had stumbled on Olive Schreiner in my dissertation work. I'd found in her passionately political, troubled, writing self, too, that visceral shock of recognition, that like-minded distaste for the freight of old submission that marriage inexorably carried with it.

Maybe I was a slow learner. I took time to read the providence in the fall of a sparrow. Harry and I quarreled, and made up, made claims on one another, corrected them, just like a married couple. But we *weren't* married. And not being married had ceased to be an accidental attribute of a situation otherwise very much like a marriage, and had become the essence of it. Perhaps I had some intuition of how soft the plastic of my identity was. His was multiform, but already shaped. I needed an openness to transformation he didn't, or didn't anymore. Perhaps this denied my life the same significance as his, but it kept it *mine* and, as such, became all the more reason to leave his alone. If being in some sorts a criminal was the price of my own self-possession, well, so be it. My sister and, I suspect, my mother read a great sacrifice of self into my situation. A vulgar error, like misreading *The French Lieutenant's Woman*.

Esta would half-jokingly say, "You're both crazy," and try to put away the part of it that vexed and puzzled her. Not much of it did, for her own reasons. Bred in the bone Jewish radical and J. Edgar Hoover hater that she was, Harry had never succeeded in convincing her that the Catholic Church was anything but one of the most reactionary forces in American society, maybe *the* most, and she wasn't above the little *frisson* of deep-down pleasure it gave her to think we were secretly sticking it to the bastards.

Her position as secret-keeper also gave her a certain power. Not that we ever feared it. She would have died under torture before saying a word to the enemy. Still, she could use the power on us, in the sort of confused, illogical way that fit the confused, illogical situation we were in. On the one hand, Harry wasn't doing right by me. I deserved better than this, this hole-in-corner humiliating thing. On the other hand—

Well, on the other hand, she had to be careful not to think like the Catholic Church, that I was just a distraction, pulling Father Browne's committed attention away from The Struggle. No, no, it *wasn't* that; it was the damned outlaw part of the thing— the— Well, what? "*Fucking* Church!" she'd explode, frankly scared. "What if—?" Jesus, too much hung in the balance now: Civil Rights, Welfare Rights, Housing Justice for the Poor, Manpower Training, the whole national Cities Movement. Sure, sure, they'd all survive if he were exposed—but they'd suffer, suffer badly, and they wouldn't be the same without him.

What could she do? She couldn't tell us to break it up. She couldn't tell Harry to quit. All she could do was needle him about being a company man. "Look at Spellman going to see the troops in Vietnam every Christmas. Same old shit. And Cardinal Sheen and his pear-shaped tones clogging up the TV airwaves with his blessed *Ave Maria Hour*. All hawks when they oughta be doves. The 'Evil of Aggression,' like it was still World War II. Oh, sure, Father Browne is doing fine, and getting away with it. Now. But just let him get out of line one more time . . . "

And then the government showcased Cassius Clay, now confidently Muhammad Ali, and sent him to prison as a draft-dodger. A protest petition appeared, full page, *New York Times*, then made the cover of *Esquire*. It carried the names of fifty religious leaders. Rev. Henry J. Browne was one of them. Spelly's office didn't call. No rebuke, no wrist-slapping. You could have knocked Esta over.

She herself was a local organizer for a peace demonstration down at the U.N. She also acted as a kind of subcontractor for the volunteers from Columbia. Peace Corps, Peace Rally—they went together like love and marriage, right? "I'll get them to hang posters, hand out leaflets, make phone calls," she told Harry. "Maybe they'll even do a little guerrilla theater."

She phoned to get the OK from the project supervisor uptown, a friend, a known antiwar activist. He refused. Waffled a little, but no, the answer was no.

She slammed down the phone, yelling into the file cabinets. "Do you know what just happened?"

"He had to refuse," Harry said. "You shouldn't have asked him."

"I shoulda just *done* it."

"Yeah, you shoulda just done it. When're you gonna learn?"

"I know," she growled, "*subvert and survive*. Only I didn't know it applied to when your friends were in charge."

Harry laughed. "*Mostly* when your friends are in charge."

Ironically, about the same time, a small group of Jesuits including peace activist Father Daniel Berrigan were moving into an apartment on the Upper West Side. No institutional shingle, no frills or fanfare. Just an ordinary apartment off West End Avenue, a place, presumably, from which to pursue the reverend Jesuit tradition of the Propagation of the Faith—or so one guessed. But they hadn't said. They hadn't had to say. Because they hadn't asked.

"Mary O'Neill has this theory about second sons."

We were sitting at the little dropleaf table with its cloth of opulent cabbage roses, drinking chablis, watching the city lights return like familiar constellations over the bridge, Harry retelling his dinner talk with Jack and children's author Mary O'Neill the night before.

"What theory is that?"

"That they're the *really* nice guys in the world. Like Jack Kennedy."

"No narcissism in this, by any chance."

He blushed a little. "Yeah, well. You wanna hear this theory?" I nodded. "OK. These are the guys who don't get spoiled with all that first-kid attention, who learn how to negotiate—cooperate, who learn how to cut a deal—how to *hondl*"—one of his favorite West Side Yiddishisms.

"You think Bim can't learn how to *hondl*?" I was feeling argumentative, but not very. I was thinking rather dreamily of the First Son, asleep nearby, dreaming, maybe about how to *hondl*.

"I mean what you don't have to learn because it's there: the sensitivity you get because you can't help it, being second string—second-class. Because you know what it means to want."

Being third of four after two boys, I guessed I knew what he meant. "All those little daily rubs—compromises . . . " I thought of my own brother, Carlo, second son too. "If it doesn't make you mean," I said, impulsively. But Carl had outgrown his meanness, hadn't he? And I remembered how good he'd been to me about Bim, receiving me in Frankfurt like a heroine on the way home from Italy. And then I remembered Jackie. That was it. He'd have talked with Mary O'Neill about Jackie.

He shrugged and hugged his arms, as his face went soft, and his voice cracked. "Frances went to see him." His nieces had just learned about the lost brother, up there in Rockland County, and the whole thing had convulsed them. It had convulsed Harry.

"Oh, Jesus."

After you'd found him, where did you put him in your mind, someone like that, a forsaken stranger who had your mother's face? A stranger you still called Jackie as if he were a boy, the boy whose brain had burst like glass? And if you were his brother, his younger brother—Second Son—what then? Did you lock him away again with the dead? Did you put his pain back inside you, in the same place you had once put his promise? Or were there mysteries of loyalty and sacrifice and terror you didn't touch, because you might snap—because you might break the deal you'd cut with life: Second Son. Redeemer. Given back to God in place of the one that was lost.

How grotesquely this web of memory floated on the current of desire. I touched him. "Good lads, second sons," he said, wistfully, with a kind of painful self-forgiveness. There was something very Irish about him at that moment, a little maudlin, sweet and sad and accepting. "*Very* good," I said. And I kissed him.

The desire that makes first sons makes second sons too. Love and sorrow met, and we cooperated with the mystery for once, in a glad, sweet, soft, floating, laughing, dizzying cocoon of reciprocal desire. *"How can you be sure it will be a boy?"* I said, and he said, very Irishly, *"I'll shlant it off the side pocket."*

Experts traced a sudden sharp rise in the municipal birth rate in August 1966 to New York's spectacular, near catastrophic blackout on November 9, 1965—first and second sons, presumably, first, second, and third daughters, all in a random *shlant*. Blessedly, Harry had appeared at the apartment door almost the moment the skyline abruptly darkened and the red vigil light on the Hell's Gate, our evening star, vanished, swallowed into a horizon the color of soot. Like couples all over the city that night, we abandoned ourselves to the velvety dark of a night before there were cities. But by then we already had a head start on the 1966 birthrate. I was in my sixth week.

There was clearly no sense now, if there had ever been, in going away to have this baby. I finished out the fall term at Hunter, and requested another leave. Bim was pretty good for a terrible two. I polished my articles, stretching our meager savings with $400 I'd won working a pilot game show on TV in the fall, a serendipity for which I had a tall, oboe-voiced graduate-student friend named Catherine Rogowski to thank. I could be very cowlike in maternity. I don't remember feeling deprived of anything—anything material, that is. I felt the shortage of Harry. At the same time that demands on him became more intense than ever, my swelling belly forced me out of all active touch with his life. We had rather alarmingly locked ourselves in.

"Burnout," Esta pronounced simply, after announcing she was engaged to somebody named Armstrong out in San Francisco and was going west in to be married in August. Nobody believed it, either the burnout or this marriage to some All-American guy. But Harry and I one-upped her with our announcement about the baby. She went pale. "You've got to be kidding." She cleared her throat and went to the edge, asking us what it . . . meant.

"It means we'll be needing a bigger apartment." She breathed. The falling bundle of lead weights had just turned out to be wiffleballs. "We're looking at New Jersey."

"New *Jersey?*" She tried to glare us down with her gypsy eyes. "You're *outrageous,*" she said. Nobody could say *"outrageous"* like Esta could say it.

"You should talk. Look at you, going to *California.*"

She beamed. "You're right. We *are* screwed up. Every last one of us. "

5

It was June, it was hot, and I was in my last month. The night before the big move, Harry showed up, fresh from some all-night strategy session on the Community Action grant, at four in the morning. I was furious—up all night packing barrels and boxes, my belly heaving into massive contractions, visions of myself going into labor on the kitchen floor. But he made me forgive him, as only he could, and soon we were all piled into the car behind the moving van, making that early morning crossing with the wings of the Hell's Gate passing out of sight behind us. It was an unforgettable sight—perhaps the earliest deep-etched memory-print of Bim's baby life.

The Shaler Boulevard Apartments in Ridgefield, just across the George Washington Bridge, were about the same vintage as the apartment blocks in Long Island City, including identical casement windows into which my faithful Fedders fit precisely. They were affordable for the same basic reason: the land-use economics of electric power: New Jersey Public Service's massive generating station stood on the banks of the river a mile away. The difference—the significant difference—was that here the facility was out of sight, and, as long as the westerly winds prevailed, out of mind.

We had chosen it because our particular captain's paradise required something cheap that was also within easy striking distance of the West Side. In time I discovered North Jersey covered with similar housing, same look, same design, same era of postwar housing boom, many of the developments managed by the same corporation and probably built by the same developer. His name was Ratner, and he knew what he was doing. His little Potemkin Villages of two-story brick-and-whitewood façades were set in underwhelming clusters around arrestingly large common green areas. They spoke a pidgin version of the local housing vernacular: one- and two-family homes, well-tended lawns, and the conspicuously inconspicuous disposal of the family car.

This was, in fact, precisely where Shaler Boulevard parted with Astoria Gardens, in a suburban potlatch of lawn and parking space. "We have space to waste," Ratner seemed to say, space to show off—the income to maintain it. When you rented here, you bought this too: the illusion, the promise—the public advertisement—that you were moving up.

But the merchandising gift box was much bigger than the bottle inside it. What Ratner gave in land he stole back from the apartments: every one, upstairs or down (renting, in housing-expert parlance for about $32 per room per month), had the same four and a half rooms, the same stingy little gentility. The showy green commons was the metaphorical glossy wrapper, always somewhat green and somewhat mown. No one walked or played on it but wandering dogs.

I noted as time passed that change of season only confirmed this strange taboo. I wondered—since there was nothing particularly off-limits about it in the lease— was it by choice? Was there some curious nexus between untouched grass and respectability? Or just an inclination to keep the daily business of life to the back door? Whatever the reason, even that summer the front quadlike lawns stood, week after week, soulless and empty, while the backyards—mere narrow concrete and grass strips along the parking lots—teemed. Kids raced each other around the aluminum laundry trees all day, butting and bumping the all-purpose plastic-webbed deck chairs, their shrill little voices echoing off the bricks walls. Moms scraped the same aluminum chairs against the concrete walks with a sound like banked anger, as the path of sticky Jersey sunshine moved around the yard. Cars spawned like roaches, not only filling all the painted stripes but overflowing to the edges of the walkways in scorn of fire laws. Tenants grew testy and hostile vying for spaces. Kids played right to the curb, sometimes off it—you needed the same vigilance as if you lived on a busy city street. Only on hot Sunday mornings did quiet reign, when the lot lay full and still, like a burning lake of steel.

What lay behind this mysterious preference for carscape over landscape? Why would this mostly housebound subculture of women and children prefer views of pitted asphalt and glinting car hoods to the cool spread of Mr. Ratner's lawn, so amiably dotted with trees and fringed with flowering laurel and rhododendron? It seemed to say something very dark about upward mobility. Green must have something to do with money in the bank. It was as if on Shaler Boulevard people could live in the daily squalor of the car park if only they believed the front yard was socked away for the future.

Or so I thought in my Spenglerian moods. Most days I could see it was actually impossible to use the front doors for ordinary comings and goings. No self-respecting commuter husband, peeling himself off his sticky vinyl car seat, would have the physical, let alone the moral, stamina for such a decisive act of the will. Visitors coming by car (and what other way *was* there to come unless you already lived in the complex?) were forced to ponder either an inelegant entrance via the back door, through the apartment's cramped galley kitchen, or a rather deliberate, long, and self-conscious walk around to the grassy side of the building to the front. A doctor, once, making what was probably one of the last house calls of the twentieth century to see my sick child, actually picked his way up the brick steps and rang my front doorbell. For several full seconds I did not know what the sound was that I had just heard.

The FBI didn't stand on any such ceremony, of course. The two agents who later flashed a mugshot of fugitive Dan Berrigan at our baby-sitter, Mrs. Halle, would have gone straight up to number 703A, scoped out the narrow back door (thick with its eleventh coat of green paint), maybe even peeked into the little curtained window, before they buzzed. Needless to say, she was mighty alarmed.

But I am ahead of my story. Mrs. Halle, our nanny-housekeeper, had become a household familiar as soon as I went back to teaching in the fall. Christopher

Robert was by then two months old. He, smilingly complaisant from the day he was born, had dallied till at least two weeks beyond his due date—also the most unforgettably, hellfire-hottest two weeks of July. But he had meant no harm, and accommodatingly broke water during one of Harry's irregular overnights so that we could get ourselves to Englewood Hospital as a family. We slipped out the front door—quite unnoticed of course—at 5:15 A.M., barely the dawn of dawn, Bim on one hand, overnight bag on the other, Harry hurrying ahead of me on the walk still clocking the time between contractions. The day promised to be another cooker, steam already rising up off the greensward grass like smoke and making corrugated heat waves on the rooftops.

"Don't worry, you'll pop him like a peach pit," Harry promised. Considering what a big baby he'd got to be, I didn't believe it. Maybe something in my atavistic Sicilian soul imagined the Lord's vengeance overdue. But pop him like a peach pit I did, at the fourteenth minute of the seventh hour of the fourteenth day of the seventh month, a true Bastille Day flower child of the spirit. The Second Son mantle lay lightly on his oversized pink-and-blond roundness. His ready monikers of "Christopher" and "Robert" were like the names the French once gave the months of the Revolution, rational, please-ourself names, declarations of the burdenless New Age, not stabs at morganatic Italian diplomacy like his brother's. We were our own family now, no one else's.

Harry had sat by me through my short labor, a kindly silhouette against the morning sun in the window, nervously watching me breathe, saying funny things. He told me later it had scared him shitless. If he was still scared, his bright eyes didn't show it. He wasn't even wearing sunglasses.

"Congratulations, Mr. Browne." *Mr. Browne.* "Mrs. Browne. Beautiful baby. Beautiful *big* baby." Nobody in Jersey knew this Mr. Browne. We were just another couple moving up on our 2.7 kids quota, justifying the purchase of a backyard plastic kiddie pool.

Thus, at any rate, was "Mr. Browne" armed with a little more family housing expertise than he had a right to, when he went to Washington later that summer.

August 29. Brown/e day before the Senate so-called Ribicoff committee, a hearing on the federal role in urban affairs. Both Claude (*Manchild in the Promised Land*) Brown and the man billed as the Reverend Henry J. had been invited because some researcher for the Subcommittee on Executive Reorganization thought the senators should know what was happening on the streets of New York before deciding which category of lawmaking it fit into.

I heard something of the exchange when he got back, of course. Like others, I caught key news clips on television. But it was not purely spectatorial for me. Never. It mattered, more and more it mattered in some vital place in my being, that the poor families—the poor *women*—I had so long empathized with from a distance, so long thought of as politically more important than myself, should be argued for at the level of national policy. But I imagine for him there was a suspicion of ambivalence in the mix. It was, yes, an exhilarating test of his gift for the sound bite, the impactful "quotable quote,"and of his capacity to engage major lawmakers in the national performance space where such policy is "staged." But it had been his whole argument from the beginning, hadn't it?, that real people didn't need *him* for a spokesperson—that they should be speaking for themselves.

But he'd been tapped. Now what choice but to face those face-offs with Abe Ribicoff from Connecticut and Robert F. Kennedy from New York, two of the preeminent liberal Democrats of the time? And they were—and are—delicious encounters, frozen by transcript now into intensely focused vignettes: politics made suddenly, incomparably human.

Claude Brown was up before him, a black former street kid from Harlem whose down-and-dirty autobiography had just electrified America, and who spent the better part of the morning in a long and emotional stint at the mike. You can see Harry's need to clear an instant space for himself in the pull-no-punches opener, where he asks the Senate committee why they talk only to men who write books or wear collars. He actually says *"men."* Was it a conscious choice, I wonder? Was he ready to think, let alone say, that the people the senators had excluded included *women*?

But he swerves swiftly into urban renewal, brashly identifying himself as someone who actually advocates it—"unlike *some* theologians." Chances are he has the eye of professional Catholic Senator Kennedy. "You know the urban crisis has arrived when the theologians have caught up with it. It usually takes them a couple of centuries."

Of course he talks too fast for the stenographer. He thinks too fast for the senators—it's as if he's trying to strike every blow and make up for every agony people have been put through since 1958. Mostly he rags the slow and mystifying technocratic officialdom: "Nobody comes into the neighborhoods and finds out what's going down." He tells them about the mortgage finance people surveying their own processing delays "like contemplating your own navel and trying to come up with the condition of your appendix." That one makes the papers.

It made the senators chuckle, too, and you can tell he is going for the unguarded jugular when he says "the only thing they've done in a hurry in our neighborhood is get the poor people out." Maybe Kennedy is nervously rubbing his chin as Harry hits away at the functionary attitude that strangles people's interest in regulations while private sector outlaws are left free to prowl. I love it when our old baby—you might say our *first* baby—the Strycker's Bay Housing Co-op, becomes a case study in government actually getting in the way of people—people building affordable housing. "We might have put up ten times the 180 apartments in this one project," he tells the senators, "and yet we were refused a second sponsorship until we took up the political bludgeon and demanded it. And now," he says, "we look around and see these luxury buildings going up and say, 'Cheez, there goes the neighborhood.'"

Another laugh. "And yet *we* can do more large apartments than any public housing ever did. We have a dozen families waiting for every single one of our nine four-bedroom apartments."

Oh, boy. It wasn't hard to imagine Senator Ribicoff getting antsy thinking about all those Puerto Rican families with twelve kids. "On that, Father, do you mind if I interrupt?"

Browne leans away from the mike.

"My understanding is that the area where you live and where you work is very heavily peopled with Puerto Ricans."

Peopled with Puerto Ricans. Jesus. Harry agrees through his teeth. "Forty percent or so."

But he can't resist bolting forward again in his seat. "And they are registering like mad."

Ribicoff smiles indulgently. "I wonder if you would give us your impression of what happens when the Puerto Ricans come to New York. What does New York do to them? I think this is important and I think you are well qualified to talk about it."

I know what Harry was thinking: *That's just the problem—you think I'm qualified.* To Ribicoff, he said, "If I try to describe Puerto Rican life on the West Side of New York, I'm gonna make about eighty thousand enemies." But Ribicoff dogs him anyway, wanting to make him explain how "white middle-class America" might better get their heads around "these problems."

Too much. "Maybe they should enter through the back door of their fancy restaurants, where as soon as you sit down you pay as much as the guy in the kitchen is getting for half a week's work."

Ribicoff shuts up. Kennedy moves in, a little testy, just as determined to define the problems in terms of race and ethnic differences. Harry won't let him, hitting on class and economic realities—won't let any of them forget that the problem is less the poor themselves than middle-class attitudes toward them. His "classic example" is recent and immediate: a group of low-income residents coming together with about thirty social workers to try to solve some problems on West 94th Street, what he called "police stuff—rubs between Puerto Ricans and the Negro community." All the social workers can see is race, the kind of friction they think they can fix. But the people turn around and take it out on "the garbage and the cockroaches and the landlords and the whole *schmeer*—no nurseries, no place to get jobs and the rest." Not what the social workers were programmed to hear.

The stenographer wasn't programmed for *schmeer* either. But there was no stopping him to ask how to spell it: his blood was up on the "middle-class attitude." You can see the personal life history rupturing through the sociology, like movie clips: "A kid with a drug problem in a 'nice' family and it's a personal tragedy. But for poor people, whatever color, it's a 'case.' It's something wrong with the whole 'target group.'" He's so hot he's got to drag all of us into it: Pop, Jackie, me and the kids. "Well-enough-off folks, you've got an out-of-wedlock kid or an alcoholic dad or somebody who's a little off his head, and you can hide it. With the poor it all hangs out. When they come up against welfare—health—public housing, they have to go through a meat chopper."

Ribicoff is resigned. "Go ahead, Father."

Well, he asked for it. "You're never going to get social agencies with realtors on their boards to listen to poor people. You've got somehow to make those boards accountable. That's what citizen's participation means. Otherwise it doesn't mean anything." Then Harry takes the real leap of conscience and says what he'd come to say. "You've got to pay, in a sense, to foment a little revolution against your own policies." You could tell he was gauging the alarm in their faces as he went on: "Statesmen are going to see this. The statesman is going to listen to the poor—to the people that haven't been heard from before."

By now I think he'd almost forgotten whether he was asking or threatening. He said—he warned—that people were getting articulate about their own needs. They might not be able to talk about nuclear fallout, he said, but they could deal with their kids and rats and nursery schools and jobs and day care. They'd learned to read statistics and knew hypocrisy when they saw it. His closing line was powerful. "We're building a People's University," he said. "People with competency speaking for themselves. And if they want to put it to me when it's all over, 'Amen' say I."

That keynote. Maybe you could only feel its poignancy if you knew where he'd come from, what he'd had, once, that had once been taken away.

You had to hand it to Senator Kennedy that day. He called Harry's statement "a very good statement" and said he agreed with all of it, said he thought probably the most difficult thing for "people in political life, or the political establishment—or the economic establishment—or the class—or just the ordinary citizen—the white citizen—to understand" was that people themselves would like to have some say in the decisions that affect them. Harry beamed, loved him from that moment. "Hope to see you on the West Side," he said.

But he didn't mean the west side of the Hudson.

No welfare mothers here, none of the people—the women—speaking for themselves he must have pictured as he spoke: Esta, Melinda, Georgia, women whose situations, multiplied exponentially, defined the feminization of poverty before it had a name. No day care for me if it wasn't supplied by mothers to the manner born. No day care for me without Mrs. Halle, that impeccably reliable old lady, already in her seventies and half-deaf in spite of the hearing aid sticking out of her right ear.

Mrs. Halle, German and Jewish, was a god of two formidable natures in one person, each at constant war with the other. She would appear unfailingly at the green door of our ground-floor flat in all weathers, precisely at the appointed hour, and maintain the most rigid discipline in every other obligation, and yet cosset a child as tenderly as if he were made of Streit's matzoh. By now she has undoubtedly closed her eyes on this weary world and its boulevard-full of babies, all of them within the accessible circuit of her dignified, stiff-legged, head-down, cautious and steady walk, ever on the alert for sidewalk treachery, a walk she took virtually every day from the little blue bungalow she shared in perpetual misery with her son and his wife.

If eternity were night court, Mrs. Halle would be an everlasting plaintiff. She carried a grievance—the same grievance—with her from home every day. A recipe given was a defense secret. A recipe taken was a challenge to conquer even if it took all the iron in her iron will, just so she could draw the line a little more firmly between herself and that slovenly, irresponsible, noncooking woman her son had had the vulgar effrontery to marry.

But Mrs. Halle, not all vinegar, told a good story, and I suppose corked up many more. Behind her alert gray eyes and under her meticulously coiffed blue hair must have dwelt a whole lending library of *Peyton Place* secrets, those tales of the inner sanctum of the families she sat for, mornings, afternoons, evenings—anything to get out of that miserable blue bungalow. Occasionally, she vented the particulars of her own exasperating family conflicts, but like all good baby-sitters she had a sacred code of internecine silence. With one exception: when she told me what the local doctor's wife had said when she, Mrs. Halle, had innocently remarked on the joy I displayed whenever I got back home to my two little boys: "She's like a child herself. She rolls around on the floor. It's a sight to behold."

"It must be guilt," said the doctor's wife, who lived in the patrician house with a swimming pool on the hillside above the apartments, and I'm sure made more use of Mrs. Halle, total hours, than I ever did.

It was like that then. It was the rare middle-class or would-be middle-class mother who worked outside the home, even as little as the three days a week I did. Around me in Ridgefield they seemed to live their domestic discipline with the austerity of a conventual vow, and I of course lived under their silent anathema. Every departure, every return was apparently watched—and condemned—from the curtained kitchen windows, or from under the fold-out laundry trees, by a surveillance corps of mothers dedicated to preserving their stubborn belief in the order of things.

Yet Mrs. Halle had stood up for me, then and always. Poor Mrs. Halle, starchy, respectable matron that she was, would have died had she known our awful secret, the disreputable arrangement she enabled with her tender labors. But she was really a feminist at heart, a Woman Warrior of the old school. Maybe it went with her generation, or what she'd suffered and escaped fleeing Germany just before the war. She had a steely self-reliance and a dread of dependency, a dread of her own impending infirmity, that was terrible, and haunting. In my ornery and perhaps unfeminine independence she saw no reason for alarm or suspicion. It was a very practical matter: *my* work assured *her* work, and that simple ecology was enough to seal her loyalty.

She didn't have to tell me she saw the exhausted vacancy in the lives of the other women in our "piazza." I knew she saw it. For all their true-believing frigidity toward agnostics like me, they were no factory-warranted Stepford wives. *We* knew they were burned to an inner crisp by their own discontent—whether they could name or even concede they felt it. It was hard to believe they represented the same generation of women I'd left behind me in Long Island City. From May to October, day's start to day's end, they appeared in a uniform of curlers and shorts, yelling savage epithets at their children from their backdoor command posts. Sullen with boredom, inspired by a mean, can-you-top-this, cell-block individualism, they would stand around the laundry trees and share each day's plans for washing the curtains, repapering the shelves, steaming the carpets, and dusting every knickknack—all this, mind you, in apartments so small they could have been spotlessly maintained from a wheelchair. The daily soaps were their only refuge. I think they *told* them, like rosaries, or monastic compline, or novenas.

It grew on me how much their backdoor subculture might further explain the spooky desolation of those empty front lawns. They were bright women, they were young women, they were women with enough education to be dogged by vagrant ambitions. Yet they were women who dared to plod only along the routes prescribed by the present definition of the American dream. Each marked her own progress every time another family "made it"—that is, moved up to a private dream house in Oradell or Westwood. You could almost hear the prayer go up like a chant: "There, O Lord, would *I* go too, if Thou hadst but a *smidgeon* of grace for me." They *needed* noise, I thought. They *needed* some illusion of fullness, however ugly the simulation of it by a full car park. Of what use was it to them to contemplate the greensward? You might miss the sight of someone actually getting away.

In some ways, perhaps, I was a yuppie a generation ahead, busy with a new job, a tenure-track appointment at the University Heights branch of NYU in the Bronx, a twenty-minute ride away over the George Washington Bridge. My brother Carl returned into my life from his stint in an engineering installation in Germany. Asking no unseemly questions, he sold us the Volkswagen hatchback he had brought back with him from the factory. We became in one stride a two-child and two-car family. On my distinguished university salary, I could soon even afford a washing machine.

Yet maybe the anger around me was a contagion, preying on my exhaustion. It seemed no matter how I tried to catch up with it, the tree in the yard grew laundry, even in winter, when the diapers and baby shirts would freeze solid as boards and I would have to rig up a line in our furnace room to thaw them out. Why hadn't somebody warned me that children only arithmetically increase, but the work they generate exponentially multiplies? My post at NYU wasn't just a job anymore, either—a stint I could do and disappear. It was a position, a commitment. It meant no longer teaching courses that came ready-made from the hands of a committee. It meant duties, committees, governance, planning, faculty meetings to watchdog my own interests or students' or colleagues' in the power struggles of university politics, all of it complicated by our being a colonial outpost in relation to the imperial Rome of NYU at Washington Square.

It meant, in the end, late nights, *very* late nights that often stopped being night before I was through, fighting to stay awake with espresso, black and thick as pitch, by the brimful pot. Mrs. Halle was all the help I could afford, and she was almost strictly a nanny. This meant weekends crammed with marketing and food and shopping for shoes and clothes and organizing meals for the week and sewing curtains and putting up bookshelves and ironing and cleaning the bathroom and scrubbing the kitchen floor and vacuuming, pressed on by some ferocious inner standard I did not yet question—not to mention the Prussian white glove of Mrs. Halle. Respectable meant inspectable. It always had. It was my version of the disease my neighbors were dying from.

It meant getting the kids to the doctor for their shots—still the doctor in New Rochelle.

It meant tending the car so it wouldn't fail me.

It meant dreading Fridays just as wholeheartedly as other people were thanking God for them, because the weekend didn't exist that wasn't infinitely more crammed with demands than my weekdays, or more minutely scheduled with physical and mental labors from dawn to midnight. It meant staggering to the bed on Sunday evenings, our lovely queen-sized bed—oh, how far we had come!—with its fresh-air scented pillowslips that my Italian Emmi would have loved. It meant lying face-down in my clothes without the energy left to take them off, and hearing rise out of me a kind of a eerie, unnatural moan from a bodily pain too deep for tears.

And yet night would blessedly follow days and weekends like these and sometimes let me steal the sweet sleep I was ravenous for. And out of this sleep, desire would sometimes come, like a dream, and out of the dream—or into it—Harry would break.

Maybe it was nothing more than the glare from the car-park lamppost, but there were nights it fell through the bedroom blinds in a radiant blue glow, touching the black-garbed figure in the bedroom doorway with something like wet moonshine.

There would be a murmur of words. A cool body, the chill of the night still on him, would slip silently between the fresh sweet-smelling sheets and fold my warmth to him with an answering desire, and for a few moments I was in the night country of the blest, instead of the damned.

I was surprised that the NYU English department secretary, besides being a woman of very imposing flesh, should prove an Irish Catholic of such fierce old breed, who kept the holy portals of the University College English House as if she were rehearsing the role of Sin in *Paradise Lost.* Her name was Mary Mullen, and she *was* the University Heights English department, the text of its continuity, to whom the rather gentle, epicene men who came and went as chairmen over the years were nothing more than footnotes.

We experienced our first close encounter as she pondered the imponderables of my being a Catholic woman with two children traveling under a name not my husband's. "What *is* your husband's name?," she put to me with the rudeness of a duchess one day, and, as off guard and bloody intimidated if she were my Mother Confessor I blurted out that it was Harry Brown with an *e.* "*Hmh,*" she murmured, as I winced inwardly. "I know a Harry Brown with an *e.*"

Harry nearly fell over when I told him. He described her as a "priests' moll" if there ever was one—by definition one of those ultra-devotees who follow clerics the way some people follow movie stars. She'd been a pillar of St. Elizabeth's, where he'd spent the year before Italy, sulking over Spellman's surprise recall and casting about for something to do with his humiliation. It was just the sort of restless brooding that would make a priest memorable to a priests' moll, even if he weren't as taking as Father Browne. "Watch out for Mary," he warned, putting rather too fine a point on it, I thought.

But there was no point too fine for Mary, who was as inexorable as Genghis Khan: two hundred pounds of force field and clearly on the lookout for *me.* I must have said something casual during one of our English House all-women kitchen, lunches, about May Dunlap's ouija board back in Greensboro and the long, laughable, and yet rather awesome magic that had nearly brought her to Rome. Mary intuited my respect for powers, and, Ph.D. notwithstanding, took me confidentially aside afterward to say that Irene, her oldest and dearest friend at the college, besides being the Irish crone who handed out the towels for the swimming pool, was the secret Witch of University Heights. "Ever had your tea leaves read?" she asked. And the next thing I knew I was having a bag lunch with both of them in a dank corner of the chlorine-scented sub-basement of Gould Library, my tea poured from a huge white porcelain pot into my white cafeteria mug, and sipping my way slowly, tremulously, to the leaves.

But you could not sip forever. When I reached the bottom, Irene—wrinkled, her stark whiteness a little ruddied, blue eyes reminiscent of Harry's Mam—took the cup expertly between the palms of her two hands. *"This first wash,"* she intoned with an unearthly shift in the register of her voice, *"is for the present."* She waited for me to nod, then: *"I see a place in New Jersey."*

Mary'd sworn she would let on nothing to her about me. "Even the little I know," she'd said, archly. But I was certain I'd been betrayed.

"I see a driveway, a large sloping driveway, full of cars."

Now this was beyond anything I'd ever said to Mary—Jesus, had she followed me home? *"Trees, like a wood."* The Great Bear Water Company grounds, behind a nearby cyclone fence. *"An old woman, a very thin old woman, with children, very young children—the old woman quite hard of hearing. I see a car,"* she went on, as I was beginning to feel queasy, *"A small white foreign car, like a station wagon."* My brother's Volkswagen. She paused. *"Another car. It comes and goes less often."*

"You're uncanny, Irene," I choked. "She *is* uncanny, Mary." She urged me to let her continue, but I'd already started for my handbag. "You scare me, Irene." Irene looked up at me out of eyes blue with the blue of eternal youth—sapphires sewn into the white muslin of her face. She smiled.

"Stay," said Mary imperiously. "Let her go on. The second cup's for the future."

Irene smiled her benevolent little smile. "I never push on where my sight isn't welcome to go." The line scanned.

Mary wasn't letting me off so easily. She breathed heavily, sweatily, all the way back to the English House, trying to keep up with my pace. "Right on the mark, was she?"

Mary knew. Something. At least that there *was* something about me, something not quite square. The more I eluded her, the more she wanted to know, and the less I could let her. I was beginning to grasp how small was the world of Irish Catholic New York, comically so in this case, but who, if I weren't more careful, might have the last laugh? From here on, I guessed, I would have to steer away from everything university-sociable I might be expected to attend with a spouse, burrow down into a protective personal silence, an icy lower circle of hell, where Mary's fiery furnace and Irene's fountain-blue searchlights couldn't follow me.

Mrs. Halle had been deeply right about me, defending me to the doctor's wife. Frazzled and anxious and sleepless though I was, trying to hold it together, I could slip down onto the floor with my babies, get inside the world down there, looking up, and just bliss out. It was almost all my joy.

Oh, I could be Mommy too. "Now you *behave*," I would say to Bim, as he splashed vigorously about in the bathtub with his toy boats. "But, Mommy," he'd correct, with the linguistic acuity of a little Noam Chomsky, "I *am* being have!"

Once, during a participatory diaper change on Christopher Robert, who kept pumping his little bootied feet into my boobs, Bim said, "He's *kicky*, isn't he," and in that moment stole the right to rename his kid brother, forever. Maybe it was his version of one of those Biblical brother myths. It is still a fallen world, after all, even for kids. I thought he'd pretty much mastered his rage at being superseded by this blue-eyed baby Buddha, until I caught him one day in a murderous gesture, about to drop something crushing on him as he slept peacefully in his basket, smelling of breast milk. This remnant of Oedipal passion turned by degrees into a sulky tenderness. Either that, or Kiki astutely learned to avoid fratricide by letting himself become Pooh to Bim's own imperious Christopher Robin. Big, chubby, gentle as rainwater, he would ingratiate himself with every lap and pair of arms within reach. He would gurgle and bleat and giggle, and blink his saucer eyes. He would drop to sleep like a slug anywhere you put him down.

But, true to genes, he had a hungry, a voluptuous heart, a heart that woke at midnight, often just as Harry came stealthily in. As the first soft murmur of our voices reached down the narrow hallway past the furnace to the ten-by-ten little bedroom he shared with his brother, he would stand up in his crib and squeal like a squeeze doll. And the two of us, I already a bit refreshed perhaps by an hour's sleep, Harry longing for a touch of baby skin, would conspire to break the Spockish law and sneak him across the hall to spend some time with us in bed.

It used to remind me of those big blowsy Renaissance paintings of Mars and Venus playing with their *putto*-Cupid. We would sing him songs and rhymes and Harry would do hugging and tossing games he had his own names for, like "Hoops of Steel" and "Blast-off." My favorite was some primal thing known as "The Hole in the Garden," evolved out of a version of Jack and the Beanstalk we were fond of reading to Bim, and ending with the baby falling scarily down out of the sky and disappearing into the bedclothes equivalent of the deep. Kiki would giggle and gurgle and bleat until he had his orgasmic fill. Half an hour later I would lay him back in his crib and watch him drop to sleep as if he'd been hypnotized.

Those pure baby blues of his absolutely daunted the brown-eyed rest of us. What a charisma they had, especially for my brother Carl, who mercifully widened our stinted social circle when I most needed it, now that Ann was hunkered down studying Greek and Esta had gone west to marry and Judy had already married and gone off to England. Back from his engineering stint in Europe and still single, he seemed glad to have a conspiratorial share in our little family. He resumed living with my parents in New Rochelle and paid good avuncular visits to Ridgefield almost just to see Kiki, second son to second son. His visits also became a way of getting solid intelligence to my mother about how things stood with us. And what she knew, I assume my father did as well. But they said nothing, shame—*vergogna*—and *omertà* sealing their lips and hearts.

Two dry years must have passed before we extended my contact with the world, going finally beyond brother and baby-sitters to a careful selection from my academic circle. There were Camille and Bill Slights, both of whom taught Shakespeare at NYU (she at the Heights, he at the Square). Harry was happily nothing more than Harry to them. They weren't Catholic, they lived in the Village, and they'd come from Wisconsin too recently to have brushed with any special Father Browne notoriety, although I think if we'd confessed the truth, neither of them would have blinked an Elizabethan eyelash. There were people like that you knew would instinctively see what was simultaneously tragic and rollicking about a situation as outrageous as ours, and cope.

The others were two unmarried friends, Carrie Silver and John Rosenberg, and they also defined just such a complex sense of things. In the midst of dinner, the night they came to Ridgefield to visit, Kiki almost convulsed himself to death with whooping cough, and Carrie and John literally helped save his life by mounting a steam tent over his bed with bedsheets. Carrie held the sheets up with her own arms.

Two couples in four years. Absorbed in the dailiness of it, I'm not sure when—or if—I knew I needed more than that, more than I had. As time went on, except for those occasional dreamlike nighttime visitations and weekend Harry-descents—his Cupid to my Psyche, Muriel might have said—I had nothing but the most attenuated contact with his worldly public life. The more it swelled into significance, the more it seemed to push mine to the margin. And then there were the nights he'd swear to save for us and forget, having made some conflicting appointment, because he just couldn't keep it all straight.

His absences had become a fact of life, a mere Hole in the Garden, a quantum deficiency in the pleasure principle I and his little boys knew that time would always partially repair. Someone gave him a tiny black pocket calendar for the Jewish year 5728, and in it, with a crudely drawn little pentagonal icon of a house, he'd legislate the dinners he swore to come home for, just to be sure to see the kids awake. This helped—nothing but the cryptic symbol, no telltale words or names if he lost the book—and penning us in sometimes actually did get him home, just in time to join hands around our little dinner table and bless the Rev-o-lu-ti-on.

For him, perhaps, we were a kind of narcotic, a warm bath of baby energy and love on which he relied after the day-to-day, meeting-to-meeting, city-to-city worlds he moved in had him stupefied. But the part of him needing us was so cauterized by the hell-hail of politics that until he arrived within the four walls of our little garden apartment on Shaler Boulevard I don't believe he could actually *feel* the need. Perhaps in back of his self-distancing there was that inescapable, self-sacrificing messianic insight—the knowledge that there was no deprivation of *his* that somebody else couldn't far exceed, all in a day's suffering, the knowledge he had transmitted to me. How could he indulge his own need? How, for that matter, could he indulge mine? To make me happy would have meant—always *did* mean—making himself happy too, a private, propertarian happiness that had the stain of self upon it. Oh, yes, Holy Mother Church was still taking her tithe.

My own tolerance of this continual sluicing away of pleasure astonishes me—for in spite of a certain natural self-sufficiency, celebrating life came to me, too, as needfully as eating and breathing. Perhaps I was repeating the anesthetized state of my adolescence, when I'd had to live my lie in a cloud of self-denial. I too was stupefied—amnesic. Even with my pain buffered by the loveliness of my beautiful little boys, there must have been times I wanted to die—of exhaustion, of loneliness, of a frustrated sense of my own need for being in the world. But then, suddenly, everything I had ever lost or desired would seem to gather itself into the honey of his mouth. He would come home and draw me into the Eden of his arms, and I would forget it all—grief, anger, shame, guilt—and my soul, more fatigued, even, than my body, would sleep inside the pure surrender of his sleep.

And it was 1967: great currents stirring, tearing us out of ourselves. What was I in the scheme of things anyway? What were you? Even just that little bit of the macrocosm that bore in on each of us then had a terrible, a daunting sufficiency. Even just the bit of it that chose to call itself the Church bore fiercely in on us. The papacy, going through institutional whiplash, already on its second Paul since the great John. In New York, Cardinal Spellman died, leaving what it would have surprised no one to call a crisis in the American Church to be dealt with by someone new.

An ecumenical movement of clerics calling itself IFCO—the Interreligious Foundation for Community Organization—had begun to stir things up at the curbstones of ministry. In Chicago, a Catholic cleric named Jack Egan made his move toward the formation of a national nucleus group called the Catholic Committee on the Urban Ministry. Nobody said so openly, but, in the face of the numbers walking away from the priesthood by now, keeping priests must have been high on their action list.

Harry, drawn into this group, used to say for a laugh that CCUM would show them all how to be "meaningful and relevant and meaningfully relevant." But he took the matter as seriously as Egan, really. And it mattered that a Catholic agenda was being set beyond them too, that Jesuit Daniel Berrigan, of the little think-tank that had emerged on West 98th Street, had by now been joined by his brother Phil, a Josephite priest, in designing effective—effectively radical—anti-war, antinuclear civil disobedience, like the public burning of draft records in Catonsville, Maryland, to be followed later by the Plowshares activism of nose-cone–hammering, blood-splashing attacks on missile installations. It was the kind of action that if you were being cautious you would say was redefining the boundary between what was inside and what was outside the Church.

And Robert F. Kennedy had decided to run for president.

So much gestating in the big womb of time, as the planet did its circuit around the sun that year, spawned by who knew what big cosmic ejaculation? Down in the microcosm—the one that slipped into Joycean reverse from Universe to North Jersey to a bedroom in Sam Ratner's gardens—Harry and me, mere atomies, after stealing crazily off to celebrate his birthday and eat and dance and get thoroughly, follow-your-blissfully smashed in a roadhouse on Route 9W, came home and quite inadvertently made Nina.

She was Irene's second cup. A sin of the purest excess. She was art itself.

That spring, Professor Regina Stalling, NYU Bible Studies 202, was giving a lecture on the creative force signified in Christianity by the Holy Ghost—the mysteriously sexless spirit Milton says sat "dovelike, brooding on the vast Abyss"—when a beige Bronx pigeon exploded through the open classroom window in a burst of noise and a small snow of dusty feathers, and flapped out again. "There you are!" she said to the class, and repeated to us that afternoon in the kitchen of the English House.

A bit of unpremeditated *shtik* that seemed, among other things, to say that it was a Reginocentric universe, with paracletes in the wings (as it were) ready to enter on cue. The more inconvenient for us, since Regina had recently been hired as the new director of the first-year writing program, and such a repositioning of the center of the universe had its way with the program: meaning more sections, more required papers, entrance and exit "outcomes" tests, a sudden and violent upsurge in the number of meetings for training, coaching, hounding, and tyrannizing the rest of us. Regina seemed to exult in the power of close reading—and close writing about it— to keep draft-age young men out of the maw of the War Machine, which was definitely to her credit. But she did it like a dominatrix, sweating those of us who taught them till we dropped. I almost longed for the boot camp of Greensboro again, with its six eight o'clock classes a week.

This may explain why 1968, "The Year Everything Happened"—when Martin Luther King Jr. and Bobby Kennedy were shot to death and the presidential conventions in Chicago and Miami became crushed revolutions and cities rose up in riot all over the globe—should have become for me a blur, a kind of dream-nightmare somebody else was dreaming. Then again, perhaps it was a little that way for everyone. We can inventory events, run them by us again like film clips, but we can't quite make them cohere, not even within the continuity of our own lives. Experience, in 1968, was not linear, and did not continue.

In the Catholicocentric universe, it was also *annus mirabilis,* the year Terence Cooke was made cardinal of New York, the year Monsignor Flanagan was put out to pasture in Dutchess County—the year Father Henry J. Browne was invited to assume the pastoral responsibilities of St. Gregory's parish. Whatever the spirit brooding dovelike on our Abyss, some gigantic amniotic wave had swept up out of the Church's fecund, oceanic belly, and Harry rode it like a surfer, hanging five.

The West Side counterculture rumored that he was getting it on with the new executive director at Strycker's Bay, the woman who'd replaced Esta. How else explain his frequent nocturnal disappearances? Father Tom Farrelly found rectory duty frequently reverting to him, and rather liked the new Browne regime—forget *televizing* the Revolution, it was more like having season tickets. Which had its drawbacks, like the night a certain peace activist with very aggressive breasts came drunk to the rectory door and insisted she and Father Browne had a date.

Tom thought she looked like Harry's type, but Harry confused him afterward by thanking him for sending her away. Who knows what she was to him? Power *is* an aphrodisiac, after all. Looking back now, *sub specie aeternitatis,* I frankly feel for the peace activist. I know just what it felt like to have Harry stand you up.

It was during Passion Week. Martin Luther King Jr. had been murdered in Memphis barely a week before. His death had launched an American passion—a sickening revulsion, a ferocious rededication to struggle. Much of the nation was in mourning, all of it in shock.

Heavy with child and sorrow, I had begun to experience contractions, though my doctor thought it was still too early for labor. Thursday evening they began to come closer together. Take a shot of whiskey, he said. See if they pass. I did, and they did. And then they didn't. I called my brother and asked him to come over and spend the night.

The boys were already sleeping. I bent over the tub daubing a color rinse over my graying hairline, and felt another contraction, that familiar syntax of the body's limited vocabulary of sensation below the navel: an elastic tightening of muscles around the pelvis like a pulled sash, followed by a curiously erotic, liquid movement of the vagina, the orgasmic erection of the nipples. I washed, rinsed, threw my head back in a towel. Again. Stronger. My mind had already gone into analog mode. *Fifteen minutes apart.*

In the deepening dusk I caught the shadowy image of myself, naked to the hips, in the long bedroom mirror. My breasts seemed huge, the veins distinct and pencil-blue, the areolas like plums. Had I splashed myself with hair color? Or was that brown mark on my stirring belly a new sign in the skin, a maculation for the not-so-*Immacolata* in her time?

I phoned Harry at St. Gregory's. I had said I would. I will *need* you, I'd warned him, the memory of my extremity in Italy a lesson I could never unlearn. I have no mother, I'd said. Remember.

He had surrounded himself with a squadron of new comrades, whipped them down the ringing grooves of change into a stirring, spirited collective. I wonder who took the phone that night and heard me say, *"Tell him Flavia is calling?"*—because now I virtually never called him, and it was the simplest code in the universe: the truth.

A brief wait. The voice returns, saying he is sorry, but Father Browne cannot come to the phone.

The world divides.

He used to say that. I considered it one of his most deeply philosophical utterances, expressing not just some bald, irreducible difference in human perception, but a rare acceptance of what we may be unable to change. In this instance perhaps the divide is deeply gendered, and women will understand, and men will not, what it meant to me that night to have Harry choose to remain out of my reach as he broke the unleavened Passover bread with his comrades. I couldn't believe it. I couldn't forgive it. I think I never have.

And yet I think I can truthfully say that I did not know some inner threshold had been crossed. I knew only that I must get help to the hospital, and turned for surrogate mother to my neighbor Margery, with seven of her own, whose oldest, Debbie, sometimes baby-sat for us. It seems almost fairy-godmotherly to say that Margery dwelt in a little blue and white cottage at the edge of the Great Bear Woods. She seldom went to bed before midnight—I could often see her light through the trees.

Ah, yes, the world divides. She came instantly at my call, her faded strawberry-gold hair as smoothly groomed as if she ran regular jitneys for birthday nights. We waited only for Carl to arrive, and clambered into her car. It was already 10:20—she had me safely to Englewood Hospital in fifteen minutes. Harry's absence she put, en route, into the pioneer-woman terms she'd been raised on from her Iowa girlhood: "Heckuvalot better hav'n' a wom'n than some *maaan* 'round at a taam like this!" I declared her the baby's godmother, fairy or otherwise, on the spot, and none too soon. It had barely turned midnight when her godchild Nina was born.

A deeply remorseful Harry came to see me in the hospital on Good Friday—apologetic, tender, tearing himself away from his first Easter weekend at St. Gregory's, which he had re-orchestrated into a major community event. That Sunday he did a three-ring circus of masses, then scurried home to give my brother some relief, dress the boys in their new red jumpsuits, and sweep them off to the hospital to see me. But children weren't allowed, and the three of them stood in the parking lot below my window—Harry, ever prudent in sunglasses—holding each of the boys in turn over his head, so they could wave.

My God, they were lovely. I could be a harpy of rage and exhaustion sometimes, but even then, *that* remained existential bedrock, Genesis 1:1. Nothing justified them more than the simple fact of their existence. What might I have said if somebody like Regina Stalling had called for an explanation of all this joyous motherhood? *It is the age of ecstasy.* Simply, sentimentally, self-indulgently, let me say it. Children seemed to me to put the seal of ecstasy and otherworldliness on love, as if they had existed before us, as if our destinies had always been inscribed on the small brows of three gift creatures, to be dipped in gold and frankincense and extra-virgin olive oil.

As for the legal issue in our case, maybe I had a deficient grasp of legal concepts, but why, I considered, should the only acceptable babies be the sealing wax of marriage contracts? I naturally took—take—an anarchist view of the matter. Babies are not made, like F14s, by contract, but only by the electric proximity of germ plasms, and no marriage ceremony can do, or has ever done, anything more to validate them.

Of course, when you are a heretic convinced, experience generally only convinces you more. Which meant that when the pastor at St. Michael's R.C. Church in Ridgefield refused to baptize Nina unless I filled out a parishioner questionnaire about who I was and to whom married and what I owned and what I earned, *et cetera*, I simply walked away, furious, exultant, prepared to trash the contractual "sacrament" of baptism with the same heathen Italian dispatch as all the others.

But Harry almost wept with rage when he heard about it, helpless rage in this instance because neither of us could safely call the pastor out and challenge him for refusing a sacrament. *I* was wild—the Church, I said, was a brute. My daughter would better be a Witch than a Christian. But my rage was balm to Harry's, who turned around and argued that it wasn't the Church, just some jerk who'd mortgaged himself too deep to his building fund. So he put Nina's tiny head under the tap in the sink and baptized her himself.

•

It was my pagan mother in me, maybe. *Mother, mother, mother:* sometimes I said the word like a spell. She was all I missed of the life before my life. Sometimes I thought, of my babies, that she was all *they* were missing. And she didn't need tea leaves or other forms of augury to know it. When she heard about the birth of my girl, that was it. *Basta.*

We agreed to meet. We chose a place in Fort Lee, just the Jersey side of the George Washington Bridge, so she wouldn't have to add fear of getting lost to her other fears. The service road near the offramp—I—we—would be there in the little white Volkswagen hatchback. And so it was that on a concrete sidewalk amid a tangle of bridge approaches, with the sloping sunlight of an August afternoon brooding on the abyss, she held each of my lovely babies in the passionate vise of her grip, against her heaving breast. She wet their faces with the rain of her tears.

Sometimes I might be just lying there in the dark. All this love-hunger and need—all this secrecy—for what? Ann's finally marrying, when Alan came home from Vietnam, only intensified the questions. I was married, as far as my neighbors were concerned—or my doctor, or my colleagues—though they had it on faith. The chairman of NYU English at Washington Square is reported to have called Professor Woodring at Columbia one day to say, "Did you know, she's married?"

Even to myself sometimes I was married. It couldn't be helped. Normal people didn't yet recognize separate identities, separate names. Mrs. Halle called me Mrs. Browne. So did salesgirls and repairmen. So did the teachers at Bim's nursery school. What difference did it make that I was *not* Mrs. Browne—that *she* was Harry's mother, or that I was not Mrs. Alaya either because *she* was mine? For most of the world I moved in, it made no difference at all. And as for me, my passing for married did not give me any corrupt satisfaction at hoodwinking the world. "Living a lie" is a bad thing I suppose, but everyone lives a lie of one kind or another, with varying degrees of intent and consistency. If there was a crime, it was rather that my lie was living *me,* stealing my true life.

Strange, how at first I had only tricked up this fiction of my faintly eccentric respectability as a gambit for survival. Now I was trapped in it. *Così è, se vi pare—* So it is, if you think so: marriage, Pirandello Style. I found I had got to *thinking* of myself as Mrs. Browne: a wife, someone to whom (within the contractual framework of legal fictions) Harry owed a debt, a conjugal "use" or "justice"—a *jus debitum.* It had been *he* who liked to play with the titillating chop-logic of that phrase, as if Latin was a seminarian boy-toy, but how much of the play was play? And how much had taken hold of his psyche too?

Still, beyond the tiny backyard playpen and kiddie-pool circle of Shaler Boulevard's gasoline alley, survival for him meant precisely the opposite kind of lie, meant reinforcing the myth of his existential freedom, meant giving the world the lie, denying me once, denying me twice. No, he had no "particular friend"—no affinity he had elected, no one person to whom he had contractually indebted himself.

And so in some sense he was trapped in *his* fiction too.

And the trap, for me, was not that I should ask something of him, something unwarranted—of course I should, under any circumstances, for love was my warrant, no? *Amor, che a null'amato.* . . . The trap was that I should *not* ask, that I should be under a kind of gag rule, unable to ask, unable to define the grounds of my expectation, unable to tell him on what terms of freedom or constraint he might answer my need, and so might either never ask him to answer it, or ask only in my silent and rancorous heart, never to be heard, assuming that, somehow, because he didn't know and didn't hear and didn't guess, he didn't care.

The trap for him was that he might take the priestly freedom his survival strategy gave him for the real thing, might indulge it even when it hurt me, even to assure *himself,* let alone assure others, that he had not failed in the vocation to which he owed his primary *jus debitum.* And if there was danger for me in idealizing my love for him, there was surely equal danger for him in idealizing, fetishizing, the bond between himself and the Church.

How strange of love to do this to us. To the two of us, sucking us up like different pebbles in different windstorms.

And so he worked his work, I mine.

But Regina, the Termagant Queen, ground me like a thresher, while the babies drained my body, and preparing to publish lest I perish drained my mind. I was a whirling dervish, catching flying bits of Harry's public life, invited to join a crowd or swell a scene or two. I met Robert Kennedy in a hotel stairwell once. Father Browne introduced us: *"Flavia. Senator."* Shy and buoyant, Kennedy blinked his sad-funny eyes and moved on. It must have been barely weeks before he was shot to death and the planet took that final lurid, panicky slide into the end of 1968. Christ, that funeral day, as television tracked the caisson train that carried his coffin, and they played the "Battle Hymn of the Republic" so many times it became the song you cried by ever after, the anthem of a generation of losses.

Then, as 1968 became 1969, the whole planet seemed to be burning. Anywhere you put your torch, you could have lit your political fire. Some of it had to be the fiery spirit of a good God. That year, in one of his—and their—proudest moments, the reins of Community Action passed, with stirring ceremony, from the hands of Father Browne to the hands of the people. That year, a woman, Doris Rosenblum, became president of the Strycker's Bay Neighborhood Council.

There were things I was in on. There were things I watched from the stands. And then there were things I simply didn't know. St. Gregory's became a stop on the Vietnam antidraft underground railroad to Canada. I didn't know, I didn't see, I didn't guess, and wasn't told. There may be many things I wasn't told, and didn't know I didn't know. There may be some I have yet to find out. There may be some I never will.

The fire that burned inside Harry's life didn't, couldn't, warm me now. He gave me what he could, or what he chose, but he couldn't bathe me in it any more, or teach me to speak his tongues. And knowing that some of what he did was outlaw, knowing that sometimes now he might be under watch, he had to—he *thought* he had to, which is the same thing—cut me out of his inmost life.

Just a minor infidelity, in the scheme of things. He couldn't do without me, without us, never altogether. He still drew those tiny Monopoly box-houses into his little book. He was still the very personification of Father-hood, Husband-hood, All-Together-Now-hood, whenever he came home. The way men are, I imagine, who work for the secret services of the world.

And when he slipped beside me in bed, his muscled body was still as sweet, his fringed earth-tinted eyes still shattered daylight before he shut them. But we both knew what we clutched so violently in each other's arms was an escape, now, and not a renewal.

7

"*Melius abbondare . . .* " *Better too much than too little.*

It might have been Harry's motto. It was certainly one of his "very few principles." And because of it, St. Gregory's dinner parties became famous—overflowing food and drink and talk talk talk, all compacted into a legendary dining-room wedge of radical celebrities and near-celebrities.

Of course his new communal regime had also announced the manumission of household slaves. No more underpaid rectory cooks and housekeepers: henceforth all cleaning and cooking would done by the *communards* themselves. This made for a narrow culinary repetoire, not to mention a long half-life for dustballs. My personal recipe for spaghetti sauce became clerically famous nationwide, better as meal for millions than loaves and fishes. And, hunger artist that Harry was, knowing now from me that how you put it together was as important as what went into it, he put it together with a purist *panache* that by some accounts approached alchemy, if not actual sorcery. Tom Farrelly scraped anathema very closely the evening he heard another guest was coming to dinner and dumped a can of Campbell's tomato soup into the simmering pot.

Everything was sacred, and nothing was. That same night, Canadian theologian Gregory Baum feasted on Harry's (and my) *bolognese* and offered the current progressive last word on the issue of the female priesthood: "No, you most certainly do not need a *penis* to say the Holy Mass"—a message that would rattle the Vatican, if not quite shift it on its foundation. In any case, it was a reminder that if the current times tried priests' souls, it was in part because the souls inhabited bodies, not unlike the souls they were supposedly set there to save. And it was women, I noticed, forcing the issue. At their recent Notre Dame conference, Jack Egan's Catholic Committee (CCUM) originally a *minyan* of ten good men, had felt considerable pressure from both lay and religious women, wanting to be, and to be seen to be, not just a presence but part of the essence, the center, the heart, the soul, the *body*, of the discussion.

That dinner party for Gregory Baum had been prologue to a parish forum at St. Gregory's on the embattled subject of abortion. You couldn't be Catholic and *not* have an opinion. It came up between Harry and me at supper one night, and we quarreled about it. I took the dogmatic feminist position. "It's *her* body. Her right to use it the way she wants to has to start somewhere." God knows, it was all in the abstract—I had never even thought of an abortion. His was the dogmatic Catholic position, abstract too: "But where does the right stop?"

"Easy enough for *you* to ask," I whipped back. "For women, it's never been anything but 'Stop—*get back, get back.*'" Just that phrase—part of an old Jim Crow rhyme that began "*If you are black*"—was like hitting him in his soft civil-rights underbelly. Not that he hadn't thought of the parallels himself. I should have let him off when he looked rueful and didn't give me a quick comeback, but once I had made it to hot, I couldn't cool down—you didn't do as much as I did day after day on five or six hours of sleep a night and not lose it sometimes. "See *this*?" I said—meaning everything, the kids, the house, the job—the whole *schmeer*, as he would have said. And I was on my feet, flinging my arm out over the tops of the kids' heads as if I could have flung it across the room. "*This* is the only thing that doesn't stop." Nina sat cowering in the high chair, her eyes jelly rolls, the boys ducking in mid-bite—they knew that warning arm. "Are *you* going to tell *me* what my rights are? To tell *women*? Jesus Christ, isn't it enough we leave it now for corporate hucksters to tell us—to *sell* us—never mind the Holy Mother bloody Church?"

One argument wasn't enough.

When I turned my back on him in bed that night, he said, "Is this what it means to be a feminist?" I threw a hard glare back over my shoulder, but the moment he had my eye, he said, "Never go to sleep on your wrath." Another principle. "St. Paul?" I said. He grinned, that impudent, satirical twisted grin of his. "Dickens?" he said. And I kissed him.

It was probably the only subject on which I taught him anything.

"You have to hear this," he announced, coming home one Sunday just after New Year, fresh from a streak of masses celebrating the feast of the Holy Family. "The last mass," he began, setting up the story. "I think I'm doing OK explaining what the hell it all means—Man, Woman, Child—but trying to see it from poor Mary's perspective—a woman with a kid . . . *you* know." I knew he was telling me how proud he was of what he knew now, what we had made it possible for him to think, to *speak*, even if he had to suppress the source. "So afterward, comes all the folks out of the church, thanking me for my precious poils of wisdom . . ."

"Yeah?"

"And comes this bent up little old Irishwoman, reminds me a little of my Mammy, wily little eyes fixed on me like gun barrels, and she leans into me and she sez . . ."

"Yeah?"

"And she leans into me and she sez, through her teeth, '*Her*, with her *one*.'"

Me, with my three, I revamped the apartment, witnessing my schizoid convictions by moving the kids into the living room and making their little bedroom into a kind of den for me: a Big Room of Their Own, a Little Room of My Own. So much for the coordinates of time and space on the west side of the Hudson.

Harry, meanwhile, was ushering in the New Age on West 90th Street, covered, physics and metaphysics, with a houseful of resident graduate students. It was agreed: no more plywood table with dropcloth for saying mass—the priest facing the people was here to stay. They moved the two-ton marble altar away from the wall where it had remained, unused for years, in quiet defiance of Vatican II. They restored the pipe organ, one of the finest in the city, and had the murals depicting the life of St. Gregory the Great retouched. They began to dismantle the eyesore clutter of devotional statuary around the church. Cries of pain arose from be-rosaried devotees. The parish committee reconsidered.

"OK, Christopher goes. Infant Jesus stays."

"We keep 'the Little Flower,' with the roses"—Saint Thérèse. "But no angels." These were two huger-than-life, resplendently painted plaster creatures. Their huge wingspans hovered like the Annunciate Gabriel's, fingertips barely, shyly, crossed on their uncertain breasts.

"Never. The angels stay."

They quarreled, they compromised. They left one angel to cast its unisex and gloriously fringed ghostly shadow on the freshly painted cream-color wall of the nave. The other would have to mutter God upon the benched parishioners in the off-street lobby.

They agreed to put scriptural texts over the three great ceremonial exit arches. The center one, a semi-gag-line, read, "Oh, Men of Galilee, why are you looking up?" Only it galled Harry, later, that they hadn't translated it *"People* of Galilee."

Eric Niemann, an accomplished local sculptor, constructed a four-story polyurethane relief of St. Gregory the Great, to be mounted onto the outer wall of the church building, over the urban-renewal playground. Viewed from Columbus Avenue, once it was seamed and painted, you couldn't tell it wasn't as solid as Mount Rushmore. Years later, huge chunks of it blew off in a great wind, and it was judged a hazard and removed. Oh, but *then*, it looked splendid. They threw a block party the day it was dedicated. Harry brought home a little wall hanging that night, woven for him by a nun friend—he didn't dare call her a "nunny-bunny" anymore, not in *my* hearing. It said "Celebrate Life by Living," a message he—we—loved to live by.

But it would have been truer to say Harry celebrated by celebrating, with a genius for liturgy revived, perhaps, out of the rush he got from the stage door at C.U. Especially the Easter liturgy, surely what he'd been scheming the April night Nina was born. Good Friday through Easter Sunday at St. Gregory's deserved advance billing as a New York theater weekend. They dramatized the Passion, Friday, by walking the streets with the cross. At services that night, the priest would take the symbolic flaming candle, burning in a well-lit church, and plunge it sizzling into water as the church went suddenly, blindly dark. Afterward, descending to the basement, they enacted a true watch of the faithful, drinking coffee and bearing personal witness to the universal spiraling Apocalypse—women's rights, civil rights, the burning cities, the Irish Troubles, Vietnam—going, resisting—some drifting in late and agonizing till dawn, others half listening, dozing in their benches, till it all flickered and buzzed like a movie and the coffee was scorched in the urn. A little sleep for the hard core, and then back Saturday, to take turns inflating a thousand balloons printed *"Alleluia!"* filling the auditorium with great bunches of them, readied for release at the curb in colorful defiance of the horse manure, in glorious celebration of life, after the last mass. Ninetieth Street on a sunny Easter morning must have rivaled the Easter parade, with hundreds and hundreds of *"Alleluias!"*

sailing up and over the wires, over the lampposts, over the tenement roofs, into the blueprint sky.

It was a glorious sight I never saw. But how brilliantly, in what fresh swift strokes Harry could tell it, and with an eye for what could make us laugh. One of those Easter weekends in the middle of his thousand days, in the sacred dark before dawn of a Holy Saturday night, he sneaked out of the rectory with a dozen of those balloon strings spooled round his fingers like spaghetti on the tines of a fork, and sped to Ridgefield. And there in our new living-room nursery, where his own lay sleeping like three Easter eggs in a nest, he tied the strings carefully to their beds and went away. Three little born-again Brownes would learn the word *"Alleluia!"* on Sunday morning, even if he couldn't be there to teach it to them himself.

Legend has it that at one of those well-attended St. Gregory's intellectual salons—a *primo piatto* of linguine with clam sauce, perhaps, a few chickens roasted with rosemary, a good Veneto white—Harry, a bit drunk, a bit maudlin, a bit conscious that *this* would someday all be history, handed around a crayon and had each guest inscribe his name on the tablecloth. Then he gave the cloth to the Altar Society, its women still skilled in the art of fine embroidery, and had them sew the scrawled names permanently into the heavy clerical linen.

I have never seen the cloth with magic in its web. Some legendarians have wondered whether it survived. Harry may have told me who was there that night, but I have not remembered—perhaps a distinguished company, for Church circles. Or maybe it wasn't the celebrated he celebrated that night. Maybe it was just the usual-unusual guys, the semi-celebrated and soon to be celebrated and never to be celebrated. They seemed to want to celebrate him back. Now, in 1969, in the year of his twenty-fifth anniversary as a priest, they had their chance.

I've heard it recalled as the bash of the decade, a thousand people at a high price a plate for those days. Mayor Lindsay, former Mayor Wagner, a glittering crowd, well-fed, well-watered. They roasted and toasted him. He gave it back—oh, how he could. An event the newspeople came out for, glad to have a crowd of nabobs enmassed, happy to display for a New York minute his light-splitting eyes and the shining white of his hair, and have the brilliant black and white of a Roman collar dance on a million television screens.

Even my mother's joy erupted at seeing him. She couldn't help herself—she called me up to say so. Daddy was in California, she said, planning their retirement to the Sun Belt, following Lou. You know how it is, when you see somebody you know on television—and better, even, when it is somebody you . . . well . . . love, yes, she *loved* him, she didn't care what anybody thought any more, she knew my father loved him too, just couldn't let himself . . . "Oh, he looked so *great*, that was so *nice*, what they did—"

What did they do?

"You didn't see him?"

I caught a twenty-second replay on the eleven o'clock news. And then I lay back on my bed and cried.

I had still imagined he told me everything—everything that mattered, some things that didn't. I had still somehow imagined I was the reason for his joy in his celebrity, that it was nothing if I didn't see it, if he couldn't, somehow, see me seeing it.

I had thought there was no risk he would take without calculating it with me. I thought there was nothing he would exclude me from without my sharing the decision to be excluded.

It was like looking into a mirror and not seeing my own face. Someone once said that about losing God. For me, the God I must have been losing for years abruptly died.

I had already been having fainting spells. I was toxic, my doctor said, from one flu after another, never getting enough rest to recover. I couldn't eat. My stomach hurt, and the hurt girdled the middle of my body, back to front. "Ulcer," the doctor told me by phone when the results of the GI series came back. It was my thirty-fourth birthday; Carl was there, Harry. I leaned against the kitchen doorway and wept.

The doctor had me in again, sat me down gently, looked at me with a tender urgency, knowing a victim when he saw one. "What has that man been doing to you?" There was something wolflike, predatory, in his tone. *That man?* He knew Harry was somebody—amazingly, nothing else. I saw *this* man, sitting here, handsome, kindly, manipulative. I searched his eyes, responded to him with a queer shiver of wayward involuntary desire, that burst into a fire of outrage and flash-froze again. I thought like a madwoman: *I have something to keep from Harry now.*

And Harry, full of sorrow that he had hurt me, took us to the Outer Banks— the first time since Bim was tiny, and he wasn't tiny anymore, he had already started school—and I sunned and swam all day and forgot what the doctor had said, washed it out in the salt sea of Harry's passion. But when we came home, and Harry went away again, I forgot that I had forgotten, and this sinister desire stuck to me like a thorn, a tooth, raced through me like a drug.

I can still smell the rank smell of the marigolds on the doctor's walk that night, still feel the tremulous swish of the silk dress I wore, the same my mother had made me for my sister's wedding. It rained, not heavily, just a wetness, a gelatinous wetness, like slime, on the roadways. Driving about, later, unable, unwilling to turn the car homeward, I stopped beside a park, and put my head down on the steering wheel and sobbed. It was the pit of the night. Time passed. Nothing changed. I thought of Debbie, home with the babies, me out of reach.

I didn't even wait to see Harry again. Now, I said, when we spoke. Now. Give it all up and come to me.

Or don't come to me anymore.

8

When I next saw his ravaged face, my heart nearly broke through my chest. But I had crossed over. To my amazement, so had he. "I'm ready," he said.

I couldn't bear it. "Don't do this," I said. "Stay. There's work for you to do."

"It's about time," he said, and again, "I'm ready."

It must have been not long after this that the FBI showed up at the green door with the mug shot and flashed it at Mrs. Halle. Both Fathers Berrigan, Dan and Phil, were on the run then, after exhausting federal appeals against their conviction for publicly burning Catonsville, Maryland, draft records in 1968. Mrs. Halle described to me as best she could the face the two trench-coat types had shown her: a thin, dark man with heavy eyebrows, looked a little bit Jewish.

Harry laughed when I passed it on. "That'll be Dan, all right." We were side by side in bed in the dark. He was leaning on his hand, and the light from the driveway lamppost fell through the blinds in faint blue stripes on his face. His eyebrows looked wickedly black and wing-tipped.

"Why would they be looking for him here?"

"They're looking for him everywhere."

From Catonsville onward, Dan had stood squarely defiant of a guilty government. He'd used the tart irony of apologizing for "the burning of paper instead of children" to evoke the horrific news images of naked and napalmed Vietnamese that only the most hardened supporters of the war could possibly erase them from their minds. Then he'd refused to accept punishment, agreeing like all the so-called Catonsville Nine with the lone woman among them, Mary Moylan, that it would constitute another kind of complicity to be marching off to jail "with smiles on their faces." Somebody said J. Edgar Hoover, possessed with seventy-seven-times-seven demons, had at least two hundred men out to get them.

That meant they were on to Harry's captain's paradise. We looked at each other, very hard. If we were going to play this out rationally, if he were going to see the school year through, find work, bring the right moment to leave into focus, now was the time to become more circumspect, not less.

"What have I got to lose?" he said, smiling, a very wet smile.

"Not me," I smiled back, sinking my face into the hair on his chest. "Not me. Not ever."

I had been turning Fiona Macleod into a book, and had a small travel grant to go to Scotland for the last bits of research in August. Harry would cover at home. "Family business," he announced to his 90th Street commune. He put Tom Farrelly in charge and disappeared, and for two and a half weeks in late August, early September, as the weather turned 'round, he took on the house and the kids, the laundry and the marketing and the cooking, woke up alone and trembling to the kid sounds in the middle of the night, often after he'd gone to sleep on the couch in the den, and then dragged himself to bed worrying about the things he'd forgotten, and the things he'd like to forget.

Uncle Carl, visiting, caught him down on his knees in his shorts, scrubbing the kitchen floor. "Great legs," he joked.

"I'm off after six," Harry shot back. "Bring money."

In his spare time—how did he always somehow manage to have spare time?—he started drafting a eulogy to his 90th Street Camelot he called "Groping for Relevance on the West Side." He asked me to edit it for him when I got home. "Needs an English professor," he said.

About a month later, when I was home and the weather was cool enough for the kids to wear the voguish argyle scarves and sweaters and hats I'd brought back from Scotland, we went to the Palisades to take pictures for my book jacket. I couldn't bear the way I looked when the pictures came back—pale and hollow-eyed, as if my ulcer were still ravening me from the inside. I thought, if only we could put the children instead of me on the jacket, looking like bouquets of chrysanthemums artfully arranged on those beds of dry golden leaves. And Harry—he stands or sits nearby, to their side, at their back, an earnest, solemn, electric presence, looking either straight into the camera or at the children, meekly absorbed in their beauty, his eyes wide open now, no more dark glasses between himself and history.

In the spring he asked Herbert Stember, his academic friend from Strycker's Bay, for adjunct teaching work. Herb, vaguely alarmed, nevertheless offered him a slot in the sociology department he chaired at Rutgers: only a few hours a week and it paid poorly, but it was a beginning. I knew—we knew—that it would take time to reestablish himself, that we could wait a little for the long future because the near time was at hand. Still, the end seemed to hang like a storm that wouldn't break, leaving me scanning the dim sky for signs, able to see only today and the stony earth, the exhausting book, the exhausting job, the exhausting war.

I ached, everybody ached, in our mournful University Heights encampment, where the bizarre calculus of draft lottery numbers came written on our students' faces, children of the largely Jewish bourgeoisie, too trained in filial piety even to grow their hair long. No one could have forced me, even on the rack, to imagine our own sons grown to draft age. How must it have been for him, slipping those frightened children of other mothers, other fathers, past the gates of St. Gregory's and sending them on in the dark? Eating the broken words of accused and condemned war resisters in Chicago, Harrisburg, Baltimore as part of his daily bread?

I knew enough not to ask him to tell me anything now. I knew only that everything that meant anything to him, or to me, was at full burn. To stay or to leave, either way, amounted to a mistake that had to be made. Beneath the hurt, and the heartsickness of hope deferred, I trusted him not to fail me either way: by taking too long to leave—by leaving too soon.

•

By April 1970, two of the Catonsville fugitives, Phil Berrigan and his friend Phil Eberhart, were ready to give themselves up. But they wanted to say one last mass, and where else to come but to the Disney of liturgists for the mass to end all masses?

Harry had explained to everybody the plan he'd worked out with the local FBI chief, Tom Walsh, who also happened to be his ex-classmate from the seminary. He'd even brought Walsh in for a preview: a weekday morning mass, an obliging congregation of a few old ladies who had more trouble than Walsh did with the chewy new communion bread. Walsh was very moved by the whole thing. "We'd rather take them beforehand, though, Harry," he persisted, the outer cop quelling the inner spoiled priest.

"Well, Cheez, Tom, don't do that."

"Don't hide them, whatever you do. It'll be harboring, all that crap."

So that was it. They had a deal.

By now St. Gregory's had obliterated all odious class distinctions. On that singular April night, while I was at home grading papers—oblivious to all of this, believe me, until the vivid multimedia versions I got of it later almost convinced me that I'd actually been there—a cohort of rumpled-looking local gang saints stood with their hands in their pockets skulking about the rectory parlor of St. Gregory's People's Republic, waiting for orders. Or they loomed in the corridor like sentries, feet apart, arms folded across their chests.

"Out," Father Tom Farrelly has since told me he told them—Farrelly, whose point of view on this wonderful and rather complicated story has always seemed to me more surrogate for my own than that of Harry himself. "You're making this thing look like a rumble."

Because of the queer fourth-floor geography of the rectory he had to lead them out down several flights of Tower of London stairs. Outside, he said, under the new planet-sized, crime-buster sodium vapor lamps they'd just installed, it was a circus: young hoods milling around everywhere, sidewalks, tenement stoops, areaways. Two FBI agents in standard trench coats and fedoras sat in a parked Chevrolet across the street. It was just then that Harry's dirty white Volkswagen hatchback turned into 90th Street—probably just back from New Jersey. When he got out, he and Tom slipped behind the street door, in the shadow of the angel's wings.

"*FBI*," Tom muttered. "I just got rid of the gang upstairs. There's a plot afoot."

"Fucking lollipop revolutionaries. Born yesterday and they got the nerve to say the system doesn't work. It took me ten years to find that out."

As the rattling elevator got them to the rectory floor, a recent graduate-student recruit, Father Phil Murnion, leaned out his room door. "Harry. There are two Jebbies waiting for you in there." "Jebbie" was priest-speak for Jesuit. "In there" meant the pastor's suite, which Harry always pronounced "*sweeeeet*," as if it were something faintly disreputable. He disappeared into it.

Rumor had it by this time that the Jesuits were going to try getting Father Berrigan out before he gave himself up. Mike Drohan, rectory security guard, was pissing mad when he heard about it: "How could they *do* this to Harry?"

Tom thought nobody would try anything that stupid. "The Feds are just panting for somebody to make a false move. They're probably hoping Dan is gonna show up." Anyway, he thought, Phil Berrigan would never go along with it. Or would he? And what about Harry?

Nobody knew about Harry.

Farrelly says he crashed about four in the morning. Whenever it was the two fugitives arrived, he missed it.

Both Harry and Tom were up early the next morning. The place was a madhouse, as if the Second Coming were here. Harry grumbled, meeting Tom in the kitchen. "Y'know what those Jebbies said? *Just have your housekeeper fix us a hamburger or something.'* I says, 'Sorry. We don't have a housekeeper.' *Man,* comes the Revolution . . ."

Tom was trying not to sound too nosy or too cynical. "D'ya know what's up?"

"Bullshit. That's what's up. Horseshit down, bullshit up. Would you believe they're in there writing their Revolutionary Manifesto? Don't get me wrong," he added, grabbing up an armload of food that looked tricky for a guy in flip-flops. "I'll be the first to yell '*miracolo*' when they get beatified."

Tom says he watched Harry fly past the chandeliers and the Tiffany lamps and the Renaissance art in heavy gilt frames and the bronze Joan of Arc and disappear down the hall and into his room again; until he was out of sight you could, as always, almost see the white of his boxer shorts through the threadbare seat of his black pants. Tom could hear the key turn in the lock, snatches of conversation—something about fucking *dynamite,* would you believe it? He was about to knock on the stained glass when Drohan suddenly announced the arrival of "*Fe-li-pe Lu-ci-ano*—the guy with the street smarts." He said the "Jebbies" had asked him to come up.

Luciano was outfitted like a Young Lord: fatigues, a black beret. He gave Father Tom a deferential bow—"Tey aks me to tek a lookaroun." Tom hesitated to cashier him without Harry's OK. "Keep it cool" was all he said. He gave Drohan a sign—*Watch this guy*—as Luciano and Drohan started down the mazy hallway to the back.

The fire-escape door banged shut and Drohan came back alone, smirking. "He's checking out the escape route."

"You think this is funny?"

"I told the little prick he wouldn't dare."

Tom pictured to himself the serried spears of the cast-iron paling along the backyard property line. "Berrigan tries going over that fence, we'll be singing the Mass of the Faithful Departed tonight."

Luciano reappeared. "Te door downstairs, she's open, right?"

"At this hour, I guess."

"I let mysel' out," he said obligingly, shooting Father Farrelly a military salute and a grinning barricade of teeth.

The house grew relatively quiet as they readied handouts for the special liturgy at six, explaining what it was all about, ecumenical service—a little offbeat maybe—

a Baptist choir in the choirloft. Tom couldn't hold back a chuckle or two as he turned out the pastoral message on the mimeo—all this "healing ceremony" stuff. Them as is already convinced won't need it. Them as isn't won't want it. He could already hear Drohan on the other side of the wall fielding the sicko phone calls: the hawks were going to be out en masse.

Still no word from the pastor's suite. Could he possibly get Harry alone? He slipped down the hall to eavesdrop again and heard muffled talk and doors opening and closing. He knocked lightly. "Need anything in there?" A voice, not Harry's, came back: "No, thanks, we're OK." He felt a little annoyed that Harry was keeping him in the dark like this, but he thought he understood why he might think he had to. Monitoring the street from his window again, he noticed the FBI Chevrolet was gone. What he didn't know, as he pulled down the shade and fell heavily into bed for a nap, was that Felipe Luciano, minutes before, had stepped out onto the ornately carved balcony just below him on the third floor, and had stood there—in full view of the FBI—shielding his eyes and cocking his black beret and looking around for signs. The way a guy does when he is street smart.

When the tooth-drilling sound of the intercom buzzer woke him, it was 4 P.M.

"FBI, Father Tom. They want up."

"Where's the pastor?"

"Still in his room. No calls. Doesn't wanna have to say anything to anybody."

"Any sign of Father Berrigan?"

A pause. "I haven't seen him yet."

"Let the Man up."

"There seems to be quite a few of 'em."

Tom looked out the window again. He didn't know that a couple of windows away, Harry was doing the same thing, and having the same reaction: *sons of bitches*. The street was swarming with cop cars. One screeched to a stop right in front of the church and all four doors opened at once. *That really happens*, Tom caught himself thinking.

Out, quick, past Joan of Arc and into the corridor. Father Murnion was suddenly there too. The first squad of trench-coated G-men stepped off the elevator. In reverence to the two priests, one, two, three, four fedoras were lifted to a silent beat above four well-groomed heads. Mike shut the gate and started down again.

They came four at a time in nine more waves. The rectory swam with them. They checked walls, poked ceilings, pounded wall paneling for secret priest-holes. The layout made for a perfect safe house—sealed staircases, blind walls—anyone who'd ever touched a nail to it seemed to have had afterthoughts. The swarming agents opened pantry closets and yanked table linens out of the carved presses in the dining room. They split into twos and threes and fanned out, slamming doors, bamming dresser drawers, flushing toilets, following each other up the spiral staircase, banging about the warren of little rooms in the penthouse with their hard leather cop shoes.

There was no talking over the din. Farrelly and Murnion watched as several G-men paused for a conference at the bronze Joan of Arc, whose profile seemed to stare off in speechless contempt. The men broke and dispersed along the corridor, jiggling doorhandles.

Only Harry's refused to yield. "That's the pastor's *sweeeet*," said Tom, helpfully. "Is he in?" Tom nodded yes. "Is anybody with him?"

"A couple of visiting Jesuit friends as far as I know."

"Why isn't he answering?"

"Your guess is as good as mine." The absolute truth.

The detective just stood there, staring at the door, with his hands shoved into his pockets and his jaw working. He was the only one not in a trench coat. He wore a light parka, the kind an ordinary family man might wear to the supermarket.

Two men suddenly started into Farrelly's room, checking under his bed and groping the walls. They opened his closet and a broken rod fell off its precarious hitch and tumbled clothes all over the floor. "Sorry, Father," the two said sheepishly, undoing themselves. "We'll fix it for ya, Father." They lifted the garments one by one and laid them neatly on the bed, went out for tools, came back, disappeared inside the closet together— *"Excuse us, Father"*—struggled with the repair for a minute or two, carefully removed the clothes from the bed and rehung them, and scuttled out like a pair of penitent ex-altar boys, which was probably, Tom thought, what they were.

There was the long belch of the door buzzer again. Just before Drohan closed the elevator, he caught Tom's eye and soundlessly mouthed the name *"Gra-dy."* When the elevator gates rattled again, out stepped the seedy little figure of John Peter, his leprechaun Irish face beaming as if he had found his potted rainbow. He had made it to Berrigan camp follower now, tattered tweeds, pink, unshaven face, twinkling blue eyes, just what the movement needed. He treated Tom to his whooping laugh the minute he laid eyes on him. "How's it *gooo*-in, *Faaather?*"

G-men filled the hallway like a crowded subway car. Grady innocently held up the package he was carrying, brown paper, no bigger than a bread bag. The bookkeeper had just come in, and she and Murnion were peering from behind the office door, mouths open in disbelief. Out of Grady's bag stuck what looked like the curved handles of a pair of wire shears called bullcutters. *"John,"* said Tom, as calmly as possible, raising his hand and trying to stare Grady's dancing blue eyes to attention. "Allow me to introduce you to Eliot Ness."

"Ain't these just the thing for the back fence, *Faaather?*"

"John. *Ahem,* John Peter Grady," Tom said again, repressing the urge to throttle him. "My *son.* Meet J. Edgar Hoover." Grady was happy to make their acquaintance. Two of the detectives were happy to make his. They clapped their hands on his arms and took away the cutters. Then they scuttled him to the parlor where they frisked him top to bottom and pushed his bony little body into a deep green sofa.

Father Doherty, an assistant, came in, and another student, Phil Murphy:

everybody formed a nervous little scrimmage, everybody's question the same: *Is Berrigan here?* Is Harry hiding him after all? The door buzzer again. A stir, a hush among the massed detectives; Mike Drohan rattled the gates and went down, came up. A thump, a whine, a slide, a rattle. Out stepped Walsh, the chief inspector, removing his hat, saying something to Farrelly that deferentially ended in "Father," moving off to the staging area in front of Joan of Arc.

Debriefed, he started down the hallway to Harry's room, and knocked, firmly but politely. Waited. Knocked again, harder. Still no answer. "Listen, Har— *Father*." He had the slightly raised, middle register voice of someone used to giving orders. "It's Walsh. We know you're in there. Open up or we'll have to break down the door."

Catching Farrelly's eye somewhere between panic and hysteria, Murnion whispered, "*I'll bet he's not kidding.*"

"I'm not kidding, Harry," said Walsh. "Unlock this door, or we'll have to kick it in."

When *he* told the story, Harry said this was the moment he'd thought, "When in doubt, go to bed." And leaving the two Jesuits in the suite sitting room, he'd taken off his shoes, locked his bedroom door, and stretched out.

When he heard the crash of the outer door he was furious—all he could see was the red of a broken deal. He shouted: "*You CAN'T come in here. You've got no WARRANT!*" But he could hear the bangs and thumps in the sitting room on the other side of his door and picture a detective fishing under a couch cushion and coming up with a *Dynamite and Its Uses* manual.

"*Where's Father Browne?*" That was Walsh.

Now it was bam, bam, on his bedroom door.

"*NO WARRANT, NO ENTRY,*" Harry shouted again, with the stubbornness of the Hell's Kitchen kid playing King of the Mountain.

"*Please*, Father," some altar-boy detective said. It was poignant.

And then he picked up the phone and called me, just as a big shoulder heaved into the door. Once. Twice. You could almost feel the demolition-ball weight of a big foot against the lock.

I heard a wavering Harry voice, a voice of love and anger and sorrow, and then a thud, the sound of the voice trailing away and the receiver crashing—

The door thrashed wide open, a few feet from the bed. Harry dropped the phone and bolted up. "*I AM THE PASTOR!*" he boomed. He later wished he'd said it in Latin. He later wished he'd taken off his pants, so the altar boys would've hung back, seeing a priest in his shorts, and given him more time to think.

One of them said, "Where's Father Brannigan?" Harry couldn't believe it. "*Who?*" They were staring at his T-shirt, with the tearhole in the middle of the chest.

Walsh came in behind them. "Sorry, Harry," he said stupidly.

"Where's your search warrant?" Harry repeated, but Walsh ignored him, and the men went about the business of thrashing around the room and stirring things up in the closet and checking under the bed. Somebody righted the telephone.

"Sounds like a hollow wall."

"All these lousy walls sound hollow."

Harry was almost in tears. "Why are you guys doing this?" he demanded. "We had a deal."

Walsh said nothing and turned back into the sitting room. Harry followed him, pleading. "You got no right, dammit!" Walsh silently gave him his back and went out. The two Jesuits Harry'd been joking with less than an hour before looked crushed. He saw his own face in theirs.

The search went on. Somebody was looking under the bed for the third, maybe the fourth time. "Hey, check under the desk," Harry said. "Nobody's checked under the desk yet." But he was crying. At least nobody's raised a weapon, he thought. He wished he felt grateful.

One by one, the detectives began to follow Walsh out, down the hall. You could hear the zesty clack of the gates as Drohan bustled again into elevator action. Farrelly and Doherty and Murnion all appeared at the suite door, hanging loose on its hinges, the leaded glass shattered. Harry, arms folded over his chest, was fixing each retreating G-man with the terrible eye of the Last Judgment. He wasn't going to waste this stuff about looking like God. Every one of the men tipped their hats and said, *"Sorry, Father. Excuse me, Father,"* as they went by him.

Somebody was still bumping luggage and thumping walls in the bedroom closet. When he came out, Tom Farrelly saw it was the guy he'd noticed before, in the jacket. "C'mon, Frank," somebody said. But Frank was still staring down the bedroom wall. "Wait up," he called, and he began to pace off the length of the wall between the closet and the doorway.

"Hey, let's go, Frank."

But Frank was into the hallway linen closet now, pacing it off. He shouted for his friend to come back. He dragged a chair into Harry's bedroom closet and stepped onto it to look over the edge of the panelled frame. Harry was pushing his right hand through his Godlike mane of white hair. When his eyes met Farrelly's, they said, *Yes.*

"I'll be damned," said Frank.

They dragged the two fugitive priests, dark-blinded and stumbling, out of their hole and into the room. Harry was weeping shamelessly. Tom felt a buzz in his ears and a terrible pain in his chest. Father Berrigan just stood there, the waning afternoon light falling on his hands as they clicked the handcuffs over his wrists, that improbable longshoreman's face of his, too craggy for a saint, wearing the look of a man used to capture. *"In the name of Christ, in the name of Christ,"* Harry kept saying, through his tears. *"You cannot do this to this man."*

Then Father Eberhart was handcuffed, and they pushed the two captives into the sitting room, up against the wall, alongside the bronze Joan of Arc. "Peace, man," Eberhart was saying. "All we want is peace, right? We can't go on making war in the name of Christ, can we? C'mon, man, can we?"

They took Eberhart away first. "Peace, brothers!" he flung back. Berrigan was next. He caught Farrelly's eye. "Take it easy, Tom."

The rectory grew suddenly, unbearably silent. The next sound they heard was the clatter of Harry cleaning the ashtrays. "Fuck," he was saying. "Fuck. *Fuck.* FUCK." Tom looked at his watch. He couldn't believe it—the whole thing had taken about forty minutes.

Cleaning up, they found the battered paper bag with the bullcutters in the kitchen. The resident art experts noted that they bore an intriguing resemblance to the Christian *icthyos,* suitable for framing, so they drove a couple of nails into the wall and hung them up as a memento. Harry called for something to drink, and they all went back to his suite sitting room. It seemed to have become sacred space.

Outside the window, down on the dusky street, the defeated troops gathered. They were holding arms, and chanting, over and over again: *"All we are say-ing, is give peace a chance."* Phil Murnion picked up a stray piece of stained glass from the broken door. "Relic, anyone?"

The liturgy went off as planned.

Or not exactly as planned. By five-thirty, the street was already massed with people stepping gingerly over the horse droppings. They were swayed both ways by anger, the doves furious that Father Berrigan had been betrayed, that they would never get to see him, the embittered, hawkish parishioners outraged that their church, *their* church, should be used for such traitorous shenanigans. Big, blowsy Mrs. Durante, whose kid Harry had got out of jail, whose husband owed him a job, whose family lived in low-rent priority housing thanks to Father Browne's sign-off, was leading the crowd around in picket circles, chanting, *"Give us back our church!"*

The 24th Precinct had obligingly sent a couple of squad cars and some DO NOT CROSS police barriers for the end of the street. They were even rerouting the horse traffic. Inside the church was everybody on the West Side owning up to a drop of political hemoglobin. Esta was there—yes, screw Haight-Ashbury—thrilled she'd had the good sense to come back to New York in time. She kept jumping up out of her seat and marching out to sidewalk face-offs with Mrs. Durante. Doris Rosenblum, Strycker's Bay's president, half-sat, half-stood in a front pew alongside Pete, her chunky lookalike husband, her excitable heart thump-thumping inside her mini-body. Things hadn't even started yet and the tears were already streaming down her face. Not far away was Sondra Thomas, a veteran of the fight to save the building known simply as 325 Central Park West; Lynn Shea, Strycker's Bay director, next to her, her wicked sense of humor in her searchlight eyes; historian Howard Zinn from Boston, readying to speak; Ruth Messinger from the FDR–Woodrow Wilson Club; Paul O'Dwyer beside her. There were Matty and Jean

Forbes, who thought sitting Father Browne at the right hand of God would have been an insult to Father Browne.

It was a multiple concelebration, the altar jammed with priests. Two empty chairs were set for the two fallen comrades. Father Browne rose to the pulpit. Over the raucous shouts at the church door he begged for calm and conciliation. He said that this had been a moral victory for the peace movement. "Of course you always say that when you lose," he added. He had them laughing through their tears.

He paid a few bone-dry respects to his friends in the FBI. Maybe he *did* say "*Fucking FBI*," he couldn't remember for sure. He remembered he said "Pray for them."

Rev'rend Kirk, the Reverend Frederick Douglass Kirkpatrick of the *Hey, Brother!* Coffeehouse, now a regular fixture of St. Gregory's basement, came out for the communion hymn with his guitar, wearing a radiant blue dashiki. He never looked more massive or more gorgeous as he bellowed out a roaring, church-rocking rendition of "We Shall Overcome" you could have heard from the 96th Street crosstown. Nobody refused communion, Catholic, Protestant, Jew, Muslim, nobody, and nobody *was* refused. They emptied the pews and filled the aisles and kept coming so fast and so long, Farrelly joked over his shoulder that he thought they were coming back for seconds. The priests hardly had time to get refills. They kept passing one another at the foot of the altar seeing that same awed mix of sweat and mystical mist on each other's faces. "Phil," Harry half-pleaded to Murnion, resident theologian, "I just gave communion to a Jew." "That's OK, Harry," Murnion said, "Christ gave it to at least eleven of 'em."

Fred Johnson, Presbyterian social worker, said afterward that he'd watched the mysteriously choreographed events at the altar with the feeling he was actually levitating. Berrigan's capture had enraged him, brought him as close to murderous thoughts as he'd ever let himself get. But now he thought he could let go of his indignation, let it be beautiful—let the brilliant lights transfigure these men and women beyond the ordinary people he knew them to be. What a powerful feeling! "*God,*" he kept saying. "*God. God.*"

The recessional began. Eight white-and-gold-robed priests flowed out from the altar, the whole church awash in the body-filling milky harmonies of the gospel chorus. Fred felt his face glow with something close to rapture as the saints went marching by him, two by two. Harry was bringing up the rear on his side, and their eyes met and locked, igniting some old flashpoint of joyous insanity between them. Something was bubbling to Harry's lips—Fred could see it the second Harry's hand lighted on his shoulder and his face leaned toward his ear. "*Did you—*"

Fred would remember the words forever.

"*Did you catch the boobs on the one in the chorus?*"

Se non e vero, e ben trovato.

But the story *is* true, as true as true can be.

And so is the story history will never believe, the one that says he was called down to the chancery six weeks later—*six weeks,* mind you—because, somebody (said somebody—somebody speaking for the cardinal—not even the cardinal, but *speaking* for the cardinal), "*Some*body," said somebody, "said *some*body in the church said *fuck*."

But is this my story that is his? Or his story that is mine? Strange how they reconverge at their farthest parting, when my Boswell eye bore no witness and my Boswell ear heard nothing more than a faraway chorus of angry voices and the clatter of a hung-up telephone.

Had it not been for the retellings time and again, how could I have told it? But Harry told it, at CCUM meetings, board and plenary, year after year, when the shouts came up, "*Tell us again about the Berrigan Bust, Harry,*" and he did. He told it at banquets, he told it at wakes, he told it at rap sessions of the Priests' Senate, he told it when Phil Berrigan's peace-activist comrade, later his wife, Liz McAlister, came to our house in Paterson, and the friends and the food were so fine, and the wine so flowing, and the noise so howling and joyfully crashing and thumping that the kids didn't bother going to bed and fell asleep under the table.

And others told it. Some, like Tom Farrelly, told it brilliantly, with that memory for poignant details that Harry couldn't have seen, and some he wouldn't have remembered if he had. But Farrelly also told it with a sense for the tragedy of the thing Harry couldn't let himself feel—a sense of the terrible knowledge of the sundering that came after, the knowledge of the tree in the garden, and the choice between goods and evils. And the knowledge that he, Tom Farrelly, journeyman to the Browne-master, would stay on, but that the master himself would go.

But the story also got repeated by people who had only heard it and were passing it on, and by people who had never heard it at all but who were pretending they had, and by would-be historians who itched to be the first print purveyors of the legend—or pooh-poohers of it. So there are as many versions of it as there are versions of it, and Harry used to love—I suppose as you might love pulling a splinter out of your fingernail—to point out that not one of the versions in print had the true facts except his own.

And seeing as the principal himself was also its historian and gave us (as Harry would have said) the *verba ipsissima* on the pages of *Cross Currents,* Hansard of the Catholic Left in those times, you'd wonder, wouldn't you, why the purveyors and plunderers and pundits and pooh-poohers of the legend couldn't go back and check it.

Is it because the fiction that Father Browne was called instantly down to the chancery and summarily sacked is so much more credible that the truth? So much more consistent with the mythology about cardinals and powers and parish priests? What storyteller who wasn't inside the clerical skin could make us believe that Cardinal Cooke actually took six weeks to respond to complaints about that tumultuous night at St. Gregory's?—complaints that hadn't come from the FBI or from Father Browne's West Side political enemies or from some punctilious monsignor who thought this *scandale* absolutely the last wound a savage black sheep of a priest named Browne should be allowed to inflict upon the majesty of the

Archdiocese, but from Father Browne's own parishioners, who'd thought the sanctity of the temple had been violated by the pronunciation of a common obscenity from the pulpit.

And who could make us believe the true fact that Terence Cardinal Cooke didn't sack him or even threaten him with sacking, but asked Harry what it was he wished to do, and Harry said, *"Your Eminence, I should like to leave. I have been planning it."*

Of course, that was probably after Terence Cardinal Cooke—referred to endearingly by fellow seminarians like Harry Browne as "Cookie"—reminded Harry Browne that J. Edgar now had a file on him, and knew quite well, and had so discreetly informed the discreet informers of His Eminence, that Harry Browne was making certain unscheduled pastoral visits to a certain 703A Shaler Boulevard in— *"Richfield,* is it, Harry?"

And then, when Harry said he'd like to leave, he'd been planning to leave, Cooke said, "Are you sure? We can still use you, Harry."

And Harry said yes, he was sure.

"When do you think that might be?"

"How about September? Academic year and all that."

"September is fine."

"And you will let me tell my own parishioners?"

"Of course. In any case, it will cause the least scandal." Ah, that Vatican *bella figura.*

Part Six

CAVALLERIA RUSTICANA

1

By June of 1970, the massacre at Kent State had handed academics like me a rather sickeningly easy way to stand up and be counted against the war: by honoring the end-of-term boycotts activist students were mounting in protest across the country and not giving exams, not turning in grades. Under the circumstances, you might be glad you didn't own a house—or owe the bank that owned it—lest the security riding on twenty or thirty years of future income put a different slant on taking a stand. As Groucho-Marxist Harry Browne was fond of pointing out, "a mortgage doth make cowards of us all."

Thankfully, we hadn't yet moved into that lily-livered company—and hopefully, mortgage or no mortgage, we never would. But the quest for a suitable house to seek a loan on was under way nonetheless. It was a quest interesting enough in the abstract for two housing specialists to find bearable. But in the concrete, in the brick and stucco and stoneface and clapboard and shingle, it was unbearable: every Saturday out searching through the Jersey boonies and burbs for a place we could call our own—*we* could call our own—and finding nothing but those "boxes, little boxes/those boxes made of ticky-tacky" Pete Seeger had long ago begged us to renounce, row upon row of them in neighborhood after neighborhood as pretty and green and quiet and lily-white as, well, one another. It made us wonder, did the commitment we were making, with all it might inevitably mean of becoming an archetypal census taker's dream family of three kids and a dog, have to drag with it so many of the other dread symbols of the bushwhazee?

And there was cost. We weren't quite a two-income family yet, and anything New York–oriented along the Hudson was already too pricey. So we were forced westward, out Route 80 or 4, up 23 or 208 and back, usually making six or seven stops a trip, till we were agog from climbing the same wall-to-wall stair-carpeted split-levels again and again, the kids hanging restless and cranky on our arms and legs. Bim would of course conduct the exit interview after each stop, as in: "Mommy, why didn't we like that one?"

There were times, outbound, as we hugged the steep flank of Garrett Mountain along Route 80 in the hazy-bright mornings, that we'd notice the brownstone spires and marble domes of the city of Paterson flashing past, hunkered down all humble-like in the crooked arm of the Passaic River, smokestacks still belching the news of things being made in the U.S.A. And in the dusk, as we hurried back to Ridgefield, we might circle around the mountainside again, when the sunset was just laying a wash of pink on the green-capped City Hall clock tower.

That same June, immediately after my Fiona Macleod book was published, came a delicately worded little note from a certain Konrad Hopkins of Paisley, Scotland, William Sharp's birthplace, telling me how timely the publication was, a recent local stir and a bit of Scottish press and telly having aroused fresh interest in my sub-ject. And back wrote I to thank him, and to say how pleased I am to hear this, and did he feel free to tell me more? Communication progressed, the letters growing ever longer, and within a few months the correspondence had climaxed in a quite favorable review of my book—by William Sharp himself.

Unfortunately, Sharp had been officially dead since 1905, so the review did not seem quite suitable for blurbing. Konrad explained that he had jotted it in auto-matic writing from Sharp's direct dictation. In fact, the handful of local press clip-pings that preceded it had pointed to Konrad himself as the original cause of the Paisley stir, when he'd raised Sharp's spirit in a clamorous seance that the newspapers hinted had done some serious physical damage to the premises.

This was funny, but it was also sad, because I liked the view Sharp took of my hunches about his problematical sex life. Out of his own mouth, *verba ipsissima*, I learned that he had *not* fathered Edith Wingate Rinder's child, whatever that *other* horny professor might think. In fact, he and his wife Elizabeth—didn't at all, you know . . . *Celibate* was the word, yes, were quite, quite celibate. Some people can be, apparently.

After that, Konrad never sent me a letter or a postcard without its little demo message from the spirit world. Olive Schreiner, my darling, author of *The Story of an African Farm* and frequent attendee at the late-nineteenth-century equivalent of New Age love-ins, took time out to tack a very sweet personal greeting to the end of a Konrad note one night whilst passing through Paisley. Oscar Wilde, same. French president General de Gaulle, only recently dead, must have considered it worth a detour en route to de Gaulle paradise, since he was just then listening to Mozart on Konrad's phonograph. When Konrad went on holiday there was always some entertaining spirit awaiting him at the hotel, and during his strenuous sum-mer romp through Eastern Europe I got postcards from places as exotic as Sofia and Budapest filled with spidery little automatic P.S.'s from Melville, Eisenhower, Cole Porter, both Kennedy brothers, Marilyn, and FDR. Budapest seemed to be especially trendy with Americans that season.

The technique was simple, he told me, if I wanted to try it. It would take only pen, paper, a comfortable place, a little time, some patience, and—of course—faith. I might actually have tried, if the exhausting house hunt hadn't still been on, or if I'd been able to muster even one of the requirements after the pen and paper.

The faith part made me particularly nervous. Harry debunked the whole thing with a passion. Yet in his heart he must have known that something mystical and superstitious and Sicilian had drawn me to this outrageous binary "Wilfion" in the first place. Perhaps it had also been what attracted me to Harry himself and, very possibly, him to *me*. Surely there was a familiar bit of both my mother and me in this impalpable busy universe of Konrad's, whose hungry-hearted inhabitants traipsed back and forth across the thin membrane of life. What was automatic writ-ing anyway but a form of prayer, I thought, with a pen instead of a pair of rosary beads? I entertained presences, I always had, even if I didn't believe in them as gods—

presences who visited in dreams, for whom life piled on death was still too little, who made all that ruckus on the other side of silence.

Of course it was not the same spirit worlds that had roared to Harry on the other side of the altar, or the pulpit, or the microphone. But he was losing those, and, who knows, maybe it was something like losing a faith.

The promised final letter to Father Browne's parishioners appeared in the parish bulletin in September on the Seventeenth Sunday after Pentecost. Among all the things it was, it was also the letter of a good historian—in this case, a historian of his own life. It opened with an evocative image of the academic identity he'd left in Washington in 1956, an image as swift, naked, and stinging as that of a cashiered warrior exposing his battle scars. It reminded its readers that when he'd been recalled from a professorship at Catholic University to teach first-year civics, he was "at the time also a priest of the archdiocese of New York."

Also a priest. The phrase had in it something—it had in it much—of that wonderful, characteristic recognition of his own *hubris*. But the revived image of this old loss, this primal punishment, was now as important to the meaning of the loss he was about to undergo as the artist's *pentimento* to the finished skin of paint. It said, "I should have known better: one is never *also* a priest." But the letter went on to say that when he was assigned to residency in St. Gregory's in early 1959, he'd written the cardinal protesting that the move would offer nothing but distraction from his scholarly work in American church history. "I moved in," he added—the *hubris* suddenly slipping to the other foot—"and have been proving that point ever since."

Now he had chosen, "freely and without anyone's coercion," to resume his old professorial role. "I shall remain a priest," he said. No uncertainty there. *Once a priest, always a priest.* "Life goes on," he said. Perhaps he should have written it with emphasis added: "*Life* goes on," so that readers might know it was not mere life, life as distinguished from death, but life piled on life, life lived, lived fully, lived in history, celebrated by living.

But that would have meant telling about *us,* and he was not ready for that yet. There was no uncertainty, but there was still a terrible, almost uncommunicative grief. Other churchmen would have understood it. Some did, or thought they did.

One of them was Monsignor John Tracy Ellis—the Church history mentor and *éminence grise* of his Catholic University days. Insiders called him "Lacy Trellis." So did Harry, with a bawdy delight that was certainly part old love and admiration and part straight Joycean joy at the gratuitous congress of language with the truth. And part small revenge. The monsignor had adored and protected him—once. He had opened to him as to few others the bejeweled private sanctuary of his mind, the vision he'd thrown back like a searchlight over the long, dynamic history of the Church. But discipleship can be pricey—to the disciple. Though nothing was ever spoken between them, Harry knew it had been Ellis who'd given the decisive voice in assuring that his wayward young disciple, too long dragging his wayward young feet on the Hughes biography, would be dragging those young feet back to New York.

They had kept a cordial distance since. Ellis had remained "Tracy" to Harry in letters and in conversations at Church history conferences. Never John, I noticed, though so many men named John had run ahead of Harry's destiny, had stood in that same indecisive masculine relation so acutely divined by the Church as the space between father and brother. When word got to Ellis about St. Gregory's, he sent Harry a pale gray covered offprint of an anti-Vietnam "coming out"—a clerical genre popular at the time. It had been originally delivered as a sermon attacking the "impermissible lies" of the government and sketching a vivid portrait of St. Thomas More, a man Ellis said had "died the King's good servant, but God's first." An interesting thing to send Harry in October 1970, so soon after the Berrigan fiasco. It appeared to assume, as others did, that it was why he'd left St. Gregory's, but perhaps also to imply, *You did well, Harry. You did the right thing.*

But bound into the same packet was another offprint, titled (with typical Ellis preciosity), "Whence Did They Come, These Uncertain Priests of the 1960s?" Another of his cutting-edge *pensées,* this one displaying his receptiveness to change, his generous feel, his sympathy, for the trials of the younger priests whose moral and theological uncertainties were then being surveyed to death. Yet finally, in the end, the stony grit of disappointment: a picture of this same uncertain priest as turncoat, forgetting "the transcendental God" and giving himself to the *immanent* God only, the God of "the streets . . . the market place . . . the inner city." Ellis's punctiliously typed little accompanying note read: "I remembered your father in the Mass I offered this morning." Remembered, presumably, because Harry himself had forgotten—and how many other "fathers" besides?

A message meant to cut straight to Harry's heart. But why not? Why not cut his heart? The Church is, after all, *Mater* and *Magister,* mother *and* teacher, and must correct as well as love. Poor male-mother Ellis. How could he have understood that, both times, Washington and New York, the greatest loss for Harry had been the loss of the scene, the theater, of his priesthood? That *this* loss had nothing to do with Vietnam, or Berrigan, nothing to do with the error of the streets, had nothing of Ellis's "uncertainty" about it. Once a priest, always a priest.

He couldn't really have known, because Harry could not yet tell him just what it was he *had* done well. Couldn't yet tell him that the "impermissible lies" had been his—Harry's—own, that the "King" he'd finally said "God first" to was Ellis's own Male-Mother Church.

Life goes on.

Harry didn't show me his parish letter, either before or after they ran it off on the rectory mimeo. Protecting the privacy of it for him, intuiting the pain of it for me. But soon after, he *did* finally give me that long-worked-on bittersweet memoir of his thousand days at St. Gregory's, "to put into English." Someone once described "Groping for Relevance" as the most readable thing he'd ever seen of Harry's in print. Maybe. Now, I read it and weep. I edited Harry right out of it, and if I can forgive myself at all, it is only because reading it now is like reading it for the first time.

I read it *then* through a wall of grief, the more impenetrable because much of it was my own.

Harry must have sent *his* offprint to John Tracy Ellis at some point, publication *quid pro quo,* and clarified things. Ellis was nothing if not loyal. He mailed an occasional open postcard to us in Paterson after that, just to keep in touch. It was the sort of thing I was bound to collect from our mailbox, containing in the sign-off just that sure bit of totem against contagion I couldn't miss: "Prayerfully, for you and yours." Never a name, never a relation. Simply *yours.*

Yes, we'd bought a big old house in Paterson, finally. "Groping" was probably the first thing to see print that either of us sent out of it—maybe the first since the house had been built, before World War I. I can remember typing a fair copy on that soft mustard-color paper we both used for drafts, up here in the big sunny bay of the front-room study he and I shared then, sitting at the shaky dark oak desk that had once stood in my brothers' old room in New Rochelle, clacking away on an Underwood upright Robert Wilde had passed down to Harry the same way he used to pass down his used cars.

Outside that room, down that long second-floor hallway, were our bedrooms. The smallest of them, at the back—a darkish, odd-shaped thing right at the top of the stairs to the kitchen—had been the maid's room in the bad old days of household slavies, or so we guessed. It began for us as a baby room when Nina was two, the walls pasted all around with the characters from *The House at Pooh Corner* I'd cut out of cardboard and hand-painted. Later, when Nina graduated to the room the two boys had vacated when they moved to the rambling third-story attic, Harry was displaced from the sunny front den to this dark back room, so that he could have a room of his own—a palimpsest, a cave—to pack-rat to overflowing with the textbooks and review copies and old news magazines and journals and clippings and letters and manuscripts and student papers he could never throw away.

It had been a stormy passage to negotiate, this move, a vastish separation of sorts, though in a house so spacious there would always be the "room to be together, room to be alone" he at last defined as the bedrock of happy communal living. I'll bet the phrase must have come to him then, in fact, just as he was cooling his sore at being dispatched to outer darkness, a bit of poetry carried with him when he left our common study. But not until he'd penned a little love poem of sorts and placed it under a golden apple paperweight that had lost its leaf but was still, he promised, "heavy with love." Next to the golden apple sat a ceramic-tile madonna from Greece "for you to put cups on. May they always runneth over." And then he signed off, "Yours for clean tops," with a jaunty X-kiss from a man whose tops would never ever be clean.

But "Groping" had also been our first household trade-off. If I edited it, he promised, he would tear out and dump all the ratty green carpeting from the living room and hallways. I know I got the best of the deal. It must have been the two blazing rosebushes on the driveway that had sold us on this old Queen Anne in the first place—plus the nine pillars on the huge veranda—because otherwise it was a mess. Cheap—on account of the Paterson riots in 1969 that had accelerated white flight from the city—very big and very cheap and a mess, with a skin of tattered sick-green carpeting upstairs and down that barely held an inch-deep sublayer of dust in check. All the grandest rooms on the ground floor had been painted pastel pink—right over the elaborate moldings and woodwork, right over the panelled walls and the coffered ceiling in the dining-room. A huge overhead fluorescent light fixture half filled the living-room ceiling. A gigantic vintage Kelvinator in the kitchen growled like a 747.

This was what my mother saw when she saw it. *Go,* my father had said. *Go.* They had been emptying the New Rochelle house then, about to make the big retirement move to California, feeling—and following—the stupendous mystery of change. Carlo brought her out to Paterson, and she wandered about the rooms holding my hand as if she were afraid she might go through the floors. At last, she stopped on the staircase landing, let go my hand and looked around and fumbled in her bag for a handkerchief, and just stood there and cried.

Life goes on.

Harry worked nights. I came, he went, with a bit of time for changing the guard.

Lashing rain out one afternoon. He meets me at the door; they all do, the kids yelling, "*Mommy!*" "Quiet," to them. To me, "Walk this way, as the bowlegged floor-walker said."

I am giggling the line about talcum powder as he leads me to the basement stairs. "I've finally figured out what's leaking down here." Periodic floods were our first major homeowner headache. You'd never have thought basements would become his specialty. Basements and roses: he sent for books on them from the USDA, called in the County Agricultural Extension Service. Back in the kitchen, he mixed me a Campari and dry vermouth and himself a Rob Roy and stirred both with his pinkie. He said, "Clayton Knowles phoned." He was the religion reporter for the *Times.* My eyebrows went up. Somebody at St. Gregory's must've given him the number.

"What did he want?"

"A story, what else?"

"What'd you give him?"

"Malarkey." The *Times* was hot on the departures of certain uncertain priests these days. The former president of Fordham University, a bishop no less, had just made the front page, leaving to get married. But Harry was adamant about not giving the world just another titillating, Church-bashing story, and I was with him.

"Did you have to . . . ?"

"Lie? 'Course not. Told him there *was* no story. I wasn't married, and I was still a priest." We smiled into each other's eyes.

"And then I sez—he's still going on, you know, what am I *really* doing, what made me do it, et cetera et cetera—I sez, 'Sorry, Clayt, I gotta get back to my baby-sitting.'"

But a leaky basement wasn't all we got for our money, or the sunny triangle of earth to plant more roses on that Harry dubbed the Fertile Crescent, the rest of the yard being known as the Gaza Strip. We got Paterson too, this ramshackle industrial bust town, historical hotbed of anarchists and socialists, big enough to matter and small enough to make a difference in. It may be difficult to believe, but it wasn't till we actually went down and stood staring into the Great Falls from Overlook Park that I suddenly remembered reading Williams's great poem: "*The Falls let out a roar. It is the poem itself that is the answer.*" Ten canyon years had dropped down between me and the poet of the Greensboro carrel. To remember words is not to know. "No ideas but in things."

Of course it wasn't stage enough for Harry—nothing could ever be again, after he'd had the one where God is made and eaten all day long. But it was pretty almighty to stand there in that pulpit of a park with the Largest Falls in the East after Niagara behind you and shout your message over the roar. A few years later some damn-fool local water authority would decide to siphon the Passaic off upriver and throw Harry Browne an irresistible chance to describe the dried-up flow as "letting the turds come marching over the Falls, two by two."

We got up a protest demo out of a crew as anarchic as any historic true believers Paterson had ever seen, including a sweet artist-drifter named Don Kommit who called himself the Count of Passaic County, and Harry helped organize them into SPLASH (Save Paterson's Living American Social Heritage), a group that managed to pull together a rally that got time on the network evening news. It was billed as a costume party of historic Paterson characters who'd come back to be pissed off at the water company desecration. Harry appeared as—what else?—a priest, "Dean" William McNulty, the redoubtable first pastor of the Paterson Irish Cathedral of St. John's. The "Dean" was one of those primal Patersonians who'd found their way into Williams's *Paterson*—who one spring day in 1880 had subdued a killing mob on Garrett Mountain and brought a murdering poor sinner from sure death to safety in a hack cab, who'd swept the beer mugs off the local bars with his walking stick and harangued a hundred Bill Baileys off their barstools and back to their homes. Harry borrowed the Dean's own cape and beretta from Mary Ellen Kramer, the mayor's wife, and made a holy fool of himself.

They'd called McNulty "Dean" because in Paterson, a town that once considered itself little more than an outpost of the English Manchester and wasn't used to larger-than-life Irishmen, he commanded the respect the immigrant English gave only to Anglican bishops. But for fifty years he'd never been anything more than a local parish priest, something of a holy fool, with Paterson before him and St. John's Cathedral at his back. Harry they called "Doctor," like the poet.

2

ot married and still a priest. Well, Harry had said that to Clayton Knowles, and he'd meant it. But here it was 1971 and now we had the full-time, same-address relationship and the three kids that seemed to say to the world that we were and he wasn't. The kids themselves were still too young to explain the difference to—Bim seven, Kiki and Nina only five and three—and somehow it didn't seem to matter . . . yet. But when would it? We had never really thought about it, or talked about it outside our own minds. And we had made no plan for telling them even when the time came to do it, out of some obscurely shared notion, perhaps, that the time *would* come, and we would know what to say when it did.

Odd to have this new seeming openness in our lives still layered with public and family duplicity, but what to do? The corollary of people's simply assuming we *were* married because of the children was that we could in some way hurt the children by challenging the assumption. So of course I went on letting schoolteachers and dentists call me Mrs. Browne, though as teacher, as publishing scholar, as what Harry mockingly, lovingly, referred to as "deanlet" because I'd taken on a new job in academic administration, I deliberately cut myself back to two names, first and last—sadly, as I see now—excising the middle *M* that had silently acknowledged my mother. But this because I'd be damned if I'd get even *close* to being one of those "three-named ladies" a male colleague at NYU had once proposed I become, to solve the dilemma of how to be married with Ph.D. and still let the world know to whom I *really* belonged.

His dilemma, of course, not mine, and not necessarily other women's either. Keeping the "maiden" name, so-called, was something married women were beginning to do. In political code, like the new honorific *Ms.*, it read *feminist*. Which is to say, defiant, but not necessarily outlaw. The fact stood that I might not have named myself any differently had I actually been married.

Besides, my name by now had become *mine*—the name that named my soul, liquid as opera, a *Gioconda* of veiled desire, a palimpsest of history, sensual and sexless, pan-Mediterranean, Greek, Jewish, Arabic, Spanish, Sicilian, Celtic, sub-Saharan, Brazilian, Old World, New World, pandemic, arcane, reversible, invocative, incantatory. The wildly inventive novelist Anthony Burgess played with it enchantingly, once, as he answered my academic plea to come and give a talk at the college, and taking a simple promotional postcard imprinted with the title of his newest novel, *M/F*, he somehow managed with a few squibbly arabesques of his pen to tease a new androgyne of my two names, reversed, out of his androgynous title. And then, when he came to talk, he publicly pronounced mine the only name he considered fit to be spray-painted on a New York subway car.

•

Burgess's visit to Ramapo College in 1972 was the exhilarating event it would never have been at NYU, though the germ of it had begun there, where one of my students had actually turned me on to reading him.

I'd left NYU in 1971, a big move in career politics terms—from a major urban private university to an upstart new public college in the metropolitan hinterlands of New Jersey—and I didn't make it without agony. But two events the previous academic year had turned not just me but many of us around. One was the sweeping, draconian nonrenewal of all untenured faculty at the Heights in winter 1970, driven *not*, they said, by retaliation for the Kent State boycott but by looming insolvency, the university having wildly overspent on a major new Heights engineering facility. Any and all reappointments were to be considered on a case-by-case basis. I was personally told I should not feel threatened. But that only made me the madder—to see a strategy so transparently designed either to make us complacent about our own survival or drive us into a cutthroat scramble to save our personal necks. Like me, most of the rehired faculty eventually resigned in anger, and in the aftermath, University College was left decimated and demoralized, factors that surely contributed to its demise a few years later.

The NYU English department during that same year, under pressure from the younger faculty as well as from the American Association of University Professors and the profession at large, had also set up a committee to study patterns of academic tenure in English, with special interest in the situation for women. I was on the committee, and frankly it was a little like Marlow sailing up the Congo to discover "the horror": in twenty-two years, the only woman ever to have been tenured at the Square was still an assistant professor, teaching mainly freshman courses. None had ever been tenured at the Heights. The department was, of course, deeply embarrassed. The tenure committee stretched itself to offer me early consideration. But I thought it a case where Harry's favorite political maxim, "*Subvert and survive*," did not apply: any such review seemed token, whichever way it fell, and no personal tenure could have been antidote to the visceral disgust I felt, as if my career had been poisoned at its source.

At the same time, here—just as we were committing ourselves to putting down roots in New Jersey—a new planet had come swimming into view: this public college whose educational mission I believed I myself could help to shape. Ramapo was part of an ardent surge of new colleges nationwide, one of two in New Jersey, instinct with political and educational vanguardism, brimful with the promise of new academic wine in new bottles. To me, in another metaphor, it held the familiar exhilaration of the blank page. Personally, too. No Mary Mullens or three-named-ladies here. I could draw Harry into it or not as I pleased—we could introduce each other guilelessly as "roommates" and never have to explain the inference. I *did* draw Harry into it, almost indifferent to the hostility he might court for either of us if he were recognized. I felt safe. I felt selfish. I loved the way he electrified my colleagues. Always, always, there was that exhilarating cachet of just being in his presence.

He *was* recognized, of course. The number of ex-clergy Ramapo hired within its first few years was amazing, and they all knew one another. It created a strange, evasive subculture, a certain forlorn and distanced camaraderie of loss in the midst of the college's early euphoria. And the subculture outlived the euphoria, to become one of the most distinctive political features of a place Harry wryly referred to as "a post-clerical institution," and the one, for me, that was most personally haunting.

Meanwhile, the new duplicity of "married with children" had one potential advantage: a possible place for those children in the Italian kinship universe. My mother had hovered on the horizon of their lives, a face, a voiceprint in their banks of baby memory, from the time of that first convulsive trip of hers across the George Washington Bridge. Might we now conceivably get beyond Carlo and Annie? Speak of my father as if they might someday come to know him, as if the dream might just come true of seeing him in the magical Oz of the West? *Mario and Maria.* Their alliterative naming held promise in itself of some ideal of parenting more fabled than our own. In some paradoxical way, in a *Waltons*-obsessed America, in a world where we two had so little that was normal to give them, it also seemed to hold the promise of a necessary, grandparently ordinariness.

I know now how stupidly we exaggerated the value of ordinariness to them— so do they, of course. Even in that more innocent time it was the last thing children of ours ever needed. But I don't think we exaggerated their need for a bond with the generation of their parents' parents. There was the greater danger that we might underestimate it, having had so little of an intergenerational remnant in our own lives to judge its value by—nothing more for me than those poignant *mustachios* and for Harry nothing more than myths. Plus, of course, whatever sorry reflections we might nurture in our hearts on a ten-year curse that had anathematized three small children. Bloody traces of hurt were well knit by now into the fibers of memory. Could we possibly pick all the threads of need apart now to make a clean weave of things?

For Harry the world of Catholic professionals and professional Catholics had always been more his family than his own. "Outing" may in some official sense have *other*ed him for someone like Ellis. It just as acutely *same*d him for the rest of his friends. Anyone who had known and loved him for his political daring was not going to love him any the less, and his priest-friends in CCUM closed him in a new embrace that testified to their own political daring—closed us both, in fact, in the same embrace, with an enthusiasm only the rebounding enthusiasms of that wonderful and troubled time could have made possible.

And then there were women—Margaret Mooney, for instance—who had loved and befriended Harry years before, when she'd been a Catholic University graduate student passionate for James Joyce and the Irish Renaissance. She had just married an outed Jesuit from Fordham, and was thrilled to learn about Harry's new life, his new defection, ready to position us all in the same gunboat.

Margaret was, besides, as Irish as Irish, brilliant, acute, opinioned, floridly pink and gold and exquisitely ladylike in dress and manners and person and housekeeping—a woman no longer young who prided herself nevertheless on the plenitude of her physical endowments, and who like Molly Bloom had said, *Yes, yes I will, yes.* I do think she frowned a little on the imprudence of our gaggle of children: a more vexed problem, after all, than her own simple defection of the Catholic heart. But children did not really interest her. She was a former priest-lover turned lover of former priests, not about to let a little urgency to procreate divide her from Harry again now that she had found how perfectly he fit into her brave new world.

Margaret continued to teach, her ex-Jesuit had found educational consulting work, and the two lived in connubial bliss in an elegantly dressed little flat in middle-class Queens. I think it was here, when she proudly presented me their bedroom on a tour of the house, that I first saw great sweeping calico bedsheets, printed all over with the tiniest roses, pasted to the wall like paper. What an extraordinary bit of material fact to remember when so little else comes back of those summer soirées and whatever it was that several dissident couples—the Catholic equivalent of Berlin Wall jumpers, I suppose—had to say to one another. I was typically glazed with fatigue. But I also felt uneasy, a little marginalized by my Italianness.

I don't mean to blame them; I have always carried my solitude with me. They meant to make a hospitable refuge for the Catholic dispossessed—certainly Margaret did, the perfect hostess, popping up everywhere, wonderfully flouncing, witty, and attentive, an orchestrating Madame de Staël of these salons of secularization, striving with all her creative might to reinvent the institution that had disowned us. Perhaps I couldn't feel quite dispossessed of something that had never fully belonged to me.

And I frankly preferred parties that *were* parties. Like our own—big, loud, full-house love-ins of the kind only our seedy, rambling mansion and tolerant Paterson neighbors made possible, plus a parking lot next door invitingly empty all weekend and big enough for forty cars. I have mentioned the time we brought peace fugitive Phil Berrigan and his activist wife, former Sister Elizabeth McAlister, home—Phil just out of the Josephites by then, and both of them just out of jail and married to each other in one of the four ceremonies they performed to clinch it. It was about as classic a rouser as this old house has ever seen before or since, when the dining-room table, drop-leafed to capacity and draped with a queen-size bedsheet, had to be moved to the wall to make enough room for the bodies, when the place became a crapshoot of good and bad priest jokes and a boombox of laughter, and no one knew what time it was anymore, until somebody lifted the tablecloth and discovered the kids we thought in bed hours ago, fast asleep between the trestle supports of its big maple legs.

This was just the high-water mark of a steady flood of celebration that embraced my own oxymoronically revolutionary academic colleagues at Ramapo—my family, then, and for a time.

But institutional passions can be short-lived, maybe the shortest—especially when you are working on the seamy side of them as I was. I had begun at Ramapo, almost without meaning to, as an administrator, head of a new academic program called Intercultural Studies. Two years later I wanted to move on. Oh, yes, it had been wonderful to reinvent educational wheels. But then, more and more, I'd found myself spinning them too. And found also that they could be Catherine wheels, racks to break you on, body and soul. I learned how good I could be as a leader, how creative, how driven, how passionate—and how bad, for all the same reasons, how unprepared I was for power, mine or other people's.

About power, they say no one gives it up willingly. But I have done so more than once. Perhaps women do. I wanted to then because I knew there were things that could make me happier. I missed the children, for one thing. The hours were long, the shallow field of focus intolerable—never more than ten minutes' uninterrupted mental time for anything, no matter how deep or demanding. I longed to get back to research, to writing, to a quiet carrel in the library, to a real blank page to start a drawing or a story on—and to finish one on, too.

An invitation suddenly arrived for me to give a paper at Bryn Mawr, part of a search process, evidently, for a new specialist in Victorian poetry. Had someone been dreaming my dream, knowing how long I had been smoldering with an idea about the Brownings in Italy? But, my God, the director's job was just too overwhelming. Where would I get the time?

"I've done the research," I told Harry. "I know what I want to say. But I'll need at least a week to write something I can bear to read."

"Do it. Stay home. Be sick. I'll cover."

He was magnificent. He'd just got word of his full-time appointment as associate professor in the sociology department at Rutgers and was radiating the triumph of his reclaimed academic identity. The world was our shared oyster now, and we were the twin shells clasping, rasping, worrying the sand grain into our single resplendent pearl.

And I *was* sick, really, as one can be sick with the joy of rapt, monomaniacal labor, intoxicated, rocking on the magic ocean of a million brilliant words. Oh, that week we two *became* the Brownings. I read and wrote on the couch like the invalid Elizabeth while he cheered and cosseted me, brought me blankets when I was cold, plied me with food and drink, swept in the children for maintenance hugs and swept them out again, speed-read me the latest brief on Watergate from the *Times* for refreshment, and was ever the robust equal of Robert B. for intellectual discourse commingled with kitchen and furnace and, yes, basement, and the inexorable dripping gutters and plumbing of our ancient, elephantine old equivalent of *Casa Guidi*.

I did not go to bed. I did not move for days, except to pee or fetch a book from the upstairs shelves. I'd had this captivating reading of the Brownings' Risorgimento politics bursting in my brain for years—notebooks crammed full of research on it. No more secret life of William Sharp. Now I could surrender myself to a new romantic universe, a perfect unsecret political and creative partnership. Lying there, day and night, I felt like E.B.B. herself big with *Aurora Leigh,* floating like a volcanic island on a sea-surround of paper, heedless of whether the day streamed through the parlor bay windows or the light burned in the torchiere lamp, my eyes swimming with the tiny texts of her poem and Robert's *The Ring and the Book*—the two longest, and surely until that week the two most unread, poems in the English language.

Finally, as if the simile were perfect and we *were* Robert and Elizabeth making for Calais or Pompilia and Caponsacchi racing to Rome, the two of us fled toward Philadelphia, Harry at the wheel pushing the accelerator like a madman even as I put the last dizzying inserts into my yellow foolscap manuscript.

I have to laugh now. If ever there had stood a redoubt of the New Criticism against the politicization of literature it was Bryn Mawr, a veritable temple of close reading by the evidence of their catalogue descriptions in English. What could I have been thinking of? Who, there, would care to hear me say that poetry was made by real people who lived in history and cared about politics and each other? Who would be captured by a still uncanonical woman poet with a disreputable history of having actually once been *popular?* Anyone with any sense knew she had nearly dragged her husband to perdition with her, that her early death had mercifully spared his genius to go on to write the great verse-novel masterpiece that dwarfed her own.

I knew the instant I set my foolscap pages on the lectern that if I had even remotely dreamt of this as a possible career move from Ramapo it had been the folly of a narcolept. But I think I also knew that I had wanted to do precisely what I was about to, which was to speak heresy in the sacred halls to the sacred cows. The cool insincerity of their kindnesses didn't dismay me in the least. The more I heard myself say what I wanted to say, the more *ardita* I became, and the more I believed it myself. Public appearances had always panicked me. Not this one. I was happy. I was right.

In retrospect the episode has the look of a staged piece of Harry-mimicry, something I would never have done without him. Maybe this is true, I wouldn't have. Just as E.B.B. would never have eloped to Italy or taken that leap into the glowing dark without the ghostly sight of Robert on the other side of the gulf, waiting to catch her and take her in his arms. I knew now that what had attracted me to this subject had been just this mutual daring, that Robert had not *caused* Ba's heretic audacity as much as he had helped her claim it, empowered her to take the very risk she had always wanted to take, just as she had for him.

We knew right after the talk that the search committee would be moving on. We took no pains at an evening party to tame our beastlier impulses to send up a few of the stiffer stiffs we'd encountered along the way. We may have made some more enemies, but we also made a surprising number of friends, and when we said we dreaded going back to our official hotel with its hardwood-frame twin coffin-beds, someone offered us a conveniently big floppy mattress in a loft living room. That night we made love as I think we hadn't since Italy, before falling off like babies to sleep.

•

The decision to take on South Africa for a breakaway summer that year marked another stage in the grinding of our mutual pearl. Olive Schreiner drew me—the writer, the dreamer, the fighter, the sexy Victorian feminist and powerful charismatic woman who had turned up in my work on Sharp, author of the daring *Story of an African Farm*, who'd brought South Africa, herself, and her manuscript together to England in the early 1880s, and later returned home to stand up to Cecil Rhodes, imperialist, to shake her tiny fist at him from a railway station of the Great Karoo, and become the sad heroine of her country's warped political destinies.

I had fallen hopelessly in love with her, this multitasking artist of dreams, of great dangling, unfinished masterpieces. Historical beings had always had more real presence to me than to Harry. He had an historian's proper sense of the *difference* that divides the present from the past, and was impervious to the silly delight of those few Olive-words scrawled *en passant* on Konrad's itinerant automatic postcards. For me it was the opposite: just to think about, to imagine Olive Schreiner, to read her, was to be *with* her, in some ways to *be* her. It still is. I know I am not alone in this delusion. This enchanting woman has done something like it, I think, to everyone who has ever had dealings with her, in life, in death, in art.

One of her apostles at the time was a professor named Ridley Beeton, a tall, mild literary scholar and poet from the University of South Africa. Literature made him my colleague, Olive my friend. We had recently been brought together by John Rosenberg, the mentor-professor from Columbia whose service at Kiki's whooping-cough tent four years earlier had written him permanently into the family narrative. John had stood as I came through the door of his little Butler Hall apartment, but Ridley anticipated introduction, saying, "Olive Schreiner, I presume?"

Olive may have forgiven him the sacrilege by now. He was one of the gentlest people I have ever known, and yet so politically acute and tenacious of principle that he dazzled even Harry's sense of justice and entered a special class of his own as our mutual hero. Ridley visited Paterson more than once, making himself a trusted source of insight into South African politics, a position Harry didn't concede easily to a white South African of British descent. Both of us saw the staring parallels between the apartheid struggle and the U.S. civil rights movement, amplified in the ugly truths of American racism being spread before us by the Kerner Commission—that we were a nation divided into two nations, one black, one white. But they were truths drawn as well on the 'scape of our own mostly black neighborhood, inscribed into the false ease of our relationship with Thelma Wheeler, the extraordinary black woman—courageous yet near exhausted by poverty—who came in now to care for our kids. The contemporary universe of South Africa seemed a twisted mirror for the lessons of our own history, of our own lives, if we could stand to look at it.

Maybe it is difficult to reimagine the explosive volatility of these days, more difficult to imagine them woven together with love and work-stress and children and sleep and waking and food and colds and shoes and dentists, things with such a repetitive sense of dailiness about them. Yet behind them all there is still Vietnam, Watergate steaming on through the summer, Spiro Agnew going down in flames, our inner cities unrecovered and smoldering—Paterson among them, and (though we didn't know it till much later, when I asked for the file) J. Edgar still keeping watch on us from a parked car forty feet away, making note of my comings and goings with the kids.

We knew we needed to get away. We knew Ridley's invitation to visit him in South Africa had been no gesture of casual hospitality. But we were not sure whether we were projecting the same wish on each other.

"Where would *you* like to go?"

"Where would *you*?"

We made separate lists. South Africa was at the top of both of them.

But going to South Africa, my Africanist colleagues made haste to remind me, was like consorting with the *real* enemy. Mary O'Neill, just back from a Peace Corps stint in Nigeria, didn't think so. She—the mother of the illicit layette in years past—came to see us, sat in our living room with the kids at her feet, they themselves bug-eyed to see the very person in person who'd written all those wonderful children's books we thought some of the best in our literature. And she, consulted on the trip, good, insightful, uncluttered soul that she was, agreed: what better time than now? Everyone needed to see Africa, navel of the world, we needed to see South Africa, navel of apartheid; our own fire next time, to see it for ourselves.

But nothing in what we were about to do was more of a gamble than our contract with Carlo to stay with the kids while we were gone. He had just left a job at Columbia University's engineering labs, working under one of those politically charged academic-corporate-military contracts, and it had not been a pleasant parting. He was restless, edgy, considering going west to see my parents. He had time on his hands. It all seemed logical enough, but with or without Thelma as backup, I don't remember how many times, the night we left for London on the first leg of our trip, I thought of turning back.

Even Harry, urgent for this adventure and not in the habit of looking backward, seemed uneasy on the overnight flight, holding my hand in his restive sleep. There was a long layover between our flights the next day, and we had time to bus into London for a swift touchdown at the British Museum. We phoned home from there. According to Carlo, everything was fine, fine—only Father Wilde had called, looking for Harry.

As Harry handled our check-in to Nairobi, there was a stir at the counter as if some alarm button had been tripped. I remember wondering if something were wrong with our passports. A captain strode up and asked if we would like to step into the VIP lounge; we followed him, stumblingly, fear whiting our brains. There he sat us down and looked straight into Harry's eyes. He said, "Your mother is dead."

He was Greek, with an accent and a carved tragic countenance, as if he were a brother bearing this heavy message to a brother. "There is time," he said. Meaning, presumably, to think. To go back.

He left to get us both a drink. Harry dropped his head onto his open hands. I waited, my heart beating thickly with that old doom of being outside his life, even outside his suffering. Because the captain was wrong. There was no time, if there ever had been, to tell her about us anymore. When he looked up at me his eyes were floating. It was as if at that moment his mother were looking out at me from behind his eyes—*my* mother Mary, too, for the first time.

"She knows everything now," he said. And he smiled. He actually looked deep into my streaming eyes and smiled his crooked smile.

We would not go back, he said. I begged him. I would never forgive him if he thought he was doing this for me. But no, he pleaded, it was not for me. It was for himself, for herself. There would be no stopping, no turning back.

What more could he do for her now? Some shamefaced appearance in a funeral tie? some para-clerical function at the ceremony? Robert Wilde was there. And Robert, more than anyone, understood—and *she*, above all, would understand. Robert knew what he would feel; Robert would feel it. Robert would send her off officially, but she had already gone, for him. It was as if she had been assumed, simply floated above the clouds, as the best reports of that old time had said the other Mother Mary had done, whose assumption into paradise, body and soul, Mother Church was barely a week from recapitulating. And in a strange synchronicity, on that very holy day a week later, we found ourselves attending mass in a Church of the Assumption, in the village of Umtata, near Durban.

We couldn't have found it because we hadn't looked for it. It had uncannily found us. We spent the rest of the day on the beach, just as she would have done had she been with us, "taking the waters" of the Indian Ocean, an alien sea into which that daring Wexford girl had never got to dabble her Irish toes.

And so our children never came to know their grandmother Mary Browne before she died. Harry could never bring himself to confess to her how his life had changed, not once in the many devout visits he'd made to her nursing home on upper Broadway, as she drew away from the world, increasingly weak and vague and indifferent. As for the rest of his relatives, well, crossing the Hudson seemed to have been decisive, to have given him a symbolic freedom from a piece of his moral identity he had long since shed. It seemed worth the price of losing them to no longer have to explain who he had become, what ten years of life in the eye of the storm had made him. He had somehow joined Jackie in that mysterious upriver exile.

It occurred to me now there was something profoundly rational in this, that if we had both been rational, we might have made some textbook-style clean break with both our families, as if not only the past had died but everyone in it too, as if we were actually the displaced persons we had once dreamed we were.

But I wasn't rational. I couldn't let go. As we traveled through South Africa, the sight of the great blank koppie-punctuated stretches of the Karoo reminded me of Arizona. I thought of my young parents, turning their backs on their old lives too, struggling to forget and doing nothing but remember. I had dedicated my book to them. My precious little book. I had signed it away as debt service. I knew that the surgery hadn't yet been invented that could cut that unmoving dark sameness deep in my blood's blood out of me, that my gesture of love only hinted at the well of my infinite capacity to mindlessly forgive and mindlessly beg forgiveness.

Especially of my father. I had no bitterness, I found, against my mother for the failure of her courage to break his law. I knew she had fought a prisoner's resistance from the beginning. I knew that in every sweating test of my own mothering I had somehow found her strength bearing down with mine. My life now, I thought, was proof of the magic of that Tosca love of hers, enduring past all will to murder it. Oh, yes, *he* would have fresh pain waiting for me, that was sure. But no forepain could quell the longing to be joined with him again, first father, father of all my lost saints, still living on the pulses of my body like an infant dream, like a dream of falling, like a self-renewing myth cycle of loss.

I wondered, as I have wondered again and again since, if I ever could be reconciled with him, the antithesis of everything I had learned of freedom, and of the freedom to love, since I had been his blindly loving child. Perhaps the time would come. I would make my children, I would make myself, a gift of my readiness for it.

We had covered four thousand miles, and we had had enough. We longed to come home. Mary O'Neill had been right—and wrong. The brutality of South Africa was bearable because we were witnessing it together, capable of processing our astonishment and pain through each other. And then again with Ridley—nothing to see that he hadn't already seen, nothing to learn that he didn't already understand. Even the sheer beauty of the land was almost unbearable, as if South Africans, having inherited paradise, must return to Genesis and begin again from the Fall.

Not a day had passed for me without the bodily need to hold my children in my arms. For Harry it was the same. The thought of actually seeing them again was as near pain as joy permits. When we arrived, the very sight of the house was a bliss of porch and pillars and trees. "*MOMMY,*" shrieked Nina with perfect high-decibel delight as we came through the door and she raced into my wide-open arms. But the boys hung expectantly back, and Christopher, our blue-eyed darling, asked the question we had almost forgotten to dread.

"Daddy, are you a *priest?*"

The little bastard couldn't wait another minute to ask.

3

I t had been Nancy O'Neill, Mary's daughter, who'd sprung our cover.
Or Nancy's kids, really—no malice aforethought. She had remarried earlier that summer and invited us to her wedding party in posh exurban Franklin
Lakes, an expansive, expensive spread under a yellow-striped tent in the yard of
her sprawling, plantation-sized house. A woman of big ecstasies, she was ecstatic
at seeing Harry again, remembering him from earlier days with her mother the way
an old fan remembers a movie star. She'd insisted that *our* kids had to come up from
Paterson and play with *her* kids. "So what's the difference if you're going away? Better
yet!"

After about a week on his own, Carlo would have grabbed an invitation from
the Fresh Air Fund just to get them out of the house. While they were there, the
kids had all slipped out to the tree house in the woods back of Nancy's place, where
her two put our three through some kind of Catholic *Jeopardy* quiz. "*You* don't know
thaaaat? and your father's a *prieeeest?*"

It wasn't exactly the way we'd planned it—but how *had* we planned it? And once
Harry'd explained as best he could what a priest *was,* and once they'd got over not
being first in on a great secret, the three of them seemed downright pleased that
some stupendous transformation had come about in our lives because of them. And
we got on with the evil of the day, which was sufficient, without taking on the behe-
moth of the marriage issue.

I began to write about the South African trip as soon as I was back, a long coiling
essay I called "In Search of Olive Schreiner," metaphor of a quest for sanity amid
the lunatic legalities of apartheid. At the killingly slow rate I usually produced work
while I was teaching, I finished it some time in mid-1974, and it was accepted by
Columbia Forum, one of the good journals of literate political opinion then coming out of New York, and indeed out of my own alma mater. But the twisted destiny in this was that no sooner had they made their back-cover announcement than
the editors wrote to say they were folding up. I took it badly. There was something
about that piece, about the connection with Olive, I couldn't bear to lose.

And yet I had in some sense already betrayed her, unwittingly betrayed her by
imitating her, beginning to feel a heady, yearning, panicky ambition that inspired
the dreaming of big literary dreams. Oh, yes, they would be "creative" and not just
scholarly: I was like Olive in that way too, my notebooks stockpiled with promising fragments of stories, novels, poems. But when the Guggenheim Foundation suggested I apply for a fellowship (in search of women—new Olive Schreiners,
perhaps, a century late?), I went over the top with the Italian theme I'd begun with
the Brownings and proposed taking on nearly every major writer who'd touched Italy
during the critical political years of the Risorgimento. It was a project that under

the best of circumstances would have taken a decade to finish.

But it seemed such a good, if grand idea, something I could *live* in, and maybe I had subliminally persuaded myself it could be done in stages, one eminent Victorian at a time, and turned out accordingly. And there was the imploding pressure for *some* writing accomplishment—the panic of three writing years already lost. *Resist beginnings,* Harry used to say, usually in connection with the latest storm at the college. Guggenheim meant not just cachet but escape, a ticket out of Ramapo's curriculum and governance struggles, if only for a year.

For in my heart, almost killing any joy in my work there lately, was an awful sense that I was vaguely complicit in some of the crueler little academic murders of that epoch, which had become as combative as it had once been exuberant. As early as the spring of 1972 there had been the loss of my wonderful friend, Michael Holden, a complex, brilliant, driven teacher who took on the most difficult remedial writing students. A half-fallen angel lurked behind that handsome, bearded face with its day-at-the-beach-blue eyes, but he was too witty, too free-spirited, too impudent a maverick not to make enemies of people with low thresholds for shock, people even pioneering colleges are full of. All his enemies needed was that flashpoint—in this case a single disgruntled student who accused him of saying "fuck" in the classroom.

We couldn't believe the charge. We couldn't believe it was taken seriously, but the student had actually taken the complaint to the state chancellor. Like some irritating zit, it seemed the more we picked at the thing the worse it got, until Michael's non-reappointment was before the board of trustees. They had to meet in the cafeteria that night to handle the overflow, but they sacked Michael anyway, over the roars of two-thirds of the student body, over the passionate protests of a steady stream of faculty friends. For some of us, then, the end of our first operating year had already become the equivalent of the expulsion from the Garden of Eden, a sign of Ramapo's betrayal of its teaching mission by killing perhaps the best teacher it had. And simply as a place it was Edenic—the loveliness, the pure landscape beauty of its mountain setting, the seductive glories of its flowering spring trees and heart-stopping gorgeousness of October—never a time of sadness for those who teach but one of sublimely gratuitous self-renewal. Oh, those brilliant hot May commencement days when we swept through the romantic, wooded grove in full academic regalia—that particularly unforgettable first one when I strode by with the faculty and Harry tossed me a single rose.

Michael had been *our* friend, too, Harry's as well as mine. Not only did they bond over a total indifference to haberdashery and a taste for scatological *shtik*, but Michael and his corn-silk blond artist-wife Edie had even moved into Paterson, passionate to get involved—in fact had been about to start an historical inner-city newsletter called *The S.U.M.Pump,* a play on the name of the Society for Usefull Manufactures that in 1792 first harnessed the waterpower of the Great Falls. Harry loved him, of course. He'd stood up before the board of trustees for him. He'd even carried his cause to Anthony Burgess when the novelist came to lecture, and Burgess, Liverpudlian guttersnipe to the core, stood before the whole student body and the august assembled in the morning and immediately struck his blow in a stentorian voice that rang against the steel bleachers of our makeshift auditorium: "I understand," he said, "that if I say *fuck,* I shall be summarily dismissed!" and brought down the house.

And yet the beauty, the poignancy, in all this for me was that Harry now saw himself as a disciple in *my* faith, in *my* mission. Sometimes he even felt a complicity in my misery, as once when a scholar he'd encouraged us to hire—an ex-priest, brother of a friend—turned out a priggish moralist whose only trick for fighting the tenure candidacy of someone he didn't like was turning it into a holy war. Harry was sick, furious that I'd been caught in the crossfire. He stalked about muttering, *"Some people will never forgive you for helping them."*

Maybe. I had my own theory, that it was another effect of the postclerical condition he'd had the insight to name. The particular tenure case, with a supporting cast that included me and several sanctimonious clerics and former clerics, a monk, two ministers, and even a former bishop—all of these, mind you, on the faculty or professional staff of the college—had given just the inflation to petty issues essential to the morality melodrama of post-clerical academic life. It was a weird flashback to the Catholicism I used to flee, mentally, before Harry, before Harry had transformed my perception of what the Church could mean, or be. It seemed to turn the college for a time into some bizarre anticipatory version of *The Name of the Rose,* a divinely comical, Manichee power struggle between the forces of good and evil. But I cannot forget that the struggle in this case was also a contest between men, with me, perhaps, the necessary woman-site of their traffic, a rather absurd Joan of Arc, really, who, by the time they had settled whether saint or witch, would be nothing more than an indifferent little stack of bone crumbs at the foot of the stake.

I had been the first woman among Ramapo's five directors of school (not to mention the lowest in rank and pay, as I discovered). This was weighty enough mantle by itself, but being the mother of three young children added dimensions difficult to reckon. Nina had been only three when I'd started, no match for the near-totalitarian demands of a new educational adventure. Even with Thelma and Harry putting in time, there were gaps, and Ramapo's little start-up child-care program couldn't possibly close them. So Nina came with me to the office. Nina came with me to class. Nina inched her little caterpillar body along the carpeting till she had done a mural in colored chalks the full length of the base of the blackboard. Then she'd crawl under the tangerine steel chairs, some with students in them, counting wads of gum, and report her findings to me afterward like a well-trained sociometrician. She'd climb up into my lap to be hugged when she knew it was what she needed—or what I did—and I would squeeze her, often in a conscious panic at the too swift and distracted passing of her babyhood, feeling almost as if in that single moment I must take the whole sweetness and beauty and sassy smartness of her in through my breasts.

Such symptoms of maternal tenderness in a woman otherwise known to bust a few chops at a faculty meeting bewildered male colleagues in those days. Even as dear a friend as Jim McCarthy—as smart and smartassed an Irishman as ever high-tailed it out of Harry's own Hell's Kitchen—even *he* admitted he'd been surprised to see me hug Nina, actually stop in the middle of the college walk and get down on my knees and fold her in my arms. I think his word was "shocked," though of course he smiled when he said it. And this was Jim, *simpatico* Jim. Couldn't put me and mothering together. It was like another version of the Scarlet Woman.

Ramapo College has such an intriguing history, it is sad that so little of it will ever be officially told. Founded in an educationally radical moment, its first president an Englishman with deep roots in the Labour Party and the British cooperative movement, the hiring net it spread for faculty and upper administrators didn't screen out some pretty doctrinaire types on both sides as then defined by the ideological structures of the Cold War. But curiously it was the conservatives who locked on to the positions of influence. It actually took only two or three of them to act out their deep mistrust of what seemed the radical drift of Intercultural Studies and other programs—or some of the people in them.

Even past my directorship, the School of Intercultural Studies had continued to enjoy a temporary little crest of success, transforming a standard foreign-service model of international studies into a new culturally oriented program with history and anthropology, even comparative literature, at the center. In the college's first five years it grew faster than any of the other four schools in the college, justifying every one of its new faculty appointments on numbers alone. I like to remember that when Harvard sociologist David Riesman came to look at Ramapo for his book about educational experiments in the seventies, he pointed to our program as perhaps the single most creative educational concept among the college's several interdisciplinary curriculum clusters.

Oh, yes, my head was in it. But so was my heart. There was no other way I could work. "SIS," as we called her, was a little universe, my own four-dimensional *Summa*, a work of art as complexly interwoven and beautifully balanced as a mobile tingling in the light. Even in retrospect it has the look of something futuristic and new, a program that thought about how people would actually do cultural work in the sped-up, shrunken, real-life global village of the future. We took it as given that undergraduates could digest the historical humanities, read Roland Barthes and Marshall McLuhan, cope with languages. We struggled to get them out to do fieldwork, travel, study abroad. We had one of the few baccalaureate-level majors in comparative literature in the country. Foreign languages were us: adding up our faculty competencies, we could have taught thirty-eight of them, living and dead.

As for the irritant of our politics, there was no question that the best talent in the Third World area studies we were out to develop tended to the left. Once I cockily suggested that we interview the notorious Stalinist, H. Bruce Franklin, recently dumped by Stanford and scouting a job in the east. Surely this was the apple-bite that felled me with the postclerical ideologues of the college, along with some others Harry dubbed its Nervous Nellies who had problems dealing with a woman in charge of anything. I added insult as a key committee chair of the Faculty Assembly when I supported the efforts of a group calling itself "Social Relations"— a clustering of openly Marxist political economists—to achieve the status of school in their own right. Ironically, this same group, which included some of the smartest and most energetic progressive talent in the college, went on to work rather hard and contentiously to "liberate" global and area studies from what they saw as the Intercultural Studies monopoly. It was a division we never had the sense to heal. Exquisitely manipulated by the right, it ultimately brought us both down.

But that was all to come. I was blinded by the brushfires. All I saw was that within its first three or four years the program I loved was being squeezed in a vise of criticism, between those who thought it went too far and those who thought it didn't go far enough.

Well, I had already bowed out as "deanlet." Though I was still piloting the curriculum, someone else was directing the program now, and those key faculty committees could do without me. I was determined to get away. *We* were five strong, five people in our regulation, *Sesame Street* family: together wherever we went from now on, because Harry and I had sworn in Africa that the two of us would never go anywhere again for longer than a weekend without them. Oh, those glory days when the fellowship came through, and we *knew* we would be leaving for Oxford in January.

And then another bolt: Catherine, one of Harry's twin nieces, saw my name on the announcement in the *Times* and dropped me a note. The twins were married now with children of their own, living in Park Slope, Brooklyn, sharing the same brownstone in a reviving old neighborhood. They suspected nothing, as far as we knew; we moved in separate worlds. How to respond? Harry and I suffered the decision deeply. Since he left St. Gregory's his connection with them had distanced— would it be too wounding to reveal the truth? Would their hurt only wound us again? In the end he gave me his permission to write back and tell all.

An odd synchronicity, that Catherine should have written as we made our plans for a summer trip to California. It made *my* family seem the lesser hurdle, suddenly. My parents had actually asked us to come see them. And yet it may no longer seem strange that I have erased the first moments of this reunion with them. I can picture heading our car into their Downey apartment complex. I have an insufferable total recall of every move we made afterward, from Disneyland to the Big Sur. But nothing of that instant when our eyes first met, when for the first time in ten years I felt my father's gracefully tapered fingers in my hand or leaned my face into his to kiss that well-shaven cheek, still as smooth as a boy's.

All this I must have done. I imagine the Mario of that moment, silvered and smaller, coolly appraising my life, evaluating my three wary children like works of art for purchase. Surely they printed kisses on those same well-tanned cheeks after me, *his* child—always—still nursing the dream of his approval. I do remember this: that even *he,* try as he might, could not spend ten minutes with Harry without being utterly disarmed. What a rush of gratitude would course through me when they laughed, as if I were bearing witness in the presence of my ancestors to the whole rebellious *Alleluia* of my life.

Home to Paterson again and a new adventure: an English graduate student to stay with us for a few months before we left for England. His name was Richard Margrave, from the London School of Economics, doing a Ph.D. on nineteenth-century silk worker migration from Coventry and Macclesfield. He arrived in late August, just in time for the Great Falls Festival—our new celebratory tactic for signifying Paterson—a sweat-funky and raucous Labor Day weekend event in the best working-class tradition of this unpoetically poetic old town. Poor Richard—it was our American trial by chasm. Nina dubbed him "Skinny Kid-do" before he'd even vaguely recovered from shock, and she had a point: he was just the thin and angley kind of Yorkshireman with shy ways about food who would have a bit of trouble coming to terms with pasta and broccoli at our house, let alone the famous local hot Texas wiener.

But he did it. He moved into the just-made-over guest room at the top of the house, and we had a lovely time, studying, talking, eating together—I already on leave doing preparatory research for the eventual trip to Oxford, Harry seizing the resident proximity to a true cliometric historian to take a fresh look at the history of the S.U.M. and massage ideas about flows of capital and labor at the outset of planned industry in the United States. And here was another one of those small-world coincidences Harry was famous for: that Charlotte Erickson, the professor supervising Richard's thesis at the University of London, had years before done her own dissertation with Harry at Catholic U.

By the time we left for England in January, it had all begun to shape itself into something exhilaratingly festive. Richard had all the student underside of London to show us, entrée to his Yorkshire family and their boatyard on the canal. There was a raft of new English friends to visit. My high-school chum, Judy, was now in England, too—James Blish, the science fiction writer she'd married, had turned out a fierce Anglophile, and they'd officially expatriated, turned their backs on post-Vietnam America. And Muriel was now living with them in Henley, not far from Oxford. I couldn't wait.

That fatal mix of exhaustion and bliss. One more time, we let down our guard.

I started ahead in January with Nina to scout for a place to live. Harry would turn in his grades in a few weeks and bring the boys. Oxford awaited: Matthew Arnold's golden-spired, venerable city, Queen of Romance. But after the first week in London it was already clear what had happened: that small orchestration of symptoms, signs on my body of what I had not allowed into all my best-laid plans.

Weeks pregnant already. Elation—gone. My little girl and I, despised American strangers, this city of beautiful towers a pitiless, dark, rainy, wretched, insolent place: Vicenza, in all its anguish, sluicing back. Every passing English sneer hurt me in my womb. In misery I put my head on the pillow, lifted it as if weights hung on my hair. No enchantment, no beauty. Just a frozen, nauseated panic, a blindness even to the gift of Nina's pitying small warmth in my hand. She, perfect in her seven-year girlhood, promise of another child as perfect, if only I could see it. But I could see nothing but the sunless days and the iron darkness. All I could feel was the cold.

Harry came. He held me in his arms and let me weep, all the dry, indignant tears that bled my ruthless self-pity. He told me I should do what I needed to do, what I wanted to do. But I could feel nothing. Nothing but the desperate meanness of the cold.

I started awake in the night, staring up into the dreary stretch of pregnancy as if I lay at the bottom of a well. So many plans—so thwarted now. Another child, another infant child, needing me, *needing* me, a fetal parasite to consume me down the years again, draining me, its host animal, of every other creation.

I couldn't believe my own thoughts. Hadn't I loved my children, didn't I love them now? Didn't I still cherish their gift of days? I cursed myself—the unspeakable pridefulness of wanting to smother this nascent life to give *me* room to grow! And yet I had loved their infancies, *their* needs, done so much for them—with them. Only now I was exhausted with birthing: children, college, new life. I couldn't go through with it. I wanted to *work*. To make something immortal.

I prayed like a child, like my mother: *Mother Mary*— But St. Ann came to me, in that image of my girlhood saints, wagging her admonishing finger, in her acid-green gown.

I was forty, not a threshold a woman ever crosses without a certain awful fear that this is all there is, all there will ever be. Not even now, a year before the great new millennium, though they tell us now that forty is quite young enough to beat a woman's unforgiving clock—if she wants to. We used to think—can it be only twenty years ago?—that childbirth at forty put mother and child at risk. So wise ones told me then, so I told myself. Was it unreasonable to rationalize an abortion this way? The cool English surgeon who finally agreed to perform it rationalized it this way. He could possibly see what I might do if he hadn't.

The agony of that choice is still as alive as it was—so vivid that I can still find it in myself to think sometimes how little it would have mattered in the scheme of things to spare that germ of life—for what great achievement, in the end, offset the pity of its loss? To see myself the Scarlet Woman after all, sick with the arrogance of ambition. To wonder if even the three I nurtured without an instant's regret might think harshly of me, remembering perhaps what I've forgotten of their pain as I withdrew from them in the anguish of my fear, fleeing like a victim, insane, savage, hysterical, down the corridors of my little time, stinking with death. To imagine how I may have crushed Harry—once, always a priest—with my certainty, with all the transparent certainty of my hysteria, that this was what I needed to do, this was all I wanted. I will punish myself with father thoughts, with mother thoughts, forever, here and hereafter. But I will never let myself forget I had to do it.

And I will never forget that this has happened to millions of women. It will undo nothing to ruminate my own private suffering, and I will still always die that little death. But I will never forget, because it is good to remember, *this:* that when I first went to English doctors, for whom abortion was then an entirely legal procedure, and sought their help and counsel, they offered me none. The U.S. Supreme Court, with *Roe v. Wade* the year before in America, had thrown our own puritan system into confusion, but it had not yet made abortion easy. These English doctors knew this, and treated me like a fugitive whose sole motive was child-murder. How I remember envying this invisible embryo they wanted so ferociously to save without a passing thought to saving the woman it came in.

It is not an English attitude, though I thought it was then. Just a cruel one, a narrow one, without nationality, and without boundaries of time.

4

Guilt is a wasted emotion.

    After that momentous decision, Harry hadn't looked back. I was glad—relieved—but my recovery was slower, harder, more intermittent, never complete—less because of the child lost than because it was a passage into my own mortality, into the true weightfulness of things. My mother seemed an inexorable part of it, perhaps a mirroring of our childbirth histories: her fourth, too, had been the one she'd suffered. My decision had been a conscious rejection of her lesson of surrender, but it had also been a rebuke to her life-lovingness. I think it was during this time that a peculiarly poignant childhood memory-image of her resurfaced: the four of us studying at the dining table—we have complained of the noise of a cricket behind the kitchen baseboard and she has just killed it, and stands weeping in the doorway, in the ensuing silence. It would not let go of me.

By March, sick of the overhanging English gloom, which I could now see *was* actually outside, and not just inside of me, the children having come down with chicken pox one after another, we agreed to start our planned trip to Italy early, to pack up a red rental Escort and head for the sun as soon as they were all well enough to travel.

    It was an exhausting, expensive, cheering, sentimental journey. Children are invisible in England. In Italy, they are the cynosure of the culture. A gross overstatement, but so it felt. My God, it was wonderful to be the mother of three again—as if I'd been released from a spell, as if we'd all come suddenly awake. The sun shone relentlessly, even when it rained, rainbows everywhere, *everywhere.*

    We went to Venice and Padua, saw Dino, Annamaria, their two boys, Gigi and Roberto, the same age as ours, in the Euganean Hills. Dino and Harry met for the first time and got on brilliantly, of course. I could imagine Dino, like me, smiling in secret self-congratulation at the choices we'd both made, the lives we'd separately created. We feasted together like gods, wrestling down the language barrier with laughter. Dino, ever the prince of Sicilian potlatch, wouldn't let us out of his driveway without a bootfull of Barilla pasta, nowhere to be found in England, and ten liters of voluptuous Veneto reds.

    We'd done George Eliot's Florence, and Robert Browning's Rome. We'd struck across the Alps going down and crawled the Riviera returning. We'd taken the ferry crossing from Le Havre, and gone from dazzling sunlight straight back into the English gloaming.

And I found myself unhappy again.

    I'd been fighting this unease and stuck to my forge, hammering away at my Italian Victorians while Harry studied the ineffable and seductive charm of Oxford, as Oxford did what Matthew Arnold said she would, and spread her springtime gardens to what little moonlight could make it through the murk. Between us, Harry seemed to have got the better of the arrangement, placing his first-ever letter to the *New York Times,* on the theme of renewing historic cities out of our little *pied-à-terre* in Squitchey Lane, Summertown. At the Oxford County Council he followed the rattling discourse on whether or not to continue the practice of caning in the schools and garnered stories that would keep him in hilarious *shtik* for years.

But my work was no laughing matter, planting my manifold of great Victorian authors like Ruskin and Rossetti and Pater against the backdrop of popular travel books of the time. Everywhere, great or small, I was appalled to find such a pattern of racism and xenophobia. Italians, of course, far from the most abused, and yet how patronized, demonized, *feminized* they were, I thought, how insufferably the British used the power of empire to distance and control and despise them—and more than them. "The niggers begin at Calais," they used to say, such a commonplace that no one could remember who'd said it first.

We had met Noel Annan the year before at a meeting of Victorianists in Florida, and in May he graciously treated Harry and me to a ceremonial visit to the House of Lords. I remember asking him once if he could recommend anything useful on the theme of British xenophobia and he astonished me by being unable to cite any study. He seemed to treat it as a rather boring idea. It may have been during the same conversation that he dismissed Raymond Williams too. I'd just fallen in love with Williams—*The Long Revolution, The Country and the City*—but I'd already been a little in love with Annan. I remember feeling like a fool, between two worlds. I never went back.

I was smoking too much. I was coughing too much. I was at sorry cross-purposes with myself, vaguely ashamed of the naïve Anglophilia that had got me here, that had set me on this quest for some way to unify my two opposed parent cultures. And yet, if not this, what? I was down on the English more and more, inflamed by mere chance remarks about *others,* especially Italians, of course. In June, after an agonized public debate, the English finally voted to join the European Common Market and the sun suddenly came out. It shone from then till we left England, for six straight, glorious weeks. It still shone after, we heard—a summer they have since touted as among the best in recorded British weather history. It made perfect sense to me, a sign from the heavens, if the English could only read it.

Deer Park, Maryland, August 1975: a CCUM retreat camp for inner-city community organizers. We had barely returned from Europe. Five priests were going to be on the altar that Sunday morning, Harry among them. The question: would he concelebrate the mass? He did. Audaciously, just that once. Peggy Roach, Jack Egan's right hand, said, "My dear, you could feel the buzz." Afterward, we seemed to have brought our own holy ghost home with us in the shape of a bat—it leapt out of the big suitcase Harry and the boys had shared in the barn they'd slept in, and flew in harmless terror around the attic bedroom. But it had to go. Harry chased it with a broom, his long white hair flying, until it fled into the eaves, and died there.

Still, always a priest. Harry's priest-friends visited like disciples, more and more. Priests from the Paterson diocese, like Paul Knauer and Pat Erwin, gathered round him and joked and worried the plight of the poor in cities. Father Russell Carroll, a Franciscan from St. Bonaventure, long-haired and besandaled, was writing an historical novel about the Irish in mid-nineteenth-century New York and needed Harry as historian as well as hero. Russell, a kind of guru in his own right, *aficionado* of all the lore surrounding the mystery of the Shroud of Turin, tried making Harry a counter-guru of this curious, mystical devotion—gave him endless holy cards he shoved semi-indifferently into the drawer of his bed table. Together they would turn our own meals into joyous Eucharistic ceremonies, with Italian bread from Lombardi's.

But it wasn't enough.

The Victorians came to Ramapo that year. Or the Victorianists, the radically cutting-edge Northeast Victorian Studies Association, having their organizational conference at the college. With my bravura gift for multitasking, I was giving a paper, working with my colleague Paul Elovitz on local arrangements, and planning a guided bus tour of Paterson on Sunday. My paper—"The Italian Garden (with Real Toads in It)," it was called—was going to test my angry new reading of some of the same writers many of my colleagues considered among our most revered prophets and forebears, flawed only as minor gods are flawed. I saw them as fallen, saw how glibly British travelers of every class had patronized and exploited Italy, made it effectively an outpost of cultural colonialism, and I wanted to reclaim it. It felt at the time like a cranky piece of vanity as well as a bold piece of iconoclasm. Did I only imagine that I vexed many of my colleagues with my theme, as if I were making a personal quarrel public? Whom would I tell this to, if not to them? How could I make them credit it?

These seem almost silly questions in light of the road nineteenth-century studies has taken since, especially since Edward Said's *Orientalism*. By now, every British "postcolonial" has said the same things about the British, and made them the clichés we all have the courage to speak. But not concerning Italy. I was a *different* kind of colonial, just as Italians are, and were, then and since, but also doubly disempowered by the diaspora, by having been nurtured in an Anglophilic culture that vaguely despised me—us—and by the moral equivocation of having found a certain warmth and shelter in its embrace. And it was true: I *was* taking a personal quarrel public. It was as if I were defending one father and shaking my fist at another. My courage failed me. It was too much. But it wasn't enough.

Some restless inattention to things had begun to show up at home in quick-tempered quarrels. It was as if somewhere, somehow, in the past year, my body had changed and my skin no longer fit. *He works his work, I mine:* I had used to say this of us. Not now. We seemed to have mislaid our work, both of us, some imperative social context in which the meaning of what we did could be blessed and redoubled. Apart from Paterson, I couldn't live in his work, any more than he could in mine. I have said he lost the theater of his priesthood. But if he lost it, I lost it too. And what I lost, he lost.

And yet it was a huge year in Paterson, its National Landmark year as well as the national bicentennial. President Ford himself had come to the Great Falls to declare the news, on a rainy Fourth of July, under an umbrella. In New York City, Harry was still in demand as historian, officially called upon for more than one "Bicentennial Minute." But I felt no thrill to see him when he appeared on television, even as the kids shrieked with joy—only a curious emptiness. He looked too crumpled, and chubby, and old.

And yet why then did I do my best work in celebration of us, revisiting the Brownings theme I had done at Bryn Mawr, so much more wisely now, with so much deeper and more informed a sense of their political partnership? Published, "The Ring, the Rescue, and the Risorgimento" was a hymn to us, to *our* mutual influence and rescue. And yet I think that more than anything else I had ever written, it had seemed like writing a novel. The rest of my Italian theme remained baffled in inconsequential anguish and buried in a file drawer.

I thought I knew what John Henry Newman meant when he said that to lose his faith would be like looking into a mirror and not seeing his own face. That register of panic and emptiness had provoked his *Apologia.* Did I need an apologia to understand myself, to write myself back into faith in my own existence? In my own relation to my work? One singular day my friend Jane Lilienfeld said, "All my most talented friends are avoiding their novels." She meant *women* friends. She meant *me.* Was it precisely "my novel" I was avoiding?

Janey visited us in Paterson that year, in the throes of her own career passions. A brilliant, vivid, wild-hearted woman, I'd first met her at an early Victorian Studies meeting in Amherst, Harry at my side. She was just finishing a Ph.D. on Virginia Woolf. It was Easter when she came, and she bore a huge white lily as a gift, with all its aura of *Lighthouse* significance. She looked at Harry and saw an archangel. She looked at us and saw two archangels. It takes absolutely no luster away from this comparison to say she also thought we were the Ramsays, sixty years after, even if she half-hinted at Mrs. Ramsay's blurred identity.

But what was wrong with me? Some smothering incubus seemed to sit on my heart. It was as if I were gestating another creature and, instead of being free to choose to take it to term, I were having its abortion forced on me. My lost Olive Schreiner essay had hung over me through most of my stay in Oxford, where I'd learned of *its* abortion. If anything, events in South Africa had only proved how timely that essay was.

I finally did what Harry said, slapped it into a new envelope, new covering letter, and refusing to aim low, sent it to the *New York Times Magazine.* It came back with a standard rejection. Several months later, they published an article by Anthony Lewis on precisely the same theme—as much better than mine as the latest news, the cachet and expense account of the *Times* and the talent of an Anthony Lewis could make it. It appeared not long before the Soweto uprising, that terrible June 16 when some of the same schoolchildren who still smiled at me from my 1973 photographs may have bled their lives away in its dirty streets. His essay had the look of prophecy. Mine was dead.

I thought I had taken it all in stride, dismissing my anger, my sense of loss. I went on pretending to be powerful. Overreaching again, I began an essay inspired by Raymond Williams's *The Country and the City,* a piece of narrative theory that had the cosmic proportions of my old curricular dreams, of my compendious study of Italy, the arrogance of a Key to All Mythologies.

But something in me as a writer felt crushed, victimized. I read Kate Chopin's *The Awakening.* I considered my sisterhood in Edna's paranoia, her longing for the act of infidelity that would make her feel alive, for that paradox of a last, triumphant self-annihilation.

We would fight in the evenings. This is when I drove his disorder out of the den, when I drove *him* out. I would say I needed more space, more time to write. And he would know what I meant and say, "Write *what?* Do your scholarship." And I would know somehow that he meant I shouldn't somehow write about our life, about anything that might expose our privacy, tell tales out of school, out of bed. It didn't matter if it were "fiction." He knew the kind of thing I wrote: he was right. But it was the risk you took living with a writer like me, who wanted to tell not lies like truth, as the literary types said, but truth like lies, with all the essential credibility and artfulness of fiction. I think he saw a kind of voluptuousness, of self-luxuriating in writing from this private source. He reminded me of my father— much too much—though he may have thought his *omertà* to be about not what was safe, but what was sacred.

He would seem to me to avoid housework, just to make me complain about it, knowing the house, the kids, were mountains to me in the way of my own mountain. And not just seem to, he really did avoid it. "Why does it have to be done on *your* timetable?" he would say, real anger breaking through against what he saw as this weary feminist commitment of mine to win our domestic wars. But the deeper truth was that in my frenzy to challenge him, I invented stables to clean and called on him as if he were the Hercules duty-bound to clean them. The kids grew perplexed, suffering. They fought too, as kids will, but now, increasingly, with a dark, sullen bitterness, especially between the two boys, that seemed to mirror Harry's and mine.

Bim said to us, "How can the only two people in this house who chose to be together be the ones who seem to want the most to be apart?"

Wise child, we could not tell you.

One night, walking around Eastside Park after a screaming quarrel, I saw a man walking a pet skunk, and it seemed to trigger some superstitious anxiety about boundaries, edges, about wildness, about my own.

What could Harry have been feeling? That he had sacrificed his priesthood for this? This sham of love, this endless struggle with a bitch of thwarted ambition?

Now what could give him back *his* meaning, the significance he had sacrificed for *me?* The message he still had to convey to the Church—about its responsibility, accountability, to the poor, to the homeless—was being conveyed better than he could do it now by other priests, by Egan and Murnion, by lay historians like Dave O'Brien and Jay Dolan and activists like Harry Fagan, who didn't have his taint of an ignominious departure. And justice to women? The irony *now* of his appearing before the National Conference of Bishops in Minnesota in 1976, and the Newark Conference in 1977 again, though he did it, and striking a blow for a noncelibate priesthood. "What does the Church's stand on celibacy do but endorse concubinage," he'd ask, with that hard searchlight way of his of dragging dirty old canonical words out into the open.

It was a powerful message, but I wonder if he could really feel his power to convey it anymore. Wasn't I still his concubine? Or was I? Hadn't he declared for me over Holy Mother Church? There was a hard knot of irony in the news Harry passed to me with a hint of tears in his eyes that Robert Wilde had just got married, a woman he'd met while he'd been pastor of St. Joseph's in the Village. It was as if Robert had been jealous of him all these years. But now maybe Harry was secretly jealous of Robert, whose love was a new, a beautiful thing. Now maybe he was afraid, afraid this challenge might prove too big for his friend, that maybe Robert had repeated his mistake. Our mistake.

But what was the mistake? Had it simply become this extraordinarily banal matter of living together—or trying to? In England I'd found a postcard image of Simone de Beauvoir and Sartre—the great couple in whose relation I'd once seen my own ideal. The photographer had caught them stepping out of a train compartment, side by side, their faces forward, their eyes bent ahead, immensely together, yet neither of them in any discernible way conscious of the other. Behind them a typical French railway car sign reads COMPLET. I attached it to the refrigerator door with a magnet so that no meal could pass without my seeing it, without estimating: how close had we come to this? how far had we drifted?

On the other hand, I sometimes wondered if we shouldn't have got married, after all—officially, ceremonially, in some way *coram publico*, as he might have said in his priestly Vulgate—"in the public face," with human respect—in a way that demanded the discipline of perseverance through the better and the worse. The principle he clung to, that he was a priest anointed, that no one would take that from him, the principle I clung to that marriage was an historical contract for the enslavement of women, what were these but hollow, repetitious dogma for either of us by now? I wondered sometimes what he really meant to say by avoiding marriage. If I wondered, surely he wondered too, what I meant to say by it.

Was I thinking that if he was a priest, I was a free woman? Not concubine? Not even that? Not wife? Not his? Free to do what I chose to do with my mind? With my imagination? With my body? Was he thinking this too, for himself?

Flashing across the scrim of my mind like a spurt of fresh blood: we are together at a party in an elegant East Side apartment. Harry is sitting across from me on a big leather couch, drunk with anger and Scotch and self-sufficiency and indifference. A woman I do not know is folded in his arms, across his chest, and before my eyes he is gently caressing the tips of her breasts.

I had not wanted to remember this.

When the Paulist Press published a biography of Hughes, Harry was asked to review it. Who else *could* review it? Who else could *write* it? He saw all his research in it. He said the author had used his manuscript at the library in the major seminary in Yonkers—no acknowledgment, not even his name mentioned in the intro. It was as if someone had just cut out a part of him. Just by itself, someone else writing—publishing—Hughes, was enough, the book that had been one of the shut rooms of his life, that famous choice of exit on the road, turning so hard yet so imperceptibly, then. And yet to Harry it had never seemed given up, let go, had always seemed still there, still his, a precious reserve of a self he had not wanted to lose, only to postpone, as if life were an infinite sequence of lives, and, done with this one, you could move on to the next.

It was then he told me more about the archbishop, about the suspect drinking, the all-too-devoted woman in his life, all of it suppressed before, such weary revelations to me now. Who cared anymore? Did I, that the Church of his priesthood was such a familiar lying parade of incontinent clerics? Always the same tragedy: that this is what we should see, this is what should keep us from seeing the good done and still to be done. In my alienation from this exhausted universe I could hardly bring myself to think about Hughes again. Later, much later, I learned for myself what Harry had not told me: that Hughes's career had stood as the bedrock of hierarchy, of absolute priestly authority and obedience in the American Church. How ironic for Harry ever to have published such a life, to have said a kind of yes to the institutionalizing of such autocratic, patriarchal power—or no to it. Either way, no option. And yet it must have given Harry no satisfaction that whatever this other writer knew he knew because of Harry.

I did not know what to do for him in his raging pain. That in itself was a sign. And I was not really there. I was sick, losing weight, unable to eat, following wandering fires. I was being robbed of a piece of my life's work too. The college administration had announced a reorganization. Intercultural Studies, they said, would be dissolved.

Something in me had walked away. I told a friend who said I was looking shining, radiant, that I was in love. "I hope you mean with Harry," he said, glaring at me queerly, admonishingly, as if I had just tossed a statue of the Virgin Mother down the stairs.

How could I have been in love? I was full of a sick, queasy, unquenchable hunger, looking luminous as people look who are dying of starvation, their thin cheeks exotically molding their cheekbones, their eyes bright and big in their faces. My need for some huge self-realization had reversed itself on my body, shrunken me like a fasting saint, supplanted my old identity like a fabulous brain-birth, or a pod, sucked on me like a freakish wild thing, wandered out now to prowl in its furious lust like a she-wolf. And other predators knew me, they knew I loathed myself and this excruciating desire they could never satisfy.

He drank more heavily now. Our quarrels became violent. I picked up a knife in the kitchen to protect myself once, and he cut his hand. He hit me, as my father had. An old grave gave up its stinking corpse.

By which imperceptible degrees of joy and heartache had things changed, had our love changed into what it had become, that I could tell him I thought I no longer loved him? By which degrees of hard miracle did it change again?

How could I no longer love him and yet not bear to lose him?

So can you understand how it was? That when we learned that Harry had leukemia, it was as though I had wakened from a nightmare? Wakened, wakened, yes, and then descended into a new nightmare, but now a nightmare that had all the comprehensibility, the curious simplicity, of scientific fact, of bodily dying, of cell death, of chemotherapies, of shunts and tubes and intravenous feedings and leukocytes and blood counts.

Of hair loss and remissions and nausea, of pain and the fragility of winter sunlight from the window of a hospital room, and of love.

I could not bear to lose him. I cannot now bear it again.

5

There are many ways to act out the kind of rage that is buried in narcotic passivity. Members of my family have found almost all of them, violent to others or violent to themselves, sometimes both at the same time. Some have also healed in the process, passing through the long and terrible night of the soul to the plain day of love and mortality, finding here in this dear world all the transcendence they need.

Let me go back, then. Through my long night, as we sped, unknowing, to that unspeakable death. For the year before Harry became ill, I slowly sank from the brink of a wild despair of thwarted energy into the depths of a self-annihilating depression, passing day after day, week after week, of my precious summer writing and rewriting the same four pages of the same introduction to the same treatise on narrative theory again and again and again, unable to escape from the symbolic prison of those four textual walls. My brother Carlo, meanwhile, seemed curiously trapped in a similar no-exit, in a bedroom in Temecula, California, at the back of the house my parents had just finished building on a godforsaken windswept tract of wild southern California desert just north of San Diego.

It seemed a bizarrely apt midlife convergence for the two of us, as if we had each come to a blind wall in the maze not knowing whether the solution were without or within, partnered or alone. For several years in the mid-seventies he had worked with Lou designing innovative clean-room technology for orthopedic surgeries, where recovery disaster can be triggered by the least nanospeck of dust. It had been the first time since boyhood they'd worked like blood brothers on a project, the kind of partnership Carlo had always dreamed of. But every old seed of rivalry or mistrust still lying unhatched in their souls, every old humiliation or betrayal denied and unforgiven, was a hidden catastrophe, a buried land mine in their new brother-bond, bursting into periodic, screaming explosions of rage, murderous confrontations, and finally threats of law on both sides as the whole project blew to pieces.

Carlo was shattered. Out of research that involved the intensest, most meticulous calculations of mega-germ-counts on door handles and light switches and in the innocuous-seeming encounters of ordinary life, he tripped into a nightmare in which only the most pristinely secure clean-room seclusion could protect him from engulfment in an imploding universe of dirt.

Perversely, I found in his trouble a reason to live. From one soul's dark night to another's we spoke by telephone, long midnight pleas from me that he not take his own life, as he was saying so wearily he must, there was no other way out. I could never forget how he had embraced me for those few lifesaving days in Germany after Bim was born, when I had the right to fear I would be banished forever from everyone's love. I begged him to come east, to stay with us if he needed for a time. I knew,

I said, there would be help for him, that we could find it together. He did not have to be alone, he did not have to die.

Harry had only reluctantly agreed to this. Sick in his own soul, greedy for his own justice, he feared the coiling tentacles of family, the curses that tracked generations, the sickening, thwarting memories, the expectations you could never fulfill, the suffocating collapse of your identity in others' disappointments, the help they would never forgive you for. He had treated the recent forgiving overtures of his own sister and nieces with a kind of neglect that left them heart-hungry. I suspect he thought it better that way—better that they outgrow any need for a persona of his that no longer existed. The twins would invite us to Park Slope, and he'd put them off with the excuse that "he always got lost in Brooklyn." But it was also a metaphor, of the wilderness of kinship itself, of his willing liberation from it, and I had reason enough on my own side to see it his way. But I thought my brother was dying. He might be the embodiment of Harry's worst fears, but we had to stop him.

We had once had a little dog, a hapless mongrel with a dose of Lab retriever in his blighted pedigree somewhere, black, shiny fur end to end, with a tail like a plume. He had wandered collarless into our backyard one fall day maybe a year after we moved into Paterson, panting with the kind of doggie joy that announced the end of his quest for home. He had put his past behind him and was not about to leave. Michael Holden happened by and he and Harry consulted.

"I have seen this dog all over Paterson," Michael said. "This is unequivocally best-of-the-show purebred Paterson ur-dog. Sent by God."

"Fido?"

"Fido, Son of Fido."

We dubbed him McFido. He and the kids ran ecstatically around the dusty yard celebrating the nearest thing Paterson could offer to the parable of the prodigal son.

McFido went mad the year we went to England, unable to survive the fresh cataclysm of our six-month abandonment. We found him a total sociopath when we returned, perverse, destructive, uncontrollable. He was exiled to the sunporch, where he pissed his relentless rage on all the doors and walls. In a passion once, Harry tried to kick him, but McFido dodged and Harry's foot struck the back door instead and for weeks he stumbled about in a state of acute toe paralysis he referred to as the curse of St. Francis.

McFido was banished to the backyard, tied to a tree at the end of a long rope, where he howled his undying resentment like a soul in perdition. But on a school day in early winter when no one else was home, I unhitched him and put him in the car, and drove him out to my friend Margery—of Nina's birth night—now relocated from the wilds of Great Bear in Ridgefield to the wilds of Parsippany. And there the two of us found an open field and let him go.

I could not bring myself to tell my children the truth about this, ever. Even now my soul flinches, confessing. I told them only that he'd broken away and disappeared, that they should be happy now that he was free, which was in its own way true. They wept. I wept. Harry wept. Until I began to write this, I did not think how much more he cried for that dog than for my brother.

Perhaps Carlo, when he came, proved Harry's wisdom after all, the wisdom that grasps the mortal degree of difference between human and animal destructiveness. Or perhaps he fulfilled his own prophecy. I know that with no conscious intent to do it, my brother drove us farther apart, creating a ménage à trois for Harry, who thought we spent too much time together, that I spared too much of my caring for him. I thought it was only that old demon possessiveness of his, flush with a new fear that in his curmudgeonly snarling late middle age I might cut *him* loose like a dog, and I in my instinctive family rage said to myself that, oh, yes, he could care infinitely for suffering, for homelessness, in the mass—and what was my brother's terrible lonely self-destructive grief but a kind of homelessness?—but for a poor brother of mine he could not care.

It occurs to me now that the postulate physicists call the "theorem of the dead cat" might just as well be the theorem of the dead dog. Actually, it is the theorem of the *live* dead cat, and it states that in the peculiar randomness and order of the universe, if we do not know whether the cat we cannot see is dead or alive, we must take both assumptions to be true at once. I look back on this time in that same quandary of paradoxical assumptions. I was right, Harry was right, both realities were true at once, and we acted as if they were, even if we could make no logical sense of it if we tried. I railed against his insensitivity to my need for family and theirs for me, and yet within that same year, on a vacation trip abroad, he'd reclaimed my mother's cousins in Sicily with an enthusiasm that bordered on lunacy. And later, in mid-1979, when my parents had their fiftieth wedding anniversary and we brought them east and gathered the whole fandangled woodlot of Alaya-Spagnola family trees into one big hall to celebrate, Harry emceed the evening's festivities as if no one in my whole Greek tragedy of a family had ever wished or done a day's harm to anyone else, as if it had all been love and tango and laughter for the past half century, and for a little while he almost made us believe it.

And my brother *did* live, happy for a time if not ever after, in some sense thanks to us. Because eventually my Italian friend Margherita Repetto from college, something of a feminist celebrity now in Italy where an amazing decade of activism had utterly transformed the relationship of Italian women to the law, made a triumphal visit from Rome while he was in Paterson, and the friend and sister my hardened bachelor brother had not been able to see when she was twenty, suddenly, at forty-something, became the lodestar of his life.

All things true at once in alternative universes. And in one such universe there is a sibling whose sex we do not even know who is also my father's child. Carlo knew this. He had apparently swallowed it like a stone for years, undigested, not daring to confront my father with it, not daring even to speak it to any of us, until it was as if he must spew it up in some total unburial of his life in one of those gravedigging midnight conversations that made Harry so jealous.

I don't remember *how* he knew it. I think I was so bedazzled with the clarity of its factoid perfection that I have forgotten—perhaps even then forgot to ask. It was as if I had been there watching, seeing the complete course of the wayward romance that had nearly killed my mother when my sister was born, the mysterious, inexorable covenant between the two of them that had sent them west, that had set into motion the whole operatic cycle of our lives, complete at last with the exquisite D'Annunzian closure of a daughter coming home to him, like a curse fulfilled, with a love child in her arms.

I had a flashback then to something Aunt Carmelina had once said to me when Bim was the spurned love child, flailing his baby arms and legs in the center of that great *letto matrimoniale* on East 78th Street. Years later, before she died, I made her confirm the story, and she let it escape from her sworn *omertà* like a breath of rot from a casket, and then slammed it shut as soon as I pressed to know more. But it was enough. I couldn't quite take it in anyway. I couldn't then, and I can't now.

How can I explain that though my father is still living, not one of us has dared to lift that iron veil of secrecy? I think it has the status of myth to us, certainly to me, perhaps to my father himself—of a truth not necessarily less true for being on a continuum of space and time that no longer fits into the universe we know, and yet remains the single, irrefutable solution to a vexing mathematical problem that in a rational world would make everything whole and right. It is the light from a distant star that has traveled light-years to reach us, though the star the light once blazed in has long since died.

But for my brother the revelation came to me out of the deeps of a frozen personal anguish. He was haunted by that rejected half-sibling child we had never known. He longed to find this child, he told me, now grown middle age like us, like Carlo himself. I remember that at the time *this* doubling became the aspect of the story that haunted me, not the tale of those mutually tormented young lovers who had long ago seemed to find a way to live by the light of their dead star, but the story of the guilt and longing of a son's quest for his double, for the son even more rejected than himself. And so I began a novel. It became in my own dark night just another of my abortive, Frankenstein dreams of delusive creativity.

Failing dogs in our little local universe, we had found cats. This was for Nina's sake, who must, *must*, have small animal life in her orbit. First, a calico beauty she named Francesca, after a character in a storybook, and we all called Chessie, to make our own character of her.

But there came a time when Chessie seemed lonely to Nina, a delicate reader of such inter-species messages, and she longed for another cat to make a pair. It had to be orange, she declared—a cat of color, as it were—and through what seemed the infinitely long fall and winter of 1979, I searched. Far and wide, when I was almost too sick to teach, too sick to eat, living on toast and tea and some bitter rue, some gall secreted not by the body but the soul. The quest buoyed me, somehow, made life unaccountably livable. I discovered a weirdly touching animal ménage in Garfield, where an Italian who reminded me of my brother lived alone with cats and gerbils and chickens and sheep, and I picked a tiny, pinkish-yellow angora kitten from a scruffy recent litter. Just old enough for me to put under the Christmas tree.

Carlo was gone by then, probably already off to Italy with his new love, shored up, no longer depressed. It was Christmas Eve—Harry, besides his usual full-time teaching, had been working with an inner-city nonprofit group called INCCA on a project for affordable townhouses in Paterson. He had gone to Trenton the day before, seeking approvals from various state departments, and come back exhausted, crusty, hostile, unable to shed a flu that had had hold of him since October. But he would give Nina this kitten—*we* would, a sign somehow of the lingering fragile life of our mortal immortal love, a precious and singular creature of this particular universe-elect, and he was bending down, nursing it in a basket by the furnace against the chill of the night, when he felt that telltale stab of pain in his chest. He was hospitalized and diagnosed by New Year's Eve.

In a curious sense, the day he went into NYU hospital Harry had his comeback on the New York stage. His fourteenth-floor room stood approximately above East 30th Street in that sprawling complex. It was his favorite joke to visitors that it had taken him sixty years to make it to the East Side. You could look from his big window out over the East River and uptown onto a glorious scrim of city bathed in cold crisp January sunlight, looking as if someone had cut the Chrysler Building tower out of the enamel blue sky with an X-acto knife.

If hard and sharp is real, reality has never looked so real before or since. And still it had that quality printers might call "second generation," the look of art. Trying to draw the view for him, time and time again, sitting on the window ledge beside his bed, I felt this, as if I were a copyist, and this, in the window, a New York Canaletto, hung in an excellent light.

It was the stageset, the theater, of Harry's dying. It is meant to take nothing from the anguish of it, for him, for me, for all of us who lost him, to say that he gave the performance of his life. "Why *not* me?" he would say, in a retake on the usual take on a death sentence, to friends who came in choking back tears and five minutes later would be herniating with laughter. He told his life story into a tape recorder, day by day, in a monologue that could put you in mind of Spalding Gray without a therapist.

I have always thought those crucifying months brought him back to me, my beloved, loved so well, so well, because I was about to lose him. Is this less true if it is also true, as I can see now, that this larger-than-life New York Harry I got back wasn't the man but the legend?

He died the following November 29. We buried him out of St. Gregory the Great on a bitter December morning, the wind driving up our backs like an open freezer as we stood in the center church doorway, waiting for forty-one concelebrating priests to make their way, two by two, down the center aisle and crowd the altar. Jack Egan came from Chicago to give one of three eulogies to at least a thousand people, which included Harry's concubine and their kids.

There was no better theater in New York that week. Someone told me, some-one Irish and well up on the lore about sainthood, that on this frozen day a rose bloomed in the yard outside of Turin House, the housing co-op that Strycker's Bay—that Harry—had created.

I suppose you could say it was his first miracle. Another, not much later, was Ruth Messinger's getting West 90th Street between Columbus and Amsterdam named for him—the block with St. Gregory's at one end of the street and the Stephen Wise Houses at the other. Until the stable moved out, it was the one street on the West Side you could count on being ankle-deep in horseshit the year-round, which would've pleased him no end. As would Harry Mario "Bim" Browne's maiden New York speech, which opened: "I called him Father, too."

Unless somebody else is keeping count and hasn't told me, all the other miracles that could put him in a class with Maria Goretti have been those he has performed for me.

6

Dorothy Day had died the same morning as Harry, the greater Catholic Worker taking the lesser with her in a way, though I confess in the ghastly watch my first child and I kept that long night in the hospital, I had hallucinated with perfectly chiseled clarity his being assumed straight into the waiting arms of his mother. Ten days later John Lennon was shot, and I realized two things: how much, even within a week of Harry's burying, I could still care for the passing of another great spirit, and how much of that caring I owed to my children.

For music, *their* music, now, the opera of the 1970s—"We all live in a yellow submarine" shading by fine degrees into "Let It Be" and "Imagine," not to mention the Stones, the Kinks, the Ramones, Pink Floyd, and the Clash—had begun to refill our lives as they grew, helping me make an obliging transition from the extravagant musical culture that had been a part of my own growing up to the extravagant musical culture that now made so deep a part of theirs. No new icon was more captivating than Bruce Springsteen, who, as I heretically saw it, had whipped the baton out of the hands of Jersey's run of great poets from Whitman to Ginsberg, and raced howling into the stardom of the E-Street Band. Bim—young Harry now—adored him because he rang out the anguish of a passion-hungered adolescence. I did too, sensing the true *ardito,* an utter self-exposure to pain in the joyous candor of his genius. But when *The River* came out in 1980 during the long hell-harrowing winter-year of Harry's dying, I was strangely abashed at how deeply Bruce's new vein of grief resonated with my own.

My son, bewildered by this sudden dark turn in Springsteen's soul, came to me with a wistful plea to help him understand. And we understood together, in our widely distant dark places—how one could love, love passionately, joyously, blissfully, desperately, foolishly, childishly, and then, growing up, fall away. And then, in the darkest night of the soul, love still again, with a pain, and sweetness too, too deep for tears. We understood, or tried to understand, how one could be alone, singular, for oneself, and still be for others, in love—because you could not otherwise be for others, in love or out of it. I was beginning to sense the emergent message of freedom in this insight. Beginning. Whether it was Harry's legacy or Bruce's didn't seem to matter—it belonged to both of us, to all of us, now.

On the crest of the Campidoglio on a blistering and boisterous Roman day in June 1981, right after the pope was shot and even tired old Rome was still quivering with shock, Carlo and Margherita were married. Michelangelo's piazza was strangely barren, the ancient statue of Marcus Aurelius on horseback—symbol of Roman *civitas* itself—having recently been removed for restoration. But we four were there, and I made witness of honor in a new red satin dress, Scarlet Woman forever, as Margherita's Italian feminist friends committed her—resentfully, reluctantly—into the care of my mad engineer brother, and him into hers.

A year later I was married. Secretly, of course—what other way to keep a secret in my life?—in a punctilious, dry little ceremony in South Carolina with no witnesses but some friends of the man I was marrying. In part the secrecy was shame, first that I was marrying at all, second that I was marrying *him*, a guy just out of prison. His name was Damian—*Damian*—there's closure for you. Why him, out of all the possible possibilities? Because he was weirdly beautiful—lust of the eye goes on forever—because he was an outlaw, and because he had come out of a mining family in western Pennsylvania, which to me was the essence of romance. It helped his case that he thought I was a goddess and had Harry nailed as a prior god.

In retrospect it has the look of a demented exercise in experimental marriage, some sick combination of personal atavisms: Joan of Arc competing with Harry for sanctity and taking on the reform and rehabilitation of a career criminal. The children loathed him, with good reason, but not good reason enough, when you think what it was I needed to do and be then, to gamble my heart again, to express in my own twisted way my taste for freedom and for love, to keep someone—and more to the point, someone outlaw—in my still half-unawakened life, to take on Harry's missions, to acknowledge his apotheosis and do his radical earthly works here for him, one saved soul at a time. But I did not expect them to understand, anymore than I fully did, which is how I rationalized the secrecy at the time. I have no hard feelings about the hell they gave me. I deserved it.

But there was another part to this. Damian had written a novel—a bad novel, to be sure, but an effort while he was locked away to come to grips with the mischances of his own life, the roads taken and not taken, the hilarity of mischievous temptations turning by imperceptible degrees into unfunny white-collar crimes. The quest for another set of limits to pure freedom. It had been how we'd met, in fact, when my brother Lou, who knew him, suggested he ask me how he might find an agent. Something in me locked on to this book, and the peculiar crippled courage that had inspired it. The best part of our marriage proved to be about writing—about *my* writing. The joy of it, the howling laughter. I rewrote the chapters of *his* book that I liked best, learning through cool imaginative distance how I might write my own.

I used to say when it was over (which was quickly): *marry in haste, repent in haste.* It was that old epistemophilia—no sooner had I learned what marriage actually felt like than I was hellbent on knowing about divorce. Maybe in the end I did save the soul of the poor bloke, with a little help from my friends, here and hereafter, though through the whole of it, my friends here were almost uniformly horrified. Much as they'd loved Harry, maybe because they'd loved Harry so much, they didn't get the bizarre necessity of comedy in my life, or understand how my peculiar narcissism required *anything* but a proper bourgeois marriage.

I lost many of them. I lost more. With the exception of his sister Kay (kind to me always, and kind beyond kind), I lost Harry's family. A slow death, but perhaps doomed from the outset. Once they were able to stop and think, without all the bedazzlement of Harry's presence, they went off me, the way you might go off a taste for anchovies without the pizza. After all, I was the woman who had messed everything up to start with, and then gone and done it again before Harry was cold, as they say. I lost all the people for whom I had luster only in the glow from Harry's light. Margaret Mooney I'm sure would have preferred I languish as his relic, perhaps in a fetching mantle of black lace. With the qualified exception of Jack Egan and his nun-assistant Peggy Roach, there were the people of CCUM, religious and lay, who knew straight off I wasn't going to carry on Harry's Catholic agenda and had no false expectations. There were *all* the people for whom the political could be personal only if it was political first. Esta was also an exception: why be sentimental when there's work to be done? But of course Esta *was* sentimental—it was her worst-kept secret. And she understood that for me the personal could be political only if it was personal first. She waited for me to come out of it, knowing she wouldn't have long to wait.

Ah, but I gained Jay Schulman. He thought I loved him because he reminded me of Harry, and he was right, and it was a lousy basis for a relationship. But he was one of the smartest men I ever met, smarter than Harry in some ways because unlike Harry he had faced his own inner pandemonium. Everybody has one, I've come to see, some bigger, noisier, more crowded. Harry's could have rivaled the Mirage in Las Vegas; Jay's *was* the Mirage in Las Vegas. Most people are afraid to look into theirs, even some saints—maybe especially some saints. Jay, who was a psychologist, wasn't afraid to look. He knew, however, that once was never enough. You had to go back on different nights.

Jay had permanently scientized the practice of jury selection with a technique invented to help the Harrisburg Eight and other civil disobedience activists during and after Vietnam, which was how Harry knew him. The principle, a kind of applied social psychology, was that socioeconomic factors could be incredibly sharp predictors of juror judgment. A careful background analysis of jury prospects and a few key questions in the *voir-dire,* and Jay's team could virtually assure that political defendants wouldn't be faced with utterly hostile juries. It began to be used in jury selections of every kind. Ironically, a lot of people benefited from Jay's genius who may have had no right to in the larger scheme of justice, and also some who did.

Like Harry, Jay was a bear. He'd been fired from City College in a drama that maybe had a few parallels to Harry's first disobedience, and looked a little like Michael Holden multiplied. He had actually come to Ramapo in a job search in the late 1970s, though I hadn't met him then. I never met him, in fact, before Harry died. He was a gravelly phone voice until we had dinner, once, and I discovered he was big and grizzled and manic, emotionally immature and politically heroic, and fell for him like an egg off the butcher block. For a time he took me and my family on as a kind of case study, thinking he knew Italians. He knew Mozart. He was tone-deaf to real Italian opera, and applied all the wrong expectations to us.

Jay worked for the legal team trying to get Rubin "Hurricane" Carter a new trial for a Paterson murder that had taken place just a few blocks from where we live.

Carter said he'd been framed for it, and the case was and remains one of the classic high-profile test cases of a black man seeking justice in a white system. It brought Jay out to Paterson once or twice for dinner. This was when Damian and I were apart, married but no longer sure why.

"Why the hell did you marry that guy?" Jay would say, truly perplexed. I wish I could have told him. He could be a ruthless hypothesizer. He'd learned just enough of my family history to theorize that I came from a family of borderline criminal self-destructives, for which somebody back there ought to be held accountable. Like any good psychologist—maybe because I hadn't been psychoanalyzed and couldn't yet talk glibly about what drove me—he thought I had the least self-knowledge of any really smart woman he'd ever met. "How," he asked in amazement, "did you get this far in your life understanding as little about yourself as you do?"

I think he was wrong about that third thing, even in this nonalternate universe. It was not so much that I didn't know as that I hadn't yet let myself, like an Ariadne whose hero hadn't quite made it out of the labyrinth, and who comes late to the news that she may have to let go of her end of the thread and head in there on her own. Not till after Harry was gone and I'd made a few more mistakes did I understand that mistakes are not always the wrong thing to make. There are the ones you make when you have lost a leg and refuse to admit you need a crutch. And then there are the transcendent mistakes, the miraculous ones that grow you wings—for a time. Mistakes you will make only once in your life if you are lucky, mistakes some people never get the chance to make and you will never get the chance to make again.

I have died my best little deaths learning to know this, when I was alone, howling down the empty space Harry left me, over and over again, as if a glacier had torn away my mountain and I could never ever be consoled for the horizon I had lost.

I sometimes let myself wonder how different the learning would have been if he had lived, but his *not* living shoved me hard through the horizon of unknowing to a place where I could finally bear to see.

The program in Intercultural Studies had been sacked and pillaged while Harry was dying. The then vice president of Ramapo called me in a few months later and avoiding my still tear-swollen eyes, announced that the administration was, as a final coup de grâce, erasing comparative literature from the roster of majors. Just like that, as if it had never existed.

It might have been worse. It might have been better—I might have got out before the ship went down. But it might have been a lot worse. Some good colleagues, refusing to let me drift, gathered me like a boat person into what is now the School of Social Science, an interdisciplinary successor program to several of those thematic cluster schools from the Age of Titans including the ill-starred Social Relations. Out of a certain respect combined with generosity and a little entropy, they have made a place for me over the years as a kind of designated hitter—or, in cases where war is a more apt metaphor than sport, a designated suicide bomber. My marginal situation has puzzled younger colleagues, who do not understand this stray literary scholar in a social science program, this lone Ariadne among the technicians of life's mazy ways.

It was soon after this, suddenly forced to feel my way among career identities, that I began this book, proving again that the margin can be creative, something the marginalized know better than anyone. I would have begun it sometime, I think, whether or not that producer from NBC ever took me out to dinner and said she wanted to make a TV movie out of our story. I was still consulting my inner Harry then, but wasn't sure what he wanted. One thing was clear: it wouldn't be our story if *they* told it. It wouldn't be *mine*.

I sought out Pat O'Connor, an editor at Basic Books. He'd met the two of us at a dinner party at the home of a Rutgers colleague of Harry's in 1979. He must have spotted me immediately for a crypto-novelist. He encouraged me to write the story myself. "You've got nothing to lose."

"Well, there's NBC," I offered—a kind of use it or lose it deadline with this producer.

He laughed. He was a roundfaced full-moon-in-a-fog kind of Irishman, who'd loved Harry's gorgeous New York Irishness. "Try it," he said.

He walked me through the process, started me on a few chapters, talked agent Charlotte Sheedy into taking me on. Macmillan wrote the contract, I bought a place in New Hampshire with some of Harry's insurance money, and slowly, sometimes in full-flower euphoria, sometimes in black agony, became the kind of writer I had always wanted to be. Separating what fate had joined together. Joining together what time had put asunder. Marrying me to my own life.

Word got out that I was writing about Harry and me, angling for the Wyf of Bath award by blabbing my sex life with a frisky cleric into a book instead of a rain puddle. I lost a few more friends, particularly scholarly colleagues who saw me pouring myself down another sinkhole. Even Esta wanted me to make it a novel, so only the people who really knew would know. A lot of people, I think, people for whom he was the life force, didn't even like to be reminded that Harry was really dead. Didn't they know it was the same for me?

My hasty marriage pudding finally done and eaten and proved, I was basically a single working mother, putting three kids through college. Bim was finishing, Kiki midway, Nina just starting, in a tripartite arrangement of financing IVs that bled me like a hemophiliac. But I was writing, when I was writing, and the kids caringly came and went, so I did not suffer much from the empty house, because an empty house is what's inside, and I was full.

Of course I could not make my contract deadline—that was expected. How do you write at a snapping pace and teach full-time, when teaching pays the bills? The advance was too small even to give me a single free term. But I researched and interviewed when I wasn't writing, and I wrote in every spare hour, day, week, month, winter break, spring break, summer break.

And when I knew I couldn't write, when the work I had to lay down still stretched as long before me as a channel swim, when I had to stop and go back to teaching in September, in February, in September again, in February again, it didn't matter how congenial the teaching assignment, how amiable the colleagues, how wonderful the students in the aggregate or how exhilarating each new school year's failsafe guarantee that there would be that one single precious one—the anarchist, the perfect, underappreciated, achieving-because-of-you former underachiever—who would make you proud to be a teacher and love you and be a friend forever. It didn't matter, none of it. I still sank back into my job the way a stone might sink in the Blackwater River, and for seven years put my poor body through a shoot-the-shoots of illness, all of it rage and resistance, I am sure, all of it color-coded red right in the DNA, reading out this message: I am doing what I *have* to do, what someone has *made* me, not what I want to do. I am not doing this out of love.

Oh, but those glorious spaces of sweetness, sometimes with Nina, sometimes alone, when I would escape for a few weeks into the solitude of that sisal-carpeted room in the north country, surrounded by glass and birch trees, the hot breeze cross-blowing through the sliders carrying the scent of New Hampshire summer on it like holy smoke, when my new little word processor cooked and steamed like a foundry and yet I molded chapters not like iron, but like bread, sweet and savory, kneaded them like loaves, making food of love better to eat than sorrel soup and blackberry tart from the bushes on Center Road, better than plum tomatoes from the backyard vines.

And when I had done a day's good work I would grab my suit and towel and ride down, down, down to the river, and plunge into the icy flow of the Blackwater, cutting into the pondlike little lake it made after racing white and warm over the rocks and before taking off down into the stream by the dairy farm, and swim out to its center and lift my eyes to the bowl-rim of trees and then to the dome of velvet sky and think that everything in my life before and after this moment had happened, I and Harry and every creature on the living earth had all done and suffered, lived and died and loved, forever and yet to come, so that I could be here, alive, afloat on this stream poised between life and mortality, between life and life and life.

7

In a fine synchronicity, the same month I became chairperson of the City of Paterson Historic Preservation Commission, I finished the book and mailed the hefty manuscript to Cynthia Merman, my editor at Atheneum. She immediately announced she was leaving to freelance.

Cynthia had been one of those rare readers who could be deliciously kind to a writer and still tell her the truth. Her milky phone voice had nurtured me and my project for over a year. It was another little death. "You'll have to find someone else," she told me sorrowfully.

My little Rome of three thousand days. She knew what it had cost me, knew I'd had a serious breakdown in the fall, the worst panic attacks of my life, as I'd approached the end, and had just fought my way through to finish by the new year. Charlotte, too, had stood by me, managed to keep the contract alive through all the Macmillan *perestroikas* of the eighties that had already almost orphaned the book once. But the market had changed, she said, and even she didn't think she could carry on.

Working so hard at teaching and writing together, I didn't have either the time or the focus then to grasp why I'd crashed, physically, emotionally, as the book was ending. For the past year I'd already begun to take up community life, to be active in the city again, and if I was only slightly present to the world, it was certainly present to me. But 1989 had been another one of those cosmic Years When Everything Happened: the uprising in Tiananmen Square, the end of the Berlin Wall, the shattering of all the tidy oppositions of the world as we'd known it. In my microcosmic life, the tumult reappeared in the shape of just-averted tragedy—a suffocating July night when I'd rushed Christopher, my blue-eyed darling, all the way from his student digs on West 110th Street to the St. Joe's emergency room in Paterson, and discovered him to be diabetic minutes before the ketosis might have killed him. A month later, while I was in California, someone broke into the house. Quite real enough events, both of them, quite painful enough as reality. But they were also metaphors of vulnerability, a vulnerability my body had not yet unlearned.

I had seemed to be looking for safety, safety even from the news. To be bunkered down, living in a well of yesterdays as I wrote, keeping myself evasively posted on the big world and its passing events by radio. I'd rediscovered Pacifica one Saturday while changing sheets in the upstairs guest room, having turned on WBAI up there for company and heard Martin Luther King's "I Have a Dream" speech end to end for the first time in my life. It felt like a lifeline to a part of me that had once stood on a soundtruck trying to make a difference, and seemed to have died with Harry.

I'd been writing, earning my living, worrying about my aging parents in California, seeing to it my kids were launched and happy, divorcing, giving up smoking, learning to use my first computer, repairing the house, weeping, shedding a few skins. I'd been slowly reacquainting myself with the British, teaching in an honors program at Ramapo that took students to Oxford before their senior year. The postwar, postcolonial British now: falling in love with them again, as I learned what it had meant to the chastened soul of a culture to lose an empire. I'd met Beatrix Campbell, the brilliant British feminist and social critic who'd followed up George Orwell's *Road to Wigan Pier* with a Wigan Pier of her own about working-class Englishwomen. We'd got her to Ramapo to speak. It took me back to Anthony Burgess, but better: a woman, a conscious writer-activist, who made me see you could give yourself and not give yourself away.

Though not precisely giving myself away, I'd been doing what people asked me to, like pen a short biographical study of Catholina Lambert for the Passaic County Historical Society. They'd remembered the work Harry and I and several others had put together a few years back on a stunningly prolific Italian American public sculptor named Gaetano Federici—a colorful tour de force spotlighting a slice of Paterson culture no one had touched till then. Lambert was better known, but still under-written. He'd been Paterson's classic autocrat silk tycoon, a rags-to-riches, self-made English immigrant in the mold that had so captivated Richard Margrave ten years before, making and losing a fortune. His surviving "Castle" seemed the single achievement worthy of celebration: a sandstone and granite Gilded Age fantasia of his own concoction hanging like a chunky pendant on the breast of Garrett Mountain. I tended to poet Williams's quick take on "the old boy" in *Paterson:* that cameo image of a hard-nosed and hard-hearted cold old man, a driven son of a bitch, really, with a passion for some kind of glory to rival the Yorkshire aristocracy that had awed him as a boy, violently hostile to unions, hero to the art-collecting fine-fettled *parvenus* of his time. But by middle age he'd lost most of his children to undiscriminating childhood diseases, and his favorite daughter, Florence, to puerperal fever when he was forty-nine—exactly my own age as I wrote about him. He had still built his castle. You had to be a little impressed.

And the editor of *Dickens Studies Annual* had asked me to write an omnibus review essay, surveying what had happened to the reading of Victorian fiction since the feminist critical revolution. The National Endowment for the Humanities gave me a summer grant to do it—brutally hard work that cost me a lot more than a summer, but good for me. For I had felt diffident, academically disconnected, both within the college and beyond it, damaged, almost scared to venture back onto scholarly turf. It had seemed as if I'd evolved downward somehow, as if I'd been squidding about in the silentest watery deeps and were being asked to breathe air again. Thin air at that. The subject sometimes seemed unbearably abstract until I found I could speak of it in two almost fictive voices: one voice for the main text, a meditatively bewildered spectator (like me) on a darkly wooded terrain undergoing incomprehensible shifts, the other for the rather densely packed endnotes, the voice of a cocksure unruffled academic (also like me, once—maybe once again), blithely marking the trees, faintly complacent, perhaps even a little glad that the forest might actually be smoldering.

In an academic profession increasingly dominated by theory, I was keeping my edge. Who, after all, knew what would become of the "Harry book" (as I was still calling it then), if ever it were finished. After losing my original Macmillan editor, I'd burrowed, on writing doggedly in a don't-ask-don't-tell kind of secrecy, while my Victorianist colleagues wondered—whispered about me, wondering if I'd have a comeback for Sandra Gilbert's interesting 1983 retake in the *PMLA* on my version of E.B.B.'s Italy. All except Coral Lansbury, who was straightforward as hell, and would reassure me when we ran into each other at meetings that I was right to plow on as I was, even at the sacrifice of more scholarly stuff: "Who needs another book of academic nattering?" she'd say—this, though she herself turned out the most brilliant scholarship with one hand and brilliant fiction with the other. Tall, brassy, magnificent, an Australian cousin of Angela "Murder She Wrote" Lansbury and a splendidly theatrical persona in her own right, Coral was any crypto–Scarlet Woman's heroine. "Keep going—write something real people will read." She meant people like you, who have made it this far.

Coral was under contract to do another novel at the time, this one set in Sicily. "Come with me," she begged. "Two weeks in the summer, translating. On me. It will be pure larx." I cannot believe I said no. My mother had just come out of the hospital, an early warning of congestive heart failure, and there they were, the two of them, old, alone, needy, out in the wilderness—a wilderness of their own choosing, to be sure, but no less a wilderness for that. Irony of ironies, I was the one child (read "*daughter*") free enough of family and work obligations to get away. "If I tell you why I can't go with you," I told Coral, "you will understand Sicily better than you could in any two weeks as a tourist."

They say you change all the cells in your body every seven years. I guess this means that, more or less, by this same time there wasn't any part of my body that had an eyewitness cell memory of Harry anymore. Maybe there is an explanatory paradox in here somewhere.

My mother's sister Joan died in September of 1988, as I probably remember because everything after seems so oddly interconnected. I went down to Atlantic City, where the family lived, meeting all her grown-up kids at the funeral, and some of Aunt Teresa's family too, though Teresa herself hadn't come. She and her brood had actually moved out to Jersey, to Glen Rock, a few miles from Paterson, years before. She'd become a recluse after Uncle Louie died—would barely speak to me when I'd phoned to invite her to my parents' fiftieth. It was as if she were waiting for a call—the one with the swelling angel music telling her that this whole stupid exercise of living without him was finally over—and I was tying up the line.

I wondered how many times she'd wished she'd gone first, as I'd heard my mother sometimes pray out loud she would, that old Tosca thing, dreading the emptiness without him the way other women dread cancer. And yet my mother, fractured with self-contradiction, also wept at the thought of leaving Mario alone, without her help—or, worse still, with time enough on his own to prove that everything she'd ever done for him, all those tenderest small offices that still gave her life its tiny pearl of meaning, could be performed just as well by somebody else. Aunt Joan had gone swiftly, mercifully, two years after her Vinnie, of leukemia.

It was a Spagnola deluge, nevertheless, with Aunt Elena, my mother's youngest sister, up from Alabama for the funeral. Elena had married Fred Dillard, brother of Ferril, Mildred's husband, back when she was just out of bobby sox and the aphrodisiac of the armistice was in the air. I could still picture them dancing the nights away at those booming victory block parties when we small kids watched from the tenement windows. I'd visited them in Montgomery once, during my year in Greensboro, where Fred gave me a boozy lecture on the mating habits of blackbirds and white birds, and Elena had seemed all too ready to take it in with the water and tolerate his racist bullshit from here to a week from Sunday.

Elena also talked like an Alabaman, "*y'all*" this and "*y'all*" that. It was the weirdest thing to hear it come out of one side of her mouth while NooYawk still came out the other. And she loved a good laugh whether or not the joke was funny to anyone but herself, running the gamut from cackle to howl in ten seconds. By the time she'd had a couple of drinks she was ready to tell me she'd nearly fainted when we'd greeted each other in the church and she'd seen how I'd lost my looks.

True, my hair had gone white, but considering nobody was looking too beautiful under the circumstances, it felt pretty cruel. I wondered if I'd ever get to the stage where I wouldn't give a stuffed fig one way or the other, even for a compliment on how good I am still looking, for which, believe me, I am still a sucker.

And that's the thought I was thinking, as I drove back home along Twelfth Avenue just before the turn into my street, and saw the old Fergusson House, a listed historic property, crashing down under the wrecking ball. Mayor Francis X. Graves had struck again, one of his now-famous sneak attacks on Paterson's great old buildings, going after this particular masterpiece because somebody had complained it was a crack house, and he wanted to be known as the Crack-Down-on-Crack King of New Jersey.

Maybe it had something to do with Aunt Elena, but my fight was up. It was as if I'd just woken up from a years-long dreamful sleep on a park bench to discover the bench being dismantled out from under me. I phoned Mayor Graves. Trading on his old admiration for Harry, I got him to see me. Then I took him on in the letters column of the local paper. Then I faced him before the city council, where he loved to preside: the King in Parliament.

"It's a crime," I said, speaking nervously into an awkward microphone for which the room seemed somehow too small, "some of the buildings that've been destroyed already—the hearts of those communities." I'd never been comfortable in front of a microphone, and I wasn't now. And maybe the gaminlike short cut of my stark white hair, if you thought about it, might put you a little in mind of Harry's, once. But frankly it didn't feel as if I were doing somebody else's duty, but that I was finally picking up where I'd left off and doing my own.

"Excuse me, Mrs. Browne—er, Dr. Alaya—?" he interrupted me. "You say this is a 'crime.' Could you tell me what law has been broken?"

"Your Honor," I said, "there are crimes that aren't yet against the law."

Two meetings later we had the historic preservation ordinance the Municipal Land Use Law had mandated for Paterson more than a decade before, when the Great Falls District had been landmarked. Two months after that we had a full-scale Historic Preservation Commission, two months later I was on it, and chairing it, as I say, a year after that.

I had successfully papered over the breakdown, you might say. I had almost buried the book. Maybe an indecent burial, but otherwise I had done everything I should.

I'd found love, become partnered again, to Sandy Feddema. Sandy: a wondrously androgynous childlike name for a wonderfully androgynous childlike yet mature human being, a crypto-poet, deeply good, but pain-stricken and joy-stricken, both, in the mold I was ever best destined to understand. He is Paterson-born, symbol in some sense of my faith, my commitment here, though for his own part he had found his way back, back here to find me, via many detours, many mazy ways of his own.

Strange how, despite his gentle vulnerability, Sandy seemed—seems—so protective, fixing things, changing things, planting an organic garden, for instance, where there'd been no more than a bit of scruffy useless lawn. And yet so free—a warrant of my own freedom. I was to him whatever I was or wanted to be to him: teacher, writer, artist, activist, mother, widowed heart, weeper, laugher, lovemaker. And he to me.

Another agent, Joan Brookbank, had taken on the book, almost without my asking. Walked it around. Nan Talese had said it was "too ornate," among other things. Joan too decided to move on, with immense kindness, but still—

I should give it up, I thought. And yet I seemed not to feel the joy of my restored direction with it buried alive that way. I was angry at myself for feeling this, just as I was angry at the college for seeming to take such little pride in what I was now doing in the world, not giving me the time off I begged for, to work on public history writing and video projects, never acknowledging the sheer press visibility I gave *them.* Why shouldn't they be proud, proud of this citizen chapter of my life—if a detour, then a detour worth the taking? Why shouldn't I?

In the summer of 1994, on the advice of Ellen Denuto, a photographer living in the historic district, I picked up Julia Cameron's *The Artist's Way* and began my "morning pages," a journal discipline familiar to devotees. Oh, I plodded through all the little exercises, from remembering Miss Ridgeway's *"normal and average"* in high school and every other awful little dig and hurt to my inner artist, to pasting up a few of the diviner things people had said about my writing. But the journal, simply putting words down every day, seemed the least mindlessly self-helpish activity, became the one thing I stuck with. It reminded me of Konrad Hopkins, his advice about automatic writing when he'd sent me William Sharp's review of my book long ago: just sit quietly. With faith. The messages will come.

Ah, faith.

It seemed to apply to writing, period. Writing even when I didn't want to, when I was feeling brain-dead. Writing about the fugitive ordinariness of life, without too carefully sifting out what wouldn't survive the test of time. And it connected me with the living and the dead, created a place to be in ordinary conversation with anyone, from whoever was God to all my old pen-pal girls, Carole and Lettie, Judy and Ann.

But it connected me with writers, too, especially women, over the whole life of literature as my feminist theory essay had shown, fictional diarists as well as real self-writers, characters in epistolary novels. It connected me with *The Portuguese Letters* and the *Sonnets from the Portuguese,* with Fanny Hill and the Wyf of Bath and *Color Purple* Celie and Moll Flanders. It connected me with the ever-renewing romance of women, and all their perpetual record of the exquisite daily pain and beauty of love and love lost. It connected me with "the tradition," with my newly defined darling, Olive again, with Kate Chopin and Katherine Anne Porter, with Katherine Mansfield and Virginia Woolf and Angela Carter and Erica Jong, women with whom I had no right to bracket myself but still, still, every right to love like sisters—no?

I had begun to think of writing another novel, a novel about Paterson, this time, for though the great poem about Paterson had been written, the great novel hadn't. I dreamed of it, days and nights. It would have Lambert in it. Federici. Gurley Flynn and the Wobblies, Carlo Tresca. The Italian anarchists—above all, a legendary woman anarchist known only as "the beautiful Teresa." Maybe Olive. Maybe Fiona Macleod.

I made notes.

> *October 2, 1994—My goal: I am a novelist. I write. I get up in the morning and I write. I have breakfast on my balcony over Lake Garda [the Mediterranean, the Adriatic], then write some more. I have speaking and lecture engagements, I teach maybe a course a year. I live in the U.S. sometimes, but get to see my Irish granddaughter more often now.*

Young Harry had expatriated to Ireland. He had uncannily met and married an Irish lass, Imelda, native of the next town over from the Brownes's Timahoe—Port Laois—where they still muttered folktales of great-uncle headmaster John's truculent pedantry and iron rule. Harry[2] (or Harry Two, as some people called him) was now a journalist, she a solicitor. They'd had a little girl, Louie, whom they had named for the early century Irish socialist Louie Bennett—an odd trick for subverting and surviving the tradition of keeping family names in the family.

My kids had learned their lesson well. Had I?

•

October 15—I seem to need some kind of desert. I could get out to Hawley and do some research on the novel there for a few days. I was oddly touched last night when Quentin Tarantino said in a Charlie Rose interview that he loved history in school because it was like a movie—stories he could see happening. He's the kind of storyteller, he says, who tells stories whatever way they happen in his mind. How do I tell stories? In overlapping weaves? In rushes forward and back? Maybe like a sculptor, in the round, everything there at once, only linear from a certain perspective. Except my life, except my life, except my life.

Hawley is a town about fifty miles west of Paterson in eastern Pennsylvania, Third World of the 1870s, where the labor was cheaper, more docile—more female—where silk industrialist Lambert had once built himself another castle to house his new silkworks. I wanted to see it, walk around it, touch it, *feel* the sense of the place, the lives lived and spent there. Yet even to plan a day trip was to carve a finer slice out of a life sliced too fine already. I'd begun to feel like my mother: *I have so much to do! There's so much to do, so many things to do!* Precisely at the time when my "doing," like hers, had seemed to have lost much of its meaning.

I thought of my own daughter, Nina, vacationing in the Berkshires at that very moment, I imagined her waking up well-slept and refreshed after a day of antiquing and apple picking with her beautiful guy. It made me swell with pride—and envy. What would it feel like, I wondered, to be uncluttered, unfettered like that? The way it felt five, six, seven years ago, when I'd had the house in New Hampshire and the Blackwater River and writing had been at the center of my life? I crazily imagined myself asking my father for money to buy time from my continuous four-course load at the college. Oh, God, my gut ached. Always. Eating had become an exquisitely calculated war, my own body the battle zone. It occurred to me that every year I had seemed to invent some illness, some exquisite little pre-death, to rescue me from the slavery of teaching—or to punish myself for stealing time from my dearest life.

Sandy and I took the trip out to Hawley, finally, on a sublimely sharp, clear, brilliant fall day, the color laid out with the cleanest of palette knives against a deep cloudless blue canvas of sky. He was patient and tender, George Henry Lewes to my George Eliot, I thought, Victorianly, as I filled my novel "quarry." I could taste and see and smell my story. But it grew by millimeters. Wanting to be written. Unwritable.

The memoir was still in the way. I asked others about who was publishing memoirs, even thought of self-publishing. I simply needed to *finish* this project, I thought, finish with it. Close. Give it a decent birth or a decent burial. At a poetry conference called "Unsettling America," a beautiful creation itself, organized right here in Paterson by Italian-American poet Maria Mazziotti Gillan and her daughter Jennifer, I heard Shirley Goek-lin Lim, the Asian-American poet. She was just finishing *her* memoir for a series being assembled by the Feminist Press.

•

I had begun to sculpt and draw again, whenever I could find time, to go to art shows.

October 24: I have just seen the work, the exquisite portrait drawings, of
an Italian-American artist, Karen Carrino, who was killed in a car acci-
dent at nineteen. Nineteen! I met her sister there, who had mounted the show.
I should write to her—tell her how much our encounter meant to me, how
good the little booklet about the work is in its honesty and understatement,
how important it is for her to live, to go on living, to free herself from the
awful grief I can still read in her face, how important to find a fracture in
the seal of heaven for Karen's joy to pour through.

I knew immediately that I was writing about myself. *"What about me? Have I cap-*
tured Harry's joy? What of my own? Is this what the memoir is about?"
More than ever, I had to know what it was about, before I could move through
it, beyond it—to see it as a story of freedom, freedom from a series of joyless thrall-
doms, his to the Church, and mine, ultimately, to him. But freedom for both of us
from the well-inscribed codes of our ethnicities in this relentlessly ethnic culture,
from our relentless families and the bondage of their expectations. From suffocating
gender expectations, for him and me.
Freedom even from our false images and ideals of one another. For I could see
Harry as a model of freedom and boldness for me, a *teacher* in the most ancient sense.
He had laid down a path and invited me, coaxed me, seduced me, *dared* me to follow him. Yet I could see there was a thralldom in his freedom, too, and it was our
common role in this reading of the freedom script to set him free of *his* bond to the
institutional church. And I was in thrall to him too, but in setting him free I began
to be able to liberate myself. *"All the conditions of our lives at the end of the book are*
our 'elective affinities,'" I wrote:

They are not pure, but they are real—the joy of the children, and the empow-
ering of another generation, Paterson and the politics of place—commu-
nity—immigration—color—

The house, the house, the solid cube of the house! All houses in it, encoding
the life livable in a concrete, geographical, spatial way, as the center of our
political lives, the yield of our labor for ourselves and for others.

"The end of the book" meant the book as it ended then, not really a life, but an episode.
Not a life, and not a death: I had kept Harry's dying out of it till then, as if he must
never die again. And yet just to think this was in a sense to let him go. I seemed
to know this—that no liberation could ever be complete, but that there was hope
in each freedom's staging, its incrementation.
I planned for months to write to Florence Howe of The Feminist Press, but

couldn't. There was, for one thing, the simple exposure to rejection again, from a source this time that might finally break my heart. There were all the fears that had ever been the circumambient atmosphere of the writing, the fear of exposure, of myself and others, the fear of breaking the codes of silence.

The fear, too, of taking that inexorable turn in my life, the turn the book would mean toward my self. And there was the excuse of busyness, a busyness that was real as well as invented—the too-heavy teaching load, the nagging oversight of the commission, the responsibility of helping administer a huge new grant to the historic district through the National Park Service, plus the duties I'd taken on as state advisor to the National Trust.

Recently, a new city fissure had opened up in the threat to sell a former Underground Railroad site for a Taco Bell franchise and the erupting community quarrel had invested me suddenly with an unaccustomed role, as mediator, bridge, between Paterson's black and white power structures. Dolores Van Rensalier, the great-granddaughter of the black abolitionist who had once protected fugitives there, sought me out, asking me to help give voice to—to empower—an activism that was not yet fully empowered. To prevent the desecration of the site. It seemed to me the essence of the work I had entered this field to do.

So it was not that it lacked meaning—only if I could not also *write* about it. And yet I seemed to be still divided from my creative self, as if nothing I did or planned to do made part of my true life, as if the very things I wanted to do, loved to do, seemed more enemy than friend. I had dreams of liberation, of doors being sprung open, suddenly. They all seemed related to the unuttered, the silent, the secret book: *I must not forget the letter to Florence Howe—*

> *November 23—Sandy's up now, feeding the cat, rattling tins, crackling the morning air. I'm in the way, here in front of the oven door, with the big chair and my book and pen, trying to get warm. There must be a dishwasher load of cups in there, since there's only one clean cup left in the cupboard. We are throwing a great Thanksgiving party tomorrow, nary a thought to the cost in any terms. Well, we shall give our thanks—to one another, to the "Creator," to the good people and good forces that have been our way lately and the love we love and the loves we treasure and the good things we have, including the weather that has left the last lettuce still in the garden to harvest tomorrow. Please God, the God whom I also thank not as an afterthought but as the not-to-be-fathomed purpose of it all, give me the courage to see this day through , and the next, and the next, so that I may feel grace and confidence again.*

November 29 that year dawned a sweet morning, as bright and clean as the one fourteen years before when Harry died. It had been cold then. But this morning was not cold.

I wondered then if Harry could possibly help me understand how it was that in every way he had been the outlaw, been damned as the outlaw, as the very embodiment of the principle of outlawry, and yet had hung in—*in*—in the Church, *with* the Church, inside the process of making things change. Was it the same with me, staying with—whatever it is I had stayed with? That I could subvert and survive, refuse to be disciplined by it, yet try to make it better? Why had I not fled the college long ago? What had seduced me to stay? Some stray, momentary kindness? The need to protect the kids? Or safety for me? How ironic that the safest place should be one that seemed to kill you, perhaps even without meaning to, to beat you to death by inches. Ironic that the quest for safety should build institutions the way bricks build walls—yet that there should remain forever that other quest, the quest of the very grass and ivy and maple sapling and anarchist within, to unbuild them.

I thought, then, that I had loved and nurtured the outlaws among my students, perhaps taught them some principles of basic fist-shaking. Perhaps I had not been loved except by the stray fist-shakers. And they had taught *me,* every one. The wild ones, especially.

Perhaps I had taught disobedience. *Non serviam.* Chafing at disciplines, yet laughing, not grieving, at the falls along the way. I thought I couldn't make people laugh, like Harry, but I had known how to laugh myself.

The Modern Language Association Convention that year-end was its usual zoo, only a San Diego zoo this time, and bearable for the sake of mid-December weather without a coat. I had missed the last couple of MLA conventions, and it felt as if I were visiting from another life. I suddenly understood the second coming. It was as if I were dividing my old universe into those I would always love to meet and those I wouldn't. There was Carrie Silver, Carrie of the whooping-cough bedsheets, reminding me about my rejected submission to the Northeast Victorians program committee, putting it all into perspective for me, the sentiment right but the love gone cold. Was I becoming such a glutton for true love? Finding Janey Lilienfeld, getting hugged and kissed amid her little Virginia Woolf mafia lovefest, made it seem so. Yes, it was precisely what I was becoming.

And then meeting Florence Howe at the book show was not the purest chance, but I hadn't really dared to dream she'd actually be there, sitting at her booth, proudly displaying her wares, leaning back in that placid unflappable way she has of looking as though she dwelt in a perpetual cloud of Zen. She glanced up at me, welcomingly, from under her long lids, smile lines sunbursting around her eyes. My poor rejected manuscript seemed less orphaned now that I had seen her, heard from her own bow-lips how she looked forward to reading something straight through as compared with the usual fifty pages at a time.

After a day or two of going to exactly the sessions I liked rather than the ones I had to, something in me longed to feel guilty and diffused, but instead I allowed the exhilaration through. My identity might include scholarship, I thought, but it didn't need to be impaled on it. There had always been that fear of losing my edge, of not knowing (as Harry loved to say) more and more about less and less, which, silly as it sounded, had come to be the definition of the life of the mind. Surely there were other models, I thought. Maybe I am kind of a poet. Maybe I am a writer of all work.

Erica Jong spoke at a special session, an anniversary celebration of sorts of the publication of *Fear of Flying.* She had talked about simply going on writing as a test of accomplishment, and it brought to mind the silences that in the early feminist days used to bring us to tears. It made me think about all the bylaws I'd written in my life, and the journal articles on the economics of urban preservation, and the letters of recommendation to graduate school, and the pleas for colleagues' promotions, and the appeal letters to foundations, along with the stuff on Matthew Arnold and Tennyson and E.B.B. and the theoretical *Prologomena to a Poetics of Place,* and where once I'd felt a bit shamefaced, as if so much of it had been hackwork, a trashing of my talent, now as this new year dawned, my sixtieth year to heaven, it suddenly seemed all right: I *had* gone on writing, and it had all been compost, a preparation, a path, the way maybe Daniel Defoe's sleazier journalism had been, so that in the end he could do anything he wanted, anything, some of it even good, some of it "art," so that he could write his *Moll Flanders,* his *Roxanne,* so that in the end I could, too.

Perhaps the time would come when I would even cease to regret ever *not* making "art"and "avoiding my novel," as Janey used to say, when I would no longer pity the little Italian American girl whose nascent little wet feathery squab of a gift could not fly because it was only the nascent little wet feathery squab of a gift of an Italian American girl.

My mother had fallen down and injured herself again, for who knows which of the many times she had done this in the last year, since Elena had died—the most terrible of all her sisterly losses somehow, her baby sister, whom she had grown up dandling in her own arms, nursing like her own.

She seemed to intuit with some silent and unspeakable logic that falling down and hurting herself would be the only way to get time off from the self-crucifying labor of caring for my father, the only way possible for him to value her. I realized how deeply sorrowful she had become, that I had not heard her laugh once since we had come this time to California.

She begged me as we were leaving not to rush away. "*Sit down by me,*" she said, and held my hand, and we nestled against each other for the first time perhaps since I was a child. Sandy told her about the orange angora cat we had to get back to. He tried to describe the color, and she remembered that she'd owned a coat with a heavy fox collar just that color once. She remembered in fact that she still owned it—it was just like her to have kept it—the very same coat she'd worn in Arizona, that night at the movies, the tearjerker Bette Davis thing that had made me soak pints into it. She actually smiled.

I wept like a baby when we parted. I felt so certain that in this moment of terrific and unblanching lucidity she knew we would never really see each other again.

She knew she was going to die, and yet she took me past my stern superiority to that place where she was ever the master of love, and me a child who did not yet want to master her. How would I ever do her justice in the writing of her in all her tenderness and beauty and genius for reaching the innocence in me?

My mother died under a great and blazing full moon in August 1996. I did get to see her after all, to hold her hand, to draw her face, to pronounce against the grand music of her unwilling departure how much I had loved her life, if I could not imitate it.

There came so many mysterious and wonderful gifts in the few months afterward, I thought there must be some deadline she was meeting for miracles.

One of them was a grant to write about the station on the Underground Railroad, which we had succeeded in making a landmark a few months earlier.

Another was Rome, where another grant sent me for nine full weeks in the spring of 1997, handpicked in a grueling competition to represent the United States in a small seminar of specialists on historic cities from all over the world. The seminar was run out of ICCROM, a wonderful palimpsest of a place, clunkily named the Center for the Conservation and Restoration of Cultural Property, and using its old teletype address as its acronym. ICCROM takes care of—is in a sense the mother of—World Heritage Sites for the United Nations. For the world. My mother knew that.

But I also brought Rome home with me when I came back. For wonders of wonders, on the nineteenth of April, the Senate and People of Rome celebrated the multimillennial anniversary of the founding of this immemorial city by placing the Marcus Aurelius monument back into its august position on Michelangelo's Campidoglio—the very statue that they had removed from the piazza at the time of Carlo's wedding, just after Harry died. Or not precisely this statue but an ersatz version of it, the original having been secured against future centuries in a less public, open, and exposed emplacement.

I had forgotten who'd told me to watch for this event, such a splendid signifier, I thought, of the meaning of memory in our cities and in ourselves, seeming so inexpressibly to *inscribe* it with name and place. Astonishingly, no one at ICCROM had mentioned it: my colleagues were all off to other historical places that weekend. I'd been preparing my final presentation on historic Paterson and hadn't even been attending to Italian news. It was only later I remembered that a young writer-friend of Christopher's, Martha Garvey, had casually mentioned it on a visit to Rome the month before, when we'd shared a classic Jewish-quarter supper of those crisp, delicate *carciofi alla giudea* and then powerwalked along the chilly Tiber afterward, back to my little rented penthouse apartment on the Aventino.

And yet, as if drawn by some invisible force, I found myself in Piazza Venezia that afternoon, caught up in the press of a thousand Romans. My old friend Judy, goddess-familiar of so many passages in my life, was with me, pleased that I had come near enough at last to her now home-city of Athens to visit, and I left her, exhausted from her shopping and sightseeing, resting on a marble bench at the foot of the great staircase, as I followed the floating sound of chamber music above us on the hill.

I couldn't get anywhere near the festivities until the players were finished, and then I met them, one by one, as I was going up, coming down those fantastic Michelangelo steps holding their instruments aloft amid the straggling celebrators. When I got to the top, as dusk came down and the moon rose, hundreds of Romans were still milling about the piazza. Some of them just stood there staring at *this,* the mere copy of their beloved and long-lost, including some who had surely been young when they last saw him in the piazza, and weren't now. They were telling their kids about him—who he was, why he was great—or having their kids tell them. Some complained that the surrogate version wasn't dirty enough; they hoped it would get dirty soon. Others recounted mangled versions of its history, all different, and all with the same imperturbable authority. A bride and groom stood at the top of the steps and had their picture taken with the statue between them, her veil blowing in the wind.

I am not ashamed to say I cried. And then there was that thin blue wafer of a moon on the indigo sky and that faintly gilded evening light of Rome, nothing else like it anywhere, touching the palazzi and the pines.

That night they banged out a big blaze of fireworks from the Circo Massimo—the most gorgeous I have ever seen. And there we were, the friend of my innocence and I, like two schoolgirls on the Staten Island ferry once, up there in my little apartment eyrie on the Aventine, with the best seats in the house.

Inside the Stryker's Bay Neighborhood Council office, corner of West 89th Street and Columbus Avenue, 1963 or 1964: Harry, Esta, Pet Slavin's back.

First Daddy photo, Harry and Bim (Harry Two). Harry trying to stay incognito in sunglasses outside Our Lady of the Sea, Kitty Hawk, North Carolina, 1965.

Father Browne with Congressman William Fitts Ryan, celebrating the "Independence Day" of the Stryker's Bay Community Action program, June 14, 1968.

Harry Browne's first family portrait, no sunglasses, fall, 1969. The children (from the top): Bim, Kiki (Christopher), Nina.

"The house, the house!": 520 East 28th Street, Paterson, New Jersey, 1972. Our gap-toothed Victorian pile, with its nine magnificent pillars. "Room to be together, room to be alone."

"Paterson Power": Harry and Harry, Great Falls Festival, Paterson, New Jersey, 1972. Big Harry's Karl Marx phase.

Blissed out with Kiki and Nina on the lawn of the English House, University College, New York University, 1970. This polaroid was snapped by student David Singer.

Pretoria, South Africa, 1973. Harry calling attention to the apartheid privilege of sitting on a "Europeans Only" bench.

Party at our house, 1974. Our photographer friend Rachel Roth catches a Harry punch line with Italian hand gestures and cigar (and my appreciative grin).

Italian Dino and his family celebrating both our families, in the Colli Euganei outside Padua in 1975. Ah, the wine flowed! Harry and Anna Maria in back, then Kiki, Dino, Gigi, Bim, and finally me holding Nina in front. Poor Roberto had to take the picture.

I think photographer friend Len Roth took this picture on my Paterson porch in 1977, as we were talking historic preservation (what else?)

"A moment's monument"—or a monument's moment: picnicking in Sicily, behind the *sassi* at Selinus, December 29, 1977.

Ramapo College, Mahwah, New Jersey, 1983. Campus photo-op. (Photo courtesy of Ramapo College.)

This shot of me in the restored Rogers Building in Paterson accompanied a long article about revitalization of the city's Great Falls Historic District in *The Record* in 1993. (Photo by Danielle T. Richards, courtesy of *The Record*, Hackensack, New Jersey.)

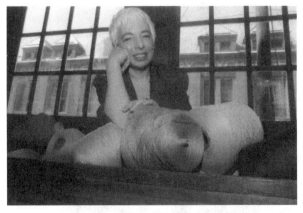

Epilogue

My father miraculously turned one hundred this past February.

Maybe it was the tofu. My mother, at some point in her crone phase of uncontaminated health remedies and witches' brews, had gone off meat completely and taken him with her into the land of the soybean.

She'd had a lot of help from Ann, fondly known as the Tofu Queen. Quite fondly, really, for Ann had got the message long before me and the rest of the sophisticated world and become a vegetarian pretty much the same time she became an artist. Both turns, however objectively justified, seemed also to have to do with defining who she was in relation to her tribal past: repudiating a family food-signature without quite repudiating food (only purging it before it became food for *her*), and, through the graphic art of calligraphy, writing herself—literally *scribing* herself—into being.

They were transformations evolved over a long period, coinciding with our numerous duty-driven visits to California—visits that were fretted, I think, with a certain symmetrical rivalry. For as we came and went there was always the stray envious comparison between us, my father protesting he liked my cooking better, urging me on to ever greater panache with zucchini, but to my unwavering annoyance eating Ann's tofu with everything. Even breakfast.

My sister and I laugh about this now, having finally grasped the little game that stole from us so many years of love and mutual recovery. I wonder if our parents ever suspected the hushed conversations at the back of their rambling ranch house, bonus of the medical emergencies that finally rushed us both to Temecula at once. We might have been girls again, whispering secrets across our darkened bedroom tower. Now the black desert midnight seemed to fly away in dazzlement at the glaring truth that we had, all of us, all our lives, been waiting for the same unachievable benediction of our father's approval.

Even the art of writing beautifully, for Ann, had clearly been homage to him, to the incised memory of our childhood nights in New Rochelle, after the dishes had been cleared from supper, when we'd leaned on our elbows to watch him prepare for sign-making: unroll the satiny white wrapping paper from the store, cut it into strips along each fold with a sharp butcher knife, set out his huge jars of tempera paint and fine long-handled sable brushes, then lay down his sales messages with pencil and rule and with masterful delicacy fill the beautifully scripted letters and numbers with brilliant reds and blues. Over the years we have learned to live with—even relish—a certain bitter but essential irony in his reproaching Ann repeatedly for "throwing up her Ph.D." in classics to do the script-work he disparaged, as he had despised it in his own wonderful, terrible hands. Until she began to win prizes for it, to surpass him utterly, and then he became the one who had encouraged her all along.

And yet he has blessed my own Nina, and Ann's Kate, both of them artists, for doing what he would not have endured to see us do. It is as if in some obscure way he knows it is too late for him to bless us, any more than to hurt us. That what's done cannot be undone. But also that what is never done will also never need undoing.

His hands are palsied now. He can hardly sign his own name. It is enough to make me cry to think of him suffering the slow agony of this loss. It has often been enough, as I have watched him time and again struggle against his shaking wrist to put the quivering pen to paper. Yet it no longer seems to trouble him. Nothing does, now that my mother's adoring pity has ceased to be the theater of his meaning. Perhaps he has come too close to dying too many times, even while she lived. *She* could sign his name then, while he still managed by TV remote and princess telephone to gamble his heart out, terrorizing her with his investment brinksmanship as she pictured him annihilating their life savings in a single day's shoot-out on the options exchange. Sandy and I still laugh about the ambulance night we hurried to his side in the hospital, when all he could say in a hoarse, pleading sputter, as I leaned into his white face for his last words, was: *"Close . . . all . . . my . . . positions."*

Of course these were not his last words, which he has yet to utter, though he has reminded us more than once of his own mother's ancestral Italian wisdom, that life, after all—even a life as long as his—is only *un'affacciata alla finestra*—a glance out of the window. He still sleeps in his own bed, hired women performing all the necessary caring offices Maria did when she was alive. His television window still opens onto Italian opera videos and masses from the Vatican or St. Patrick's Cathedral. And his real window is still there to glance out of, literally and otherwise, with its incomparable view of hillsides as rockbound and spiny, and skies as nearly unchangeably blue, as those that look immemorially down on his mother's grave in the Vesuvian foothills of Sperone, along the Appian Way.

We thought he was dying of pneumonia last year, just before his ninety-ninth birthday. Even as he fought through he seemed finally, hopelessly old, old beyond old. I sat beside his hospital bed, drawing him again and again in pencil and chalk, trying to capture that queer mix of granite and grace that had carried him so far. He has only begun to admit his hearing is failing. Lou and I, tired of shouting, finally bought him a little chest-hung amplifier with earphones, and I would sit there, beyond any fear of him now, holding his smooth hand, talking, listening. For knowing somehow that I had been writing of him, *he* would talk, mostly, about his childhood, his family, his boyhood in Libya, his near-drowning once on the African shore where he'd stopped for a dip in the sea, his stint with D'Annunzio's *Arditi* in the Great War. I ask how he translates *ardito* and he instantly snaps back: *foolhardy.* He tells me of his immigration, his businesses, his mother. He seems to want to tell me everything—everything—before he goes. For memory, he seems to know at last, is all he will take with him.

Something confessional clung to this moment, inspiring me to want to help him go shriven and clean, if it was what he wanted. And yet, in a strangely guilty reversal, it was my own shriving that spoke almost unbidden from my heart when I spoke, needing to know if he could forgive me the hurts I had done him, that perhaps I was still to do. And unhesitatingly he shook his head and sighed and said, "I should sooner ask that of you."

For moments after, I couldn't speak. When I found my voice again and asked if there were anything he had still to tell me, he replied with such imperious finality, "I have said what I needed to say," that I was forced to laugh. And understanding I meant, "No secrets?" he smiled at me with a sad irony, as he does now. "My life is my life," he said. "Nothing about it is secret. Only things . . . at a certain point . . . no longer spoken of."

Well, evasive to the end, I thought. And yet it flashed on me, like a swift glance of light off a mirror, that he *knew* I knew.

But he did not go then. He rallied beautifully. We celebrated his ninety-ninth birthday in the hospital. Ann followed me to California, but he said no more to her. Then he returned home. Months passed. We lamented, at intervals, that after all he would take his story to the grave.

In September he was sick again, and again I arrived in Temecula, just as he was declared out of danger and back in his own bed, to find him looking pale and weary, his spotty pinkness the skin-deep flush of cartridged oxygen. I dug the amplifier out of a dresser drawer and placed it around his neck like an amulet.

It was as though our conversation had never been interrupted. He continued the saga of his young life, bringing me to New York City now, to Yorkville, where he had roomed in the 1920s, to the young German couple who'd taken him in as a boarder. She was a very good cook, he said—and then, abruptly, as if he must blurt it out or never say it: "You have a brother." I took his meaning without ambiguity. He looked straight into the unstartled look on my face. But I think at that moment no look of mine could have stayed him.

It had happened just before he was married, he said. In her husband's benighted innocent affection for him, the child had actually been named Mario. He told me his surname, when and where he'd been born. The odd but significant fact that the doctor who'd delivered him had been the same who later delivered my brothers and me—but not Ann.

Ah, but this, for him, was an emotional old country. He had left it behind him. He would not venture back—not now, not any more. He let me go alone, imagining my guess true, that she had come to know while she was pregnant with Ann and had wanted to die. Maria's venerated ashes sit there on his bureau in a beautiful bronze and silver box, their double portrait beside it, smiling—still lovers.

Time has been merciful to my father's face, it wrinklelessness a wonder of the world. I marvel that it can still tell his emotions like a boy's, show such changeful sweeps of inner sorrow. Only there is this terrible thing: his tear ducts have dried—he can no longer cry. Even after this confession he seemed unrelieved, shutting his eyes as if in pain, opening them again and again, blinking dryly.

At last he resumed in a rough whisper, taking gulping breaths, staring straight ahead of him: "A few years later—we arranged to meet—an uptown subway station—on the West Side." He paused. "I had not seen her since my marriage," he went on. "It was the worst of the Depression—her husband out of work." Again he paused. "She had come to me—desperate—begging for help—" his voice broke and he squeezed his eyes helplessly shut. "I refused her," he whispered.

Suddenly, uncannily, I could see her—the young mother standing before us both in that cold tunnel, her child clinging to her hand.

His chest heaved. "I turned her away." I knew he had entered the purgatory of those who can no longer weep. My heart caved with pity as he repeated: "*I turned her away.*"

I wept for him. I wept for her. I wept for me.